SOCIAL WORK
Themes, Issues and
Critical Debates
THIRD EDITION

Co-edited titles by Robert Adams, Lena Dominelli and Malcolm Payne:
Critical Practice in Social Work, 2nd edn
Practising Social Work in a Complex World, 2nd edn
Reshaping Social Work Series (series editors)

Other titles by Robert Adams
Prison Riots in Britain and the USA* (2nd edn)
Protests by Pupils: Empowerment, Schooling and the State
Self-help, Social Work and Empowerment*
Skilled Work with People
The Abuses of Punishment*
The Personal Social Services: Clients, Consumers or Citizens?
Social Policy for Social Work*
Empowerment, Participation and Social Work*, 4th edn
Foundations of Health and Social Care

Other titles by Lena Dominelli
Beyond Racial Divides: Ethnicities in Social Work (co-author)
Feminist Social Work Theory and Practice*
Social Work: Theory and Practice for a Changing Profession
Women and Community Action
Revitalising Communities in a Globalising World
Anti-Racist Social Work*
Introducing Social Work
Anti-Oppressive Social Work Theory and Practice*
Revitalising Communities in a Globalising World

Other titles by Malcolm Payne
Social Care Practice in Context*
Globalization and International Social Work: Postmodern Change and Challenge
    (co-author)
What is Professional Social Work?, 2nd edn
Modern Social Work Theory, 3rd edn*
The Origins of Social Work: Continuity and Change*
Anti-bureaucratic Social Work
Teamwork in Multiprofessional Care*
Social Work and Community Care*
Linkages: Effective Networking in Social Care

* Also published by Palgrave Macmillan

EDITED BY ROBERT ADAMS
LENA DOMINELLI AND
MALCOLM PAYNE

SOCIAL WORK

THEMES, ISSUES AND CRITICAL DEBATES

THIRD EDITION

palgrave
macmillan

First edition 1998
Reprinted six times
Second edition 2002
Reprinted eight times
Third edition 2009 published by
PALGRAVE MACMILLAN

Palgrave Macmillan in the UK is an imprint of Macmillan Publishers Limited, registered in England, company number 785998, of Houndmills, Basingstoke, Hampshire RG21 6XS.

Palgrave Macmillan in the US is a division of St Martin's Press LLC, 175 Fifth Avenue, New York, NY 10010.

Palgrave Macmillan is the global academic imprint of the above companies and has companies and representatives throughout the world.

Palgrave® and Macmillan® are registered trademarks in the United States, the United Kingdom, Europe and other countries.

ISBN-13: 978–0–230–21865–9
ISBN-10: 0–230–21865–2

This book is printed on paper suitable for recycling and made from fully managed and sustained forest sources. Logging, pulping and manufacturing processes are expected to conform to the environmental regulations of the country of origin.

A catalogue record for this book is available from the British Library.

A catalog record for this book is available from the Library of Congress.

10 9 8 7 6 5 4 3 2 1
18 17 16 15 14 13 12 11 10 09

Printed in China

2/oo/10

Contents

PART 1   Knowledge for social work practice   11

Contents

List of figures and tables

Notes on the contributors

Robert Adams worked in the penal system for several years before running a community-based social work project for Barnardo's. He has been an external examiner on qualifying social work programmes in the UK since the mid-1980s. He has written and researched extensively in youth and criminal justice, social work, the personal social services, protest and empowerment. He has edited more than 80 books and written more than 12 books. He was Professor of Human Services Development at the University of Lincoln and has been Professor of Social Work at the University of Teesside for more than a decade.

Norma Baldwin is Professor of Childcare and Protection (emerita) at the University of Dundee, based in the Social Dimensions of Health Institute (Universities of Dundee and St Andrews). She is Chair of the Trustees of Circle, a charity supporting some of the most marginalised families in Scotland. Her research interests are in the links between disadvantage and harm to children and in population-wide and individualised assessments of need and risk.

Lorna Bell is a freelance trainer and consultant. Previously she was Reader in Social Work at Kingston University/St George's Hospital Medical School, London. She teaches aspects of child welfare and child protection and critical thinking, evidence-based practice and research methods. Her research interests have focused on interprofessional and interagency working, and her PhD explored multidisciplinary child protection teams in New Jersey, US. She has a particular interest in trying to ensure that her research impacts on practice.

Suzy Braye is Professor of Social Work at the University of Sussex. She has written widely in the field of social work and the law, community care provision and professional values, and is editor of the *European Journal of Social Work*. Her research interests include the relationship between law and social work, e-learning and the pedagogy of professional education, welfare policy implementation and practice, and the participation of experts by experience in policy, practice, education and research.

Beverley Burke is Senior Lecturer at Liverpool John Moores University, UK. She has practised as a social worker in the field of childcare and has published in the areas of anti-oppressive practice, values and ethics. Beverley is co-editor of the practice section of the international peer reviewed academic journal *Ethics and Social Welfare*.

Cecilia L.W. Chan is *si yuan* Professor in Health and Social Work, Director, Centre on Behavioral Health, as well as Professor, Department of Social Work and Social Administration of the University of Hong Kong. She worked as a social worker for over 30 years. She is renowned for her creative innovations of integrating Eastern concepts into her holistic therapy as well as her work on psychosocial oncology, end-of-life care, death and bereavement studies. She has published and edited more than 30 books and over 200 journal articles and book chapters. She received the 2008 Leadership in Oncology Social Work Award from the Oncology Social Workers Association, the 40 Distinguished Alumni Award of the Faculty of Social Sciences 40th Anniversary, HKU, 2007, and the 2008 Lydia Rapoport Distinguished Visiting Professorship to the School of Social Work, Smith College, Massachusetts, as well as being elected as board member of the International Workgroup on Death, Dying and Bereavement from 2008.

Helen Charnley is a lecturer in Applied Social Studies at Durham University. She has worked as a social work and social action practitioner and researcher in the UK and West and Southern Africa. Her areas of research are the involvement of children and young people in social work education and participatory research with older people on the benefits and challenges of personalised models of care.

Viviene Cree is Professor and Head of Social work at the University of Edinburgh. She has spent 16 years working in community work and social work, and another 16 years as an academic and researcher. Recent publications include *Becoming a Social Worker, Social Work: Voices from the Inside* (with Ann Davis), and *Social Work: Making a Difference*. She is co-editor of the international journal *Social Work Education* and joint series editor of the BASW/Policy Press series, 'Social Work in Practice', launched in 2008.

Jane Dalrymple is Senior Lecturer at the University of the West of England. She trained as a generic social worker and her practice and research interests are focused on children's rights and advocacy. Her doctoral thesis is on advocacy for children and young people.

Lena Dominelli is Professor of Applied Social Sciences and Head of Social and Community and Youth Work at the University of Durham. She is an academician in the Academy of the Learned Societies for Social Sciences. From 1996 to 2004, she served as President of the International Association of Schools of Social Work. She is widely published, with a number of important sole-authored books to her name, particularly in the areas of feminism, anti-racism, globalisation and social policy.

Pat Hanley qualified as a social worker in 1984, working for the probation service for ten years and then as a children's guardian for five years. Pat is Chief Executive Officer of Families in Care, a registered charity, providing independent social work services for birth families involved in child protection and family court proceedings. Pat has acted as a tutor and practice teacher for the Durham University social work programme since October 2000.

Margaret Holloway (formerly Lloyd) is Professor of Social Work at the University of Hull. She was previously Senior Lecturer in Community Care at the University of Sheffield. Her practice experience spanned a wide range of settings, including in criminal justice, but as an academic, she has specialised in adult services. She undertakes research into death, dying and bereavement, with a particular interest in spirituality, and service delivery at the health and social care interface for older people and people with Parkinson's disease.

Nigel Horner is Deputy Head of the School of Health and Social Care at the University of Lincoln. His practice background includes residential childcare, child and adolescent mental health, community work and substitute family care services. He has written texts on social work intervention for the Open Learning Foundation, and his recent publications include *What is Social Work?* and *Social Work in Education and Children's Services* (with Steve Krawczyk), both for Learning Matters, and *Values in the Helping Profession*, with Adam Barnard and Jim Wild.

Bill Jordan is Professor of Social Policy at Plymouth and Huddersfield Universities. He worked for 20 years in frontline public sector social work, and has carried out consultancy work for local authorities and voluntary agencies. He is the author of more than 25 books on social work and social policy, political and social theory, poverty, exclusion and migration, and has held visiting chairs in the Netherlands, Germany, Denmark, Slovakia, Hungary and the Czech Republic.

Joyce Lishman is Professor and Head of the School of Applied Social Studies at the Robert Gordon University, Aberdeen. Her practice experience is with children and adolescents and their families and as a Malcolm Sargent social worker working with children with cancer and their families. Her research was primarily on client perceptions, the analysis of social work interviews, the work and organisation of volunteers in social services and more generally on evaluation of social work and social care, and practice learning. A recent publication is the *Handbook for Practice Learning in Social Work and Social Care* (2nd edn). She is General Editor of the 'Research Highlights in Social Work' series.

Hugh McLaughlin is a registered social worker who worked as a practitioner, manager and senior manager in local authority social work before entering academia. He is the Director of the Salford Centre for Social Work Research. He is the author of *Understanding Social Work Research* and has published widely in journals, where his research interests include participatory research, childcare and the development of the learning organisation.

Gabriela Misca is Lecturer at Keele University where she teaches the human growth and development and 'working with children and families' modules for undergraduate and postgraduate social work programmes. She comes from an interdisciplinary background, having researched and taught in the fields of psychology, child development and their interface with social work and social policy (child abuse and neglect, residential and foster care and intercountry adoption). She is leading a longitudinal research study on evaluating progress and outcomes in a recovery programme for children who suffered abuse and neglect.

Siu-man Ng is Assistant Professor, Department of Social Work and Social Administration, and Associate Director, Centre on Behavioral Health, the University of Hong Kong. With training in both psychiatric social work and Chinese medicine, his key research area is mental health and traditional Chinese culture and medicine.

Malcolm Payne is Policy and Development Adviser at St Christopher's Hospice, London, having been Director of Psychosocial and Spiritual Care there for more than five years. He is Honorary Professor, Kingston University/St George's University of London, Visiting Professor, Opole University, Poland, and was formerly Head of Department and Professor of Applied Community Studies at Manchester Metropolitan University. Recent publications include papers and research on aspects of palliative care, including *Creative Arts in Palliative Care* (edited with Nigel Hartley). He is author of *What is Professional Social Work?*, *Social Work Practice in Context* and *Modern Social Work Theory* (3rd edn).

Stella Perrott is a writer on social policy matters, having previously been a Deputy Director with the Scottish government and a Deputy Chief Inspector of the Social Work Services Inspectorate. She was a Probation Officer for many years and has also taught MBA students.

Michael Preston-Shoot is Professor of Social Work and Dean of the Faculty of Health and Social Sciences at the University of Bedfordshire. He is a founding editor of *Ethics and Social Welfare* and Chair of the Joint University Council Social Work Education Committee. His research interests revolve around outcomes: of teaching, learning and assessment of social work law, of service user involvement in social work education, and of services for older people and for looked-after young people.

Grace Roddam is Young Persons' Training and Development Mentor for Sunderland Children Services. She is a leader in the development and evaluation of children and young people's involvement in qualifying and post-qualifying social work programmes in the northeast of England and serves as an adviser to a National Study of Interprofessional Practice in Safeguarding Children funded by the Department of Health.

Steven Shardlow is foundation holder of the Chair of Social Work at the University of Salford, England, where he is Director of the Institute for Health and Social Care Research. He has held academic appointments in Norway and Italy; he is Visiting Chair Professor at Hong Kong Polytechnic University. He is founding Editor-in-Chief of the *Journal of Social Work*. He is a registered social worker in England and has worked extensively in international social work, through research, consultancy and development work. Research interests are: welfare and social capital; evidence-based policy and practice; professional ethics; comparative practice in the social professions; and professional education. He has published widely in these fields, including 14 books, and his work has been translated into several languages.

June Tilling has been the Practice Learning Coordinator for Social Work Studies at the University of Southampton for the past 19 years. She has also been the Admissions Tutor for both the MSc and BSc social work programmes and contributes to the teaching of the assessed 'safety to practice' year 1 academic unit.

Alan Walker is Professor of Social Policy and Social Gerontology in the Department of Sociological Studies at the University of Sheffield. He has researched and written extensively on the fields of poverty, inequality, social exclusion, disability, ageing and European social policy.

Carol Walker is Professor of Social Policy in the Department of Policy Studies at the University of Lincoln. She has researched and published widely in the fields of poverty, inequality, social exclusion, disability, ageing and European social policy.

Linda Walker is Senior Lecturer in Social Work at the University of Dundee. Her research interests include collaborative inquiry and practice, organisational transformation and the development of learning cultures. She recently completed a secondment with the Scottish Institute for Research and Innovation, where she successfully managed a wide range of national change projects.

Jane Wistow (formerly Simmons) is a qualified social worker specialising in children's participation. She is undertaking doctoral research in this area and teaches communication skills to postgraduate social work students.

List of abbreviations used in this book

AASW   Australian Association of Social Workers
AOP   anti-oppressive practice
ASSD   adult social services department
BASW   British Association of Social Workers
BME   black and minority ethnic
CAF   Common Assessment Framework
CDT   community drug team
CHAI   Commission for Healthcare Audit and Inspection
CMHT   community mental health team
CPA   care programme approach
CRB   Criminal Records Bureau
CSCI   Commission for Social Care Inspection
CVS   council for voluntary service
DCLG   Department for Communities and Local Government
DCA   Department for Constitutional Affairs
DCSF   Department for Children, Schools and Families
DETR   Department of Environment, Transport and the Regions
DfES   Department for Education and Skills
DGH   district general hospital
DH   Department of Health
DSS   Department for Social Security
DWP   Department for Work and Pensions
EBP   evidence-based practice
EU   European Union
GP   general practitioner
GSCC   General Social Care Council
HEI   higher education institution
IASSW   International Association of Schools of Social Work
IB   individual budget

IFSW   International Federation of Social Workers
IS   income support
JUC   Joint Universities Committee
LA   local authority
NASW   National Association of Social Work
NHS   National Health Service
NICE   National Institute for Health and Clinical Excellence
NSF   national service framework
OECD   Organisation for Economic Co-operation and Development
PAF   Performance Assessment Framework
PCT   primary care trust
PHCT   primary healthcare team
PLC   practice learning coordinator
PMSU   Prime Minister's Strategy Unit
QAA   Quality Assurance Agency for Higher Education
RCT   randomised controlled trial
SAP   single assessment process
SCIE   Social Care Institute for Excellence
SIESWE Scottish Institute for Excellence in Social Work Education
SSD   social services department
SSI   Social Services Inspectorate
SWEC   Social Work Education Committee
Topss   Training Organisation for the Personal Social Services
UN   United Nations
UNICEF United Nations Children's Fund

ROBERT ADAMS, LENA DOMINELLI and MALCOLM PAYNE

Introduction

What is this book about?

This book provides a core of material for your social work studies in the early stages of the professional qualifying degree programme for social workers, as well as foundation material for students and practitioners on higher level courses. Our purpose is to introduce the distinctive and sometimes unique character of social work as a social profession by developing our critical understanding of:

- the different knowledge bases and subject disciplines to which social work relates (Part 1)
- the basic tasks and processes that it entails (Part 2)
- the settings in which it is practised and the kinds of policies and structures that professionals can expect to work with (Part 3).

As its title indicates, this book is not just about developing criticality but also about highlighting key themes and issues that are threaded throughout and sometimes appear in several of the chapters. For example, although poverty is dealt with in Chapter 7 along with social policies, it is an important factor in people's lives and we refer to it in several other chapters.

How does this book fit into our trilogy of social work books?

This book, *Social Work: Themes, Issues and Critical Debates*, is the first of our three books designed to help students and beginning practitioners in social work to explore their profession and the settings in which they work. The second book is titled *Critical Practice in Social Work* and the third is *Practising Social Work in a Complex World*. Practitioners need to develop their practice by reflecting critically on what they do and integrate within their thinking and practice an understanding and analysis of social work values and a capacity for personal professional development. This first book in the trilogy introduces the distinctive character of social work in its different settings. It tackles social work values, locates social work in its different contexts and begins to explore some of the lasting debates that arise in different practice settings.

Critical Social Work Practice moves from exploring what practice entails to developing actual expertise in practice, as a critical practitioner. It examines what it means to develop critical practice in social work. We argue that without a capacity for critical analysis of aims, outcomes and practices in social work, it is impossible to respond flexibly and with understanding to the needs and wishes of the people social workers serve.

In *Practising Social Work in a Complex World*, we argue that a good understanding of themes, issues and debates in contemporary social work and the capacity to practise social work critically need to be integrated with more complex professional skills. These include dealing with complex situations to enable practitioners to develop confidently a partnership with service users, their families, carers and communities, with other agencies and with colleagues in other professions. They also include management and leadership skills and research-based practice skills. Partnership working is essential to achieving the fundamental objective of social work: to increase the resilience of individuals, groups and communities in dealing with the problems in their lives through solidarity and equality in society.

Readers of previous editions of the three books in this series will find that the topics covered in each volume have changed to reflect feedback and our own judgement about the order in which particular topics should be introduced when readers use the books in sequence. We have included 'critical concept' boxes in the narrative of this first book, *Social Work: Themes, Issues and Critical Debates*. These are designed to provide compact definitions of terms referred to occasionally by authors which contribute to the theoretical bedrock on which the book sits. As editors, we are aware that different disciplines carry their own conceptual vocabulary and, given the particularly strong multidisciplinarity of this book, we appreciate that no single reader should be expected to be familiar with the full range of concepts drawn on here.

Towards a critical understanding of social work

People often confuse social work with other 'socials' including social security, social services and social care. In this introductory chapter, we clarify what social work does and how it relates to social care. We also clarify what the 'social' in social work refers to. We show how expertise in being 'social' is one of the unique features of the profession of social work.

Chapter overview

What is social work and what do social workers do?

Social work aims to improve and facilitate the working of society, the environment of relationships and social institutions developed from relationships, in which human beings live. In its most general aspects, this is about improving human cooperation because this helps human beings to survive and develop. This means improving social relationships, facilitating the development and use of both kinds of social institution – those such as families, which develop from relationships, and those such as residential homes, which aim to improve people's lives – and generally improving society as a social environment for human life. A word that expresses these linkages between people and their environments is 'connectedness'. Care can contribute this aspect of connectedness to different dimensions of people's lives – social relationships, families, organisations and institutions.

The aim of social work, therefore, is improvement in social life, increasing cooperation among human beings and increasing solidarity in society. This has been expressed in a variety of ways by social workers and others over the years (Payne, 2006). The most-used formulation currently is the international definition of social work devised jointly by the International Federation of Social Workers (IFSW) and supported by the International Association of Schools of Social Work (IASSW):

The social work profession promotes social change, problem solving in human relationships and the empowerment and liberation of people to enhance well-being. Utilising theories of human behaviour and social systems, social work intervenes at the points where people interact with their environments. Principles of human rights and social justice are fundamental to social work. (IFSW, 2000)

The above definition identifies three aspects of social work, also identified by Payne (1996, 2006):

■ Social change – *transformational*
■ Problem-solving in human relationships – *social order*
■ Liberation of people to enhance wellbeing – *therapeutic*.

Good social workers maintain a critical, that is, questioning, attitude to their work. We can see this threaded through these aspects. The first of these aspects is work that emphasises the social improvement and social solidarity objective, regardless of whether a social worker is working with individuals, groups or communities. In work with individuals, it includes advocacy for users' and carers' needs within social, education and healthcare services and enabling individuals to understand how social arrangements oppress and disadvantage them and, within their limits, to do something about that. In work with groups and communities, this aspect of social work aims to bring people together to support each other for mutual help and in action to change disadvantageous and oppressive aspects of the way in which society affects them. A good example of individual, group and community interventions within this aspect of social work is working with women affected by domestic violence (see Adams et al., 2009c, Ch. 3). Individually, practitioners help women to accept the need to change their lives to avoid the risk of violence, perhaps leaving their present home or excluding a violent partner. Group and community work involves creating and supporting refuges, changing legislation to enable it to support non-violent social relationships, and trying to develop appropriate services to enable women and their children to re-establish a more satisfactory way of life.

The second aspect of these definitions is providing personal help, advice and support in difficult situations and packages of services that help people to deal with the difficulties in their lives. A good example is the care manager role in local authority adult social services for older people (see Chapter 23). Practitioners give advice and information and organise basic services in the home as older people become more frail. Eventually, practitioners will organise extensive packages of help with the ordinary activities of life from paid carers alongside the service user's family and friends. Some people might argue that this includes practical help with bathing, dressing and food, connected with healthcare services aimed at keeping a service user in good health, while others maintain that this is the job of a healthcare or social care worker. Because social work is particularly concerned with how interpersonal relationships help people and create security and solidarity in their lives, social work's role in these services is to personalise them, assessing each individual's needs and the help that their informal carers need and tailoring the package of services to those needs. New patterns of service, such as self-directed care using independent, personalised budgeting, allow service users a high degree of control of the organisation of these services to fit their preferences. Social work also has a role in supporting people in making these decisions, advocating for their wishes in the system of services and facilitating arrangements that make them feel secure and connected to their existing social network and community (Payne, 2009).

The third aspect of these definitions is empowering therapeutic help. Examples of this might include helping an older person in hospital to think about the consequences of their increasing frailty and decide to how to reduce the risk of being alone at home, or helping a young person who is addicted to heroin make the decision to change aspects of their lifestyle that are keeping them in the 'drug culture'.

Social work is not only about social relationships and institutions, it is practised socially. An important characteristic is that its work to improve social solidarity is done by providing social relationships and institutions as a substitute for weak relationships and institutions, or as a learning experience, or to help existing relationships at a particularly difficult time. Here are some examples. Foster care and adoption of children whose parents cannot care for them are a substitute for poor parental relationships or an unhelpful family. Cognitive behavioural social work might provide a learning experience that would help someone with anxiety or depression to find ways of managing their problems. Palliative care in a hospice, for someone who is dying, provides extra care and support at one of the most difficult times in a family's life. All these use interpersonal relationships and social institutions to help people to deal with their social difficulties.

One of the best examples of how this is done is social work in residential care. Whitaker et al. (1998) carried out a study of practice in children's residential care. They found that residential work took place on three 'fronts' between staff and young people. The first front involved containing and controlling the young people so that they led an orderly life in a way that encouraged acceptable behaviour. This means that there was an attempt to improve social behaviour and relationships at the time in the residential care situation, with the aim of developing improved social behaviour and therefore improved social relationships in the future. This first front also involved maintaining the viability of the relationships in the residential care home, a social institution, reducing the possibility of difficulties affecting the managers of the care home or people in the local community.

The second front involved working individually with young people to meet needs that will allow their life situations to improve. This focused on individual social relationships, with the aim of improved social relationships in the future outside the present social institution, the care home.

The third front involved providing experiences that repaired the relationships the young people had missed or lost, such as good relationships with parents or authority figures. Staff did this by trying to increase the occurrence of group situations that help residents and by reducing occurrences of group situations that were damaging and repairing the consequences of group situations that had produced difficulties. Their practice tried to avoid mixes of residents that might cause difficulties, noted and responded to early warning signs of difficulties in group relations and avoided behaving in ways that might escalate a difficult situation.

Social care and social work as social professions

In this book and this trilogy, we aspire to social work in the UK being prominently located in a constellation of social practices, known as the leading social profession, in the sectors of services for children, young people, families and adults. It is perhaps the only one that situates people in their social and physical environment. Social work is an international profession, and operates within a range of social provision that differs in every country, according to the political and social debate and the social institutions in each society. Most countries have a number of 'social professions', with varying descriptions and differing systems of training. In mainland Europe, for example, you might find social pedagogues, social educators and in many countries around the world you would find social development workers.

Similarly, in the UK, social workers practise alongside residential workers, youth and community workers, education social workers and a range of social care workers. Many of these practitioners, such as youth and community workers, would be regarded as social workers in some other countries. Others, such as education social workers, are regarded as specialised social workers. Many social care workers, such as registered managers of care homes or social care workers in various community care projects, may or may not be social workers.

The governments in the UK are increasingly using the term 'social care' to describe this range of services that in most other countries would be social work services or social services. This reflects a particular social ideology:

■ A public choice or modernisation agenda that argues that people receiving social services should have a choice of provision from public, private and voluntary sector agencies, rather than feeling that they are dealing with monolithic state services that reflect the interests of the professionals that provide them with what they think is best rather than taking into account their personal wishes and feelings.
■ An emphasis on 'care' rather than social or behavioural change.
■ A focus on providing services, rather than an emphasis on therapeutic work.
■ An emphasis on helping people experiencing difficulties with the social conse-quences of long-term issues or disabilities in their lives, rather than short-term problem-solving.
■ A close integration of the work and services with service users themselves and people in their families and social networks who care for them as they try to deal with the issues that affect them (Payne, 2009).

These activities are still social work according to the international definition, with a focus on trying to personalise help with the social consequences of long-term difficulties in people's lives. This personalisation aims to help people to be more in control of their lives, more self-directing. Social care workers are social workers who need just as many skills in assessing and working through interpersonal and social relationships to do this kind of work, as someone who sees their work as trying to change behaviour or change the depressing social environment of a housing estate where people experience exclusion and poverty. Social care services are just as likely to be trying to help people experiencing poverty and social exclusion as, say, a children and adult mental health service that works with young people with emotional and behavioural difficulties, a youth worker organising day centre activities for a range of young black minority ethnic groups, or a community worker trying to help people in a run-down urban area prevent rising levels of violence and crime in their community.

All these types of work require partnership between practitioners, a range of agencies and professionals, great interpersonal and social relationship skills and a commitment to meeting the needs and responding to the values of services users, carers, their families and communities. They are all social work and we treat them all as such in these books.

What is social about social work?

The social in social work engages with social relationships or interactions between people as they go about their daily lives in the context of the society in which they live. This covers the social aspects of social policy and the social aspects of living in a society in which some individuals, families, groups and communities encounter problems in their lives which are so major as to require help, support or intervention. The word 'social' appears in different guises, as we shall see below. It refers to social work's simultaneous responsibilities for working with the problems of individuals and families, while maintaining an awareness of the context of social problems and issues to which they relate. This is equivalent to the health professional working with the illnesses and conditions of individual people, while promoting and developing the health of the community. However, the tensions of managing the personal and the social dimensions of people's problems are more acute in social work than in most other professions. Halmos (1978) characterised them in terms of a tension between the personal and the political dimensions of a person's circumstances. They are not separate. Social workers work with people who experience complex problems that are multifaceted. They engage with 'the personal dimensions of multiple problems such as urban and rural squalor, deprivation and degradation in communities and societies, while attempting to empower and sometimes intervene' (Adams, 2007: 32–3). In this sense, many people regard social work as an intrinsically critical profession. Social workers are expected to maintain an open-minded, critical view of inequalities in society and, where necessary, to advocate on behalf of people to empower them to acquire the services to which they are entitled.

These responsibilities require social workers to maintain an awareness of the social policies in which public services are rooted. In the latter stages of the Second World War, Sir William Beveridge (1879–1963) set out proposals to tackle the five giants of want, idleness, squalor, disease and ignorance (Beveridge, 1942). Today, we would term these a lack of financial means, requiring social security; being faced with insufficient work to create a need for employment; poor housing or an unsound physical environment; poor health; and inadequate education, respectively. Beveridge was convinced that many of these problems required tackling through new social policies. He viewed poverty as a social problem rather than a symptom of weaknesses of the individual. This touches on the uniqueness of social work today, because as social workers help individuals and families, they do so aware that many of their problems are generated by poverty and inequality. Social workers work with individuals, families, groups and communities in the knowledge that many of their problems can be tackled by some form of external or social intervention. Social work values refuse to blame people for this; they require practitioners to try to change things so that the effects of poverty and inequality do not oppress people and aim to empower people to overcome the barriers that poverty and inequality put in their way.

In the early twenty-first century, we no longer refer to the legislation following the Beveridge Report that set up the welfare state, but we still refer to welfare services. In the UK, the word 'welfare' has acquired a particular meaning since the formation of the welfare state. It refers to the policies and services developed during the 1940s, which provide a range of education, employment, health, housing, social security and social services for people who are unemployed, older, sick and disabled or vulnerable. Increasingly, we use the word 'wellbeing' to refer to something wider than welfare, to describe a consistent experience in an individual, family or community that they are happy in themselves and that the life they lead is satisfying and worthwhile. This sense of their lives being worthwhile derives from people feeling that their relationships with the people and the social institutions around them are good and that they are making a useful contribution to aspects of social life that are important to them. In Chapter 6, Jordan explores this concept further and connects it to social work practice and social care services.

We also attach the word 'social' to some other important ideas, which relate to social work but which have a different focus:

- *Social problems* are social ills that raise concerns in a society, such as disability, crime, unemployment, mental health, child and adult abuse and old age.
- *Social policies* are all around us, every time we switch on the TV or radio or pick up a newspaper or magazine. They are the measures that governments take to respond to our needs throughout our lives, from the cradle to the grave, such as services for children, older people, disabled people and people with mental health problems.
- *Social issues* include social inequality, disadvantage and discrimination, including age, ethnicity, gender, disability, wealth and poverty, inadequate income.

■   *Social care services* refer to provisions that aim to meet the needs of people who are disabled, older and/or vulnerable.

Let us return to explore the 'social' in social work. Practising to achieve solidarity and equality in society requires an understanding and commitment to the 'social'. This is an aspect of social work that is often not discussed, and therefore not criticised. It is also a term that colleagues in other professions find unclear, and it often adds to their uncertainty about what social work is and what social workers do.

The 'social' implies several different things:

■   The social, as an area of experience or study, is concerned with the experience of human beings, in contrast to the natural, physical world, for example the geology and geography of our planet.
■   Human beings are 'social animals', that is, they live cooperatively in groups. They do so because collaboration confers a social advantage that goes beyond natural selection in the natural world in which the fittest survive. Thus, helping each other enables human beings and other social animals to survive better.
■   The social is also the relationships between human beings and the traits and skills that help human beings form, build and continue those relationships. These relationships help to maintain the cooperative groups in which human beings most successfully live.
■   These relationships develop into social institutions of two kinds:
    –   the common pattern of relationships such as kinship, families, communities and organisations
    –   planned and managed organisations that might include political institutions such as parliament, and collective institutions such as residential care homes.
■   Society is the complete set of relationships, including cultural, personal and social relationships, that form the human social environment in which human beings live.

Social work focuses on and works with all these aspects of the social. This means that social workers may be concerned, for example, with the environment and sources of power for heating and cooking, because this is necessary for human survival; aid agencies and social agencies concerned with welfare rights may well want to make sure that homeless people or older people in their own homes can receive food and warmth. However, they are not professionally responsible for the physical alternatives that protect the environment or for finding oil and gas or generating electricity. Social workers' responsibility is for the human consequences of the way in which society and social institutions expressing that society's culture and social values make those physical provisions.

How this book is distinctive

This book is presented in three parts, which deal with distinctively different but closely related aspects of social work, responding to three questions:

1 From which areas of knowledge do social workers draw their understanding and expertise? Our response to this question takes the form of a survey of the different contexts to which social workers relate. These refer us to areas of knowledge rooted in knowledge of the social sciences, including sociology and social policy as well as politics, philosophy and psychology, the law and the organisation and management of services through central and local government.
2 What is the nature of social work? The response to this question takes us into an exploration of the distinctive character of social work, through its processes and the key stages of assessment, planning, intervention, review and evaluation.
3 In which sets of circumstances and settings do social workers carry out their work with individuals, families, groups and communities? Early in a professional qualifying course in social work, it is apparent that the core of the learning lies in developing expertise in different settings and working with different groups of people who use services at different points in their lives. These include adult and children's services, which also involve work with families. Clearly, these are not comprehensive categories and involve an emphasis on some areas and the omission of others. As we write, the commissioning and procurement of services is increasingly distancing local authorities from direct provision, as local trusts and the third sector of independent voluntary and private organisations and groups become more involved in providing services.

How this book is structured

This first book in the trilogy provides the foundation of knowledge required for the first stage of the qualifying programme. It enables you, the reader, to locate social work in relation to its social, policy, legal, psychological and values knowledge bases (Part I). It illustrates the character of social work by introducing the idea of process and taking you through its basic stages (Part II). It gives you an overview of what social work entails in its three main settings: adult services, children and families services and third sector work with voluntary and community groups and organisations and introduces material relevant to undertaking a period of practice learning in an agency (Part III).

For a critical context for social work, see Chapter 2, and for different perspectives on social work process, see Chapter 13.

Dominelli, L. (2004) *Social Work: Theory and Practice in a Changing Profession*, Cambridge, Polity Press. Explores the impact of globalisation, professionalisation and social work's dependent status on the development of professional practice.

Ferguson, I. (2008) *Reclaiming Social Work*, London, Sage. Explores the impact of the market on social work's commitment to social justice and solidarity.

Payne, M. (2006) *What is Professional Social Work?*, 2nd edn, Bristol, Policy Press Reviews a range of debates on the nature of social work, including an extensive historical review of definitions of social work.

Payne, M. (2008) *Social Care Practice in Context*, Basingstoke, Palgrave Macmillan. Seeks to theorise and develop social care practice as a social profession alongside social work and using many social work skills.

Part 1

KNOWLEDGE FOR SOCIAL WORK PRACTICE

Social work occupies a lead position among public sector and human service professions by engaging not only with the personal but the social aspects of people's lives. Part 1 of this book locates social work in its different contexts, concentrating mainly on the range of perspectives that the social science disciplines bring. It is important to recognise that social work occupies an intrinsically contested territory in these areas of knowledge and that this is reflected in practice itself. The chapters in Part 1 show how social work tackles essentially contested areas (Chapter 2) and how it is changing (Chapter 3). Chapter 4 explores social work's fundamental value-base and, in the following chapters, we see how social justice and human rights are central to the challenges the profession can pose for oppression and discrimination (Chapter 5), how they can contribute significantly to human wellbeing (Chapter 6) and how they harmonise with policies intended to engage with persistent problems of poverty (Chapter 7).

Nevertheless, social workers have to be grounded in the ever-changing legislative and regulatory base for practice (Chapter 8) and in realistic, yet critical, understandings of organisational life (Chapter 9). They also need to draw on a range of perspectives on the life course, both in work with children from their earliest years into adolescence (Chapter 10), and in the relatively neglected aspects of the middle and later years of life (Chapter 11). Throughout, social workers need to maintain an evidence-based practice which is critically aware of the limitations as well as the potential of particular research strategies and methods (Chapter 12).

Repositioning social work

2

British social work is being repositioned to meet the challenges of globalisation, service user empowerment, professionalisation and research-based practice. I explore their practice implications in a context wherein the nation-state is subservient to external economic pressures, but responsible for the ensuing social problems without necessarily having the capacity to resolve them.

Chapter overview

Contemporary social work practice in the UK is facing considerable challenges and opportunities as government seeks to implement a modernisation agenda in the context of **globalisation** that initiated a worldwide credit crunch and economic recession in 2008, pressures from services users for person-centred services, increased managerial control predicated on new technological mechanisms, and practitioners' desire for further professionalisation and autonomy. The opportunities and tensions for service user-led practice that these trends can underpin or undermine have been evident for some time. They have acquired renewed emphasis as structural changes in local authorities fragment social services departments (SSDs) and subject social workers to working within organisational frameworks often in health and education that place them in a minority. This besets the profession with new contradictions that locate social workers in an ambiguous position vis-à-vis defending their role and status in society, retaining their commitment to social justice and enhancing people's wellbeing.

> **Globalisation** refers to the processes by which institutions, markets and cultures are assisted by the new information technologies to become increasingly global in their reach and impact. Globalisation entails the movement of power away from localities and towards globally controlled corporations and organisations. While it has some features that allow relatively powerless people who lack significant resources to join forces for a stronger voice, especially if they use the internet to communicate with like-minded others, it is generally acknowledged that large corporations representing the strongest interests benefit most from globalisation.

In this chapter, I examine the new positioning of social work in Britain within the context of a globalising world wherein the nation-state is subservient to economic pressures originating outside its borders, but is called upon to resolve the ensuing social problems without necessarily having the capacity to do so. This has had profound implications for the positioning of social work within the UK, both as a country made up of four separate nations (England, Scotland, Wales and Northern Ireland) and in relation to other professions. I consider these issues by focusing on the challenges and opportunities presented by:

- Globalisation
- Service user empowerment
- Professionalisation
- Research-led practice.

Globalisation redefines the terrain of social work practice

Neoliberalism This political viewpoint advocates liberalism expressed as market-driven imperatives in economic policies and practice as a means of advancing the economic wellbeing of individuals, communities and societies. Thus neoliberalism needs to be understood against the backcloth of liberalism. In the classic economic theory of Adam Smith, liberalism referred to a belief in the so-called 'natural' laws which ensured that in a free-market economy, market forces would operate to the benefit of both producers of goods and services and the people who bought them. Neoliberals tend to reassert versions of this position in the modern world and expect the market to distribute goods and services effectively. A key limitation of this approach is that it excludes those who cannot play the market because they lack funds through which to 'choose', that is, purchase, the best services in meeting their needs.

Globalisation has been defined primarily as the economic integration of national economies into one global market. This is a narrow view of the forces of globalisation that now encompass the social, cultural and political domains (Dominelli, 2004a). In its current formation, globalisation has been termed **neoliberalism**. This variant of globalisation has promoted the deepening of capitalist social relations in all arenas of social and personal life in and through the routines of everyday life – everyday life practices. Social workers have been drawn into the ambit of globalising forces in various ways. Some have been focused on external relations, others on internal developments. These include:

- Promoting the privatisation of public service provision and managerial control of the workforce
- Promoting forms of practice that are linked to a particular nation-state as if they have universal applicability
- Being part of a colonising process
- Responding to people during times of natural or human-made disasters
- Engaging in exchanges to foster developments in local practice
- Having an impact on the international stage
- Being part of a migratory workforce (Dominelli, 2007; Payne and Askeland, 2008).

These trends can overlap and although some are part of social work's past, their tentacles can reach into the present. For example, there is a link between assuming that social work theories and forms of practice have universal validity and the potential to engage in colonising processes. British social workers went to the colonies in missions to embed welfare practices that privileged British nationals over local populations, as occurred in South Africa where the majority was excluded from welfare provisions pre-1994. In Canada, Australia and New Zealand, indigenous children were placed in residential schools where they were denied their own cultures and languages under the explicit aim of 'turning them into English men and women'. Equally pernicious in Germany was the use of social workers to affirm Nazi eugenicist practices. These implicated social workers in the formation of the nation-state (Lorenz, 1994), at the expense of ethical and moral practice. Resistance to these ventures was extensive, although usually ineffective. The business of recovery from these oppressive forms of social work remains unfinished, even though indigenous welfare systems have begun to flourish in Canada, Australia and New Zealand/ Aotearoa. Indigenous endeavours have created innovative models of practice. For example, Maori social work practitioners and educators in Aotearoa have given their family group conference (FGC) model to the world as a less oppressive form of practice in working with children and families. First Nation peoples in Canada have created their own child welfare system to promote indigenous community-based ways of working with children and families. These models display a community development focus on the uplift of a people rather than individuals as a prime aim.

These new encounters between those in the global North and the global South represent practice exchanges that are more egalitarian, and where the flow of information and illustrations of good practice flow from Southern peoples to Westerners. They also indicate a transfer of practice paradigms and knowledge from the global South to the global North instead of the other way round. Other instances of social workers helping human development are provided by the profession's role in the United Nations (UN). The International Association of Schools of Social Work (IASSW) has held consultative status in the UN since 1947 when this organisation was formed and was an important player in getting the Universal Declaration of Human Rights approved by the General Assembly in 1948. Since then, the IASSW, International Federation of Social Workers (IFSW), and International Council on Social Welfare (ICSW) have participated in UN summits and the formulation of policies affecting the rights of poor people, older people, women, children, migrant workers and others. Members from these organisations work alongside others including Oxfam and the Red Cross to alleviate suffering during natural and human-made disasters like the 2004 tsunami in the Indian Ocean. Additionally, these organisations promote workshops and conferences that attract educators, practitioners and policy makers from all over the world to share models of good practice and learn from one another's curricula and research projects.

Social workers, like other workers, are part of migratory populations. In some cases, social workers living in countries in the southern hemisphere have been specifically targeted for work in the UK (Devo, 2006). This has prompted calls for the British state to pay these workers' countries of origins for their training, as their departure marks a transfer of educational resources to the West and creates serious shortages of personnel in places where further funding for training is scarce (Dominelli, 2004b). It has also led to demands for protocols to regulate employment practices involving overseas workers. These efforts produced the social care code of practice for international recruitment in 2006 (GSCC, 2006).

Social work is a part of the welfare state understood as the symbolic representation of people's collective commitment to assisting others who are not members of their immediate or extended families through the mediation of the state. It has recently been subject to market forces that have had an extensive impact on practice in the relationship between service users and professionals, between professionals and their employers, and citizens and the state. The British state's commitment to fund social work through public monies has never been universal, unlike health and education, where, for a period, these were available as unstigmatised services to all at the point of need. However, the introduction of user fees in both education and health in recent years has undermined their universality. Coupled with the growth of private providers, this is likely to dilute their universality further. The personal social services have been residual ones targeting those most in need from the beginning.

Government has supported these initiatives through a modernisation agenda that has subjected professionals working in the public sector, whether social workers, doctors, nurses or teachers, to further regulation that covered training, workforce planning, performance management and managing need in order to curtail demand for what were construed as limited public resources. Included in this were measures to promote interdisciplinary teamworking, common assessment frameworks, tighter regulatory mechanisms at both professional and individual levels and a restructuring of social services that placed it in subordinate positions vis-à-vis larger bodies in health and education and splitting work with children and families from work with adults. The separation of social work from probation practice in England and Wales except that involving young offenders had occurred earlier in 1998 in a measure implemented by Jack Straw as home secretary under a New Labour administration.

Neoliberalism has produced the growth of market provisions in the welfare arena, a trend that is intensified under the General Agreement on Trades and Services, which requires the opening up of public provisions in health, education and the personal social services to the private sector. The privatisation of public services in the UK began under Thatcher's government. This initiated the purchaser–provider split whereby the state lost its status as a near monopoly provider of welfare services. From that time, the state reduced most of its provider functions to become a purchaser, the entity that bought or commissioned services from other providers including those located in the voluntary and commercial sectors.

The expansion of the private sector in residential homes for children and older people, the prison service, young offender services, and health and social care services is a reflection of globalisation's impact upon the welfare state in Britain and elsewhere. In the UK, this development has shifted the welfare mix to one in which private and voluntary provisions dominate many areas of practice. The latter sector provides 40 per cent of personal social care and receives 37 per cent of its funding from the state which has required that it become more businesslike through 'contract government' (Greer, 1994). The voluntary sector employs 1.5 million people and has 6 million volunteers (Dean, 2005). Privatisation has been accompanied by intensified managerial control of workers, using computer-based information technologies that have shaped record-keeping, managerial processes, support provision and worker–service user relationships. These have often left social workers on the sidelines, implementing bureaucratic procedures that they have often critiqued (Dominelli, 2004a). Had privatisation increased the range and quality of services and met the needs of service users, there would be little reason to complain about their spread.

This is often not the case as profit motives override welfare concerns. For example, Sedgmoor, a venture capital company, closed 47 children's homes on the grounds that it was losing money, thereby exacerbating young people's vulnerability. Private homes for older people are exempt from the Human Rights Act, and so older people living in these cannot use this legislation to address their grievances. The exclusion of private establishments from protecting the rights of many vulnerable people in society exposes the imperative of making a profit out of meeting people's needs for social care and the crisis of profitability at the heart of neoliberal relations as capitalists seek to exploit welfare provisions as sites of capital accumulation that they can drop like hot potatoes when profits falter. The crisis in profitability has been exacerbated by the 2008 credit crunch caused by failure in the American subprime market to make money by inflating prices paid by consumers, especially in housing and the personal social services, and by speculating in future provisions in which production does not equate to the value ascribed to goods. This example also indicates the crises engendered through the 'internationalisation of the state' (Dominelli, 2004a) as the nation-state is drawn into saving the financial system and its institutions, especially the banks, while withdrawing money from individuals requiring welfare state assistance, for example by proceeding with its plans to reduce the number of people claiming incapacity benefit by one million by 2015 and toughening up the requirement to work for all those seeking income support.

Reducing people's expectations for welfare services as a right is part of the struggle to curtail the spread of publicly funded provisions as citizenship entitlements. Moreover, the commitment to individual responsibility for welfare, initiated under Thatcherism, has continued under New Labour. Under it, self-sufficiency and market provisions aim to affirm quality resources while bureaucratic controls over social workers assure quality care. That this is not what service users want is indicated by surveys of public commitment to public welfare. However, this insight has escaped New Labour, which has intensified the rate of privatisation of welfare services, from foundation hospitals that will employ social workers, to the idea of private social work practices floated in early 2008.

The new managerialism or public sector management that favours bureaucratic forms of control over a professional workforce draws upon corporate management techniques, often introduced through the importation of managers without social work qualifications to manage social services and ensure that taxpayers get value for money through the efficient, effective and economic delivery of services. Managers utilise performance management tools including Best Value frameworks – the statutory indicators that local authorities use to plan, review and manage workers' performance, in the expectation that this will deliver continuous improvement for all services and meet service users' expectations and needs for better services – national standards, league tables, audits and inspection regimes to exert greater control over social workers and reduce space for exercising professional autonomy. In turn, these managerial practices allow managers to become more accountable to politicians for how resources are used under their watch. Performance management has become part of a surveillance regime that bureaucratises trust and, in so doing, breeds mistrust. It also indicates that policy makers have lost touch with the intricacies of practice and sensitivity for the lives that people in straitened circumstances live. A social worker quoted in Dominelli et al. (2005: 1133) puts this aptly by demanding:

> Can you get down here … deputy minister and talk to us about … the real day-to-day issues … young moms are having difficulty raising their kids because we don't fund them. We don't support them.

Care management for older people has been subjected to corporate management for several decades now. And it has been accompanied by the growth of 'contract government', the private finance initiative (PFI) (Greer, 1994) and public–private partnerships (PPPs), which have aimed to change professional culture through a quasi-market and turn social services organisations into better managed businesses. Another objective of these changes has been to increase consumer choice. Interestingly, a study conducted by Khan and Dominelli in 2000 reported that social workers and managers had divergent views of what had happened. Managers thought these reforms had delivered consumer choice and freed practitioners up to deliver services more effectively, while social workers claimed that choice was virtually non-existent and that budgets rather than needs determined what service users ultimately received (Dominelli, 2004b).

Service user empowerment

Notions of empowerment, social justice, human rights and anti-oppression are central to placing service users in charge. The modernising agenda (DH, 1998a) claims to promote these values by turning service users into consumers who can exercise choice and access the services they want. The involvement of service users in social work education and in research projects has given reality to these assertions. However, the involvement of service users as co-producers of public services may be little more than tokenistic, given resource constraints in funding innovations, increasing service availability or paying for the time that service users expend on such work.

The bureaucratic welfare state has been challenged by service users, particularly those comprising the new social movements led by women, black minority ethnic

(BME) groups and disabled people since the 1960s. They have demanded services that they design and control and highlighted oppressive responses that demeaned their personhood and failed to meet their needs. They called for empowering practice by which they meant self-directed, personalised provisions and practitioners who responded to them as whole human beings or citizens in charge of their daily lives. Oliver (1990) argues that social workers should desist from disempowering disabled service users because they are unable to empower them by being the experts who know better than them how to lead their lives. Activists in the new social movements also demanded changes in legislation to ensure that their rights and dignity were upheld, money to purchase their own services and alternative services that they had developed to be incorporated into mainstream ones so that these could be transformed and become responsive to their agendas. Their interventions have led to person-centred practice where service users are involved in drawing up care plans and the provision of direct payments and individual budgets that are under their control. These developments in person-centred practice are core elements in the modernisation agenda being promoted by New Labour.

Eliminating structural poverty was a crucial empowerment issue for the new social movements including those led by older people in organisations like the Gray Panthers in the US and the British Pensioners and Trade Union Action Association in the UK who demanded incomes that enabled them to purchase what they wanted rather than means-tested benefits or vouchers, as these were stigmatising and humiliating. New Labour promised to tackle poverty, but its success in the past decade has been limited. It had reduced the number of poor people in Britain by 2 million by 2004, primarily among families with children and pensioners – a 3 and 5 per cent drop respectively. However, poverty remains at twice 1979 levels. For disabled people of working age, it rose by 3 per cent (Palmer et al., 2005). By 2007, 3.8 million children remained in poverty, as compared with 4.2 million when Blair took over from the Tories. The failure of the poverty strategy meant that Prime Minister Blair presided over a period in which British children suffered more deprivation, poorer relationships with parents, and more drug and alcohol misuse than in any other rich country (UNICEF, 2007).

Labour saw waged work as key to eliminating poverty for people of working age and affected this policy through New Deal programmes aimed at young people, older people, unemployed people and single mothers, for example Connexions, the New Deal 50+, New Deal for Unemployed People and New Deal for Lone Parents respectively. This approach failed to address non-waged and low-paid work, which was eschewed by men who needed employment but sought interesting long-term jobs and reasonable rates of pay. Nor did it raise women working on low wages out of poverty. The New Deal attempted to change individual behaviour but not the corporate structures or social relations demanded by many in the new social movements, including those in the anti-globalisation movement. The state's emphasis has resulted in anti-oppressive or empowering practice focusing on micro- rather than macro-level issues, thereby limiting its potential to transform wider social relations.

A plethora of policy initiatives with a punitive, authoritarian populist orientation have demonised certain client groups (Jordan and Jordan, 2000; Dominelli, 2004a), for example antisocial behaviour orders (ASBOs) for young offenders, detention and limited access to welfare benefits for asylum seekers, moralising attitudes to teenage mothers, and patronising approaches to poor parents who are held responsible for young people's transgressions, as occurred to Patricia Amos from Banbury. She was imprisoned (under the 1996 Education Act) in 2002 and 2004 when her children truanted. These approaches aim to manage risk and uncertainty by setting boundaries around individual behaviour. None of these responses address the structural inequalities that frame people' lives in deprived, disenchanted neighbourhoods with limited job opportunities and schools that lack stimulation for alienated young people. These government initiatives have complicated social workers' interventions as they often contradict empowering approaches to practice. A critical practitioner would engage with these complications to support this mother in turning her life around by enabling her to see how her life had been configured around them, the role her behaviour played in reinforcing their impact on her family, the constraints it placed on what work practitioners could do with her, and, working in collaboration with others, to identify these weaknesses in policy and resource availability for policy makers and the public more generally.

Professionalisation

Social work has struggled to establish a professional identity since its inception in the late nineteenth century when it was denied professional status because it did not have restricted entry to its ranks, its own body of knowledge and autonomy in regulating members as did established professions like medicine and law (Flexner, 1915). This definition of professionalism ignored social workers' attempts to develop new ideas about professional identity because the profession was formed and dominated by women who were interested in involving their 'clients' in improving their lives. The founders of the profession were also aware of its dependent status and moral basis. These latter two points eventually converged under the auspices of the Charity Organisation Society (COS), which took the lead in developing social work practice and training in the UK and was then copied in other English-speaking countries including the US (Kendall, 2000). The COS approach to social work practice focused on individual 'cases' that were 'carried' by a practitioner and gave it a moralising dimension that held people responsible for their plight, including structural problems such as unemployment and poor housing. The COS view was opposed by those involved in the settlement movement (Gilchrist and Jeffs, 2001), who were concerned about the lack of opportunity for poor people in both employment and housing and highlighted the structural nature of this absence.

Social work's lack of status has been a source of tension and is expressed as the public's lack of confidence in social workers' capacity to intervene appropriately in difficult and complex situations and its location at the bottom of any professional hierarchy. This has resulted in other professions, particularly health, psychiatry and psychology, appropriating as their own many areas of practice that had been developed by social workers. This is likely to increase under the modernisation agenda or New Labour's attempts to make public services more responsive to the wishes of service users and bring practitioners under managerial control. This is because the replacement of local authority personal SSDs with multiprofessional teams based in education for children and health for older people has left social workers in the minority in these teams dominated by other professionals and lessened their status by being positioned at the bottom of the multiprofessional labour pyramid. Social work is characterised by permeable borders that can initiate conflict over terrain that can be appropriated by others who redefine its boundaries differently. The loss of SSDs as an identifiable institutional base for the profession has left it homeless and liable to lose its sense of purpose as broader organisational priorities begin to drive the work they do. For example, this can occur if social workers are employed in agencies not committed to service user empowerment because breaking even financially supersedes other considerations. Commentators such as Clarke (1996) were concerned that these developments would lead to the demise of social work as a profession. Lymbery (2005) argues that the modernisation agenda can lead to new opportunities for social workers to redefine their interventions if they grasp these wholeheartedly and work with service users to create new paradigms for practice. A critical practitioner would reflect upon ways in which new opportunities are opening up to strengthen its professional claims. These would include aiming for excellence, empowering service users, utilising scarce resources wisely and obtaining recognition for its skills in working with vulnerable people on complex problems.

CASE EXAMPLE

Jenny was a volunteer in an older people's home trying to gain experience before she began studying for an MA in social work. She was tidying up when she overheard a conversation between the family members of an older woman who had died earlier in the day. The brother was saying: 'I think we should use [name of funeral home] because the social worker said it was a good one to go for.' The sister replied: 'I don't know, she didn't convince me.' As the arguments went back and forth, Jenny felt uneasy. She decided to ask the social worker why she recommended [name of funeral home]. 'Wasn't it against the code of ethics to recommend one particular provider over others?' she asked. The worker responded that in private establishments, this was permissible because their employer had a network of providers with whom he had good relationships, albeit he had not provided evidence to back up the assertion. Jenny was appalled because she felt strongly that this was wrong and wondered what she should do. What action(s), if any, would you advise Jenny to take?

In the UK, employers and government have been dissatisfied with the capacity of social work educators to deliver practitioners who could turn up in the office the day after they completed a course to engage in office routines effectively and efficiently and without further need for training or supervision. The three-year degree introduced in the UK in 2003 was an attempt to respond to these concerns by raising the time spent in practice to 100 days a year. However, the government did not ensure the funding for local authorities to provide sufficient high-quality placements, and programme providers (as they are now called) are struggling to meet demand. The qualification in practice teaching is no longer compulsory and statutory placements are living off previous expenditures in preparing practitioners for this highly skilled, but underrated task. Placements in the voluntary sector also have difficulties in providing qualified practitioners willing to supervise students. This issue threatens to overwhelm programme providers and might increase litigation as students seek to ensure that they meet the requirements to successfully complete a course when they are paying a significant proportion of the fees for their education.

Having professional qualifications should increase an individual's potential to exercise skills, criticality and professional autonomy in ways that effectively support service users, facilitate their search for excellence in what they do, and acquire employment in a global market. Portability of qualifications and employers being able to assume that a particular qualification means a certain level of skills and knowledge are essential in a world of mobile, migrant workers including practitioners. Professional and highly skilled workers can make mobility a matter of personal choice rather than being forced into it through poverty, natural disaster or armed conflict. The European Union (EU), which has made labour mobility a centrepiece of its economic prosperity and stability, has promoted harmonisation across different educational systems and enshrined it in the Bologna Process. For social workers, this has meant that a three-year qualifying award is to become the norm, a move that is advantageous in countries where social work had not been taught in universities, but disadvantageous in those where four-year degrees were the norm (Juliusdottir and Petersson, 2004).

Research-led practice

The evidence base on which practice is founded has been low and the research base of the profession needs further development (JUC SWEC, 2007). The government has promoted evidence-based practice (EBP), but this has been associated with narrow views about evidence, namely, that which is empirical. This development has enabled service users to ask important questions about who does research and what role it plays in responding to needs and developing services. But it has devalued experiential practice, which is a source of knowledge that service users appreciate and have successfully used to develop alternative services that meet their needs. Service users, particularly disabled people, have demanded training in research methods and insist on 'no research on us without us' (Barnes, 2003).

User-led research can contradict government policy, which has sought to routinise knowledge through bureaucratic measures that record and keep track of what constitutes 'good practice', defined largely in terms of 'what works'. In England, the creation of the Social Care Institute for Excellence (SCIE) to disseminate research and good practice was a move in this direction. It was paralleled by the Scottish Institute for Excellence in Social Work Education (SIESWE) in Scotland. Both bodies were based on the NHS's National Institute for Health and Clinical Excellence (NICE), which promotes EBP in the health service. These organisations have been critiqued for the narrowness of their research base and politicised funding that is given only for specific projects.

Conclusion

Social work is in exciting if fraught times. Its future is uncertain, but there is a lot to play for as it seeks to reposition itself in changed and changing conditions that are not primarily of its own making. Growing inequalities, housing shortages, rising food and fuel prices and the threat of unemployment can combine to confine social work interventions to the dustbin of history as irrelevant or parasitic, in the way that mass action against poverty in nineteenth-century London tolled the death knell for the COS that invented 'scientific case-work' (Stedman-Jones, 1971), unless practitioners find new responses to the new circumstances they face. Globalisation offers opportunities and challenges that can enhance social workers' reputation for promoting human wellbeing. At the same time, globalisation threatens social work's value orientation by privileging profits before people. However, social workers can resist these pressures through collective action in which they either take the lead or act as allies in struggles organised by others, for example the anti-globalisation movement, through demands for social accountability and responsibility from global corporations. Additionally, social workers can use their professional organisations and their endeavours to raise ethical actions and standards in professional practice, for example the IASSW and IFSW's global standards and ethical documents, and lobby for changes in national legislation to enhance human wellbeing for both local residents and asylum seekers and refugees. These are activities that social workers can use to promote social work as a profession rooted in interdependence, solidarity and citizenship entitlements that must transcend national borders to ensure human wellbeing. Engaging in critical, reflexive practice is one way of addressing these wider issues and the complexities of contemporary social work and assist in repositioning the profession in more emancipatory directions.

Modernisation is equally ambiguous. It promises consumer choice that seductively offers freedom to make decisions about services while it disenfranchises those who are considered socially deviant and/or income poor and manages workers through regulatory and supervisory regimes that are rote and bureaucratic instead of supportive and conducive to the development of good practice. Structural inequalities continue to shape the lives of service users despite policy commitments to eradicating these and social workers continue to focus on micro-level interventions while forgetting the meso- and macro-levels because they seem out of reach. In this, they can receive the reward of a 'job well done' as individuals, be thanked by service users for practical help that eases their lives a little (Beresford et al., 2006) and continue to leave structural issues for someone else to address while expecting marginalised people to prove resilient in the face of enormous odds. Tackling the complexities imposed on their work in changing inappropriate forms of personal behaviour and reducing structural inequalities is possible if practitioners reflect upon what they do through a critical reflexive lens.

Other chapters extend the dialogue begun here by focusing on specific issues, dilemmas and controversies. These indicate that the contexts within which social work is practised and developed are constantly shifting in circumstances that respond to external forces, activities generated by service users and policy makers, and the aspirations of practitioners and academics. Readers are invited to contribute to this process by reflecting upon their own life experiences in relation to what has been written. To give you, the readers, maximum space, there is no predetermined order in which to read the chapters that follow. Your choice will prevail. Hence, I have resisted describing the structure of this section in sequential order, preferring instead to encourage you to read the content of a particular chapter as an element within an organic whole at the point at which you choose to explore a specific topic. This way of proceeding means that chapters from other sections of the book can be brought in without erecting artificial boundaries between one part and another. Through this means, I hope to encourage you to make links between the different chapters in the book for yourself and consider the specific meaning of critical social work in contexts that are examined for their relevance to particular situations.

For a broader critical context for social work, see Chapter 6 and for wider changes affecting social work, see Chapter 3.

Tomlinson, D. and Trew, W. (eds) (2002) Equalising Opportunities, Minimising Oppression: A Critical Review of Anti-discriminatory Policies in Health and Social Welfare, London, Routledge. Encompasses a range of authors who explore the difficulties that social workers have in changing practice and repositioning themselves in contradictory discourses about what social work is about.

Dominelli, L. (2007) *Revitalising Communities in a Globalising World*, Aldershot, Ashgate. Contains a collection of chapters examining major challenges to social work under globalisation in the UK and other parts of the world. They include a range of marginalised voices from survivors of disasters to indigenous peoples creating their own forms of welfare practice.

Ferguson, I. (2008) *Reclaiming Social Work: Challenging Neoliberalism and Promoting Social Justice*, London, Sage. Explores social work's commitment to social justice in trying circumstances and concludes that it is important to be rooted in social movements if social work is to be true to its commitment to liberating values.

VIVIENE E. CREE

3 The changing nature of social work

Chapter overview

This chapter discusses the changes taking place in social work in the UK, while setting these in the context of European and global developments. In particular, it focuses on political and organisational changes and those taking place at the level of the individual practitioner.

Threading through the political, organisational and individual changes taking place in social work in the UK are a particular set of discourses – ideas and practices – that determine what social work is and should be, and what society is and should be. These are not, of course, peculiarly UK discourses. Similar debates are taking place within social work in the US and Europe, where similar – and sometimes different – resolutions have been found. The scale of change has been such that it has been necessary to make choices about what will be discussed in this chapter. In consequence, some issues have either been left out, or touched on only in passing. This says as much about the diverse and complex nature of social work as it does about my selection.

Political changes

Political changes have transformed Europe in the past 20 years. The break-up of the former Soviet Union in 1991 led to new alliances and the formation of new nation-states. In the UK, political change was expressed in the drive for a form of devolution within the current constitutional settlement, as well as a concerted effort to achieve a peaceful resolution to the long-running 'Troubles' in Northern Ireland.

In 1999, the first elections to a Scottish Parliament and the National Assembly for Wales were held, marking a culmination of years of campaigning for some kind of constitutional change in Scotland and Wales. In Scotland, devolution was not simply understood as an exercise in administration. It was charged with a mission to bring about real changes in Scottish society: to 'promote social welfare', as promised in the Social Work (Scotland) Act of 1968. The actual management of the new constitutional settlement suggests something rather less ambitious in scope. Some matters that have great significance for social work and society (notably social security and employment) remain 'reserved' ones: they apply to the UK as a whole and are dealt with by the UK government based at Westminster.

The UK Parliament continues to have power over the constitution, foreign policy, defence, the UK fiscal and economic system, common markets, employment legislation, social security, transport safety and regulation and other areas that are subject to regulation by the UK. Some matters remain devolved issues. The Scottish Parliament has powers to make primary legislation on a wide range of devolved matters including social work, health, education, housing, criminal law, prisons, police and fire services, food standards, sport, arts and local government. The Welsh Assembly has neither tax-raising powers nor full law-making powers. It does, however, handle hundreds of pieces of secondary legislation each year. Political changes in Northern Ireland have been longer in coming, and have been the focus of much activity in recent years. The so-called 'peace process' began in 1994 with the Provisional Irish Republican Army (IRA) ceasefire. From this time on, determined efforts were made to reach a political settlement between the UK government and politicians north and south of the border. This was not a straightforward process. Serious acts of violence and atrocities were committed at various points along the way, and, as a result, early attempts to bring a form of self-government to Northern Ireland broke down. Devolution was finally achieved for the Northern Ireland Assembly on Tuesday 8 May 2007, following the election of a four-party Executive of 12 ministers. The Northern Ireland Assembly is now widely regarded to be working well; a new committee for health, social services and public safety undertakes a scrutiny, policy development and consultation role with respect to the Department of Health, Social Services and Public Safety and plays a key role in the consideration and development of legislation (see www.niassembly.gov.uk/).

The new constitutional arrangements across the UK have been the subject of much debate. Critics point out that devolution took place within the context of strong, centralising government, and was only ever intended to be partial. It is claimed that devolution was principally an exercise in regulation; it was 'a way of ensuring that local authorities perform up to the centre's standards' (Jordan, 2000: 68). But, writing as someone who has lived through the changes in Scotland, I believe that the impact of devolution has been more than this. The creation of a parliament in Scotland brought with it a new confidence in the idea that Scotland might develop its own approaches. The advent of a degree of proportional representation in the new structures has also led to the arrival of new voices within the devolved structures, including the voices of more women. So, for example, although only 20 per cent of UK Members of Parliament (MPs) are women, 40 per cent of members of the Scottish Parliament are women, as are 50 per cent of the National Assembly for Wales (EOC, 2007). Decision-making has also been made more transparent by the introduction of committees with 'lay' (non-politician) representation; politicians from all sides of the political spectrum have demonstrated a commitment to consultation and participation. Devolution in government has led to devolution of power in other areas too, so that large UK voluntary organisations such as Barnardo's followed the lead of the UK government in introducing greater autonomy for their Welsh and Scottish offices.

The new constitutional arrangements in the UK have led to the possibility of a greater diversity of approaches towards social care. There are, however, developments taking place on a global scale that are more likely to lead to convergence, not just within the UK, but within industrialised countries as a whole. The impact of economic organisation on an international scale has been that individual countries can no longer function as closed societies, if this was ever truly possible. Decisions taken at international level govern the capacity of individual countries to act in all spheres of life, political, economic and social. This can have positive spin-offs for countries and individuals within them. For example, the adoption of the UN Convention on the Rights of the Child in 1989 led to important changes in legislation and childcare practice in all the member states that have signed the declaration. Two articles in the UN Convention have proved particularly influential to policy makers, practitioners and researchers in the UK: Article 12, the right of children to express an opinion and to have that opinion taken into account, and Article 13, the right to information and freedom of expression. Both the 1989 Children Act in England and Wales and the Children (Scotland) Act of 1995 demonstrate this new concern for children's views being heard and being taken into account in social work and legal decision-making processes, as does the Children (Northern Ireland) Order 1995.

Similarly, the European Convention on Human Rights 1950 has led to major realignments within the organisation of social and legal affairs in the UK, as demonstrated by the enforcement in October 2000 of the Human Rights Act 1998. The Human Rights Act 1998 makes it unlawful for a 'public authority' to behave in any way that is not compatible with the provisions of the European Convention on Human Rights. The 'public authority' includes all courts and tribunals, central and local government, the NHS and any organisation whose functions are of a public nature – likely to include voluntary and independent, as well as statutory, social work agencies.

The effects of globalisation are not, however, always experienced as benign. The benefits of globalisation increasingly flow directly into the global market and no longer serve to create jobs or augment tax revenue in the countries where the activities originated (Adams, 2000; Barrell et al., 2006). In consequence, even within the European Community, members compete with one another 'as global, economic and technical rivals' as globalisation generates new opportunities for 'both competition and harmonisation across increasingly fragile national boundaries' (Adams, 2000: 1). The influx of migrants to the UK from the former Eastern European countries demonstrates the reality of this. Over 200,000 workers from the eight EU accession countries (the 'A8': the Czech Republic, Estonia, Hungary, Latvia, Lithuania, Poland, Slovakia and Slovenia) came to the UK in 2005 and 2006, filling gaps in the labour market, particularly in business and management, administration, hospitality and catering, agriculture, and the food manufacturing industries, and contributing to the success of the UK economy. Meanwhile, the migrants' countries of origin have experienced serious labour shortages and the loss of younger adults to provide informal care for their elderly relatives (Home Office, 2007).

Organisational changes

Changes at an organisational level in the UK reflect the changes that have been taking place across Europe and in other continents. The mechanism of the market – familiar in US social services for many years – was introduced in the late 1990s throughout public sector agencies: social services, transport, higher education and the health service. Statutory social work agencies saw the creation of a split between 'purchaser' and 'provider' roles, and the introduction of charges for services, the contracting out of services and the promotion of competition between the statutory, voluntary and private sectors (Pinkney, 1998: 263). The Labour government, which came to power in May 1997, began with a **modernisation** agenda: what was described as 'modern', 'joined-up' government, with national strategies for combating issues such as social exclusion and unemployment. But for all the rhetoric of change, the government continued the previous Conservative administration's strategies of ever-tighter control of public spending, increasing involvement of the private sector in public services, and intensifying regulation, inspection and centralised control of social work and social workers. And it was legislation that proved to be the mechanism

> **Modernisation** refers to the use of new policies, strategies and methods to bring about progressive change, usually driven by a political and economic agenda. For example, the Labour government that came to power in the UK in 1997 introduced a swathe of public policy initiatives under the headline 'the modernisation agenda', with the aim of regulating the performance of agencies delivering public services, through partnerships between the public and private sectors.

through which changes in policy and practice have been managed, as the government led a whole programme of legislation affecting work with adults, children and families and offenders (see, for example, the 2004 Children Act and DH, 2006).

The Third Way for social care: modernising services

The government White Paper, *Modernising Social Services* (DH, 1998a) set the scene for the future direction of social work and social services in the UK. The stated driving force behind the White Paper was the urgent need for change; social services were accused of 'failing to provide the support that people should expect' (1998a: 5). The recommendation was for a '**Third Way** for social care': one which would promote independence, improve

> **Third Way** The Third Way is a label for a particular cluster of political beliefs that offer a compromise between centralised state solutions to public issues and heavy reliance on the free market. The appeal of Third Way politics to modern political parties seems to be that it offers a means of revitalising support around middle-ground policies that break with the extremes of traditional left or right-wing politics.

consistency, ensure equality of opportunity to children (especially in relation to education), protect adults and children from abuse or neglect in the care system, improve standards in the workforce, and improve delivery and efficiency. This was to be achieved principally through the reorganisation of social work services and greater scrutiny and control of social work and social workers. A key priority of government was to seek to break down the organisational barriers that existed between services and create 'new shared ways of delivering services that are individually tailored, accessible and more joined up' (DH, 2000a: 30). New partnerships were encouraged, with users and carers, between health and social care, across the local authority (between housing and education), and with private and voluntary sector agencies. Health and social care services were early targets for change, as outlined in the Health Act 1999 and taken forward in the Health and Social Care Act 2001. There has been considerable debate about the eventual outcome of these changes. Some commentators have foreseen the end of social work; it is suggested that the profession would simply be swallowed up by its larger and more powerful partners in the field of health and education. Others suggest that the organisational changes have the potential to benefit service users, if they lead to more multidisciplinary working and greater coordination of service delivery (Bywaters and McLeod, 2001). In reviewing the changing scene, Morris (2008) acknowledges that some multi-agency working rests heavily on the role of social work, but, she argues, there are tensions too, particularly around the pressures on social work to develop new skills and practices, as well as the need for social work to consolidate its identity vis-à-vis other professions.

Statutory services are not the only agencies to have demonstrated new joined-up thinking. The call for change was also for new partnerships between statutory, voluntary and private sectors, as well as between agencies, service users and their carers. The voluntary sector in the UK has always been a key provider of social work services, and, increasingly, the private sector is also making a contribution to services, particularly for older people and those with mental health problems (Lewis, 1996). New multi-agency groupings have been formed to manage services (such as the new care trusts for health and social care). Perhaps even more significantly, the private sector is being invited to fund key statutory services, including aspects of education and health services. The consequences of this are, as yet, unknown, but critics assert that corporate cultures are the exact opposite of the idea of 'public' service. Lessons from social work in the US give credence to such a view. In 2000, Meinert et al. argued that the public sector was increasingly being co-opted by the private sector, through the managed healthcare movement. Reviewing the situation again in 2005, Clark and Woods-Waller note that all social programmes in the US are under attack. One of social workers' responses has been to mount a highly visible public education campaign as a way of 'selling' the importance of social work.

Modernising is, of course, about more than joined-up services. Modern social work also means the increasing use of information technology (IT) for managing information and service user data and for controlling the workforce, for communication and for web-based enquiries. Social workers today use computers for a wide range of service-related activities, from accessing research databases to inputting service user details. Again, this development is not without consequences, which might be both positive and negative, as social work practitioners struggle to apply applications and computer programs that are not always either easy to use or even fit for purpose (Cree and Davis, 2007; Burton and van den Boek, 2008). While bringing the possibility of easier communication and the creation of new social networks, IT has also brought with it the capacity for surveillance and control to a degree unthinkable in the past. Networked computer systems, electronic 'tagging' and DNA screening bring evermore sophisticated ways in which the 'disciplinary society' can 'police' its members (Foucault, 1977). More fundamentally, Meinert et al. (2000: 62) argue that the increasingly elaborate forms of microtechnologies available to ever-larger numbers of human professionals have 'eroded the centrality of face-to-face conduct'. This will be considered further as we explore individual changes.

Regulation and inspection

Organisational change is evident in the explosion of different ways of measuring and directing standards in social work and social care, targeted at both services and service providers. This process began with the introduction of 'performance indicators' to a large number of social service functions, and the creation of new service frameworks and targets for measuring 'Best Value' outcomes. The Best Value regime, which was introduced in the 1999 Local Government Act and came into force in April 2000, replaced compulsory competitive tendering in local government, compelling social services to scrutinise the services they provide and justify their effectiveness and efficiency. In April 2002, inspection and regulation units previously run by local authorities transferred to new non-departmental public bodies answerable directly to central government. The National Care Standards Commission (NCSC) is responsible for the inspection and regulation of almost all forms of residential and domiciliary care in England, including care homes, children's homes, nursing agencies, schools, adoption and fostering agencies, and private and voluntary hospitals. Similar arrangements exist in Scotland, with the Scottish Commission for the Regulation of Care (SCRCC), and in Wales, with the Commission for Care Standards (CCS).

While social work practice has become more regulated, so new arrangements have been put in place for the regulation of service providers (social workers and social care personnel) and social work training. The Care Standards Act 2000 and Regulation of Care (Scotland) Act 2001 required that all qualified social workers should be registered. Social workers were invited to register from April 2003, then from 2005, the title of 'social worker' was protected for the first time, so that only those with an 'entitling qualification' (set at degree level) could call themselves social workers. Registration became increasingly important as social work in the UK moved closer to other professional groups, all of whom had been registered professions for many years; the first professional body to be registered in the UK was the General

Medical Council, formed as a result of the 1858 Medical Act. The question was inevitably asked: if doctors, teachers, health visitors and psychiatric nurses were registered, why not social workers? Four new social work registration bodies were instituted in 2002: the General Social Care Council in England (GSCC), accountable to the secretary of state for health; the Scottish Social Services Council (SSSC), accountable to the Scottish Parliament; the Cyngor Gofal Cymru/Care Council for Wales (CGC/CCW), accountable to the National Assembly for Wales; and the Northern Ireland Social Care Council (NISCC).

Alongside registration for social workers in the UK came the upgrading of the social work qualification from a two-year diploma to a three-year honours degree (four years in Scotland). The new degree was introduced in 2003 in England and in 2004 in the rest of the UK. In keeping with the 'modern' agenda, its standards and requirements are set in the context of the National Occupational Standards for Social Work (Topss, 2002), which offer a set of descriptions of the functions of social workers. The standards were developed from a detailed analysis of what social workers do through consultation with employers and practitioners and they include service users' own statements of their expectations of social workers. New statutory codes of practice for social care (social service) employers and employees have also been incorporated into the National Occupational Standards. They are for all kinds of social workers, statutory or independent sector, working for health, education or for social services (and from justice agencies in Scotland), regardless of whom their service users are (Cree and Myers, 2008: 6).

The pressure for these changes was both internal and external. Professional associations and social work educationalists had campaigned for many years for change which, they believed, would lead to the upgrading of the social work profession. Since the 1980s, the growing service user and patient lobby had also pressed for improvements in the training and practice of social workers; registration became one part of this wider programme of demands for reform (Beresford and Croft, 2004). At the same time, membership of the EU brought with it the free movement of workers between member states, and, in this way, drew attention to the different educational requirements for social workers across Europe. While the minimum requirement for a social worker in other parts of Europe was a three-year undergraduate degree, the UK two-year diploma looked increasingly out of step. The movement of workers had another influence, as social work agencies in the UK sought to fill vacancies by recruiting staff from developing countries and other English-speaking countries, notably Australia and New Zealand. As a result, employers had to find new ways of regulating the workforce, for the safety and protection of all.

All these developments have the potential to provide positive outcomes for social service delivery. Standards in the workforce may improve, as social workers develop methods and systems based on good practice, rather than local custom. The so-called 'postcode lottery' may be less apparent, as those using services become more aware of the services they should expect, and as services become more standardised across the UK. Again, those using services may feel some reassurance that those working with them are trained to degree level and are registered to do the job. But there is an undercurrent running beneath these developments suggesting that a more circumspect approach should be taken. The increasing regulation and inspection is very 'top down'; it is an exercise in government, not peer control, and the centralised monopoly of power may have a detrimental effect on local autonomy and accountability. It also implies more surveillance and external management of social workers and social work education. This is, in large measure, a response to the 'risk society' (Beck, 1992). The realities of risk and uncertainty are managed by the introduction of new systems for organising professional practice and new mechanisms for predicting future risks and their potential negative outcomes. The end result is that the social work task becomes increasingly broken down into discrete units which can be measured and controlled. The push within social work towards evidence-based practice similarly seeks to provide answers in a world that is increasingly complex and uncertain (Webb, 2001, 2006).

Individual changes

Just as social work has been transformed by constitutional and organisational changes, so there have been important changes at the individual level, at the level of service users and service providers.

Increasingly, social work 'clients' have become 'customers', and the introduction of direct payments has given service users more power over the nature of the services they receive, transforming the role of the social worker to that of adviser and facilitator. This has been experienced extremely positively by those using services and their carers. So-called **personalisation** means that support services can be organised in ways which are user, not provider or agency, led (Leece and Bornat, 2006; Priestley et al., 2007). Meanwhile, many social workers have become budget holders: they work as care managers, assessing need and arranging packages of care; a small number have become inspectors regulating standards in care. This process has been referred to as the 'McDonaldisation' of welfare (Powell, 2001). The settings in which social workers are located have also changed. They are as likely to be working in a GP surgery, school or hospital, as in a local authority social work or social service department, and their colleagues in the future will be nurses, health visitors, occupational therapists and teachers as well as social workers. Some social workers have 'jumped ship' altogether, leaving the statutory sector to become care providers in the volun-

Personalisation Personalisation has acquired a distinctive meaning in UK social policy and legislation in the early twenty-first century, reflecting the political trend towards developing welfare policies that meet people's needs by transferring responsibility (and associated risks) for delivery from the state to the individual. Personalisation can be viewed positively as an opportunity for the individual who needs services to share in the management of their delivery. It can also be criticised for allowing the market to dominate the supply of care services, misrepresenting the interests of carers and people who use services, while deprofessionalising qualified practitioners.

tary or private sectors. Interestingly, this plurality of identity is much closer to the European model, where social workers are more likely to be scattered among a range of central and local government agencies and civil society organisations (Lorenz, 1994; Campanini and Frost, 2004).

Social workers have experienced the changes in a variety of ways. Some have described feeling high levels of anxiety and pressure, as they strive to maintain the social work role in the face of challenges from other care professionals, such as occupational therapists, district nurses and community psychiatric nurses. Others have complained that they can no longer use their social work skills as they would wish. There are simply too many forms to complete, and practitioners struggle to maintain individual discretion and creativity in their work. The reality of this was explored by Cree and Davis's (2007) text, *Social Work: Voices From The Inside*. This study did not shy away from criticising aspects of social work practice that were seen as negative and perhaps even damaging to service users and social workers alike. But it also demonstrated the resilience of practitioners, their willingness to continue to take risks, to try new approaches, and to build supportive and democratic relationships with those with whom they were working. In an earlier study of social workers working in local authority social services departments, Jones (2001: 551) suggested that the manifestations of stress and unhappiness were 'various, serious and pervasive', with the greatest source of stress coming from above – the agency – and not from the clients. While this picture of social work practice remains evident in Cree and Davis's research, there are also more hopeful accounts here of the positive value of social work to those giving and receiving services.

Recent reviews of social workers' roles and tasks have been conducted across the UK. In Scotland, *Changing Lives: Summary Report of the 21st Century Social Work Review* (Scottish Executive, 2006a) highlighted that social work needed to change because 'our lives are changing'. It noted the lack of time available for social workers to develop therapeutic relationships with clients, yet social workers themselves valued this highly. The report described social service departments as 'risk-averse' in their decision-making, and social workers as 'overly driven by processes' rather than outcomes. A similar evaluation in England was conducted by the Commission for Social Care Inspection, which published its first report in December 2005, *The State of Social Care in England, 2004–05*. This review stresses the positive difference that social care can make, but suggests that, most of all, people want independence, choice and control in their lives, and to be treated with dignity. It was followed up in 2007 with a public consultation on the roles and tasks of social work, with the aim of defining 'a profession with service users at its heart, capable of meeting the challenges of 21st century society' (GSCC, 2007). The findings from this consultation present a largely positive picture of social work in England and define the social work profession as being committed to enabling every child and adult to fulfil their potential, working in partnership with them whenever possible and embodying values including equality and human rights. Wales has carried out its own review of social work, *Social Work in Wales: A Profession to Value* (ADSS Cymru, 2005), which asserts that it is not pay which is the driver in encouraging practitioners to remain in social work, but the culture of the organisation; this is therefore where improvement needs to take place. This is mirrored in the recent review of public administration in Northern Ireland, which anticipates a major overhaul of the way the workforce engages with other professionals and service users.

Key questions remain, however. While there is little in any of the review reports that anyone could disagree with, where is the space for debate, ambiguity and different perspectives in this rather 'motherhood-and-apple-pie' picture with which we are presented? And what about the absences in the reports? The vision of social work in all the reports seems more concerned with the promise of concrete knowledge and evidence-based research than it is with the more messy world of ideas and theories. And on a more specific level, how achievable is the aim of 'personalised services' in a context of limited (and perhaps even declining) resources? How can social work contribute to community building while focusing on high-risk/need cases? What additional resources are going to be needed, and for how long, if social work is to live up to its promises?

Conclusion

'We live in a society defined by risk, polarisation, global markets, chronic change and fragmentation' (Powell, 2001: 14). Social work, situated as it is between the individual and society, inevitably reflects the wider society within which it is located (Cree, 2002). It is not surprising, therefore, that social work in this postmodern age should be undergoing major change and reformation. But there is more to consider here. Social work demonstrates a compromise solution – a compromise between liberal ideas of freedom and personal autonomy and the need for the state to safeguard the functioning of society as a whole (Parton, 1996). As this compromise solution is always being challenged and modified, so social work itself has a contingency about its being, its task and direction by no means self-evident (Cree, 1995).

Looking ahead, it seems likely that we will see increasing convergence and diversity in the nature of social work across Europe, the US and beyond. Global economic forces and ITs mean that there will be an increasing transfer of resources, personnel and information in the years ahead, leading to some standardisation of practices and systems. At the same time, new alliances across Europe and the world as a whole suggest that there will continue to be different kinds of solutions to shared problems such as immigration and refugees, poverty and social exclusion, humanitarian disasters and wars. In 2001, Lymbery argued that social work in the UK was at a crossroads: it could either continue to fight to hold onto its nascent professional status, in the face of the encroachment of other professional groupings and the steady march of managerialism, or it could take a step back and try to recover its purpose and its expertise. Social work remains 'at a crossroads'.

It has a strong tradition of working alongside people, valuing difference and showing concern for social justice and inequality. I believe that these are the aspects of social work that we must build on in the future, wherever social work is located.

For an examination of the wider significance of social work, see Chapter 6, and for a discussion of policy-making links between poverty and social work, see Chapter 7.

www.csci.org.uk/PDF/state_of_social_care_summary.pdf   *The State of Social Care in England* Report.

www.socialworkscotland.org.uk/resources/pub/ChangingLivesSummary Report.pdf   Scotland's *Changing Lives* Report.

Cree, V.E. and Davis, A. (2007) *Social Work: Voices from the Inside*, London, Routledge. Presents the narratives of 59 service users, carers and practitioners.

Cree, V.E. and Myers, S. (2008) *Social Work: Making a Difference*, Bristol, Policy Press. Explores social work across diverse settings through case studies.

Morris, K. (ed.) (2008) *Social Work and Multi-agency Working: Making a Difference*, Bristol, Policy Press. Outlines multi-agency practice in different settings.

Values, ethics and social work

4

This chapter examines the difficulties surrounding the task of trying to answer three main questions: How should social workers treat the people with whom they work? What is the purpose of social work as an activity in modern society? Why do we have social work? These resolve themselves into one principal difficulty – namely, the gap between the neatness and simplicity of abstract generalisation and the complexities of the real world of practice.

Chapter overview

Introduction and context

Social work across the UK has been a regulated profession, with the title 'social worker' being a protected title from 1 April 2005, such that only those who are professionally qualified and registered with the appropriate regulatory body may use the term to describe themselves. In other countries, social work has been a regulated profession for a much longer period (for example in France, the equivalent title 'assistant de service social' has been protected since 1953. Being a regulated profession requires that social workers in the UK must adhere to a code of practice, which is managed by the respective regulatory body for each of the UK countries: England (GSCC, 2004); Scotland (SSSC, 2004); Northern Ireland (Northern Ireland Social Care Council, 2004) and Wales (Cyngor Gofal Cymru/Care Council for Wales, 2004). Ideally, these codes of practice offer the prospect, tantalising if theoretical, of resolving value and ethical issues in social work. In practice, they do not, as the real world is complex, imprecise and messy. Getting to grips with social work values and **ethics** is rather like picking up a large, live wet fish from a running stream. Even if you are lucky enough to grab a fish, the chances are that just when you think you have caught it, the fish will vigorously slither out of your

Ethics refers to aspects of philosophy concerned with the principles of right and wrong that guide conduct. Professional practice is guided by a code of practice that reflects ethical principles based on generally recognised values.

hands and jump back into the stream. Values and ethics similarly slither through our fingers for a variety of reasons:

- we don't try hard enough to catch them, preferring the practical business of doing social work
- the subject matter, if we really investigate it, may sometimes seem complex, hard to grapple with and possibly obscure
- there is a lack of conceptual clarity about many of the terms used that form part of the lexicon of social work values and ethics
- the boundaries of social work values and ethics are imprecise and ill-defined, so the notion of what should constitute social work values and ethics is itself part of a discussion about the nature of social work values.

No doubt there are other reasons for not picking up this particular fish. Yet despite these difficulties, there is something that intuitively suggests that social work is bound up with values and ethics. According to the *Oxford English Dictionary*, ethics is 'the science of morals in human conduct', and surely social work is about human relationships and behaviour? Social workers have a professional duty to understand ethics and values, not least because social work practice contains a terrible potential for the misuse of power (Payne and Littlechild, 2000). In recent years, there has been a growth in popular interest in values and ethics and similar subjects that are part of the philosophical tradition (for example de Botton, 2000).

This chapter is grounded in the presumption that no consensus exists about value questions in social work. Evidence of the contested nature can be seen by looking at long-standing debates, for example concerning:

- the extent to which social work is grounded in Kantian ethics, that is, the view that it is sufficient for social workers to reach their own reasoned view about the ethical basis for social work (Downie, 1989; Webb and McBeath, 1989, 1990; Gould, 1990)
- the significance of **ideology** and knowledge in social work (Dominelli, 1990–91; Webb, 1990–91a, 1990–91b; Smith, 1992)
- the extent to which a social worker is responsible or accountable when something goes wrong (Hollis and Howe, 1987, 1990; Macdonald, 1990a, 1990b; Guthrie, 1998)
- debates about the spirituality and religiosity in social work (Rice, 2002).

Ideology refers to a set of related beliefs and ideas that justify a particular set of policies and actions. It excludes any others that are inconsistent with these.

These debates are inevitably open-ended where social work itself is intrinsically political, controversial and contested, and where the nature of practice is subject to constant change, for example through the dismemberment of social services departments and the consequent restructuring of the organisational landscape for the delivery of social work across health trusts, education departments and the growth in importance of voluntary agencies. Of particular importance has been the Labour government's 'modernisation project' and the introduction of performance management at organ-isation level (DH, 1998a, 2000a, 2006), as discussed by Dominelli in Chapter 2.

Understanding the scope of social work values and ethics

If, as suggested, the boundaries of the subject 'social work values and ethics' are them-selves subject to different interpretations, understanding the scope of such interpretations may be the first step to clarifying the ethical basis for social work prac-tice. A narrow or 'restricted description' of the scope of social work values and ethics might focus on:

- social workers' behaviour with clients, that is, professional ethics.

A 'mid-range description' would add to the above:

- the interface between social work and the law (see Chapter 8)
- the relationship of social work to religious belief systems, that is, theology
- the nature and form of social work knowledge – the knowledge we possess about social work and with what degree of certainty we hold that knowledge, that is, epistemology. This is perhaps the most fundamental issue faced by any discipline; for a recent discussion of the key issues, see Reid (2001)
- the nature of social work as a professional activity, that is, the sociology of professions
- the characteristics of social work organisations and their influence on the behav-iour of individual social workers, that is, managerial and organisational theory (see Chapter 9).

A 'broad definition' might further add:

- the function of social work in society, that is, political philosophy and political sociology (see Chapter 6)
- the construction of social work as a social activity, that is, social theory, for example postmodernism.

This delineation of three different interpretations of the scope of social work values and ethics, illustrated in Figure 4.1, is indicative of a broad range of notions and disci-plines that might legitimately fall within the rubric of social work ethics and values.

It can also be seen that this conceptualisation is itself potentially fluid and subject to possible future modification and debate. From these interpretations (some of which have received greater analysis than others) , it is evident that the subject matter of social work values is frequently, although not exclusively, defined by the interac-tion of different domains of knowledge (in particular those reliant upon philosophical forms of thinking) and social work practice.

Philosophy is about asking questions and is as much concerned with finding the best questions as with providing complete or incontrovertible answers. Likewise, in trying to understand values and ethics in social work, we should be as much concerned with the questions we ask as the answers we might find – not perhaps a satisfying position for the busy practitioner in search of help in dealing with a particular client. Over time, the questions that philosophers ask have changed, similarly, for social work values – a dynamic and evolving subdiscipline within the broader field of social work itself. In the rest of this chapter, two central themes in social work values and ethics will be examined, as examples of the issues embedded in different domains.

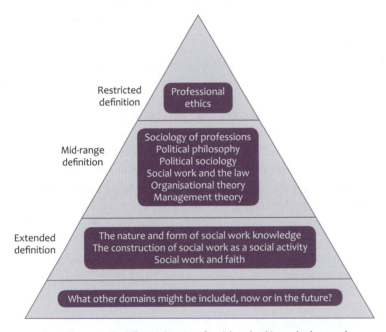

This figure illustrates the different domains of social work ethics and values: each section represents a different conceptualisation of the scope of social work ethics and values, from the most restricted to the most extended. You, the reader, might like to speculate upon these conceptualisations: are they sufficiently comprehensive, do they concur with your perceptions and how might these domains expand in the future?

Figure 4.1 The scope of social work values

Ethics and work with service users: a restricted description

The first question to ask ourselves might be:

How should social workers behave towards their clients?

This is obviously a useful question and one that social work practitioners need to answer for their everyday practice. Others might be: What are the boundaries of acceptable behaviour, either for themselves or their clients? For example, is it acceptable for a male social worker to provide comfort to a female client in distress by touching her (Doel and Shardlow, 2005)? To what extent does an older person, who is not caring for themselves, have the right to live as they choose (see, for example,

Horne, 1999: 39)? Should a child be removed from a carer who is a drug addict (Clark, 2000: 14)? Such apparently simple and straightforward questions immediately spawn a whole raft of other more problematic questions. Is the language in which these questions are framed sufficiently neutral or are terms used that have powerful emotional connotations, prejudicial implications for individuals or groups, highly contested meanings and so on (see, for example, Webb, 1994)? If any of these factors apply, it becomes even more difficult to think carefully about how to answer questions about how to behave with clients or when to intervene in clients' lives.

In this example, the word 'client' is problematic and other terms such as 'service user' or 'customer' might perhaps be preferred by some. The problem about using any of these words – 'client', 'service user' or 'customer' – is that they all carry implications about how people should be treated in everyday discourse. For example, 'customers' have certain legal rights and expectations about treatment when receiving services – increasingly, social work is, rightly or wrongly, being defined by legal requirements. Assuming that we can frame questions about how social workers should behave towards their 'clients', both in respect of personal interactions and more broadly about when to intervene in people's lives, in ways that do not presuppose answers on account of commonly held understandings of the terms used, then other definitional problems arise, such as, who are the clients: is it people who are receiving help from social workers, clients' families, those who might receive help and so on? Thus, to make sense of the original question, we need to be able to define carefully the situations and people to whom the question refers.

Despite the apparent prevarication about meaning and not wanting to wallow in difficulties, we can turn our attention to how others have sought to answer these questions concerning how social workers ought to behave towards their clients (using 'clients' as a generic term to refer to all who do or who might use social work services) by examining three of the most important types of response: the 'traditional list' of values, the professional code of ethics and the 'principle' approaches.

Lists of values and professional codes of ethics

Reamer (2005) distinguishes four distinct periods in the development of social work values and ethics in the US:

1 the morality period – late nineteenth and early twentieth century
2 the values period – 1950s–60s
3 the ethical theory and decision-making period – 1970s–80s
4 the ethical standards and risk management period – 1990 onwards.

This historical categorisation is a useful aid to understanding the nature of literature in this field and can be applied to the UK.

First, the morality period: during the early years of social work in the UK, practitioners, often motivated by Christian religious conviction or political zeal for social reform, tended to judge their clients' morality and behaviour (Younghusband, 1981). The individual practitioner's moral stance would be, to a large extent, the determinant of action.

Second, in the immediate postwar period, initial codified injunctions to social workers to adopt certain modes of behaviour towards clients emerged, often underpinned by US models of professional practice. Famously, Biestek (1961), a US Catholic priest, stands as the originator of a set of values that specified how social workers ought to behave with their clients; these included the following 'headline terms':

- individualisation
- the purposeful expression of feelings
- controlled emotional involvement
- acceptance
- a non-judgemental attitude
- client **self-determination**
- confidentiality.

Self-determination by service users is a widely accepted principle of social work practice. Self-determination commonly refers to a person's right to make choices and decisions and to act on their own behalf while exercising the same freedoms and rights possessed by other people.

Each of these implies a moral imperative that is determinate, apparently absolute and grounded in Christian faith. To know how to treat clients, a social worker only has to act in accord with the headline principle. How can a claim be made that such a list of principles has universal applicability for the social work profession? Similarly, how can the list be justified? Does it represent anything more than one individual's beliefs – a personal view of what social work values ought to be? Others developed similar but not identical lists. For this reason, Timms (1983) extensively criticised what he termed 'the list approach' to social work values. Nonetheless, some of the values contained within the 'lists', such as 'confidentiality' or 'self-determination', chime persistent chords within the social work profession.

Third, there is the ethical theory and decision-making period, or use of fundamental ethical principles. Answers to questions about how social workers ought to behave towards their clients can be found in the use of a fundamental moral principle to determine desired behaviour. For example, within professional social work practice, 'respect for persons' has been a frequently employed principle. This moral notion was fully explored by Downie and Telfer (1969), and is derived from Kant's moral principle of the categorical imperative. This is variously written, but among the best-known formulations are:

> I ought never to act except in such a way that I can also will that my maxim should become a universal law. (Kant, 1785, in Paton, 1948: 67)

> Act in such a way that you always treat humanity whether in your own person or in the person of any other, never simply as a means but always at the same time as an end. (Kant, 1785, in Paton, 1948: 91)

Through following these two principles, social workers are 'respecting persons'. Rather than having a set of prescribed or proscribed actions, this approach requires that if social workers wish to know how they ought to behave with their clients, they should consider the proposed action in the light of these two moral principles. This type of approach requires that social workers are fully able to engage in moral reasoning to determine how they ought to behave with their clients. The application of Kantian approaches in caring professions has been fully developed in the UK by Downie and Telfer (1980) and in the US by Reamer (1990).

Fourth, there is the ethical standards and risk management period, the current period, during which there has been a steady growth in the number of statements of ethical standards, sometimes termed a code of ethics, a code of conduct, a code of practice, or practice standards. These have been produced by various national professional associations, for example Australia (AASW, 2003), the UK (BASW, 1996), and the US (NASW, 1996, 1999); at international level by the International Association of Schools of Social Work jointly with the International Federation of Social Workers (IFSW, 2004); and by government agency as in the UK (Cyngor Gofal Cymru/Care Council for Wales, 2004; GSCC, 2004; Northern Ireland Social Care Council, 2004; SSSC, 2004). Often these codes are to be read in conjunction with a series of other documents such as the National Occupational Standards for Social Work (Topss, 2002). These various documents, some of which relate to the requirements of individual practice and some of which are concerned with organisational responsibilities, create an interlocking framework of required professional behaviours, some of which are located within an ethical domain. To know how to act towards clients/service users, social work must act in accord with these statements. Failure to comply with these codes of practice may lead to a social worker being brought before the respective professional disciplinary body that has the power to remove the social worker's registration and therefore the right to practice. Implementation is new and at the time of writing no research evidence was available about effectiveness. The codes of practice in the various UK countries contain various prescriptions such as: 'As a social service worker, you must protect the rights and promote the interests of service users and carers', which 'entails treating each person as in individual'. This has echoes of both Kantian philosophy and Biestek's list of values, but does not give guidance as to what is intended or how, for example, to reconcile conflict between two individuals. Similarly, certain actions are proscribed: 'in particular you must not ... put yourself or other people at unnecessary risk'. This is well intentioned and difficult to disagree with but does not state the nature of risk to be avoided. As can be seen from these examples, and more particularly the codes themselves, the contents of the codes of practice are highly general and do not in themselves provide much help to the social worker, or client for that matter, who wants to know how social workers ought to behave towards clients. For example, the codes do not provide any immediate answer to questions such as: 'Is it a social worker's duty to inform the police if they discover that a client has committed a crime?' The statements in the codes of ethics seem to prompt other questions, such as: 'How do I respect clients as individuals?' Such codes of practice have as much to do with the establishment of a sense of professional identity as providing answers to questions such as: How ought social workers behave towards their clients? Yet the codes purport to provide such help. They do offer some guidance, but at a very general level.

Having explored these different examples as ways of approaching the question, we may legitimately ask whether we are any nearer to being able to answer the question: How should social workers behave with their clients? The answer is yes we are; we now know some of the different ways in which the question has been approached. What we do not have is much of an answer about what a social worker should do in any particular situation – which is just the answer the practitioner needs. Answers may also be found by looking to clients themselves, who have defined their expectations of social workers, as evidenced in a series of research studies dating back to the seminal work by Mayer and Timms (1970) and more recently to practice guides such as that on the Dignity in Care campaign by Cass et al. (2008). One can also look to legal or procedural guidance provided by the government, as exemplified in the fields of safeguarding children (DH/DfEE/Home Office, 2006). Some such governmental statements tend to reduce professional autonomy and restrict the arena for independent professional decision-making and might, therefore, be seen as an attempt to deprofessionalise social work, removing the need for decision-making based on professional values by substituting a bureaucratic and procedural requirement (see Chapter 6). More practically, these procedural requirements may leave social workers fearful of making mistakes.

Social work and society: an extended definition

Our second group of questions is concerned with the function of social work:

> What is the purpose of social work as an activity in modern society?

> Why do we have social work?

Is it possible to conceive of a society without social work? Some of the newly emergent states of Eastern and central Europe functioned under communism without a social work profession (Deacon, 1992; Constable and Metha, 1993). In recent years, these states have moved quickly to establish social work – just as they are seeking to develop non-command-style economies and introduce market mechanisms (see, for example, Munday and Lane, 1998). This drive to develop social work in such states does not of itself establish that social work is a necessary function of modern industrial societies. However, it may well be that there is a functional need for social work in modern industrial societies, for example as Lorenz (1994: 4) writes:

> Broadly speaking, social work's origins coincide with the formation of modern Western nation states and are directly related to the internal stability that these states need.

Thus he argues that social work is necessary and contributes to the maintenance of social order, while Cannan et al. (1992) point to comparative and historical similarities in the emergence of social work in northern Europe in parallel with urbanisation and industrialisation. Perhaps the most persuasive argument that social work is functionally necessary to modern society has been propounded by Davies in *The Essential Social Worker* (1994). He argues, from a humanist perspective, that the function of social work is to help to maintain the fabric of society, a fabric that would otherwise be brittle and likely to fracture, as exemplified in the following quotation:

> In so far as there are common elements in social work they are best described by the general notion of maintenance: society maintaining itself in a relatively stable state by making provision for and managing people in positions of severe weakness, stress or vulnerability; and society maintaining its own members, without exception by commitment to humanist endeavour (Davies, 1994: 40).

Interestingly, in the second edition of the book, Davies (1985: 3) continued with a bold statement about the underlying purpose of social work:

> and its [social work's] emphasis on the idea of respect for the client, optimism for the future, and faith in the essential or at least potential unity of society.

We can only speculate about the reasons for the lost vision of a social work striving for a unified and harmonious society. Yet, Davies's vision of the function of social work emphasises the need to maintain the social order while seeing the operation of the state in the promotion of social work as being to further humanist ideals. The 'maintenance theory' of social work found in Davies's writings is essentially benign: he expresses a broad approval of the motives of the state and the consequent role of social work to maintain the social fabric. When a similar argument (in the sense that social work helps to maintain existing social structures) about the role of social work in society is advanced from a Marxist perspective, the timbre alters dramatically:

> Since its modern origins in the middle of the last century, social work has been one of the many strategies developed and deployed by the ruling class and the state for intervening in the lives of working people ... social work has to be considered as one of the agencies of class control and regulation. (Jones, 1983: 9)

Leonard (1976: 261) developed this argument further, suggesting that social work promotes a more compliant labour force and seeks the re-education of the 'underclass clientele who are seen as irresponsible and immature'. Here, social work is portrayed as a malignant force assisting dominant elites to maintain political and economic power over groups in society who are deemed to be a threat. In such a vision, social work is not acting in the interests of those it helps but is part of a set of social structures that oppress. However, these two different opinions – the Marxist and the maintenance theorist – do not diverge over what social workers actually do in society. It is in the significance, meaning and value of those actions, not for individuals but at the level of sociological or political explanation, that they differ. The type of position adopted by Leonard, which is critical of the position and role adopted by social work within society, leads relatively easily to the view that social work should strive for social change, in other words to refute the notion that social work is about the maintenance of society. Similar critical and radical views about the function of social work in society are located within a variety of other intellectual traditions, notably feminism (see, for example, Graham, 1992; Wise, 1995) and anti-racism (see, for example, Ahmad, 1990; Dominelli, 2008).

Looked at from the vantage point of the early years of the twenty-first century, these debates have a rather anachronistic feel. It is difficult to argue that social work is primarily concerned with social change. Rather it appears to be a functional part of the welfare system that meets specific needs of particular individuals and groups in given circumstances – the child who may have been abused or the older person who may need care – and so each is dealt with in its category. The fragmentation of social work into so many technical subdivisions within a highly regulated and performance managed world leaves little room for these debates, which were, until relatively recently, the fire in the belly of social work.

Highlighting of new values: netting the fish

In the past 20 years or so, a set of ideas, such as advocacy, self-advocacy (for example Simons, 1992), consumerism (for example Allen, 1988), empowerment (for example Adams, 2008), participation (for example Biehal, 1993), partnership (for example Marsh and Fisher, 1992), user involvement (Office for Public Management, 1994) and so on, have influenced social work ideology. Braye and Preston-Shoot (1995) characterise these new and emerging social work values as 'radical' values, which are concerned with challenging oppression as distinct from 'traditional values', which emphasise the individualised nature of the relationship between the social worker and the individual receiving help. Yet there should be no presumption that the emergence of these new values or the development of older, more traditional ones will lead to changes in professional practice.

Let us take empowerment as an example. It is centrally about people taking control of their own lives and having the power to shape their own future. For Braye and Preston-Shoot, empowerment seems to imply a general broadening and deepening of citizenship and implies structural or political change, as in the large body of work of Beresford and Croft that draws upon liberationalist ideologies (see, for example, 1993), and is closely linked to self-advocacy (see, for example, Simons, 1992) and the assertion of users' rights (see, for example, Morris, 1997). For others, the context of empowerment is more circumscribed and refers only to the technical articulation and meeting of needs (Stevenson and Parsloe, 1993). Here, then, empowerment becomes a social work tool for the achievement of high standards of professional practice. Hence, in essence, in its more restricted sense, 'empowerment' as an idea may not be so very different from 'self-determination' as proposed by Biestek (1961). The social context and the social construction of professional social work practice are different, but when we use words such as 'empowerment' or 'self-determination', we should ask how these professional concepts are linked or related to long-standing philosophical debates about the nature of freedom or liberty. Part of the difficulty with terms such as 'empowerment' is their very slipperiness – just like our fish! These values are defined in different ways and hence mean different things to different people.

Conclusion

From this brief overview of professional values and ethics in social work, we may emerge in despair about the possibility of providing definitive answers to the questions posed. If this is so, however, the nature of the enterprise is misunderstood; it is not so much final answers but better refined questions that are required – which fit into the skill set of the critically reflective social worker. This will help to establish an ethically mature professional stance for social work. Moreover, there is a great diversity and liveliness about the emerging topics for debate in this field: see, for example, the role of social workers in organ donation (Geva and Weinman, 1995), the need for social work to adopt a pacifist stance (Verschelden, 1993) or the importance of religion in social work (Amato-von Hemert, 1994; Clark, 1994; Patel et al., 1998). There have recently been an increasing number of published materials concerning postmodernism and social work (for further discussion of this aspect of values, see Adams et al., 2009b, Ch. 20). There is an inevitability that 'professional values', however defined, will mediate between forms of social work practice that are essentially procedural and forms of practice that are individualised and highly creative. Forces such globalisation and managerialism are strongly changing the nature of social work practice. Discussion about professional values and ethics has yet to respond to these challenges – perhaps that is for the future.

For a values-led discussion of anti-oppressive issues in social work, see Chapter 5, and for a critical examination of social work values, see Adams et al., 2009b, Chapter 2.

http://bubl.ac.uk/link/r/researchethics.htm   BUBL Applied Ethics Resources.

http://socialworker.com/jswve/   *Journal of Values and Ethics* (free access).

Banks, S. (2006) *Ethics and Values in Social Work*, 3rd edn, Basingstoke, Palgrave Macmillan. Brief general overview of social work values intended for practitioners.

Beckett, C. and Maynard, A. (2005) *Values and Ethics in Social Work: An Introduction*, London, Sage. An introductory text.

Reamer, F.G. (2006) *Social Work Values and Ethics*, 3rd edn, Berkeley, CA, University Presses of California, Columbia and Princeton. A US perspective on values and ethics.

Chapter

Anti-oppressive practice: the challenges of the twenty-first century

5

Anti-oppressive practice (AOP) has developed over several decades and mainstreamed as empowering practice in response to critiques from those in the new social movements who highlighted oppression in social work practice. Its meaning and relevance are contested, but it seeks to enhance human wellbeing by drawing upon notions of **citizenship**, solidarity and social justice.

Chapter overview

Anti-oppressive practice, with its strong commitment to people's holistic wellbeing and service user-led agendas, has become part of mainstream social work practice in Britain and many other parts of the world. Its main components, **social justice** and **human rights**, have become commonplace. Social workers talk about these as being central to their work and encapsulated by the term 'emancipatory' or 'empowering practice'. The international definition of social work, jointly compiled by the International Federation of Social Workers (IFSW) and International Association of Schools of Social Work (IASSW), reflects this and has been accepted as such since 2001 (see Chapter 1). However, the shifting context of global politics since the 9/11 attack on New York's World Trade Center in 2001 and the Madrid and London bombings that came

> Citizenship refers to the notion of a person belonging to a community, usually involving some conditions of membership, with rights and responsibilities attached to this. Citizenship is a double-edged concept. It may be applied in social policy not just to include people but to exclude them, for example, from access to employment, education, housing, health, social security and social services.

> Social justice refers to individuals, groups and communities having rights and entitlements based on the notions of equality of treatment, access, inclusion and treatment.

later have complicated this picture. The Islamic world has been demonised through the 'war on terror' as the response to a murderous onslaught on people going about their daily lives. The accompanying encroachment on the civil liberties of citizens, from the Patriot Act which perceives every visitor to the US as a potential terrorist to the surveillance society of CCTV that monitors activities

Human rights refer to basic freedoms and liberties to which all people are entitled as human beings. There have been many statements of human rights for children, adults and other groups, internationally through the United Nations, through the European Union and through the Human Rights Act 1998 in the UK. It is easier to legislate than to achieve full human rights for all people, because in some circumstances, one person's rights can be in tension with those of another.

on British streets, challenges the idea of the independent citizen going about life's routines without interference from an overbearing state. These measures also complicate social workers' relationships with 'clients' as they become heavily implicated in the state's surveillance activities, particularly with groups like asylum seekers when they become drawn into immigration control procedures as another arm of the immigration service.

These developments have profoundly altered the meaning of social justice and human rights. Other complications include the internationalisation of the state that has brought privatisation into the heart of welfare provision, the global impact of climate change on the poorest people, rising food and fuel prices, and increasingly inaccessible credit that is absorbing an enlarging circle of the earth's inhabitants. These limit the space for alternative discourses and are making it harder for social workers to respond effectively to need within a framework that sustains human rights and social justice.

I focus on AOP in this chapter because this book is committed to assisting readers in understanding and engaging with the knowledge base and tools that social workers use to respond in empowering ways to the needs of people whose lives are configured by struggles against structural inequalities like poverty, sexism, racism and disablism. Progressive practice is but one paradigm for practice that vies for social workers' attention. Anti-oppressive practice draws on social work's historical concern with the underdog, so it is not as new a paradigm as its opponents attest. Practising the principles of AOP is hard work and requires commitment. Its reception and spread have been problematic. Anti-oppressive practice is contested practice with varied meanings and disputes about its place in the profession. It remains to be firmly embedded in practice in constantly changing social contexts that provide new opportunities for individual and group wellbeing while raising new hurdles for anti-oppressive practitioners to transcend as they seek to empower people in need.

Locating anti-oppressive practice within social work

Anti-oppressive social work has evolved largely in response to critiques of traditional social work with the avowed aim of reconciling practice with social justice issues and the empowerment of those receiving services. As a result, there have been three key approaches to practice that have pronounced on the role and purpose of social work (Dominelli, 1997; Payne, 2005; Dominelli, 2009). These are the:

- maintenance approaches
- therapeutic approaches
- emancipatory approaches.

While these are evident in social work globally, the picture is slightly more complicated in England and Wales (but not Scotland) where probation has been removed from social work since 1998 and care management has become the dominant paradigm used in work with adults, especially older people, from 1990.

The *maintenance* approach was initially explicated by Martin Davies (1994) in his book, *The Essential Social Worker*. In it, he argued that a social worker's main goal is to ensure that people can cope or deal adequately with their lives. Today, it is recognisable in proceduralised and bureaucratic forms of practice exemplified by 'contract-based approaches' to professional practice. Under this approach, social workers do not adopt a therapeutic helping role. Their interventions are more pragmatic – usually passing on information about resources and possibilities. Their interventions are guided by 'practice wisdoms' or the accumulated experience of 'what works'. Probing deeply into the individual's psyche is not an issue in this approach. The maintenance approach relies on an expert practitioner adopting a neutral attitude towards 'clients', although this may involve the use of authority that clients may resist, for example when a social worker takes a child into care or a probation officer recommends custody for an offender. I use the word 'client' here in quotation marks to denote the problematic usage of this term. It is better recognised internationally, and so I use it here. Engaging in political issues, particularly those that challenge the existing social order, falls outside the remit of the maintenance practitioner, who views society as basically benign, a view upheld by Davies (2004) in critiquing Dominelli's (2004a) *Social Work: Theory and Practice for a Changing Profession*. In English social work today, the tenets of the maintenance approach are more likely to be expressed in care management approaches to older people, where practitioners known as care managers expend budgets in purchasing 'packages of care' from voluntary and/or commercial providers.

Therapeutic approaches to social work are exemplified by counselling theories, of which Carl Roger's work stands paramount (Rogers, 1980). In these, a client is assisted by the counsellor to better understand themselves and their relationships with others, especially close relatives or friends, and move on to deal more effectively with their situation. Therapeutic approaches focus on individuals and their psychological functioning as the basis of intervention. The role of the counsellor as helper is to listen actively to what is being said and facilitate a process of exploration that enables people better to address their life circumstances. Any change that takes place occurs in the individual who is being assisted as they learn to develop more effective strategies for dealing with problems they encounter. Their long history and wide currency means that therapeutic approaches are readily understood by practitioners. The link between social work and counselling evident in British social work several decades ago has been discontinued, as counsellors seek to establish their own profession, but the person-centred basis of this approach lives on in English social work as strengths-based practice, cognitive behavioural practice, narrative-based practice and solution-focused practice.

Emancipatory approaches cover a wider spectrum of practice than either maintenance or therapeutic approaches. Anti-oppressive practice, with its value commitment to realising social justice, is a variant of these. Others focus on single social divisions like class (Corrigan and Leonard, 1978), 'race' (Dominelli, 1988; Ahmad, 1990; Graham, 2002), gender (Dominelli, 2002a; White, 2006), disability (Barnes and Mercer, 2002; Swain and French, 2008), age (Phillips et al., 2006), and sexuality (Myers and Milner, 2007). I use 'race' in quotation marks to highlight the social construction of racial and ethnic attributes. The term 'black people' is used in a political sense and should not be taken to mean a homogeneous and ungendered category. Empancipatory approaches engage in processes of empowerment that alter service user–professional relationships by moving away from a professional as expert orientation to:

- examine the impact of power relations on the specifics of daily routines
- value people's existing strengths and experiential knowledge
- explore situations and enable people to acquire skills and knowledge for controlling their lives
- understand the links between positions in social structures and opportunities available
- connect one's personal plight to that of others.

Understanding complex social relations draws on consciousness-raising techniques advocated by Freire (1972) to probe underneath surface realities and expose how power configures social relations into those of domination and subordination.

Some emancipatory approaches see service users as 'victims' of unjust social relations (for example Bailey and Brake, 1975); others focus on strengths (for example Collins, 1990, 2000). Regardless of orientation, all are explicitly committed to social justice and challenging welfare practices that thwart this goal. The search for social change at individual and societal levels affirms the explicitly political orientation of emancipatory approaches that popular critiques articulated by Pinker (1993) and Phillips (1993) have exploited to devalue its contribution to service user empowerment. These authors conflate AOP with poor practice, which cannot be condoned whatever approach it purports to follow. Others like Davies (2004) are concerned that an overtly political stance undermines social workers' professionalism. These critics ignore the impact of new social movements led by women, black activists, disabled people, gay men, lesbian women and older people in developing forms of practice that empower them as users capable of creating and running their own services.

CASE EXaMPLE

Ron lost his job when the coal mines in northeast England closed and has been doing odd bits and pieces on the side to augment his benefits ever since. He has two children by his second marriage as his first one failed to survive the first bout of unemployment. He recently reached his 50th birthday and became moody, changing between bouts of depression and aggression. One night he returned home drunk and assaulted Jane, his wife, in front of the children. The neighbours, hearing her cries, called the police, who in turn called social services to investigate potential harm to the children. Consider the differences in responses that a social worker makes when following each approach: maintenance, therapeutic and empancipatory.

Anti-oppressive practice as transformational practice

Anti-oppressive practice seeks to understand and deal with the structural causes of social problems and address their consequences by altering social relations at all possible levels, from the macro-level to the micro-level, although it may not be the same practitioner who attempts to do this all in one piece of work. Anti-oppressive practice encompasses all aspects of social life – culture, institutions, legal framework, political system, socioeconomic infrastructure and interpersonal relationships, which both create and are created by social reality. It aims to improve the quality of life or wellbeing of individuals, groups and communities (Dominelli, 2002b). In Ron's case, this would have included the issues of low income and gender relations, including an exploration of his notions of masculinity in relating to Jane and the children. Dominelli (1993: 24) has defined anti-oppressive practice as:

> a form of social work practice which addresses social divisions and structural inequalities ... to provide more appropriate and sensitive services by responding to people's needs regardless of their social status. Anti-oppressive practice embodies a person-centred philosophy, an egalitarian value system concerned with reducing the deleterious effects of structural inequalities upon people's lives; a methodology focusing on both process and outcome; and a way of structuring relationships between individuals that aims to empower users by reducing the negative effects of hierarchy in ... the work they do together.

Anti-oppressive practice is transformational because its comprehensive orientation espouses social change through holistic practice, the elimination of structural inequalities, social relationships, a concern with inputs, outputs, processes and collective working (Dominelli, 1993, 1996, 2002b; Ferguson, 2008). Anti-oppressive practice challenges maintenance-inspired views of professionalism in which a neutral expert exercises power over a client and workers lower down the labour hierarchy through rules that call for deference to those in 'superior' positions. Anti-oppressive practice's structural dimensions cover working relations and citizenship rights. Working relations have become embedded within a new managerialism that turns social workers into techno-bureaucrats who are bogged down by endless form-filling and checklists. Citizens rights have been overwhelmed by rising levels of poverty globally and natural disasters that they are poorly equipped to handle. About 2.8 billion of the earth's population lives on less than $US2 a day, while the top 3 out of

946 individual billionaires hold more money between them than 48 low-income countries put together. The anti-globalisation movement links this poverty and exploitation of the earth's resources by the few to neoliberalism and demands that it be replaced by a socially responsible and accountable social order.

Anti-oppressive practice also reveals that social existence and individual identities are more complex than indicated by a focus on a single social division (Dominelli, 2002b; Fook, 2002). Anti-oppressive practice:

- celebrates diverse identities as being equal to one another
- rejects the fragmentation of social life and hierarchies of oppression, with the ensuing isolation of individuals that this endorses
- promotes people-oriented social environments.

These goals produce a search for bonds of solidarity to cover the different starting points held by groups of people working towards a common aim (Hill Collins, 2000), encourage interdependency between peoples (Basu, 1997), and form ecologies that enable each person, group or community to develop their full potential, cherish their cultural traditions, and respect the rights and dignity of others. Anti-oppressive practice fosters the development of new practice paradigms. These transcend a maintenance practitioner's traditional goal of controlling clients so that they might 'cope' with life as they find it and adjust to existing power relations. Working through egalitarian principles, moral and ethical positions, AOP social workers facilitate both coping and change strategies by understanding and engaging with the harsh realities within which clients live and work and seek to change them. Its liberationist stance locates AOP within long-standing traditions of humanism and transformation (Howe, 1992).

Rooted in people's lived-in reality, AOP responds to concerns identified by oppressed individuals and groups rather than practitioners imposing their views on reluctant service users. Professionals providing anti-oppressive services redefine professionalism within an egalitarian power-sharing framework and explicit human rights-based value system. Client-centredness validates everyday experience as a legitimate source of information in designing services and endorses experiential knowledge as a key source of both experiential and empirical data. Research following approaches endorsed by AOP provides an empirical base for experiential reality and facilitates the development of a change-oriented practice that addresses the needs of poor and often disenfranchised peoples. Researchers can systematically collect data for those advocating transformative change and challenging normalised political hostility to marginalised groups. As Humphries shows (Adams et al., 2009c, Ch. 25), research expands the repertoire of a reflective practitioner in improving practice and monitoring compliance with anti-oppressive principles.

Process considerations about how relationships are conducted and on whose terms are crucial to the realisation of AOP. Process becomes the means for expressing ethical anti-oppressive relationships that place service users in charge. This contrasts with traditional client–worker relationships in which ethics focus on the ends to be achieved rather than the mechanisms whereby these are reached and the power relations involved. In AOP, being client-centred acquires meaning through egalitarian power-sharing, empathetic connections with the client's position, and a practitioner's ability to work with clients' messy realities in more sensitive and relevant ways. Anti-oppressive practice uses relationship-building to secure change, interrogate practice value systems and reveal ambiguities contained in seemingly straightforward statements about social work's value base and ethical stances. As Shardlow demonstrates in Chapter 4, this complexity is a strength that social workers constantly utilise to revisit their own values and practice.

Understanding social relations and how power operates within them enables practitioners to apply the principles of egalitarianism to the relationships they establish with clients. Practising equality involves practitioners in valuing 'difference' in lifestyles and identities instead of demanding uniformity. Lorde (1984) comments that without this, individuals' reactions will not be to value difference, but to exercise the wish to control, dominate, copy or exterminate it. Valuing 'difference' goes against common-sense socialisation, which portrays difference as 'inferior' or pathological and a deficit to be made up. Casting people different from oneself in a subordinate status is central to 'othering' processes (de Beauvoir, 1974; Rutherford, 1992). 'Othering' individuals or groups withdraws them from the circle of humanity and jeopardises their human, social and political rights. It also configures oppressed people as passive, dependent victims unable to act on their own behalf. Such views permit their 'superiors' to make decisions for them, allegedly for their own good, without having to justify this claim. 'Othering' people is, therefore, inimical to AOP.

Reflexivity and social change are the bedrock upon which anti-oppressive practitioners build transformative interventions. Empathetic reflection transcends common-sense attitudes about 'difference' by developing a deepened understanding of the other person's position while reflecting on the privileged nature of one's own. Self-knowledge is a central component of the repertoire of skills held by a reflective practitioner (Schön, 1983; see Adams et al. 2009b, Ch. 8). Knowing oneself is crucial to working in empowering ways with others who are different. As Lishman explores in Chapter 26, this is essential when carrying out anti-oppressive practice, but immensely difficult to do. Knowing oneself better equips individuals to transform social relations and challenge inequality. Practising equality is extremely difficult, given the competing practice discourses identified by Parton (see Adams et al. 2009b, Ch. 20) and calls for an open acknowledgement of the constraints that hinder its implementation. This may mean that securing egalitarian relations in a pure form is impossible and that the best that can be achieved is a lowering of power imbalances by continually identifying power differentials and eliminating obstacles to power-sharing. The tensions that social workers who implement AOP have to address are evident throughout this book. Their impact in client–worker relationships is explored by Doel (Adams et al., 2009b, Ch. 15), where he unpacks power in task-

> Reflexivity refers to awareness of the contribution of theory and research to the ways meanings are constructed and interpreted.

centred social work. Social workers can explore these issues in an open and frank manner that engages clients in partnerships they feel they can own.

Those advocating AOP have a responsibility to develop theories and concepts that reflect its principles in practice and lead to innovations in the academy and the field. As Burke and Harrison show (Adams et al., 2009b, Ch. 19), this requires academics to move beyond dualistic (either/or) thinking and approach their studies in a holistic manner. Uniquely among social science disciplines, social work maintains the link between theory and practice. Anti-oppressive practice retains the integration of theory and practice. Working in one area of AOP can lead to innovation and theory-building in others. For example, feminist work with women has contributed to rethinking masculinity (Bowl, 1985; Connell, 1995; Barker, 2005), black and anti-racist perspectives have paved the way for rethinking white identity and whiteness (Roediger, 1991), and disabled people have added new insights to the meaning of 'expert' knowledges and affirmed experiential ones (Wendell, 1996).

The struggle over anti-oppressive practice

Anti-oppressive practice began in the late 1960s as a critique of casework methods in social work practice when practitioners writing *Case Con* and community workers challenged class-based privileges within the ambit of social work itself (Corrigan and Leonard, 1978; Loney, 1983). This critique spread during the 1970s to encompass women (Brook and Davis, 1985; Dominelli and McLeod, 1989) and black people (Dominelli, [1988] 2008). The spread of AOP in academic social work circles was slow, but it achieved greater prominence in the late 1980s when the Central Council for Education and Training in Social Work (CCETSW) responsible for social work training published *Paper 30*. This concentrated mainly on 'race', the area in which black and white practitioners had been organising to redress CCETSW's neglect of the topic. The impetus for expansion in anti-racist practice was threefold:

■ pressure from the new social movements, particularly those involving women and black people
■ the requirements of *Paper 30*
■ the implementation of equal opportunities legislation and policies:
   – the Race Relations Act 1968 (amended in 1975 and 2000)
   – the Sex Equality Act 1975
   – the Disability Discrimination Act 1995 and 2006
   – the Equalities Act 2007.

These pieces of legislation also turned the law into a site of anti-oppressive practice (Dalrymple and Burke, 2006). Anti-oppressive practice gained a strong foothold in the field and equal opportunities policies expanded it across welfare sectors during the 1980s. Greater awareness of oppressed peoples' demands for justice supported it.

The theory and practice of confronting structural inequalities in and through social work also had generalised support among academics.

Market forces and debates about 'political correctness' have distorted discussion about the nature of AOP and the contexts in which social workers operate. These include the impact of globalisation (Dominelli and Hoogvelt, 1996), the privatisation of the welfare state including the personal social services (Oakley and Williams, 1994), and a deepening polarisation in the social structures of British society as marked by an increasing gap in wealth between rich and poor (Oakley and Williams, 1994; *Social Trends*, 1996, 2007). Poverty, a principal manifestation of the structural inequalities that social workers encounter, is exacerbated by globalisation (Dominelli, 2004a, 2007).

The British government is using social policy and legislative instruments to restructure where social work occurs and how it is practised. Promoted as the modernisation agenda, this is encapsulated within the Green Paper *Every Child Matters* (DfES, 2003), the Children Act 1989 and 2004, the National Health Service and Community Care Act 1990 and the Crime and Disorder Act 1998, and has fundamentally altered the statutory environment in which social work practice takes place. Aiming to give consumers more choice and casting this in terms of citizens' rights and the 'personalisation' of services, these developments should support AOP (Braye and Preston-Shoot, 1995). However, these initiatives have been promoted at a time that has coincided with a rolling back of the welfare state as a service provider and a significant expansion in privatisation measures driven by 'contract government' (Greer, 1994). The market rationale that underpins these has undermined their progressive thrust by excluding those without resources from the marketplace and replaced it with a conservative one based on economic not social priorities. Anti-oppressive workers who seek to reverse this trend through practice have been caught in the crossfire.

Social policy has a crucial role to play in endorsing AOP. As Carol and Alan Walker argue in Chapter 7, social policy can assist social work to make a major contribution in reducing the 'growing divide' between rich and poor people in the UK. Policy analysts can identify the plight of poor people, pinpoint their survival strategy and skills, and provide data that strengthen their case for securing social justice. In supporting such efforts, social policy can make a substantial contribution to placing AOP on a firmer footing and embedding it in the political arena. Anti-oppressive practice can achieve more rapid progress if there is political support from those currently controlling society's political and economic resources, and if there is a legal structure that underpins it (Dalrymple and Burke, 2006).

The structural changes being brought about by powerful economic and political forces unleashed by globalisation give the issue of welfare for all a new potency, with more at stake than services for needy people. At the heart of the matter lies the question of how the postwar welfare state has been transformed into a fertile breeding ground for entrepreneurs who foster capitalist relations in a hitherto sacrosanct area and capital accumulation under new conditions in new arenas (Dominelli and Hoogvelt, 1996; Delgado, 2000), with the credit crunch and failure of long-standing financial institutions hitting the headlines during 2008, making people wary of accepting the many claims made for it to offer freedom, choice and services that were hitherto unavailable. The anti-intellectualism of popular consciousness (Jones, 1994) and performance management exacerbate tendencies that force professionals to comply with government diktat rather than explore new responses to the concerns of society's most marginalised groups. That poor people lose out in the struggle over welfare is an unfortunate consequence, possibly unintended, of developments that flow from restructuring the welfare state as proposed by free-market advocates.

Prioritising the market undermines anti-oppressive principles and practice because poor people cannot engage on its terms to access provisions, take control of their lives or meet their welfare needs. The illusion of choice mystifies existing inega-litarian social relations and bureaucratic forms of empowerment now actively endorsed by the state. Bureaucratised empowerment operates through appeals and complaints procedures activated after services have been delivered, thereby ignoring questions about what is delivered and how. The apparatus for processing customer complaints and agency compliance is outlined in the National Health Service and Community Care Act 1990 and the Citizens' Charter originally promulgated by John Major. These mechanisms are consistent with top-down forms of control exer-cised by those in power. They are neither intended to nor do they challenge inegalitarian social relations or the supremacy of the market in distributing goods and services. Braye and Preston-Shoot (Chapter 8) suggest that the law has similar ambiguities. Law is useful in challenging individual unlawful inequality but has limited relevance to restructuring social relations or collective injustices. Its tendency to individualise collective problems hinders its capacity to support claims for redis-tributive justice aimed at addressing structural inequalities and social injustice experienced by groups as demanded by black activists, women and other oppressed groups. The law also provides the base for bureaucratising rights as occurred in various citizens' charters which proceduralise empowerment in consumeristic rather than social justice terms (Dominelli, 2000). Free-market ideologies enhance consumer-ism, promote citizens as consumers (Clarke and Newman, 1997) and intensify this trend (Dominelli, 2004a).

The 'backlash' against anti-oppressive practice

Market-led approaches to welfare allow only those with money a real choice about what personal social services they can have. The economic relations underpinning these developments are camouflaged under an ideological cloak that focuses on the value system of those supporting AOP. The mass media provides the terrain for conducting the struggle over the role of social work and privileges traditional power holders and media pundits in defining opposition to AOP over the voices of margin-alised groups that have created and supported it. Criticisms of market-based welfare policy led to a backlash against AOP. A backlash is resistance to change that those accustomed to having privileges initiate as part of the struggle to preserve these. The high-profile media backlash against AOP in Britain in 1993 rested largely on 'race', the field in which black activists had been mobilising since the 1960s. Government ministers at the highest levels endorsed this backlash because AOP resisted the use of the welfare state to enhance business priorities. The solidarity shown in pooling risks to ensure that all members requiring services receive them free at the time of need is a collective strategy for welfare and anathema to a privatisation (Gilder, 1984; Murray, 1984, 1990, 1994) that seeks to consolidate market principles through the commissioner–provider split. Limited by a market economy, AOP can be co-opted to promote bureaucratic responses rather than empowering social relations. In its more ideological form, it is resisted and mistrusted by those who are antipathetic to the idea that there is such a thing as oppressive social relationships in an otherwise democratic society (personal communication from a service user, 2008). These reactions highlight the significance of dialoguing across differences in order to understand the complexities in social relationships being explored by anti-oppressive practitioners.

Generalised support for AOP limited the scale of reversals following the 1993 attack on replacing the academic head of CCETSW's governing council with a lawyer, abolishing the Black Perspectives Committee that had spearheaded CCETSW's anti-racist initiatives, and abolishing the paragraph stating that racism was endemic in British society, that is, the statement in Annex 5 of *Paper 30*, which regulated the requirements for the DipSW. *Paper 30* was revised to expunge anti-racist ideology from its midst (Black Assessors, 1994). Probation, an area of social work that had endorsed AOP and over which government had financial control, was withdrawn from social work training despite almost unanimous resistance to this plan of action (Sone, 1995). These measures were deemed to have effaced AOP from social work training and, in consequence, from practice.

Reality is, and was, more complicated. The opponents of AOP did not realise that AOP achieved popularity because it responded to the needs of oppressed people who objected to the failure of state services to meet their needs as they defined them, not because a few academics and practitioners wrote texts that identified what it was and proposed guidelines for social workers to follow. By catching the imagination of academics, practitioners and policy makers alike, AOP represented a small attempt by service users, social work academics and practitioners to respond to the agendas for practice being set in the field by members of the new social movements led by women, black people and disabled people. Oppressed people had created their own organisational entities to challenge the inadequate services being meted out to them under the mainstream statutory system.

The new social movements and their demands for relevant services will not go away just because a government decrees that they should. Nor will they die just because professionals fail to support their demands through AOP. Activists will continue with action that produces oppositional forms of practice irrespective of mainstream systems and exert pressure on mainstream policy makers and practitioners to respond to their agendas until they reach the outcomes they seek. A good current example of this trend is the disability movement. Disabled people have asked social workers to step aside if they cannot support their demands on their terms (Oliver, 1990; Barnes, 2003). Unless practitioners support these, they are deemed to be working against them. Disabled activists maintain their prerogative to criticise whatever professionals do or claim to do on their behalf. Collective action is a crucial aspect of the anti-oppressive practices endorsed by the new social movements (Noble, 2007). As Mayo demonstrates (Adams et al., 2009b, Ch. 11), community organisers have a long history of working collectively to challenge the status quo by subjecting professional practice to public scrutiny. The attack on AOP begun by the Thatcherite administration has been replaced by the co-option of its key principles at the individual level under the Third Way (Giddens, 1998), while a rhetoric of addressing structural inequalities, especially poverty among children, has given AOP a new twist by subsuming it in an authoritarian populism and surveillance society.

Personalised care, direct payments and individual budgets have become part of the repertoire for AOP now endorsed by the New Labour government. Its main limitations are that it individualises responses to social problems without addressing structural inequalities, and increases surveillance by turning service users into employers who collect tax and national insurance contributions and record keepers whose performance is ultimately scrutinised by social workers. In this way, AOP is being sucked into the mainstream as an offshoot of maintenance approaches that aim to enable service users to 'cope' with their circumstances while the inegalitarian social structures in which their lives are embedded remain intact. Personalised care and individualised budgets have a progressive potential based on freeing service users to purchase their own services and affirming self-determination. However, these developments have to be monitored by anti-oppressive researchers to ensure that they do not simply turn service users into consumers who become commodified agents seeking ever-cheaper services to save the state money and bear the brunt of privatisation on their shoulders, particularly if they chase ever-dwindling supplies of inexpensive care or rising costs are shifted onto unpaid carers within their family or friendship circles.

Structural constraints on the spread of anti-oppressive practice

Structural constraints, particularly the lack of resources and training, limit the spread of AOP and its capacity to permeate an organisation's culture and structures, inspire its workforce and include clients. Teaching AOP in a thorough and reflective manner requires skilled specialists who know their material and can explore fears about work that fails to keep to its principles and meet aspirations for better practice. CCETSW sought to introduce AOP in the DipSW without providing appropriate training for either practitioners or academics teaching this subject. The net result was a patchy and inadequate outcome, as poorly prepared academics and practice teachers tried to teach students and assess them on something that many could not deliver, despite a desire to do so. Tokenistic responses and partial learning occurred as people grasped the form without knowing the substance. These failures confirmed the hostility of those who had rejected the whole enterprise.

CCETSW's Northern Curriculum Development Project produced useful curriculum materials for anti-racist practice. The General Social Care Council (GSCC) that followed CCETSW has not built on this initiative. This has hindered the development of AOP as a specialism with specialist knowledge that has to be learnt. However, AOP differs from other specialisms in that everyone needs to know about it and have the skills to practise it and infuse their work with anti-oppressive principles. A dialogue about AOP is essential to carry the hearts and minds of those committed to it and engage those opposed to it in confronting and reflecting upon its content. Individual practitioners commit to AOP at the intellectual and emotional levels and implement it in practice by integrating their understanding of AOP on three levels:

- practically to implement the principles they have learnt and own their practice
- intellectually to grasp its central principles and methods of working
- emotionally to feel secure about and confident in working in anti-oppressive ways, or at least to be able to own up to and learn from mistakes when reality falls short of their ambition to work in this way (Dominelli, 2002b).

Reflexive work in small groups is essential to exploring the complexities of AOP in sensitive ways. Such work is also costly compared to mass teaching in lectures. It is unlikely that resources will become available in the current political context. The busy work of getting through each day is a substantial barrier for those wishing to develop AOP and live up to its principles because it reduces time for development work and individuals have to overcome the obstacles it places in their way. New ways of addressing the issue will have to be invented. One could be a system of secondments whereby academics and practitioners with the requisite skills could train other colleagues. Another could be the active exchange of models of best practice, not as exemplars, but as models for discussion. These exchanges would examine the possibility of adapting them to the specific circumstances of those struggling to develop them or those constantly seeking to improve them. Forging collaborative partnerships between hard-pressed agencies and universities is asking a lot in today's pressured climate and privatised marketplace whether in the field and or the academy. These partnerships can be formed if agencies can encourage such initiatives by being creative about obtaining additional resources in improbable situations. Social work academics can develop new paradigms for practice that count in teaching quality assessment and research assessment exercises.

Anti-oppressive practitioners engage in organisational change within agencies and universities to promote anti-oppressive working environments. Such change will make demands of everyone within an institution regardless of rank and include service users as equal participants in the enterprise. As Perrott argues in Chapter 9, changing inegalitarian cultures in an organisation is a structural constraint to be transcended to realise AOP in the workplace. This goal is problematic to achieve as it requires management and workers to move in new directions, including rethinking how people relate to one another as individuals and collectively to promote egalitarian relations as the norm. Reaching this point requires the transformation of existing organisational cultures and value systems that devalue 'difference' and perpetuate structural inequalities (Broadbent et al., 1993). Changing organisational structures is about promoting a different vision of an organisation and how it can be (re)organised to accomplish new aims successfully.

Changing existing managerial structures and including service users are central to securing change. Management relations, workplace relations among employees and relationships between workers and clients have to incorporate more egalitarian ways of working with each other. A flattening of hierarchies followed by the ultimate goal of reducing them to the lowest possible level can enable egalitarian relations to flourish as a source of creative energy and innovation in developing better and more relevant services. Anti-oppressive practice relies on teamwork in the best sense of the word and is hard work. Being aware of the obstacles that have to be overcome can counter views that embarking on AOP is an easy option.

Conclusion

Anti-oppressive practice is occurring in controversial contexts and continues to develop despite hostility towards it. Its continued growth depends on more work being carried out to ensure that it meets the needs of those whom it is intended to serve. This can extend its remit widely and assure its long-term future. However, for anti-oppressive practice to fulfil its potential in social work, its supporters have to raise its profile as a model of good social work practice and raise the numbers supporting it. I am cautiously optimistic for its future because it is rooted in the needs of oppressed people and their visions for alternatives to mainstream or statutory services. The future of AOP will not be assured without a struggle because the forces undermining it are socially, ideologically, economically and politically dominant and powerful. In this context, those favouring AOP can engage in a dialogue over controversies about its meaning and substance. This will require its proponents to develop initiatives to transform social relations and publicly present their case for AOP, thereby winning new adherents to the cause. I outline these initiatives below.

The supporters of AOP can form stronger alliances between professionals who advocate AOP and activists in the new social movements (Bishop, 2001). This can enable them to understand their critiques of existing services, know of their ideas for improving them and support them in eradicating structural inequalities and introducing transformational change in welfare provisions. Anti-oppressive services should 'belong' to service users. This requires anti-oppressive practitioners to become accountable for their professional behaviour and establish credibility with them. User involvement becomes empowerment when there is a level playing field between professionals and service users. Professional relationships with users can model anti-oppressive service provision and AOP as a citizenship entitlement. People accessing the personal social services should not feel like charity cases begging from the bowl of mercy. Their welfare needs should be met as a right with relevant services. Requests for assistance should not act as barriers that disenfranchise them. They should be responded to with dignity and respect.

Academics and practitioners can present arguments to turn this state of affairs into reality. Achieving this objective would be easier if anti-oppressive practitioners and educators could research this area and establish better relationships with the media. A supportive media would facilitate proactive publicity for progressive social work, promote knowledge of good practice and encourage debates begun by anti-oppressive practitioners and not just of those opposing them. Anti-oppressive social workers can develop AOP in new areas. Their cause can be strengthened if its adherents also become more involved in research and theory-building to develop theoretical bases that draw on AOP carried out in the field. This can enhance the status of social work theory and practice. Social work practitioners acting as social anthropologists who have a strong research orientation can amass data to argue for AOP that responds to the needs of service users as they define these. If this were to succeed, social workers acting as intermediaries between policy makers and clients could more powerfully serve disenfranchised groups.

On the training front, anti-oppressive practitioners can perform more effectively than they have done to date. Courses that have established good practice in this area are encouraged to share models with other courses that are struggling to implement AOP. Such exchanges can assist the process of learning from the mistakes made by others without having to revisit them in their own practice. Dialogue between courses can enrich existing models of good practice. This could block complacency, a barrier to reflexive practice, and foster constant improvement in anti-oppressive practice.

Anti-oppressive practitioners need a coherent professional organisation that has the support of the profession and capacity to defend its interests in the political arena. To do this effectively, it will have to be independent from government and encompass academics, policy makers, practitioners and service users who endorse its activities. A continuous dialogue about the role and purpose of social work in society ought to feature constantly on its agenda. Organising on this basis can play a crucial role in promoting AOP, advocating its adoption and regularly monitoring its achievements.

For an approach to intervention rooted in anti-oppressive principles, see Chapter 19, and for an examination of an anti-oppressive approach to social work, see Adams et al., 2009b, Chapter 19.

Dalrymple, J. and Burke, B. (2001) *Anti-Oppressive Practice: Social Care and the Law*, 2nd edn, Buckingham, Open University Press. Although this book focuses largely on using the law as a tool for progressive practice, it threads the principles of anti-oppressive practice and the empowerment of service users throughout the discussion. Thus, it can be used by readers to deepen their knowledge and understanding of anti-oppressive practice in a particular area of practice.

Baines, D. (2007) *Doing Anti-Oppressive Practice: Building Transformative Politicized Social Work*, Halifax, Fernwood Publishing. Considers how social work can be implemented as transformative, politicised practice. It shows that AOP can both address individual needs and challenge structural inequalities.

Payne, M. and Askeland, G.A. (2008) *Globalization and International Social Work: Postmodern Change and Challenge*, Algershot, Ashgate. The title hides the concern with AOP covered in a book that explores the links between local practice and national and international contexts that practitioners have to navigate to develop relevant forms of practice for the specific group(s) of people they work with.

Dominelli, L. (2009) *Introducing Social Work*, Cambridge, Polity Press. Introduces basic concepts in social work and highlights practice in a range of settings from an emancipatory or anti-oppressive perspective.

Reaffirming the value of social work

6

This chapter builds on preceding chapters by arguing that global trends create challenges and, to some extent, threats to the wellbeing of citizens in some communities, groups and families. However, at the same time, these new conditions create new challenges and opportunities for how social work is practised.

Chapter overview

In this chapter, I shall argue that the latest stage in the historical evolution of social work provides a vivid example of the tension between the way value is understood in social and commercial relations, and allows a new opportunity for social work to improve human wellbeing. Globalisation, in turning the world into one big market and accelerating the movement of finance, technology and people across borders, threatens every kind of human collective membership unit, including nation-states themselves. As national governments strive to gain some control over global economic forces and to offer some protection to their citizens least able to adapt to new conditions, theories of public policy and the social order have evolved, prescribing new approaches to social work organisation and practice, which are breaking down in the face of a crisis in financial institutions.

Social work as an occupation came into existence to bridge the gap between communal societies, ordered mainly by kinship and faith, and commercial ones, organised through firms, markets and bureaucracies. It has deep connections with both sides of this divide. On the one hand, the social needs and problems that gave rise to social work activity (and eventually its professionalisation) can be traced to the negative consequences of the industrialisation, urbanisation, mobility and fragmentation associated with economic development. Social work seeks to protect vulnerable individuals, families and communities from the worst effects of these transformations. On the other hand, it is motivated by values (such as individualisation and self-determination) and principles (such as rationality, planning and management) that are derived from the modern project for the commercialisation of social relations and for efficiency in government administration (Jordan, 1984).

The tension between these two sides of the historical legacy of social work practice has shown itself in different ways during the two centuries of its spread within the developed, and then to the developing, countries. In its earliest phase (in Europe and North America), voluntary workers (mostly female, religious and middle class) struggled for recognition and respect, as much from local and national governments as from the urban poor whom they sought to serve. As socialist political parties and labour organisations grew in strength at the end of the nineteenth century, the new social work profession was more closely allied to the idealist and liberal approaches to working-class emancipation than to the Marxist, materialist or Fabian ones. With the birth of welfare states, the profession became part of the public service structure in the UK and the Scandinavian countries, and closely allied to public policies in the other affluent states. It struggled to maintain an independent, critical voice on behalf of unrecognised minorities and oppressed groups. Finally, with the collapse of Soviet-style state socialism, social work has become an instrument in a new, global approach to economic development, pursued through international non-governmental organisations (NGOs) and funds; it has also been recreated in the post-communist countries. In all these settings, it seeks to respect traditional practices and bonds, while channelling the small donations of money and technology from the wealthy countries to those most at risk from global economic integration.

But the economic model that underpins these innovations is itself in trouble, as much from evidence of stagnating levels of wellbeing (Kahneman et al., 1999; Frey and Stutzer, 2002; Layard, 2005) and the growth of problems such as depression, drug and alcohol abuse, obesity and delinquency as from recession and the 'credit crunch'. In affluent Anglophone countries, social work has been restructured in line with the model, yet its fundamental practice methods and ethical commitments still lie in the substance of affectional, associational and civic bonds, and in services promoting social justice.

I shall show that all these issues are closely linked. The new economic approach to government relies upon a theory in which relationships are modelled as contracts, which are based on the information held by each party about the other, and the incentives for compliance given by the contract's terms. The government's role is to design contracts for all society's agencies (from banks and businesses to the public services) and, ultimately, for the actions of citizens themselves. In this sense, it is no longer the arbiter of social justice between organisations and their members (as during the era of the postwar welfare state), but the 'insurer' of the economy and regulator of its functioning, trying to affect or control all agents, to make them 'act more in accord with social objectives' (Stiglitz and Greenwald, 2003: 209). What justifies state intervention is not so much inequality or oppression as the incompleteness of the information (relevant for greater efficiency) held by firms, households and individuals (Stiglitz et al., 2006: 47).

To this end, government accumulates huge databases about the economy and society. It uses these to define the tasks and targets of the public services, which in turn design contracts and guidance for their staff, giving them incentives to produce the desired outcomes. For example, children's services and social care are supplied or contracted out in carefully costed units, each intended to contribute to a policy objective.

But the achievement of higher levels of efficiency and output does not correspond to an improvement in wellbeing among populations. I shall argue that the divergence between (rising) incomes and (stagnating) average levels of self-assessed overall happiness (subjective wellbeing – SWB) reflects the failure of economic models to capture the social value of emotional support, respect and the sense of belonging, communicated in interpersonal interactions (Jordan, 2007). Social work has always been primarily concerned with wellbeing and the relationships that sustain it (Shulman, 1999: 22; Adams et al., 2005: 2). These new phenomena present an opportunity to readdress the tensions between the two sides of its original functions, and a challenge of individual economic welfare and relational wellbeing.

Social value and wellbeing

It may seem outrageous to try to separate wellbeing from the income-based welfare that sustains the economic approach. If it does, this is because, particularly since the 1970s in affluent Anglophone countries, people have been led to understand society as a set of interactions through which they seek individual self-realisation, through choice, competition and exchange. Government's role is to facilitate citizens in their quest for autonomy and the pursuit of their projects, in markets and in public services. The contract between the state and citizens requires the former to 'make work pay' and the latter to be self-responsible, and avoid being a burden on others (DSS, 1998: 80). By enabling each individual to identify and develop a 'project of self' (Rose, 1996), welfare becomes the province of self-realisation and self-improvement, through education, employment, earning, saving and consumption.

But this whole approach ignores the creation and communication of meaning and value that is central to social interactions. The social order is produced by everyday interpersonal processes, which sustain and transform cultures and build institutions. Like language and morality, these collective resources represent the frameworks in which people gain social value, in the form of intimacy, empathy, respect and the sense of membership, or suffer the losses associated with rejection, stigma or exclusion. As Goffman (1967) pointed out, these processes have a 'sacred' or 'ritual' element; they stem from our deepest collective understandings of our societies and our relation to each other (Durkheim, 1912). The anthropologist Mary Douglas (1970, 1978, 1987) insists that economic concepts, such as consumption, saving and debt, should be understood in terms of the production and exchange of these forms of social value:

Whenever consumption goods change hands, someone is communicating with someone else. Commodities define social categories ... We define inclusive and exclusive categories by rules about degrees of sharing and giving of commodities. No amount of welfare grants … will cancel meanings which the language of commodities declares. Poverty is not a lack of goods but exclusion from esteem and power. (Douglas, 1978: 181) **"**

The point here is that research on subjective wellbeing (SWB) shows that it is more closely correlated with supportive relationships, participation and inclusion than with income or consumption (Argyle, 1999; Myers, 1999; Helliwell, 2003). Even employment satisfaction and health, the other two main contributors to positive SWB, are clearly beneficial in terms of the relationships they enable. Economists themselves are confronted with data that defy their fundamental assumptions about rational individual behaviour – that citizens of affluent societies seem addicted to work and consumption that gives them less than the full value for their choices (Di Tella et al., 2003; Bruni and Porta, 2005; Layard, 2006).

All this should make social workers reappraise their role in societies. According to the economic model, there are two primary reasons for interventions in social relationships. The first stems from legal and quantitative ('objective') assessments of need, risk and harm, such as the abuse of vulnerable individuals, or the lack of personal capacities to sustain independent living. Social workers uphold society's official standards, through assessments and negotiations with those in such situations (Sheppard, 2006: 116–31). The second concerns the lack of adequate links, either between members of communities or between a deprived community and mainstream society, which indicate a deficit or fault in 'social capital' (Putnam, 2000). This diagnosis justified the **communitarian** elements in Third Way programmes in the US and the UK (Driver and Martell, 1997), and in the World Bank's development projects (World Bank, 2001).

> **Communitarian** refers to the political culture of communitarianism that prioritises meeting the needs of the community rather than merely the needs of individuals.

Both these justifications for social work rely on the idea that individuals can be restored to full functioning as rational (choosing) agents, and social interactions can give rise to more efficient outcomes, through the provision of fuller information and selected material resources, or (where this fails) through corrective training or treatment. In the case of **social capital**, members of communities are assumed to need facilitation for better communication and self-organisation so as to make them more able to access the benefits of markets and public facilities, such as schools and hospitals.

> **Social capital** refers to the shared stock of individual and collective resources available to enable people to relate with each other and take part.

But the evidence on wellbeing challenges all these assumptions and justifications. It suggests that it is the quality of relationships, the emotional and social value they create and distribute, and their inclusive effects, which contribute most to people's sense of worth and overall satisfaction with their lives. In a highly individualistic culture, shaped by the economic model, people seek material gratification and the symbols of celebrity and status, but are haunted by insecurity, emptiness and depression, mainly because competition for advantage over others undermines the very sources of relationally derived wellbeing (Jordan, 2008).

All this suggest that social work's focus should not be limited to the realisation of the potential for self-development of individual children (DfES, 2003), or the choice and independence of disabled citizens (DH, 2005a), or even the economic opportunities of marginal communities (World Bank, 2001). It should also embrace the relational factors that, in 2006, put the UK's children 21st out of 25 European Union (EU) states (Bradshaw et al., 2006), and bottom among 21 Organisation for Economic Co-operation and Development (OECD) rich countries (Innocenti, 2007) in terms of wellbeing – notably, low quality of relationships with parents and peers, and risky behaviour. It should also address the question of whether all disabled people benefit from the emphasis on employment and earning now adopted by the UK government, and whether participation, membership and belonging are well captured by the concept of 'social capital' in international development policies (Fine, 2001).

Contract or culture?

These issues crystalise around the puzzle about how the social interactions that make up societies are best understood and regulated. It is fundamental to the economic model that dominates public policy in both the US and the UK and the development strategies of the World Bank (Stiglitz et al., 2006) that information and incentives are the key elements in the design of contracts, which supply efficiency, stability and growth (and hence maximum welfare), and reliable institutions (Stiglitz and Greenwald, 2003: 4).

However, there is an alternative to the regulation by contract that is now the basis for the funding and management of social work in both public and voluntary sectors in the UK, and also the rationale for most practice with service users. Even diehard neoliberal economists concede that anything which can be regulated by contract can alternatively be regulated by culture, but with different costs, benefits and outcomes (Buchanan and Tullock, 1962: 42).

A research report illustrates the differences between the two approaches. Gneezy and Rustichini (2000) investigated outcomes at an Israeli children's nursery, when the management decided to impose a financial penalty on parents who were late collecting their children at the end of the day. The consequence of this charge was that the incidence of lateness grew significantly, and remained at the new, higher level after the penalty was withdrawn. The researchers' explanation was that, before the penalty, parents knew that 'something might happen' if they were late, but their contract with the nursery was 'incomplete', because they did not know what. Once they had full information (the 'price' of lateness), they could calculate when it was advantageous to continue in whatever they were doing and pay the penalty, rather than observe punctuality.

The alternative explanation is that, before the penalty, parental norms of behaviour were regulated through a culture of respect, consideration and concern for children's wellbeing, among parents and staff. The new rule introduced a calculated, contractual relationship between the parties, such that parents could increase their welfare by choosing to do more gainful things, rather than be punctual. Staff could also gain, as overtime could be funded out of the 'fines' paid. But the new approach undermined the former culture and weakened the standards governing interactions. This could lead to a loss of social value communicated through everyday processes among the adults, and hence a decline in their, and their children's, wellbeing.

All this is particularly relevant for the services provided through social work; indeed, the story might serve as a kind of parable of the 'modernisation' of these services undertaken by neoliberal and Third Way regimes. In their analysis of society's needs and the role of the profession, the goal was to make the costs associated with 'cultures of passivity' and 'the public service culture' transparent (DSS, 1998) – to promote the independence, choice and cost-effectiveness possible only in quasi-market contractual systems. This meant that social work activities must be costed in terms of specific units of service, each of whose outcomes can be quantified by evaluating its impact on behaviour or risk. To inform this 'packaging' of care and measure its quality against targets and tasks, practice must be tightly managed, both to assure Best Value (Fletcher, 1998; Thompson, 2002: 101) and to improve future performance. To this end, most social work activity is regulated through checklists and bullet points, which strongly influences interactions with service users. The contractual approach has spilled over into the regulation of the voluntary sector, ensuring that these agencies can be held to tasks of implementing government policies, such as intentionally deterrent and restrictive conditions for asylum seekers in the UK (Humphries, 2004).

The point here is that there is a real danger that this approach to practice undermines cultures of mutuality, participation and membership, among both service users and social workers. The attempt to individualise social care, and to quantify all kinds of service, along with the slicing of interventions into specific, costed items, cuts across the processes by which social value is created and shared in interpersonal relations. As in the example of the Israeli nursery, the cultures through which people gained the sense of belonging, sharing and maintaining standards of childcare, as a group or community, are undermined by the introduction of an approach focusing solely on the costs and benefits to individuals, according to financial criteria (Jordan, 2007, 2008).

Furthermore, from the perspective of practitioners, the contractual, checklist approach deskills staff, focusing their attention on the gathering of information and making decisions against quantified criteria, rather than reflection, learning from experience, and the exercise of judgement. It also undermines the values and standards that come from cultures of sharing expertise and the everyday ethical dilemmas of practice, substituting 'abstract statements of principle' (Sennett, 2008: 50), which have little felt application, within a mechanical, impersonal regime.

Proponents of the economic model would argue that it is well able to encompass the social elements that I have suggested it excludes. Theorists like Coleman (1988) and Becker (1996) have specifically extended the scope of the economic analysis of human behaviour to theorise social and cultural influences on individual choices. Under the catch-all category of 'social capital', they have attempted to take account of how these considerations affect interactions among groups and communities. These in turn have entered the strategic thinking of the World Bank's development programme, through the work of Amartya Sen (1999) and Joseph Stiglitz (2002).

But the theory of social capital is framed within a model in which the first-best outcomes are always available only through markets or government (contractual) regulation (Durlauf and Fafchamps, 2004: 15). People resort to informal, associative and communal ways of meeting their needs when they lack the information, skills or material resources to achieve the same ends through commerce or official political channels. Hence the work of NGOs and self-help projects operate at a 'second-best' level and seldom challenge the exclusions and injustices of unequal distributive shares. As Fine (2001: 94) says:

> Social capital becomes the academic equivalent of the Third Way in politics. You can have whatever you want, although we would prefer you to draw a hard line against certain factors – such as class, power, conflict and control (social capital without the capitalist system, in other words).

EXaMPLE

In the US and the UK, the notion of social capital has inspired a policy move towards faith schools and welfare agencies. There is nothing inherently wrong with this approach, but it generalises about the benefits to society of faith-based organisations, and carries with it at least two risks. If the agencies concerned are successful in supplying improved provision for their members, as with many religious schools in the UK, they are quickly colonised by the aspiring groups who seek economic advantage. If they serve deprived users, they may consolidate and institutionalise prejudices and conflicts on faith lines.

The theory of social capital claims that those who participate in religious activity gain resources through learning skills and acquiring networks. But in neglecting the influence of power and solidarity, the theory fails to recognise that faith can be mobilised for competitive advantage, and can provide the focus for prejudice and hatred.

Conclusion

The notion of a political struggle between the claims of economic value (individual welfare) and those of social value (wellbeing, including collective cultures and standards) is not a new one. We can find it in Ruskin's (1860) denunciation of John Stuart Mill's political economy, in Marx and Engels' (1847) account of the corrosive effects of capitalism, in Durkheim's (1912) analysis of collective conscience, and in Polanyi's (1944) history of resistance to the 'utopian project' of global commercialisation. All these authors have argued in their different ways that the substance of society's collective life should provide the standards by which we evaluate economic development, and not vice versa:

> Indeed, Polanyi defines socialism as the *subordination of the economy to society* and of economic goals to the societal goals which accompany them and assign them to their subordinate place as a means to an end. Economic activity must be put to the service of ends which go beyond it and which establish its usefulness, its meaning. (Gorz, 1989: 130)

In this chapter, I have argued that the interest in wellbeing sparked by the publication of critiques of consumerism, individualism and marketisation (Layard, 2005; James, 2006) gives an opening for social work to reassess its heritage. In recent years, under pressure from government and international agencies towards contractual and commercial approaches to organisation and practice, it has veered in the direction of individualisation in service provision and an uncritical fostering of self-help among marginalised communities. It has also been drawn into coercive practices with many 'deviant' individuals and groups in the name of reintegrating or retraining them for the world of work and earning, and into the service of oppression and injustice in its dealings with outsiders such as refugees and asylum seekers (Humphries, 2004).

The wellbeing perspective invites social work to re-engage with the other part of its heritage – the maintenance and promotion of the social value that stems from relationships in informal interpersonal interactions in membership units and in wider communities. This demands a willingness to step outside the limitations of contracts and the paraphernalia of risk and eligibility assessments, and to revive the skills of listening, empathy, engagement, mobilisation and collective action.

There are even deeper concerns in the struggle between economic and social value. Many commentators have come to believe that competitive individualism creates a culture that lacks basic civility; it breeds public behaviour and underlying behavioural strategies that subvert the trust and cooperation on which all societies depend. The defence of 'democratic values', which is claimed to inspire the 'war on terror', is for an increasing number of observers a thin veil for the imposition of the economic model through military power. And the logic of ever-increasing consumption threatens survival through climate change. In relation to all these aspects, social work's links with quality of life through social value should be developed, not neglected.

For further discussion of radical and critical ideas about social work, see Adams et al., 2009b, Chapter 17 and for postmodern perspectives, see Adams et al., 2009b, Chapter 20.

McMurtry, J. (2002) *Value Wars: The Global Market versus the Life Economy*, London, Pluto. Provides a passionate if flawed attack on economic versions of value in the globalisation process.

Gorz, A. (1989) *Critique of Economic Reason*, London, Verso. A more reflective analysis.

Harris, K. (2006) *Respect in the Neighbourhood: Why Neighbourhoods Matter*, Lyme Regis, Russell House. Provides a local perspective.

7

Social policy, poverty and social work

Chapter overview

This chapter focuses on the social policy context within which social workers practice and service users live. It considers the impact of the range of welfare services but concentrates particularly on the impact of poverty on families and individuals. A broader social policy awareness is paramount in delivering critical and reflective social work practice.

In this chapter, we focus on the social policy context within which both social workers operate and their service users live. Social policy is of particular importance because it sets the framework within which professionals work and the type and level of service they can provide. It also has an impact on the number of people seeking or being referred to the social services. It has a direct bearing on all service users and potential users in terms of their living standards, wellbeing and ability to cope independently. This chapter considers, in particular, how **poverty** affects the majority of people with whom social workers and other social care staff work. Poverty is a key defining characteristic of the lives of many social work service users (Smale et al., 2000). Nine out of ten users of social work services are benefit claimants and most of them are on means-tested ones (Becker, 1996). Poverty increases the likelihood of children being looked after by care services, older people being admitted to residential care and admission to acute psychiatric care (SEU, 2004). It is impossible to practise mainstream social work without encountering poverty. Thus poverty awareness or, preferably, a broader social policy awareness is an essential part of a reflective and critical approach to practice. Commonly, however, professional and organisational concerns with coping strategies within external constraints exclude such awareness.

Poverty is the state of deprivation of income and resources, whether material, social and cultural. It affects health and life expectancy, as well as access to social networks, employment, learning and respect. It is difficult to envisage a universally agreed definition of poverty, given the inextricable way in which poverty, policies and politics are bound together.

The current social policy context

Over the past three decades, there have been major changes in British social policy. Under the Conservative governments, 1979–97, welfare policy aimed to roll back the frontiers of the state in order to:

■ increase individual and family responsibility
■ replace public with private provision
■ reduce public spending on the welfare state.

All these objectives had their greatest impact on the most vulnerable people in Britain because it is they who require total or partial support from the state: they were, therefore, the main losers. These changes occurred within the context of huge cuts in social spending, which led to a diminution of confidence in public services and to increasing numbers of affluent people opting into the private sector, for example in health, education and pensions.

The New Labour government came to power in 1997 and, in contrast to its predecessor, was committed to a programme of welfare reforms (Labour Party, 1997), which included, first, increasing investment in public services, particularly in the areas of health and education and, second, reducing poverty. These positive welfare aspirations were heavily constrained in New Labour's first term of office by a commitment not to increase income tax and to stick to the previous Conservative government's stringent plans for spending for the first two years. However, once released from this electoral commitment, there were substantial increases in government spending across a number of welfare programmes. The government's commitment to reduce poverty and, specifically, child poverty, was a reversal of the policies of the previous Conservative administrations during which time the numbers in poverty in the UK nearly doubled (Walker and Walker, 1997). Despite Labour's radical shift in goals, there was also considerable continuity with the Conservative years in the welfare mechanisms adopted.

Successive Labour administrations have remained heavily committed to the involvement of the private sector in the provision and delivery of public services. This includes using the private finance initiative (PFI) to fund large public building projects, private treatment centres to offer operations on behalf of the NHS and private finance to underpin the academy programme in secondary education. Considerable emphasis has been given to offering citizens choice in public services through diversity in types of schools, choice of hospitals and consultants, and individual budgets in social care. All these policies have critics as well as advocates. Together they represent a fundamental recasting of the welfare state towards a more pluralistic and individualistic and, therefore, less secure form. Rather than being a direct provider of welfare, the state (national and local) is being reconstructed as an enabler, manager and funder of alternative providers, including self-care – in other words, the managerial state (Clarke and Newman, 1997).

Before considering how government policy in other areas of welfare state provision has affected vulnerable people, we will look at the growth and persistence of poverty in Britain and its implications for social work.

Policies on poverty

In 2006/07, 13.2 million people in the UK (24 per cent) were officially living in poverty. Despite such prevalence, poverty is often marginalised in social work training compared to 'race' and gender, with which it also overlaps (Walker and Walker, 1997). In social work practice, there is a danger that poverty and deprivation are overlooked precisely because they are so common and may be seen as 'normal' for social work service users. However, the fact remains that a significant proportion of people are living on incomes substantially below the average for the rest of the population and are, as such, at risk of malnutrition, hypothermia, homelessness, restricted educational opportunities, poor health, earlier death and being victims of crime. A child born into a poor family is four times as likely as a child from a better off family to die before the age of 20. At the other end of the age range, there is a 16.9 year gap in healthy life expectancy between the richest 10 per cent of electoral wards and the poorest 10 per cent.

Under the previous Conservative governments, the UK experienced an increase in poverty and income inequality unparalleled in the industrialised world, with the sole exception of New Zealand (Hills, 1995). Despite this, Conservative governments were reluctant to acknowledge the problem, to the extent that, in the 1980s, the word 'poverty' was banned from official publications. By contrast, the incoming New Labour government took the issues of poverty and **social exclusion** on board.

Social exclusion is the denial of basic rights, including equality and access to services.

The Social Exclusion Unit was created to monitor and coordinate policies across a range of government departments until its abolition in 2006. *Opportunity for All*, the government's report on poverty and social exclusion, has been published each year from 1999 (www.dwp.gov.uk/ofa). Also Tony Blair, prime minister from 1997 to 2007, made a public promise to end child poverty within 20 years and pledged his government to an anti-poverty strategy comparable to that of the Beveridge Report of 1942, which led to the creation of the welfare state (Howarth et al., 1998).

In the postwar period, the political debate generally had shifted away from the problem of poverty towards the 'problem' of the poor. Consequently, policy tended to concentrate on influencing the behaviour of the poor, in particular to reduce their dependence on state benefits, rather than tackling the underlying factors that cause poverty, such as unemployment, barriers to work, and a lack of affordable childcare. New Labour has shifted the balance back, but only a little, and mainly in relation to children. New Labour's first welfare reform Green Paper, *New Ambitions for Our Country: A New Contract for Welfare* (DSS, 1998), set out its reform agenda and redefined the contract between the government and citizens. 'Work for those who can;

security for those who can't' was the slogan. Most of the government's reforms have concentrated on the first half of this pledge, 'making work pay', by the introduction of the national minimum wage and a complex range of tax benefits, as well as a number of reforms to encourage/cajole people off benefit into work (Becker, 2002). A series of welfare-to-work schemes have gradually been rolled out to cover young people, the long-term unemployed, older workers, lone parents and people with disabilities. Two key aspects of the Conservative approach have been maintained. First, benefits for adults have become increasingly conditional upon meeting income and other work tests. Means-tested benefits now account for almost one-third (£39.5 billion) of the total social security spending of £134 billion in 2006/07 administered by the Department for Work and Pensions (DWP). An additional £18.7 billion is paid out in means-tested tax credits by Her Majesty's Revenue and Customs (HMRC).

Overarching its unprecedented commitment to reduce child poverty was New Labour's ambivalence towards welfare and the poor. The frequent use of the US slogan, a 'hand up rather than a handout', reinforced the stigma of benefit receipt and avoided the question of the adequacy of benefit levels (Craig, 2002). Much of the government's income maintenance policies, like those of its Conservative predecessor, are based on the premise that many people are reluctant to work. The government eulogises a new family type – 'the hard-working family'. Such labelling immediately disadvantages in the public mind those people who are unable to work. Most disappointing is the government's decision to continue to vilify benefit claimants:

> there is a tendency to 'balance' progressive social measures with a populist rhetoric which often stigmatises benefits claimants ... the drive against poverty in the twenty-first century needs to leave behind the divisive language of the deserving versus the undeserving poor. (Fimister, 2001: 104)

The government has continued the previous Conservative strategy of high-profile, big brother-style advertising campaigns to combat benefit fraud (www.dwp.gov.uk/benefit-thieves), while being far more reticent at helping the over 4 million people eligible for social security benefits to obtain the £3–5 billion that are unclaimed each year. This emphasis is of the utmost importance to social work, as the profession concerned with the poor. It helps to set the moral climate in which social workers practise and, as well as influencing public opinion, is likely also to challenge the self-esteem of many service users (an issue we return to below).

New Labour, poverty and inequality

The 1997 election of New Labour marked an end to the Conservative administrations' complacency towards the rapid growth in poverty. Major improvements were made, first in financial support for children, through the tax credit system and child benefit, and later for people's retirement pensions, again through the tax credit system and some in-kind payments. Levels of poverty (60 per cent of median income after housing costs – AHC) fell in each consecutive year from 1996/97 until 2004/05 after which it rose by three-quarters of a million to almost 13 million people. This increase affected children and working age adults, while pensioner poverty continued to fall. Another concern is that government policies have done little to relieve 'deep poverty'. Since 1996/97, the numbers with incomes below 40 per cent of median income have remained at around 5 million per year (Palmer et al., 2007). As well as the increase in poverty rates, income inequality has also worsened. In 2005/06, income inequality reached its highest level since 2001/02 and was statistically higher than when the government came to office in 1997 (Brewer et al., 2007).

The poverty measure used by the New Labour government in setting its poverty targets is 60 per cent of median household income (adjusted for household composition). In 2006, the government changed the baseline from income *after* housing costs (AHC) to income *before* housing costs (BHC), which, as Table 7.1 shows, reduces the numbers in poverty. Such misleading and cynical manoeuvring of poverty statistics had been common under the Conservative administrations but was a surprise from a government committed to abolishing poverty (Palmer et al., 2007).

Following Blair's public commitment on child poverty (reiterated by his successor Gordon Brown at his first party conference as prime minister in September 2007), the following targets were set: to cut child poverty by a quarter between 1998/99 and 2004/05, by half by 2010/11 and completely by 2020. As Table 7.2 shows, the government succeeded in reducing child poverty but failed to meet its target. In order to meet the 2010 target, the number of children in poverty would need to fall twice as fast as has been achieved so far. Many are sceptical that this can be achieved, especially in the light of the modest additional steps that have been taken in this area and growing pressure on the nation's finances. The Institute for Fiscal Studies estimated that new spending of around £4 billion per year would be needed by 2010/11 for the government even to have a 50/50 chance of meeting its target (Brewer et al., 2007; Palmer et al., 2007).

Table 7.1 Relative poverty: percentage and numbers of individuals in households with incomes below 60 per cent of median income (BHC), UK

	1996/97		2005/06		Change 1996/97 to 2005/06
	%	Million	%	Million	%
Children	26.7	3.4	22.1	2.8	−4.6
Pensioners	24.6	2.4	20.8	2.2	−3.8
Working age parents	20.2	2.5	18.2	2.3	−1.9
Working age non-parents	12.0	2.5	13.3	3.0	1.2
All	19.4	10.8	17.6	10.4	−1.8

Source: Based on Brewer et al., 2007, Table 6

Table 7.2 Number and percentage of children in poverty, UK

Year	Before housing costs		After housing costs	
	Millions	% of children	Millions	% of children
1998/99	3.4	26	4.4	34
2004/05	2.7	21	3.6	28
2006/07	2.9	23	3.9	30

Who are the poor?

The risk of poverty is not shared evenly: economic status, household structure, age, gender and ethnicity are key indicators of vulnerability. Secure employment is the surest way to avoid poverty: those in full-time work are at less risk than those working part time, who are in turn at less risk than a household where no one is in paid employment. Unskilled and semi-skilled workers, those from certain minority ethnic groups (especially Pakistani and Bangladeshi people – see below) and those living in low employment areas are most likely to be affected. However, work is no guarantee of freedom from poverty. Although, overall, people in work are better off than those not in work, there is considerable inequality within the working population. In 2006/07, one-fifth of all poor households had at least one person in full-time work (one-third of all poor households had at least one person in full- or part-time work), and 57 per cent of poor children lived in working households. The minimum wage, introduced in April 1999, raised the incomes of 1.5 million workers, two-thirds of them women. However, it remains low at, from October 2008, between £5.73 (over 22 years old) and £3.53 (under 18 years old).

Having children increases the risk of poverty for couples. Thirty-four per cent of those in poverty in 2006/07 were in couple households with children against 10 per cent for childless couples. The similarity in the figures for lone parents and childless single people (20 per cent and 19 per cent respectively) can be explained by the improvements that have been made to benefits for children paid to the former but not to the latter. Child poverty in the UK exceeds 20 per cent of all children in the UK, and is greater than most other comparable EU countries. In a UNICEF (United Nations Children's Fund) analysis of *Child Poverty in Rich Countries* in 2005 (www.unicef.org/sowc06/pdfs/refcard6e.pdf), which uses a standardised poverty measure, the UK was placed 20th out of 26 countries. Of those households with children, lone parents – the majority of whom are women – are at greatest risk of poverty.

Other factors predisposing groups to poverty are age, gender, disability and 'race'. Retirement pensioners, especially single women pensioners and older pensioner couples, are also highly vulnerable to poverty. As lone parents and retirement pensioners, women are more likely to experience poverty but in general, the gap between men and women living in low-income households has narrowed considerably (Palmer et al., 2007). Poverty rates for all minority ethnic groups have fallen since the mid-1990s but remain markedly higher than for whites, with the rates for both Bangladeshi and Pakistani families being above 50 per cent (Palmer et al., 2007: 28). People from minority ethnic communities are more likely to be unemployed and, if in work, to earn poverty wages. The poverty of disabled people is exacerbated by extra costs related to their illness or disability, which are not reflected in their incomes, and also by their limited participation in the labour market. Disabled adults are twice as likely to live in low-income households as non-disabled adults and the gap between the two groups has widened over the past decade (Palmer et al. 2007).

But are the poor really poor?

Research has tracked the increasing polarisation between 'a prosperous majority and a growing minority of people living on low incomes' (Hills, 1995). A synthesis of qualitative research studies examining the lifestyles of people living on low incomes confirmed the persistence of poverty and the deprivation of poor families (Kempson, 1996: ix). Irrespective of how they define 'poverty', no one reading this report could be left in doubt that life on a low income in the mid-1990s was a stressful and debilitating experience. People who relied on income support and related benefits, in particular, faced a struggle against encroaching debt and social isolation, where even the most resilient and resourceful were hard-pressed to survive. This was the situation which the Labour government inherited in 1997, and which, given its commitment to reduce child and pensioner poverty, should have begun to change.

Up until 1997, the social security system was the main mechanism for helping people in poverty. The benefit rates have always been insufficient to lift people out of poverty and were substantially lower than average wages. In 1980, the Conservative government restricted the annual uprating of benefits to the level of price inflation, leading to benefits falling further and further behind the incomes of the working population. The Labour government did not change this uprating formula. The failure to uprate benefits beyond inflation means that any improvement in income is at the government's whim. It has made real increases in both the level of child benefits, paid to all families with children, and to the children's additions paid with income support, the means-tested state safety net.

Since April 2001, the flagship strategy for boosting the incomes of poorer people has been the tax credit system. Child tax credit (CTC) and working tax credit (WTC) were introduced in April 2003, replacing earlier versions and some other forms of financial support for families with children. WTC extended in-work financial help to families with children, people with disabilities and some people without children. Pension credit is available to people over retirement age. The aims of the tax credit system were set out in the chancellor's budget in 2002:

- Supporting families with children, recognising the responsibilities that come with parenthood
- Tackling child poverty, by offering the greatest help to those most in need, such as low-income families

■ Helping to make sure that work pays more than welfare and people have incentives to move up the earnings ladder (HMRC, 2008).

The take-up rates of CTC and WTC – 80–84 per cent and 59–63 per cent (of caseload) respectively – are higher than those achieved for the social security benefit (family credit) they replaced. However, even at these higher levels, in 2005/06, up to 1.4 million people did not claim the CTC to which they were entitled and 1.2 million did not claim WTC (HMRC, 2008). In the previous year, 2003/04, a further 700,000 people were underpaid a total of £464 million. As well as sharing the traditional problems associated with means-tested benefits, including insufficient take-up and underpayments, a major difficulty with the tax credit system has been overpayments. In 2003/04, £1.9 billion was overpaid to one-third of all families receiving tax credit. Eventually, a substantial proportion of overpayments had to be written off by the government but thousands of the poorest families found their tax credit reduced in the subsequent year as they were required to pay back overpayments, which were not their fault (www.citizensadvice.org.uk/pdf_debranded_tax-credit-takeup-e-2007-01.pdf).

As well as using means-tested systems, rather than increase national insurance benefits, most notably the state retirement pension, the government has also extended benefits in kind for many older people – free television licences, free travel, increases in the annual fuel allowance and a one-off payment towards council tax. The pensioners' lobby has been highly critical of such benefits in kind ('handouts') in place of the freedom an increase in the real value of their pensions brings.

Throughout the three Labour administrations since 1997, welfare reform has been a key feature. The emphasis has been on 'work for those who can'. While poverty campaigners and the government both agree on the importance of work in helping people out of poverty, there is concern when schemes designed to help people back into work are made mandatory rather than voluntary, as recommended in the Freud Report (DWP, 2007). In autumn 2008, the government announced further proposals to increase conditionality in the benefits system, which include 'working for benefits'. Welfare-to-work schemes can help to fight the discrimination facing some groups, be they long-term unemployed people, those with caring responsibilities, disabled people or those from black and ethnic minority communities, but implemented insensitively or coercively, they can create longer term difficulties and jeopardise the government's goal of 'security for those who can't'. The government is gradually reducing the age of children above which lone parents are expected to return to work. The Welfare Reform Act 2008 introduced a new, more restricted, system of financial support for those registered as long-term sick or disabled, which will radically reduce the numbers eligible and the amount of benefit received.

Living on a low income

The above discussion has considered the prevalence of poverty as revealed in the official statistics. However, bald statistics can convey little of the reality of daily living on a fixed low income. What is remarkable is not that some people in such circumstances fail to make ends meet but that many of them succeed against the odds. Judgements about an individual's inability to cope often overlook material factors, such as length of time on benefit and debt that can reduce capacity to zero (Walker, 1993; Kempson, 1996). The fact is that people respond differently to poverty, with some being able to manage on very low incomes while others are driven quickly to despair. In time, however, even the most resilient can be undermined by the combination of poverty and debt. Beset by constant worries, deprivation has a cumulatively negative impact on poor people's self-identity. High levels of stress, fatigue and poor mental health are common among the poor. Rather than examining the social causes of their deprivation, however, poor people are more likely to blame themselves by thinking that they have failed. In such stressful circumstances, it is remarkable that relationships survive but, when they fail, this is likely to reinforce a personal sense of guilt. Thus it is essential for social workers to recognise these hidden injuries of poverty and not to stereotype or pathologise the poor. How people are treated is vital to how they regard themselves. Some of the popular stereotypes surrounding poverty, which usually 'blame the victims', are especially pernicious. They are a double-edged social policy device: diverting attention from the social causes of poverty and the need to raise the levels of benefits and access to them, while making the poor themselves feel worse as they internalise what they see as society's moral attribution of blame and, therefore, their outsider status or 'otherness' (Walker, 1990; Beresford et al., 1999; Lister, 2004).

The Poverty and Social Exclusion (PSE) survey reveals the everyday impact of poverty on people's lives (Gordon et al., 2000). People on low incomes go without a range of essential items because they cannot afford them. Many cannot afford to have insurance, decorate their homes, replace electrical goods or replace worn-out furniture (Flaherty et al., 2004). The greatest struggle relates to essential expenditure such as food and fuel, which accounts for a much higher proportion of their weekly income compared to more affluent families. Food, normally one of the most basic essentials, is, in practice, often the most flexible part of family expenditure. When money is short, the food budget suffers; cheaper food is bought and families cut down on fresh fruit and vegetables. The diets of those on low incomes are nutritionally poor as they rely on cheap, but filling, processed, low-cost food instead of fresh fruit and vegetables (Christie et al., 2002).

The inadequate diets of the poor have often been blamed on ignorance, famously so by the former Conservative government minister, Edwina Currie. According to research sponsored by Age Concern, the minimum income for healthy living in old age (at 2007 prices) was £135.58 for a single person and £212.82 for a couple (excluding housing costs and council tax) – £21.53 and £36.77 per week respectively above pension credit levels (Morris, 2005). Poor diets lead to a greater risk of malnutrition, failure to thrive, vitamin and mineral deficiencies and poor dental health (Cole-

Hamilton and Lang, 1986; Leather, 1996). Following the 2005 Channel 4 series featuring Jamie Oliver, which highlighted the poor quality of school dinners, the government reintroduced basic nutritional guidelines and provided £200 million to improve kitchen facilities and staff training. Poorer children, in particular, benefit because the school dinner is often their only proper meal. The government also introduced free fresh fruit to schools.

Even before the massive increases in fuel prices in 2007/08, the proportion of the weekly income spent by the poorest fifth of the population on housing, fuel and power was three times that of the richest fifth (Botting, 2003). The UK-wide figure for those in fuel poverty (defined as households spending over 10 per cent of their income on energy costs) rose by around 0.5 million in 2005 to 2.5 million households, of which 2 million were deemed vulnerable. Although this represents a significant decrease from the 1996 figures of 6.5 million and 5 million respectively, it is a major setback to the government's target to eliminate fuel poverty by 2010 (BERR, 2007).

Debt and poverty are now inextricably entwined:

 No matter how resourceful, those living on social security benefits generally find that no amount of forward planning and bill juggling is enough. They face a difficult choice between cutting back drastically on food, fuel and other essentials or falling into debt. (Kempson 1996: 26)

Kempson (2002) found that a third of households with incomes of less than £9,000 had debt problems. Poor people's debts are most frequently for basic household bills – rent, mortgage, gas, electricity, water and council tax – therefore they are at risk of serious sanctions, such as disconnection of essential services or the loss of their home (Kempson, 1997). The unsecured debt of people in poverty is considerably larger than the general population, and they are also significantly disadvantaged in relation to their access to credit (Mitchell et al., 2005).

Social relationships

One of the first sacrifices that poor people make is to cut out 'luxuries', even if they might not be defined as such by the general population: these include leisure and social activities. This self-imposed exile means that many people lose contact with family and friends. They cannot afford to go out and may be reluctant to visit other people's homes because they cannot afford to reciprocate. Such isolation, together with the constant worries about making ends meet, can put a strain on family relationships. This can be a contributory factor to a couple separating or to an older child leaving home:

Little things that never mattered before are suddenly major issues and you fight over them. I fight with him [her husband], I shout at the kids, he does as well and the kids cry. (Kempson, 1996)

The wider impact of poverty

Government social policies relating to social security, tax credits and employment have a direct impact on poverty. However, there is also a close relationship between poverty and other social policies, in particular health, housing and education.

Health

There has been a growing body of evidence on inequalities in health since the publication of the Black Report in 1980. The link between poverty and health is symbiotic: ill health makes people vulnerable to poverty because sick and disabled people have a tenuous relationship with the labour market and may have higher costs related to their condition. However, poverty itself can contribute to ill health. Poor diet and homelessness or inadequate housing are major contributory factors to ill health. Money worries, together with the circumstances that cause them – job loss, onset of ill health, relationship breakdown – may affect people's mental health and can lead to anxiety and depression.

Despite nearly half a century of the NHS – providing healthcare free at the point of access on the basis of need – a health gap between rich and poor persists. Life expectancy for people in social class V (manual workers) is, on average, seven years shorter than that of those in social class I. Children in social class V are five times more likely to die in an accident and 15 times more likely to die in a fire than children in social class I (DH, 2002a). People who live in disadvantaged circumstances have more illness, greater distress, more disability and shorter lives than those who are more affluent. Adults in the poorest fifth of the population are around twice as likely to be at risk of developing a mental illness as those on average income (Palmer et al., 2007).

The greater propensity of the poor to ill health is not reflected in their use of health services. Health resources are still not distributed equitably between areas in proportion to needs and formal healthcare services do not respond appropriately to the healthcare needs of different social groups (Benzeval et al., 1995). As a result, poor people receive less healthcare relative to their health needs than do better off people: they are less likely to see a doctor, more likely to have shorter consultations and less likely to have their children vaccinated or receive health screening. The Conservative governments' health reforms made matters worse by creating a two-tier health service (Wilkinson, 1996). The Labour government opted for a similar, although differently named, system. The continued use of charging, for example for prescriptions, which have increased in price over fourteenfold since 1979, and for optical and dental charges, also puts an extra burden on many poor people. The British Association of Pharmacists estimates that one-third of the prescriptions that are not presented are due to the patient not being able to afford the charge. New Labour policy on the NHS has prioritised structural changes, increasing 'choice' for patients and a growing role for the private sector, over rigorously pursuing policies to increase the health chances of the poor.

Housing

Housing is a key parameter of social exclusion. In 1997/98, 102,430 people were accepted as homeless by local authorities, with a further 47,520 in temporary accommodation. Under New Labour, the number of homeless peaked at 135,430 in 2003/04 before gradually falling to 73,360 in 2006/07. The number of people in temporary accommodation peaked at 101,070 in 2004/05 and fell to 87,120 by 2006/07. In Britain, renting is regarded as a poor second best to owning one's own home, and housing tenure is therefore an important source of social division and an important indicator of deprivation. The rapid rise in property prices has increased the inequalities in wealth between homeowners and tenants. The Conservative government's main housing policy was to increase the number of homeowners and this was done, primarily, through an actively pursued and heavily subsidised 'right-to-buy' scheme, which led to the loss of 1.9 million units (Hills, 2007). As a result of this decline in the stock of social housing and the slowdown in building new social housing inherited and continued by Labour, the number of people moving into social housing declined from 250,000 per year during the 1970s, 80s and 90s to 170,000 post-2000. A review of social housing undertaken for the communities secretary (Hills, 2007) concluded that the pressures on social housing had got much worse since 2000 and would continue to do so. The number of people on council or housing association waiting lists in 2007 was 1.5 million, 500,000 more than when the government came to power 10 years earlier. The government has made various announcements relating to increasing the stock of affordable housing but very little progress has been made. Housing is a critical determinant of wellbeing and social exclusion in later life. Two-fifths of older people live in housing that does not meet decency standards and one in three people aged 75 and over are in unfit housing (the worst housed subgroup). Older people who do not own their housing are more likely than those who do to experience multiple forms of social exclusion (Barnes et al., 2005).

Education

On coming to office in 1997, Tony Blair said that his first three priorities were 'education, education, education'. The Conservatives had introduced several important education reforms, to finance, structure and curriculum. The reduced educational opportunities open to children in poor families were not addressed. Partly because of the social segregation caused by housing, the children of poorer families tend to go to schools in poorer areas. They often have access to the worst, most deprived schools. Their parents are unable to subsidise school funds and activities to the extent that this happens in more affluent areas. Children from poor families are less likely to stay on at school beyond the minimum school-leaving age and are much less likely to go on to higher education. Evidence indicates a link between educational performance and social disadvantage, both among junior school pupils (Brooks et al., 1996) and at GCSE (General Certificate of Secondary Education) level:

> Educational opportunities and results have become more unequal in social terms. It cannot be the case that 'every child, regardless of background [now has] the chance to progress as far as his or her abilities allow'. (Smith et al., 1997)

Reducing educational disadvantage has been a key goal of the New Labour governments and is a key plank in its tackling social exclusion (DSS, 1999); however, there is still much more to be done. In 2006, in England, 61 per cent of children not entitled to free school meals obtained five or more GCSEs at grades A*–C; this is nearly double the 33 per cent of children who were entitled to free school meals (www.dcsf.gov.uk/rsgateway/DB/SFR/s000708/index.shtml, Table 8). A study of **social mobility** conducted for the Sutton Trust found that for a cohort of children born in the early 1980s, the gap between those staying on in education at age 16 narrowed between different socioeconomic groups but inequality of access to higher education widened further: while the proportion of people from the poorest fifth of families obtaining a degree increased from 6 to 9 per cent, the graduation rates for the richest fifth rose from 20 to 47 per cent (Blanden et al., 2005).

Social mobility describes the extent to which people's social status can change for the better or worse through upward or downward movement within a given society's class structure.

Social care

During the Conservative administrations in the 1980s and 90s, social care did not feature high on the political agenda. A significant development was made in relation to long-term care. Local authorities were required to reduce their role as providers of services and instead to commission residential and domiciliary provision from a mix of providers from the private and voluntary sectors. This resulted in a huge increase in residential and nursing home provision and a massive rise, from £10 million to £3 billion, in social security payments for board and lodgings. The NHS and Community Care Act 1990 was introduced to rein in this expenditure. As a result of changes following the Act, community care was driven to a state of crisis:

- too little home care and no preventive work, which meant that many older people had to enter residential homes, despite the government's rhetoric of supporting community care
- a lack of choice between providers
- a lack of consultation with users and carers about appropriate provision
- an overreliance on family carers, often to the point of breakdown
- some 40,000 older people each year having to sell their houses to fund their long-term residential care.

The New Labour government's response to this crisis was to appoint a Royal Commission on Long Term Care for the Elderly (1999). The resulting report, *With Respect to Old Age,* was a major contribution to social care policy but the government rejected its radical proposal to fund all personal care. Instead, unlike the Scottish Parliament which provides free social care, the *NHS Plan* (DH, 2000b) opted for the cheaper policy of funding only 'nursing care' – defined as the time spent by a registered nurse in providing, delegating or supervising care in any setting.

The issue of how best to meet the long-term care needs of older people and other vulnerable groups such as people with physical and learning disabilities and mental health problems, as well as the needs of growing numbers of family carers, remains an urgent one on the political agenda. The Labour government launched a number of strategies. *The National Service Frameworks for Mental Health* (DH, 1999a) and *National Service Frameworks for Older People* (DH, 2001a) aimed to raise the standards of care available to these vulnerable groups. Other important policy initiatives included *Valuing People* (DH, 2000c), *Caring about Carers* (DH, 1999b), *Independence, Well-being and Choice* (DH, 2005a) and *Putting People First* (DH, 2007a).

These various policy initiatives reflect themes similar to those in education and health: first, the involvement of the private sector in the delivery of services and, second, offering greater choice to the service user. In particular, the government is moving towards a system of individual budgets (IB), under which, in theory at least, service users will be able to purchase directly the package of care of their own choice. Direct payments, the predecessor to this scheme, and pilot individual budgets schemes have found that they can provide creative and innovative packages, which transform the lives of vulnerable people. Caution must be exercised, however, as the responsibility for creating and managing complex packages of care can be too great a burden for some groups of family carers and service users. There are expectations in some quarters too that social workers will take leading roles to assist in IB arrangements. In general, though, social work has been marginalised under New Labour social care reforms (Jones, 2001).

While the social care sector has been highlighted by the Labour government, the various initiatives have not been allocated sufficient resources to restore years of underfunding or to cope with the rising needs of an ageing population. There are still tensions between health and social services, for example over the discharge of (normally older) patients who are deemed to need only 'social' care, with social services departments being obliged, but unable, to fund suitable care packages for all those assessed as being in need. Whether or not the massive 2006/07 reorganisation of the NHS into larger primary care trusts and the promised development of integrated health and social care trusts will overcome these barriers to seamless care is, at the moment, an open question. There is no sign of the major increase in resources necessary to create high-quality, responsive and user-empowering community care services.

A review of social care services for older people conducted by Sir Derek Wanless (2006) concluded that there needs to be a sharp increase in funding to keep pace with need. Simply keeping pace with population changes caused by increasing numbers of older people, without any improvement, would require total spending on social care for older people to increase from the 2002 level of £10.1 billion to £24.0 billion by 2026. The review found serious shortcomings in social care provision and in the funding arrangements; it was particularly critical of the means-tested system. Nine years on from publication of the Royal Commission Report on Long Term Care, in May 2008, the prime minister announced a new six-month consultation on the future of long-term care based on *Caring Choices* (www.caringchoices.org. uk/?p=88).

Conclusion

Social policy provides the context within which social work professionals and service users live and work. State welfare is particularly relevant – but not the beginning and end of social policy. If housing, employment, income or health needs are not being met by the relevant service, the individual is more likely to turn to social services departments as the last resort. The key to social workers finding a resolution to family crises may involve addressing a material need, such as inadequate housing, without which family stress cannot be relieved. In practice, however, the fact that the majority of social work service users are poor is not given sufficient weight in social work training, thought and practice.

Because social work is at the front line in dealing with the consequences of a society that condones high levels of poverty and inequality, in effect discharging society's moral responsibility for the disadvantaged, it is essential for it to be aware of the importance of social policy. On the one hand, it concerns the rules by which the lives of service users (and social workers) are regulated and, on the other, the social processes that create the disadvantages that lead to poverty and social exclusion, such as poor health, disability, frailty, unemployment, ethnicity, location, lack of education and so on. Armed with this social policy awareness, the development of a critical and reflective approach to practice means being mindful, constantly, of the problems faced by individual service users and the social origins of those problems. It is particularly important for those working with the poor to look beyond individual hardship, and sometimes personal inadequacy, to the structural factors that exclude the poor from sharing in the lifestyles of the wider society.

This suggests an even more important role for social workers in seeking to go beyond the amelioration of poverty and the promotion of social justice at the individual level towards becoming agents of progressive social change. The fact that social workers know much more about the consequences of poverty and inequality than any other profession provides the potential basis for advocacy and community education in favour of social justice for all service users. As agents of the state, many social workers are in positions to empower service users. This is a big challenge for social workers individually and collectively.

To respond adequately to this challenge would need not only commitment on the part of social workers themselves but also support in terms of resources and the freeing up of some of their time taken at present by bureaucratic tasks. But, if social workers do not take the lead in combating poverty, inequality and discrimination and in promoting social justice, who else will do so?

www.dwp.gov.uk/ofa   *Opportunities for All* annual reports, by government on progress to combat poverty and inequality against a wide range of indicators.

www.poverty.org.uk   Comprehensive data and information on current debates on poverty.

For a discussion of policy and practice with poorer children and families, see Chapter 22 and for wider work with communities, see Adams et al., 2009b, Chapter 11.

Beresford, P., Green, D., Lister, R. and Woodard, K. (1999) *Poverty First Hand: Poor People Speak for Themselves*, London, CPAG. Accessible accounts of people's own experiences, which complement statistically based studies.

Flaherty, J., Veit-Wilson, J. and Dornan, P. (2004) *Poverty: The Facts*, 5th edn, London, CPAG. Easily accessible information on current measures, definitions and statistics of poverty. The sixth edition is imminent. Updates can also be obtained online (www.cpag.org.uk).

Gordon, D., Townsend, P., Levitas, R. et al. (2000) *Poverty and Social Exclusion in Britain*, York, Joseph Rowntree Foundation. Report on the PSE surveys in Britain and Northern Ireland, which reveals the extent to which people lacked items that the majority of the population perceive as essential because they cannot afford them. An alternative measure of poverty to the official statistics.

Howarth, C., Kenway, P., Palmer, G. and Street, C. (1998) *Monitoring Poverty and Social Exclusion: Labour's Inheritance*, York, Joseph Rowntree Foundation. Provides a baseline of a number of indicators of social exclusion against which to map future government progress. Most recent is Palmer, G., Macinnes, T. and Kenway, P. (2007) *Monitoring Poverty and Social Exclusion 2007*. York: Joseph Rowntree Foundation/New Policy Institute.

SEU (Social Exclusion Unit) (2004) *Mental Health and Social Exclusion*, London, SEU. Project focusing on how people with mental health problems can enter and retain work and have equal access to services.

Walker, A. and Walker, C. (eds) (1997) *Britain Divided: The Growth of Social Exclusion in the 1980s and 1990s*, London, CPAG. Comprehensive collection of articles based on the record of the Conservative administrations of the period showing how poverty leads to social exclusion and disadvantage.

SUZY BRAYE and MICHAEL PRESTON-SHOOT

8 Social work and the law

Chapter overview

This chapter critiques the structure and purposes of the legal rules that govern social work. It explores how legal rules interface with professional values, and how both are mediated through a challenging organisational context. We argue that competent and confident practice derives from knowledge-informed critical reflections on policy and decision-making.

Students and practitioners can experience contact with the law and legal system as stressful. They may be anxious about being found wanting or uncertain. They may lack familiarity with legal procedures, methodology and language or, conscious of the breadth of knowledge to be acquired and retained, be unaware of developments in the legal rules. Indeed, one feature of social work law is the permanence of change in the primary legislation, regulations and policy guidance that shape both the organisational structures through which social work and social care services are delivered, and the mandates for intervention with different service user groups. This vulnerability is amplified by concerns that practitioners feel unable to retain their professional values in the face of work pressures, procedural and bureaucratic forms of decision-making, increasing control and regulation of practice, and growing managerialism (Preston-Shoot, 2000a; Braye et al., 2007). Judicial scrutiny of practice may further provoke feelings of vulnerability, particularly in the context of diminishing resources and infrequent post-qualifying training (Preston-Shoot, 2000b).

The relationship between social work and the law is complex. One tension that endures is whether the law (Beckford Report, 1985) or an ethical duty of care (Stevenson, 1988) is social work's defining mandate, or whether practitioners and managers must negotiate the interface and determine the balance to be uniquely struck between these polarities in each situation (Braye and Preston-Shoot, 1990, 2006a).

Another tension surrounds purposes and outcomes. Law is a product of political and moral debates or controversies. It speaks volumes about the society in which it exists. The law can be used to preserve power structures and maintain structural inequalities, for example in childcare, family life and mental health. It can be used for social engineering, identifying norms of behaviour and creating sanctions for nonconformity. Another aspect of social control, which illustrates the relationship between moral panics and legal developments, arises from the law being employed to 'solve' social problems, such as youth crime or asylum-seeking. The law may also be used to shape attitudes and behaviours, as in legal rules to promote equality of opportunity. Reflecting their nature as a social construct, the legal rules contain muddled images of competency, for example of children, and potentially oppressive images of moral worth, which present challenges to practitioners. The legal mandate also contains conflicting imperatives:

- needs versus rights
- welfare versus justice
- autonomy versus intervention (Braye and Preston-Shoot, 2009).

Practitioners and managers must negotiate the resulting dilemmas at the interface of practice and law, where professional values and knowledge are sometimes in uneasy juxtaposition with legislative requirements or intentions.

Intersecting law with social work practice

A distinction may be drawn between social work law, which includes those **legal powers** and **legal duties** that expressly mandate social work activity, and social welfare law, comprising statutes with which social workers must be familiar if they are to

> Legal powers are actions that the law makes it possible to carry out.
>
> Legal duties are actions the law makes it necessary to carry out.

respond appropriately to service users' needs, but which do not permit or require specific actions by them (Preston-Shoot et al., 1998a). The two 'territories' exist in close proximity, as when duties towards children in need (social work law) interface with legislation affecting homeless families (social welfare law).

Social work law defines the individuals towards whom social workers have **legal responsibilities**. It determines the nature and extent of preventive, protective and rehabilitative intervention. It sets out

> Legal responsibilities are actions that the law makes it our role to carry out.

the conditions under which compulsory intervention is possible, together with the safeguards and mechanisms for redress that place boundaries around, and seek to ensure, the accountability of professional practice.

The legal rules contain absolute and discretionary duties, and powers in relation to particular service user groups. These may be delegated to voluntary organisations and independent sector providers. Examples include residential care for older people (National Assistance Act 1948) and family support services (Children Act 1989). They are accompanied and amplified by secondary legislation (regulations, directions and approvals) and by central government guidance. Sometimes this is advisory (practice guidance) but, when issued under section 7, the Local Authority Social Services Act 1970 is directive (policy guidance) and must be followed. Courts are often required to interpret this mandate and sanction or monitor its use. Consequently, case law becomes an important component of understanding how the legal rules can shape social work practice.

Usually, these powers and duties are delegated to social workers who must adhere to statute and, when lawful, to their employers' procedures for its implementation. Occasionally, as with approved mental health professionals performing functions under the Mental Health Act 2007, powers and duties are designated to individual practitioners who are then held personally accountable (Table 8.1).

Table 8.1 Legal rules and agency

Acts of Parliament	Outline duties and powers
Regulations	Provide further detail on duties and powers
Guidance	Is issued by government to inform agency policy and practice
Agency procedures	Interpret the duties, powers and guidance Give instructions to employees on practice
Courts	Interpret the legal rules and apply them to cases, creating case law Monitor the legality of practice and may lead to changes in agency procedures May require Acts of Parliament to be reviewed if incompatible with the European Convention on Human Rights as integrated into UK law by the Human Rights Act 1998

The legal rules are translated into operational policies and procedures by local authorities and other agencies undertaking statutory duties. Case law indicates that health and social welfare organisations, in their interpretation and/or implementation of the mandate, sometimes act beyond the boundaries of the legal rules (Preston-Shoot, 2008). Organisations can be held accountable for the definition and administration of policy, and for social work practice derived from it, through complaints procedures, judicial review and the commissioner for local administration (ombudsman). The appeals mechanisms available to service users are limited in that, in the event of finding illegality or maladministration, they can quash or criticise decisions made but not ensure or reinstate service provision. Complaints procedures, as one component of maintaining and improving the quality of services, are weakened because service users and carers lack information about them, are sceptical or fearful about the outcomes of using them, and have low expectations of services and, possibly, high tolerance thresholds (Preston-Shoot, 2001). More positive is the influence of Article 8 (the right to private and family life) and Article 6 (the right to a fair hearing/trial) of the European Convention on Human Rights. These were incorporated into UK law by the Human Rights Act 1998, which means that they may be used explicitly in arguments before UK courts. Together with Article 13 (the right to

involving the exercise of authority within complex and contested frameworks of accountability and ethical and legal boundaries (QAA, 2008). Social workers must be able to identify and justify the need for legal intervention (Topss, 2002) and be able to challenge discrimination (GSCC, 2004; QAA, 2008). The Human Rights Act 1998 merely reinforces the importance of this obligation, since it is concerned with political and civil rights, which, while important, contrast with the social and economic rights with which social workers are concerned through the impact of poverty, ill health and social exclusion on people's lives.

Conflicting purposes

Central to social work is a commitment to a value base. Whether this is interpreted traditionally as a commitment to respect for persons, equal opportunity and meeting needs, or radically as a concern with social rights, equality and citizenship, the focus is on social change. Social work law and social welfare law may facilitate this focus. For example, courts have stressed the importance of compassion, humanity and dignity in community care law (*R (A & B by their litigation friends X & Y)* v. *East Sussex CC and Disability Rights Commission (interested party)* [2003] 6 CCLR 194); the welfare of the child must not become secondary to resource considerations (*R (L and others)* v. *Manchester CC* [2002] 1 FLR 43; *R (CD) (a child by her litigation friend VD)* v. *Isle of Anglesey CC* [2004] 7 CCLR 589); and asylum seekers must not be left destitute (*R (Limbuela and others)* v. *Secretary of State for the Home Department* [2006] 9 CCLR 30). However, social work law is largely expressed as discretionary duties, whether towards groups or individuals. Entitlement is often to unspecified services, such as assessment or a care plan, rather than to a particular service or one of specific quality. Moreover, the local authority may define the extent to which it will exercise discretion, for example in defining need and taking resources into account (*R v. Gloucestershire CC and the Secretary of State for Health, ex parte Barry* [1997] 2 All ER 1). Provided local authorities act reasonably in their exercise of discretion, it is difficult for service users to challenge their decisions. The present emphasis on standards, outcomes and consistency, through *Fair Access to Care Services* (DH, 2002b), assessment frameworks (DH/DfEE/Home Office, 2000) and national service frameworks (for example DH, 1999a, 2001a), which seek to improve services through tighter focus, regulation and monitoring, does not alter this position fundamentally.

Additionally, notwithstanding the broadening of equalities legislation to include enhanced provisions in respect of disability (Disability Discrimination Act 2005) and gender (Equality Act 2006), and new legal rules regarding sexuality (Employment Equality (Sexual Orientation) Regulations 2003) and age (Employment Equality (Age) Regulations 2006), the law can still express objectives that oppress or marginalise people rather than counteract discrimination and meet needs. Enactments on asylum, youth justice and contact are examples. The Asylum and Immigration Act 2004 allows for the withdrawal of support from failed asylum-seeking families. Provisions in the Powers of Criminal Courts (Sentencing) Act 2000, including antisocial behaviour orders and detention orders, seem more intent on controlling young people than addressing the causes of crime. Legislation (Children and Adoption Act 2006) continues to enforce contact between children and non-resident parents, even where this might destabilise the care being given by the resident parent.

The law, then, embodies value judgements and ideologies (such as increasing punitiveness, demonisation and authoritarianism towards young offenders) that social work might wish to challenge but to which, because of their position, practitioners are expected to conform. Indeed, the purposes of the law are multiple and sometimes contradictory. The law may be harnessed to preserve power structures or prescribe or proscribe certain lifestyles (for example the strong presumption in favour of contact between children and separated parents, even in situations of violence and hostility). It may be used to shape behaviours and attitudes, as in anti-discrimination legislation, or express ideology (for example the primacy of the market in the NHS and Community Care Act 1990). The question for social work is how to respond.

Legalism

Social work is increasingly being regulated through national standards, volumes of guidance and constrained resources. Increasingly, too, it is being judged through inquiries based on the norms and practices of the legal system. This emphasis on legalism is problematic. Essentially, this is because legalism conflates good practice with 'procedurally correct' practice, the latter emphasising apparent certainties rather than acknowledging the imprecisions and choice points inherent in social work tasks.

Legalism refers to excessive or strict adherence to the law, or adherence to the letter rather than the spirit of the law.

Roles and responsibilities may be defined in law but many situations are unpredictable and decisions require skilled professional judgement (GSCC, 2008). Additionally, legalism presents inherently conflictual notions as if they were complementary and thus minimises debate on the balance to be struck between conflicting imperatives such as rights and risks, needs and resources, autonomy and protection. In response, social workers need to challenge assumptions about the relationship between law and practice, including the belief that the law provides a clear map for welfare practice, which is all that is necessary (Braye and Preston-Shoot, 2006b).

The statutory mandate is neither consistent nor comprehensive; it is confused and ambiguous. A child's welfare is not always paramount (compare family proceedings under the Children Act 1989, to which the paramountcy principle does apply, with financial and accommodation questions in divorce and domestic violence proceedings (Family Law Act 1996), in which the needs of, often male, adults can predominate). Children are sometimes denied the right to seek to initiate proceedings – contrast appeals to special educational needs tribunals (Education Act 1996), which children have no right to initiate, with section 8 orders (Children Act 1989), which they may seek, and their right to instruct solicitors (*Mabon* v. *Mabon* [2005] 2 FCR 354). Government exhortations to alter the balance between child protection and preventive services towards the latter (DH, 1995a; DfES, 2004) have not been accompanied by acknowledgement of either the complexity of practice or the social context in which practitioners operate. Policy guidance on assessment (DH/DfEE/Home Office, 2000) offers signposts about how to intervene in families where children are in need but cannot guarantee the right answers.

The adult services mandate boasts choice, personalisation and needs-led assessments, yet resources control questions of service provision, while the differential meanings of partnership, empowerment, choice and quality obscure rather than clarify the objectives to which services should aspire. Judges (*R* v. *Gloucestershire CC and the Secretary of State for Health, ex parte Barry* [1997]; *R (Grogan)* v. *Bexley NHS Care Trust and South East London Strategic Health Authority and Secretary of State for Health* [2006] 9 CCLR 188) and inquiries (Ritchie et al., 1994) have criticised government guidance for its lack of clarity, and central government for the wretched position into which it has placed councils. Practitioners inherit a legal mandate still characterised by poverty of provision and meanness of spirit (Utting, 1996), in that it guarantees few social and economic rights, is severely restricted by resource constraints and, through the language of need, limits its horizons regarding quality of life.

Legalism does not necessarily safeguard service users. First, reliance on the law for resolving welfare questions may be misplaced because of its adversarial nature and narrow emphasis on questions of evidence and procedure (King and Trowell, 1992). The proceduralisation and regulation of valued practices, such as advocacy, can destroy their very value and utility to service users (Boylan and Braye, 2006). The more that the law becomes the main form of admissible knowledge in social work, the more difficult it may become to address awkward questions about the purpose of provision and highlight the limitation of judicial procedures in supporting vaguely defined objectives of choice, needs-led assessments and empowerment.

Second, the legislative mandate continues to marginalise the social. The policy emphasis is on individuals rather than the wider systems that frequently contribute to the difficulties that people experience. Social work should connect the personal and political, public and private, and, from individual cases, identify those political and structural issues that require social change as part of problem resolution. Legalism fragments this perspective, offering officially sanctioned procedures but leaving unaltered the current alignment of power and relationships.

The location of social work

Social work's predominant location in local authorities has always meant the negotiation of multiple accountabilities (Braye and Preston-Shoot, 1999) – between employers, professional values, professional self, service users and the public. The challenge has always been to hold the dynamic tension that this involves rather than succumb to bureaucracy, and to find the room for manoeuvre within agencies for anti-oppressive practice and promoting service users' rights and needs. The problem here is less the law but rather how it is interpreted in policy and practice, and how registration of social workers (GSCC, 2004) has yet to impact significantly on the balance of power between social workers and their employers.

Evidence continues to accumulate (see Preston-Shoot, 2000a, 2008) that agencies are failing to follow policy guidance and meet their statutory obligations to both children and families and adults needing care or services. Social work is being drawn into practices that are ethically or legally suspect – withdrawing services from vulnerable adults without the required reassessment and when their needs have not diminished, giving undue primacy to the resource position when reviewing care packages for older people or disabled children, or attempting to evade obligations in the legal rules, for example in respect of young people leaving care. Judges have been sharply critical of practice standards, delays in providing services and the attitudes and values expressed by local authorities through their decision-making.

This is not to underestimate the impact of the consistent underresourcing of local authorities compared with growing social need and mounting legislative duties. Indeed, government has acknowledged underresourcing (DH, 1998a) and that effective safeguarding and quality social care require that funding issues are addressed (DH/DfES, 2006). However, ongoing resource constraints, together with increasing regulation, mean that managers and practitioners still face the unenviable discomfort of continuing to struggle with irreconcilable demands and tighter targets or performance indicators. This can result in acquiescence to the degradation of social work as the only means of survival (Jones, 2001). That sensitive and innovative practice remains in evidence is a tribute to the strength of commitment and imagination still derived from the professional social work ethos of public service. This discussion must highlight, however, the evidence of services and practitioners under strain. It must caution that the emphasis given in social work training and practice to social work law (legislation, regulation and policy guidance) should not amount to acquiescing to a rationing role and bypassing political and ethical questions about the purposes of welfare and social work, and about the quality of life that services should promote. Social workers should challenge degrading and inhumane social policies and legal rules (Humphries, 2004).

Critical debates

How, then, should social work interface with the law and social policy, and their expression in agency procedures? An empowering context for practising social work law requires a social work that is confident in interacting with legislative and local government systems, and active in initiating and contributing to debates about the goals of practice. This requires frameworks for understanding, which together construct a theory for practice and can strike the balance in the relationship between the law and social work uniquely in each situation. The emergence of the discipline 'social work law' (Preston-Shoot et al., 1998a) is one such framework. Another is the construction of a conceptual frame wherein practice decisions are informed by knowledge of the legal rules alongside ethical dimensions of applying the law in practice and the role of the law in promoting rights (Braye and Preston-Shoot, 2006a).

Appraising social work law

The different purposes to which the law can be harnessed result in contradictions which, for social workers, formalise around conflicting imperatives. Thus, some procedures in child protection have to balance welfare with justice, where the requirement to promote the child's welfare conflicts with the parent's right to the justice of a fair investigative process and trial. The conflict between needs, resources and rights appears endemic within community care and services for children with special educational needs. The tension between the rights of the individual to autonomy and the rights of the state to intervene is present for adults lacking mental capacity and/or experiencing mental distress, and within the Children Act 1989 and its associated guidance.

These conflicting imperatives are encountered in practice as dilemmas, for example rights versus risks, care versus control, needs versus resources, professional power versus partnership with users, and professional versus agency agendas. Determining the balance to be struck in each situation will require an understanding of social work goals and legal goals, clarity about where social work and legal purposes overlap and where they diverge, and an approach to decision-making that weighs up the claims of each polarity. It requires consideration of proportionality (Human Rights Act 1998) – where an individual's rights are to be restricted or limited, the public authority must show how such action is prescribed by primary legislation and proportionate to the aims being pursued. It requires an understanding of the nature of the interaction between social work and the law, a continuum characterised by the extent to which either legal or social work language, methodology and values dominate (Preston-Shoot et al., 1998b). Increasingly, action should be guided by the principles outlined in statute (Children Act 1989; Mental Capacity Act 2005; Mental Health Act 2007).

Creative practice in the arena of social work law is thus characterised by the identification and exploitation of the spaces created by the legal rules and accompanying principles for practice. It connects different areas of the law, and utilises case law, advocacy provisions and appeals procedures – all with the purpose of pushing the law's boundaries to maximise a service user's rights and access to services.

Defining welfare

When social work and legislative goals diverge, this separation should be introduced into debates about the purpose of welfare. Social work has at least three frameworks for understanding to advance here:

1 An understanding of oppression and how social work risks being co-opted into the task of preserving power structures rooted in inequalities. This understanding is derived from research and service users' experiences. It informs practice based on values that emphasise rights and equality, and that adopts the outcomes emphasised in social policy for children (DfES, 2004) and for adults (DH, 2006) to argue for services that strive for an optimal satisfaction of basic needs.

2 A critical appraisal of the concepts that underpin social policy – partnership, empowerment, choice, quality and need – with particular reference to how the concepts can be recruited to serve both a New Right and an anti-oppressive agenda. This focuses on the quality of the lives of less powerful people by reference to key values and basic needs, and addresses awkward questions about the issues involved in need satisfaction, rights and resources, autonomy, protection and empowerment. It explores how social workers' accountability to different stakeholders should be managed, what a professional ethical duty of care should be, how welfare should be interpreted and needs defined, and how the legal mandate might be used with and for users. Practising social work law will involve accessing research on need in order to argue for services. It will involve enabling people to gain access to political processes by developing partnership and advocacy skills that place service users centre stage in articulating need, expressing choice and advocating change. Recent emphasis by government on the development of advocacy services (Adoption and Children Act 2002; Mental Capacity Act 2005; Mental Health Act 2007) and the involvement of service users in inspections and reviews supports this endeavour.

3 The third framework also draws from research and from listening to users. It identifies and actively promotes the core elements of good practice and delineates the contextual features that presently undermine that practice. Welfare is often presented as ineffective. Social work can reclaim its effectiveness – what is valuable and important between practitioners and service users.

Reviewing organisational behaviour and practice ethics

That agencies, far from solving problems, can maintain or exacerbate them is well known. Healthy organisations, therefore, require staff who will challenge received ideas and explore different possibilities, and who can identify the elements that can combine to render agencies dangerous or abusive (see Wardhaugh and Wilding, 1993; Waterhouse, 2000; CHAI, 2006). The emphasis now given in policy guidance to whistle-blowing procedures (for example DH, 2000d), following the Public Interest Disclosure Act 1998, endorses such staff activity. Equally, given the complicated and contradictory mandates inherent in social work law, competent organisations must engage with, rather than defend against, the dilemmas posed by their mandates and roles. Practice here may include forming alliances with other organisations and with service users to advocate for change, and providing clear direction about the principles that are to take precedence in practice. It should name the contradictions, for example between the Children Act 1989's emphasis on welfare and the Crime and Disorder Act 1998's emphasis on individual responsibility, reparation and rehabilitation. It should articulate the impact on people's lives of contemporary social and economic policies. It should incorporate acknowledgement of the feelings that the work engenders in practitioners and managers. The challenge is to create an organisational culture where responsibility is shared through structures of support, supervision and consultation, and where it is accepted that accountability to an employer can only be fulfilled with integrity where it is consistent with the higher order principle of effective, ethical and legal practice. This approach to practice is fully in line with the obligations on registered social workers (GSCC, 2004) to highlight resource and operational difficulties that affect the delivery of safe and effective care, and to uphold standards of practice by working lawfully.

To intervene in organisations requires a factual understanding of decision-making and policy-making structures and how to gain entry to these. It requires knowledge of law and policy guidance, which relate to the concerns to be raised in order that the challenging position being taken can be justified. It demands an understanding of how organisations respond to demands for change and, therefore, sophisticated change agent skills, together with constructing alliances or constituencies for change. Such practice requires skills in using legislation and policy provisions to achieve clearly expressed outcomes informed by social work values, theory and knowledge, and to advance ways of understanding and tackling issues that enable organisations to perceive room for manoeuvre and respond positively.

Conclusion

A common question is how social workers might practise anti-oppressively in the context of social control functions, resource and employment constraints, and the absence of a legal mandate in key areas of inequality. The answer partly centres on knowledge and skills that integrate social work and the law. Knowledge includes relevant statute, case law and guidance, together with learning from other disciplines that helps to make sense of the 'what' and 'why' of each practice situation. Skills, using this knowledge, include:

- Using law and guidance that endorse anti-discriminatory practice
- Using provisions to achieve outcomes informed by social work values
- Challenging how authorities approach decision-making and interpret the legislative mandate
- Presenting a clear rationale for practice, based on connecting knowledge with social work goals and tasks.

The challenge is to address the tensions and dilemmas inherent in social work law, and in the relationship between social work, social policy and the law, through a legal, policy and organisational literacy. This engages not just at the level of practice – the 'what', 'why' and 'how' of individual situations – but also at higher levels of context about the objectives of policy and the means by which they will be realised. If social work loses its ability or willingness to question and comment, it will lose its position to promote and empower a difference at the levels of individual and collective experience, and will become identified with policies, procedures and practices that evade awkward questions, mask inequality and perpetuate disadvantage.

For further discussion of using the law in work with children and families, see Chapter 22, and in adult services, see Chapter 23.

www.childrenslegalcentre.com   The Children's Legal Centre provides legal information, advice and advocacy concerning the rights of children and young people.

www.imhl.com   The Institute of Mental Health Law provides specialist information on mental health law in England and Wales.

Braye, S. and Preston-Shoot, M. (2006) *Teaching, Learning and Assessment of Law in Social Work Education: Resource Guide,* London, SCIE. Offers a range of resources for academic and practice teachers, students, practitioners, service users and managers. Provides examples of innovative approaches to teaching and practising social work law, and describes how legal knowledge can be linked to promoting an ethical and rights-based orientation to social work.

Braye, S. and Preston-Shoot, M. (2007) *Social Work Law: E-Learning,* London, SCIE. Ten e-learning objects are available for download (www.scie.org.uk/publications/elearning), covering perspectives from service users and carers, court room skills, knowledge of different mandates within social work law, and orientations to practice.

Braye, S. and Preston-Shoot, M. (2009) *Practising Social Work Law,* 3rd edn, Basingstoke, Palgrave Macmillan. Explores the tensions and dilemmas in the complex relationship between the law and social work, and offers guidance to practitioners and managers for legally competent social work practice.

Roach Anleu, S. (2000) *Law and Social Change,* London, Sage. Explores the relationship between law and social life. Considers the social conditions under which laws emerge and change, the values incorporated by law, and the degree to which a legal mandate might lead to social change.

Social work and organisations

This chapter provides an overview of the most significant organisational theories and developments that impact on social work and the wider public sector. It considers the implications of recent developments in management practices for the future organisation of social work.

Chapter overview

Understanding organisations and organisational change is a key knowledge area for social work service managers and practitioners, although not all organisational theorising has been of any long-term consequence. This chapter intends to fill a gap in the social work literature by providing an overview of organisational theory and trends, drawing out their relevance to developments in social work and the wider public sector. In this context, social work refers to any social work task undertaken in local authorities, probation, the voluntary sector or other agencies such as health and prisons that are funded in part or fully by the state.

Organisational theory

Organisational theory has a long history. Initially, it primarily focused on manufacturing processes and tasks but at the start of the twentieth century, following the work of Max Weber, there began a growing interest in organisational structures. After the Second World War, researchers became more interested in people and work motivation, culminating, by the end of the millennium, in attention to personal contributions such as sexuality, personality or emotional labour. Alongside this, the early interest in processes, structure and functions continued but with a new focus on quality and excellence in the 1970s and in communication technologies and their impact on work and organisation from the 1980s onwards. Recent 'wiki' approaches to product development challenge the whole notion of organisation, as networks of people – paid and unpaid, in and out of the 'organisation', users and providers – jointly develop new products for members or for the market. Although new organisational forms and approaches to work organisation have brought about paradigmatic shifts in thinking about organisations, the reality and practice are more residual and sedimentary, especially in the public sector. Most public sector and social work organisations are an amalgam of different organisational forms accrued over time, and to understand the modern-day organisation, it is necessary to understand its history.

Scientific management refers to theories and systems of management based on analysing processes of work in order to improve production.

Early observers of organisations focused their activities on manufacturing processes and in 1911 Frederick Taylor advocated **scientific management** and deconstructing tasks into their smallest possible elements to allow for improved process redesign. It was the job of managers, according to Taylor, to find the most efficient manufacturing practice and to cease tasks that did not add value. His ideas were instrumental in the development of highly specialised and divided labour, exemplified by the assembly lines of the mass-produced motor car manufacturer Henry Ford.

Taylorism was coined after the founder of scientific management, Frederick Taylor. It refers to a highly segmented division of labour that tends to increase efficiency at the cost of a deskilled and even dehumanised workforce.

Fordism is generally used to refer to systems of mass production and mass consumption typical of industrialised economies. Derives from the entrepreneur Henry Ford, who drew on Taylorist principles to develop his system of mass motor car production in his factory in Detroit.

Although professional occupations were not so highly divided as those in manufacturing, the influence of **Taylorism** or **Fordism**, as highly deconstructed production tasks came to be known, can be seen, even today, in the public sector. Benchmarking – comparing against other organisations – the most economic and efficient production methods is now a routine part of Best Value reviews (reviews, required in law, to be undertaken by public agencies to demonstrate that services are of good quality and are economic and efficient). The creation of 'public value' (Moore, 1995), including the concomitant removal of tasks that do not add value or could be better done by others, is reminiscent of Taylor's urging to focus on the essentials. Within the professions, there is now increased specialisation; sequential administrative and computational tasks, for example transferring client information, routine letters and data collation, have all but disappeared, and tasks are broken down into their constituent elements in order to 'process re-engineer' them and make the best use of technological advances. The introduction of technologically supported diagnosis and decision-making in professional tasks through tools such as computerised risk assessments has brought the work of professionals much closer to those of workers in manufacturing.

After the Second World War, interest grew in how organisations were structured and the role of managers. Henri Fayol is particularly known for his identification of five functions of management, but in the field of organisational studies, it is his theory of the 'unity of command' that has had most influence. He argued that each worker should have one supervisor and only one from whom they should take instructions, thus supporting a hierarchical organisation with a 'span of control' being no greater than that which could be managed by one person (Pugh and Hickson, 2007). Max Weber's ([1947] 1978) view that bureaucracy, characterised by a hierarchy, specialisation and role boundaries, was the 'perfect' form of organisation for large-scale administrative functions gained ground in organisational thinking in the UK. Weber identified the requirements of an impartial public service prior to the development of the modern welfare state when a range of professionals began to be absorbed into public services. Later, Henry Mintzberg (1979), developing Weber's thinking further, identified a range of organisational forms including that of a professional bureaucracy where the power lay with expertise rather than within hierarchical roles. Unity of command, traditional spans of control, appointment and promotion on merit and a bureaucratic organisational form remain dominant in the public sector and large charities. Increasingly too, the rules and procedures are determined by the employing organisation rather than by the professional body, if only to safeguard against negligence claims. This is especially true in social work.

> The human relations school of management comprises a cluster of initiatives and methods of improving productivity or effectiveness, by taking into account a variety of human factors affecting people's performance, individually, in groups and across the organisation as a whole.

From the 1950s, the negative effects of Taylorism and the developments in occupational psychology prompted an interest in worker motivation and wellbeing, especially social solidarity. **The human relations school of management** included theorists such as:

- Maslow (1968) who identified a 'hierarchy of needs', starting from the basic physiological needs of food and shelter and rising to the highest level of 'self-actualisation' – reaching one's fullest potential and creativity
- Hertzberg (1959) who argued that work motivation was intrinsic to the job, for example interest, challenge and value, but that conditions of employment and relations in the workplace had the capacity to demotivate
- Mayo (1933, 1975) who identified group cohesion, the 'Hawthorne effect', as a major factor in worker satisfaction and productivity and suggested that managers should encourage it.

Although there was some scepticism about the extent to which employers subscribed to any of the new theories (Braverman, 1974), the work of the human relations school influenced the new human resources corporate function, which, from the 1960s onwards, was beginning to replace the personnel or 'industrial relations' functions in large corporations. Over time, organisations began to pay more attention to the employment conditions, needs and motivations of their workforce.

In the late1960s, focus turned again to the structuring of organisations and the organisation of work but, rather than identifying an ideal or effective structure or organisational form, theorists concluded that degrees of formalisation, bureaucracy or hierarchy were outcomes of the industry's technology (Woodward, 1970) or size (Hickson et al., 1974). Unsurprisingly therefore, the bureaucratic form has continued to dominate organisational structures and although there has been a lack of faith in its capacity to further increase productivity or quality in a competitive global environment, two new directions emerged in the organisational literature. First, during the 1970s, the West looked to Japan, a market-driven rather than production-driven economy in which products were manufactured 'just in time' – the delivery of products and parts at the moment of need – by 'lean manufacturing' processes – paring all processes to the minimum necessary to deliver the product. Japanese products were noted for quality (simplicity), attention to detail, and speed of innovation. Success was attributed to teamworking, workforce flexibility and focus on innovation and quality through 'quality circles', all supported by a strong company culture (Schonberger, 1984).

Although Japanese manufacturing was subsequently to take a downturn, the approach radically changed thinking in the West about organisations as a conglomerate of functions to understanding them as a system of processes for meeting customer needs, including non-production processes such as marketing and complaint handling. This outward-looking, customer-focused way of doing business, the antithesis of 'you can have any colour you like as long as its black' Fordism, resulted in more modular production, choice and a greater number of business partners or 'co-producers'. Yet, although teamwork and empowerment, as organisational resources, continue to be valued by managers, it has not brought the increases in productivity that were envisaged by the West, possibly because it took hold as an idea during the 1980s and was accompanied by 'downsizing' and redundancies.

Second, theorists explored aspects of organisational life, such as emotions, creativity, commitment and solidarity, previously considered 'inimical to rational, efficient capitalism' (Clegg, 1990: 150). Religious, feminist, gay and lesbian and anti-hierarchical organisations in the black and green movements had long built on the personal experience and commitment of staff and volunteers, and the professional discourse had always emphasised personal commitment above and beyond the call of duty but few for-profit organisations had pursued this route consciously. Bringing a personal and emotional commitment to 'excellence' into the organisation was largely driven by the work of Peters and Waterman (1982). *In Search of Excellence*, their bestselling book, has been one of the most influential management books ever written. They called for senior managers to capture the hearts and minds of their workers through their own passion and commitment. This marked a new trend in valorising the personal and the emotional along with the scientific and rational in management. The key attributes of 'management excellence' – vision, innovation, commitment and energy – are now understood as 'transformational leadership' and Peters and Waterman prompted a rethinking of leadership and management as two different disciplines; leaders looking to the future while managers were managing the present. *In Search of Excellence* marked the final death knell of production-driven rather than customer-driven manufacturing.

At about the same time as the inherent weaknesses of traditional hierarchical bureaucracies were being articulated in the private sector, the Conservative government, elected in 1979, identified the same weaknesses in the provision of state services. In addition to seeking to reduce public expenditure, the government was critical of welfare services that were producer driven and unresponsive to the 'customer' as taxpayer or service user. The new 'public management' (Hood, 1991) that emerged over the following decade ushered in the notion of the citizen as consumer and taxpayer, the three Es (efficiency, effectiveness and economy), greater competition (quasi or real) and private sector styles of management including performance incentives. Choice, voice, redress and (later) personalisation became the watchwords, if not always the reality, of public sector provision (Leadbeater, 2004). Agencies and professionals were increasingly split between purchasers and providers or case managers and practitioners, and a greater multiplicity of providers from the public, voluntary and private sectors competed for state business.

Under the Conservative government, the market and competition was at the heart of the public sector reform project. In 1997, with the election of New Labour and the ideology of the Third Way (between the extremes of the market economy and the state providing all services) (Giddens, 1998), a more pragmatic approach to the delivery of public services was introduced. The government continued to value plurality of provision as a means of creating choice and competition, while seeking greater collaboration and cooperation between public sector agencies and profession-als. 'What works' was expected to drive organisational arrangements based on effectiveness and Best Value, with no bar to or any requirement for any sector becom-ing a provider of public services.

More recently, in the business world, as more established companies have strug-gled to compete against new online and other service-based or information-based businesses, a new paradigm for organising has emerged. It is built not on personal commitment to the work of an organisation, or indeed to work at all, but to a commitment to complex problem-solving where the rewards are intellectual and personal recognition for skills, simply 'because they are fascinated by a problem and want to contribute to solving it' (Gloor, 2006: 13). In particular, the success of Linux (the development for free of free software by technically skilled programmers) and electronic 'freeconomics' (matching of free goods or services to potential recipients) has challenged much of the orthodoxy about what a successful organisation should look like. The products of Linux (and Wikipedia and many other networked organ-isations) are made by unpaid people who are totally absorbed in problem-solving. They work cooperatively, share intellectual property and change each others' work to improve on it.

Some people may have political motives such as anti-capitalism (or they may start that way) or are sufficiently concerned about the global ubiquity of certain products to commit to creating competition without pay, but secure in peer respect. This shift has also been paralleled by the growth of religious or political networks, where a strong ideology, but little to speak of in terms of organisational infrastructure, is suffi-cient to achieve change (for good or ill). Terrorist organisations such as al-Qaeda are an example of this. Within this model, leadership is more personalised but also dispersed and there can be little control over who can emerge as a sector leader or collaborator.

In an increasingly specialised world, a greater number of collaborators with different skills are needed to develop a product or service. The end 'provider' may only coordinate and 'badge' the efforts of a range of contributors, although entirely dependent on them for the final product. Contributors may be both users and developers. A system may be free for use so long as any developments made by those using the system are also made freely available to others. In this way, the webs of interdependency are strong and self-supporting. This approach is not yet as well developed in the public or voluntary sector. Yet, given their purpose of improving social outcomes and being resourced from the same public purse, these sectors should be ideally placed to work in this new way. Resources such as parenting education, offending desistance programmes, healthy eating programmes or children's education resources would benefit from a collaborative approach, making freely available resources that at present are either unobtainable to service users or at a cost that only certain sectors of the population can afford.

Social care professionals are increasingly developing user-generated or uploaded web-based information and learning resources for their own professional development, resources that are updated in real time, for example BUBL and Intute. The Wikipedia approach to developing site content (user-generated material developed according to agreed standards with editing controls limited to the minimum necessary to meet the standards) is radically changing and democratising information (Tapscott and Williams, 2006). The boundary between user and producer is blurred and no single contributor is the sole repository of expertise.

Behind these changes is an underlying assumption that, in a fast-moving information and knowledge economy, each individual professional has a personal responsibility for updating their knowledge and skills from easily accessed e-resources. This assumption is beginning to be reflected in the organisational literature. The 'learning organisation' (Senge, 1990), in which it was assumed that workers would need to constantly adapt their skills according to new demands, is now being replaced by the 'adaptive organisation' in the discourse (Chapman, 2002). An adaptive organisation's members are so in tune with the changing environment that the organisation is in a state of constant adjustment without individuals having to undertake targeted learning and relearning to change the way they behave. An adaptive organisation assumes that there are no ready-made solutions and success is dependent on changing and mutating in an experimental fashion, discovering what works on the way (Bently and Wisdon, 2003; Brafman and Beckstrom, 2006). Some firms, for example Google, expect R&D staff to spend part of their time pursuing their own projects, some of which will be successful, others not. One intention is to stimulate the characteristics of the adaptive organisation – enthusiasm, creativity, innovation, learning and the development of problem-solving skills – rather than solely as a means of generating new products.

In a global market-driven economy where consumers can purchase a wide range of services, including healthcare, from providers all over the world or move to countries with better social care provision, the traditional role of local and central governments as providers of services is being severely challenged. Public sector agencies must 'add value' beyond that which can be provided through the market or the third sector to be secure in having a future role. Given the pace of economic and social change and the potential casualties of that change, the role may be as much an influencing one as providing a service (Moore, 1995; Cabinet Office, 2002). For social workers in any sector, their influence may be at an individual or family level but for social work organisations, this may extend to influencing community or corporate behaviour where it has the potential to enhance or is detrimental to the wellbeing of citizens.

New organisational forms

The current organisational literature suggests that the twenty-first-century successful organisations will be dependent on innovation, speed to market and customisation. With increased globalisation and the growth in communications and manufacturing technologies, the focus is on the organisation as a network of people, working together cooperatively but at a distance for a common good (Castells, 2000). Valued professionals are those who combine expertise with the technical capacity to solve problems, particularly major global problems such as health and the environment (Brint, 1994). With the growing standardisation and mechanisation of some professional tasks, status in organisations will continue to shift from those professionals working directly with service users to those who are responsible for developing solutions to current social problems, be they managers, policy advisers or innovative technicians (Brint, 1994). Increasingly, business managers are seeking to harness the creativity evident in peer problem-solving networks, either by directly employing those who are known among their peers as innovators or by recreating the essential elements of networks that appear to be delivering success.

Moynagh and Worsley (2005) surveyed the current organisational landscape with an eye to the future and suggest that the organisations most likely to emerge in the future are:

- *the virtual corporation*, 'a network of contractors held together by legal bonds' or joint venture agreements, coordinated through a 'strategic centre'
- *the boundaryless organisation,* or one with 'highly porous' boundaries and greater use of internal and external networks, in which 'information will flow freely across its "borders" and people will work easily on either side'
- *the project-based (or team) organisation*, made up of temporary groups of people that will disperse as the project ends
- *the modular (or cellular) corporation,* in which small teams with standard operating procedures combine and recombine in different configurations

- *the process-based (or horizontal) organisation*, which will manage processes not functions (Moynagh and Worsley, 2005: 118–19).

In the public sector, Williams (2002) has argued that successful organisations will need a 'commitment to the building of inter-organizational capacity' and the language should reflect 'relationships, interconnections and interdependencies – holistic thinking'. He goes on to say that:

> Bureaucratic forms of organization which champion the virtues of rationality, professionalism and compartmentalism are anathema to the challenge of interdependencies. Forms of organization and governance that are designed around collaboration, partnership and networking appear to be more suitable for this task. (Williams, 2002: 105)

The observations of Moynagh and Worsley, and Williams about the organisations of the future are already evident in the field of social care where there is a considerable amount of interagency and intra-agency working from the top to the bottom of the organisation. Multidisciplinary teams based around a person or service user or a problem-solving project are increasingly common, with different team members and configurations according to the task. At a more formal level, agencies have been required to work together through partnership Action Zones, or for the purposes of improving regeneration, child protection or community safety. Some are statutory, for example community safety partnerships under the Crime and Disorder Act 1998. However, statutory partnerships generally require plans, annual reports and formal processes, which may be in tension with the aspirations for greater collaboration, flexibility and speed of development and delivery.

New forms of organising work may be adopted by organisations because they appear to be successful elsewhere and offer a solution to identified problems of productivity. However, the choice of organisational form is often contingent on the task, the context, sector technologies and the options available and may not emerge as a deliberate choice but one that evolves over time. Wikipedia, for example, now has rules about contributions and some of the entries cannot be edited by any one other than those authorised to do so. In the third sector, Women's Aid has shifted from being a democratically organised feminist collective to a mainstream public service with hierarchies, differential pay rates, processes and procedures and annual planning. These changes may come about because of the power of the dominant (purchasing) sector and the pressures on the smaller/newer organisation to conform to the expectations of the older more established funders, or it may be that beyond a certain size, managers believe that some tasks are better served (or more easily controlled) by bureaucracy, especially those tasks that are routine and where consistency is required. This contingent and incremental approach to organising is likely to lead to a complex mix of older forms of organising coupled with new elements. Even within a single organisation, we might expect to see networked, hierarchical, functional and process-driven practices.

As organisational shapes and arrangements change, so too do employees' relationships with their employing organisation. There has been a significant increase in the proportion of the workforce who are self-employed or working on a contract basis, and highly marketable employees may be able to negotiate contracts that provide greater flexibility. A number of people have 'portfolio' careers, earning their income from a range of sources. For example, there has been a significant rise in the number of social work professionals working as self-employed report writers, associate inspectors, critical incident reviewers and independent chairs for children's reviews. Increasingly, many organisations are seeking to provide a better work–life balance for employees and in this regard the public sector leads.

The private sector is more able to reinvent its purpose and products than the public sector, which will remain constrained by legal requirements to provide particular services. The public sector does not have the same freedom to innovate, particularly if innovation could lead to a greater demand for services, nor can it opt out of uneconomic provision, and so the public sector is likely to remain as the 'cushion' for market failure. Nonetheless, there is considerable scope for innovation, innovation that will change the skills mix in the social care sector. We are likely to see continued development of technological solutions such as electronic self-help guides, which will require the inclusion of technical expertise in IT systems, presentation, communication and learning as well as expertise in the theoretical or practical programme content. Likewise, the expansion of new developments such as electronic monitoring of offenders will lead to a different range of professionals being involved in the 'core team'.

One further development linked to the new networked organisational paradigm has been the growth in the number of social entrepreneurs. Individuals, sometimes with considerable venture philanthropy capital at their disposal, can identify potential solutions to social problems and work with others, across a range of backgrounds and disciplines, to create a new service. Social entrepreneurs believe they can combine the innovation and entrepreneurship of the private sector with the social conscience of the voluntary sector. They have much greater flexibility than the public sector and so are attractive to government in the overall mix of provision.

Which way for social work?

There are some real tensions in developing a more flexible and innovative public sector. The competition and business ethos that has replaced the bureau professionalism of the welfare state has led to a greater focus on costs and controls, which is inimical to innovation and responsiveness to human needs (Harris, 2003). This is probably why new social entrepreneurs are able to be more innovative and responsive. Even the core principles (challenge, consultation, comparison and competition) of the Best Value regime in England and Wales (which replaced compulsory competitive tendering in 2000) implies doing the same but better, rather than innovation.

The focus remains on the three Es of economy, efficiency and effectiveness, with comparator services being those in the same business, not those that might radically meet need but in an entirely different way (DETR, 1998). Increasingly, social work is about risk management in a 'risk society' (Beck, 1992). A blame/fear-driven culture is a risk-averse one and public agencies are managing risks by increasing the number of procedures that, if not followed, leave staff exposed to accusations of negligence (Hood et al., 2001). Additionally, the introduction of performance indicators against a background of star ratings and the potential for public exposure has led to some professionals distorting practice towards that which will meet targets, even at the expense of good outcomes, for example in keeping children in suboptimal placements (Munro, 2004a).

The public sector also remains largely dominated by the professions working within professional boundaries, and working in partnership with other agencies and disciplines has been challenging (Rushmer and Pallis, 2003; NFER, 2001). Working in partnership with the public and service users has been no less a challenge, especially in determining whose voice should count and in working with 'counter-publics' such as Fathers for Justice or parents of abused children (Barnes et al., 2003). Moreover, central government bureaucratic requirements can, of themselves, stifle the very partnership behaviour it wishes to encourage (Public Service Productivity Panel, 2001).

Traditionally, national governments, although more evident in England and Wales than in Scotland, have sought change by tackling structures from the outside through, for example, requiring compulsory competitive tendering, restructuring local boundaries or seeking health providers from outside the NHS. Although the option of structural change remains firmly on the political agenda, the governments of England, Wales and Scotland have all sought to encourage greater flexibility and responsiveness through 'decluttering' the performance landscape by reducing the number of inspectorate bodies, seeking greater synergy between them and requiring agencies to focus more on outcomes than processes through local outcome agreements. Even then, the performance targets for local authorities remain numerous and poor or failing councils are still subject to the formal engagement of government officials.

The reporting burden on social workers and other public sector professionals cannot be overestimated. Social workers appear to be particularly burdened by bureaucracy and organisational constraints, judging by the responses provided to the Audit Commission in 2002 in its report on recruitment and retention of local authority social workers. The primary reasons for leaving were bureaucracy, paperwork and targets, followed by insufficient resources and unmanageable workloads, lack of autonomy, feeling undervalued and pay. A great number of those leaving the statutory sector join voluntary organisations and increasingly there are opportunities in the private sector. As well as legislation with which social workers must comply, there are also national standards, performance indicators, Best Value indicators, local guidance and policies and inspection requirements. Additionally, they may have to provide information about particular client groups for local planning purposes. Technology is reducing the burden in terms of information-gathering, processing and collating but a significant burden remains.

The demands of central government coupled with the very traditional environment of local government, especially with its lack of flexibility in the recruitment and deployment of staff, have resulted in some authorities encouraging innovation by 'floating' parts of the organisation into trusts or other structures that give some entrepreneurial freedom to develop the organisation in ways that best suit the task. Social housing provided through housing associations is one example and there are others such as the Community and Safety Service in Glasgow that deals with all crime prevention concerns. The voluntary sector and social entrepreneurs will be well placed to provide the flexibility that government needs to ensure service provision can more rapidly adapt according to changing demography or demand. The current direction of travel suggests that in future, there will be more joint production of goods or services between private and public organisations (and service users) and, perhaps, less commissioning and contracting. Undoubtedly, however, contract management will remain a feature of interorganisational relationships.

Reports from social work inspectorates across the UK have noted that local authority social work services are riddled with experiments and practices that have been discontinued once short-term funding ceases as well as mountains of guidance and bureaucracy, much of which has not been revised for a good number of years. Any organisational form, including entrepreneurial and bureaucratic forms, will not achieve the potential to support staff without attention to sustainability. New ways of organising may be successful because of the commitment of those developing them but may fall into ignominy without longer term assiduous attention and resources. Staff then see change as 'just another fad'.

This is not to suggest that social work organisations should ignore new ideas for improving organisational capacity but decisions about organisational structures and staffing need to be based on some knowledge of different organisational forms and the environments in which they work best. For example, the assessment of needs of older people leaving hospital may require a different organisational form to that of developing of a new service for asylum-seeking families, who have few material resources and cannot speak English. The former may require a more bureaucratic organisation so that the social worker knows what money is available, how it is accessed, with whom they must liaise and the timescales for delivery. On the other hand, the refugee social worker may need to 'organise' a wide and varied network in order to begin to understand the problem. A highly rule-bound organisation is unlikely to be helpful, whereas in the first illustration, too much innovation and entrepreneurship might lead to instability and interagency confusion.

Conclusion

In spite of all the difficulties and constraints outlined above, the current trends in organisational thinking provide many opportunities for social work practitioners in any agency. The current discourse of outcomes, personalisation, entre-preneurship and innovation coupled with new developments by 'communities of interest' may provide opportunities for change previously only available to those designated as managers. Those who can suggest improvements and see the way forward to delivering them with realistic plans and proposals are much more likely to succeed than those who adopt formal methods of raising matters about existing services or processes and await their formal resolution through working parties or policy groups and so on. 'Coalitions of the willing' are more in tune with today's environment than involvement on the basis of roles. Additionally, new methods of organising that require practitioner collaboration between disciplines and service users provide opportunities for radically empowering service users and enabling them to have a greater input in service design and delivery than hitherto. This is not to say that, in a traditional bureaucracy, roles and hierarchies can be bypassed, they remain powerful, but with increasing pressures to deliver better services, those who can provide solutions will be more likely to be heard than ever before.

For further discussion of the management dimension, see Adams et al., 2009c, Chapter 11, and for how practitioners manage the workload, see Adams et al., 2009c, Chapter 12.

www.tomorrowproject.net/   The Tomorrow Project is a not-for-profit organisation that analyses emerging social, economic and demographic trends and offers insights into what they will mean for us all in the future.

www.workfoundation.org.uk/   The research section of this website provides up-to-date, easy-to-read reports on current public sector trends (for example on public value and collaboration) and implications for work.

www.iriss.ac.uk/   The Institute for Research and Innovation in Social Services for all those in the social care fields in Scotland provides information on e-learning and e-information relevant to all UK students and practitioners.

www.bubl.ac.uk and www.intute.ac.uk/socialservices/   These two academic sites provide access to research papers and other documents, useful to those working in the social care and justice sectors.

Burke, W.W. (2008) *Organization Change: Theory and Practice*, Thousand Oaks, CA, Sage. Good, general, up-to-date book on current thinking and practice in organisational change.

Handy, C. (1999) *Understanding Organizations*, London, Penguin. Widely read, popular book by an admired author and thinker, which still offers refreshing insights into organisational behaviour.

Morgan, G. (2006) *Images of Organization*, Thousand Oaks, CA, Sage. Influential book in the field of organisational studies, and an interesting read, using metaphor to understand and decode organisational behaviour and practices.

Moynagh, M. and Worsley, R. (2005) *Working in the Twenty First Century*, Leeds, The Tomorrow Project/ESRC. Examines social, economic and technological trends and explores what these mean for the future of work and its organisation.

Pugh, D.S. and Hickson, D.J. (2007) *Writers on Organizations*, London, Penguin. Summarises the work of the most influential organisational theorists from Max Weber to the present day.

10 Perspectives on the life course: childhood and adolescence

Chapter overview

This chapter focuses on human development in infancy, childhood and adolescence. In the light of recent research findings, it revisits some long-standing debates about the importance of early experiences to later human development and the ways in which individuals cope with adversity. It indicates some of the complexities in understanding human growth and development as well as some directions for further study.

The relevance of human growth and development for social work

The effectiveness of social work interventions in the here and now depends on the understanding of what has come before and what will happen next in the lives of those who are the target of such interventions. Thus knowledge of human growth and development plays an essential part in assessing, planning and intervening in a successful, positive way in people's lives.

This is reflected in the international definition of social work devised jointly by the International Federation of Social Workers (IFSW) and supported by the International Association of Schools of Social Work (IASSW) which is quoted on page 2 of Chapter 1 of this book.

Moreover, theories of human growth and development are seen as a central body of knowledge among the theory base of social work:

> The social work profession draws on theories of human development and behaviour and social systems to analyse complex situations and to facilitate individual, organisational, social and cultural changes. (IFSW, 2000)

The study of human growth and development is identified as a key knowledge requirement, reflected in the academic standards as set out in the social work subject benchmark statement:

The relevance of psychological and physiological perspectives to understanding individual and social development and functioning. (QAA, 2000) "

In the current climate of evidence-based and research-informed social work practice, the challenge of the human growth and development body of knowledge is to provide relevant, scientific and evidenced-based frameworks for those who are training to be or are social workers. This implies recognition of the contribution that many academic disciplines make to the field of studying human growth and development (Sugarman, 2001). Although the current trend is to view social work as a distinctive academic area, with its own recognised body of research – the Economic and Social Research Council is taking positive steps in promoting change in the breadth, depth and quality of the UK research base in social work; and social work research is closely aligned with other disciplines in the government's Research Assessment Exercise – there is still debate as to the extent to which empirical social work research contributes to generating the theoretical base (Trinder, 1996; Berridge, 2007). Human growth and development remains a substantive part of the social work theoretical knowledge base that is drawn or 'borrowed' from other disciplines, mainly developmental psychology, but also sociology, biology, anthropology and so on.

The theories of human growth and development across the life span address several complex questions: What are the mechanisms or processes that bring change in development? How do the physical, cognitive, emotional and social functions of the individual interact in the course of development? How relevant are early experiences for later development? How do the environment and social context influence individual development?

The central theme of this chapter is reviewing, in the light of recent research findings, the long-standing debate of how relevant early experiences are to later human development and how individuals overcome adversity and continue normal development (the ability or process known as **resilience**). The debate is highly relevant to social work practice. We know that the experiences of children, families and adults with whom social workers work are likely to fall outside the 'normal' range of developmental issues and they are likely to experience or have experienced adverse environments at some point in their development. The debate will be supported by recent theoretical developments and research evidence from studies of individuals who suffered early deprivation, intercountry adoption studies as well as longitudinal studies on **attachment**. The issues discussed in this chapter span the first three life stages – infancy through childhood and adolescence – and are

Resilience refers to the ability of individuals, families, groups and communities exposed to harm to resist its negative consequences and develop positively regardless.

Attachment relates to the feelings of warmth and security that accompany being well looked after by another person. It represents a key means by which babies and children, when most dependent and vulnerable, gain a sense of security and are protected from risks and anxieties that otherwise might adversely affect their emotional, mental or social development.

intended as initial steps in exploring the complexities of human growth and development that the reader may wish to take further.

Early experiences and later development

One of the most enduring debates in the study of individual human development is that of continuity versus change. Initially, it encompassed the assumption that early years have long-lasting, even irreversible, effects on later development and functioning in later life. Early theories of human development were based around this assumption. For example, both **behaviourism** and the psychoanalytic theories argue – albeit for different reasons – that outcomes in adulthood are predicted from infancy. **Psychoanalytical theory** suggests that early experiences are extremely relevant for later development, as basic patterns of personality upon which subsequent experiences are based are formed by the age of six (Newman and Newman, 2007). Behaviourists saw development in terms of environmental influences on the child, and the earlier the input, the more crucial (Schaffer, 2006). Therefore, the impact of trauma, abuse and deprivation during the early years was thought to have irreversible, lifelong consequences.

Behaviourism refers to psychological theories and practices based on changing behaviour by conditioning to ensure that new behaviour is learned.

Psychoanalytic theory relates to psychoanalysis, a cluster of theories and practices developed by Austrian physicians Sigmund Freud, Carl Jung and their followers. Psychoanalytic theory has produced numerous ways of understanding and treating human problems, most commonly using the method of the patient verbalising thoughts, dreams and fantasies that the analyst uses to understand and treat inner emotional, mental and unconscious processes contributing to the problems.

Support for the argument in favour of the irreversibility of early experiences came from early studies on children brought up in severely deprived environments, such as institutions. Orphanages functioned for centuries as a solution for 'tidying up' the problem of abandoned infants (by hiding them from public view). Well into the twentieth century, in major Western countries, placement of an infant in an orphanage was equivalent to a death sentence, with mortality rates exceeding 90 per cent during the first years of life (Johnson, 2002). Consequently, it was only in the late 1930s and 40s, after improvements in sanitation and medical care in these institutions, that concerns about the development of children living in orphanages were raised. Evidence of 'hospitalism' and severe developmental delays resulting in physical and mental deficits such as motor retardation, rudimentary language, grossly retarded perceptual and motor skills, paucity of emotional expression, lack of attachment behaviour and social withdrawal became linked to the experience of institutional rearing in infancy (Clarke and Clarke, 1976). The postwar years saw the emergence of the concept of **maternal deprivation** (Bowlby, 1951), with claims being made about the irreparable consequences of, and the subsequent mental health difficulties caused by, an interrupted mother–child relationship in infancy. Studies of institutionalised children (comprehensively reviewed in Clarke and Clarke, 1976) seemed to support these claims and documented the preva-

> Maternal deprivation refers literally to the separation of the infant from the mother. However, it commonly carries the implication of the negative consequences following from this.

lence of chronic impairments in multiple areas of functioning, including physical, cognitive and emotional development, unless the children were placed in a family environment during infancy. The belief that early experiences, and especially early separation from the mother or early lack of mothering, have permanent and damaging effects rapidly became widespread. One influential application of this theory is the fact that it was followed by a marked reduction in the use of residential care for children, especially in the early years of life, and other alternatives such as foster care or adoption were promoted (Tizard, 1977). However, theoretical and research developments in the area of children's identity development and wellbeing (Owusu-Bempah, 2007) have since challenged the practice of moving children from their birth families and current practice encourages supporting children to be cared for within their birth or kin families wherever possible.

Challenges to the irreversibility assumption

In the 1970s, new studies began to challenge both the concept of maternal deprivation and the irreversibility of the effects induced by early deprivation experiences. The hypothesis of 'maternal deprivation' has been extensively examined by Rutter (1972) in a book entitled *Maternal Deprivation Reassessed*, in which he argues that the nature of the separation experience and the range of associated psychosocial risks are important, and not the separation per se. Evidence contrary to the hypothesised irreversible damaging effect of maternal deprivation also emerged from case studies of children rescued from extremely severe adversities, such as children who had been isolated, neglected and abused for prolonged periods of time (Hall, 1985; Skuse, 1984a, 1984b, 1985; Thompson, 1986). These studies showed that if rescue is followed by strong intervention and if there is an absence of congenital damage, the prospects of recovery are very positive (Clarke and Clarke, 1976, 2000).

At the time the orphanages were closing in the UK, giving way to foster care and adoption, Tizard and colleagues (Tizard, 1977; Tizard and Hodges, 1978; Tizard and Rees, 1974, 1975; Hodges and Tizard, 1989a, 1989b) initiated a longitudinal study of the developmental outcomes of institutionalised children who were placed in foster care, adopted or reunited with their birth families before the age of two. The important feature of this research is that the children in the study were living in good-quality institutions, which provided them not only with good physical care, but also with a stimulating environment, even though it was impersonal: they were cared for by a large number of staff, who made deliberate attempts to minimise emotional involvement between themselves and the children. This study, unique at that time in its comprehensive longitudinal assessment of the outcome of institutional rearing on child and adolescent development (the children in the sample were followed up to the age of 16), not only showed that adoption could reverse some of the deficits associated with early childhood institutionalisation, but also pointed out that adoptive children were faring as well as, and in some areas better than, those restored to their birth families (Tizard and Rees, 1974; Hodges and Tizard, 1989a). For example, by the age of 16, no effect of early institutionalisation was found on IQ, and early institutional rearing did not seem to prevent the adolescents from forming strong and lasting attachments to parents once they were placed in families. The study also indicates that there are some long-term effects of institutionalisation, especially in the area of social and family relationships: the ex-institutionalised adolescents were more oriented towards adult attention and had more difficulties with peers and fewer close relationships than the non-institutionalised adolescents used as comparison (Hodges and Tizard, 1989b).

Even though caring for children and infants in large institutions has diminished greatly in most Western countries, studies of the outcomes of children who are 'looked after' in substitute care arrangements (small children's homes, foster placement and so on) continue to be reported. They tend to illustrate a higher rate of emotional, social, behavioural and educational problems for these children overall compared with the general population (Brand and Brinich, 1999; Roy et al., 2000; Rutter, 2000; Triseliotis, 2002). However, there is less consensus regarding the reasons for these difficulties. Studies have shown that these children also come from families with parents with multiple problems in parenting and diverse psychopathologies (Quinton and Rutter, 1984a, 1984b). Rutter (2000) suggests that when considering the adjustment of children in various substitute care settings, it is important to take into consideration factors such as the biological background of these children, which may include genetic vulnerabilities and the experiences of the children before entering care, as they are likely to have experienced adverse environments, for example poor or inadequate parenting and family conflict.

Early deprivation and resilience

The topic of 'early deprivation and later development' was revived in the 1990s by the opportunity to study children who grew up in impoverished institutions in Eastern European countries, particularly Romania, and who were subsequently adopted by Western couples after the fall of the communist regimes. Research studies were conducted in the main receiving countries (the UK, the US and Canada) and particular references to 'Romanian orphans' seem to attract the attention of numerous segments of the international research community. This 'natural experiment' provided a unique opportunity to readdress the question of relevance of early experiences on subsequent development. One of most rigorously conducted study was the English and Romanian Adoptees (ERA) Study conducted by a team at the London Institute of Psychiatry. A longitudinal sample of 111 Romanian children aged under 2 at the time of their adoption into the UK were followed up at 4, 6 and 11 years of age and compared with a sample of 50 within-UK adoptees (Rutter et al., 1998, 1999, 2007a, 2007b, 2007c).

The conclusions reported to date point towards a remarkable resilience in development (Groothues et al., 2001; Rutter et al., 2007a), although with certain caveats. The physical and cognitive development of many Romanian adoptees showed impressive catch-up after their adoption, resulting in functioning that was in the average ranges within a few years of their adoption (Rutter et al., 1998). However, the improvement of children who had spent a considerable time in Romania (mostly in institutions) was not as great as that of children who had spent less time, and their overall levels of development remained lower. The assessment at age 11 confirmed further continuity and change in cognitive catch-up (Beckett et al., 2006). There were, however, concerns that the attachment patterns of these children showed features of 'indiscriminate friendliness' (O'Connor et al., 1999, 2000a, 2000b) and a small proportion of children also showed 'autistic-like' features (Rutter et al., 1999). Moreover, attachment problems, inattention/overactivity, quasi-autistic features and cognitive impairment were associated with a longer duration of institutional privation, but emotional difficulties, poor peer relationships and conduct problems were not (Kreppner et al., 2001; Rutter et al., 2001; Beckett et al., 2002). Overall, 'duration of exposure to severe global early privation' was the most powerful predictor of individual differences in developmental outcomes. However, the frequency of disinhibited attachment was reduced at age 11 (Rutter et al., 2007b) and a quarter lost their 'quasi-autistic' features (Rutter et al., 2007c).

Before these conclusions can be accepted with confidence, certain limitations of these studies have to be considered carefully. Research on international adoption usually involves the design known as 'natural experiment' (Serbin, 1997), in which a group of children who have been placed in adoptive homes, without any random assignment or other experimental control procedures, is identified. These types of natural experiment allow researchers to examine the effect of interventions that cannot be carried out ethically using true experimental designs. There is considerable potential for learning about human development and its limits from these situations. However, research questions should be addressed by the careful selection of certain groups. For example, in order to examine the effect of early privation on subsequent child development, the best comparison group to use would have been the children who remained in Romanian institutions and who were not adopted, but to date none of the studies has included such a comparison group.

Nevertheless, the overall findings from studies on Romanian orphans adopted in the UK highlight the remarkable resilience of development following 'rescue' from early and severe deprivation (Schaffer, 2000). Although the extent to which these findings could be generalised to less severe forms of deprivation is yet to be ascertained by further research, there are important lessons to be learned about the resilience of human development in the aftermath of early deprivation.

Resilience is conceptualised as an ability to recover from negative experiences rather than invulnerability to stress (Rutter, 1999). Other authors (Olsson et al., 2003) make a distinction between resilience as an outcome and resilience as a process. The perspective of resilience as an outcome will emphasise the role of individual variables – such as self-esteem, social competence, internal locus of control and so on – in coping with adverse experience(s). Seen as a process, resilience takes into account the mechanisms that act to modify the impact of the adverse experience, that is, the protective factors that may moderate or mediate the impact of risk factors. The concepts of risk and resilience have been applied to understanding the variety of disadvantages that might be experienced by adolescents in today's society and how young people can overcome adversity and how professionals can facilitate this process (Coleman and Hagell, 2007).

Attachment from infancy through adolescence

Attachment theory remains one of the influential developmental theories in social work (Howe, 1995), particularly in child welfare, although its scientific basis and practice relevance has been and continues to be challenged (Barth et al., 2005). Attachment is generally defined as an enduring affectional bond of substantial intensity (Armsden and Greenberg, 1987; Ainsworth, 1989). Traditionally used to describe affectional bonds between infants and their primary carers (Bowlby, 1951), the term has been broadened to include other developmental periods, such as adolescence (Allen and Land, 1999), and adulthood (Hazan and Shaver, 1987; Bartholomew and Horowitz, 1991). This section will critically examine the continuity assumption of attachment formed in infancy across childhood and adolescence.

The developmental period in which the attachment is studied has a direct influence on the way attachment is conceptualised. During infancy, attachment is assessed as a behavioural dimension reflecting the extent to which attachment figures are used for support and proximity (Ainsworth, 1989).

Acquiring the capacity for symbolic representation enables the child to form representations of 'secure base' experiences and expectations about their own and other people's behaviour; about the acceptability and social effectiveness of the self, and about the emotional interest and availability of others. It is considered that if the quality of parenting is 'good enough', children develop a broadly positive mental representation about the likeability of self and the psychological availability of others, these children being classified as 'securely attached' (Howe and Fearnley, 1999). Children who experience less sensitive, consistent and responsive caring are less able mentally to represent themselves as lovable, effective and worthy, or other people as emotionally available, caring and protective. This 'psychological loss' of the carer results in patterns of insecure attachment behaviours (Howe and Fearnley, 1999).

In adolescence and adulthood, a person's 'internal working model of attachment' is a mental representation of self, attachment figures and their relationships based on experiences with several attachment figures over time, and these form the affective/cognitive dimension of attachment (Armsden and Greenberg, 1987; Brown and Wright, 2001). A growing body of research in recent decades has extended attachment theory into adulthood (Hazan and Shaver, 1987; Bartholomew and Horowitz, 1991).

Attachment in infancy and childhood

Most studies on attachment have focused on infancy, and the 'traditional' patterns of attachment that emerged from studies using Ainsworth's 'strange situation procedure' (Ainsworth, 1991) comprise:

- *the secure attachment pattern*, characterising infants who make successful use of their carer as a secure base from which they can explore and interact with the environment
- *the insecure-avoidant pattern*, consisting of a representational model in which the carer will reject child attachment needs and thus children attempt to keep their attention directed away from their attachment figure
- *the insecure-ambivalent or resistant pattern*, resulting from the experience of a carer who inadequately meets a child's attachment needs through passive, unresponsive and ineffective behaviour and thus children display anger and/or ambivalence towards their carer.

Recent research studies have identified other 'atypical' attachment classification categories particularly among high-risk groups such as abused, neglected or maltreated infants. Being fearful of the attachment figure, or having an attachment figure who is frightened (experiencing domestic violence, for example), is thought to be a common experience of children who develop a *disorganised/disoriented attachment pattern* (Vondra and Barnett, 1999), with prevalence among social risk samples, particularly maltreated children. The *disinhibited/diffuse attachment* behaviour characterises children who show apparently affectionate, 'indiscriminately friendly' behaviour to strangers whom they approach when in distress. This form of attachment behaviour has been reported as strongly associated with institutional upbringing (Chisholm et al., 1995; Chisholm, 1998; O'Connor et al., 1999, 2000a).

Attachment in adolescence: from parents to peers

One of the most important changes in adolescence is a decreased reliance on parents as attachment figures, and the development of the ability to function with greater social, cognitive and emotional autonomy from parents is recognised as a critical developmental task of adolescence. Traditional notions of adolescence as a period of 'storm and stress' (Rutter et al., 1976) and of adolescents' purposeful flight away from their attachment relationship with parents have given way in past decades to the realisation that most adolescents achieve autonomy not at the expense of attachment relationships with parents, but against a background of secure relationships with them that are likely to endure well beyond adolescence (Allen and Land, 1999). Recent longitudinal studies on adolescence (Allen et al., 1994a, 1994b, 1996a, 1996b; Allen and Hauser, 1996; Allen and Land, 1999) support the idea of gradual change during this developmental period, suggesting that previous theories of 'storm and stress' supported by clinical cases of pathological adolescents were inappropriately generalised to the normal population of adolescents (Greenberg et al., 1983). By early adolescence, friends, teachers and other people with whom the child is close may be used selectively as 'secure base' figures of convenience in specific contexts (Waters and Cummings, 2000). In this context, it is crucially important to take into consideration multiple attachment relationships experienced both within (with family members other than parents) and outside the family (for example in child-care settings).

There is a lack of systematic investigation of the relationships that children and adolescents have with adult figures to whom they may become attached, and who may play an important role in their lives, especially in the case of young people who find in these figures the security they could not achieve with their own parents. These potential attachment figures or 'parent surrogates' (Mayer, 1972; Ainsworth, 1991) might include an older sibling, another relative (such as grandparents), or an especially perceptive and understanding teacher and so on.

Early theories concerning the relative shifting influence of parents and peers during adolescence present a picture of a major swing from parent to peer salience, but recent research has considerably revised this approach (Greenberg et al., 1983). Research on adolescent autonomy processes (Allen and Land, 1999) suggests that growing autonomy from parents during this period creates 'healthy' pressure to begin to use peers as attachment figures, so that attachment needs can be met while autonomy in relationships with parents is established.

From this perspective, adolescence may be viewed as a period in which attachment needs are gradually transferred to peers, so that by mid-adolescence, interactions with peers begin to take on functions such as the provision of sources of support, intimacy, social influence and, ultimately, attachment relationships (Markiewicz et al., 2001). Often, by late adolescence, long-term relationships can be formed, in which peers (both as close friends or romantic partners) serve as attachment figures. In accordance with attachment theory, Weiss (1991) argues that adults' attachments to their peers are characterised by a seeking out of attachment figures when under stress, by the experiencing of anxiety when these figures are inaccessible, and by the experience of feeling comforted when in their company. Similarly, during adolescence, close and emotionally significant peer relationships can be considered as a type of attachment relationship, the particular importance of which is the peer's ability to provide adolescents with needed emotional resources, relevant role models, instrumental assistance and self-esteem support (Greenberg et al., 1983; Cassidy et al., 1996; Felsman and Blustein, 1999).

As relational theories have suggested, close relationships in late adolescence have some of the qualities of attachment bonds, in that they provide an enduring sense of closeness and felt security (Ainsworth, 1991). Research that has examined attachments in adolescent peer relationships suggests that the nature of developed peer attachment relationships derives from prior attachment relationships with parents as well as from prior relationships with peers. Armsden and Greenberg (1987) found that individuals who report secure attachments to their parents also reported high-quality attachment to their peers.

Continuity assumption in attachment

Exploring the 'legacy' of early attachment on subsequent psychosocial development has been one of the enduring questions of developmental psychology addressed by attachment theory and research (Thompson, 2000), with important implications for practice. Recent attempts to reformulate attachment theory suggest that Bowlby's ideas of the importance of early care in the onset of attachment and the long-lasting impact of early experience are challenged. Many longitudinal studies have failed to confirm continuity in attachment classification from infancy to childhood, adolescence and early adulthood (Bar-Haim et al., 2000; Lewis et al., 2000; Waters et al., 2000, Weinfield et al., 2000). Moreover, evidence from cross-cultural studies (Rothbaum et al., 2000; Robinson, 2007) reveals that attachment relationships with single attachment figures are not the most salient factors in socialisation and social adjustment in all communities or cultures. Most studies concerning the problem of stability and change in attachment indicate that children vary significantly regarding whether early attachments have an enduring impact (Thompson, 2000). In other words, it is impossible to identify a normative level of consistency in the status of attachment over the life span. The same is true when considering the 'sequelae' of attachment relationships: there is great variability in early attachments predicting later outcomes (Lewis et al., 2000).

These recent developments, made possible by advancements in the assessment of attachment over the life span and the use of longitudinal study designs, bring important revisions to the basic prediction of continuity in attachment theory. The relevance for practice of these findings reflects a mixture of pessimism and optimism. On one hand, secure attachments in infancy or childhood do not necessarily provide immunity from adverse social outcomes throughout later development, as originally thought. Equally, early attachment difficulties do not inevitably pose risks for subsequent developmental problems, but intervening experiences play an important part.

Childhood and adolescence as social and cultural constructions: signposts

As stated at the beginning, this chapter takes a developmental psychology perspective on childhood and adolescence, illustrating how elements of social work theoretical knowledge are 'borrowed' from other disciplines. However, it is important to acknowledge the psychological perspective's limitations and alternative perspectives, such as the sociological and life course frameworks. This section will briefly signpost the reader towards areas of further exploration in understanding the life stages of childhood and adolescence.

Albeit recognised as essential underpinning knowledge for social work practice in childcare and child protection work (Daniel et al., 1999), critiques of the developmental psychology perspective (Burman, 2007) emphasise the need for social workers to engage in a more meaningful and reflective way with the child development literature (Taylor, 2004). Moreover, over the past decades, influential work, drawing on multidisciplinary studies of childhood, shows how childhood is constructed in society (James and Prout, 1997; James and James, 2004).

The life course perspective views individual lives embedded in historical times, using concepts such as 'life path' (as opposed to 'fixed' developmental stages) and 'life transitions', all interlinked with other individuals' life trajectories (Newman and Newman, 2007). This perspective is pertinent to the study of adolescence, which is a life stage remarkably difficult to define, because of historical and cultural variations as well as a lack of a unified theory of this phase of life (Durkin, 1995). For example, although there are certain social stereotypes, there are no universally agreed ages as markers of the beginning (for example there is great variation in age when major physical changes, such as menarche, occur) or ending (for example an increasing number of young people continue education into their twenties and beyond and therefore the economic criterion is difficult to apply) of adolescence as a life stage. Historically, adolescence as viewed in the Western culture is a relatively recent phenomenon and its complexity is augmented by the nature of the societies in which adolescents live (Durkin, 1995).

There seems to be a consensus that adolescence is a dynamic period of change and transition requiring adolescents to negotiate the impact of their early experiences and their relationships with parents or carers, families and peers, as illustrated in this chapter. For some adolescents, there are additional challenges, such as developing their ethnic (Robinson, 2007) and gender (Golombok and Fivush, 1994) identities, negotiating a disability (Priestley, 2003), or coming from the looked-after system (Biehal, 2005). Some of these will need support in successfully negotiating the transition into adulthood.

Conclusion

Human growth and development is regarded as essential underpinning knowledge for social work practice. However, in the current climate of 'research-informed' social work practice, conventional assumptions about human development need to be reviewed in the light of continuously emerging evidence. The issues discussed in this chapter indicate that long-standing assumptions of continuity and change in development are challenged by recent research findings. Understanding of the impact of early experiences upon later development has been further enhanced by studies of children who suffered deprivation in early years, such as intercountry adoption studies, and the recent longitudinal studies on attachment continuity over the life span. Grasping the complexity of the relationship between previous experiences and later outcomes in the lives of those who social workers aim to intervene in a positive way is essential to enable a better informed professional practice.

For further discussion of perspectives on the life course of adults, see Chapter 11 and for crosscultural and black perspectives, see Adams et al., 2009b, Chapter 13.

www.**resilienceproject.org/**   Resilience Research Centre led by Dr Michael Ungar at Dalhousie University, Canada, coordinates a number of different research projects on children and youth resilience, bringing together leaders in the field of resilience research from different disciplines and cultural backgrounds.

www.**people.virginia.edu/~psykliff/index.php**   Virginia Adolescent Research Group led by Professor Joseph Allen at University of Virginia, US, studies the psychological and social development of adolescents and young adults. Virginia Institute of Development in Adulthood (VIDA) is an ongoing longitudinal study examining the influences of social relationships, autonomy, and attachment to parents on young adult development.

Clarke, A. and Clarke, A. (2000) *Early Experiences and the Life Path*, London, Jessica Kingsley. In this sequel to their acclaimed 1976 book, the authors revisit the early experiences assumption in the light of new research findings.

Coleman, J. and Hagell, A. (eds) (2007) *Adolescence, Risk and Resilience: Against the Odds*, Chichester, John Wiley & Sons. Brings together international research on how the concepts of risk and resilience relate to adolescence.

Grossmann, K.E., Grossmann, K. and Waters, E. (eds) (2006) *Attachment from Infancy to Adulthood: The Major Longitudinal Studies*, New York, Guilford Press. Brings together first-hand accounts of the most important longitudinal studies of attachment.

Robinson, L. (2007) *Cross-cultural Child Development for Social Workers*, Basingstoke, Palgrave Macmillan. Offers an introduction to cross-cultural perspectives on child development including attachment theory and adolescent identity development.

Schaffer, R.H. (2006) *Key Concepts in Developmental Psychology*, London, Sage. Discusses the main developmental concepts in relation to their theoretical, historical and empirical background.

Perspectives on the life course: later life

This chapter explores some of the debates about how adults change during the course of their life and considers the variety of social, psychological and physiological factors that affect people's lives during adulthood, in order to help social workers understand how these affect the people with whom they work.

Chapter overview

How we understand adulthood

The nature of people's lives is not determined in their childhood but continues to be shaped throughout adulthood. Therefore, in this chapter, we build on the discussion of child development in Chapter 10 to explore changes in personality and identity in later life. Looking at later life, though, requires a broader perspective than examining children's development.

Teaching and thinking about human growth and development tends to focus on the developmental psychology of children and young people. This is partly because children experience rapid physiological growth and psychological development. Meanwhile, adults accept responsibility for children's psychological development, education and socialisation and the important social institutions of education and social care accept responsibility for protecting children. Therefore, children's psychological and social development is accepted as an important social responsibility, engaging and motivating both parents and other adults. Social work professionals have historically given great importance to their role in this field. There is also a historical reason: ideas of childhood have changed and developed over the centuries. Christianity sometimes viewed children as coming into the world invested with original sin, needing to be civilised into adult society. At other times, for example in the work of the philosopher Locke, children were thought to need loving care and education, or they were treated as small adults and forced to work long hours in the factories of the Industrial Revolution. From the beginning of the twentieth century, psychoanalytic theory was also influential, because it saw the course of adult psychological problems in inadequate development in childhood. Vestiges of this idea remain in modern-day attachment theory, supported by a growing body of research.

Stages and complexities of the life course

The analogy with child development leads to the idea that there are 'stages' in adult development and that the main determinant of the character of each stage of adulthood is the reality that people age. Some psychological and psychoanalytical writers, notably Erikson (1965), suggested that adults moved through a series of phases, with each transition between phases having the potential to cause problems in social and psychological adjustment. The idea of studying the life cycle of a human being as part of their social context is an important part of this movement in thinking. Human beings pass through recognisable phases in their lives, marrying, having and bringing up children and then living into old age.

Some sociologists, such as Talcott Parsons (1942), have studied this tendency to use age as the main factor shaping people's movement through their lives, despite the fact that people's lives during childhood and adulthood are diverse and changes over these periods are shaped by many factors. Theories of age stratification rely on the argument that biological ageing is connected with social roles and status, which are often age related. Theories of age integration and age segregation are associated with this, since they help us to understand how some activities such as schooling, employment and retirement accommodation are age segregated, that is, more or less exclusively tied to particular age groups, while others, such as adult and lifelong education are age integrated, meaning that people can take them up flexibly throughout their (adult) lives.

There has been criticism of all these ideas, because of inherent variability. No analyses of life phases or cycles apply to all human beings and all societies. Moreover, all these ideas assume a socialisation into existing social structures and roles, such as families, communities, heterosexual marriage. Simple life cycle descriptions rejected the value of later life and positive views of retirement and old age, focusing instead on a cycle of reproduction and the socialisation of children; whatever happened after that might be viewed as less important according to such ideas. Even the idea of development, which assumes that people will inevitably progress and places a social value on some progressions rather than others, might be questioned. Also, phases or transitions related to particular ages seemed inappropriate and rigid.

As Western societies have grown more complex, they have incorporated a wide range of possibilities for different roles in variable sequences. Moreover, stage theories of psychological development seem an unsatisfactory way of incorporating a wide range of knowledge about the way in which human beings live their lives and sociological and social psychological knowledge about how social structures develop and groups form and interact with each other. For social workers, the neglect of some aspects of adulthood heightens the need for family maintenance in order to support child education and development. Also, practice with adults often has a lower status than work with children and families, perhaps arising from the stigmatisation of adult client groups as deviant or presenting social problems, through mental illness, crime, undesirable or 'imperfect' human states such as physical or learning disability, or the deterioration and frailty associated with growing older.

In spite of all these difficulties, it is important that social work practitioners should be aware of evidence about how adults change during the course of their life, as a background to being able to understand psychological and social factors affecting the people with whom they work. Rather than looking for patterns of development like stages, understanding personal changes in adulthood requires practitioners to explore influences that have constructed the personality and identity of each individual and those that influence them now and will or might influence them in their future. Paying attention to the impact on individuals of the following is often helpful:

■ Social and cultural factors in their life history
■ Psychological reactions to those factors as people's lives change
■ Social relationships and structures that often affect people.

We look at each of these areas in turn.

Social and cultural factors

If age-related ideas are an oversimplification of adult experience, exploring instead a range of factors shaping people's lives allows us to see people's potential in a more flexible and open way, as part of a life course, in which people may pick up influences in many different ways and at many different times. Examining the social and cultural factors in people's life histories also helps us to criticise and problematise **stage theories**. We can examine the important factors that influence them and explore when and how these factors had their influence, rather than expecting a sequence of development related to age. There is a complex variety of influences on the span of our lives, including historic and societal, social and cultural, demographic, lifestyle, geographical, genetic and biological, psychological and early life factors, which we often refer to as 'the life course'. We can use this term as long as we recognise the variety and complexity of the above ingredients in our understanding of it. This should contribute to redressing what we regard as a widespread imbalance – the tendency for social work educators and practitioners to attend more to 'human growth and development' in infancy and childhood and to neglect the many reasons why some adults become

> Stage theories are somewhat rigid perspectives on human growth and development, based on the assumption that people pass through a succession of more or less fixed stages from birth to death.

vulnerable during adulthood and have needs that could and should be attended to by welfare services, including those provided by social workers.

Quadagno (2005: 50) writes of 'the life course framework' as 'an approach to the study of aging that emphasizes the interaction of historical events, individual decisions and opportunities, and the effects of early life experiences in determining later life outcomes'. To this, we can add the range of physiological and social factors, noted above, which we now briefly consider.

Historical factors

Some historical factors that affect individuals and families arise before a particular adult was born and may still affect family members. For example, a Bosnian mother with two babies arrived in Yorkshire in 1992 and in the first decade of the twenty-first century is struggling to build up a life for her and her two children in England while remaking relationships with relatives in her former country of residence.

Societal and social factors

Social divisions and inequalities shape the adulthoods of diverse groups of people differently. For example, there are gender inequalities, ethnic inequalities and factors contributing to cumulative disadvantage. Social policies mitigate to a greater or lesser extent these inequalities, risks and uncertainties experienced by adults. We may assume that major shifts in patterns of vulnerability among adults – indicated, for example, in morbidity (illness) and mortality (death) rates – occur because of changes in society. However, we should beware of making such generalisations. Reductions in mortality in the UK since the late nineteenth century do not correspond with the development of better social networks and supports for individuals and families.

Policy and practice regarding health and welfare services for adults are rooted in the realities for people of these patterns of early, middle and late adult life and their relationships with family characteristics. The character of families also changes through the decades, with the diversity of family forms increasingly recognised and accepted throughout the countries of the world between which people migrate to and from the UK. At the same time, the distinctive character of family forms can be recognised longitudinally throughout the lives of adults with roots in a particular household and set of family relationships (Allan et al., 2001).

Demographic factors

Demographic factors significantly affect the shape of people's lives in adulthood. Features of the life courses of adults cannot be considered in isolation from social factors such as the demographic features and cultural realities of the lives of adults from the age of 18 until death. One particular demographic factor affecting adulthood is the increasing longevity of people, particularly in Western countries. Within this group, increasing longevity is associated generally with improved health. However, at the same time, there is a tendency towards an extended period of decline of physical and mental faculties among older and much older people.

Lifestyle factors

It is often asserted that people's vulnerabilities are determined by differences in their lifestyles, for example in the incidence of smoking and alcohol consumption. They can also be affected by social factors such as the fragmentation of social groups as people grow older, move house, lose touch with former friends and work associates and suffer social disintegration as people die.

Geographical factors

Lifestyle factors do not account for geographical differences between people's lives during adulthood. These include those 'ecological' factors that impinge on people's lives simply by virtue of the area in which they live and/or work. In some localities, for example, there are climatic and atmospheric pollution factors that contribute to a higher incidence of particular health conditions and diseases.

Genetic and biological/physiological factors

Growing attention is being paid by researchers to establishing correlations between people's genetic inheritance and their current circumstances. There is growing evidence of the persistence of these factors into adulthood.

Psychological and early life factors

The huge literature on child development carries forward into the understanding of adulthood and confirms the many ways in which childhood experiences influence the development of people in adult life.

Structural factors

Poverty, 'race', gender, disability, mental ill health and other social divisions shape the experience of age and complicate the opportunities made available to individuals throughout the life course. Sometimes, these persist, despite various strategies aimed at reducing them. For example, a girl child is more likely to be poor in childhood and to experience poverty in old age, for structural reasons linked to her gender and child-care responsibilities. As a mother, she may go into part-time work or take a period off work to care for her children, thus losing out on pension contributions that mean that not only is she earning less while she is a mother, but her pension will be less than a man of similar age who has worked all his life in paid employment. The situation may be more complex for an Asian Muslim woman who works in a low-paid factory job while caring for her children and husband if she entered the UK as a sponsored immigrant. She will not be entitled to claim benefits if she is laid off her waged work. Social workers, in responding to claims for services from women in either of these situations, would have to examine their situations carefully to ensure that the women were helped to maximise their incomes without falling foul of the law.

We can see from the above brief list that the interaction between the multiple factors contributing to health and illness, independence and vulnerability during adulthood is extremely complex and some popular assumptions are not borne out by critical research. In the contemporary picture of genetic and biological research, for example, it would be tempting, but erroneous, for historical and societal factors to be ignored in the face of seemingly universal genetic and biological truths. In similar vein, biological and psychosocial perspectives on adulthood tend not to take account of geographical differences and trends that contribute to health and wellbeing. Thus it would be a mistake to assume that social factors can be 'reified into pathophysiological mechanisms' (Davey Smith, 2003: 448). We should beware of adopting one perspective to the exclusion of others.

No single viewpoint will accommodate the variety of adulthoods we encounter in social work, given the cultural diversity of individuals and families with whom social workers practise. Davey Smith (2003: 448) emphasises the contribution of research in 'understanding the particular factors which act together to produce the patterns seen in any one specific instance'. This discussion emphasises that it would be misleading to present a single framework for understanding the multitude of factors that influence people's lives to death from the onset of adulthood – notionally set at 18 in many Western societies, but in different parts of the world varying up to a decade either side of this. Consequently, there is scope for a plurality of perspectives on adult life. We may use the term 'life course' to refer to the more or less equally important three life stages of a person's life span from birth and childhood, through adulthood and old age without acknowledging that even this seemingly obvious and 'natural' division breaks down as we scrutinise it. For a start, as we indicated above, the boundaries between the different stages are blurred to the extent that there is no hard and fast clarity about what marks a person's transition from childhood to adulthood. We saw in Chapter 10 that adolescence is a problematic social construct, and in India, Pakistan and some Arab and African countries, girls and boys often marry at the onset of puberty, whereas in Western countries, marriage is generally delayed for several more years.

Similar blurring occurs in the later life course. It is questionable whether the customary assumption that there is a unidirectional and linear decline from the onset of adulthood to old age can be sustained in the face of evidence that transitions and sequencing of changes may be interrupted and even reversed. So we should recognise that a plurality of perspectives applies to the term 'life course', rather than there being just one framework, which we must accept in order to move forward.

These changing features of people's lives in adulthood interact with each other in complex ways. Demographic characteristics of family and individual adult life both create and are responsive to people's decisions about their relationships with life in their households and at work. The UK shares some demographic features with other countries that have dramatic consequences – whether for good or ill – on the lives of adults. Most men and women in European countries become parents at some point in their lives and, like France, the UK since the 1970s has had consistently high total fertility rates, at 1.7 to 1.8 (Kiernan, 1998: 63). At the same time, since the 1980s, European countries, including the UK, have seen a decline in women having children in their twenties and an increase for women in their thirties (ONS, 2006; *Social Trends*, 2006). One consequence of the social and economic pressures on households with children has been the tendency for mothers to return to work while the children are growing up. Despite this, women's employment patterns reflect their caring roles – for children and older dependent relatives – and, not helped by the relatively poorer pay for women, levels of child and lone-parent poverty remain stubbornly high in the UK. A further consequence is problems of stress and ill health that affect parents and lone mothers in particular, in their middle years. Fathers are not exempt from these pressures in their middle years, working an average of 47.1 hours per week in contrast with 43 hours for non-fathers (Kiernan, 1998: 71).

Demographic changes affect older adults as well, principally through steadily increasing longevity throughout the second half of the twentieth century. Unfortunately, the fact that people are living longer has extended the period during which their physical and mental faculties are in decline, associated not only with physical illness and chronic conditions but also problems of social isolation for older people living alone. It has also led to problems in financing lengthening periods of retirement, which may also include the healthcare costs of increasing frailty in later years.

Psychological reactions to life course factors

Gross (2005) usefully identifies a number of different psychological approaches to thinking about adulthood:

- *Normative age-graded approaches* focus on the accepted, expected personal and social changes during adulthood associated with different ages
- *Normative historical approaches* focus on the accepted, expected personal and social changes associated with particular historical contexts, for example epidemics, war, economic depression
- *Non-normative approaches* focus on particular events in people's lives that create personal and social change for people, but which are not considered to be expected in life, for example divorce, unemployment, illness.

Without accepting that any of these could be taken as complete explanations of human variation, these different approaches suggest aspects of life on which we could reasonably focus to understand the psychological reaction to experiences within the life course of adults. It suggests that while there might be a pattern that mainly follows different ages, this is markedly influenced by events in the world that affect social groups and populations; current issues might be climate change, for example. As well as this, commonplace smaller scale human events can also be explored for their impact on individuals and the families and communities around them.

Thus, a woman born in the UK after the Second World War went through childhood during the 1950s, affected by the aftermath of war, a period of economic growth and the development of the welfare state, came to young adulthood and probably marriage during the late 1960s or early 1970s, lived and perhaps had her children during the period of economic retrenchment and political conservatism during the 1980s and 90s, and is now approaching retirement during a period in which the average life span has increased markedly, so that she will be one of the increasing proportion of older people in the population during the period 2010–30. Women born at the same time in sub-Saharan Africa and Russia would have lived through the same phases of life, but in very different economic, political and human circumstances. The Russian woman might have experienced an effective social state and political oppression, and the African woman's family might have been more affected by HIV/AIDS than the others. Men born at the same time and in these places would have widely different experiences.

Two well-known age-graded analyses of adult development are important. Erikson's (1965) account of life stages proposes that at each stage of life, people typically experience fundamental human conflicts deriving from commonplace social experiences. Briefly, there are:

■ During their twenties, they experience a conflict between intimacy and role confusion, deciding whether they will continue to live as an individual, perhaps being in competition with others, or enter a relationship with a partner, perhaps being cooperative in their relationships; an important quality of strength that they use in this phase is the capacity for love.
■ Between their thirties and late fifties, the conflict is between generativeness (contributing to the welfare of others, especially children) and stagnation, to identify life goals in work or in their partnership. Their focus may be on their divided activities and lives or on a shared household. Caring is a quality or potential strength that may be present or lacking in the family.
■ After their late fifties, the conflict is between ego integrity or despair, in which people come to a conclusion that they have become part of humankind or are part of a family and community; the quality of strength that may influence their happiness and social reactions is wisdom.

This analysis does not differentiate well between the different phases of life, middle adulthood being treated as one phase, and makes excessive generalisations about social and psychological reactions. Levinson et al.'s (1978) research on males, with later studies on females (Levinson and Levinson, 1997), focused on the transitions people made as they grew older and developed a pattern of relationships with their social surroundings, which was then disrupted by later transitions:

- A transition in early adulthood from childhood to enter the adult world and at around age 30, another minor transition into a 'settling down' phase
- A midlife transition follows, leading through a minor transition to a culmination in late adulthood of family and work achievements
- A final late adult transition occurs in the sixties.

An alternative conception is Gould's (1978) idea that adult consciousness and identity evolve as we lose the psychological constraints of earlier aspects of life. For example, we might gain greater confidence and experience that allows us greater flexibility and opportunity in our social and interpersonal relationships. All these accounts focus not only on the content of the phases but on the processes that lead to the transitions.

Particular areas of psychological and social development that might be relevant to age-graded analyses are evidence about aspects of social life that occur within particular age phases. These areas might include:

- Marriage and divorce
- Parenthood
- Old age
- Dying.

Physiological, psychological and social factors affect all these. Psychological and social behaviour is substantially affected by biological issues; thinking, emotion and social interaction all occur using the physical senses and neurological mechanisms of bodily sensation, body rhythms and perception. Marriage, parenthood and divorce involve both sexual relationships and behaviour and social institutions and conventions.

Human communication includes nonverbal communication, hearing and perception, but is significantly conditioned by learned skills and behaviour that people develop according to the assumptions and conventions of their society and ethnic and social groups (Hargie and Dickson, 2004). Ageing and dying are physical processes, but how people experience them is constructed by their social life. For example, old age may be affected by changes in work patterns for many people on retirement from employment, and is also affected by changes in housing. People may not have enough money to maintain a home to their previous standards, or lose physical capacity to do things for themselves. They may also have to move to older people's sheltered accommodation or care homes, which leads to differences in their lifestyle (Bytheway et al., 1990).

Although ageing may lead to changes in intelligence, memory and personality through physical and social changes (Stuart-Hamilton, 1991), there is wide variation and the issues are complex. For example, Gross (2005: 669) draws attention to the difference between crystallised and fluid intelligence. Crystallised intelligence includes things like accumulated wisdom and the capacity to reason, which may increase and be retained by many older people, while fluid intelligence is the capacity to solve new problems, which many people lose slowly from early adulthood. Some people may experience dementia, a group of diseases that progressively affect the brain, eventually leading to considerable physical frailty affecting the whole body; it is different from occasional memory losses that may occur in normal ageing. Although the incidence of dementia increases with age, only 1 in 14 people over 65 years of age and 1 in 6 people over 80 years of age has a form of dementia (Knapp and Prince, 2007).

Dying processes and the experience of the end of life are inevitable for everyone. Lynn and Adamson (2003) suggest that there are three main trajectories at the end of life:

1   In the *typical cancer trajectory*, there is a slow decline in patients' ability to function over a few years, but a rapid decline over a few months leading to death.
2   In the *long-term conditions trajectory*, typical of people with heart and lung failure, capacity to function is at a lower starting point, and declines slowly over three to five years, with intermittent crises, followed by an apparently sudden death.
3   In the *frailty trajectory*, again from a low starting point, patients mainly suffer from prolonged dwindling of function, usually because of dementia and general physical frailty. This continues over perhaps six to eight years with no sudden decline until death.

These different experiences are likely to lead to different experiences of dying and death.

Glaser and Strauss (1968) identified the importance of awareness in the variation of experiences of death. While everyone knows that they are going to die at some time, becoming aware that someone is suffering from a life-threatening condition such as cancer may change awareness of the closeness of death. Accounts of dying processes that suggest phases of adjustment, such as that of Kübler-Ross's (1969) description of the stages of denial, anger, bargaining, depression and acceptance, have not been supported by later research; there is considerable variation in reaction. Similarly, there are no clear patterns of bereavement, although Stroebe and Schut's (1999) dual process model of grief proposes that bereaved people oscillate between focusing on the loss and on restoration of an active life.

Social relationships and structures

We have argued so far that although there are some changes in people's social and psychological lives during adulthood, it is more fruitful to look at how a range of psychological and social factors affect people's behaviour and life. Among these factors are:

■   Critical historical events in the surrounding society
■   Critical life events such as childbirth, bereavement and other losses

- Major social and personal differences such as gender and ethnicity
- Important social processes such as social perception and attribution, attitude change, prejudice and discrimination, conformity and group influence, language and moral development, obedience and resistance
- Important individual differences such as intelligence, motivation, and capacity for perception, information-processing, pattern recognition (for example of faces), behavioural consistency, memory and cognition or capacity for processing thoughts and reasoning.

These individual factors are also affected by social factors, such as the resilience of the individual and family to adversity (Greene, 2002). Fraser et al. (1999: 136) usefully define resilience as 'unpredicted and markedly successful adaptations to negative life events, trauma, stress, and other forms of risk'. This analysis points up that we only talk about resilience when people do better than expected at responding to adversity, or to the risk of adversity. Families in particular may have strengths that support their members in dealing with challenges to individual members (Walsh, 1998). The same may also be true of communities. The impact of social and individual stresses may be particularly important for individuals, since there is considerable evidence of a socioeconomic class gradient in death: the wealthier people are, the healthier they are and the longer they are likely to live (Siegrist and Marmot, 2006).

We highlight here four particular issues arising from the study of people's adulthood, which have relevance to social work in practice. Many of these are linked with trends towards new family forms and the consequences of families breaking up and being reconstituted, as relationships between partners break up and one or both partners move on to form new relationships and families. This often leaves other relatives – children and grandparents – struggling to find their places. In families that bear additional strains through poverty, unemployment, poor housing and discrimination through a range of other circumstances, the consequences of lack of support and resources can be disastrous for individuals and can lead to family break-up. The following discussion may help us to appreciate the significance of what is happening in the lives of adults with whom we are working.

Transitions and counter-transitions

There are social expectations about when adults should partner up, have children and retire. However, we can no longer assume that as people move through adulthood, they experience changes in their roles – from partner to single person, employee to retired pensioner – that are irreversible. These transitions used to be age graded, that is, closely tied to the chronological age of the individual. However, nowadays, while some people retire earlier, others go on working into their eighties and nineties and may also remarry and parent children over the legal age they become pensioners. Improvements in healthcare make it more common for people to reverse major transitions they have made in adulthood, for example moving into retirement and later moving to another dwelling in a new area or country and taking up a second career.

Trajectories

In the same way that dying may have a trajectory, so do other aspects of life. Several counter-transitions may combine to create a new direction in the lives of individuals and other family members, which affect the trajectories of their lives. We can see how one person's counter-transitions affect other people. A man's marriage at 66 makes his new partner's older parents into 'in-laws', and a woman having a child in her late forties gives her existing children in their twenties a new sibling and her parents a new grandchild. These changes affect how people view themselves in what used to be called 'middle age' and 'old age' and are likely to have both positive and negative consequences. In the twenty-first century, trajectories that a couple of generations ago were regarded as relatively unchanging are nowadays subjected to major changes, which destroy existing patterns of relationships between generations of people in family and other networks.

Sequencing

The issue of sequencing is closely related to transitions, since sequences are tradition-ally assumed to apply through people's life course, with a degree of inevitability and standardisation. For example, in the traditional family, we would expect to find that grandparents are older than parents, and uncles and aunts are older than sister and brothers. However, intermixing between cultures brings different customs regarding the age of first marriage together and whereas in some UK communities, young people are delaying marriage till their thirties, they may be neighbours to East and Southeast Asian families where marriage customarily takes place at 16 and the first children are born at 17. A woman may be a grandparent by her mid-thirties and a great-grandmother by her early fifties. Family forms change when adults have differ-ent partners and children in these relationships through time and this affects sequencing. A woman may have a number of children by different partners and different grandparents may relate to different siblings, creating a serial family and serial extended family.

Timing

It used to be the case in the eighteenth and nineteenth century in many Western countries, including what we now call the UK, that there was some stability and predictability about the timing of the main transitions in people's lives – the expec-tations when children would pass into adulthood, upper-class girls would become 'young ladies' eligible for marriage and those older people who survived beyond middle age would retire. There is some evidence that despite trends towards some people challenging these deep-seated age-related norms, many of these expectations are still predominant, illustrated perhaps by such widespread remarks as 'she married late' and 'he's a bit old to be taking on young children and a new job.' Neugarten et al. (1965) identified the strength of many people's assumption that major life events should be linked with their age.

The above assumptions may lead to people pressurising other people to conform to social norms that are outdated – because societies are changing – and discriminatory – because they reflect prejudices that can lead to people in some communities being treated unjustly and unequally. The consequences of adults taking on parenting roles over a longer period and with different groups of children of widely separated ages include an increased tendency for overlap between roles traditionally associated with one age. This can lead to role conflict, that is, tensions between different responsibilities in the family, and heightened financial and emotional stresses, for example in the case of a mother whose childbearing years are extended into her forties and who still supports children and young people at home at a time when her parents are becoming more dependent and in need of support and, perhaps, caring.

Conclusion

Human change goes alongside ageing; both occur throughout the life course and social workers need to take account of the many different factors affecting the entire life course when working with people, as individuals, in families and in other groups. Our understanding of the life course of adults continues to grow and develop as the patterns of people's lives change. Maintaining our understanding of how adulthood changes is a crucial ingredient in our social work expertise; we cannot learn about adult development, instead we must continue to explore how adults' lives change as social change affects their life course. This is an area of study that is not static and is affected by changes within societies, as populations move between countries and contribute to both social continuities and changes. Social workers have a vital role to play in helping people to manage such change in their lives and relationships; therefore an understanding of the impact of present changes on future adult lives is a crucial continuing aspect of social workers' learning.

Social work remains selective and somewhat unbalanced in its focus on particular parts of the life course, to the neglect of others, concentrating too much attention on children and problems affecting older people. There is a relative neglect of the transitions and traumas of middle age. Teaching of what is traditionally known as 'human growth and development' on social work qualifying programmes tends to focus on the entry to life (birth and early childhood) and exit from life (terminal conditions and illnesses and dying), with relatively less attention paid to the traumas and vulnerabilities of adulthood in between. A more thoughtful perspective might include important changes at many other stages of the life course. For example, many individuals and family members experience middle adulthood as a time of uncertainty and stress as they encounter the menopause, the so-called 'midlife crisis' and the complexities of contributing to the lives of families that are breaking up and being reconstituted.

We urge on all social workers, then, a continuing concern for keeping in touch with knowledge development in adulthood and later life.

For further discussion of ethical aspects of work with people in later life, see Adams et al., 2009b, Chapter 7, and for safeguarding adults, see Adams et al., 2009b, Chapter 27.

www.statistics.gov.uk   A uniquely useful source of authoritative data, providing the evidence base on continuities and changes.

Gross, R. (2005) *Psychology: The Science of Mind and Behaviour*, 5th edn, London, Hodder Arnold. A well-established and comprehensive textbook of psychology that includes a well-referenced and critical section on adult development.

Priestley, M. (ed.) (2001) *Disability and the Life Course: Global Perspectives*, Cambridge, Cambridge University Press. A wide-ranging collection of essays tackling disability and the life course.

Quadagno, J. (2005) *Aging and the Life Course: An Introduction to Social Geron-tology*, 3rd edn, London, McGraw-Hill. Provides a useful resource to follow up the range of factors impinging on adult development.

Researching social work 12

This chapter argues that practitioners underuse research evidence to support their practice. The chapter highlights key themes in social work research, including its context and distinctiveness and its methodologies. It also offers a critical look at evidence-based practice, the development of the research-minded practitioner, service user involvement in research and interdisciplinary research.

Chapter overview

Pawson et al. (2003) have identified five sources in which knowledge could best be identified in social care:

- *Organisational knowledge* – to do with governance and policies
- *Practitioner knowledge* – personal, context specific, often tacit
- *User knowledge* – first-hand experience and reflection, often unspoken and undervalued
- *Research knowledge* – the most 'plausible' source but requiring a 'broad church' interpretation of research
- *Policy community* – concerning societal and political drivers determining the issues of significance.

They argued that none of these different sources was inherently better than any of the others, but neither should we assume that all the sources are of equal merit on all occasions. Research can thus be viewed as one of the five key contributors to social work knowledge and, by implication, practice. As D'Cruz and Jones (2004: 2) state:

We teach research to social work students because we believe that social work practice is more likely to be effective when social workers are able to draw on and evaluate previous research.

This is not to deny that the worlds of the researcher and the practitioner are often viewed as contentious and problematic. There are a number of potential incompatibilities in relation to timeliness, the accessibility of research, differing views of the value of research and differing expectations of how the product will be utilised. However, neither social work nor research exists in isolation, both are mediated, value-driven political activities. Social work research exists not only to support practice but to transform it (McLaughlin, 2007a). As such, social work research is an applied research discipline charged with achieving the dual standard of being relevant for practice and credible within the academic community. This is captured by Shaw and Norton's (2007) notion of 'relevance-with-rigour'.

Evidence-based practice refers to practice that is informed by research evidence indicating the most effective form of intervention to be used in specific circumstances. A widely advocated form of evidence-based practice relies on research based on random controlled trials.

In this chapter, we will explore the context in which social work research operates, the colonisation of **evidence-based practice**, practitioner research, the development of service user research and interdisciplinary research.

The context for social work research

It was only in 2005 that the Economic and Social Research Council in the UK recognised social work as a separate discipline for which doctoral students could train. Prior to 2005, social work doctoral students had to compete under the more established disciplines like psychology or sociology. While this has been a major step forward, social work remains poorly funded in comparison to health research. For social work, the overall spend per workforce member is £25 as opposed to £3,400 in health (Marsh and Fisher, 2005). The UK government has established a target for research and innovation of 2.5 per cent of gross domestic product by 2014. Health funding of research has already achieved this target, while funding for social work research would require an eightfold increase to achieve the target.

The Joint Universities Committee Social Work Education Committee (JUC SWEC, 2006) developed, adopted and published a research strategy in 2006 to address the impact and reach of social work research, to increase the number of research active academics and to promote research collaboration with other disciplines and stakeholders. In particular, the strategy aimed to:

- increase the resources available for social work and social care research to 2.5 per cent of the total social services budget by 2014
- increase research capacity and capability
- increase the visibility and impact of social work research
- ensure social work has full institutional recognition as a research discipline and establish robust research governance arrangements (JUC SWEC, 2006).

Qualitative research refers to a cluster of research approaches based on gathering mainly verbal information, often from a small number of respondents.

Social work tends to favour **qualitative research** at the expense of quantitative. Shaw (2007) reminds us that it can be self-limiting and primitive to suggest that qualitative approaches are more in line with social work values and quantitative approaches are inherently positivist, a term that is almost universally viewed negatively within social work. It is worthwhile looking at these two major methodological categories in more detail. Payne and Payne (2004: 180) state that:

> " Quantitative methods (normally using deductive logic) seek regularities in human lives, by separating the social world into empirical components called variables which can be represented numerically as frequencies or rate, whose associations with each other can be explored by statistical techniques, and accessed through researcher-introduced stimuli and systematic measurement. "

Quantitative methods are therefore concerned with accounting for regularities in social behaviour that have been separated into variables represented by numbers, which can be statistically manipulated to identify associations. Quantitative studies are also keen to show that the findings from the specific can be generalised to other situations and use data collection methods like surveys, questionnaires and structured interviews. Such approaches have contributed to social workers' practice, for example the work of Parker (1966) who showed that the closer in age of foster children to the foster carers own children, the greater the likelihood of placement breakdown. **Quantitative research**, although good at identifying patterns, is less good at explaining what these patterns are about. Quantitative

> Quantitative research is based on measured scores and tends to be gathered from larger groups, creating data that are statistically analysed.

researchers are charged with failing to address subjective experience and focusing only on those aspects of behaviour or circumstances that can be numerically manipulated and statistically analysed.

On the other hand, the focus of qualitative research is to interpret and construct how ordinary people observe and describe their lives in natural settings. In so doing, qualitative methods generally produce detailed non-quantitative accounts and use induction to interpret the meanings that people make of their lives (Payne and Payne, 2004). In particular, qualitative methods tend to be less structured and concepts are seen as emerging from the data rather than appearing at the outset of the research. Qualitative researchers tend to favour semi-structured or unstructured interviews. Other types of qualitative data collection techniques include focus groups, ethnography and participant observation.

It has been argued that quantitative and qualitative research methodologies are derived from incommensurate philosophical paradigms (Hughes and Sharrock, 1997). Quantitative methodologies are viewed as predicated on a positivist paradigm, making it heresy to use qualitative approaches that are predicated on social constructivist approaches. **Positivism**, in general terms, involves the belief that scientific knowledge can be positively verifiable and is thus based on sure and certain foundations and

> Positivism is a set of philosophical beliefs in the sciences emphasising observed facts and aiming to reduce understandings of aspects of reality to core, or essential, truths.

on the discovery of general laws (Delanty, 2005). Constructivism rejects this view of human knowledge. Constructivism represents a number of approaches that all share the view that you cannot research the social world in the same way you research the natural world. Human beings, unlike atoms or simple harmonic motion, are engaged with their world; we are all born into a world of meanings bestowed upon us by our culture and seen through our historical and social lenses (Creswell, 2003). For the constructivist, there is no objective truth waiting to be discovered. There is no measurement without meaning.

In recent years, this incommensurability has been challenged and we have seen the development of pragmatism. For the pragmatist, it isn't the methods that are important, it is the problem. Researchers need to use whatever research methods are required to address the problem. Mixed methods come from the pragmatist view of research methodology where what matters is 'what works'. There is some debate about whether this inevitably leads to a lack of 'analytical clarity' (Snape and Spencer, 2003). Ritchie (2003: 43) takes a more measured view:

> When using qualitative and quantitative research in harness, it is important to recognise each offers a different way of knowing about the world. Although they may well be addressing the same research issue, they will provide a different 'reading' or form of calibration on that issue. As a consequence, it should not be expected that the evidence generated from the two approaches will replicate each other. Instead the purpose of interlocking qualitative and quantitative data is to achieve an extended understanding that neither method alone can offer. It is then up to the researcher to explain why the data and their 'meaning' are different.

This view acknowledges that qualitative and quantitative methods can be combined in the same study to discover more than would be possible with just a qualitative or a quantitative approach. It also highlights that we should not expect qualitative and quantitative methodologies to provide the same answers but should expect differences. It should also be acknowledged that using mixed methods is not an excuse for not struggling with the implications of different methods and their respective knowledge claims.

Social work research has tended to favour qualitative approaches to knowledge creation and is criticised by Shaw (2003) for allowing a decline in quantitative approaches. Shaw and Gould (2001) also note that much of the qualitative research tends to be routinised and less complex. Social work's interest in qualitative research should not be surprising, given social work's interest in understanding client's perspectives. Dominelli (2005) argued that there is a characteristic research approach that can be identified as social work research, whose distinctive features include:

■ A change orientation
■ A more egalitarian relationship between those who undertake the research and those who are the objects of the research
■ Accountability to clients/service users for the products of their work

■ A holistic engagement with the different aspects of the problem(s) of the people they are investigating.

Whether these are differences of degree or kind is open to question. None of the above characteristics can be exclusively associated with social work, although together they represent a claim for a distinctive claim to an area of knowledge. Like other applied disciplines, social work has a commitment to influencing and being influenced by practice. Social work traditionally has had an ethical commitment towards challenging social injustice and promoting a 'respect for persons' (Downie and Telfer, 1980). This respect has been variously interpreted in how social workers relate to others in a holistic, anti-oppressive way that promotes mutuality, interdependence and working from people's strengths. While it is attractive to argue that there is a distinctive social work research approach, this is not universally accepted and Wilson et al. (2008) identify social work research as being less about distinctive features and more about research methods and orientation towards social work recipients:

> Social work research ... involves systematic investigation, which is conducted using the most appropriate research designs and verifiable methods and analysis. It seeks to find answers relevant to social work about which there is disagreement, uncertainty or a lack of knowledge and to contribute to reducing social problems and distress and promoting well-being. (Wilson et al., 2008: 238)

From one contested terrain we move on to another, evidence-based practice.

Social work research and evidence-based practice

Although not a recent phenomenon (Sheldon et al., 2005), evidence-based practice (EBP) now has a global standing and has transferred from its original conception in medicine to cover mental health (Geddes, 2000), nursing practice (Blomfield and Hardy, 2000), education (Hammersley, 2000), management (Briner, 2000), probation and social work (Sheldon and Chivers, 2000; Newman et al., 2005), has gained endorsement by government (DH, 1998a; DH/DfEE/Home Office 2000) and is embedded in the guidance for qualifying social work courses (DH, 2002c). The reach of EBP is truly impressive.

Evidence-based practice developed in medicine to bridge the gap between research and practice, which is often significant. For example, Antman et al. (1992) highlighted that the majority of textbooks recommended treatments for myocardial infection that were of proven worthlessness. Closer to home, Macdonald (2008: 438) reminds us that as social workers:

> We assume that 'helping' is a good thing but the history of social work bears testimony to the fact that well-trained, well-supported, well-resourced and well-intentioned people doing what appear to be perfectly sensible things can do more harm than good.

Neither social work nor social work research is without risk and both have the potential to do harm as well as good. It is thus imperative that the social work practitioner should be as well informed as possible that their intended intervention will bring about the desired changes and leave their client, family or community no less worse off than when they intervened. From a common-sense perspective, it is hard to argue that social work should not be evidence based. However, EBP has come under critique from within social work (Trinder and Reynolds, 2000; Webb, 2001) as being wed to a particular view of science and in particular to positivistic and behaviourist approaches. Within this view, there is a clear hierarchy of knowledge, with **randomised controlled trials** (RCTs) viewed as the 'gold standard'. Randomised controlled trials require the random allocation of participants to a control or experimental group. In some trials, the treatment group is further divided in two, with one group receiving a placebo rather than the treatment. Ideally, this is done as a 'double blind', where neither the patient nor the doctor is aware of who is receiving the placebo. Similarly, the treatment evaluator should not know who has and has not received the treatment. In doing this, it is possible to maximise the control for competing explanations of outcomes and to be able to say whether a treatment has, or has not, clinical significance. Becker and Bryman (2004) identify the following hierarchy of evidence based on explanatory power:

> **Randomised controlled trials** are the research method designed to evaluate the effectiveness of a therapeutic intervention or a drug in tackling particular illnesses or conditions. Specific interventions are allocated randomly to groups of individuals, one of which is designated the control group. The control group receives the equivalent of no treatment (sometimes in the form of a placebo) and thereby offers a baseline against which to measure the effect of the intervention.

- Several systematic reviews of randomised controlled trials or meta-analysis
- Systematic review of randomised controlled trials
- Randomised controlled trials
- Quasi-experimental trials
- Case control and cohort studies
- Expert consensus
- Individual opinion.

It is clear from the above that quantitative research is valued more highly than qualitative. From a social work perspective, this emphasis upon EBP has led to a useful focus on 'what works' in, for example, child protection (Macdonald and Winkley, 1999) or leaving care (Stein, 1997). There are, however, currently very few RCTs in social work and part of the reason for this is the complexity of social work. McDonald (2008) argues that such complexities are merely technical not epistemological challenges. However, these complexities should not be underestimated – social work is not medicine. Social work is not able to control the practitioner or service user environment. Service users are not passive recipients of interventions – they may even view well-intentioned interventions as unwanted interference. Each service user is unique; each has their own history of personal and interpersonal difficulties located within a social world which they are both shaped by and help to shape. They will also have a view of their own needs and how these can best be met. By its very nature, social work exists in a world of complexity, paradox and contradiction, where workers grapple with intervening in people's lives within knowledge, ethical, legal, policy and professional parameters. If we develop this to look at the educational outcomes for looked-after children, the inadequacy of RCTs comes to the foreground. In seeking to identify 'what works' for achieving educational outcomes for looked-after children, we also need to consider the child's pre-care school experience, the length of time in their placement, their parents'/carers' advocacy of education, the care provided within their placement, the stability of the placement, the commitment to education of the other children in the placement, the educational commitment of the school to looked-after children, whether the child had an advocate/supporter in relation to their education and the child's own commitment to education. On top of these we also need to consider the educational attainment of the other pupils in the school and the value-added performance of the school against its demographic profile and intake. While doing all this, other key features of educational attainment maybe overlooked, such as social class, the mental health of the young person or contact with parents. This is not to suggest that RCTs cannot or should not be used in social work, but that they have a place alongside other methodological approaches and should not necessarily be privileged over other forms of knowledge claims. Macdonald (2008: 437) appears to accept this position when she writes:

> There are different hierarchies of appropriateness for different kinds of research question. It is only in relation to evaluations of the *effects of interventions* that one might wish to argue for 'in principle' superiority of random controlled trials over others. If we want to improve our understanding of how it feels to be a child looked-after then a survey of children using in-depth qualitative interviews is much more appropriate.

At one level, McDonald appears to accept that RCTs can only claim to be the most appropriate kind of research for 'evaluation of the effects of interventions'. Such a view certainly has some purchase with the emphasis of RCTs on the importance of outcomes, but the effects of outcomes will also include the subjective experiences of service users that RCTs are poorly equipped to capture. In social activities, processes can often be highly influential in achieving important outcomes. Service users are more likely to follow intervention programmes that build on their strengths, acknowledge their worth, begin from where they are and are aimed at helping them to achieve their goals. Also, we need to be wary of accepting that the 'ends will justify the means'.

One of the difficulties of the healthcare domination of EBP has been the colonisation of the term as it has increasingly become associated with a positivistic scientific view, whereby EBP has become a technical, rational exercise in solving problems. As Trinder (2000: 236) comments:

> Evidence-based practice tends to fit solutions to problems into its own world view, providing more and better information, further refinement of methodological criteria

or incorporating consumer perspectives into an evidence-based framework. The result is there are major outstanding issues that the rational scientific model is ill equipped to handle, and would appear unlikely to resolve. "

This section of the chapter has sought to unpack some of the assumptions behind EBP and in particular to highlight that although the term has brought a welcome interest in outcomes, it has also had a negative impact on professions outside the clinical world. Evidence-based practice has sought to secure a primacy for RCTs that is inappropriate within social work. This is not to say that RCTs and EBP have nothing to offer social work but that they are limited and are only part of how research can support practice. This is why some commentators have decided to adopt terms like 'research-informed practice', distancing social work from the health-led colonisation of EBP practice while still seeking to highlight the importance of research, all types of research, to supporting practice.

The research-minded practitioner

In seeking to develop a more research-minded profession, Walter et al. (2004) identified a tripartite model: the research-based practitioner, the embedded research model and the organisational excellence model. Before exploring the research-based practitioner, it is worthwhile identifying the other two models. The embedded research model is based on the view that research use is achieved by embedding research into the systems and processes of social care including such things as procedures, policies, standards and performance indicators. In this linear instrumental model, it is the policy makers and service delivery managers who have responsibility for ensuring that research is translated into practice. The organisational excellence model is based on the development of an organisational culture that is 'research minded', where there is local interpretation of key research findings and where social care agencies proactively develop partnerships with local universities to facilitate the creation, dissemination and use of research knowledge. This model is dependent on the leadership and management within the organisation.

The research-based practitioner model assumes that it is the responsibility of the individual practitioner to keep abreast of current research and to ensure that it is used in their day-to-day-practice. This model assumes that research use is a linear process of accessing, appraising and applying research and that practitioners have high levels of professional autonomy to be able to change their practice. Walter et al.'s model (2004) is dependent upon professional education and training to develop the appropriate research literacy skills. Within the quality assurance framework for social work courses, there are a number of benchmark statements relating to research, including: 'appropriate use of research in the evaluation of practice outcomes' and using 'research based concepts and critical explanation for social work theory' (www.qaa.ac.uk/academicinfrastructure/benchmark/honours/socialpolicy.asp#18). While all social work programmes have to meet these degree benchmarks, there has been a growing trend away from social work students engaging in empirical research. This is under-standable, given the difficulties in negotiating research governance committees (DH, 2001b) and issues concerning the ethical value of student research projects for service users. However, it is still to be lamented that fewer social work students are having the opportunity to experience empirical research at first hand. More worryingly, this is not being addressed at post-qualifying levels where the General Social Care Council has so far refused to include a social work research post-qualifying award.

A special case of the research-minded practitioner is the practitioner researcher. The practitioner research is a social worker who either in their spare time or for part of their employment undertakes a small-scale research project that is locally based and directly related to the services they deliver. Such projects are generally heralded positively as an example of promoting research-informed practice. Employers may support such projects by providing time, access to files or other staff and, potentially, service users, and in so doing, this type of research runs the danger of being employer led and agency owned (Shaw, 2004). There is also the danger that practitioner research is often methodologically naive, a solitary activity insulated from wider issues and therefore unlikely to influence social work policy and practice.

One other issue that should be mentioned here is that practitioner research is likely to be 'insider research', both in terms of location and standpoint. As Shaw (2004: 125) notes, 'where I work and where I stand' are often conflated in practi-tioner research. While it may be possible for practitioners to 'defamiliarise' themselves from their work context, it has also been argued that research understandings can be enriched through 'insider' perspectives (White, 2001). This is also an issue for service user involvement in research, discussed in the next section.

In trying to rescue practitioner research from its limitations, Gould (2008: 431) notes:

> It is likely that practitioner research will continue to develop as part of overall aspira-tions to evidence-based practice, but that the quality of such research is dependent upon having a supportive organizational climate for research, effective partnerships with universities to enhance methodological rigour and mechanisms for dissemina-tion that ensure that findings add cumulatively to the knowledge base.

At the start of this section, we identified Walter et al.'s tripartite model (2004) of the research-based practitioner, the embedded research model and the organisational excellence model. For social work to become a research-based profession, it requires not one or two aspects of the model but all three.

Involving service users in research

The push within social work to include service users derives from the consumerist tradition of the 1990s and the democratic tradition of developing participation in order to improve the quality and effectiveness of services (Beresford, 2005). In the UK, user involvement has been a central tenet of the modernisation agenda of the

Labour governments who have sought to put service users at the heart of health and social care research (DH, 1998a, 1999a, 2000a, 2000b). With this approach, there is a change in the way that services users are conceptualised, moving from service users as merely the objects of research to becoming co-creators or sole creators of knowledge.

Arnstein (1971) famously identified an eight-rung model of citizen participation, but McLaughlin (2007a), building on the work of Hanley et al. (2004), reduced this to four points on a continuum. The continuum consists of tokenistic involvement, consultation, collaboration and service user-controlled research:

- *Tokenistic involvement* occurs when the researcher claims to be involving service users but manages the research in such a way that the involvement is a mere façade.
- *Consultation* is often viewed as the first rung of participation. However, consultation is a usefully ambiguous term that is open to abuse, as it can mean nearly anything to anyone. Consultation does not require those who are consulting to act on any of the consultee's views, only to hear them.
- *Collaboration* is where service user involvement becomes consequential. Collaboration implies an ongoing relationship with the research project and the potential to influence decision-making and implementation of the research project. Service users may participate collaboratively in some or all the research project, they may be members of the steering group, involved in the research design, act as interviewers, engage in data analysis, participate in writing up and or partake in the dissemination of the findings.
- *Service user-controlled research* takes service user involvement to its logical conclusion, whereby it is the service users who are in control of the research. In contrast to the other points on the continuum, here the power resides with service users. While service user involvement in research is relatively new, service user-controlled research is still in its infancy. Turner and Beresford (2005) found there was a difference of opinion between service user groups as to whether service user-controlled research meant that service users should undertake the research themselves or whether they could employ traditional researchers.

There is a growing awareness that knowledge about service users, or the services they use, is incomplete if it does not include the knowledge that service users have of the services they experience. Service user experience is what is valued but, as in the last section, it can be claimed that service users, like practitioner researchers, are too close to the subject they are studying. This is based on the belief that objectivity, neutrality and distance are prerequisites for valid research evidence. This is not necessarily always the case and Glasby and Beresford (2006) have argued that emancipatory disability research and service user-controlled research have identified gains by involving service users who have been close to the area under inquiry and challenged notions of distance and neutrality. In this instance, it is possible to suggest that what we need here is not to be too close so that we cannot see the big picture or too distant that we cannot see the individual parts that make up the bigger picture. Just as service user researchers can be too close, traditional researchers can also be too distant.

From our analysis, service user involvement in research can only be described as meaningful at the collaborative and service user-controlled end of the continuum. It is not the case that service user research should be privileged over other types of research, but that it offers a dimension that is missing in other research approaches.

The claimed benefits for involving service users in research include:

- Service users can offer a different perspective
- The range and quality of research data can be enhanced
- Service users can help with the identification and prioritisation of research questions and areas
- Service users speak a common language and can help with ensuring the accessibility of research questions and interviews
- Service users can often help with the recruitment of their peers, which is especially helpful in contacting hard-to-reach groups
- Service users can help with the dissemination of results
- Involvement in research can empower service users
- Service user involvement in research helps to meet the growing political priority for involvement (Hanley et al., 2004; Kirby, 2004; McLaughlin, 2007b).

Given the claimed benefits, it is not surprising that there has been a significant interest in this style of research, but there are also significant associated costs:

- Increased resources necessary to undertake research
- Increased time needed to complete research especially if co-researchers require training
- Extra ethical dimension to research process
- Need to manage issues of remuneration of service users and interface with benefits system
- Restriction on types of research that are possible
- Impact on publications and researcher's career (McLaughlin, 2006).

One of the constant criticisms of any participatory process is the need to avoid 'the usual suspects'. This is to miss the point of involving service users in research that does not claim to be representative but aims to provide an alternative experiential perspective.

Involving service users in research is not a cost-neutral activity and needs to be considered in light of the research question under investigation, the resources available and the skills of the research team. It is quite clear that it would not be sensible to consider that service user researchers or co-researchers would be able to undertake advanced quantitative or qualitative analysis and this may limit the types of research that can be undertaken and the knowledge claims that can be derived from the research. Currently, service user involvement in research is more honoured in rhetoric than in practice. Carr (2004) found that a successful outcome was often associated with service users feeling positive about the process rather than achieving particular outcomes or changes in service delivery. There is a current danger that service user involvement in research has the become flavour of the moment. If it is to be more than a fad, there is a need for service user involvement to maintain its integrity and neither to overclaim nor underclaim what can be achieved and to develop knowledge claims with demonstrable outcomes.

Interdisciplinary research

One other aspect of social work research is worthy of mention here and that is the drive towards interagency or multi-agency working. It is suggested that in the future social workers are more likely to be co-located with other professions than with other social workers. It is quite common today to talk of health and social care where both terms become merged into one. There is, however, a worrying trend in publications purporting to cover health and social care. Recently, I looked at two such edited text-books; one on ethics by Long and Johnson (2007) contained no social work authors whatsoever, and the other on service user research by Nolan et al. (2007), in which only 2 of the 34 authors were from a social work background. The use of the term 'health and social care' is in danger of becoming a form of colonisation of social work by health-based academics. There is also a fear that a similar experience may occur with education in the future.

This is not to argue that we need to incorporate research that goes beyond social work. As Roe (2006) so accurately observed:

Social work services don't have all the answers. They need to work closely with other universal service providers in all the sectors to find new ways to design and deliver services across the public sector.

This also identifies the two challenges for social work in a multi-agency or interdisciplinary perspective. The first of these is to research attempts at multi-agency working to identify how this can create added value and to identify when and where it is not to be recommended. Second, there is a need for social work researchers to consider working with other disciplines to share approaches, develop understandings and create synergies to promote new understandings. It is quite clear when we consider the safeguarding of older people that we also need to work alongside colleagues from health including gerontologists, psychiatrists, psychologists and nurses. Similarly, in research terms, we also need to work with colleagues from these same disciplines to understand their contribution to safeguarding older people, including their understanding of the ageing process, physical health, mental health, mental capacity and nursing needs to promote an environment in which older people can be safe. The challenge for social work research is to gain disciplinary credibility within academia while effectively contributing to the potential solutions of 'wicked problems' without becoming subservient to more established academic disciplines.

Conclusion

This chapter has sought to establish why it is essential that social work practitioners become research literate. Research can help to improve practice, but also practice can help to challenge research and suggest new directions of inquiry. While we have examined issues concerning social work research distinctiveness, methods of research, evidence-based practice, the research-informed practitioner, service user involvement in research and interdisciplinary research, it is clear that social work research is a contested and contestable arena rich with challenge and debate. However, research, in all its forms, provides practitioners with a key and often underutilised support in undertaking a difficult and demanding task while navigating the realities of everyday practice.

For a discussion of other aspects of work with service users, see Chapter 15, and for a detailed discussion of doing research in social work, see Adams et al., 2009c, Chapters 20 to 26. For discussion of the further development of social work research, see Adams et al., 2009c, Chapter 26.

www.rip.org.uk   Research in Practice, a nationally based research dissemination site for research in relation to work with children and families.

www.ripfa.org.uk   Research in Practice for Adults, a sister organisation to RIP focused on adult services.

www.invo.org.uk   INVOLVE, the website for public involvement in health, public health and social care research. Provides a useful free collection of materials on involving service users in research.

D'Cruz, H. and Jones, M. (2004) *Social Work Research: Ethical and Political Contexts*, London, Sage. Well-written introductory text that makes a case for research as another social work method.

Lowes, L. and Hulatt, I. (eds) (2005) *Involving Service Users in Health and Social Care Research*, London, Routledge. Provides a useful series of case studies in involving service users in research.

Macdonald, G. (2008) 'The evidence based perspective', in M. Davies (ed.) *The Blackwell Companion to Social Work*, Oxford, Blackwell, pp. 435–41. Concise and highly readable account in favour of evidence-based practice by one its most active advocates.

McLaughlin, H. (2007) *Understanding Social Work Research: Key Issues and Concepts*, London, Sage. Considers research in relation to a number of key social work themes and argues that research is an underused but essential tool for busy social workers.

Part 2

SOCIAL WORK PROCESS

Part 2 of this book deals with the ideas which the word 'process' in social work conjures up. It explores the stages of what is generally recognised as the social work process in some detail. In social work, process refers to a connected series of interactions between practitioners and service users, as the practitioner builds up a picture of people's social relationships and needs, decides between different courses of action and carries out particular interventions (Chapter 13). Before proceeding through the stages of social work, two chapters are spent considering two crucial aspects. Chapter 14 discusses communication skills, which are essential to the quality of interaction between the practitioner and people who use services. Chapter 15 examines the complexities of 'service user involvement' – a somewhat inadequate shorthand term used to refer to both policy and practice efforts to engage people who use services in various forms of participation. Chapters 16 to 21 deal in turn with the main stages of practice, beginning with assessment (Chapter 16) and then showing how planning is more than a one-off event and contributes dynamically throughout the entire process of practice (Chapter 17). Three chapters are devoted to the relatively neglected area of intervention, beginning with generic ideas about intervention (Chapter 18), looking next at how the tensions between intervention and empowerment are worked out in practice (Chapter 19); and concluding with a view of intervention drawn from outside the inevitable constraints of Western philosophies and assumptions (Chapter 20). This sequence concludes with an examination of how the activities of monitoring, review and evaluation are embedded throughout the entire process of practice (Chapter 21).

Understanding social work process

13

Social work process is a series of connected activities, including assessment, interventions and evaluation, not a collection of separate services or events in someone's life. Using ideas of process, practitioners can understand the connectedness and integration of different objectives and the context of practice.

Chapter overview

What is process?

One way of understanding social work is to see it as a process. This means that we treat social work with an individual, group or community as a whole: it is a series of connected contacts between a social work practitioner and the people who the practitioner is trying to help. The process takes place within the auspices of a social institution called an agency; we look at some of the main agency settings for social workers in the UK in Part 3 of this book. The chapters in this second part of Book 1 start from communication and working with service users and carers, which are relevant to all aspects of process, and then follow the process through a well-established cycle of practice, starting with assessment, moving through planning, various kinds of intervention, and finally monitoring, evaluation and review. My aim in this chapter is to explain what the idea of process is and the different ways in which social workers have applied it in their practice.

I start with an example of my practice. Among my responsibilities in the hospice where I work is the protection of vulnerable adults. A common situation is conflict between spouses, really angry exchanges between husband and wife. The multiprofessional team that I work with – doctors, social workers and other healthcare professionals – are sometimes uncomfortable about such events. Is a particularly violent outburst aimed at getting the spouse's own way emotional abuse? If so, our local multi-agency procedures for the protection of vulnerable adults say that we should take action to protect the person affected.

Our starting point is the present position of the family: we are involved with them because someone is dying and usually there are social consequences for their family members. Therefore, an outburst might easily be a reasonable expression of what they are all experiencing. But what view do we take if there is continuous hectoring? We might look into the history of the marital relationship. Perhaps this is a particularly edgy or tempestuous relationship, in which outbursts are accepted as part of the family culture. There are two ways of seeing this: we might say that both parties have accepted the continuing nature of their relationship; alternatively, we could see one spouse as the unthinking object of long-standing abuse. Another factor is the overall task that we are there to carry out. Our service aims to help people to maintain a good quality of life until they die, and assist family members with the process of bereavement afterwards. If we protect our patient by removing another family member, will we interfere with our main aim? What if the patient says they want their spouse with them, while we think they need protection?

I have set out some of the things going on in this situation in Figure 13.1. At least five factors are relevant:

1   The patient is dying, which is part of a 'disease trajectory': the disease has built up from minor changes in their body, to physical changes that have produced symptoms. These have been treated, perhaps with some success, but eventually their illness is leading to death. How they die, however, is not only defined by the disease, but by their life history. Are they satisfied with their life and relationships? What is their view about death? Do they still have tasks to perform?

2   The marital part of the family history of constantly evolving relationships leads to the conflict that concerns us. It will continue until death and beyond it, because it will affect the surviving partner in all future relationships, looking back and perhaps reassessing the marriage continuously after the death. The illness and the death, the conflict and the marriage interact with our multiprofessional services.

3   Doctors, nurses, nursing assistants, chaplains, complementary and creative therapists, physiotherapists, social workers all have their duties and are part of a philosophy of palliative care and treatment policies, regulated by the requirements of our funders and the government regulator of hospices. How these people interact together and how their occupations see their roles and activities constantly changes and develops as professional knowledge and policy decisions accumulate and interact with each other.

4   There is a reporting and investigation process in adult protection, following multi-agency guidelines set up and administered by our local authority, according to government guidance. These have been built up over time by the multi-agency working party, and are constantly monitored and developed.

5   The conflict exists as part of these continuing streams of social relations. How each party perceives it depends on the social relations they are involved in. Their perceptions then colour how they will react.

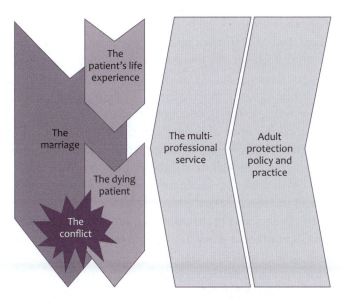

Figure 13.1 Complex processes in an adult protection case

At any one time, all these factors contribute to a 'situation'. We can try to understand their contribution and define what is going on in order to decide how to act. However, looked at over time, each factor changes at its own pace, responding to the relationships and social changes that affect it. For example, the marriage may have been a rather edgy compromise for the spouses a few years ago, but constant conflict may have altered the balance of power between them and turned one into an abuser. Another example, the multiprofessional team might have concentrated on the wishes of their patient a year ago, but have been forced to balance this with the risks to a vulnerable adult by the development of the protection policy. We call these continuous changes 'processes'.

Process has several connected meanings. A *proces*sion brings to mind people in uniform or ritual dress entering to take up their positions; industrial *proces*ses mix chemicals, or machines manufacture something; in offices, lines of clerks *process* application forms. More generally, *a process is a series of actions and the factors affecting them that go towards making or achieving something.*

This account of the idea of process suggests, first, that it refers to an accepted way of doing things. In the ceremony, there is an order of precedence; the office worker 'goes through' documents; inside a computer, a 'processor' carries out a series of tasks in logical sequence, similar to the officials at their desks but more quickly. The formal church or academic procession, where people enter, go to their places and perform tasks, has many features in common with the informal process of a family entering a sitting room and settling down to watch television. They go to their normal seats, settle down, agree about the programme to watch and fiddle with the remote control. In both, there is an accepted way of doing things that grows up in social relationships. In social work, this idea helps us to understand how a marriage, the experience of dying, the professional task or the organisational policy sets social expectations so that people know how to behave and how to react in different circumstances. The 'way of doing things' comes from both formal procedures and socially accepted conventions.

Second, process refers to complexity and connectedness. We do not see separate events but the connections between them. This is, of course, a human interpretation of events: it is how we understand connections and complexes that create process. In social work, people's stories or narratives of what has happened to them connect apparently separate matters together in their minds and the connections then affect how they act. For example, a woman dying of cancer may connect her weight loss with her husband's sudden lack of interest in sexual intercourse.

Third, process is time based. Events and the factors that affect them occur in sequence, over a period of time. Seeing social work as a process, rather than, say, as a packages of services or as separate episodes in people's lives, makes connections between events in the client's life and the social worker's assessments and reactions to them, and between what the worker does and the effects on their clients. For example, a package of services including a daily delivery of meals, visits by carers in the morning and evening, a daily visit by district nurses, twice-weekly shopping and domestic help are experienced by the service user as a sequence of stimulating and mutually support-ive visits, or perhaps irritating interruptions to their own life sequence. The care manager may interpret them as a complex whole, covering different risks or needs, rather than separate events and services or a sequence. How people see the process may help or hinder them. For example, the care manager who sees a total package may not have thought to check that it works for a service user who sees it as a sequence, or an occasional visitor who may not realise that there is a care plan and thinks the support is random.

Fourth, a process is structured and organised. Part of the structure is the time-based sequence, but other parts of it may be the people involved, the place where they interact or the organisation that they are a part of and the accountabilities that participation in an agency and service involves. The process of deciding what to do about a family in conflict in a hospice involves various members of the multiprofessional team coming together. There is an acknowledged and partly written down procedure for doing so. For example, in my hospice, if there is a worry about family relationships, rather than a ward management issue, a social worker will be called. If there is concern about abuse, I will be called. If there is concern about a risk of falling rather than a risk of abuse, a physiotherapist might be called.

Fifth, there is an outcome to processes. The procession arrives at its position and then events begin to happen, the factory produces goods, the office produces completed documents. The multiprofessional team will decide the best thing to do, people will take on tasks, plans will be made. These will then form part of a process of intervention, a new process, and the decisions and actions will begin to incorpo-rate themselves into the longer running processes of dying and marriage.

Social work as a process

At a general level, social work as a whole is a process. Considering process makes social work a whole, one activity. Aims, starting points, processes and interactions with other aspects of life are made whole by our interpretation of them as a process, rather than as separate events. Several writers have described it in this way: Table 13.1 outlines some of their contributions.

Table 13.1 Social work as process: alternative interpretations

Type of process	Writer	Aims
Critical	Fook (2002) Healey (2000)	Move towards transformation of social relations through dialogical, shared relationships
Developmental	Smalley (1967)	Help people to 'grow' in understanding and skill
Ego-supportive	Goldstein (1995)	Strengthen people's will to plan and organise life
Empowering	Solomon (1976) Lee (2001)	Strengthen people's ability to overcome social barriers
Person-centred	Rogers (1967)	Release individual's capacity for self-actualisation
Problem-solving	Perlman (1957)	Help people to specify and overcome problems
Psychosocial	Hollis (1964)	Help people to identify and respond to psychological and social stresses
Process knowledge	Sheppard et al. (2000)	Make assessments and decisions through cognitive processes
Systems	Evans and Kearney (1996)	Phases that place work tasks in sequence, according to connections in time

Process differs from content and outcome; the three integrate together as social work deals with the whole situation. Many writers referred to in Table 13.1 present an aim, such as critical social change or problem-solving, connected to a process for achieving it: helping, strengthening or releasing, for example. Process focuses on how to practise and what happens during practice, rather than the aims and outcomes of social work activities. The empirical research of Sheppard et al. (2000) and Sheppard and Ryan (2003) identifies social workers' thinking processes as they work. They make a critical appraisal of situations, focusing attention on important aspects of it, querying and evaluating information and then make causal inferences. This first stage then links to hypothesis generation. Partial case hypotheses propose ways of understanding particular aspects of the situation: is a husband's aggressive behaviour towards his wife due to stress of life or psychiatric illness, for example? Whole case hypotheses are propositions about the case as a whole: is it an adult protection case, requiring the application of formal procedures, for example? Finally, there are speculative hypotheses about proposed actions: could I persuade the husband to moderate his behaviour, for example?

Process describes social work generically, rather than referring to the content that the process deals with, for example child or adult protection, disability, ageing or family conflict. This suggests that social work is all three aspects of social work: to miss out process misses an important aspect of practice analysis. Aims and content can only be understood fully by including how it works, and what it works on – critical dialogue, understanding, skill, the will to plan and organise, the ability to overcome barriers, self-actualisation, overcoming problems and responding to psychosocial stresses.

In social work, to set an outcome is not the end of the matter. If we want to improve someone's childcare skills, where do we start from and how are we going to achieve our aim? If a single-parent father provides effective physical care to his daughter, but finds it hard to deal with her emotional needs, we start from a different place than if he can do neither. If he can learn through discussion, the process is different from the situation where he needs to practise interpersonal skills first. Another factor is that other processes will be going on in his life, as with the dying patient discussed at the outset of this chapter. If he is being criticised at work because he is taking too much time out for his family, the process of relationships with his boss will be proceeding at a different pace and in a different place from our attempt at helping, but will interact with it. The social work intervention has to take into account its interaction with other processes in his life.

All these processes are social. Doctors might be concerned about the body and its physical processes, with the mind and its mental processes, or teachers with developing personal knowledge and understanding. Social workers, on the other hand, are concerned with capacities to deal with other human beings and the social assumptions or relationships that follow from that and are required in order to do that.

Ideas about process

The idea of process as an important part of social work comes from a variety of different sources, both within and outside social work. It is useful to explore these because they bring to the surface some of the thinking that we sometimes take for granted or even are unaware of when we casually say that 'social work is a process'. In this section, I identify four important sources of process ideas in social work:

- Whitehead's process philosophy of science
- Psychodynamic social casework
- Groupwork
- Feminist and critical theory.

The mathematician and philosopher A.N. Whitehead (1861–1947) saw process as a complex of factors that achieve unity through a distinct series of stages or changes taking place through a time dimension and an organised structure that we can understand and define. In the early 1900s, contrary to many scientific approaches to knowledge at the time, he proposed that it is as important to think about reality as events and occurrences as well as being about objects and substances. So, what is important about a building or a human being is not only what they are made of or look like, but also what has happened to them, what is happening or might happen to them and how they might be used. Thus it opens up options and possibilities for change, rather than focusing on what simply exists in the present (Rescher, 2002). It is also about including holistically all the factors in a situation, as in our consideration of social work process.

Psychodynamic theories of social casework drew strongly on Whitehead's ideas. Discussing 'psychosocial process' in an early casework text, Hamilton (1951: 3–4) described social work as a 'living event' incorporating and integrating the person, their situation, social experiences and their feelings about their experiences. Functional casework theory sees process as central to achieving social work purposes that are expressed in the aims of the agency or service. Hofstein (1964: 15) defines process in the functional view as a 'recurrent patterning of a sequence of changes over time and in a particular direction'. Process ties together work with service users to indirect work with the agencies and people around them (Irvine, 1966; Smalley, 1967: 16–17), achieving unity of purpose between different aspects of the work. Smalley's (1970) principles for the practice process include workers using relationships to engage with and act on clients' choices, consciously using time phases – beginnings, middles and ends – and gaining direction, focus, accountability and clarity for the work from the agency's function. These aspects are combined by a constantly changing interaction with the client.

The importance that functional casework gives to relationships also emphasises the way in which social work requires the interpersonal as a basic aspect of its practice. Psychodynamic social work sees process as a cycle of interactions between worker and service users, tied together by growing mutual understanding in their interpersonal relationship (Perlman, 1957: Ch. 5; Ferard and Hunnybun, 1962: 48–81; Butrym, 1976: Ch. 5). Social work requires more than the superficial bedside manner. Workers' dealings with clients must have integrity, and must therefore be integrated with their authentic personal reaction to the client and the situation. Communication of feedback between the worker and client on reactions to the other's actions and thoughts is a crucial part of process working. All these writers put forward a model of process in which the worker and client demonstrate their personalities and ways of behaving to each other. This then leads to an interpersonal engagement with each other, in which difficulties are raised and identified and ways of dealing with them planned and executed.

From its earliest days, groupwork relied on ideas of process. Mary Parker Follett (1868–1933), one of the historical sources of groupwork ideas, writes about being part of a group:

> " I go ... [to a group] in order that all together we may create a group idea, an idea which will be better than any one of our ideas alone, moreover which will be better than all of our ideas added together. For this idea will not be produced by any process of addition, but by the interpenetration of us all. This subtle psychic process by which the resulting idea shapes itself is the process. (Follett, 1918) "

Expressing this 'subtle psychic process', Thompson and Kahn (1970: 13–14) say:

> " In order to try to understand ... [group] interaction, it is necessary to take all the individual pieces of behaviour, the contributions of each different member, and treat them as if they were part of a meaningful whole ... It is necessary to treat the group as a distinct psychological entity, but this does not alter the fact that it has no existence apart from the activity of its individual members ... If we are to assume that some connection exists between all the events taking place in a group, then we must also assume that, at some level, forces exist and exert an influence over every single thing that happens. To these forces we give the name of group processes. "

This quotation emphasises that process always involves bringing together different elements and dealing with the differences that arise. This is clearer in groupwork than in other forms of social work, but it applies to all process. If social work is a process, it is, therefore, about trying to be inclusive when dealing with difference. A process seeks out and tries to respond to everything that affects what is going on. It is thus particularly relevant for anti-discriminatory and anti-oppressive practice, because these forms of practice examine and try to respond to difference.

Thompson and Kahn (1970) also make it clear that process is a metaphor, a human interpretation of what is going on in complex situations. It is treating events 'as if' they were connected and that 'forces exist and exert an influence'. The metaphor of process allows us to understand how events are connected, to make a 'story' or narrative that offers explanations that can be adapted to reflect more information as it arises during our engagement with the client and the situation as it changes.

This aspect of groupwork continues to have its influence. Mullender and Ward (1991) discuss self-directed groupwork as an endeavour to help to empower oppressed groups. They describe process as a development from workers setting up and starting the group, through a series of stages leading to the point where the group operating as a inclusive whole takes charge of its future. Here the process is not just a sequence in time, it is a sequence from powerlessness to empowerment, through learning self-direction in the group.

Critical and feminist theory (Fook, 2002) draws many of these different points together. Feminist theory emphasises a particular aspect of integrity and integration – between the personal and political. Politics is about groups contending for power. We experience power being used in relationships. Sometimes, this is to achieve personal ends. For example, the wife of a dying man prevents his children by the previous marriage from seeing him, by showing him that she is upset by the reminder of the previous relationship. They experience this as frustrating; a direct application of power against them. As well as personal power, politics is also expressed in our personal experience; through discrimination, people experience personally how social and political divisions affect society. Personal experience is an expression of political relationships, but a political reaction – to form groups for mutual support or to seek change – also involves personal commitment.

Process in practice

Why should we use the idea of process in practice? There are three main reasons. First, the idea of process treats workers' actions with people as wholes, rather than separating different aspects of what they do. So, for example, when you ring the social security office to sort out entitlements, the idea of process tells us that this is part of a more general attempt to take the pressure off a single mother whose child has a serious disability. Better social security will make her feel that she is more in control of her weekly budget, and free her from some money worries to focus on caring for her child. Perhaps this is in the early stages of working with her, in which case getting her some practical help may improve your relationship with her and make her more willing to work with you in more emotionally difficult areas later on, such as her fear of letting her child gain more independence. We can see the connections, how everything affects everything else, and our planning (Chapter 17) identifies and makes use of those connections. The relationships with the other agency are also wholes: how they experience us in this case will affect how they respond to us the next time.

Second, process makes clear and takes into account the complexity of the connections between different aspects of the situations we are dealing with. Ideally, everyone should trust that a social worker will be of benefit to them, but most people want us to prove it before they will let us in on the more complex parts of their problems. So, a disabled woman will ask us to sort out her social security entitlements and, if we seem responsive, might be prepared to come up with more personal issues.

Third, process allows us to connect theory with practice and practice with theory in a critical way. Identifying processes begins to make explanatory narratives about the client's situation and our intervention. As our connection-making continues, we see more and more aspects to the narratives that allow us to criticise our earlier explanations and adapt them to the new information. Thus, explanation becomes a process of making meaning from what we see and participate in, not deriving an assessment from a set body of information about the client and then acting on it (Chapter 16).

Although the idea of process comes from psychodynamic and critical theories, it is now used as a general idea in social work. We can use a range of social work theories (for example those discussed in the Adams et al., 2009b, Part 2) as ways of guiding our practice.

Connectedness, communication, context

Accepting that the idea of process may help us to practise, how can we use it? The definition of process given above, as 'a series of actions and the factors affecting them that go towards making or achieving something', offers a starting point. This definition draws attention to how we must bring together both the actions of various people involved, factors that affect those actions, movement towards achieving something and the outcome we want to achieve. My discussion of process so far sets the objective of identifying and bringing together as many relevant factors as possible. A good process identifies relevant people and agencies and brings them together in the interaction.

A social work process is one human event made up of a variety of elements. Figure 13.2 identifies a series of elements within the overall process, a sequence of social work activities. The elements are themselves processes, which draw different elements of the whole into the main. The overall social work process takes place in the context of the processes going on in the lives of the people and the agencies who take part. For the social worker, this might include their personal life, their professional development, and the agency's policies and conventions. For example, they might not be prepared to work with the client late at night, and how they behave would be different if they are a student rather than a seasoned worker. The clients' context might include continuing social relationships, the social environments they live in and the issues they bring to the social work process. Process brings together aspects of the environment through these elements as worker and client find or make connections between these elements, intellectually and in practice in our relationship with the people involved. They need to understand that we are taking the right factors into account, and our relationship will develop so that we can help them better if we can demonstrate our efforts to incorporate what they see as relevant factors.

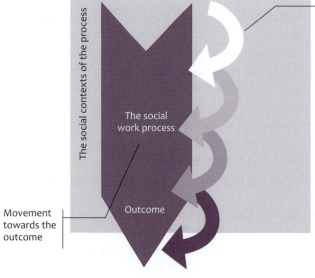

The social contexts of the process

The social work process

Outcome

Movement towards the outcome

A series of social work processes are elements of the overall process and draw different issues into the complex overall process

Figure 13.2 Social work process

The elements are connected in social work interventions (Chapters 18–20) by the following factors:

- *The context in which they take place:* For example, I made a home visit to a couple recently, and the experience is socially different from when the wife visits my office in the hospice. Their involvement with our agency comes from his serious illness; this brings them to us rather than some other agency, and dictates the focus on their support for each other and relatively brief changes in relationship, rather than long-term family change. We sit on comfortable chairs in both cases, but one environment is domestic and controlled by the clients, the other is professional and perhaps medical and is more in my control. Clothing is different, relationships are revealed differently.

- *Communications between the human beings involved:* When the wife visits my office, she gives accounts of, among other things, marital interactions between her and her husband and I try to demonstrate, by interest, commitment to our time together and intelligent responses, that I understand something of her perceptions of the difficulties and value her interpretation of them. I try to get her to make plans to respond differently to some of the human communications. When I visit their home, I can see the interaction, although I am not party to all of it, and I am more balanced in my understanding between her and her husband's perceptions. When the nurse in the multiprofessional team visits, she focuses more on the management of the husband's symptoms, and therefore sees different aspects of the relationship and attempts different interventions.

- *The human understandings developed by the communications:* My communications with the wife aim at her managing her interactions with her husband, choosing particular times for difficult interactions and controlling her behaviour, for example. Together with the husband, my work helps them to understand how each might respond to particular behaviours in the relationship and plan how it might be better to relate to each other.

- *Human reflection on the understandings:* Seeing through experience what works better in the relationship also helps them to reflect on and see their long-term relationship differently.

- *Human action that communicates based on the reflection:* As a result of changes in how they view each other's behaviour, they act with more consideration to each other.

The process elements, then, form a **reflexive cycle**: the context and what takes place in it affect – through communication, human understanding and reflection on that understanding – actions that communicate, changing the context and understanding of participants. It is reflexive because it allows each participant to put themselves in the shoes of the others and find out about how they are

Reflexive cycle refers to a process of reflexive activities, each stage of which involves engaging with oneself: self-reference, self-analysis, self-interpretation and self-criticism. While the strength of the concept lies in its focus on specific parts of a process, its weakness is that it tends to imply that rather than flowing flexibly, the process cannot deviate from a fixed sequence.

thinking, so that they can readjust their own thinking. This starts off another cycle, in which they gain further understanding about the other person and their environment and can make further adjustments. A sequence of cycles forms the wider process; because it moves forwards, it develops from a cycle into a spiral. The cycles change during the sequence. Early on in the overall process, I was more inclined to explore, to try to understand how each party saw the relationship and how they wanted to change it. Later, I use the events of the process elements to try to change perceptions and reactions that may lead to changing behaviour.

As it is one event, a process has boundaries, which are defined by the context. Among important boundaries are:

- *The agency's responsibilities* to its political or managing body, which may set its priorities and funding, and to regulators, who set standards of practice
- *The worker's (my) accountability* to the people they are working with and the professional regulatory bodies for professional standards of practice
- *The different personal identities* of the individuals involved and as part of a family and community
- *The interests of other stakeholders*, including individuals, such as neighbours, and organisations, such as the client's employer.

Understanding boundaries is important because it is always important to how social workers exert professional control over their participation in other people's lives. Making boundaries clear helps people, both service users and colleagues in other agencies, to understand and manage their interactions with the social worker. One boundary lies between the social worker as a professional and as a person. Social workers will disclose aspects of themselves as a person. Part of this will be natural, for example the way they pay attention to what clients say and express concern will enable clients to make judgements about what kind of person the social worker is, whether and in what ways they can be trusted. However, workers may also introduce information about themselves as a person. For example, they might talk about how they have experienced similar events to those of the client, as a way of helping the client feel that the worker has empathy with their experiences. However, it is easy to step across the boundary between disclosing similar experiences to achieve empathy for the client's benefit and disclosing information to feel good about ourselves for our benefit. Perhaps we want to see ourselves as open to and equal with the client, when the client is clear about our different status as a powerful professional rather than a friend. Worse, the client may be unclear and our disclosure may make it even more confusing.

Process requires us to take into account the accepted ways of doing things. They cannot be ignored because they will have an important emotional and practical effect on the people involved. Accepted ways include the following:

- *Social and emotional conventions and expectations:* For example, when a family member dies, there will be a period of bereavement. The emotion and behaviour that people express will reflect what is expected of bereaved people in the family and culture (Smith, 1982).

■ *Legal and administrative requirements:* For example, children must go to school during the years of compulsory attendance. Such requirements place pressures on families. Where there is a disabled single mother, for example, children in the family might be expected to care for her and this may conflict with the legal requirement to attend school.

■ *Agency requirements and procedures:* For example, to provide help to a frail older person means that they must meet either the social services department's criteria for providing 'packages' of care in the community or the primary care trust's criteria for funding 'continuing care' packages (see Chapter 23 for more information about this).

Each system of social provision across the world has similar criteria fitting with their welfare system. For example, in the US, a similar aspect of service is called 'managed care'.

Process brings together all the elements that might have an impact on the situation. Important elements that the worker will consider are the people and agencies involved. Often, these elements are lumped together as 'stakeholders'. This term implies that they are likely to be affected by the issues being dealt with in the process. How might they be identified? Factors might include their present participation, their relationships with the client or the issues involved and their official responsibilities. For example, one of the issues for the hospice multiprofessional team is referring cases of abuse of vulnerable persons to the local authority for investigation, under the local multi-agency guidelines. The local authority has a 'stake' in such matters, because of its role in government guidelines, but its staff often have no other involvement with a person to be referred, so they have no stake as far as the patient or other professionals are concerned. This means that careful arrangements for explaining and gaining consent for referral are important to maintaining the trust of the client.

Time, sequencing, structure

How process connects elements involves seeing a structure in the events that we take part in, how the different elements fit together. The structure may develop from a client grouping. For example, social work processes are established by present-day trends such as managerialism, competence-based practice and the 'contract culture', in which services are commissioned by public authorities, rather than provided directly. Various writers then divide social work into work with children and families, adults and offenders. This points to the agency whose legal and administrative roles form an important structure that constructs our work. Other ways of looking at structure include the special interests of particular client groups, using theories to decide how to connect the different aspects of cases together, and using a perspective such as feminism or social values; all these are discussed in various parts of these books.

A common approach to structure in social work, however, is sequencing. The following are examples of social work sequences and time phases:

1 Beginnings – middles – ends
2 Study – diagnosis – treatment
3 Intake – assessment – intervention – outcome – evaluation
4 Problem specification – contract creation – task planning – task implementation – ending
5 Assessing need – care planning – implementing care plans – monitoring – reviewing
6 Critical appraisal – hypothesis formation.

The first of these is used in Golan's (1978) account of crisis intervention. The second was a common description of social work in the 1950s and 60s, and the third is a more managerial or research account of social work process sequences. The fourth is the conventional task-centred practice sequence (Reid and Epstein, 1972). The fifth is the sequence of care management described in the British government guidance on care management and assessment (SSI/SWSG, 1991). The sixth reflects in outline the stages of process knowledge disclosed in Sheppard et al.'s (2000) research into process knowledge.

Although all these structures for social work process have been commonplace in social work at various times, and elements of the sequences connect, they each carry different implications. For example, ideas such as 'diagnosis' and 'treatment' imply connections with the medical assessment of patient, whereas looking at tasks and problems implies a different approach. To focus on structures such as beginnings, middles and ends draws attention to the way in which workers and clients may behave differently at different points in the process. Both may be anxious or uncertain at the outset. They may have established a way of relating in the middle that may be difficult to break out of if change is needed. An end might imply anxiety about the future or a feeling of loss. 'Intake' implies an administrative and professional stage of taking a case into the agency as well as 'taking in' the implications of its initial presentation for the worker. Many accounts of social work sequences ignore this element of the sequence, focusing on assessment first. But the pathway by which the client arrives at the agency, how the agency treats them and how the worker reacts to them in the first instance can be important factors in how the rest of the process goes. For example, a family with relationship problems may go to a criminal justice agency and the initial focus will be on offences committed by one member, or it may go to a housing agency and the initial focus might be on their behaviour as tenants or the maintenance of their property. In either case, their social security entitlements may be an issue to remove the need to commit offences or give them resources to manage their property. Family relationships may become an issue or not.

Similarly, to refer to 'endings' implies a concern for the relationship aspects of finishing a process, while 'outcomes' refers more to achievements, measuring by evaluation or monitoring and review (Chapter 21). In between, activities such as planning, intervention and implementation form other activities of social work, designed to create change.

Although I have referred here to interpersonal social work, the same account of process may be applied to residential work, community work, groupwork and social care management. All involve processes made up of elements, and our understanding of them as whole, overall processes is crucial to making plans and interventions with purposes and aims. When we run a group, we organise a series of meetings with purposes, selecting members appropriate to the purposes within the context of the agency's practice. We see the connections between the different groups, consistencies between group members, connections between their behaviour in the group and behaviour in the community, and try to draw these together and make links for the groups' members. A manager or a community worker has a strategic sense of where they want to go with the activities they are organising. In the same way, therefore, they see themselves as taking part in a process.

Conclusion

Process is important in thinking about practice in social work because it provides a universal way of conceiving what we are doing as we practise. It allows us to think of the many different elements of what we are doing as connected, and therefore to make sense of them, both for ourselves and the people with whom we work. Most social workers do not think about particular theories or value commitments when they are working with people in everyday practice, but they do have plans and strategies that make sense of their work as a sequence or pattern of activity that will benefit the client.

Process has several important features as a way of thinking about social work practice:

- It makes clear that social work is not a series of episodes or 'packages' of service, but seeks to integrate them into a whole.
- It makes clear the continuing contexts, those things that are already going on in the life of the agency, the worker and the client, within which the work takes place. These move continuously. This does not mean that they necessarily progress, in the sense of improving, but they do move on.
- It identifies the importance of structuring and sequencing practice so that many different factors can be incorporated into the practice we are undertaking.
- It emphasises that how we do things is as important as what we do and what the aim and outcome might be.
- It helps us to understand and deal with the complexity of the range of people, stakes, ideas and values that we usually have to struggle with.

After two generally applicable chapters on communication and working with service users and carers, this part of the book makes use of a conventional time sequence, starting with processes around assessment, moving on to intervention and then review. We include three chapters on different approaches to intervention, to illustrate different ways in which intervention may be approached, including a non-Western approach. You can use the discussion in this chapter to examine critically what each author says about the element of the structure they are dealing with. For example:

- How does an assessment or intervention integrate different elements?
- How does it deal with contexts and their movements?
- How does it use structures and sequences?
- How does it deal with aims, processes and outcomes?
- How does it include complexity and the range of potential stakes?

You can ask the same of your own practice.

For further discussion of what critical practice means, see Adams et al., 2009b, Chapter 1, and for links between this and practice approaches, see Adams et al., 2009b, Chapter 8.

Butrym, Z.T. (1976) *The Nature of Social Work*, London, Macmillan – now Palgrave Macmillan. Chapter 6 provides a good account of 'traditional' views about process and is still a valid and useful account.

Compton, B.R., Galaway, B. and Cournoyer, B.R. (2005) *Social Work Processes*, 7th edn, Pacific Grove, CA, Brooks/Cole. This widely used American textbook only minimally discusses the idea of process (on p. 3) (astonishing considering its title), but in its presentation of many aspects of social work, it demonstrates how social work processes may be understood in some complexity. Is a current update of ideas that draw on Perlman's (1957) account of casework as a problem-solving process.

Sheppard, M. and Ryan, K. (2003) 'Practitioners as rule using analysts: a further development of process knowledge in social work', *British Journal of Social Work* **33**(2): 157–76; Sheppard, M., Newstead, S., Di Caccavo, A. and Ryan, K. (2000) 'Reflexivity and the development of process knowledge in social work: a classification and empirical study', *British Journal of Social Work*, **30**(4): 465–88. These two papers report an empirical study about how social workers develop rules for thinking about what they are doing and show how this becomes a process for gaining understanding and making decisions about their work.

Communication skills in social work

14

This chapter considers the nature of communication and explores how communication skills can be learned and applied in practice.

Chapter overview

Communication is central to interpersonal relationships and interviewing. Good communication lies at the heart of empowering social work practice. Communication skills have been defined as: 'The verbal and nonverbal exchange of information, including all the ways in which knowledge is transmitted and received' (Barker, 2003: 83). In Britain, students need to learn about communication theories and practice and acquire good communication skills before working with people, as set out by the General Social Care Council (GSCC).

Different types of communication

Social workers have a vast range of theories and methods of intervention from which to choose in developing their communication skills. Different theories influence the language used with service users and shape the interpersonal relationships between them. For example, those adhering to postmodernist paradigms use language to mirror the story or narrative through which a service user constructs their world view or story. Intervention will take the form of helping the service user to restory their narrative account. This may involve an emphasis on the service user's strengths and the worker's ability to reframe negative situations into positives ones or find a window of hope for the future. This entails looking for what Bateson (1956) calls a difference that 'makes a difference' rather than more of the same. Egan (1982: 181) describes this thinking as 'questioning assumptions to get rid of distortions, relabelling, reframing and making connections'. Egan calls these 'developing new perspectives' and argues that the terms imply a cognitive restructuring that 'while painful at times tends to be prized by clients'. Language, a key medium of communication, can open or close doors and influence action. It is also embedded in power relations that have to be unpacked and understood for empowerment to occur (Dominelli, 2002b).

Communication covers a wide range of active possibilities like talking and passive ones like silence. Communicating involves interpretation to derive meaning and significance. 'One cannot not communicate' (Watzlawick et al., 1967: 48) is a famous axiom that is illustrated with examples of how it is impossible not to communicate so that even when sleeping, the message received by the observer is of a person sleeping. Silence conveys powerful messages that have to be reflected upon and analysed (Kadushin, 1990: 252–64). For example, we can ask: 'Why is this person silent? Are they unsure, distressed, angry, unhappy or simply bored?' Silence may be interpreted as contemplation, thinking or simply savouring the moment. Some people are silent listening to music, others like to sing along. Body language might help inform us as to the motivation underlying silence. For example, a child silently creeping on tiptoe may be interpreted as behaving in such a way to surprise an adult or another child. The context and shout of 'Surprise!' gives the game away.

CaSE EXaMPLE

Meeting with a birth father for the first time, a student social worker believed that he would demonstrate respect by addressing the service user as 'Mr'. The student was surprised to discover that this angered the man, who accused him of trying to assert power over him by using a formal title. The student was able to calm the situation by asking the man how he would prefer to be addressed.

Consider how the student might have been better prepared so as not to make assumptions that could undermine his objectives when meeting a service user.

Not all communication is easy to interpret. Students and practitioners can use silence or employ more imaginative approaches with service users unaccustomed to talking things through. Whatever the circumstances, making assumptions about those being communicated with should be avoided. Lishman (1994) identifies four types of communication: symbolic, verbal, nonverbal and written.

1 *Symbolic communication:* this examines aspects of behaviour on how we present the self, for example being on time, how we dress. Punctuality with service users appears to have slipped from social workers' lexicon due to pressures of work as practitioners become preoccupied with meeting organisational timescales and deadlines. Dirty waiting rooms and being late convey symbolic and literal meanings to service users. The message is that they are not valued. Organisations have a long way to go to improve facilities for service users. These include simple 'do not disturb signs' on doors to interview rooms to prevent constant interruptions from staff seeking an empty room.

2   *Verbal communication:* oral or spoken communication involves asking questions, including *open questions* like 'How do you feel today?' This invites a range of replies, whereas *closed questions* like 'Is it raining?' will generally elicit 'yes' or 'no' replies. Direct and indirect questions provide ways of questioning service users. *Direct questions* are followed by a question mark and *indirect questions* are more like a statement, for example: 'It must be difficult bringing up four children on a limited income.' The *limited choice question* is used in market research and magazine quizzes, for example: 'Do you prefer red or green?', when the person may actually prefer another colour. The 5WHs expressed by Rudyard Kipling (1902) as what, why, when, where, who and how are useful. The use of why in working with children and young people is best avoided as it sounds accusatory and a child or young person may experience blame for something they have not done. Teaching micro-communication skills requires attention to group processes as these may be daunting to master during interviews. Encouraging students to try out different types of question in role plays and referring to their notes as prompts can assist them in acquiring the necessary skills in the safe environment of a classroom.

   Probing questions can encourage service users to talk about themselves. These are usually open or indirect questions. Finally, *scaling questions* can attract less threatening responses. Asking a young person where they would rate themselves on a ranking scale of 1 to 10 is less emotive than asking them: 'How unhappy/happy are you?' The *miracle question* from de Shazers' (1985) work is popular with students who utilise solution-focused approaches in practice. It is necessary to be cautious in applying any theoretical approach in difficult situations, for example a social worker cannot magic away child abuse or broken bones in a domestic violence context. Students need to plan the questions to be asked appropriately with their practice teachers.

3   *Nonverbal communication* is divided by Lishman (1994) into two: *proxemics*, concerned with distance and closeness or personal space; and *kinesics*, concerned with movement, gesture, expression and eye contact. Egan's (1982) SOLER mnemonic provides an alternative to Lishman's conceptualisation of nonverbal communication:

   - S – straight position facing the client
   - O – open body position
   - L – leaning towards the client
   - E – eye contact
   - R – relaxed position.

   Exercises that model nonverbal communication conveyed through body language can include commenting on messages given when:

   - staring when standing close to a person while holding one's hands on one's hips
   - sitting slumped in the chair with head and eyes down
   - sitting with folded arms and swinging your foot.

Lack of congruence between what is said and body posture illustrate confusing messages. Students can provide examples of congruous and incongruous behaviour. A favourite one is the look of contempt while looking a person up and down and saying: 'Well, you look great.' Here, body language is incongruent with what is being said. Another anecdote that students appreciate covers Brian Cades' famous use of metaphor about the intimate behaviour involved in gazing lovingly into the eyes of one's partner while enjoying an intimate meal. In it, Cades describes the process of having a meal as a metaphor for sex. Some people begin slowly with a starter leading up to the main course. Others enjoy going straight to the main course then winding down with desert. There are several variations on this metaphor, and the author apologises for any errors in the translation by quoting Oscar Wilde in *Conversation:* 'I may have said the same thing before … but my explanation, I am sure, will always be different.'

4   *Written communication:* this assumes a variety of forms, ranging from informal note-taking, formally recorded notes, reports to courts or other officials to research reports and articles for publication. Each has its own style and is tailored for the audience(s) it is intended to reach. Thinking about who comprises the audience being targeted will assist the process of writing appropriately. Regardless of audience, written communications should be clear, concise and easy to follow.

Communication skills are central to interpersonal relationships and interviewing

Empathy is a sense of sharing emotions, feelings and experiences with another person. While it may be claimed to be a social work skill, it could be argued that it is a human quality which is beyond skill, in that it is hard to learn or acquire through other means.

Being a good communicator is central to social work practice. Communicating effectively requires skills, knowledge, **empathy** and constant critical reflection. Practitioners have simultaneously to ask good questions, listen actively, convey information, exercise scepticism, and reflect on the interaction. Good communication requires skill and constant critical reflection in the following areas:

- Ability to engage
- Ability to put another person at ease
- Awareness of cultural issues
- Awareness of potential for differences in power between workers and service users
- Clarity regarding the purpose of an interaction
- Ability to pose questions clearly and unambiguously
- Ability to check comprehension and clarity
- Being aware of the need for alternative forms of communication where necessary
- Active listening skills
- Appropriate responses to service users' concerns
- Awareness of one's own body language
- Awareness of and appropriate responses to the body language of the service user
- Ability to structure, summarise and conclude an interview appropriately.

Listening skills

The ability to communicate effectively is at the heart of social work practice and before interacting and responding, it is good practice to actively listen (Egan, 1982) to what has been said (verbal communication) or not said (nonverbal communication) (Kadushin, 1983). Not listening comes at a cost, including loss of face for a manager or worker as indicated below.

CASE EXAMPLE

A senior colleague firmly believed in the philosophy of management by walking around, greeting people by name and asking how they were. Regardless of the response, he would say 'Good, good' and walk on, giving him the nickname, 'Goody two shoes'. I was working with a colleague in this statutory setting and recall watching a woman approach the office. She was wearing a bandage around her arm and appeared to be in pain as she walked. Arriving at reception, the woman asked to see this colleague and took a seat to wait. To my horror, this colleague approached reception and greeted the service user in a happy voice, telling her how wonderful she looked and invited her to follow him into his office. Clearly, he hadn't looked at the woman who hobbled past my office door saying: 'Actually, I feel dreadful. I've been in an accident.'

Consider the failure to communicate in this scenario and think about how this manager could improve his communication skills.

Becoming a good communicator

The Social Care Institute for Excellence (SCIE, www.scie.org.uk) has produced the following guidance for social workers to use in being good communicators. These social workers:

- are courteous
- turn up on time
- speak directly to service users, not carers or personal assistants
- don't use jargon
- 'open their ears' and 'think before they talk'
- listen and 'really hear' and accept what carers are saying
- explain what is happening and why
- do what they say they are going to do and don't overpromise
- say honestly when they can't help
- are patient and make enough time to communicate with disabled service users
- don't assume anything about a user's abilities simply because of a disability

- recognise the loss of dignity that people experience when approaching social services for the first time – the 'cost' of this – and respond sensitively
- understand the importance of privacy, peace and quiet and users' and carers' choice of meeting place
- check that they have been understood
- know that closed questions can be easier for service users with communication difficulties to answer
- find a mode of communication that works
- remember that young people may prefer to talk while doing something else
- build trust, empathy and warmth
- work in organisations that help them to do all these things.

Many of these points are relevant in both written and spoken communications.

Knowing oneself aids communication, especially across differences

Self-knowledge is a form of knowledge that enables practitioners to explore their own understandings of the world and their own and other people's places in it. Knowing oneself is central to communication processes that involve transcending difference and initiating change in individual behaviour and institutional structures (Dominelli, 2002b). Egan (2002: 184) suggests that workers should not only look at their own assumptions but invite service users to 'challenge themselves to change ways of thinking and acting that keep them mired in problem situations and prevent them from identifying and developing opportunities' by focusing on learning rather than helping. Looking for connections can assist this process.

CASE EXAMPLE

Mrs Smith, a woman from northeast England, is being assessed as a full-time carer for her granddaughter. During the assessment, she becomes distressed and informs the social worker that she has been having an affair with a married man for several years. She is concerned that Criminal Records Bureau (CRB) checks carried out at his address might reveal the affair. Mrs Smith doesn't want to jeopardise her chances of looking after her granddaughter or lose her friend as they have been together for over 10 years.

How would you use your communication skills to address the following issues?

- Approaching Mrs Smith's concerns sensitively
- Finding out how Mrs Smith might be feeling
- Examining your feelings about the situation
- Obtaining the information you need to intervene appropriately

- Exploring the relevance of your own personal attributes, for example ethnicity, gender, age, religion, culture, and your understanding of their potential impact on your interaction with Mrs Smith
- What you will say to Mrs Smith in response to her immediate concerns
- Seeking advice, including any legal advice, you need in order to respond appropriately
- Ending the interview appropriately.

In considering these points, it is important that practitioners and students engage with their own beliefs and values as these will impact on their responses to this situation. The importance of empathy and acceptance in devising responses and developing appropriate communication skills are highlighted in Lishman (1994), where service users claim how much they value not being judged. Acceptance is defined as 'a preparedness to try and understand a client's subjective world, without conveying rejection or disapproval' (Lishman 1994: 51). Empathy is one of the core skills that Joyce Lishman claims is necessary to build and maintain relationships and communicate effectively. She defines empathy as the ability of the worker to enter the 'client's subjective world, to feel what it must be like for the client, to understand what s/he might be thinking, and convey this understanding back to the client' (1994: 53). Lishman adds a caveat in her explanation of empathy: 'I have to be able to understand my client's confusion without being confused myself' (p. 53).

Practitioners and students who hold strong beliefs may find it difficult to be non-judgemental, or their life experiences may lead to bias in practice areas like child abuse, abortion or arranged marriages. Their attitudes should be explored and discussed openly and honestly. Tutors may share their approach or perspectives regarding commitment to empowering practice like anti-oppressive practice and feminist approaches to theory and practice (Dominelli, 2002a). In explaining the latter, Trevithick (2005: 281) claims: 'This is sometimes called a woman-centred perspective, where the commonalities that women share as women are incorporated.' Male students may feel excluded by feminism and ask questions about their position on gender issues. They are encouraged to develop a gender perspective that they feel comfortable with and can draw upon literature to help them in this (Connell, 1995; Wild, 1999; Shakespeare, 1999; Dominelli, 2002a).

Feminist theory has a rich and diverse 'herstory' that is intertwined with anti-oppressive practice and empowerment theory. This can become a starting point for practitioners, tutors and students to undertake research and reading that will enable them to reflect upon their own gender and that of service users. Those who explore and reflect upon their own values and perspectives will be able to respond more effectively to diversity and communicate better with those who are different from them without drawing upon stereotypes and other biased perceptions of people.

Managing 'the self' is about how we present to others

In-depth reflection on the 'presentation of self' is crucial, as failure to do this can, in some circumstances, prevent children and adult service users from having a voice. The example below illustrates this point. In it, the author draws on previous experience as a guardian ad litem working with children and families.

CASE EXAMPLE

In talking with a little boy who had just finished drawing a picture, I was about to say 'Oh that's a good rocket!', when I remembered my training and asked instead, 'What's that?' His response was: 'That's David's willy.' I replied in a casual, matter-of-fact way: 'What does David do with his willy?' The little boy then went on to disclose abuse by his stepfather. It was important not to react in a shocked manner to this disclosure as doing so could have prevented the little boy from continuing his story, or else he may have thought he had done something wrong.

Similarly, when adults tell you about distressing events, it is important not to react instinctively, which might be to express your own distress at what has happened to them. Think before you speak and use your training to avoid 'kneejerk' responses. Reflect back what the service user has said, and if possible use some of the actual words spoken by the service user. Also, acknowledge the emotional content in their disclosure. For example, in the above scenario, you might reply: 'You are right to be upset and you must be very angry. How did you feel when …?'

Techniques that can help service users to voice their own opinions include circular questioning. This involves asking questions about differences in relationships. An example of circular questioning is: 'Since your son began acting in this way, has your relationship with your partner been better or worse?' Another is: 'How did you feel when the hospital asked you to talk to your mother about the possibility of residential care?' and then asking the mother: 'Were you prepared or surprised by this option?' Developing a sequence of questions about difference gradually builds a pattern of information about family relationships. Family members are curious about responses that comment on how things happened and what the other persons' thoughts or feelings were at the time. A similar way of asking questions can be used with individuals. This is often referred to as the 'empty chair' technique. An example of this is: 'If your partner were here today, what might they say?'

Students need to acquire confidence in trying out questions about difference and are encouraged to read up on relevant theories prior to testing out these skills in the safe environment of a role play in the classroom. Burnham (1986) provides a useful starting point, to which the author adds a cautionary note on using these questions. Service users may find them useful in opening up new avenues for exploration, especially when the family or social worker feels 'stuck'. Some students may feel uncomfortable asking one person to comment on another in their absence. In these circumstances, communication skills can provide alternatives ways of encouraging an absent person to attend. Another way of pursuing this might be to ask: 'Who would be the best person to get your partner to come along, as their opinion is important to this work?' Pamela Trevithick (2005) emphasises the 'sensitive use' of these questions including comparison and ranking questions in gauging service users' reactions to them.

Seeking help

Practitioners and students can feel vulnerable at times. If this is the case, it is appropriate to share this with another person. For students, this could be tutors, practice teachers or a confidential resource like the university counselling service. Caring for and about your own personal feelings is important, as individuals have to feel strong in themselves to communicate with others, reach out or assist other people. Sometimes, a student or practitioner may feel 'stuck' and not know what to do or how to respond effectively in a particular situation. This can happen when students are keen to help but have no knowledge of the available services or resources or experience of working in this type of situation. Obtaining the relevant information is an essential first step, and may sometimes be all that is required. Reassurance may also be needed. Learning about the policies, procedures and resources available in an agency and having access to colleagues in the team and formal supervision can help to reassure those new to the job or organisation.

Using metaphors to reframe communication

Metaphors can transcend the spectrum of nonverbal and verbal communication by conjuring up pictures and images. The *Oxford Dictionary* defines metaphor as 'the application of a name or descriptive term or phrase to an object or action to which it is imaginatively but not literally applicable'. Objects, relationships and activities can have metaphorical meaning and relevance to service users. Metaphors can enable service users to describe thoughts and feelings. The example below shows how metaphors can be devised and told as stories that fit with a service user's language and context.

CASE EXAMPLE

A social worker found it difficult to engage with a Southeast Asian family in improving their eight-year-old son's behaviour in school. Their son was in danger of being excluded for being aggressive with other children and the family's relationship with the school had deteriorated. The mother and father viewed the school as rough. Although they didn't think that their child had been subjected to racism, they felt that the school was like a jungle where you had to be tough to survive. It was evident that the little boy was much loved by the couple who had tried to have a family for many years. Discussions on having rules and boundaries around what constituted good behaviour for the child simply made the family more protective of him.

The social worker created a metaphor using the story of a lonely lion cub in the jungle. This described how the little cub was shunned by the other lion cubs for playing too roughly and how he felt isolated and lonely. And, it showed how it was up to his parents, the adult lions, to teach him how to behave properly so that he would eventually grow up to be a strong lion who wasn't lonely. The parents responded immediately to the story, which led them to setting rules and boundaries and teaching their son to be less aggressive and demanding. The school also responded well to the child's improved behaviour and were told how this much-loved little boy carried the whole family's hopes for the future. This reframing of the child's and family's situation enabled the teacher and parents to work together. The reframing was crucial to creating a positive ethos that removed blame, repositioned the family's image with the school and allowed a new relationship to develop between them, in contrast to the previous meetings that had been extremely acrimonious.

Complex communications and relationships

Interviewing is the most common format for communication used in social services to solve problems and gather information for assessments and reports. Good communication involves negotiation of multiple issues and extensive reflexivity to work effectively in complex situations. Engaging with distressed service users and exploring complexity with care is evident in the scenario below. The initial referral information revealed that engaging Caroline from the outset was crucial for her to make an informed decision about accessing family support services.

CASE EXAMPLE

Caroline is the 35-year-old mother of two children who were adopted when they were five and three years of age. Caroline was sexually abused as a child by her mother's partner, a fact never accepted by her mother who continued her relationship with her partner. Caroline was in great distress when referred because her children had been removed by social services and placed for adoption. The referral describes Caroline as reluctant to engage and hostile to social workers.

Although Caroline spent part of her childhood in local authority children's homes, social workers decided to return her to the care of her mother when she was 11 years old. On her return home, Caroline was further sexually abused by her mother's partner who eventually became the father of her first child. He has never been prosecuted. Caroline's subsequent relationship with the father of her second child did not last and was complicated by the fact that he misused heroin. Caroline is angry that she was returned home to live with an abuser and has little respect for social workers. When she 'fell through' the office door of the family support service, she presented as very distressed and angry, with signs of serious self-harm. This is how the social worker conducted their first meeting:

- *Engaging with:* As Anne, the social worker, engaged with Caroline during those first moments, she was aware that her verbal and nonverbal communication would set the tone and influence the quality of their longer term working relationship. Under the circumstances, Anne paid particular attention to her own facial expressions, eye contact, posture, language and tone of voice. Caroline already had negative expectations of social workers, given her life experience, and Anne was aware that she was communicating nonverbal messages even before she started talking. In an effort to ease Caroline's distress, Anne wanted to communicate her willingness to engage with her. Being aware that Caroline is a survivor of abuse, it was important that Anne did not present as oppressive. So, she asked Caroline her name and asked what name she would like to be called by, because a number of parents change their names to try and cope with the abusing experiences they have suffered.

- *Vital information:* Anne, mindful of Caroline's presenting behaviour and the need to help, put her at ease without missing vital information she might provide. Advising her colleagues of Caroline's arrival, Anne asked another member of staff to offer to make Caroline a drink and requested that they were not interrupted during the meeting.

- *Showing respect:* Inviting Caroline into a warm and comfortably furnished meeting room, Anne asked her where she would like to sit. Anne felt it was important to offer her this choice as a sign of respect, and a willingness to act in an empowering manner. Caroline chose a seat that enabled her to see out of the window.

- *Safe space:* Anne was aware of the importance of creating a safe space for Caroline in terms of the physical environment and in her presentation as a worker. Being sensitive to Caroline's earlier experience of being sexually abused, Anne sat near her without being too close. She sat opposite Caroline to enable her to maintain eye contact without staring. Anne ensured that her posture was open, arms unfolded, legs uncrossed, leaning forward to communicate interest. Although Anne felt it important to let Caroline dictate the pace of the communication, she was aware of her subsequent appointments and knew that she would have to explain this and agree a time limit. Anne was also aware of the need to explain confidentiality and its limits. For example, she needed to let Caroline know that she would talk to her colleagues about the work she would undertake with her. Given the agency's work, Anne explained its children protection policy to Caroline.

■ *Silence:* As Caroline was crying, Anne allowed for a period of silence, accepting the need for her to cry. Anne did not feel that it would have been appropriate to fill the silence with words. She waited until Caroline was able to speak and, sensing her hesitation, helped by opening up the dialogue.

■ *Asking questions:* Anne was aware of the need to ask questions. These included:
  – Explaining why she was asking a particular question
  – Using open questions to let Caroline tell her story in her own words
  – Letting the questions offer Caroline permission to explore her feelings.

  Anne was aware that her intonation and interest in Caroline's answers were likely to influence her response. She was mindful that she could create a particular reality by the questions she asked, the areas of interest she identified. and those she ignored.

  Anne's aim was to assess Caroline's situation and determine how the agency could support her.

■ *Listening:* Listening to Caroline, Anne became attentive to the language that she used and on occasions used similar words and phrases in an effort to connect with Caroline and build rapport, as this could benefit their future working relationship. Anne could see that she was listening not only with her ears but also with her other senses.

■ *Paraphrasing:* In an effort to check out that she had understood what Caroline was saying, Anne used paraphrasing techniques, repeating back the meaning of what she had said. This technique let Caroline know that Anne was actively listening to her.

Working with difference

Kadushin's (1990: 304) work comments on working with difference. His writing style is not always appropriate, but he has written in-depth analyses of communication in social work interviews. He describes cross-cultural interviewing where a 'culturally sensitive social worker is aware that there are similarities and differences and that both need to be given consideration in the conduct of an interview'. For him, every person is, in certain respects:

■ like all other people, that is, there are panhuman features across all groups

- like some people, that is, there are common aspects of groups, for example ethnicity, class, colour, membership
- like no other person, that is, each individual differently manifests affiliation with other human beings and members of a particular group.

Kadushin warns against taking a colour-blind approach and refers to the 'myth of sameness' as well as the danger of the worker who emphasises difference at the expense of all else. In the context of an interview, Kadushin (1990: 305) argues for a balanced approach and insists that 'knowledge of the client's milieu is necessary'. Awareness of cultural difference 'is necessary in formulating interview objectives'. Students, tutors and practitioners can be concerned about political correctness and fear using words that may inadvertently cause offence. These issues need to be addressed early in training, preferably in the first session where agreement to speak freely is reached, with the caveat that each person is challenged if inappropriate words creep into their conversations or descriptions. Applying this enables all participants to learn from each other.

Practice examples can illustrate points and reinforce learning that is not based on making assumptions about sexuality, disability and ethnicity. Lena Robinson (2007: 172) argues strongly for social workers to 'be alert to the impact of culture on speech and style of communication'. Robinson suggests that Asian families value interdependence and prefer directive counselling rather than non-directive styles. Each situation has to be appraised as unique to avoid slipping into cultural relativism by making allowances for cultural differences. This insight is crucial in fields like child protection, as highlighted by the murder of Victoria Climbié, and working with older Asian people where social workers neglect them by assuming that their family will look after them. Robinson (2007: 174) makes a strong case for more research in examining social work theory and practice with black children. This 'needs to be more reflexive, inclusive and cultural'. Dominelli (2008) has also argued that white social workers' practice with black families has too often defined 'difference' in child rearing practices as 'inferior'.

Use of interpreters

> Black and ethnic minority communities value staff who understand their religion and culture; staff who can communicate with them in their own language; staff who can deal with any communication barriers by acting promptly and getting interpreters when required. (www.scie.org.uk)

Good practice guidelines can assist students and practitioners using interpreters. These include:

- allowing more time for interviews involving interpreters
- checking out the registration status of interpreters
- ascertaining their understanding of the relevant culture
- ensuring that they are skilled in the requisite specialist vocabulary, especially in mental health or child sexual abuse contexts.

It is important to find out if the family knows the interpreter personally, as can happen in small minority ethnic communities, in order to avoid complicating matters.

Linking theory and practice in learning and demonstrating communication skills

The GSCC requires that students are formally assessed on their fitness for practice. This implies that the student develops competence in communication skills prior to going on placement. The student will need to practise first in the safe environment of the classroom, using case studies, role plays, simulations, videos, DVDs, and new information technologies, such as online learning materials, to analyse content and process issues. This will enable the student to learn through experience and develop a range of communication experiences and styles. There should be opportunities to use various techniques to self-assess performance, linking placement activities with observation, interviewing and recording skills. A range of tools may be used to judge the acquisition of communication skills and feedback on performance will normally be sought from service users.

Creating a safe learning environment

Feeling safe, having clear expectations and being able to practise in a setting that does not endanger the lives of others or oneself make teaching communication skills in the classroom a good idea. Tutors are responsible for creating a safe environment that is fun, participative and informative as this facilitates learning. Role plays, case studies and videos can be utilised to ensure that this learning simulates real-life situations. Family therapists, such as Burnham (1986), highlight the advantages of using role play in learning situations. Role play and audio visual aids are useful not only with students but also with families to enact life events.

Juliet Koprowska and colleagues (1999: 4) at York University use role play in teaching communication skills and have devised useful teaching aids for students and tutors in the Interviewing Skills and Direct Observation Project. Their practical advice to students includes: 'Your main role is to practise the skill, not be perfect or to come up with some dazzling solution at the end of ten minutes' (1999: 3). They advise tutors to help students 'become used to viewing themselves, so they can begin to concentrate on the work being done'. Thus, the tutor's role becomes that of enabler in assisting students to observe, analyse and review their work. 'Tutors ... model the kinds of reflective practice which they aim to help students achieve' (Kropowska et al., 1999: 10). Evans and Kearney (1996: 50) argue that an advantage of role plays is that

> they do not rely on verbal reports and instead can allow ... access to the visual image of the interaction, as well as some sense of the emotional content ... and more particularly the blocks that are interfering in this process.

At Durham, tutors, students and practice teachers use the 'York model of observation' developed by Koprowska et al. (1999). It is prevalent in social work education throughout northeast England. This model emphasises the planning process and evaluative feedback from students, service users (or students role-playing service users) and practice teachers. A video outlining the process is shown to them.

This process can be aided by adult learning theory that enables educators to address a diverse range of student experiences and needs. Acquiring effective communication skills is one of these. Honey and Mumford (1992) and Kolb (1976) focus on types of learners or learning styles. Freire (1972) analyses learning and the pursuit of knowledge in terms of liberationist theology and the pursuit of freedom. Lishman (1994) and Smale et al. (2000) emphasise working in partnership with students while acknowledging the power imbalances inherent in relationships between students and teachers (Braye and Preston-Shoot, 1995). It is important to develop critical thinking and the confidence to challenge assumptions and explore alternatives.

Making links with practice

Planning a role play is analogous to the process of students planning their observation sessions with practice teachers. Clear instructions are provided for making a DVD and opportunities to practise are provided for sessions that occur when the tutor is not present. Students are encouraged to be creative and to practise role play scenarios by generating ideas or hypotheses about what is happening to an individual or family and allowing new meanings to emerge from these scenarios.

Extracts from role play scenarios can highlight the teaching and learning points to be covered in communication skills sessions. Role plays are more effective if based on real practice with service users, with names and identifying features changed to preserve anonymity and confidentiality. Students discuss confidentiality, including its contingent nature (Dominelli, 2002b) within an agency context and the legal powers and duties that impact upon them. Ethical dilemmas are essential ingredients in case examples. Sara Banks' (2006) book, *Ethics and Values in Social Work*, can inform this teaching. Case studies can reflect the diversity of service user groups including minority ethnic groups, older people, disabled persons and children and families.

Learning expectations and outcomes should be presented and discussed during the first session so that students are aware of expectations and the outcomes to be achieved by the end of the skills sessions. The end point, effective communication in practice, can be reached in multiple ways. As Oscar Wilde said in *The Devoted Friend*: 'Every good storyteller nowadays starts with the end, and then goes onto the beginning, and concludes with the middle. That is the new method.'

It is common to feel reluctant to engage in simulations and role plays at first. Fears, for example, may include not knowing how to operate a video camera, 'drying up' or looking silly on the DVD. It is useful to develop contingency plans in the classroom to deal with 'drying up', which can also be practised in the placement, and perhaps linked to the observations of practice which are part of the assessment requirements.

It is positive if the learning encourages the attitude 'I don't know but I will try and find out', with notes taken of important points to help to keep on track. Obtaining service users' permission for taking notes is required for ethical practice, and asking them: 'Is it OK to take notes as I don't want to miss anything important?' is one way of doing this. The cliché, 'failing to plan is planning to fail', is a truism that can impede good communication in social work practice if students or practitioners feel pressured by meeting agency timescales and deadlines.

Communication skills are important in conducting a role play and in giving feedback about it. Students and practitioners can develop these skills by working together to help each other learn in pairs or small groups of three. The third person can be part of the role play or act as an observer giving feedback off-camera. Agreed guidelines for the role play should cover issues ranging from selecting a partner to using their own names if role-playing the social worker or a fictitious name if playing a service user. Participants may amend the gender of the service user to fit their own if necessary. Debriefing at the end of the case example or simulation is crucial to the learning experience. Debriefing begins by participants stating who they are and declaring that they are not the service user in the case example. If the role play is recorded, for example on DVD, presentation of the DVDs to a group of 10–12 people can provide excellent material for peer group discussion and feedback. However, time constraints or individual reluctance may preclude this from happening. On the Durham social work qualifying degree, all DVDs are formally assessed by tutors, while around 60 per cent of students opt to present a DVD for peer review and structured feedback.

Information and empowerment theory

Preparing students by familiarising them with communication skills and theories in advance of their practice fits with empowerment theory (Braye and Preston-Shoot, 1995; Dominelli, 2002b) and can allay student apprehension/anxiety regarding expectations about practice. Exploring these issues mirrors good practice with service users who may be apprehensive or anxious about contacting social workers. Clarifying expectations at the beginning can reduce their anxieties. The idea of role-playing an interview and making a DVD raises apprehensions that need to be addressed right away. Juliet Koprowska et al. (1999) define apprehension as an alert state that does not prevent learning. Anxiety can become a barrier to learning if it prevents students and service users from hearing what is being said.

Diverse forms of assessment

Assessment occurs in a variety of forms. Self-assessment, peer assessment, service user assessment and tutor and practice teacher assessments are integral to the learning process. Students' communication skills are evaluated by tutors in the classroom and practice teachers and service users in the field. Ethical assessment requires negotiation to acquire the signed permission and cooperation of service users and an awareness of the distress this process might cause to service users. Seeking permission from service users is an integral part of ethical practice and consistent with the National Occupational Standards and value requirements that students have to meet in their practice. Assignments covering communication skills can encourage students to explore interactions with a service user through process recording, audio recording or DVD recording.

Self-assessments facilitate the setting of individual learning goals and areas for future developments by drawing on previous knowledge of communication skills and experiences of interviewing or being an interviewee and establishing a benchmark of skills held at the beginning of a particular learning opportunity. They also enable students to comment upon what they have learned about communication skills and identify areas they need to develop further. This constitutes an essential element in demonstrating the ability to practise reflectively and understand the issues they have to engage in if they are to see their learning as a process that continues throughout their professional career, rather than a one-off event. This task constitutes part of transferable learning. Transferable learning from one context to another is still a contentious subject in social work (Trevithick, 2005).

Tutors also assess students carrying out role plays and provide individual feedback. To undertake this task, the tutor can circulate round the room observing and listening to the interview conversations. Students quickly become acclimatised to the tutor sitting next to them and carry on unphased. This process can also prepare students for being observed on placement by practice teachers and their colleagues. An advantage of doing this work in the classroom is that they receive immediate feedback and can repeat a series of interactions if necessary. Thorough attention to process and context issues at the beginning helps to create a safe learning environment in which students reflect on their communication skills, and immediately amend their conversation/body language to make a difference in the interview context.

Structured feedback

Giving and receiving feedback should be positive and constructively critical. It should begin by highlighting positive aspects of the interaction before moving on to the critique. Communicating information that is precise and to the point structures feedback in a constructive, if critical manner. Feedback might cover the following:

- *Constructive criticism:* See yourself as part of a learning context and don't take things personally. Challenge the idea, not the person.
- *Focus on overall skills then look at specifics:* Give concrete examples rather than mind reads. For example: 'Overall, that was a well-executed interview. Now we need to

look at how you ask questions. You used a closed question towards the end of the interview by asking: "Are you happy at school?" How could you have rephrased this as an open question, or could you have used another sort of question?'

■ *Avoid assumptions/opinions:* Focus on what was said and check it out with the other person.

■ *Avoid being overcompliant or too negative:* Base your comments on the here and now.

Be respectful to each other and help each other to learn. Remember that it is possible to learn more from mistakes than from things that are done well.

Conclusion
Communication skills are a core element of practice. Learning how to become a good communicator is essential to practising effectively and working in empowering ways. Skilled practitioners will be able to use their knowledge about themselves to work across differences with sensitivity and expertise. If supported, students can learn these skills in both academic and practice contexts.

For further discussion of managing tensions between intervention and empowerment, see Chapter 19, and for different approaches to communication through counselling, see Adams et al., 2009b, Chapter 9.

Dominelli, L. (2008) *Anti-Racist Practice*, Basingstoke, Palgrave Macmillan. Considers the significance of differences in working effectively with diverse service users. Explores the impact of power relations, language and culture on communication between different actors.

Sue, D.W. and Sue, D. (2003) *Counseling the Culturally Different: Theory and Practice*, New York, Wiley & Sons. Includes the issue of communicating in situations where a counsellor and the person being counselled are culturally different and covers the issues to be addressed.

Thompson, N. (2003) *Communication and Language: A Handbook of Theory and Practice*, Basingstoke, Palgrave Macmillan. A basic text on communication skills. It also covers the issue of ethical communication.

Turner, F.J. (2008) 'Interviewing skills', in W. Rowe and L.A. Rapp-Paglicci (eds) *Comprehensive Handbook of Social Work and Social Welfare*, vol. 3: *Social Work Practice*, Hoboken, NJ, Wiley & Sons, pp. 29–45. Discusses interviewing, a key intervention in which communication skills are practised as talking to others in a purposeful manner.

Working with service users and carers

15

In this chapter, we examine the contested notion of 'service user involvement' in social work. We identify the drivers, processes and outcomes associated with service user involvement in social work policy, practice, research and education, and present a reflective case study based on our recent collective experiences of working with children and young people as educators of social work students.

Chapter overview

There is a strong rhetoric about the importance of working with people who use social work services. But the reality suggests a complex maze of political ideology and action (or inaction), terminology and discourses, theoretical frameworks and empirical evidence (Scourfield, 2007). The complexity deepens as public sector social work practice in the UK is relocated within multidisciplinary children and adult services involving education, health and allied disciplines. There is also much debate surrounding the terminology used to articulate the individual and collective experiences, views and actions of people who use services. Acknowledging its strengths and limitations, we use the term 'service user' to refer to people who use, have used or are entitled to use services as well as those who live with or care for people using services (www.shapingourlives.org.uk/).

Contemporary 'histories' of service user involvement

In the UK context, Braye (2000) distinguishes three sets of mandates for service users' participation and involvement in contemporary social care: legal and policy mandates, professional mandates, and service user mandates. These are held in tension as the interests of the state, professional practitioners and service users are represented and recreated through action and reaction informed by wider considerations of political ideology, professional values and human rights.

Commentaries on the role of legislation and policy in facilitating service user involvement (for example Braye, 2000; Warren, 2007) cite increasingly lengthy lists of legal and policy instruments that underpin service user involvement. They range from anti-discrimination, equalities and human rights legislation to government documents that inform or define policy. The 1989 UN Convention on the Rights of the Child, ratified by the UK in 1991, articulates the right of children to be consulted and to participate in decisions that affect their lives. An example of children's participation in policy-making is found in *Every Child Matters* (DfES, 2003), a government discussion document in which children and young people defined the desired outcomes of integrated services for children: be healthy, stay safe, enjoy and achieve, make a positive contribution and achieve economic wellbeing. In the field of adult care, national service frameworks that set standards for tackling discrimination and providing services were developed with reference to advisory groups of service users and carers.

Professional mandates are heavily influenced by principles and values. Expressed in different forms at different times, social work principles and values have made consistent reference to the importance of human beings as individuals and the right of service users to self-determination and self-direction (Biestek, 1961), principles that are still evident in the General Social Care Council (GSCC) (2004) code of practice for social care workers. The international definition of social work (IFSW, 2000) reminds us that the social work task is linked to principles of empowerment, human rights and social justice. But despite these principles, social workers can be constrained by the cultures and practice models of their employing organisations and show varying degrees of commitment to empowering practice (Banks, 2006).

Service user mandates have emerged as a result of hard-fought campaigns involving collective action, in which experiences of oppression and discrimination have been, and are still being, shared and articulated to produce new knowledge and influence theory (Beresford, 2000; Beresford and Croft, 2001). Adult service user movements led by disabled people, collectives of mental health service users and survivors, and people with learning difficulties have been enormously influential in lobbying for the development of equalities and anti-discrimination legislation, and articulating visions of user-led and user-controlled services (Barnes and Mercer, 2006). Following the establishment of Voice for the Child in Care in the 1970s, there are now numerous collectives of children and young people who are users of social welfare services. They are less visible than their adult counterparts, due not only to the position of all children outside the boundaries of political democracy, but also to their specific position within the world of the welfare services where ethical and safeguarding considerations constitute barriers to children's involvement in public discussion.

Who are service users, how are we conceptualised and theorised?

For those of us living in the economically privileged North, a simple answer to this question is 'all of us', at some point in our lives. But while using education services by going to school or health services by visiting a GP or practice nurse are considered to be everyday experiences, making use of social work and social care services is popularly associated with an inability to cope, an unwillingness to conform or the presence of a threat, real or imagined, to the wider social order. Social work has a long history of dual purpose and dual identity in which it attempts to support and enable individuals, families and groups to function more independently, but also intervenes in situations where 'vulnerable' individuals are considered to be in need of protection from themselves or others.

An intriguing multiplicity of words has been used to describe people who use social welfare services or, as McLaughlin (in press) argues, to describe the relationship between those who control access to services, those who provide them and those who use them. 'Client' and 'patient' have been associated with the passive receipt of services prescribed by powerful professionals with specialist knowledge and skills. 'Client' has largely disappeared from the social work arena in the UK, but 'patient' is alive and well in the fields of health and mental health. 'Customer' and 'consumer', terms that joined the vocabulary in the 1980s, reflected the market ideologies of the New Right in which individuals were to exercise choice from a range of service products. But the customer analogy did not work well in social work since:

■ the choice of services was extremely limited
■ there was little if any provision that matched the preferences of minority groups, for example those based on ethnicity and sexual orientation, whose needs and preferences were largely ignored
■ those who were statutorily obliged to be part of the social services system under childcare or mental health legislation could not choose to withdraw their custom.

Moreover, measures of customer satisfaction were widely acknowledged to have weak validity, since expressions of dissatisfaction were associated by many service users with ingratitude or fear of losing services (Nocon and Qureshi, 1996), an uncomfortable reminder of the relative powerlessness of people using services.

Resistance to experiences of powerlessness by people who had been subjected to oppressive welfare structures gained strength during the 1980s and 90s. The widespread adoption of the term 'service user' indicated some measure of public and political acknowledgement of the distinct and positive roles and contributions of service users, individually, collectively and in partnership with professional practitioners. The achievements of social movements have informed academic debate on the changing relationship between structure and agency and, drawing an analogy with Sen's insights into the nature of development, service users have been reconstructed, not simply as having entitlements, but as people with capabilities, who still require freedom to realise their full potential (Sen, 1999). The term 'service user', however, remains contentious. Current critiques are largely directed at its exclusive focus on one element of an individual's identity, one that places the service user as the 'other' in a relationship with one or more 'professionals', where power resides largely with the professionals. The words of a GP, describing his own experience of being a patient, offer a powerful example of this critique:

> As someone with experience of depression (I am NOT a depressive), I actually resent the term [patient], since it enforces a modus operandi on those who relate to me when I am using medical or health care services; it strains everything else I am through the arse of a gnat and may well prevent those who deal with me thinking about solutions outside of their own methodological or entrained mental mindsets. (Manning, 2002: 1264)

The national network of service users, Shaping Our Lives, distinguishes two broad understandings of the term 'service user'. Popular understandings serve to 'restrict your identity as if all you are is a passive recipient of health and welfare services', while members of Shaping Our Lives understand 'service user' as an active and positive term, always based on self-identification but embodying experiences of:

- unequal and oppressive relationships with the state and society
- past or present entitlement to receive welfare services
- long-term use of services that create popular perceptions of inferiority
- recognition of shared experience with other people who use services, that confers power, creates a stronger collective voice and greater influence in shaping services (Levin, 2004).

Each of these meanings of service user reminds us of the power that resides with professionals. A significant source of professional power lies in the specialist or 'expert' knowledge that is the essence of professional status. By contrast, the specialist knowledge or 'expertise' of service users has only recently been acknowledged in mainstream debate. Challenges to the exclusive expertise of professionals have given rise to the term 'expert by experience', which recognises the specialist knowledge that can only come from individual experience. Spaces for consideration of service users' experiences, knowledge and skills have historically been closed and the voices of service users silenced. But the achievements of service user movements and continuing campaigns for services to be led and controlled by service users have seen the emergence of new spaces for service users' experiences and knowledge to emerge through involvement in research, policy, practice and education, leading to new theoretical approaches (Beresford, 2000). Two well-known examples are the **social model of disability** (Oliver, 1996) and **the recovery model** in mental health (Repper and Perkins, 2003), which focus on methods and approaches for removing barriers to social inclusion rather than on medical responses to physical or psychiatric conditions. Both models demand fundamental shifts in thinking on the part

The **social model of disability** refers to a set of sociological perspectives on disability, which emphasise the social factors that disable people. One consequence of the application of this model is the representation of disability as purely the consequence of socially constructed barriers and processes. This is a contested aspect of the social model, since some argue that to claim that people's impairments are only disabling as a result of social factors may exclude them from eligibility for resources required to sustain their independence.

of professionals to see the world from different viewpoints. But, as Carpenter (2002) has argued, these models are informed by values and beliefs that are closely aligned with the principles and values of social work.

While language is undoubtedly important in its power to empower and disempower, we argue that the focus on language can serve to detract from getting on with the business of service user involvement in the same way that focusing on barriers to involvement can be misused to rationalise non-action. Unlike the barriers to involvement experienced by service users such as physical and financial access, or the hostile attitudes of professionals, the barriers often cited by professional practitioners and researchers are expressed in terms of the additional time required, poor evidence of positive outcomes, the non-representative nature of service user involvement, and the absence of 'hard-to-reach' groups (Curtis et al., 2004). The phrase 'hard to reach' offers an example of the ways in which language is used oppressively to place responsibility with service users rather than with professionals and their employers who, lacking the flexibility, skills or resources to reach some service users, reinforce their sense of exclusion (Morris, 1998; Harris and Bamford, 2001).

> The recovery model of treatment consists of building resilience and resistance to a mental health problem or illness. It is commonly used to refer not to complete recovery from mental health problems, but to a specific approach involving the person taking control of their life. In the process, the person focuses on managing their symptoms and building up resilience and resources to support them. The emphasis is on a holistic view of the person's needs rather than just on their symptoms of mental illness and on maintaining the journey of recovery rather than arriving at a cure.

Situating involvement

The literature on service user involvement shows many attempts to differentiate degrees or levels of involvement, from no involvement, to consultation, participation, partnership, involvement and user-led and user-controlled services and how these relate to social work's central theme of empowerment. Ladders (for example Arnstein, 1969; Nocon and Qureshi, 1996; Hart, 1997), circles (Treseder, 1997) and pathways (Shier, 2001) conceptualise service user involvement and empowerment as linear processes. More recent research in the area of children's and young people's involvement has concluded that meaningful and sustainable participation depends on the capacity of organisations to develop cultures of participation (Kirby et al., 2003). Hierarchical models of participation have been superseded by 'whole systems' approaches that require attention to organisational culture and structures as well as practice and reviewing processes (Wright et al., 2006). Kirby et al. (2003: 22) stress the importance of:

- adults listening to children and young people and taking their views into account
- shared decision making between children, young people and adults
- sharing of power between children, young people and adults
- children and young people making autonomous decisions.

They remind us that no level is assumed to be better or worse than another, and the appropriate level must be determined by circumstances and by the children and young people involved.

Situating service user involvement is also concerned with the processes in which service users may be involved. The most commonly identified processes are policy (Simmons and Birchall, 2005), practice, research (Fisher, 2002; Kellett et al., 2004; Kellett, 2005; Balen et al., 2006; McLaughlin, 2006), knowledge production and theorising (Beresford, 2000), education (Levin, 2004; Cairney et al., 2006) and democratic processes exercised through active citizenship in the community (Barnes and Shardlow, 1997). Analysis of the involvement of service users in social work practice can be usefully linked to identifying involvement across the social work process that has been (narrowly) defined by the Department of Health as assessment, planning, intervention and review. Different social work models, theories and methods (see Trevithick, 2005) are more or less likely to achieve genuine involvement of service users. For example, the **exchange model of assessment** (Smale et al., 1993), in which service users are considered to be the experts of their own experience, supports empowerment through involvement.

> **Exchange model of assessment** is used in care management to refer to a model of practice with two assumptions: the service user and/or carer is regarded as the expert, through experience, on their own situation; the practitioner is regarded as the expert on the available services and the negotiating of resources. The process of assessment consists of the practitioner and the service user and/or carer each exchanging information from their own vantage points and constructing the assessment between them.

Involving service users, sharing power

Permeating our discussion so far are themes of power and power relations between service users and professional practitioners. Space does not permit a detailed analysis here, but it is important to recognise that power may be used in different ways and it is the use of power that is crucial in evaluating the relationship between service users and professionals. Tew (2006) draws on changing concepts of power to present a matrix of power relations in social work. He distinguishes between:

- productive and limiting modes of power
- power that is used over others, and power that is used together with others.

In this way, he acknowledges the possibility that professional practitioners may use power over service users to gain advantage for themselves (limiting, oppressive power), but also to gain an advantage for service users (productive, protective power). Similarly, he acknowledges that power may be used with others, either valuing commonality and difference to achieve collective goals (productive, cooperative power) or valuing commonality but suppressing difference in order to exclude 'others' (limiting, collusive power). While limiting modes of power are based on a 'zero-sum' concept of power, in which one party's gain in power involves another's loss of power, productive modes of power allow for the possibility that power can be used to achieve positive outcomes for all parties.

It is not simply these different forms of power that are important, but the dangerous ease with which productive modes may slip into limiting modes and cooperative modes into collusive modes. For example, while it may be possible for a social worker to employ protective power to meet the identified needs of a service user in the short term, it is important to ensure that this use of productive power does not spill over into limiting power by restricting the service user's chances of gaining control over their own circumstances in the longer term. Similarly, the use of cooperative power through collective action may run the risk of transforming into limiting, collusive power if failure to recognise diversity results in such an uneven distribution of power that it leads to exclusion and powerlessness for some.

'Othering' of and 'connecting' with service users

'Power over' and 'power together' are useful ways of identifying the challenges and opportunities of working with service users. For a social worker, having 'power over' is often associated with processes of disempowerment, while using 'power together' has strong potential for empowerment, a central concern of social work. One of the ways in which service users continue to be disempowered is through a process of what Fanon (1990) described as the constant erosion of a sense of positive identity. With the closure of long-stay institutions in the 1980s and 90s, and the growth of community-based services, more subtle forms of marginalisation are used. One of these is 'othering', a process that identifies people on the basis of their difference from the mainstream, reinforcing and reproducing positions of domination and subordination (Johnson et al., 2004). 'Othering' in the context of health and social care professions is related closely to Foucault's (1973) notion of the medical 'gaze', a concept that Ellis (2000) has extended to a social care 'gaze', in which service users are seen through particular professional lenses that ascribe them to convenient medical or administrative categories.

In the context of difference based on ethnicity, Canales (2000) develops the concept of othering to distinguish exclusionary and inclusionary othering. As with Tew's categories of oppressive power and cooperative power, Canales draws attention to the difference between:

- recognising and focusing on the specific differences between one person (for example nurse, social worker, teacher) and another (patient, service user, pupil/student) in ways that lead to the use of power to dominate and subordinate
- recognising the fact of difference as a route to the use of power to build relationships and coalitions.

Drawing on research in schools with Anglo-Australian and indigenous Australian children, MacNaughton and Davis (2001) outline a set of principles to avoid slipping from inclusionary to exclusionary othering:

- avoid homogenising others into a collective 'they'

- avoid building knowledge of others that focuses solely on differences from the majority
- help practitioners to develop strategies that avoid simple binaries (for example social worker/service user)
- seek to identify and challenge practices that present service users in ways that reflect earlier oppressive practices.

Focusing on positive practice, we offer two brief examples of inclusionary othering. One is taken from the work of Pain et al. (2007), who facilitated an anti-bullying art project that connected the places and lives of young African refugees and young British residents of Byker, Newcastle. Brought together to discuss questions of fear and hope, the young people identified bullying and racism as their major concerns. The art project acted as a vehicle to promote positive images of Africa and Newcastle (both subject to negative imagery in the popular media) and the connections between them. One outcome of the project was the establishment of positive links between the children of the different communities that in turn created a means of 'breaking the ice' between the established and new residents. A second example illustrating the use of cooperative power and inclusionary othering is Hill's (in press) study of relationships between professionals, parents and children in the context of children's therapy following child sexual abuse. The combined expertise of service users and professionals is necessary to enhance the power to achieve positive outcomes. Aiming to understand the complex triangular dynamics in situations where blame and responsibility are negotiated, Hill highlights the use of 'interactional expertise' as the professional brings together their own knowledge with the expertise of the family. He argues that in order to build trust with service users, professionals must recognise and value the role and expertise of service users and find ways of presenting their own professional expertise that encourage service users in turn to contribute their expertise to produce empowering, rather than disempowering, experiences. Importantly, Hill argues that the interactional expertise he identified in the therapists was not 'high status' expertise characterised by glamour, but the ability to enable the production of observable and measurable outcomes, the kind of expertise that is consistent with the value base of social work.

Experiencing involvement: 'R U Getting It?'

This section of the chapter is dedicated to our experiences of working with a range of children and young people to inform and educate student social workers (and academic staff) about their lives and issues of importance to them. A condition of approval of the new degree in social work (GSCC, 2002) was consultation with service users about the design and development of courses, the involvement of service users in delivering and reviewing courses, and ensuring that resources are available to meet these requirements.

Following one year's experience of involving children and young people in the degree, in 2006, two local authority agencies and two voluntary sector organisations joined forces with three social work education providers in an attempt to overcome two significant barriers to participation:

- the availability of adequate financial resources to support children and young people in building the confidence to be involved in social work education
- the limited availability of children and young people during the school day.

Several groups of children and young people participated, some with experience of social care services, some without. They included young parents, young carers, young travellers, children and young people in foster care and residential care, children and young people who had experienced mental health problems, substance misuse and bullying, young people from sexual minorities and young people involved in volunteering. They chose to call their work 'R U Getting It?', reflecting the sense that adults, particularly adults delivering services, did not always 'get it'. They chose the messages they would like to convey at a one-day conference and presented workshops on experiences of bullying, young parenthood, different backgrounds, mental health, young carers and volunteering.

There is little literature on the involvement of children and young people in social work education, but drawing on documented accounts of the experiences of adult service users (Bassett et al., 2006), it was possible to identify the following strategies that were adopted to overcome potential barriers.

Table 15.1 Barriers to service user involvement and strategies employed by R U Getting It? for overcoming them

Barrier	Strategies for overcoming
Hierarchies that exclude	Children and young people prepared for the experience and were represented at all levels
Stigma and discrimination	Children and young people controlled the agenda
Meetings and boards	Children and young people chose how meetings took place
Academic jargon	Agencies/individuals encouraged not to use jargon and monitored by young people
Clever excuses	Partnership agencies and individuals actively promoted the involvement of children and young people through a culture of encouraging and facilitating involvement
Knowledge as king	Children and young people acknowledged as experts of their own experiences
Universities individualising people	Development of partnership over time (four years and ongoing) to build strong dynamic groups of young people
Gaining access	Working in partnership with children and young people from the initial stages facilitated access
Bureaucratic payment systems	Budget held by non-university agency
Lack of support for trainers	Support systems within agencies form an integral part of the project

Feedback from social work students included a mixture of positive learning, admiration for the young people's abilities, and expressions of frustration that young people did not all present like professionals. Serendipity presented an opportunity to support the young people in learning evaluation skills in order to be able to undertake their own evaluation of the conference (see Simmons, 2006). All young participants were invited to join the evaluation and the final group of 11 was self-selecting. Following clearance by university and local authority ethics committees, a participatory approach was adopted and the young people identified the key areas for evaluative research, and chose the precise methods: direct observation of the evaluation group, a discussion group, and photographs to record the evaluative process. A secrets box was added by the facilitator to offer individual young people the opportunity to express views that they did not feel able to express in the group. Discussion groups were audio taped, fully transcribed and then analysed by the young people who identified the key themes. The young people were not involved in writing up, but presented and disseminated findings to the wider group and beyond.

In common with research across a wider range of service user involvement in professional education and other areas of public services, the evaluation generated more information about processes than outcomes. The following quotes by the young evaluators offer a flavour of the positive messages about participating in social work education:

'It is interesting for everyone and helps everyone understand where development can be made.'

'Sees students on the right path.'

'Children and young people are the future and students are the future social workers, so if we all work together, we get to understand and learn from each other.'

'I was interested in the cause of raising awareness and to give valuable ideas.'

'To help deliver a better understanding of what we can do.'

'To get the points of view of students and ensure young people give the correct materials and help the students in different areas that will be required in their working role.'

'You get more experience for yourself, more confidence.'

'When I first went to the group, I sat and said nowt, but now I've done training, I've done interviews, I done all sorts.

The evaluation also identified challenges. The positive experiences of some young people in gaining confidence and skills raised important questions of how young people can be supported to move on, building their skills to participate in wider forums. Some controversy arose in relation to questions of payment. The R U Getting

It? initiative was informed by the principle that the participants should be paid, in cash, on the days of attendance at meetings and the conference. The evaluation group worked on the same principle, but individual participants indicated different views about payment, as illustrated by three different participants:

> Some of them do just go for the fact that you get paid.'
>
> 'I think it is an incentive and I think it does work.'
>
> 'I reckon there should be rules on which people get money and that.

We are not able to explore these issues in detail here, but further work by the young people who wanted to extend their influence in the public arena experienced problems of funding flows so that some payments were made in arrears. Although this had different impacts on different young people, it led to the clear expression of views that while payment is important, it should not be the only reason for participation. Although no one did forgo payment, several young people were clear that they wished to continue whether they were paid or not.

Our 'adult' conclusions from the R U Getting It? experience (Roddam et al., 2007) were that:

- Evidence of processes of involving children and young people in social work education is slowly emerging
- Successful involvement is characterised by:
  – Children and young people taking the lead
  – Appropriate adult support
  – The development of collaborative partnerships
- It is important to identify the barriers and take a 'can do' approach
- Young people welcome support in developing skills for educating social work students
- There is rarely a 'right' or a 'wrong'. Many issues are controversial, for example payment
- Young people must be supported to 'move on', keep an eye on the path ahead, realise new activities, and respond to new opportunities
- Involving young service users is not always comfortable
- But it is exciting.

Young people leading the agenda: Help Us Help You

Moving on from the evaluation of R U Getting It?, the group was joined by others to form 'Help Us Help You', a group that has organised events to share public platforms with a local MP and the children's commissioner. The latter event offered a live opportunity for community action when a group of young people came to lobby the commissioner about the closure of facilities for young people in their town. Young people from different areas and circumstances engaged in mutual learning and mutual support. But a cautionary tale for the young presenters was that, despite carefully negotiated consents for the young people to talk to the media about their work, the press only had ears for the children's commissioner, a timely reminder that some children and young people are still expected to be seen but not heard.

The Help Us Help You initiative is dynamic, and is developing by:

■ reaching out to include new groups of young people who have not previously been involved in preparation for teaching social work students (Freeman, 2000)
■ consolidating and developing involvement in the assessment of social work students and decision-making structures of social work programmes.

Our aspiration is that the first steps in creating a culture of participation can be nurtured to achieve a culture in which children's and young people's involvement becomes the normative expectation (Kirby et al., 2003).

What difference does service user involvement make?

The evaluation of children's and young people's involvement in social work education reflects a common critique of service user involvement that focuses on the relative importance of 'process' and 'outcome', and the common confusion in social work between ends and means (Braye, 2000). In the UK context of newly configured multidisciplinary services for adults and children, it is important to examine the evidence from a range of disciplines to see what is known about the outcomes of service user involvement.

A systematic review of patient involvement in the planning and development of healthcare found that involving patients had contributed to some positive changes in service provision, improved accessibility to services, and led to the development of new services including advocacy and crisis services (Crawford et al., 2002). Staff attitudes to involving service users were more positive and cultures had changed. The impact of these changes on the quality of care was not clear, but the authors caution against mistaking lack of evidence for lack of effect. Fudge et al. (2008), reporting on an ethnographic study of user involvement in the development of stroke services, identified personal gains for those involved as satisfaction of feeling listened to by professionals, social opportunities of meeting others in a similar situation, and increased knowledge about strokes and the services available. Doel et al. (2007) argue that establishing clear outcomes of stakeholder participation has been hampered by the same barriers that inhibit service user involvement. Participation in evaluation is, they contend, subject to:

■ unequal power relations between professionals and service users
■ unclear expectations of evaluation since, for service users, involvement is simply 'like breathing'
■ a lack of planning for evaluation.

Concerns about the wider 'costs' of service user involvement (for example McLaughlin, 2006) remind us that care that must be taken to ensure that the act of participation does no harm. But neither must such concerns be used as excuses for continuing to exclude children, young people and adults who use services from being involved in social work policy-making, practice, research and education.

Conclusion

Our starting point for this chapter was the contested nature of service user involvement in social work. We have examined service user involvement through the lenses of power and empowerment to identify positive developments and persistent barriers. The tensions that surround service user involvement can all too easily transform into negative forms of power in which service users and professionals adopt stand-off positions. But as Beresford and Croft (2004) remind us, professionals are also subject to processes of othering, linked to gender, 'race' and ethnicity, class, disability, sexual orientation and service use. Social workers and teachers, doctors and nurses, police officers and probation officers and other professionals also experience physical and mental illnesses, disability, substance misuse, serious difficulties in parenting and other challenges. Manning's contribution to the debate, which focused on professional perceptions of his identity as a 'depressive', is balanced by his plea not to expect patients to become experts overnight, any more than doctors do. The term 'expert', he argues, has accounted for the demise of many a professional and organisation and he urges that we should not damn service users with faint praise (Manning, 2002: 1265).

Social work, as a regulated profession, demands a careful balance of skills underpinned by strong values to act as an anchor in negotiating the roles of enabler, and sometimes protector, of individuals, families and groups who use social work services. Learning to engage, assess situations and needs, plan the way forward, implement and review plans with service users is about learning to share power. It is about building alliances and learning to combine knowledge and skills in ways that benefit people using services. It is about sharing responsibility, neither abrogating professional responsibility by locating all power with, nor removing all responsibility from, service users (Kirby et al., 2003). But alliances built at the front line of social work must be supported and nurtured by organisational cultures and structures that value the involvement of diverse service users not only in practice but in policy-making, research and evaluation, and training and education. Ultimately, service user involvement is about being accountable to those who use services. Achieving that accountability requires change, and changing organisational cultures and individual practices is seldom a pain-free process. As Carr (2007) argues, traditional power relations become unsettled by change and disturb the existing order. But this is to be expected and we should not recoil from the discomfort of confronting the 'unsettling relations' that push us to more considered understanding of the power relations associated with difference (Church, 1997). Leung (2008: 531), writing of the challenges and responses of service providers to calls for accountability to welfare service users in Hong Kong, reminds us that it is a mistake to consider service user involvement as an effective measure of accountability to service users, since welfare professionals can easily accommodate requirements to involve service users by 'manoeuvring the accountability discourse'. His argument is that involvement is a necessary but not sufficient condition to achieve true accountability to welfare service users. Similarly, Hodge (2005), using discourse analysis to understand the power dynamics at work in service user involvement in a mental health forum, shows that even where specific efforts are made to ensure that the interests of service users are served by placing service users in leadership positions and having 'service user involvement' as a standing agenda item, the persistent discursive inequalities between service users and officials simply reinforce the wider institutional inequalities of power.

Let us return here to the purpose and values of social work. Drawing on the IFSW definition of social work, Sewpaul (2005) describes the common core of social work as affirming humanity and human dignity, and argues that this core can be applied in any social work setting, locally or globally, without oppression or the misuse of power. These wide claims are echoed in a large-scale qualitative study of palliative care with individuals with life-limiting illnesses and conditions and those facing bereavement by Beresford et al. (in press). They found that the most highly valued aspects of social work practice were related to concepts of humanity:

■ the positive relationships between service user and the worker – warmth, empathy, respect and listening – described as 'friendship'
■ the qualities and skills of the worker.

We conclude that the excitement, enthusiasm and optimism of service user activists and their allies (some of whom are social workers and social work students) are readily experienced as threats by many in positions of power. But examples of practice in which the tensions between different stakeholders are confronted and reframed as positive opportunities for creative engagement show us how power can be shared effectively (Postle and Beresford, 2007). Such examples remind us that failure to use the talents and skills of people who use services is to lose an opportunity to increase the chances of achieving the goals of social work, defined by the International Federation of Social Workers (IFSW, 2000) as: 'the promotion of social change, problem solving in human relationships and the empowerment and liberation of people to enhance well-being'.

For further discussion of advocacy service users rights and service user perspectives, see Adams et al., 2009b, Chapter 16 and Adams et al., 2009c, Chapter 8.

www.hbr.nya.org.uk/ Hear by Right presents a framework for organisations to assess and improve policy and practice in involving children and young people.

www.involve.org.uk/userempowerment INVOLVE is a national advisory group that supports and promotes active public involvement in NHS, public health and social care research.

www.shapingourlives.org.uk/ Shaping Our Lives: National User Network is an independent, user-controlled organisation that supports the development of local user involvement to deliver better outcomes for service users.

www.scie.org.uk/publications/index.asp Social Care Institute for Excellence (SCIE) provides knowledge reviews, practice guides, research briefings and resource guides on a wide range of topics including service user participation and involvement.

Barnes, C. and Mercer, G. (2006) *Independent Futures: Creating User-led Disability Services in a Disabling Society*, Bristol, Policy Press. Offers a description and critical analysis of the development and control of services for disabled people, by disabled people.

Kemshall, H. and Littlechild, R. (eds) (2000) *User Involvement and Participation in Social Care*, London, Jessica Kingsley. Useful in setting a clear framework for considering service user involvement and drawing lessons based on empirical studies involving a range of service users.

Repper, J. and Perkins, R. (2003) *Social Inclusion and Recovery: A Model for Mental Health Practice*, London, Ballière Tindall. A re-examination of the balance of power between mental health service users and professionals. Offers a clear argument for valuing service users' experience and knowledge as an effective way of challenging discrimination and social exclusion through the promotion of service users' rights and citizenship.

Tisdall, E., Davis, J., Hill, M. and Prout, A. (eds) (2006) *Children, Young People and Social Inclusion: Participation for What?*, Bristol, Policy Press. Drawing on different disciplines, it examines theoretical and practical questions that inform the inclusion and participation of marginalised children.

Warren, J. (2007) *Service User and Carer Participation in Social Work*, Exeter, Learning Matters. This introductory text is a useful starting place for social work students. Each chapter is linked to the National Occupational Standards for Social Work and provides case studies, research summaries and activities.

Kirby, P., Lanyon, C., Cronin, K. and Sinclair, R. (2003) *Building a Culture of Participation: Delivery and Evaluation, The Handbook*, London, Department for Education and Skills. A practical guide to participation by children and young people, well illustrated with examples. A parallel publication by the same authors ('The Research' rather than 'The Handbook') deals with the research underpinning the guide.

Acknowledgements

We would like to thank Becky, Ben, Carl, Claire, Dan, David, Emma, Gemma, Kim, Kirsty, Kyle, Nicki, Sam and Thomas who played central roles in the delivery and evaluation of the 'RU Getting It?' and/or 'Help Us Help You' initiatives; Dave Laverick, children's participation officer, Sunderland children's services, for his active support and commitment; and Kelvin Rushworth whose experience and wisdom has informed the development of service user involvement on the Durham MSW programme.

Assessment 16

Chapter overview

This chapter uses an ecological framework to address the complexity of assessing service users' circumstances. The aim is to see individuals in context and take account of the wide range of influences on any individual situation. An ecological approach enables us to balance the assessment of need and risk with an evaluation of strengths and resources, in order to determine the potential for and possible routes to change. We consider how key principles of social work and other professional practice inform this approach.

Assessment is the foundation for all effective intervention: as such it needs to be grounded in evidence from research and theory in disciplines such as sociology and psychology, which illuminate human needs. Evaluations of the effectiveness of practice will inform general approaches, but individual cases need to be assured of attention and sensitivity to their unique situations.

Where services are to be provided in situations of **risk** or need, accurate and realistic assessment of all the relevant information needs to be undertaken before judgements and decisions are made about action and resources. A simple question for all professionals in social work, health and welfare services, who are engaged in caring, supporting or **safeguarding** vulnerable children and adults, is:

> Risk is a generic concept based on the assumption that the likelihood of loss, harm or other negative happenings can be estimated or even quantified. When applied to social work, the complexities of the factors correlated with people's vulnerabilities and problems tend to make the assessment and management of risk a matter of qualitative judgement.

> What does this person need in order to maximise wellbeing in all key areas of their life?

This is the starting point for any assessment. The question may be simple, but solutions that match the reality of people's lives are likely to be complex. Key areas will vary according to age and stage of development, personal and social circum-

Safeguarding is a term commonly used in the public services generally and social work and social care in particular. It refers to the protection of children or adults from abuse or harm.

stances, aspirations and achievements and whether any risks are posed for or by the service user.

While we focus on the assessment of individuals and families in this chapter, the logic of an ecological approach demands that the implications of individualised assessments will be looked at alongside population-wide assessments, informing the strategic planning process throughout children's services and the health and community planning mechanisms for services to children and adults, attempting to ensure that the pattern and range of services matches local needs and priorities. It also guides us to look for the causes of and solutions to problems across all aspects of an individual's situation and experience, avoiding assumptions that change should only come from the service user and looking at the need for change within institutions such as schools, hospitals, care homes, and within the structures of society.

Why is assessment important?

In social work services, workers are concerned with support, care, guidance and control. They have responsibilities towards some of the most needy, disadvantaged and vulnerable people in society and responsibilities for trying to respond to unmet personal and social needs and to risks that may be posed for or from service users. They deal with issues of public safety – through mental health services, the justice system, child protection and some aspects of community care. For services, teams and individual workers, these issues of risk and how they may best be managed are as important as the expectation that they will work to maximise wellbeing in all aspects of service users' lives. Drawing on best evidence from research and principled practice is essential in a systematic attempt to plan interventions that have the greatest chance of achieving success in all these services.

The needs and risks in individual situations must be assessed in detail before judgements can be made about the most appropriate interventions, services and resources. There is increasing emphasis from government on the need for evidence-based practice (EBP) and increasing attention to 'what works' in literature and research, relating to all aspects of social work, social care and the justice system (McGuire, 1995; Little, 1997; Acheson, 1998; Buchanan, 1999; Macdonald with Winkley, 1999; Davies et al., 2000; Farrall, 2002; Nutley et al., 2007, Ch. 7). (See Chapter 12 for more discussion of EBP.)

Human situations, however, involve many interconnected, frequently changing variables, not all capable of accurate measurement. Black (2001: 33), discussing the limitations of evidence, argues that not all situations lend themselves to the gold standard test of randomised controlled trials (RCTs), where a carefully measured and controlled treatment can be compared with a placebo or non-intervention. He emphasises the prior intellectual analysis of the problem, a planned search for all relevant evidence and continuing review. He recognises that art as well as science is involved. Sheppard (2006) makes similar points, emphasising that deductive logic is needed in drawing on all types of available evidence, as well as emergent understandings that may be related to the art of assessment. He argues that all these aspects must be rigorously explained, analysed and contextualised.

In circumstances where people's lives are complex, it is difficult to balance the holistic assessment of needs against the uncertainties of predicting future risks. Outcomes will be uncertain. The pressure to adopt an actuarial approach to the assessment and prediction of risk is not well supported by evidence about human behaviour in complex, varied and changing circumstances (Kemshall and Pritchard, 1997; Baldwin and Spencer, 2000; Munro, 2002). Where events of relatively low probability – such as child abuse or child homicide – are involved, Alaszewski and Walsh (1995) question whether it is possible to derive objective measures of risk. Baldwin and Spencer (2000), Munro (2002) and Reder and Duncan (2002) draw attention to the large number of false negatives and false positives involved when attempts are made to ensure that screening covers all those potentially at risk. There are also ethical problems in relying on predictive tests that may label and stigmatise individuals and families (Taylor et al., 2008).

McDonald and Marks (1991: 120), in their review of risk factors used in a wide range of risk assessment instruments, found that less than half the variables used had been empirically tested. They concluded that a common approach was to adopt and adapt an available instrument and put it into practice without testing. Even where extensive testing has taken place, predictive tests and screening instruments are likely only to be able to give a guide as to *proportions within a given population* where the risk may come to fruition, rather than pinpoint precisely the individuals where that risk will lead to harm. Yet social work and social care professionals have the responsibility to reach judgements about intervention, protection, safeguards and resources in a wide range of situations where evidence may be unclear or contested. This is the background to an emphasis on systematic, critically reflexive assessment, drawing widely on theory, research and professional judgement.

Other criticisms of a preoccupation with risks to the detriment of a wider process of assessing needs suggest that this preoccupation has been concerned with 'bureaucratic and organisational needs' (DH, 1995a), rather than those of the vulnerable service user. Calder (2003: 44), however, identified an apparent 'jettisoning' of the concept of risk and risk assessment in favour of needs-led assessment. He speculates that this may be due in part to the term 'risk' frequently being misused in social work because it focuses exclusively on the risk of harm, whereas in any other enterprise, a risk equation also includes a chance of benefits. Calder draws attention to a shift from terms such as 'protection', 'abuse' and 'risk' to 'safeguard', 'promote', 'welfare' and 'need'. Social workers and others in the caring professions have the task of managing the uneasy tension between these trends. An ecological approach, recognising a web of multiple, disparate, interacting factors, provides a holistic framework for understanding, analysing and acting on them.

Given the complexities of individual situations and organisational arrangements, it may not be surprising that there is a poor record in social work of high-quality assessment and purposeful planned intervention (DH, 1995a; Scottish Executive, 2000a; Horder, 2002; Petch, 2002, 2008).

Munro's research into child abuse reports (1999, 2002) found that there was a lack of recognition of known risk factors and a lack of systematic investigation and assessment of all the available information. Workers tended to concentrate on the immediate, current incident or episode, rather than carefully evaluating both long- and short-term evidence relating to behaviour, risks and safeguards. She also found a reluctance to revise initial assessments in the light of new evidence. Workers were not drawing all the complex information together, documenting sources, considering the impact over time on the child and synthesising updated information. All these activities are core features of assessment.

The consequences of the inadequate assessment of need and risk are demonstrated in the numerous child protection inquiries held when things have gone tragically wrong (Reder et al., 1993; Laming, 2003; O'Brien, 2003: Scottish Executive, 2005a). There are similar examples from mental health, work with older people and people with disabilities (Scottish Executive, 2005b). Often the result of inquiries into cases where there have been serious failures in the system and in professional practice has been an upsurge of criticism of agencies and individuals – a culture of blame that can lead to defensive practice and undermine the principle of user-centred assessment and intervention.

Our aim here is to encourage practitioners to increase their confidence, skill and professionalism in assessment as a basis for intervention, ensuring that it is a collaborative process undertaken within a legislative and organisational framework. National standards (Scottish Executive, 2001; GSCC, 2004) identify the centrality of assessment to the social work task and link it with the core values of social work. We hope to show that systematic, evidence-led assessment is a straightforward process, drawing on the core principles and skills of social work and social care.

Key principles

Human rights legislation, such as the Human Rights Act 1998 and the UN Convention on the Rights of the Child (UN, 1989), mental health and community care and children's legislation provide a framework for the code of ethics for social work (BASW, 2003), the codes of practice for social service workers (GSCC, 2004) and the codes of practice for social service workers and employees (SSSC, 2001). Underlying principles support assessment that is firmly based within an **ecological framework**, with the service user centre stage, a player in a collaborative inter-professional process.

Ecological frameworks offer a conceptual basis for exploring an aspect of research or practice. They reject single factor approaches and maintain that the many contributing factors interact in four domains: within the individual; through interpersonal relationships; in the community; in wider society.

Effective assessment should:

- Be centred on the service user – not agency or resource driven
- Be built on partnership: with individuals, families and across agencies
- Recognise the service user within the context of family, material circumstances, culture and social networks
- Respect dignity, individuality, privacy and human rights and adhere to social work and other professional ethical codes
- Recognise conflicts of interest and power differentials
- Seek alternative explanations, judgements
- Balance protection and safeguards for the user and family members and members of the public with the right to autonomy.

An ecological framework

These principles are best supported by an ecological framework that addresses the context within which needs, risks and problems arise (Bronfenbrenner, 1977; Belsky, 1980; Garbarino, 1992; Acheson, 1998; Baldwin, 2000; Calder, 2003). Such a framework takes account of research on human needs and is readily applicable in health and social work practice (Walter, 2007).

Individuals do not live in a vacuum, rather they exist within complex systems that include their immediate surroundings, social networks and cultural communities, set within a wider social structure. An understanding of ecological systems will encourage systematic information-gathering, drawing on observations and factual evidence, taking account of intra- and interpersonal factors, alongside social, organisational and economic influences on situations where assessment is required. It allows the possibility of recognising the unique influence and relevance of the immediate environment and interconnecting systems on an individual's situation; how strengths within them may be mobilised to support positive change, as well as how deficits and problems may be addressed.

Figure 16.1 shows these interacting systems. The Department of Health assessment triangle, the Scottish Executive version of it (Figure 16.2) and the guidance for Single Shared Assessment in community care (Table 16.1) follow this approach.

These models illustrate the importance of recognising and understanding the complexity of any given situation and of individual circumstances and avoiding a concentration on any single factor. The web illustrates how a complex range of inter-related factors impacts on any individual's life and requires to be addressed within any assessment process. The two assessment triangles (Figure 16.2) recognise that children's lives and development are influenced by their own needs and capacities, by parenting and caring styles, capacity and resources and by their wider social environments.

Jack and Gill (2003) criticise the Department of Health, however, for not backing up the third side of the triangle – family and environmental factors – with the same range of materials as made available for the other two. This is particularly important, given the connections between disadvantage, poor material and social circumstances and the range of risks (Acheson, 1998; Wilkinson, 2005; Dominy and Kempson, 2006; Save the Children, 2008). An ecological approach must ensure that all aspects of a user's life are taken fully into account within available timescales. Francis et al. (2006) argue that comprehensive assessment tools may sit uncomfortably within crisis-driven contexts because of lack of time.

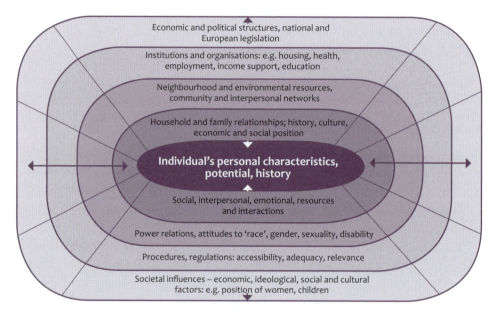

Figure 16.1 The web of interacting factors influencing individual situations

Source: Baldwin, N. (2000) *Protecting Children and Promoting their Rights*, reproduced with permission of Whiting and Birch

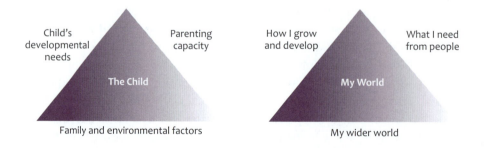

Figure 16.2 Department of Health assessment triangle and Scottish version

Source: DH/DfEE/Home Office (2000) *Framework for the Assessment of Children in Need and their Families*; Scottish Executive (2005c) *Getting it Right for Every Child*

All dimensions need to be considered in assessment. Although expressed in a different format here, the Single Shared Assessment framework (Table 16.1) adopts similar principles, recognising that an interprofessional coordinated approach to assessment should capture and address the complexity of individuals' lives and allow those involved in the assessment to address issues from a wide range of perspectives (Mansfield and Mayer, 2007). Powell et al. (2007), in a study of older people's experience of Single Shared Assessment, suggest that interdependence, rather than dependence, should underlie any approach to assessing older people's needs, if we are to appreciate and build upon the complexities of older people's strategies for actively managing their lives.

Table 16.1 Single Shared Assessment in community care

Single Shared Assessment:
1. is person-centred and needs-led relates to level of need is a process, not an event
2. seeks information *once* has a lead professional who coordinates documents and shares appropriate information coordinates all contributions produces a single summary assessment of need
3. actively involves people who use services and their carers is a shared process that supports joint working provides results acceptable to all agencies

Source: Scottish Executive (2000a) Community Care: A Joint Future

These approaches are fundamentally interdisciplinary, assuming a systematic gathering of information from diverse, evidence-based, sources, which will be critically evaluated and used to develop a structured, purposeful intervention plan.

In a critical comparison of four different assessment frameworks, Crisp et al. (2007) suggest that an increasing commitment to the use of standardised assessment frameworks reflects the pressure on practitioners to draw out the evidence on which they base decisions, as research evidence has rarely been found to underpin social work decisions. They caution against seeing assessment frameworks as a panacea, however, arguing that effective assessment depends on a combination of systematic inquiry, backed by probing, supportive supervision that recognises the importance of multidisciplinary and specialist aspects of assessment. Skilled critical analysis of the information available and alternative theories relevant to the particular needs and circumstances are crucial for both assessor and supervisor, before judgements are reached about the most appropriate action to be taken. Stanley (2005) highlights the effectiveness of supervision in assessing and managing risk when the culture is one of 'learning from mistakes'.

Here we outline a brief case example, which we shall use to illustrate how key principles may support assessment within an ecological framework: gathering and analysing information, assessing needs and risks, reaching judgements about action and evaluating outcomes.

CASE EXAMPLE

- Cathy (mother) 37, unemployed

- Sanjit (Cathy's current partner) 35, unemployed

- Dennis (Cathy's father) 69, retired

- Jonnie (son of Cathy and Gary) 11, at primary school

- Jason (son of Cathy and Gary) 8, at primary school

- Gary (Cathy's ex-partner and father of Jonnie and Jason) 39, unemployed

- Zac (son of Cathy and Sanjit) 6 months old, in full-time local authority daycare

Cathy is currently living in local authority housing with her partner Sanjit and two of her children, Jason and Zac. Her third child Jonnie lives with his father Gary and Gary's mother. Cathy is six months pregnant.

Dennis, Cathy's father, also lives with her. Dennis retired from work on medical grounds when he was 52 and has lived with Cathy for the last four years. His health has deteriorated recently and he requires a wheelchair to get around the house. He does not go outside. His GP has expressed concern about his deteriorating mobility and restricted lifestyle.

Cathy and Sanjit are regular users of cannabis. Sanjit is suspected of supplying others.

Cathy left her previous relationship because of domestic violence, which was frequently witnessed by the older children. There has been no suggestion of violence in her current relationship with Sanjit.

Cathy has previously sought help from the drug and alcohol team at times when she has used alcohol as an escape from problems: she has recently contacted them again to ask for general support.

The health visitor has had concerns about Zac's overall development and has been talking to Cathy about the inadvisability of leaving the children – particularly the baby – in the care of her father Dennis.

We work from the starting point of a social worker from the drug and alcohol team responding to Cathy's request for support. However, the request could just as easily apply if it was a social worker from a children and families team responding to a request by a health visitor to talk to Cathy about her support needs or a request from the GP to a community care team in relation to the disability issues of Cathy's father.

Collaboration with service users

Principles of respect and partnership are central to the social work task and must begin with the assessment process. The unique contribution that each service user can make to the process, in relation to their history, personal circumstances, feelings, priorities and understandings, needs to be fully recognised. A partnership approach can recognise individuals' rights to autonomy, safety, inclusion and having their voice heard, without denying power differentials.

Kemshall (2008) discusses the increasing recognition of the need to move from a deficit model in understanding individual situations to a model that emphasises strengths, broader networks of support and community resources.

In the case of Cathy and her family, with their diverse needs, as in any complex situation, substantial time will be needed to engage with the individuals and the family group. If all are to understand why professionals are showing an interest in their welfare, then they and the professionals involved need to understand the concerns as well as the resources and interventions available – honesty, openness and transparency cannot be achieved instantaneously, they depend on empathetic inter-action and exchange. McLeod et al. (2008), from their study of user feedback on the process of reintegrating older people discharged from hospital into their social networks and social resources, emphasise the importance of sensitive, individualised interventions and objectives that reflect users' priorities. They discuss the human face of social work. Yet Forrester et al. (2008), in a study of taped interviews between social workers and simulated service users, found many closed questions, little reflec-tion and few identified positives. They found that the workers achieved clarity about what the concerns were, but rarely demonstrated high levels of empathy. Yet they noted that the factor most likely to reduce resistance and increase the amount of information disclosed was empathy. Platt (2007) stresses that the greater the congru-ence between the understandings a social worker has of the situation of children and their families, the more likely it is that cooperation will be achieved.

The Single Shared Assessment (Scottish Executive, 2000a) and the *Framework for the Assessment of Children in Need and their Families* (DH/DfEE/Home Office, 2000) are based on these principles. The framework for children is well researched, well resourced and extensively used. Yet critics suggest that its guidelines are being too rigidly applied, leading to a requirement for set piece assessments, within unrealistic timescales, with the continuing problem that families will experience 'things being done to them', rather than being 'engaged' in a collaborative process (Calder, 2003: 25; Booth et al., 2006).

Some initial questions to address when engaging with the family within the case example might be:

- What are the strengths, aspirations and priorities of the individual members of the family?
- How do they – singly and collectively – characterise their current

- personal needs
- interpersonal needs
- social needs
- material needs?
- Do they identify any points of vulnerability or stress about their daily lives, routines, living arrangements?
- Has a professional – health visitor, social worker, teacher, carer – identified any reasons for concern, and if so, what are these specifically?
- Have any concerns been shared previously with appropriate family members and any legal and resource implications discussed?
- Do they know why the worker is discussing these matters with them?
- Do they understand the purpose of any further discussion, information-sharing, assessment?
- If caring arrangements for the baby are a reason for concern, has the substance of this been explained, for example feeding patterns, baby-sitting arrangements? Have any child protection issues been considered?
- If the health and personal care of Dennis is a source of difficulty, has the worker had preliminary discussions with the appropriate team about how they may proceed in a coordinated way?

It would be possible to focus on any one member of the family in a narrow, discipline-related way, for example are there child protection issues for Zac? Are there issues about accommodation for Dennis? Are there problems of drug and alcohol abuse for Cathy? Targeted, specialist assessments for individual services would risk a one-dimensional, fragmented approach. An ecological approach – no matter which service initiates it – offers a broader and more realistic perspective.

Interprofessional collaboration

The development of a Single Shared Assessment in community care and the *Framework for the Assessment of Children in Need and their Families* have both been driven by the recognition of a need for joined-up approaches to common human needs and problems. Yet our health and welfare services are enormously complicated, often with labyrinthine bureaucracies and funding arrangements.

Many child protection inquiries have shown that a contributory factor to negative outcomes and sometimes irreparable harm to children has been the lack of coordination and cooperation between agencies (Reder et al., 1993; Laming, 2003; O'Brien, 2003). Assessment that engages with the complex realities of service users is an essential starting point in accessing appropriate services and ensuring that they operate for the benefit of users. When gathering and sharing information for an assessment, it is essential that professionals coordinate their efforts and cooperate with one another. A study by Francis et al. (2006) found that social workers agreed on the centrality of information-sharing across professions, but this was not routinely practised. Routes for prompt information-sharing – with or without consent – need to be clearly set out and agreed across agencies. Information should be held and shared in ways that best promote and safeguard individuals' interests. Human rights legislation rightly stresses privacy and confidentiality, but not to the extent of over-riding safeguards for the vulnerable.

The format of record-keeping should be simple, flexible and usable across professional boundaries. Assessment and other records should be capable of expansion to take account of complex, changing needs over time and the involvement of new agencies. However comprehensive the record-keeping system and sophisticated the guidelines about content, workers need to be clear that they are only tools to be used with and for the benefit of service users. A Scottish government report (2007) quotes Stanley's caution that the use of assessment tools, whether completed collaboratively or not, can result in information not being seen as context specific but technical or scientific fact and therefore not open to critical scrutiny.

Interprofessional collaboration carries undoubted benefits in improving coordination, consultation and decision-making. However, its hidden costs include the time required for professionals to begin to understand each other's ways of thinking and working and engage in the process of working more closely together (Hallett and Birchall, 1992; Hallett, 1995; Wilson and Pirrie, 2000; Leathard, 2003). Although current governments in Scotland and the UK demand joined-up working and promote integrated services through the provision of specific funding streams (Single Shared Assessment, Joint Futures, Changing Children's Services Fund, *Getting it Right for Every Child* and so on), there are practical problems in many areas about allocating the time necessary to support these collaborative arrangements, such as workforce and recruitment problems, inexperienced staff and managers and infrequent supervision.

Many have argued that from initial training onwards, different professionals become embedded within their own 'camps' and are reluctant to look at alternative perspectives (Wilson and Pirrie, 2000). Others argue that professional jealousies, status issues and alternative value bases all contribute to frequently poor working relations between differing professions (Wilson and Pirrie, 2000; Leathard, 2003; Weinstein et al., 2003).

Any worker attempting to help Cathy and her family will need to be sufficiently aware of these issues to handle them constructively and engage with the family in assessing and meeting their needs. Initial issues to be addressed when working across professions are:

■ Who has relevant information about the members of the household:
   – individual family members
   – health professionals
   – drug and alcohol team
   – local authority carers
   – social worker
   – primary schools?

- Who needs to make information available?
- Who is the most appropriate person to coordinate information with the family?
- Who will deal with issues of confidentiality, consent for information-sharing?
- How will evidence, facts and observations be verified and separated from opinion?
- What timescales will be set for gathering and analysing the information and using it to arrive at an assessment of strengths, resources, risks and needs?
- Who will take responsibility for recording, updating, sharing the range of information with this family and professionals involved, ensuring their continual engagement in the collaborative process?
- Is there a local system of 'core group' advice, discussion and collaborative working that an individual worker can activate, or does the worker have to create the most appropriate mechanism to match the needs identified?
- Are there conflicting professional priorities that need to be made explicit and agreements made about resolving them?
- Are there legal or funding issues that need to be checked out, for example child protection, arrangements about payments for community care?

Instruments and tools for the assessment process

Smale and Tuson (1993) describe three main types of assessment within social work:

- *the questioning model,* where a social worker will be seen as the expert, drawing out and processing information
- *the procedural model,* where a social worker gathers information to assess whether the service user fits predetermined criteria for services
- *the exchange model,* where all people are seen as 'an expert on their own problems' and the emphasis is on the exchange of information. The social worker attempts to help service users to mobilise internal and external resources to meet the goals defined by them.

This third model is the one that best fits the values and principles of social work. It recognises principles of empowerment, setting the service user at the centre of the assessment process. Principles of empowerment can be seen in the widest context – including issues of safety for and risk to others, power differentials and conflicts of interest.

Social workers have an enormous range of assessment tools to guide their work, some concentrating on general risk factors, others emphasising specific aspects such as mental health, alcohol use, disability or domestic violence. Each of these instruments should be guided by the principles of social work and human rights legislation and located within the wider ecological framework. A positive aspect of such a diverse range means that methods can be closely aligned to an individual's situation. However, the diversity and range of methods and approaches can lead to confusion about how they should be applied, or result in key principles of assessment being subordinated to the priorities of a particular method.

Which instrument to use, how to use it and how well it has been evaluated are all questions to tax individual workers and their organisations. Although clear guidance may be issued with an assessment tool (DH/DfEE/Home Office, 2000), this still needs to be interpreted locally within individual agencies and translated for staff in the form of training, policies and more specific guidelines. Calder and Hackett (2003) discuss further tensions arising from local training and guidelines, where there can be multiple interpretations of the method, and confusion on the part of workers in relation to the administration of the tools and their effective outcomes. We are not yet at a point in social work where the evidence base neatly points to the validity of a few all-encompassing assessment tools. The skill of workers in drawing systematically on the best evidence available relating to the general circumstances they are assessing will need to be backed up by skill in analysing and judging the unique situation and its specific strengths, needs and risks. The expertise of workers also arises partly from reflections on their own situation.

If workers are guided by the set of principles previously outlined in relation to assessment and locate their work within the wider ecological framework, Maddock and Larson (1995) suggest that they also need to take cognisance of their own position within the assessment process. The worker has to address how and where the individual being assessed is located within an ecological framework and also 'pay attention to his own place in the total ecology of the client's presenting situation, choosing an appropriate ecological niche from which to make some useful contributions' (Calder, 2003: 33).

This allows all those involved to operate within a systems framework where conflicts of interest and tensions are commonplace and recognised as the norm within a complex set of interlinked relationships. The 'ecological niche' from which workers make their contribution will be affected by their ability to make sound professional judgements. These judgements are made against a backdrop of limited knowledge, time pressures, high emotions and conflicting objectives (Munro, 2002). In these circumstances, assessment tools should be seen as working documents that should be transparent to all involved, with decisions and actions being continually measured against the available evidence and updated accordingly.

Recognising the fallibility of assessment tools is important, as studies show that professionals seek certainty, have a tendency to choose one option rather than checking out several possibilities, and dissent is often discouraged (Munro, 2002). McCarrick et al. (2000) raise further criticism by arguing that many assessment tools rely far too heavily on verbal exchanges. They suggest that this can accentuate power differentials and fail to engage service users in genuine participation. They propose a wide range of interactive exercises and methods of observation as essential tools of assessment.

Following any system, or relying on a particular tool, will inevitably constrain the assessment process, reducing its flexibility. Here the issue of exchange becomes crucial – openness to the realities of the service user's situation demands critical flexibility in skill and professional judgement.

Supervision that supports critical reflection is a crucial part of the overall systemic approach to assessment (Morrison, 2001). Opportunities where workers within complex cases can challenge and be challenged on their assumptions, question their decisions and analyse their understanding of information received are essential to the assessment process.

Assessment as inquiry

Assessment itself can be seen as a method of inquiry, to be adapted to respond to the unique situations of service users. Professionals assess individual circumstances in relation to risk, need and potential change, from within organisations where tensions exist between the allocation of time and the time required for assessment. Workers require time not only to assess and intervene as appropriate in relation to potential risk and need but also, taking an ecological approach, to think about and question their decision-making. Such reflective practice is essential to the assessment process and decisions about intervention and the provision of services and resources.

We support Heron's model of inquiry (Heron, 1996; Heron and Reason, 2001) that harnesses cycles of reflection, review and active participation to improve the assessment process. Within the process of assessment, workers are required to 'act' in relation to gathering information from a wide range of sources, through collaboration with others, and then intervene where appropriate. They need to continually 'reflect' on information obtained, on their judgements and the decision-making based on it, then on any action to be taken as a result. They need to analyse, review and make sense of it. Figure 16.3 illustrates this inquiry process linked to assessment.

When reflection is built into each stage of the assessment process, any follow-up action taken by workers will be based on up-to-date information and grounded in current reality. Reflecting on information gathered allows workers and others involved to question their assumptions, challenge accepted givens, frame and reframe further questions, and analyse information in a collaborative attempt to gain new 'common meaning structures' that lead to greater common understanding (Dixon, 1999). Within complex situations where there may be conflict, power differentials and space for misunderstanding, this mechanism is essential to provide clarity and transparency and deal with a diverse range of opinions about potential direction and possible outcomes.

Within any assessment process, there are likely to be many cycles of reflective and active practice as workers seek to update information and obtain more pieces of what, at times, seems like a complex jigsaw puzzle. Coulshed and Orme (1998) suggest that assessment requires administrative and interpersonal skills. Parker and Bradley (2003) add communication and observational skills, and an ability to organise, synthesise and rationalise information-gathering. A cyclical model of reflection and action that allows time to process material in this way recognises workers' need to be reflexive, in order to help to discourage bias in their assessment (Cooper, 2000). It can support holistic assessment, taking account of diversity, complexity and the need for a balanced approach.

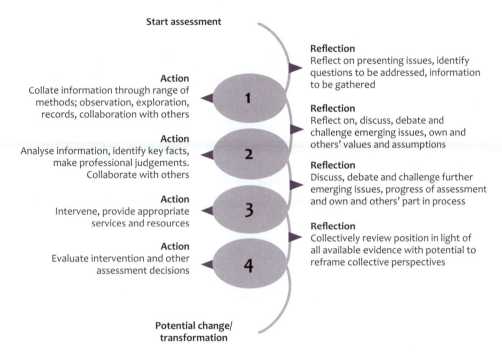

Start assessment

Action
Collate information through range of methods; observation, exploration, records, collaboration with others

Action
Analyse information, identify key facts, make professional judgements. Collaborate with others

Action
Intervene, provide appropriate services and resources

Action
Evaluate intervention and other assessment decisions

1
2
3
4

Reflection
Reflect on presenting issues, identify questions to be addressed, information to be gathered

Reflection
Reflect on, discuss, debate and challenge emerging issues, own and others' values and assumptions

Reflection
Discuss, debate and challenge further emerging issues, progress of assessment and own and others' part in process

Reflection
Collectively review position in light of all available evidence with potential to reframe collective perspectives

Potential change/ transformation

Figure 16.3 Assessment as inquiry

The use of a cyclical model, which recognises the complexity of unique human situations, provides safeguards within which information can be continuously assessed, collective understanding questioned, and potential interventions and outcomes revisited. It allows the possibility of the individual service user being centre stage, recognising the potential for individual and collective change through active participation in a process.

Although within any assessment process, depending on the complexity of the situation and the number of variables involved, there are likely to be multiple cycles, within this example, only the four key steps are shown to illustrate the model. Within each step, smaller cyclical processes will occur as information is gathered and ideas framed and reframed within the process.

Cycle one

The first cycle within the assessment process requires workers, in partnership with service users, to set the scene and begin to frame the parameters of the assessment. Taking an ecological perspective, this should encompass the key principles of assessment as outlined previously, showing respect for individuals while recognising the imperative to address safety and immediate issues of risk to or from service users. These are some questions that might be addressed and action that might be taken in cycle one.

Reflective phase:
- What information is available at the outset?
- Is intervention required immediately or in the short term?
- What further information do we need?
- Where might this information be obtained?
- Who needs to be involved in a holistic assessment?
- What timescales are we working to?
- What systems of communication will be employed to keep everyone informed during the assessment process?
- What resources might we need to carry out this assessment?
- Who might need to be contacted regarding resource allocation?
- Where will supports come from for service users, carers, workers?

Action phase:
- This involves active collaboration with individuals, families, wider groups and other professionals to obtain information, for example through discussion, observation, reading records and collating photographic and other evidence.

Cycle two

These are some of the questions that might be addressed and action that might be taken in cycle two.

Reflective phase:
- What issues/concerns are emerging about disability, drug and alcohol use, pregnancy, developmental and health issues?
- What evidence do we have?
- Does the evidence match the emerging issues/concerns?
- What value judgements are being made and by whom?
- Where can these be checked out?
- What mechanisms are in place to support, challenge and question, for example in relation to prejudice about race, disability, child development and parenting capacity?
- What assumptions are being made and by whom, for example in relation to past requests for support, current circumstances, 'norms' and 'stereotypes'?

Action phase:
- Collating information from a range of sources, analysis of the information obtained

in collaboration with service users and professionals, resulting in professional judgements based on the presenting evidence and evidence from research.

Cycle three

The reflective phase provides quality assurance, by allowing workers to step back and assess the situation. Compton and Galloway (1999) caution that workers can never fully understand what others are saying, doing or feeling and should not attempt to do so. However, taking time to make sense of information provided and seeking to understand the context within which it is located goes part way to gaining greater understanding. Similarly, within the action phase, active participation by family members in identifying strengths, problems and solutions recognises the key principles of collaboration, partnership and respect.

Particularly in child protection cases, where workers are often faced with the 'resistant client', some degree of creativity and flexibility is required to skilfully engage the individual or family concerned (Calder, 2003). These are some of the questions to be addressed and action to be taken in cycle three.

Reflective phase:
- Are the facts gained so far correct and how might we know this, for example in relation to Dennis's health, the mother's and father's past and present drug and alcohol use, and Zac's development?
- Has everyone who needs to be included within the assessment been included and how would we know this? Has an opinion been sought from the GP, health visitor, other relevant health professionals, extended family members, nursery, school and so on?
- What changes do the individuals within this family want?
- What do they consider achievable and sustainable?
- What is your professional judgement and what do other professionals think?
- Have assumptions and 'givens' been challenged?
- What mechanisms exist to debate and question emerging issues and reframe thinking?

Action phase:
- By this stage intervention should be agreed and include a wide range of options for this family. Their inclusion in relation to identifying strengths and solving problems is essential in achieving effective outcomes.

Cycle four

Within an ecological framework, cycle four emphasises the collaborative nature of the process, concentrating on collective perspectives through reframing in the light of specific current evidence and research evidence. Workers here need to review the information gathered and interventions made so far, checking that thorough attention has been paid throughout the assessment process. It has been suggested that in the stepwise model of assessment by Samra-Tibbets and Raynes (1999), workers frequently skip the planning stage to progress to a later information-gathering stage (Cleaver and Department of Health, 2000). These are some of the questions to be addressed and action that might be taken in cycle four.

Reflective phase:
- Has the assessment process been completed to everyone's satisfaction – in relation to Dennis, Cathy, Sanjit and the children?
- If not, what are the gaps or unresolved issues?
- Have the issues of risk, need, problems, targets and potential change been identified?
- What mechanisms and resources will need to be in place for these to continue to be addressed?
- How will this be agreed and outcomes reviewed?
- Who will continue work with the individuals within this family, if continuing involvement is agreed – drugs team, school, GP, social worker, health visitor and so on?
- Has the coordination of professional contact been identified and agreed by everyone?

Action phase:
- This stage requires workers to be clear with individual family members and each other about future planning and expectations, agreeing specific outcomes, who will be responsible for particular actions, resources, review and assessment.
- Transparent, honest communication in appropriate formats is essential, which respects individual rights, confidentiality and privacy. This needs to be balanced with the imperative to have accurately assessed the degrees of risk and need for all in the household and to have made clear what consequences may follow if agreed – or required – expectations for care and safety are not met.

Conclusion

In this chapter, following a brief discussion of the underpinning theory, we set out a working model of assessment, which we elaborated through a case study. While we have both had experience of working with adults and children, our recent experience has concentrated on work with children and families. Inevitably, this influences the references we draw on. We believe, however, that the principles, content and processes of assessment are broadly generic, and that specialist assessments for particular settings or groups should build on these, elaborating more fully and probing more deeply. Generic and specialist assessment should connect, recognising the uniqueness and expertise of each individual, maintaining their centrality in the process.

Robust systems to support a process of assessment that can take all these factors into consideration are required across all sectors of care services. Professional judgements need to be made, based on a balance of complex relationships between risk, need, safety and autonomy. An ecological framework provides a structure from within which workers can consider the impact that interconnected layers have on an individual's life.

Professional judgements are based on evidence relating to specific sets of circumstances unique to the individuals involved and from wider studies and perspectives. Inquiry processes that harness cycles of reflective practice and active participation provide workers with a model to collate and assess evidence systematically. All assessment processes, whether they be in relation to children, families or adults, should place the service user at the centre of the process, valuing their perspective as a contributing partner.

Professional support mechanisms, allowing time to reflect and encouraging the development of skills to evaluate and challenge practice, should be embedded within and across organisations, with active supervision being a vehicle to aid this process. Balancing risk, need and safety requires a complex set of skills, involving the cooperation and collective understanding of a range of individuals in seeking positive outcomes.

When workers have the opportunity to work collaboratively with service users and other professionals, to address power differentials and potential conflict through a systematic approach that draws together and evaluates strengths, needs, risks and the potential for change, the effectiveness of services is likely to be improved and the outcomes for service users more positive.

Professionally oriented services, driven by the principles of social work and drawing on best evidence from research and practice, will ensure that these approaches and skills are developed and supported throughout organisations, as the foundations for effective assessment and intervention.

For further discussion of assessment in practice, with children and families, see Adams et al., 2009b, Chapter 25, and with older people, see Adams et al., 2009c, Chapter 7.

Calder, M. and Hackett, S. (eds) (2003) *Assessment in Childcare*, Lyme Regis, Russell House Publishing. An overview and critique of a broad range of assessment frameworks used with children and families.

Heron, J. and Reason, P. (2001) 'The practice of co-operative inquiry: research with rather than on people', in P. Reason and H. Bradbury (eds) *Handbook of Action Research: Participative Inquiry and Practice*, London, Sage. Provides theoretical frameworks and practical examples of cooperative enquiry.

Hudson, B. (2002) 'Interprofessionality in health and social care: the Achilles' heel of partnership?', *Journal of Interprofessional Care*, 16(1): 7–17. Explores the pros and cons of interprofessional collaborative practice.

Jack, C. and Gill, O. (2003) *The Missing Side of the Triangle: Assessing the Importance of Family and Environmental Factors in the Lives of Children*, Ilford, Barnardo's. Emphasises the importance of assessing wider social and economic contexts of need.

Kenny, G. (2002) 'The importance of nursing values in interprofessional collaboration', *British Journal of Nursing*, 11(1): 65–8. Discusses nursing values and their importance, alongside research evidence, in interprofessional collaboration.

Lishman, J. (ed.) (2007) *Handbook for Practice Learning in Social Work and Social Care*, London: Jessica Kingsley. The chapters by Daniel, Fook, Kemshall and McIvor raise key practice issues in assessment with different client groups.

Petch, A. (2008) 'Social work with adult service users', in M. Davies (ed.) *The Blackwell Companion to Social Work*, Oxford, Blackwell. Discusses current issues in assessment and interventions in services for adults.

Worth, A. (2001) 'Assessment of the needs of older people by district nurses and social workers: a changing culture?', *Journal of Interprofessional Care*, 15(3): 257–66. Covers the organisational, educational and resource constraints affecting similarities and differences in assessment practice.

Planning 17

Care planning has developed from being a task that links assessment with intervention to being an integral part of the social work process and the focus of initiatives driven by the UK government's modernising agenda. Planning is a crucial instrument to achieve effective partnerships with service users, who increasingly are encouraged to plan their own care.

Chapter overview

Planning, once seen at best as a bridge between assessment and intervention, has come to occupy centre stage in contemporary social work. Originally seen as primarily the province of the service manager, skills in planning are now a key requirement for every practitioner. For example, the shifting emphasis in the UK's Department of Health over the past decade on outcomes rather than process incorporates, often explicitly, the notion that these must be planned outcomes based on evidence from research (McNeish et al., 2002). The national service frameworks (NSFs), published to guide the development, delivery and regulation of health and social care services for children and adults, each contain within them a substantial emphasis on the notion of care that is planned and systematically reviewed (for example DH, 2001a; DH/DfES, 2004), and the same notion underpins the Care Standards Act 2000. In many ways, this emphasis on what at first sight may appear merely a technical process is the automatic outcome of professionalising trends over 30 years, which have sought to establish social work as a logical, ordered and defensible activity. To many social workers, however, it appears that their skills in human relations, their flexible, intuitive use of mechanisms for change and their ability to respond at the user's pace are all being subsumed to the planning machinery. Yet when it comes to their day-to-day case management, these same social workers find themselves reaching for 'planning' as the tool that may help them to reduce a complicated, multifaceted problem to a manageable situation. This chapter explores this process through the implementation of legislation and policy directives in the UK, yet its messages increasingly resonate globally.

CaSE EXaMPLE

Planning at the heart of practice

Janice is a 35-year-old woman with severe and multiple impairments. She has very limited verbal communication. She lives with her parents, now in their late seventies, and is supported by home carers who attend to her personal care needs. This arrangement was put in place before the introduction of direct payments and this option has not been discussed with Janice's parents. Janice goes to a day centre from Monday to Friday. Her overall care has not been properly reviewed for years. The last time a full day centre review procedure was conducted (two years ago), the resulting plan was subsequently withdrawn because it was deemed that hers was not a priority case for the more intensive social programme recommended. This was because, simultaneously, a programme of one-to-one working for the more 'able' users was being implemented, leaving insufficient staff resources to develop programmes for users such as Janice, who, it was felt, would benefit far less from such dedicated resources. However, no alternative plan was put in place to address her identified need for greater social stimulation. Janice's parents, concerned about the future, contact the social worker for information to help them in making plans. They express some dissatisfaction that the centre isn't working as well for them as in the past. Janice has developed a sore on one leg, apparently caused by the use of leg restraints, which staff argue is in the best interests of both Janice and other users as she is constantly kicking in an agitated fashion.

The weaknesses in Janice's care package and arguably her limited quality of life can be seen to stem from systematic deficits in planning:

- Her basic package of care developed in an ad hoc fashion. She has never had an overall assessment of need or an integrated care plan devised on the basis of that assessment.
- Previous care plans have been partial. The home care was targeted at her physical care needs and there was a failure to set any broader objectives relating to her social or emotional needs.
- There have been repeated failures to review her care and revise the care plan in line with her current needs. Thus, new 'problems', such as the agitated kicking, have been dealt with via an isolated response designed to contain the problematic behaviour.
- There has been no attempt to work in partnership with Janice's parents, or for the different formal carers to pool their knowledge and understanding to create the optimum caring environment. Janice's 'voice' is lost, as she does not have the one-to-one attention that might help her to communicate her needs and wishes.

Planning and the policy–practice interface

The driver in this new emphasis on planning is the policy–practice interface. Although social work theorists have only recently been particularly concerned with planning as part of the social work process, policy makers and service providers have for some time been increasingly preoccupied with its importance in social services delivery. The relationship between service planning and individual **care planning** is an important one that increasingly impacted on the work of frontline practitioners in the UK throughout the 1990s. The Children Act 1989 highlighted the responsibilities associated with planning for children 'in need', and subsequent guidance detailed the procedures and skills to be employed by the social worker. The National Health Service and Community Care Act (NHSCCA) 1990 introduced care management as the 'cornerstone' of health and social care delivery, in which the production and monitoring of an individual care plan are a key task of the care manager. The care programme approach in community mental health services preceded and has continued to run alongside care management, and the production of a care plan, which is periodically reviewed, is central to the approach. The 'modernising services' agenda, which began in the late 1990s, has created a series of policy directives, giving increasing weight to the planning task for the frontline worker and to joint planning between different agencies and workers. Not only have practitioners found themselves increasingly planning their interventions within statutory frameworks and government guidelines, they also have to set objectives and make plans that can result in demonstrable outcomes and will be subject to regular review. The balancing act between professional considerations and management imperatives that the individual practitioner must achieve becomes crucially located within the planning task. Moreover, the dominant emphases in current policy and practice are intrinsically tied up with care planning.

> **Care planning** refers to the stage in the process of introducing a service user or carer to community care services where each person's expectations and intentions are set out in an agreed statement.

The role of the service user

Although this chapter focuses on the planning role within the context of UK policy and practice, it is worth noting that the key emphasis in the current agenda is one that reflects a global trend in service delivery. This is the goal of achieving the highest degree of autonomy and choice for every service user with the principle of person-centred care firmly established (Holloway and Lymbery, 2007). In the UK, this goal has resulted in a significant change in the way in which planning is understood. Care planning, in adult services at least, is no longer to be primarily a professionally led task, with varying degrees of involvement of the service user in partnership with the professional, but service users and carers (including parents) are charged with the responsibility of planning their own care and being accountable for their use of resources, which they directly manage. A series of UK government initiatives (DH, 2005a, 2006, 2007a) combined with the 'in Control' service user movement (www.

in-control.org.uk) have steadily developed the principles, parameters and mechanisms of this shift. There is, however, acknowledgement of the continuing role of social workers and care managers as 'enablers' in this service user-led planning process, providing information and support to assist the user in the making and implementing of choices (Hatton et al., 2008). In complex situations and at crisis points, it is suggested that social workers may create an interim plan to enable a person to progress to a situation in which they are more able to take control over future decisions.

In children's services, the role of parents and young people themselves in future planning is increasingly recognised and promoted in policy directives and guidance (DH, 2002d; DfES, 2007).

Person-centred planning

For adults who have continuing, lifelong needs, such as those with complex, multiple disabilities and many people with learning disability, the emphasis on holistic care and lifelong planning was retained alongside the introduction of care management. This has developed into a mode of practice termed 'person-centred planning' (DH/SSI, 1995, 1996; Burton and Kellaway, 1998). **Person-centred planning** provides a widely adopted framework for supporting people in the community who have continuing and often intensive needs, grounded in the notion of developing short- and longer term goals, based on the things in life that are important for this individual service user in their particular social context. It is at the heart of the UK modernisation agenda and enshrined as a key standard in the *NSF for Older People* (DH, 2001a) and the *NSF for Long-term Conditions* (DH, 2005b). Coupled with the extension of direct payments – the UK version of the European-wide move to replace direct care with cash payments to enable service users to arrange their own care (Ellis, 2007) – to older adults, and the development of individualised budgets, promised in a series of government policy documents (DH, 2005a, 2006, 2007a), person-centred planning to deliver person-centred care looks set to occupy centre stage for the foreseeable future. It is a trend shared by all the health and social care systems of the developed world (for example Institute of Medicine, 2001). At the heart of childcare policy in the UK is *Every Child Matters* (DfES, 2003), which focuses on a holistic view of the individual child and their welfare.

> Person-centred planning is an approach to planning services that starts from the individual receiving services and puts them at the centre of the planning process.

Multiprofessional and interagency planning

Since the 1970s, a growing emphasis in health, social care and criminal justice services has been the need for different professionals and services to work together. Without exception, the different types of plan discussed later in this chapter are built around the assumption of multiprofessional working. The most recent developments – shared assessment procedures – take as the starting point that it is in the best interests of the service user for health and social care perspectives (and in the case of children, education) to be brought together at the earliest opportunity into an integrated assessment and intervention plan. A series of policy initiatives have been concerned with creating the agency structures and implementation procedures to achieve better joint working. In adult services, government has adopted a 'levering' approach, whereby additional resources may only be accessed on the basis of joint planning. In children's services, driven by the child protection agenda, joint assessment and planning is mandatory. Professionals are expected to align their plans to the five objectives set out in *Every Child Matters* (DfES, 2003). Thus, when we come to consider the 'on the ground' implementation of these initiatives, it becomes clear that, for the frontline worker, multiprofessional working is primarily carried out through the planning task.

The core task

Planning as a core task can be simply stated. It involves the setting of objectives to meet the needs and/or address the problems identified through the assessment, followed by the development of a plan for intervention to realise those objectives. However, as already discussed, the complexities of the situations with which social work is concerned, and the relationships in which it must engage in intervening in these situations, make the reality of planning far less simple. Payne (1995) delineates six stages in the 'planning interaction': introduction, in which the relationship is established, assessment, formulation, agreement, implementation and operation. Hughes (1995) also emphasises the importance of preparatory planning, taking account of factors specific to this situation that are likely to be significant. Thus, to undertake the planning task, social workers must employ a range of analytical and human relations skills:

- assessment
- design
- creative thinking
- review

alongside the generic interpersonal skills of:

- communication
- negotiation
- motivational/enabling
- sustaining.

The plan needs to specify the purpose, requirements and timescale for each element. The mechanisms and schedule for evaluation and review should be built in. User groups emphasise that plans must be 'explicit, action orientated and practical' (National Schizophrenia Fellowship, 1992: 10). Importantly, the planning process should be shared by worker and service user and the objectives agreed or disagreements recorded. Finally, although planning is clearly a task whose execution requires the use of a number of core skills, it should never be conceived of as atheoretical. As Brown (1996) has pointed out, implicitly or explicitly, social workers use knowledge and theoretical models all the time in planning their interventions, and this is better done as a conscious integrated process than one which exerts an unconscious and perhaps biased influence. Arguably, as the balance shifts in favour of the social worker's role being one of assisting the service user in their own planning process, this form of critical reflective practice becomes even more important.

The generic planning task takes formal shape in a number of specific types of care plan in the UK. It is primarily through these frameworks that multiprofessional and interagency planning are conducted at practitioner level. These sorts of care plan fall broadly into two categories – need and risk.

Care planning and need

In both children's and adults' services, all intervention is to some extent built around the devising of a plan to meet assessed needs. The following tasks, however, formally devise a plan on the basis of a needs assessment.

Community care plans

Under the NHSCCA 1990, tailored packages of care are arranged for disabled or older adults or people with mental health problems on the basis of a needs assessment. The *Care Management and Assessment Practice Guidance* (DH/SSI, 1991) outlines seven stages in which the core tasks are carried out, of which stages four to seven are concerned with the design, implementation, monitoring and review of the care plan. It is the responsibility of the care manager, in conjunction with the service user and/or carer, to design and put in place this care package, which is formalised into a written care plan. A key feature of community care plans is that each element has to be costed (DH, 1994), and this costing may be included in the written plan. Another common element, favoured by disability groups, is the incorporation of a daily/hourly time-table (Gathorne-Hardy, 1995).

Single assessment process refers not just to the assessment stage of care management, but to a process of treating people as individuals and maximising their choice. This is intended to be achieved through ensuring that the commissioning and delivery of services is carried out by agencies and professionals working together. The outcome is intended to be a holistic provision with the full involvement of service users and carers.

The single assessment process (SAP)

The single assessment process, introduced between 2002 and 2004 in conjunction with the *NSF for Older People* (DH, 2001a), may in time replace the community care assessment procedures for older people. There are four levels and types of assessment:

1 *Contact* – initiated at the first identification of significant health and/or social care needs
2 *Overview* – encompassing all or several life domains
3 *Specialist* – requiring one specific professional expertise
4 *Comprehensive* – specialist assessments in all or most domains.

Each level, however, is intended to produce a care plan that fully integrates health and social care needs. From the point of view of the service user, the significant factor is to what extent a more integrated assessment process results in holistic plans that meet their overlapping needs.

The Common Assessment Framework (CAF)

A similar shared assessment framework has been rolled out in children's services (DH/DfEE/Home Office, 2000). It determines that the needs (and also the protection) of all children and young people should be addressed as a result of a multi-agency assessment and planning process along three dimensions:

- Child development
- Parenting capacity and adaptability
- The extended family and wider environment.

Child in need plan

The Children Act 1989 laid down that a child may be deemed to be 'in need', whether as a result of neglect, abuse, deficiencies in their environment or their own special needs arising from physical or intellectual impairment. In such circumstances, the local authority has a duty to address those needs, employing a multi-agency, multiprofessional plan as appropriate (DH, 1991a). The increasing emphasis on partnership working has led to guidance on the inclusion of parents in this planning process (DfES, 2007).

Care plans

A child who is in the care of the local authority has a care plan that must identify immediate and longer term objectives. Here the notion of 'permanency planning' is particularly important to reduce the risk of children drifting around the care system or in and out of care (DH, 1991b). The current emphasis is on the participation of the child or young person in this planning process, alongside the promotion of self- and peer advocacy (DH, 2007b).

Pathway plan

A young person preparing to leave the care system will be involved in drawing up their individual pathway plan with a worker, usually in a specialist team, designated to work specifically with them on making that transition, this support being available until they reach the age of 21. However, research indicates that contact is frequently lost with young people leaving the care system (Wheal, 2002), and there are proposals that foster care should continue until the age of 21 if desired, and support be extended until the age of 25.

The above three types of plan, all stemming from the Children Act 2004 guidance, are designed to prevent children remaining in situations that fail to meet their needs, or that fail to foresee and prepare for their changing needs. They are examples of the way in which planning may be used to structure medium and longer term caring situations while introducing purpose and therapeutic potential.

Care planning and risk

The escalating concern about risk assessment and risk management in all branches of social work has brought with it the notion of 'risk planning' (Titterton, 1999). The dominant view, which derives from the concept of risk as 'bad', a threat, sees planning as an essential element in preventing and managing risk posed to a vulnerable party.

Child protection plans

A child protection plan will be drawn up at a multidisciplinary case conference where there is evidence that the child is at risk of 'significant harm'. Although initiated under the Children Act 1989, child protection procedures have undergone significant revision principally designed to ensure that plans do not drift and children become more vulnerable as a result (DfES, 2006). A 'lead professional' (in practice, usually a social worker) has responsibility for coordinating the refining, implementation, monitoring and reviewing of the plan.

The other approach sees risk as an essential part of life and the right to take risks as an essential part of taking control of one's own life. This approach incorporates into care planning the notion of informed choice concerning risk. In children's services, a major dilemma for the social worker developing a pathway plan with a young person leaving care lies in achieving a balance between supporting that young person in making choices and developing independence and safeguarding against risks (the 'choice' of drifting into prostitution being one such example). In adult services, we see a tension between the protection of vulnerable adults and their right to take risks. There has, nonetheless, been little development of the concept of risk planning. For example, risk assessment procedures for older people are largely concerned with managing risk as conceived as a threat to safety stemming from the service user's frailty or incapacity (for example Lawson, 1996) rather than the risks posed to the service user from an inadequate support package.

Geoff is a 51-year-old man who sustained cerebral damage following a heart attack, causing severe memory problems and visual impairment. As a further consequence of the cognitive damage, Geoff has limited insight into his difficulties and frequently puts himself at risk in everyday situations. He is divorced and has no children, but has been supported by his parents and a few friends and former colleagues throughout his period in hospital. He is now ready for discharge from the neuro-rehabilitation unit. The social worker joins the multidisciplinary team of doctors, nurses, psychologist and therapists who have been involved in his rehabilitation treatment to plan his discharge into the community.

The social worker has a dilemma at the heart of this care plan. While his professional instinct is to balance needs and risks and utilise Geoff's own resources and strengths to the full, the priority given to risk management in local resource distribution means that he must emphasise the risks inherent in Geoff's returning home, in order to activate a care package at the level that he feels is necessary to meet Geoff's needs. This may be concentrated on objectives that are not a priority for Geoff. He manages this dilemma by establishing the twin aims of risk management and the achievement of a degree of independence as of equal importance in delivering the desired outcome of Geoff's rehabilitation into the community. Thus it is possible to devise a plan that:

- Establishes Geoff's eligibility for the service
- Allows for a flexible, holistic approach but ties each element to an objective that may be monitored
- Has the potential to achieve the desired outcome, which in itself is a shared objective for both the service user and service providers.

Without such a plan, there is a danger that risk management will dominate to the point of exclusion of other quality of life elements. To devise and implement such a plan, a range of skills must be employed:

- Skills in communicating with other professionals, formal care providers, informal supports and a service user who has cognitive difficulties
- Skills in negotiating between parties so that there is agreement on principal objectives and a shared understanding of the strategy to achieve these
- The ability to think creatively, since Geoff has very particular needs and there is no dedicated community rehabilitation service available
- Skills in setting up adequate monitoring systems for different components of the package
- The ability to sustain a creative dialogue, in which the service user remains involved, about the effectiveness of the care package and the possibility of adapting the plan in line with changing needs.

Further dilemmas in the planning task

The planning task appears to be a straightforward process on paper, but it is at the planning stage that most of the classic dilemmas in social work practice emerge. Four main areas are highlighted and discussed in more detail.

The problem of inadequate resources

A common frustration expressed by practitioners is that undertaking a needs-led assessment is pointless when the care plan is predetermined by the available resources. Part of the problem here is that planning is perceived as a mechanistic activity, rather than a creative strategic process that harnesses the combined skills and resources of the worker and service user in problem-solving. Thus it may be that alternative solutions can be devised, or a staggered response may be planned, which includes making use of the less than ideal, while pressing for the required resource. However, the frontline worker may be caught in the contradictions existing between government policy and implementation guidance. For example, although *Fair Access to Care Services* (FACS) purports to support person-centred planning, in fact it establishes an eligibility framework that categorises individual need in terms of its relative severity (DH, 2002b).

Overtaken by events ... crisis

O'Hagan (1986) argued that social services departments are characterised by crisis-driven responses in situations of danger and uncertainty. He goes on to argue that social workers have a duty to bring this 'dangerous chaos' down to manageable proportions, in which 'good' decision-making, on the part of both worker and service user, replaces the frequently 'bad' decisions that have long-lasting deleterious effects. The potential of planning to contribute to this chaos reduction, as both a therapeutic and pragmatic process, should not be underestimated. All planning involves splitting up the problem and setting boundaries of time and responsibility within which the situation will be managed. However, some practitioners feel that it was all for nothing when some external event causes the plan to 'fall apart' or at best appear redundant. This falls into the trap of viewing planning as a static event rather than a dynamic process subject to continuous modification. Many people become service users precisely because crises, or negative events over which they have no control, are regular features of their lives. To engage with them in developing the planning skills to manage these events is a crucial professional task.

Managerial versus professional objectives

It has been argued that throughout the 1990s, managerialism triumphed over professionalism in the community care sphere in particular (for example Cowen,

1999). A culture in which quantitative, material outcomes override qualitative factors such as a 'good' working relationship has an immediate impact on care planning. The practitioner may assess an older person as grieving the death of their spouse and therefore neglecting self-care. They may wish to offer counselling and/ or other forms of social contact such as a volunteer visitor, while monitoring the risk from neglect, but the GP's referral is for home care. One hour's home care per day is possible within current resources, demonstrates a response to the assessment made by another professional, and contributes to area statistics as an identifiable outcome in a way that ongoing emotional support does not. This is precisely where the skilled use of planning allows the merging of a number of objectives. The service user, previously very independent, may be happy to accept home care for a trial period since it represents some company. The care manager may use the planning process to allow the older person to air their feelings about 'not wanting to be bothered anymore'. The home carer brings to the situation another listening ear. A planned review suggests to the service user that they may not always feel like this and can consider whether or not they need the service to continue; it allows the care manager to monitor the level of risk and whether the need continues, has changed or has now been met. What is important is that each of these elements is identified within the plan and that objectives are set, which can be monitored and result in identifiable outcomes.

Problematic partnerships with users

The age-old problem of disagreement about the terms of the working contract between worker and service user becomes particularly acute when there is a requirement to draw up a written plan. However, the explicit nature of a plan is also its strength. So, for example, a child protection plan, which is imaginatively put together and skilfully used in the ensuing interactions, provides the framework that both supports the worker in carrying out their statutory duty and gives a clear agenda for the parents.

CASE EXAMPLE

Lisa is 19 years old and has a daughter, Melanie, of 15 months. She had spent most of her teenage years in care. Lisa has a history of heroin use and is currently on a methadone maintenance programme, supervised by the community drugs team (CDT). Although Lisa managed to stay mostly drug free once she knew she was pregnant, Melanie does appear to have some degree of developmental delay and six months ago was put in the care of the local authority because Lisa was leaving her alone at night while she worked as a prostitute. There are a number of workers involved. By agreement between agencies, Lisa herself is primarily supported by her key worker from the CDT, although a pathway plan (of sorts) had been drawn up before she left care. Melanie's case is carried by a social worker from the children and families intake team, but consideration is being given to moving her case on for permanency planning.

A number of formal plans have been, or are currently, in place:

1   A contract has been drawn up between Lisa and the CDT, which governs her continuing on the methadone programme.
2   Melanie was originally the subject of a child in need plan, but now has a care plan for a child in care. These arrangements are overseen by the children's guardian and independent reviewing officer.

There are thus parallel planning processes going on. From one perspective, the key to the overall management of this case, given the interdependence between Lisa's and Melanie's welfare, the principle of involving Lisa in planning for Melanie's future and the interrelationship of health, social and emotional needs, is the plan agreed between the key worker and Lisa as part of the ongoing intervention process. It is from the perspective of the objectives of this plan, and the review of its progress, that the CDT worker will contribute her knowledge and professional assessment to multidisciplinary discussions, will support and empower Lisa to be actively involved in planning her own and Melanie's care, and will sometimes negotiate with other agencies on Lisa's behalf. Moreover, the relationship that develops between Lisa and the CDT worker as a necessary ingredient in the planning process has the potential to be, of itself, of therapeutic benefit and an agent for change. Social workers and officers managing Melanie's care planning, on the other hand, will have primary concern for her immediate and longer term welfare.

The plan

Aims:

1   For Lisa to detox from methadone and ultimately become drug free.
2   For Lisa to stabilise her lifestyle so as to be able to offer parenting to Melanie.
3   In the short term, this means that Lisa should develop her understanding of Melanie's needs and contribute to discussions about Melanie's care options.

Strategy:

1   To identify 'risk' factors in Lisa's lifestyle and explore options for managing these.
2   To identify activities that both act as a diversion and enhance Lisa's social networks and skills.

Actions:

1 The CDT worker identifies and introduces Lisa to a 'street' project working with women in the sex industry.
2 Lisa begins to regularly attend sessions concerned with parenting young children at the women's drop-in centre run by project workers from the New Deal for Communities.
3 Lisa identifies that she would like to attend a gym, to increase her fitness and boost her self-esteem and hence confidence. The CDT worker agrees to explore options for funding this.

In the course of developing and implementing this plan, the worker has to draw on counselling skills and motivational interviewing techniques. Throughout, she offers constant encouragement and emotional support. However, despite a coherent plan, developed in partnership with Lisa, progress is hampered by a number of the issues and dilemmas identified in this chapter:

1 The relationship with Lisa has to be managed in the context of national and local drug strategies. Thus, the outcome that is most important to Lisa – regaining a parenting role with Melanie – has to be related to the outcome that is of prime significance for the agency, that she should in the longer term become drug free. While the worker is able to use the aim of being seen as a responsible parent as a powerful motivating factor for Lisa to pursue the detox programme, it is also necessary to find shorter term objectives that could demonstrate outcomes which in themselves are of less significance for Lisa but are important to the agency. So, for example, a counselling programme aimed at relapse prevention assumes priority over discussion of Lisa's feelings about herself as a parent. However, by focusing on Lisa's problems with low self-esteem, it is possible to integrate these two objectives to an extent.
2 There is a clear conflict between rehabilitation objectives for Lisa and permanency objectives for Melanie. Melanie's review at six months had concluded that it was important to start planning for her longer term future now, while Lisa had at this point not long entered the methadone programme. It is necessary for the different professionals to work hard at using their specialist expertise as complementary contributions rather than competing perspectives. A compromise is negotiated in which the pursuit of the CDT's plan of intervention forms part of a contract between Lisa and the childcare team governing contact arrangements until Melanie's next review.
3 The only suggestion volunteered by Lisa was that she would like to attend a gym. Despite this being linked to the boosting of her self-confidence, the worker is unable to obtain funding to enable Lisa to pursue this activity. To some degree, this is compensated for by the worker liaising with the women's centre to iden-

tify other confidence-boosting activities and supporting Lisa in getting involved with these, but they lack the 'fun' element and access to a mainstream lifestyle that Lisa desires.

Planning and the reflexive practitioner

This chapter, and Lisa's case example, has emphasised that planning is much more than a technical exercise used to link assessments to interventions. Payne (1995) argues that it is a human interaction. It occupies the core ground in many frontline service delivery dilemmas and utilises a range of social work skills. The setting of objectives and agreement about desired outcomes requires a conscious reflection on the inherent value position and tests and stretches the practitioner's commitment to working in partnership with the service user. The creation of the elements in the plan and its implementation require a diverse knowledge base spanning human behaviour, social structures, policy frameworks and local resources. Thus planning is very much the business of the reflexive practitioner. It incorporates Schön's notion of 'reflection-in-action' (Schön, 1983) and demands the critical thinking skills of 'reflective scepticism' (which challenges the notion that there is only one way of doing things) and 'imagining and creating alternatives' (Brookfield, 1987). It does so cognisant of policy and social context.

Conclusion

Social work has at its heart the tension of intervening in a rational, ordered way, which can demonstrate what it has done and why, in contexts that are marked by instability and crisis at both individual and corporate levels. This chapter has discussed the planning task as one which facilitates the practitioner holding onto core values and essential objectives, while maintaining the goal of creative, empowering interventions in situations marked by constraint and dilemma. As such it holds the key to practice that is, at the same time, a reflexive and a managed response.

For further discussion of care management, see Adams et al., 2009b, Chapter 28 and for discussion of working with care plans, see Adams et al., 2009b, Chapters 29 to 32.

www.in-control.org.uk   A good example of a service user-led movement.

DH (Department of Health) (2001) *Children Act Now: Messages from Research*, London, TSO. Analyses the links between legislation and policy implementation.

Hatton, C., Waters, J., Duffy, S. et al. (2008) *A Report on in Control's Second Phase: Evaluation and Learning 2005–2007*, Birmingham, in Control Publications. Detailed account from the perspective of service users involved in planning their own care, which highlights key issues and dilemmas and suggests some ways forward.

McNeish, D., Newman, T. and Roberts, H. (eds) (2002) *What Works for Children? Effective Services for Children and Families*, Buckingham, Open University Press. Provides a good overview of an evidence-based planning process in children's services.

Parker, J. and Bradley, G. (2003) *Social Work Practice: Assessment, Planning, Intervention and Review*, Exeter, Learning Matters. A handbook for practice, focused on the requirements for the social work degree.

Payne, M. (1995) *Social Work and Community Care*, Basingstoke, Macmillan – now Palgrave Macmillan. Provides a detailed discussion of care planning in adult services following the introduction of care management and locates this in a broad discussion of social work intervention, traditional social work relationship skills being described as the 'glue' that holds the care plan together.

Wheal, A. (ed.) (2002) *The RHP Companion to Leaving Care*, Dorset, Russell House Publishing. A guide written for practitioners, carers and young people.

Acknowledgement

I am grateful to my colleagues Dave Marsland and Caroline Humphrey for their observations on current policy and practice in adult services and children and families respectively. The responsibility for incorporating this is, however, wholly mine.

NIGEL HORNER

18 Understanding intervention

Chapter overview

This chapter acknowledges the somewhat ambiguous situation of intervention, viewed as a distinct phase in the practice sequence, and as beginning from the moment a practitioner takes on a new case. We begin the process of understanding what is entailed in intervening by discussing what is involved in intervention and evaluating different models of practice used by social workers as forms of intervention.

The *Online Medical Dictionary* defines intervention as 'the act or fact of interfering so as to *modify*'. However, we need to acknowledge that beyond the general definition of intervention:

> We have only the most general ideas of what we are trying to produce, what constitutes the essential skill of the social worker, and consequently still more varied ideas of how to set about it. (Younghusband, 1959: 28)

When Dame Eileen Younghusband produced the report on the roles and tasks of social workers at the end of the 1950s, few would have guessed that half a century later, the profession is still grappling with the same questions, albeit framed in different language. In order to address Younghusband's conundrum today, we need to know what it is social workers are trying to achieve. Indeed, once such clarity of purpose has been established, then the necessary skill set follows, as does the requisite training. So, the key question for us to consider is: 'What is it social workers are trying to achieve?' This question has routinely been addressed by reference to the concept of intervention.

For many years, writers have conceived of the social work process as a sequential – be it linear or circular – set of stages or tasks, which have often been referred to by the acronyms of APIE (assessment, planning, implementation and evaluation), APIR (assessment, planning, implementation and review), or the composite ASPIRE (assessment, planning, intervention, review and evaluation) (Sutton, 1999). This is how social work is presented in this series of chapters.

In this chapter, we will examine whether intervention – seen as a core component in this practice sequence – can indeed be realistically seen as a distinct phase, or whether it is more the case that practice intervention in fact begins from the moment that a practitioner is made aware of a referral, supporting the assertion of Compton and Galaway (1999) that 'intervention begins on day one'. Moreover, one could suggest that an agency's intervention begins from the moment it allows a referral to be made to it (Walker and Beckett, 2003: 22). We will consider the models of practice used by social workers as forms of intervention and evaluate their effectiveness or fitness for purpose within contemporary social work practice formations.

Why we need to talk about intervention?

'Social work is not an exact science and will never be an activity that could be performed satisfactorily simply by mechanically applying rules' (Beckett, 2006: 197).

In one sense, it might be more profitable to refer to the 'idea' of intervention, because of its representing the essence of what we as social workers do. Social work is a 'doing' profession: it is not an academic activity that can languish in the relatively calm backwaters of theoretical observation and analysis, it is a vocational practical activity. By giving itself the epithets of 'social' and 'work' – and the consequential associations with the arenas of tasks and labour within an interactive human setting – it announces itself as an expression of a commitment 'to do something'. Such an imperative for action flows not only from an internally generated moral obligation to 'help', but also from a contractual requirement to act arising from the social worker's generally salaried position within the labour market.

The internationally endorsed, adopted and generally accepted definition of social work affirms that it intervenes in people's lives to achieve changes:

> The social work profession promotes social change, problem solving in human relationships and empowerment and liberation of people to enhance well-being. Utilising theories of human behaviour and social systems, social work *intervenes* at the points where people interact with their environments. Principles of human rights and social justice are fundamental to social work. (IFSW, 2000, emphasis added)

So, it is fair to assume that social workers are engaged in intervention behaviours, not least by virtue of the nature of the task, but also because people other than social work practitioners themselves largely determine what they actually do. Social workers are usually employees – traditionally of local and central government structures, but increasingly of independent and voluntary organisations, or even now of service user groups and individuals – and those who pay expect results. Employers expect a difference to be made, a transformation of circumstances, a change in the situation; in other words, they want to see results and value for money.

In one sense, it has long been recognised that social work is a chameleon-like activity, with a proven capacity to change its identity to suit its purchaser. It appears to be easily bought, readily switching from an emancipatory, liberationist position to one of social control and the regulation of otherness. As David Howe (2002: 86) observes: 'In the broadest sense, the purposes of social work are determined by prevailing political ideologies', and the Quality Assurance Agency (QAA, 2008) social work benchmark statement likewise affirms that:

> Social work adapts and changes in response to social, political and economic challenges and the demands of contemporary social welfare policy, practice and legislation.

So, at one level, the answer to the question 'What is social work intervention?' can be 'It is whatever the employer tells you it is.' Increasingly, practitioners in social work and related agencies – such as youth offending services or the probation service – are delivering interventions that are prescribed by the service as evidence of 'what works'. In other words, the emergence of an expectation of research-informed, evidence-based practice has resulted, in some areas of work, in a narrowing of the palette from which intervention options may be drawn. In reviewing these intervention options, government policy has asserted increasingly that decisions should be informed less by personal or professional preference and 'opinions' and more by an appreciation of 'what works' and relevant 'evidence' of practice effectiveness (DH, 1998a).

The meaning of intervention

From the outset, we acknowledge that the term 'intervention' itself merits some analysis. In social and political terms, the word 'intervention' indicates the moment when powers react to a problem, and move in to interrupt a set of adverse situations, such as crowd trouble, a 'domestic incident' (usually a euphemism for domestic violence), a rising sense of tension in a public domain, such as a gathering of young people in public space, or a public protest at a meeting of world trade leaders. Those empowered to act within such a scenario, such as police officers, weigh up the situation (an assessment of risk) and try to balance the merits of action (intervention) against the merits of inaction (or non-intervention).

On a macro-political scale, governments – either alone or in alliance with others – assess the merits and risks of intervention in the domestic affairs of other states. Their 'intervention levels' may range from public comment, diplomatic influence, economic sanctions (or incentives), military threats and finally to limited or extensive military intervention, with the implicitly or explicitly articulated objective of 'regime change'.

To adapt the macro-political analogy to the micro-social arena of social work practice, we can see that the process of assessment (in answering the question: what's going on?) forms the basis for considering a range of intervention options (in response to the core question: what are we going to do about it?). This key question also leads to a set of other questions for the social work practitioner:

- Do I have to do anything?
- Do I wish to do something?
- What is to be gained by doing nothing?
- What is to be gained by doing something?
- What are the likely outcomes of any of my interventions/actions?
- Who decides which interventions I can offer?
- How I do know which ones are effective?

We will briefly review the historical antecedents of practice interventions before exploring the relative merits of intervention approaches.

From treatment to intervention: a historical perspective

> You and your doctors with your appalling so-called professionalism, which is nothing more than a series of verbal tricks to prevent you relating to your patients as human beings. (Clark, 1993)

In Brian Clark's play, first published in 1972, the 'patient' Ken Harrison is faced with an enduring life of ever-increasing dependency and physical deterioration. He rails against the consequences of medical professionalism that leads to the dehumanisation of patients. Yet social work as an emerging profession has often been seduced by the attractiveness of the apparent certainty in medicine. Mary Richmond, one of the earliest theorists of social casework, produced her seminal text *Social Diagnosis* in 1917 (Richmond, 1917). The deliberate and studied use of medical language is significant, in that traditional Western medicine had developed a positivist version of practice that claimed to progressively establish a body of knowledge that would be characterised by evidence, facts, classification, a claim to objectivity, universalism, and proof. Such practice was not to be contingent on engagement with the patient, in fact, quite the reverse.

An essential tenet of scientific modernity asserted that a skilled medical practitioner would, with the appropriate set of knowledge and skills, be able to correctly and repeatedly diagnose a set of conditions or symptoms – such as an inflamed appendix – and that their colleagues would, with similar knowledge and skills, repeatedly come to same conclusion. Consequently, diagnosis – the medical model equivalent to assessment – is seen to logically lead to a prognosis, or a preferred intervention (or procedure). The medical profession has a lengthy, laudable and celebrated research tradition, developing the fields of epidemiology (patterns of incidence of disease), the study of causation and strategies for prevention (often leading to public health initiatives), and the evaluation of clinical effectiveness (to promote 'best practice' in terms of intervention and procedures).

To summarise this legacy of modernity, Fook (2002: 11) asserts that:

> the characteristic feature of the modernist world is the belief that conditions can be progressively bettered through the establishment of reliable, universal and generalisable knowledge, developed through the use of reason and scientific methods.

We can therefore consider the question as to whether such a modernist view pertains to the business of social work practice. Walker and Beckett (2003: 22) state that 'the orthodox literature tends to emphasise the separation of assessment and intervention in social work practice, while practice guidance from central government unwittingly reinforces the impression', yet the same authors go on to suggest that this is neither helpful nor an accurate reflection of what actually occurs in practice. Indeed, Lishman (2007a: 9) offers a sequence of sections that move from 'understanding' to 'assessment' to 'intervention' and then to 'an appropriate intervention', but rightly cautions against seeing this as a simplistic linear or causal process, and suggests 'that we need to be careful not to assume that an initial assessment automatically leads to a specific method of intervention'. They are not in reality separate events, but are interlinked, interwoven and often enmeshed.

Parker (2007: 118) suggests that 'intervention follows from and is bound together with assessment and planning and relates to the methods and models to be used to achieve changes or outcomes that have been identified and agreed'. Thus by using Sibeon's typology of theory (1989), we can see intervention as essentially an exploration of theories of how to do social work (as distinct from theories of the client's world and theories of what social work is).

Table 18.1 Applying Sibeon's typology of theory to practice with disabled people

Theories of the client's world	Theories of what social work is	Theories of how to do social work
1 The social model of disability 2 Living in a disabling society 3 Theories of personal construct and identity politics 4 Social exclusion and disadvantage 5 Educational and employment inclusion	1 Social work is a discipline that promotes social change, problem-solving in human relationships and the empowerment and liberation of people to enhance wellbeing 2 A profession with a value base that promotes inclusion and challenges discrimination 3 An activity that promotes user empowerment, resulting in user and carer-led services	How are we going to achieve change? 1 By working with the individual (counselling/personal brief therapy)? 2 By working with the individual and their context (systems working, networking, advocacy)? 3 By working with those with connected needs facing common challenges (groupwork, collective action)? 4 By working with users and carers at a macro-political level to challenge discriminatory and disabling processes (structural action)?

Interestingly, when introducing the requirements for the new social work degree in 2003, Jacqui Smith, the former UK minister for health, stated that social work 'is a very practical job not about being able to give a … theoretical explanation of why [people] got into difficulties in the first place' (quoted in Horner, 2006: 3). In other words, it was being suggested that theories of the client's world are less important than knowing what you are going to do about it. This is indeed an entirely fallacious assertion, as the appropriate selection of an intervention flows inexorably from and reflects the assessment, which it turn should always be based on theories of explanation, of understanding.

The dominant canon of intervention literature

In recent decades, social work has celebrated its detachment from the dominant medical discourse, particularly as it has historically pertained to people with learning disabilities, physical disabilities, sensory impairments and mental health issues. Thus social work has advanced its own sequential model of assessment leading to planning, intervention and review – as distinct from diagnosis, prognosis and treatment. That said, the advent of a social model discourse has tended to produce literature that has significantly enriched thinking about how service users are made into clients, how their rights are largely ignored, how processes of discrimination and oppression perpetuate their dependent status, but there has been remarkably little change in the literature concerning intervention as such.

Most textbooks purporting to summarise and examine the range of social work intervention models have certain methods in common. Task-centred practice, crisis intervention, groupwork, psychosocial or psychodynamic work, systems approaches, counselling, behavioural/cognitive behavioural approaches were all central features of the core texts of 20 years ago summarising theory and methods (Howe, 1987; Lishman, 1991; Payne, 1991) and they appear again in one form or other in Trevithick (2000), Payne (2005), Beckett (2006) and Lishman (2007a). What is remarkable, in fact, is the level of consistency across the decades, but we can see other ways of conceptualising practice when we consider less Eurocentric or Anglo-centric paradigms.

To this end, it is worthwhile considering a significant portion of the definition of social work as produced by the International Federation of Social Workers (IFSW, 2000):

> Social work interventions range from primarily person-focused psychosocial processes to involvement in social policy, planning and development. These include counselling, clinical social work, group work, social pedagogical work, and family treatment and therapy as well as efforts to help people obtain services and resources in the community. Interventions also include agency administration, community organisation and engaging in social and political action to impact social policy and economic development. The holistic focus of social work is universal, but the priorities of social work practice will vary from country to country and from time to time depending on cultural, historical, and socio-economic conditions.

From a British perspective, this extract is illuminating for two reasons:

1 Interventions at the macro-level of policy, planning and development are seen as of equal status alongside more traditional person-centred psychosocial interactions.
2 The illustrative list of interventions includes social pedagogy, groupwork and counselling, which have been largely eliminated from British social work's established toolbox of activities.

The result of intervention: the concepts of effectiveness and outcomes

The purpose of an intervention is clearly to achieve an effect, to produce change, to achieve an outcome. An outcome may be defined as: 'the final condition of clients and/or their situation after the intervention as compared to this condition and/or situation at the start of the intervention.'

Clearly the outcome will be determined by the intervention method used, as different interventions will have different objectives, to which we will turn soon. Nevertheless, in spite of these differences of approach, McNeill et al. (2005) found three consistently identified elements in successful interventions that lead to behaviour change or reduction in problem behaviours:

- empathy, respect or warmth and therapeutic genuineness
- establishing a therapeutic relationship or working alliance, that is, mutual understanding and agreement about the nature and purpose of the intervention
- an approach that is person centred, or collaborative and client driven, that is, taking the client's perspective and using the client's concepts.

Similarly, the Shaping Our Lives organisation (2007) emphasised the importance of relationships as the cornerstone, the bedrock, the foundation of any form of intervention, stating that:

> People value a social work approach based on challenging the broader barriers they face. They place a particular value on social work's social approach, the social work relationship, and the positive personal qualities they associate with social workers. These include warmth, respect, being non-judgemental, listening, treating people with equality, being trustworthy, open, honest and reliable, and communicating well. People value the support that social workers offer as well as their ability to help them access and deal with other services and agencies.

O'Connor et al. (2006: 107) are entirely vindicated in asserting that intervention begins with 'building relationships and the purposeful use of self'.

We can therefore propose that the term 'intervention' refers to a planned set of actions that are inextricably linked to an initial contact phase in which needs are identified and assessed, establishing the grounds for action, and that the mode of intervention itself, by virtue of being a human interactive process, is a key determinant in the achievement of desired, successful outcomes. But is this how students and practitioners see things?

A research summary: what do students understand by intervention?

A small-scale research activity undertaken with 68 second- and third-year students enrolled on the social work degree course sought to explore their understanding of the concept of social work intervention, to examine what interventions they thought they had been using while engaged on their practice learning opportunity (practice placement) and to examine the literature used by practice assessors to help them understand intervention options.

The results revealed significant difficulties in grasping the concept of intervention.

Finding one: For most of the respondents who had been placed in the voluntary and independent sector, the term 'intervention' had not been used at all by practice supervisors, mentors, assessors or others.

Finding two: For the majority of those students who did refer to the term 'intervention' (whether placed in the statutory or independent/voluntary sector), its meaning was most likely to be seen as synonymous with statutory, that is, legal, action. Furthermore, the term 'intervention' was used repeatedly to describe activities that fall into four broad categories associated with the operation of statutory responsibilities:

1 Assessment and planning, using the Common Assessment Framework, risk assessment and management systems, safeguarding plans, community care assessments, care planning
2 Packages of service delivery, associated with commissioning and securing such services as family support, home care, respite care, daycare
3 Principles of service provision, such as partnership working, establishing user-led services or working collaboratively
4 Models of practice intervention, as listed below, with the number in brackets indicating the frequency of identification:
   – **Crisis intervention** (15)
   – Task-centred practice (3)
   – CBT (1)
   – Pro-social modelling (1)
   – Counselling (1)
   – Play therapy (1)

Crisis intervention refers generally to methods of providing short-term help to those faced with sudden problems, including not only illnesses or bereavements but also natural disasters or flight from armed conflicts. In social work, crisis intervention originated in the mental health practice of two community psychiatrists, Erich Lindemann and Gerald Caplan, in the 1940s and has since become more multifaceted.

Finding three: When asked to identify relevant sources of literature, students readily listed authors who help in 'understanding the service user's world' by offering theories of explanation – such as authors of lifespan or human develop-ment models, or theories about life course events, such as attachment, loss or bereavement. Students found it much more difficult to identify authors who are more usually associated with models of intervention, treatment or therapy. The notable and significant exceptions to this finding came from students who had had practice learning opportunities in focused service settings (such as substance misuse services, youth offending teams or child and adolescent mental health services). Such students were readily able to identify the relevant practice literature that underpinned the interventions as learned, practised and evaluated.

Taking the debate forward

So how is the concept of 'intervention' to have operational value within complex, multiprofessional working environments that characterise the reality of contempo-rary social work practice?

Higher education institutions, as programme providers, have made important strides in ensuring the acquisition of an acknowledged base for informed practice in terms of theories concerning the nature of problems and issues, but are perhaps less adept at meeting the QAA (2008) benchmark requirement concerning 'approaches and methods of intervention in a range of settings, including factors guiding the choice and evaluation of these'.

Students and practitioners need to be empowered to recognise social work inter-vention for what it is – an intervention into the lives of others that represents one of a number of different options. The key question needs to be: 'What is the evidence base for this being the preferred and most effective way of working?' As Whittaker (1974: 108) recognised over 30 years ago, this all matters because 'the choice of theo-retical orientation has a great deal to do with shaping the atmosphere of the therapeutic encounter between client and worker'.

Intervention levels and categories

One way of trying to effectively manage the demand for interventions is to establish priority or eligibility processes based on an assessment of need. We can see, in the example below, that Dennis's access to drug treatment services would be determined by an assessment of need in relation to a four-tier framework.

CASE EXAMPLE

Dennis

Dennis, aged 30, has been engaged in long-term, persistent use of heroin. He has had periodic casual employment and has usually lived in shared accom-modation with other drug users. He has moved around Britain and Europe and has now returned to the town of his childhood, mainly because his mother is critically ill. He is trying to balance his new role as a carer with efforts to manage his drug habit. To this end, he has approached a drugs and alcohol agency for help. Dennis is also keen to re-establish a relationship with his 12-year-old daughter, who lives five miles away. He has not seen her for nine years.

Intervention issues

For many services, an initial assessment will seek to identify the appropriate response in terms of graded tiers or levels of intervention. Accordingly, the National Treatment Agency for Substance Misuse (2006) has split the different types of service available into four tiers:

Tier 1: Non-substance-specific service providers – this tier consists of a range of interventions that can be provided by generic providers, including social workers, depending on their competence, and partnership arrangements with specialised drug services.

Tier 2: Open access drug services – interventions that are geared to engaging people in treatment, supporting people through to more structured treatment, providing aftercare services and working with people to keep drug free. For example, advice and information services, drop-in services, needle exchange, outreach, **motivational interviewing** and brief interventions.

> **Motivational interviewing** is a counselling approach based on collaborative exploration, in a supportive rather than persuasive way, enabling a person to grow and change rather than attempting to change them.

Tier 3: Structured drug services – interventions that require a greater degree of structure and care planning than tier 2, for example structured counselling, day programmes, detox programmes, prescribing, offenders on drug treatment and testing orders, regular key working and case management, related aftercare.

Tier 4: Residential services – interventions include inpatient detox and rehabilitation services, residential crisis services.

Dennis would almost certainly enter at tier 2 – his relationship with the service would be voluntary, he currently seems motivated to address his levels of substance misuse, and the time might be opportune to effect a change, given his commitment to his mother's needs and his stated desire to establish contact with his daughter. He may even progress to tier 3 intervention programmes. However, the tier of intervention merely identifies a cluster of treatment options, but still does not identify what actual form of intervention would be most helpful for Dennis. (We will return to intervention options later.)

Triage and prioritising intervention

For many agencies engaged in active service delivery (intervention), the matching of demand with resources means a daily or even hourly reappraisal of need, which in emergency health settings results in a triage process – defined as the prioritisation of patients according to their problems within A&E departments (Mackway-Jones, 1997). Interventions are prioritised so that maximum effort and resource are directed to those in group 1 (to be seen immediately) down to group 5 (who will only be seen once those in groups 1, 2, 3 and 4 have been seen).

In social work terms, the equivalence of such systems operates in the allocation of cases in relation to child protection and safeguarding, and strategies for the protection of vulnerable adults.

Choosing modes of intervention

Although triage or levels of priority may indicate the levels at which intervention may be offered – and indeed the speed at which action may be taken – as noted in the case of Dennis, the perplexed practitioner may still have to identify an appropriate intervention method. We will consider below, in relation to the case of Dorothy, how this process might unfold.

◇◇◇ CASE EXAMPLE ◇◇◇

Dorothy

Dorothy is aged 92. Although widowed over 30 years ago, Dorothy has lived a full, active and satisfying life. In her youth and early adulthood, she was involved in various amateur operatic societies, and although she would have liked to have had children, sadly this never happened. She lived for 25 years with her only sister, who died 15 years ago. She then lived on her own in a flat until two years ago, when she was hospitalised with a perforated bowel, and subsequently had a colostomy. She was admitted to a nursing home as she has high-dependency needs in terms of personal and medical care. Dorothy has periods of feeling very low and depressed – she finds her current life entirely devoid of meaning and periodically she refuses to eat, as if she is trying to end her life through starvation.

Humanistic psychology or counselling stems from the 1950s, when it challenged both psychoanalytic and behavioural approaches. It is based on the assumption that the practitioner should assert the worth and dignity of other people.

Intervention options

The relevant intervention activity has to be in terms of existential, humanistic practice, for instance, drawing on **humanistic psychology** in interviewing. We can, in part, demonstrate its relevance by systematically eliminating other options.

This is not a crisis, as it is an ongoing, 'meaning-of-life' issue that confronts Dorothy. Task-centred work is not relevant as no tasks are to be achieved. Groupwork would be neither relevant nor ethical, as the issues confronting Dorothy are essentially and undeniably personal, private and intensely difficult. This is not an ecological/systems problem in terms of the lack of available resources or difficulties in accessing such resources. It is not a psychosocial problem rooted in the past, other than in terms of the fact that Dorothy might, conceivably, have found greater meaning in her continued existence if she had had children, grandchildren and other relatives around her, although that remains conjecture. There is no need for a cognitive behavioural intervention, as we are not trying to address problematic thought patterns, unless we are trying to suggest that Dorothy's thoughts are in themselves problematic. Empowerment or advocacy models are not relevant as Dorothy is not trying to achieve more power in terms of her rights or access to resources.

By a process of deduction, we can arrive back at where we would probably have started – confronted by a humanistic, existential and spiritual dilemma. The main problem for Dorothy is that the nursing/care staff do not want to talk to her about these deep issues. Their responses – often exhorting her to cheer up, to join in the centre's activities, to look forward to better days, to 'look on the bright side' – are experienced as well meaning yet infantilising and patronising.

The required intervention is a human relationship that acknowledges and does not deny or minimise the existential struggle of the 'other', that allows a space in which such thoughts, feelings and ideas can be explored, without censure or critique, and which carries the hallmark of self-determination. Such practice can only operate within a system that can embrace risk, rather than being risk averse. Indeed, Beresford et al. (2006) show that creative, humanistic social work intervention is at its most effective in the underresearched arena of palliative care.

Multidisciplinary interventions: identifying common ground

The work of John Heron (2001) identifies broadly six different intervention strategies that pertain to any helping roles, whether undertaken by those engaged in medicine, nursing, teaching, counselling, medicine, social care, or social work itself.

These six intervention modes fall into two groups:

Authoritative interventions

- *Prescriptive interventions:* Directive, giving advice, setting goals and plans
- *Informative interventions:* Imparting knowledge, interpreting and sharing information

■ *Confronting interventions:* Addressing issues of behaviour, challenging unaccept-able or undesired patterns or presentations.

Facilitative interventions
■ *Cathartic interventions:* Enabling the release or discharge of complex, difficult, emotional issues in a safe enabling environment
■ *Catalytic interventions:* Facilitating self-discovery, self-actualisation and empowerment
■ *Supportive interventions:* Seeking to affirm worth and value of the individual, family, group or community.

Heron's model enables interventions to be evaluated in terms of their meta-meanings, and to acknowledge that service providers need to evaluate their practice in terms of whether there is a systemic consonance or dissonance between the service user's expectations and the service provider's mode of intervention delivery.

Although, as we have seen, the term 'intervention' may have lost its potency in many social work practice settings, it remains a core concept in medicine, nursing, mental health practice, in addressing special educational needs, and in housing and community work (as we will see from later examples). The research summary earlier shows that social work students have become accustomed to seeing only statutory, legal, mandatory work as being an 'intervention', and thus only operating with Heron's notion of confronting interventions. The other five modes of practice would often not be described as interventions, but indeed they are. Because social work, particularly in childcare settings, has come to see prevention as meaning 'the preven-tion of children coming into public care', then earlier involvement in terms of family support is not seen as an intervention, although it might be highly facilitative, and, most importantly, effective.

◇◇◇◇ CASE EXAMPLE ◇◇◇◇◇◇◇◇◇◇◇◇◇◇◇◇◇◇◇◇◇◇◇◇◇◇◇◇◇◇◇◇◇◇◇◇◇

The McIntosh/Johnson family

The family comprise Kirsty McIntosh (aged 27), Jake Johnson (aged 25) and their two children Ashley (aged 7) and Jessica (4). For some time, concerns from various agencies – health visitor, the children's centre, GP, community psychiatric nurse – have been recorded about the welfare of the children and the general functioning within the family unit. Kirsty has been treated for depression for the past three years. The identified areas of concern relate to poor (negative) parenting skills, the impact of Kirsty's depression on the children's wellbeing and neglect in terms of problematic hygiene standards.

Intervention levels and options

Before we consider intervention as a response to developing concerns, let us reflect upon prevention as a form of early intervention. The common distinction between 'prevention' and 'intervention' can be problematic, as it implies that preventive strategies are not themselves an intervention. Conversely, early intervention strategies have been absorbed into broad notions of prevention. Writing from a health perspective, Williams et al. (2005: 93) differentiate between the two as follows:

> Prevention refers to strategies or programmes that prevent or delay the onset of health and behaviour problems, while early *intervention* refers to strategies and programmes that reduce the harms and health consequences of behaviours that have been initiated.

Little and Mount (1999: 48–9) made a similar distinction in relation to services for children in need:

- *prevention:* activity to stop a social or psychological problem happening in the first place
- *early intervention:* activity aimed at stopping those at highest risk of developing social or psychological problems, or those who show the first signs of difficulty from displaying unnecessarily long or serious symptoms.

Furthermore, the same authors identified two other types of activity:

- *intervention or treatment* that seeks to stabilise or achieve realistic outcomes among those seriously affected by a problem
- *social prevention*, which is aimed at reducing the negative effects of a child's social or psychological problems on themselves or other people.

Thus we can see that for the McIntosh/Johnson family, all agencies need to develop a shared language to locate and define their interventions. Although agency representatives are beginning to talk in terms of high levels of concern about the children's welfare, the response could be seen as early intervention (recognising that the time for prevention has passed). What modes of intervention could be considered?

In relation to treating depression (as in Kirsty's scenario), Golightley (2004: 101) notes that the 'the most likely success will come from a treatment approach that will embrace a combination of anti-depressants and psychosocial support'.

By psychosocial support, we mean 'talking therapy' and engaging with Kirsty using cognitive behavioural therapy, task-centred work or solution-focused work.

We will explore the essential features of these intervention models by considering the case example of Jed.

◇◇◇◇ CASE EXAMPLE ◇◇◇

Jed

Jed (aged 15) lives with his mother Clare, her partner Errol and their daughter Charmaine (aged 12). He has no contact with his birth father.

Jed has had various difficulties in recent years. He has a poor school attendance record and the family have been involved with the Education Welfare Service. He has had two periods of suspension from school, on both occasions arising from verbal aggression towards teaching and support staff. Jed's behaviour has also been a source of concern for the police and the youth offending service, mainly to do with his membership of a 'street gang' who often verbally taunt and abuse members of the public in the evenings. Concerns about his behaviour have led to conflicts with neighbours, leading to the police being involved in managing public disorder incidents. There are now allegations of racist attacks on the family.

Intervention options

The Education Welfare Service is required by statute to promote school attendance, which is non-negotiable. However, this is a family that merits a holistic, systemic approach, given that Jed's behaviour – and the family's response to it – is leading to an uneasy and unstable relationship with others in their community. To that end, the family could be referred to an intensive parenting programme. In recent years, there has been a significant investment in such programmes, which provide parents with an opportunity to improve their skills in dealing with the behaviour that puts their child at risk of offending. The programmes offer parents and carers one-to-one advice as well as practical support in handling the behaviour of their child, setting appropriate boundaries and improving communication.

On such programmes, the intervention methods may combine:

- The Webster–Stratton 'incredible years' programme
- Mellow parenting
- The 'strengthening families' programme
- Multisystemic therapy.

These approaches are rooted in a nexus of specific theoretical frameworks:

- Changing problem behaviours by empowering parents/carers to engage in positive parenting – behaviour modification approaches
- Equipping parents/carers with skills in boundary-setting, positive communication, rewarding appropriate behaviours – empowering parents through acquiring behaviour modification strategies
- Emphasising what the family already does well and building upon those capabilities – strengths-based work

- Challenging negative thought patterns and developing positive thinking (changing schemas) – CBT work
- Breaking down desired goals into small, manageable, bite-sized chunks of work – task-centred work
- Working with the 'minimum sufficient network' of parents/carers/relatives/siblings to change the system of family functioning – family systemic work
- Promoting support systems and connectivity to reduce isolation, loneliness and to share coping strategies – neighbourhood development, groupwork, networking.

Evaluating parenting programmes

By improving the parenting skills of parents/carers, parenting programmes are addressing one of the major risk factors associated with young people at risk of offending. In the eyes of the government: 'Intensive family based interventions are essential if the deepest rooted anti-social behaviour (ASB) problems are not to be recycled from one area to another' (DCLG, 2006).

Sheffield Hallam University conducted an evaluation of six family support projects in northwest England. The study revealed:

- An 85 per cent reduction in complaints about antisocial behaviour
- A 36 per cent improvement in school attendance
- An 80 per cent reduction in the risk of homelessness.

Conclusion

In this chapter, we have considered intervention as a part of a process, and recognised that any response to a social problem or situation is indeed a form of intervention itself. That said, we have sought to demonstrate that within the wider language of health, education and social care services, the term 'intervention' is synonymous with treatment or therapy, in other words, it is the mode of providing a response to a need. We have seen that assessment is the process of identifying the needs of individuals, partners, families, groups and reaching decisions about whether and how to intervene. Therefore intervention flows from the assessment process itself, and should be based upon the best evidence of what works is certain situations. Such knowledge, or evidence, is always changing, and research-informed practice will continually demand a critical analysis of service models and the development of new ways of working. As Ferguson (2008: 159) notes:

> Best practice in any case or system is always socially constructed and therefore open to debate, and arguably there are always ways in which improvements and different approaches can be suggested for all interventions.

As Wilson et al. explain (2008: 341), intervention has to be understood as a synthesis of thinking, doing and being: it is about understanding, about practical actions, and equally about the ways of doing, the values and principles that underpin and support our actions within a helping relationship.

It behoves social work to keep up with the evidence-based nature of practice in other countries, where interventions are frequently researched to establish their impact and efficacy. In the UK, multidisciplinary mental health services and similar agencies working with offenders are leading the way in adopting modes and levels of intervention based on research-informed evidence. For many other service sectors, the predominant concerns of risk assessment, risk management, and case surveillance and monitoring have led to interventions that can readily answer the question 'What's going on?' but are much poorer at being able to respond to the questions 'What are we going to do about it?' and 'How are we going to do it?'

Hopefully this chapter contributes to enabling students and practitioners to develop confidence in being able to carry a serviceable toolbox of intervention skills for use in practice.

For further discussion of aspects of intervention with looked-after children, see Adams et al., 2009b, Chapter 24, and of decision-making, see Adams et al., 2009c, Chapter 16.

www.21csocialwork.org.uk   Scottish 21st Century Social Work Review explains the statutory social worker's role in prevention and early intervention with children.

www.toolkit.parentinguk.org   Parenting UK provides a commissioners toolkit, for information on parenting programmes.

www.instituteoffamilytherapy.org.uk   The Institute of Family Therapy provides a helpful summary of systemic family work.

Beckett, C. (2006) *Essential Theory for Social Work Practice*, London, Sage. This helpful text enables the reader to make the links between theories of understanding and theories of intervention.

Marsh, P. and Doel, M. (2005) *The Task-centred Book*, London, Routledge. The foremost authors on task-centred work provide a wealth of examples of this intervention model.

Roberts, R. (2000) *Crisis Intervention Handbook: Assessment, Treatment and Research*, Oxford, Oxford University Press. Offers a helpful seven-stage approach to crisis intervention work.

Stepney, P. and Ford, D. (eds) (2000) *Social Work Models, Methods and Theories: A Framework for Practice*, Lyme Regis, Russell House. Popular and helpful summary of the main approaches used in current social work practice settings.

Trevithick, P. (2005) *Social Work Skills: A Practice Handbook*, 2nd edn, Buckingham, Open University Press. Addresses core skills that underpin the effectiveness of all modes of social work intervention.

Critical intervention and empowerment

19

Chapter overview

In this second chapter on intervention, we present an alternative to the dominant approach discussed in the previous chapter. Here, the authors seek a specifically critical perspective on ways of understanding intervention: critical of the dominant model of intervention and critical in the sense of seeking to empower fellow human beings in their dealings with the world around them. As with the Chinese body-mind-spirit model presented in the next chapter, this is both an alternative to intervention approaches and a development, a modification and an expansion of them.

Critical practice is based on an understanding of how the concepts of power, oppression and inequality determine personal and structural relations. Practitioners are required to analyse how the socially constructed divisions of 'race', gender, class, sexuality, age and disability, and the impact of differential access to resources, interact to define the life experiences of individuals and communities. Critical practice is informed by a political perspective, which takes account of diverse experiences of oppression, is critical of existing social and political institutions and is 'emancipatory in intent' (Mullaly, 1997: 109). The critical practitioner recognises that the claim that practice is 'emancipatory' (Tew, 2006) has to be made with care, as there is no guarantee that intervention will always improve the conditions of the lives of those most vulnerable to oppression – even if carried out by competent practitioners working in **partnership**. However, by engaging in meaningful dialogue with service users

> **Partnership** refers to a formal agreement between two or more individuals, groups or organisations to work together to achieve shared goals. There are many types of partnership in social work, between professionals, and between professionals and carers, service users, adults, children and young people.

to facilitate the telling of their stories so that, in the process, their situations can be better understood, the critical practitioner can develop and utilise more creative and less oppressive intervention strategies. Fundamental to these strategies is the idea of promoting structural change. To achieve this aim, the critical practitioner needs to be ethically aware, political, reflexive and critically reflective (see Chapter 1).

As writers, our theorising regarding critical practice is rooted in an understanding of how service users experience social work intervention (Mullaly, 1997; Parton, 1999; Healy, 2000; Beresford and Croft, 2004). To help us in writing this chapter, we asked Dawn, a mother with learning difficulties, to share her story and allow us to use her narrative. In telling her story, she gives voice to the experiences of parents with learning difficulties. People with learning difficulties face a range of oppressions and, in common with other minority groups, their voices can often be marginalised (Coles and Connors, 2008) and lost, particularly those who are unable to read and write (Atkinson and Walmsley, 1999), raising the complex question of whose voice is finally reflected in the text (Clifford, 1998). The challenges are to ensure that Dawn's narrative is true to her account and is heard and respected, while acknowledging that she is not an equal party in any ongoing dialogue concerning intervention and **empowerment** strategies (Cedersund, 1999).

> **Empowerment** is the capacity of people, individually, in groups and communities, to help themselves by exercising power, taking control of their lives and achieving the goals they set or share with others.

The testimony of Dawn in this chapter illustrates how professional intervention can be experienced as disempowering and oppressive. This highlights the challenges of defining empowering practice when intervening in people's lives, particularly within a practice context that is characterised by bureaucratisation, resource constraints (Healy and Meagher, 2004), is concerned with managing risk (Parton, 1999; Stepney, 2006) and places limitations and restrictions on social workers (Fook, 2000). Competing discourses around concepts such as risk and need, parenting, rights of parents with learning difficulties and children's rights add to the complexity of practice. If practitioners are to engage in critical practices that promote the rights of service users (Stepney, 2006), they have to be aware of the organisational context, deal with a range of situations involving many players with competing and conflicting interests, and be cognisant of how the competing discourses shape the practice context in relation to defining priorities and intervention strategies.

We have interspersed the text with excerpts from Dawn's story as told to us through her advocate. She relates her experiences with various professionals: Anna the social worker, who is based in a children and families team, Clover, a community nurse specialising in working with parents who have learning disabilities, and Bernie from a family centre. While placing Dawn's story in the foreground, we are aware that her children also have their own stories to tell, and the professionals involved will also have different and sometimes competing stories and perspectives. However, we justify the parent- and child-centred focus on the basis that although 40 per cent of parents with learning disabilities interviewed in a national survey were not living with their children, this still means that 60 per cent are living with their children. Furthermore, it seems that often they are involved with child protection procedures when professionals are worried about their children's welfare (SCIE, 2005).

Intervention and empowerment in critical practice

> " I know that I did everything I could to get my kids back, you must fight back. It's still not any easier living without my children and I still want them back. It's so painful and I still feel really angry that I've been let down by not having more support. (Dawn) "

Practitioners critically reflect on how they are intervening in the lives of others on a daily basis and many interventions could be described as positive, affirming and creative (Coles and Connors, 2008: 199). Equally, it could be said that the term 'intervention' also has oppressive connotations (Dalrymple and Burke, 2006), as it indicates the moral and political authority of the social worker to invade 'the social territories' of service users (Payne, 1996: 43). Many of us find it difficult to reconcile the invasiveness of our professional role with the concepts of critical and empowering practice and have developed terminology such as 'working together', 'partnership', 'participation' or 'user involvement' in our attempt to portray a more equal and cooperative relationship between ourselves and service users. Examination of the term 'empowerment' indicates conceptual disagreements, rooted in how power is conceived (Dalrymple and Burke, 2006). Given its hybrid political ancestry, the notion of empowerment practice in contemporary social work creates ethical, moral and practical dilemmas for practitioners (Lupton and Nixon, 1999). However, we argue that the radical potential of empowerment practice cannot be realised if professionally driven intervention strategies are seen as key to the promotion of empowerment (Croft and Beresford, 2000; Stepney, 2006). We concur with Simon (1990) that service users 'who are empowered by their social workers have, de facto, lost ground ... in their battle for autonomy and control over their own environment and existence'.

> " My partner would hit me in front of the children and I'd try to move out of the way when it happened. It was terrible for the children to see. I was too scared to tell anyone at first as he said he would knife me. The children were getting naughtier and they would sometimes copy him. They would hit, kick and bite me and each other. "

Actively involving Dawn in decision-making will be difficult, as this has not been part of her experience. Dawn has not only been silenced by the violent environment in which she lived, but also her status as a young, white, heterosexual, working-class mother from the north of England who has learning difficulties contributes to her marginalised position and experience of oppression. Self-location and reflexivity are essential elements of empowerment practice (Dalrymple and Burke, 2006). Therefore, Anna, the social worker, actively needs to consider how her social class, personal experiences, training and practice experience with adults who have learning difficulties will affect her relationship with Dawn.

Children and family work in statutory agencies is dominated by legislation and policy mandates built on welfare principles, with the notion of partnership as a central tenet. The dilemma for Anna in developing partnership practice is that she is working within systems and procedures that create tensions between herself, Dawn and the children through coercive and legalistic approaches. As a case manager, this forces her to assess risk and monitor and evaluate progress. Anna may find herself driven towards defensive and reactive forms of practice (Parton, 1999; Lupton and Nixon, 1999; Healy, 2005; Ruch, 2007), where intervention becomes focused on collecting information or evidence, rather than working with Dawn and trying to understand the situation of her children (Cooper and Hetherington, 1999).

Constructing critical practice with Dawn and her children

Countering bureaucratic, mechanistic ways of working, Parton and O'Byrne (2000) posit a constructive social work approach, which focuses on dialogue, listening to and talking with the service user. It is concerned with narratives of solutions to problems, which are necessary for change to occur. Instead of focusing on gathering information about the causes of Dawn's problems in order to make an expert assessment, Anna should help Dawn in the difficult process of telling her story so that she can gain control and meaning. It will only be an empowering process, however, if Anna is aware of the potential for language to reflect power differentials; it is important to use words that Dawn understands and are meaningful to her and can use to define herself and her situation. So, for example, if Anna described the behaviour of the boys as 'disturbed', this would indicate her theoretical and value perspective and impact on her ability to understand Dawn's narrative.

> The children had a social worker, Anna, and me and the children went to the family centre twice a week. I had a key worker there called Bernie. Eventually, I told Anna and Bernie what was going on and they were concerned about the boys' behaviour. At this time, I got a community nurse, Clover, and a social worker of my own.

Numerous professionals with different personal and professional values, membership of diverse social classes and varying levels of experience and training are now involved in Dawn's life. However, children's services obviously focus on the needs and welfare of the children concerned and both legislation and research indicate that Anna also needs to work together with adult services to ensure that Dawn's needs are addressed (Goodinge, 2000; SCIE, 2005). It could be argued that Dawn is actively contributing to the assessment process by attending the family centre and talking openly about the difficulties she is experiencing. Dawn believes that by complying with the social worker's plan, she is getting help to be a 'good parent'. Eventually, as she says, when she feels able to trust them, she talks to Anna and Bernie about her concerns. But her insight and the act of her telling also provide the evidence for possible care proceedings. This experience is not unusual for parents in Dawn's position. Some parents consulted for a SCIE research briefing (2005) agreed to attend parenting courses as part of a package of care to ensure that their children were able to continue living with them. However, they did not find these useful and the desired outcome was not achieved. The various players are gathering information in relation to their roles and responsibilities. As the key worker managing the complexity of the situation, Anna needs to take into account how far her own assessment of the welfare needs of the children and Dawn's parenting capacity, that is, the professional assessment of how capable she is as a parent, is confirmed or disconfirmed by other specialist assessments. How does Anna evaluate information provided by workers promoting the rights of Dawn as a parent as compared with those holding a more protectionist perspective regarding the children's right to welfare? Whatever decision is eventually made, Dawn needs to be constantly involved in the planning and decision-making process. This requires Anna to have an ongoing honest dialogue with Dawn.

Interagency sharing of information in child protection focuses on the welfare of the children, which marginalises and excludes Dawn. The dilemma for Anna is that she cannot directly empower Dawn. Anna's **advocacy** role is compromised by her location within the agency and her legal mandate regarding the welfare of the children. However, by linking Dawn with Clover and ensuring that she has her own social worker, Anna is recognising the need for Dawn's voice and agency. The engagement of an

> **Advocacy** is a term with roots in legal practice. It refers to the activities associated with negotiating or representing on behalf of a person.

independent advocate drawn from a local group with expertise and experience of working with people with learning difficulties would contribute to Dawn's power resources (Mullaly, 1997). A study of two specialist advocacy services for parents with learning difficulties found that not only did the support of an advocate help them to understand the child protection process and have their voices heard but also they felt they were treated with more respect by the professionals concerned. Furthermore, the advocates also 'inspired some local professionals to improve their practice in working with parents with learning disabilities' (Tarleton, 2007: 5).

> " Anna said I should leave my partner, either make myself homeless or go to a refuge. But I was too scared that my partner would find me and hurt me if I did this. I was also scared to go to a place where I didn't know anyone. I felt Anna wasn't helping me because I wanted me and the boys to be protected but she was only interested in the boys. I wanted to stay with my children; no one else had ever looked after them and I thought they would be scared. "

Oppressed groups 'experience obstacles to develop their capacities and participate fully in society' (Mullaly, 1997). Domestic violence reduces the ability of women to make life-changing decisions. Dawn's experience is that no choices have been offered, because she does not understand the notion of a refuge or making herself technically homeless. Anna's use of language here is disempowering, indicating an assumption that Dawn has a particular level of understanding and ability to seek ways out of domestic violence. Hence Dawn has been denied the opportunity to consider all the information presented to her, which in turn has implications for any decision she might make. Dawn's decision-making capacity is compounded by her learning difficulty. So Anna needs to consider different forms of communication. The narrative approach discussed above would provide Anna with the opportunity to examine with Dawn her previous decision-making experiences and identify and develop her skills in this area.

> I think I need help with parenting. There are some things I can't do very well and I needed advice. I didn't get this from Anna. I also can't read or write, so when Anna wrote to me or sent me anything, my partner always had to tell me what to do. I don't think that Anna really thought about the help I needed, and sometimes I find it hard to explain myself properly to other people. I did all that Anna had asked me to do.

Evidence from international research on parenting by people with learning difficulties shows that they receive a service that is characterised by an 'over zealous' approach to the assessment of risks (SSI, 1999). Booth (2000) suggests that professional practice serves to undermine rather than support parents with learning difficulties wanting to care for their children. They are scrutinised and policed, their vulnerabilities exposed rather than their abilities worked with. The difficulties they face when they find themselves involved in the child protection system have been described as 'system' or 'institutional' abuse (Tarleton, 2007). This is Dawn's experience. Anna's focus on the children should not be at the expense of Dawn's needs. Dawn's wishes and feelings appear to be overlooked, her right to parent denied. Dawn asks for help with her parenting, but this support is not initially provided, and the children's right to experience improved parenting by their mother is therefore also denied.

The problem for a practitioner attempting to work from a child-centred perspective is balancing the range of needs identified within the family. The interconnectedness of these needs should be explored, focusing on the whole family rather than solely on the children (SCIE, 2005) and should inform the assessment and intervention strategy. The question to be considered is the precise nature of Dawn's parenting and the justifiability of judging it adequate or inadequate. Is Dawn providing minimum standards of care for her children to thrive, and is her parenting comparable to other women in similar social circumstances? Dawn has to be respected as a person and her human right as a woman to be a mother to her children also has to be respected. But this has to be balanced against her ability to 'parent'. If Dawn is doing all that is asked of her, then it could be said that she is doing all that she can to be a good parent. Ultimately, she will never be able to fulfil all the 'dimensions of parenting capacity' identified in guidance for social workers (DH/DfEE/Home Office, 2000: 21). However, Anna, in partnership with the family centre, could work with Dawn to identify the positive aspects of Dawn's relationship with her children. Guidance recommends that the needs of disabled parents are acknowledged and supported (DH, 2002b) and particularly that the needs of parents with learning disabilities are recognised (DH, 2000c). So, for example, Dawn can provide basic care and secure attachments, but due to her own cognitive ability, she finds it more difficult to facilitate the children's intellectual development. By undertaking a comprehensive assessment of her strengths, an empowering strategy for 'working with' Dawn could then be identified.

> " Eventually Clover contacted my sister who my partner had not allowed me to see for quite a few years. She helped me leave with the children. I was really scared during this time, but I knew I had to do it. Anna then said that the children had to go and stay with foster carers. I was upset about this and so were the boys. I visited the boys several times a week, and we all got really upset; it was very sad. I felt angry towards Anna and Bernie because I felt they should have helped me with the boys sooner. "

At this stage, Clover, in her specialist role, has used a different approach to help Dawn leave the violent situation. The language used by Anna in suggesting options to Dawn earlier was not facilitative or helpful in eliciting an informed response from Dawn. Research indicates that with the right help from services, parents can develop confidence and engage more positively with professionals and the systems concerned with safeguarding their children's welfare (Tarleton and Ward, 2007). By listening to and engaging with Dawn's narrative, Clover has established not only that a sister exists but also that there is somewhere for Dawn to go. It needs to be recognised that leaving situations of domestic violence 'involves changes of such magnitude' (Wilcox, 2006: 739) and so it is important that Dawn is able to access a range of formal and informal support systems and networks. The act of leaving is an empowering first step for Dawn. Dawn's networks are developing and her social situation changing, which will have an impact on her life experiences. These changes are an indication that Dawn is attempting to take control of her life and resolve her own relationship problems. Booth (2000) reminds us that in focusing on the needs of the children, practitioners often overlook the needs of the parents who may be unable to do their best by their children until their own problems are resolved. At this point, intervention could be refocused to recognise Dawn's resilience, moving practice away from a problem-solving approach towards a strengths perspective (Jessup and Rogerson, 1999; Healy, 2005).

A family group conference (FGC; see Adams et al. 2009b, Ch. 24) could be an alternative decision-making process. The FGC approach emphasises collective family decision-making and, through the use of an independent coordinator, tries to manage the tension between compulsory intervention and family choice (Lupton and Nixon, 1999; Holland et al., 2005). Messages about the empowering potential of FGCs generally indicate that professionals and family members find it a more enabling process (Bell and Wilson, 2006; Holland and Rivett, 2006; Ashley and Nixon, 2007). Using such an approach with Dawn could be problematic by replicating her feelings of powerlessness if her learning difficulty is not taken into account. However, it could also provide the opportunity for the telling of her story and modelling a more constructive and democratic way of working with professionals as well as developing supportive familial and social support networks. Identifying such networks could provide opportunities for Dawn to access both practical and emotional support (SCIE, 2005).

A supported parenting model also offers an empowering perspective on working with families headed by parents with learning difficulties (Booth and Booth, 1998).

This requires moving from a punitive to a positive approach and rejecting traditional deficit models of service delivery. For Dawn, it would mean focusing on her strengths and resilience (already demonstrated by her) rather than on risk. Anna would need to move from a concern about promoting dependence to the goal of building Dawn's competence, and work in partnership with her rather than maintaining the role of detached 'expert'.

> " I then found out that Anna wanted my children to be adopted and this made me feel even more upset and angry. I felt I was losing control but wanted to fight to keep them even though this was hard and I was scared. There were lots of meetings and trips to court and I didn't always understand what was going on. Clover and my solicitor spent a lot of time trying to explain. I had to make decisions about what to do – I wanted to fight. There was a lot of arguing in court and my solicitor fought hard for me but it wasn't enough. "

It could be argued that although the children are the most vulnerable in the scenario, once the child protection system becomes activated, they are subject to the protective gaze of professionals charged with the responsibility of ensuring that they are adequately cared for (Booth et al., 2005; Parton, 2006). Their vulnerable position is now transformed, because their welfare is supported and maintained by a powerful legal system and professional surveillance. Dawn does not have the benefit of such support, instead she is subject to a system that appears to be, in her view, intent on destroying her family.

Too often empowerment means reconciling people to being powerless (Langan, 1998). If this is to be avoided, Dawn needs to be made aware of the realities of practice in order to avoid unrealistically raising her expectations. Dawn was invited to attend 'lots of meetings and trips to court'. This professional-led attempt at empowerment actually meant that she was complicit in the state's intervention into her life and that of her children. Professionals wanted to be supportive and Dawn acknowledges this. However, Dawn still felt that she was not given a chance. Any attempts at empowerment were negated by the system and Dawn eventually felt that she was losing control despite wanting to fight. Although the support of an independent advocate may not have changed the situation for Dawn, it would have helped her to overcome the 'system' abuse that she experienced (Tarleton, 2007).

In terms of assessing Dawn's parenting ability, it is likely there would be sufficient evidence to indicate that the children's welfare would be better served by their removal. However, this decision has to be balanced against research evidence which shows that corporate parenting fails to provide stable consistent care once children are removed from their family of origin (Jackson et al., 2000). Having left a dangerous relationship, Dawn has demonstrated her commitment to being a 'good' mother and making life changes to enhance the welfare of her children. With a supported parenting package, and cooperation between adults' and children's services (SCIE, 2005), Dawn could continue to be a mother to the best of her ability and share the parenting tasks with others.

The welfare of the children and that of Dawn are not entirely separable and the future placement of the children has to be considered in the light of the existing bonds and the culture and ethnicity of the children. Therefore management of the process to ensure Dawn's involvement is essential from both her own and the children's perspective, in order to maximise the potential for continuing constructive involvement of the one parent who is able to maintain links with their past.

> They are now looking for parents to adopt my boys, I don't think I'll ever get over it (Dawn cries). I feel like I wasn't given a chance. I was with my partner all the time the children's behaviour was bad and I wanted a home of my own with the kids. I needed some help with parenting on my own, but if I had got this help, I would have managed.

Dawn does not accept the decision to remove her children and the ideological, professional and structural power, which Anna and Bernie use to achieve their desired result, served only to crush Dawn. She feels the full power of the invasiveness of professional intervention.

Continuing reflections

Anna had to assess and balance the risks to the children and the needs of a mother with learning difficulties who clearly wished to care for her children. As a critical practitioner, Anna will now need space in supervision to deal with feelings generated by the situation and support to reflect on and evaluate her experiences, and further develop her practice. This should be the start of a dialogue, which could contribute in the future to the development of policy and practice. Clover used the energy generated by her anger and frustration immediately after the court case to write a discussion paper for the community learning disability team concerning practice with parents with learning difficulties. Through this, she aims to bridge the organisational gap between child protection teams and adult services for people with learning difficulties. While a number of structural models and guidance have been put forward for improving policy and practice, there remains a need to provide more support for parents with learning disabilities to enable them to keep their children or to help those whose experiences reflect those of Dawn (SCIE, 2005).

How far we have facilitated Dawn telling her story can only be confirmed by her. Our personal histories, ethnicities, values and experiences of being social workers and service users have had an impact on our deliberations. The writing of this chapter presented us with the opportunity to consider the contradictions of empowerment practice that is provoked by the intrusiveness of intervention. Dawn's experiences provide the impetus for us all to engage in practice informed by the politics of challenge and resistance.

For further discussion of empowerment models and practice, see Adams et al., 2009b, Chapter 16 and for radical and critical perspectives on social work, see Adams et al., 2009b, Chapter 17.

www.familyaction.org.uk Formerly the Family Welfare Association (FWA), Family Action gives emotional, practical and financial support to families.

www.learningdisabilities.org.uk The Foundation for Learning Disabilities, part of the Mental Health Foundation, gives support to learning disabled people, carries out research and works to improve learning disability services.

Booth, T. and Booth, W. (1998) *Growing Up with Parents who Have Learning Difficulties*, London, Routledge. Challenges taken-for-granted ideas about the process of parenting, the roles of parents, especially disabled parents, and the needs of children.

Healy, K. (2005) *Social Work Theory in Context: Creating Frameworks for Practice*, Basingstoke, Palgrave Macmillan. Outlines critical theoretical perspectives and approaches including the strengths perspective and anti-oppressive practice as well as looking at the links between theory, context and skills.

Jones, K., Cooper, B., and Ferguson H. (eds) (2008) *Best Practice in Social Work: Critical Perspectives*, Basingstoke, Palgrave Macmillan. Promotes a new practice paradigm that identifies and celebrates critical best practice and encourages readers to reflect on their diverse practice experiences.

Lupton, C. and Nixon, P. (1999) *Empowering Practice? A Critical Appraisal of the Family Group Conference Approach*, Bristol, Policy Press. Examines the nature and meaning of empowerment, which is evaluated and operationalised using the family group conference approach as an example.

Parton, N. (2006) *Safeguarding Childhood: Early Intervention and Surveillance in a Late Modern Society*, Basingstoke, Palgrave Macmillan. Analyses how thinking about child abuse has changed and argues that the 'preventive state' involves systems of intervention characterised by increased regulation and surveillance.

Alternative intervention: a Chinese body-mind-spirit perspective

20

Chapter overview

This chapter presents intervention as a proactive means of enabling people to empower themselves to take action to improve their situation. The holistic approach proposed integrates the physical, cognitive and spiritual aspects of the person, with a view to developing strengths and enabling wellbeing rather than focusing on pathological problems. The aim is to build on harmony between the body, mind and spirit as a means of promoting growth and transformation.

Social work intervention to embrace holistic wellbeing

This chapter offers an alternative approach to intervention, drawing on experience and ideas from China. Intervention may call on many different cultural viewpoints; an alternative perspective helps to highlight our own assumptions and offer ways of working that can contribute to other forms of practice. Although some of the ideas may be unfamiliar to Western readers, they can experience some of the alienation of readers from other cultures faced with social work based on the English-speaking world's cultural assumptions. At the same time, it is also possible to see many parallels in practice that can enrich all social work experience. Although this model of practice accepts that intervention follows assessment and planning, as in many Western accounts of social work, their relationship is not necessarily linear or sequential as some Western presentations of social work conceive it, although Horner (Chapter 18) also rejects this linearity in the social work process in Western social work. By fostering growth and transformation, intervention may achieve the social work ideal of 'helping people to help themselves'.

The scope of social work intervention is extremely wide, ranging from the remedial to the developmental, and even the transcendental. We can conceptualise it as a four-level model, which is summarised in Table 20.1.

Table 20.1 Scope of social work intervention

Scope of intervention	Key intervention strategy	Social workers' primary roles

4 Holistic wellbeing	■ Responding to clients as an integrated whole
	■ Achieving body-mind-spirit harmony
	■ The SMART principle:
	  ■ Strength focused
	  ■ Meaning reconstruction
	  ■ Affirmation of self
	  ■ Resilience training
	  ■ Transformation
		Coach and counsellor

3 Psychosocial distresses and pathology	■ Problem-solving and a task-centred approach
	■ Psychosocial therapies:
	  ■ Individual therapies
	  ■ Marital and family therapies
	  ■ Group therapies
		Counsellor and therapist

2 Basic needs and physical illnesses	■ Mobilisation of resources
	  ■ Medical service
	  ■ Rehabilitation service
	  ■ Support for the underprivileged or disabled
		Case and care manager

1 Personal safety	■ Crisis intervention
	■ Exercising positional duties and statutory power in relation to:
	  ■ Child abuse
	  ■ Domestic violence
	  ■ People with mental disorders in an unstable mental condition
	  ■ Negligence in caring for people with mental incapacitation
	  ■ Victims of crime/violence
		Official agent in implementation of welfare legislation

1 *Personal safety:* in cases where personal safety is under imminent threat, the primary objective of intervention is to ensure safety. Common examples include social work for coping with child abuse, domestic violence, dealing with people with mental disorders in an unstable mental condition and negligence in caring for people with mental incapacitation. Crisis intervention skills are often necessary in these situations.

2 *Basic needs and physical illnesses:* when basic needs are unmet and physical illnesses untreated, the primary objective of intervention is to ensure that the necessary resources are mobilised to address those needs. Resources can include medical services, rehabilitation services and other tangible support. Competence in case management is required in such situations.

3 *Psychosocial distresses and pathology:* a social worker's most prominent role in such cases is that of counsellor and therapist. Competence in problem-solving training, task-centred approaches and various counselling and psychotherapy approaches is required.

4 *Holistic wellbeing:* 'holistic' refers to the integration of the whole in terms of the physical (body), the cognitive and emotional (mind) and peace of mind and life meaning

(spirit). 'Wellbeing' refers to a positive state and growth, rather than pathological problems. The focus of intervention at this level is on strengths rather than problems. A social worker's most prominent role here is as a coach and counsellor.

Most, if not all, social workers work under immense pressure and spend most of their time struggling with the problems of their clients at levels 1 and 2. Some more fortunate individuals can also afford to play a role at level 3. Level 4 is focused on strength and transformation-oriented intervention that can speed up the recovery process.

Intervention is about inducing change in the client. Change can involve the reduction or extinction of the negative or the increase or synthesis of the positive. Research and clinical experience suggest that the former is far more difficult to achieve than the latter. Inducing positives is often more rewarding. In making positive changes, clients will gain more capacity to cope or live with the negatives. Therefore, adding level 4 intervention at an early stage can help to free social workers from the entanglement of intervention at levels 1 to 3.

Responding to clients as an integrated whole: body-mind-spirit interconnectedness

A common fault in social work intervention is that of reductionism and a compartmentalised view of the total wellbeing of individuals and groups. Such an approach fails to address the multidimensional and interconnected nature of the problems, or bring about meaningful benefits to clients' lives.

Traditionally, social workers are shy of working in the bodily and spiritual domains. However, there is growing evidence that the body, mind and spirit are interconnected. This evidence includes research findings in diverse areas such as biofeedback, psychoneuroimmunology, holistic body work such as tai chi and yoga, mindfulness training and spirituality in clinical care. There is a strong indication that social workers should incorporate bodily and spiritual dimensions in their interventions, so that they may respond to their clients in an integrated way.

Inspired by the conceptual framework of traditional Chinese medicine, Chan (2001) developed the Eastern body-mind-spirit approach, which aims at fostering a harmonious dynamic equilibrium within clients, and between clients and their social and natural environment. This approach has been applied to various target groups such as cancer patients, infertile couples, divorced women and adolescents. Systematic outcome studies were conducted for the approach, and evidence of its efficacy and potential for generalisation are growing (Chan et al., 2000, 2001; Chan et al., 2004).

Chan (2001) developed one-second techniques that are simple for counsellors to learn and easy for clients to follow. Table 20.2 provides some examples of these interesting techniques. By working with the body, the client can develop a sense of control because they are doing something to help themselves physically and emotionally. The mood changes as clients focus on the physical movements and massage. Tai chi and qigong practice can also be used as a psychological distraction for clients who are troubled by an obsessive indulgence in pain.

Table 20.2 One-second hand techniques

Health is in our hands. According to Chinese medicine, all the twelve meridians pass through the hands, feet and ears. Massage of the hands, feet and ears can activate our self-healing capacity.
1 *Palm rubbing*: with palms facing one another, fingers to fingers, palm to palm, rub the palms and fingers hard until they are warm. Close your eyes and feel the tingling sensation between the palms.
2 *Healing hands*: rub the hands until they are warm, then place the hands over the body parts that feel pain or discomfort. Pass the heat and healing energies of the hands onto the part of the body that needs nurture and love. Put the hands on the abdomen when going to bed, imagining calming and soothing energies going into the body and go to sleep with such comforting energies.
3 *Clapping qigong*: for people who are prepared to work much harder on their hands, clapping qigong is a simple technique to try. With fingers and palms facing each other, hold the fingers upward with palms in front of the chest like hands folded in prayer. Open the palms to shoulder width and make loud forceful claps. Do this for five minutes, three times a day for effective results.
4 *Roll the wrists with hands like a lotus flower*: there are acupuncture points along the wrist that can be calming and stabilise the heartbeat. Roll the wrists in big circles so as to stimulate the acupuncture points. Do this 50 times, twice a day.
There are also techniques for the ears, eyes, mouth and feet in Chan's (2001) book.

Source: Chan, C.L.W. (2001) *An Eastern Body-Mind-Spirit Approach: A Training Manual with One-second Techniques*. Hong Kong: Department of Social Work and Social Administration, University of Hong Kong

Reflection on and sharing of spiritual issues should not be too alien to social workers or their clients. Reflections on growth through pain, as well as the search for a meaning of life are core components in the spirituality interventions.

In the following sections, the body-mind-spirit approach will be introduced in more detail. The essence of the model is represented in Figure 20.1.

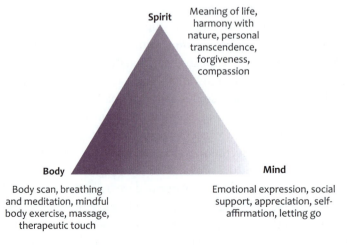

Figure 20.1 Body-mind-spirit transformation

The body-mind-spirit approach in therapy

Basic assumptions and therapeutic goals

Inspired by traditional Chinese medicine and philosophies, the model has a number of basic assumptions:

1 *Everything is connected:* human existence is a manifestation of physical, psychological and spiritual being. The different domains are inter-connected and come together to form a whole.

> Yin and yang are terms in Chinese philosophy that refer to some of the opposites or complementary qualities of many phenomena in the world. They do not refer to conflicts or tensions but to dual relationships that, in some circumstances, may counterbalance each other.

2 *Life is the eternal dance of **yin and yang**:* life is ever-changing, and the interflow of energy maintains a harmonious dynamic equilibrium. The disruption of such harmony is the cause of life problems.
3 *Healing comes from within:* therapy aims to ignite the client's innate healing power that will bring them back to a state of balance. Intervention looks for strength rather than pathology.
4 *Restoring harmony:* this not only cures illness and resolves problems, it also opens up opportunities for growth and transformation.

The future of social work should be strength focused and growth oriented. It should go beyond coping and symptom reduction and aim for transcendence to a higher level of connectedness within the self, with others and with the universe.

Body processes and emotional healing

Body scan

The healing process can start with getting in touch with the body and connecting it with the emotions. Body scanning is a useful technique. In a relaxed and mindful state, clients are instructed to use mental imagery to scan through their whole body to check if any part is experiencing pain or discomfort. They are then encouraged to talk about the physical pain and discomfort, and explore the relationship with their emotions. The process enhances clients' awareness of their physical discomfort and emotions, and the connection between them.

This systemic perspective on emotions is a reflection of the deep influence of the yin yang theory on Chinese medicine. A brief account of this theory now follows.

The yin yang theory

The yin yang theory was first described in the ancient book *Yi Jing* – also known as the *I Ching*, the *Book of Changes* – which was written around 7 BC and had a great influence in the conceptualisation of the original theories of Chinese medicine. Yin and yang are opposites and are a mutually facilitating but also a mutually repressing pair. Yin signifies substance, stillness, storage, darkness and softness. Yang signifies energy, movement, transporting, brightness and hardness. Examples of such yin yang pairs are earth and sky, day and night, moon and sun, winter and summer, woman and man and so on. The yin yang theory proposes a universal model depicting the pattern of interaction and change within a yin yang pair. Some core relationships are as follows:

1 Yin and yang are mutually facilitating as well as mutually repressing.
2 Yin and yang are mutually dependent. They cannot flourish on their own.
3 Yin and yang are relative but not absolute concepts. For example, among a group of yin subjects, there can be subjects that are relatively yang, as well as subjects that are extremely yin.
4 At either extreme of yin or yang, there can be sudden qualitative change, that is, extreme yin changes to yang, or extreme yang changes to yin.

Yin and yang working in a harmonious dynamic equilibrium are considered to be fundamental to good health.

 This classic yin yang logo shows the mutually embedded nature, dynamic interflow and dual metamorphosis of yin and yang.

Inspired by the conceptual framework of this ancient theory, a social worker in the role of therapist may stimulate clients to explore their own body-emotion connections.

Breath is life

Breathing can be used as a powerful tool to bring stability to the body and mind. Mindful breathing helps us to get in touch with our deep emotions, whether they be feelings of pain, fear, anger, joy or contentment. In deep breathing meditation, a person moves to a state of total concentration and consciousness.

During breathing meditation practice, a therapist may verbally guide clients to achieve harmony within themselves and with the external world. Values such as appreciation, self-affirmation, forgiveness and compassion can be cultivated in clients during this practice.

Breathing exercises do not necessarily have to be practised while the body is still, but can be practised along with movement and mental imagery. Tai chi, qigong and yoga are good examples of this type of body-mind-spirit exercise. Through mindful movement and breathing, clients get in touch with their true total being and develop an appreciation of themselves and their environment. Simplified tai chi, qigong and yoga are practical options for use in counselling work. If these exercises are practised in a group, they can provide the additional benefits of social support.

Acupressure and light massage

Acupuncture and light massage were originally conceived based on the meridian theory of Chinese medicine. There is evidence that acupuncture and light massage are effective for a number of conditions such as insomnia, depression, pain and peri-menstrual problems. For social work intervention, acupressure, rather than acupuncture, and light massage are more appropriate alternatives. Chan (2001) simplified these practices into easy-to-learn techniques. Mastery of these techniques can help clients to regain a sense of control over both the body and the mind.

Prescribing acupressure and light massage to couples or families can help to enhance marital and family relationships, as massaging one another is a way of communicating and expressing concern and love. Sometimes it can work more quickly and better than words.

The power of the mind

The corresponding Chinese word for mind is Xin, which literally means 'the heart'. We believe that the power of the heart is more important and ultimately greater than the power of the brain. The concept of mind (Xin) is a complex construct that encompasses willpower, vision, hope, emotion, human sensitivity, passion, cognition, or the whole of humanity in one word. Techniques for mobilising the power of the mind include mindfulness practices, meditation, letting go, forgiveness, compassion and loving kindness. The process of transformation in our body-mind-spirit model involves five As – three of them related to the mind and two related to the spirit:

- Acknowledge vulnerability
- Accept the unpredictability of life
- Activate one's self-healing capacity
- Affirmation
- Appreciation.

- *Acknowledge vulnerability:* we help clients to normalise suffering as an inevitable part of life. By acknowledging our own vulnerability, we can face pain and loss with tranquillity. Trauma and loss can result in ultimate spiritual growth.
- *Accept the unpredictability of life:* acceptance means fully embracing whatever is in the present. The yin yang metaphor inspires us to understand that gains and losses are embedded in each other. People who embrace loss are more ready to appreciate gain.
- *Activate one's self-healing capacity:* by letting go of intense emotional attachment, we can free our energy for self-healing. Letting go and genuine forgiveness are the ultimate solutions to our emotional problems. In our experience of working with Chinese cancer patients, bereaved widows and divorced women, we have found that clients' self-healing power is largely ignited from their determination to let go of the victim role and maximise their own healing capacity.

Affirming spirituality and a new appreciation of life

The remaining two As are *affirmation* and *appreciation*: affirming the meaning of life and a renewed appreciation of life through suffering help to recreate the once-disrupted harmony of body, mind and spirit. Traumatic events may shatter a person's world view and self-identity. The cognitive reappraisal of a traumatic event, the search for meaning and the integration of the experience into one's life help people to adapt to the loss brought about by the event. The reconstruction of meaning after loss involves the process of 'sense making', 'benefit finding' and 'identity reconstruction' (Neimeyer, 2002). We engage clients in a process of restoring their lives to develop a more coherent narrative of their life experiences. The body-mind-spirit model uses the concept of impermanence to help patients to reconstruct their experience of illness or loss and make sense of their misery. Our recent study of cancer survivors confirms our belief that life affirmation (for example 'I can face life challenges with a peaceful mind') and appreciation of life (for example 'I enjoy life every day') are two important factors constituting spirituality (Chan et al., 2004).

While Western forms of therapy largely work to help patients to master, control and overcome their problems better, Buddhist teaching encourages the individual to detach and let go, so that they can flow with the here and now, the 'moment-by-moment experience', instead of being controlled by, or preoccupied with, desire. Paradoxically, one gains control by letting go of control. By practising emotional detachment and letting go, people find it easier to forgive. Forgiveness is the ultimate solution to emotional disharmony.

The SMART principle

The body-mind-spirit model is a multidimensional and holistic approach that can be used to guide social work intervention. Its uniqueness can be summarised by the SMART principle. The SMART principle is consistent with the theoretical shift from psychosocial pathology to positive psychology and empowerment interventions. The five SMART components are:

- Strength focused
- Meaning reconstruction
- Affirmative and appreciative
- Resilience
- Transformation.

- *Strength focused:* intervention should focus on identifying, assuring and enhancing the strength of the clients. By actively identifying strength, a social worker can truly respect the healing capacity of their clients.
- *Meaning reconstruction:* the therapist may help their clients to emerge from the victim role, and obtain meaning from and transcend the suffering. The ability to

find meaning in suffering can be a motivating force for perseverance and the generation of healing strength.

- *Affirmative and appreciative:* the therapist helps the client to affirm and appreciate themselves as well as the external world of both their social and natural environments.
- *Resilience:* this is not only about coping ability, but also about the ability to acknowledge vulnerability, accept adversity and unpredictability, recognise impermanence and let go.
- *Transformation:* this is a state of body-mind-spirit harmony that enables a person to live fully and completely. With transformation, individuals can develop a personal capacity of self-sufficiency in life and are able to formulate selfless goals to help other people.

Evidence-based practice and the future of social work intervention models

Evidence-based medicine is taken as a gold standard in the health and social services. To adopt evidence-based practice (EBP) in social work intervention, social workers need to master practice research skills, and continuously keep up to date with the latest developments in evidence-based interventions, regardless of whether they originate from within social work or another discipline. As roles within the caring professions merge, social workers can maintain role differentiation by truly asserting basic social work values and objectives. At the same time, social workers need to maintain a critical attitude towards EBP.

Conclusion

All too often, social work intervention is restricted to dealing with tackling issues of protection and personal safety, basic physical or emotional needs, or problems perceived as pathological. This chapter has proposed a much broader and holistic approach, based on a four-level SMART model of the scope of social work intervention. This expands the conventional model to cover the holistic treatment of clients. The body-mind-spirit approach facilitates growth and aims to foster a harmonious equilibrium within clients, and between clients and their social and natural environment. The model illustrated in this chapter significantly enhances the conceptual coherence and completeness of social work intervention. We have seen how a strength-oriented holistic approach can speed up recovery and help to shorten the entanglement in problem-focused intervention.

For further discussion of critical ideas about practice, see Adams et al., 2009b, Chapter 17, and for challenges to the medical model in disability practice, see Adams et al., 2009b, Chapter 31.

Abramson, R.J. (2003) 'The unity of mind, body, and spirit: a five-element view of cancer', *Advances in Mind-Body Medicine*, **19**(2): 20–1. Shows how the body-mind-spirit approach is applied to an aspect of medical treatment.

Chan, C.L. (2001) *An Eastern Body-Mind-Spirit Approach: A Training Manual with One-second Techniques*. Hong Kong: Department of Social Work and Social Administration, University of Hong Kong. A useful handbook with detailed guidance on how to carry out the body-mind-spirit approach.

Chan, C.L., Ho, P.S. and Chow, E. (2001) 'A body-mind-spirit model in health: an Eastern approach', *Social Work in Health Care*, **34**(3/4): 261–82.

Engel, G.L. (1977) 'The need for a new medical model: a challenge for biomedicine', *Science*, **196**(4286): 129–36. Gives information about the application of the body-mind-spirit approach in healthcare and argues for a new look at the medical model of treatment.

Ng, S.M., Cheung, K.Y. and Chou, K.L. (2004) Application of Chinese medicine yangsheng in community health service. Paper presented at the Fourth International Conference on Social Work in Health and Mental Health, 23–27 May, Quebec City. Deals with community health service applications of the Chinese medicine approach.

Monitoring, review and evaluation

21

This chapter illustrates the importance of reviewing and evaluating practice. These are carried out in an embedded way as practice proceeds, rather than interrupting practice at formal points of review and evaluation at which decisions are made. Practitioners need to move back and forth between review, evaluation and other activities, as practice takes place.

Chapter overview

There are three elements of review and evaluation of practice. Monitoring checks how service users have responded to services and whether and how planned services have actually been delivered. Reviewing builds on monitoring and periodically 'looks again' at the work done in practice as a basis for planning what to do next. It may also lead on to evaluation, which examines more comprehensively whether the planned programme of work done over a period has been valuable in meeting the aims set out in the plan. These aspects of practice decision-making are often presented as the terminal stage of a sequence of processes starting with assessment, moving on to planning, intervention and review. However, each is embedded throughout practice. We never stop assessing, and so therefore we are always reviewing.

Below is a case example, which will be referred to throughout the chapter to highlight the various points being made along the way.

CASE EXaMPLE

Sam, aged 4, lived with his mother, Judy, aged 27. She is a single parent who drinks excessively and takes non-prescription drugs for depression. Sam was removed from Judy's care a year ago after he had been found in the house alone on four separate occasions. The assessment of Carol, the social worker, was discussed at an initial child protection conference, which decided that he was a child at risk of significant harm and as Judy's family have rejected her and her son, he was placed in foster care;

a child protection plan on Sam was devised. The intention was to rehabili-
tate Sam with Judy; she was encouraged to spend time with him and attend
parenting classes. Judy was also receiving help from the community mental
health team (CMHT), whose members were concerned about her depression
and use of drugs.

After six months, it was noted that Judy had not been attending classes, only
visited Sam sporadically and did not engage with him when she did visit. The
visits were increasingly upsetting Sam. An interim care order was applied for
and granted and Judy and Sam were provided with intensive family support.
However, Judy has continued to show little interest in Sam and Carol is now
considering placing Sam for adoption.

Monitoring practice

Monitoring during a period of work aims to see if interventions are happening as
planned. Monitoring may focus on service users' and carers' needs or on the agency's
requirements. The first aspect checks that users and carers feel secure in their present
situation. Deterioration or variation may occur, but security means that users and
carers are able to manage changes themselves. Monitoring is supportive because it
enables users and carers to feel confidence that there will be a response to crisis; practitioners can only achieve this security if service users and carers are actively aware of
and involved in the monitoring.

Various services offer this kind of monitoring, for example supported housing
with support workers, to provide the confidence of regular checks to identify deterioration. Continuous knowledge of clients is important in order that changes can be
identified, so monitoring often involves regular checks by visits or telephone call, or
programmed activities that will involve a check on someone in residential care. Also,
some care services are from serial carers, that is, a succession of carers from an agency,
and different personnel visit clients' homes throughout the day to perform different
tasks, and it is useful to intersperse these with visits from staff who have a continuous relationship with service users and carers. This enables someone who knows the
person to identify problems and also to integrate serial carers' contributions carefully
with care plans, by offering guidance and supervision on an everyday basis. Respite
or periodic care in a care home or day centre or drop-in provision enables regular
checks on capacity to attend and on service users' physical and psychological condition. For older or disabled people, having radio and telephone call systems that
enable frail people to call for assistance if they have a sudden crisis can also be a
useful, non-intrusive monitoring device. Again, in residential care where personnel
change with shifts, it is important to monitor what has happened in each period, to
form the basis of a handover to the next group of staff responsible for care.

For people with severe or long-term difficulties, several of these monitoring
devices can be used in combination. Monitoring provides an opportunity to reduce

all kinds of risk faced by people with long-term care needs. However, as with all risk situations, it is important to think about how surveillance may intrude upon people's privacy. We can see this working in Sam and Judy's case, because constantly looking again at what is going on enables Carol and her colleagues to see where progress is not being achieved and take action.

Review and evaluation before, during and after

The aim of review and evaluation is to ensure that practice is effective and efficient over a longer period than monitoring. Practice is a continuous process (see Chapter 13), therefore practitioners should review and evaluate their aims, assessments and practice continuously before, during and after their work with service users. The starting point is practitioners' gathering and considering evidence about how effective potential interventions might be, so that they can negotiate using effective interventions with the service user. This is the principle of 'evidence-based practice'. There are a number of problems with evidence-based practice (Calder and Hackett, 2003). Powell (Adams et al. 2009c, Ch. 26) considers the issues succinctly; they are concerned with conflicting views about the purpose of research, the nature of evidence, how data should be collected and how potential bias should be viewed. Academics and researchers have been engaged in a long-established debate about the relative merits of qualitative and quantitative methods of inquiry and the quality of the evidence generated by such methods (see Chapter 12). Practitioners may, therefore, feel ill-equipped to disentangle the issues sufficiently to enable them to appraise evidence from studies about an intervention.

During and after a piece of work, practitioners gather evidence about their interventions, to monitor how efficiently their plans are being implemented, review their impact and see if changes are required and finally to evaluate their effectiveness in meeting service users' needs. This is 'reflective' or 'reflexive practice', because it brings together a range of factors affecting the situation and applies practitioners' thinking to the intervention.

Reviewing research evidence

According to Hamer and Collinson (1999: 6):

> Evidence-based practice is about finding, appraising and applying scientific evidence to the treatment and management of healthcare. Its ultimate goal is to support practitioners in their decision-making in order to eliminate the use of ineffective, inappropriate, too expensive and potentially dangerous practices.

In other words, when the practitioner is about to begin work with a service user, they should start by searching for evidence about what has been shown to work and what has been shown not to work in similar situations. The practitioner should then critically appraise the evidence to determine what intervention is most likely to be effective and then negotiate the implementation of this with the service user. Thus, the decision to place Sam for adoption might be based on research that suggests that the younger a child is placed for adoption, the more successful that adoption is likely to be (DH, 1999c).

Research in practice

Reviews are conducted by practitioners at specific decision points, in periodic meetings during or at the end of their work with the service user. For this review, practitioners 'research' or 'evaluate' the progress of the work and its outcomes for the service user. This requires:

> the application of a common core of research skills: in formulating research questions or hypotheses, in collecting or utilising data and analysing it in ways which address the questions, in interpreting the findings, and in communicating the results in writing or orally. (Fuller and Petch, 1995: 4)

It then involves the practitioner using the information gained from the research to inform their practice, both with this service user and in general. The importance of this is highlighted by Laing (1969: 4), who argues that:

> without time for critical reflection we may become dogmatic in theory and keep repeating ourselves in practice. We may even keep repeating a story about what we repetitiously do which does not even match what we do; especially if we do not have sufficient time to scrutinise what we are actually doing.

Combining evidence-based practice and reflection demonstrates how reviewing research before intervening and reflecting during and after intervening informs practice (see Figure 21.1).

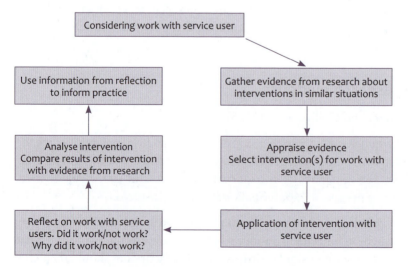

Figure 21.1 Combining evidence-based and reflective practice

Despite the importance of research for practice (Adams et al., 2009c, Part 3), social workers often appear reluctant to use it prospectively or retrospectively to inform their practice. While, as we suggested above, this may be because they are made to feel confused and uncertain by the debate about methodology or they are sceptical about the process of research and the findings that emerge from it, it may also be because they see research as ineffectual, remote from the real world, exploitative of service users and politically naive. Or it may be because they feel daunted by research, intimidated by the language typically used by researchers and deskilled by the prospect of engaging in it. In their study examining the connections between research evidence and social care practice, Hughes et al. (2001) argue that the potential users of research were put off if:

■ The style of the research was not adapted to the audience
■ The report was overly long
■ The policy and operational implications were not made clear
■ It was not seen as immediately relevant to practice
■ The study produced inconclusive or conflicting evidence.

Given the importance of evidence-based practice, how can practitioners be encouraged to embrace it more wholeheartedly? Macdonald (2000), Hughes et al. (2000) and Sheldon and Chivers (2000) stress the importance of improving training and staff development in critical appraisal skills and understanding research on both basic and advanced courses. Where such training has been provided, such as the practitioner research programme at Stirling University (Fuller and Petch, 1995) and the programmes at the Centre for Evidence-based Social Services at Exeter University (Macdonald, 2000), the outcomes appear to be positive. The more recent development of collaborative organisations, such as Making Research Count, Research in Practice and Research in Practice for Adults (see web addresses at end of chapter), has allowed practitioners, managers and researchers to work together on projects of interest to each other. An example of such collaborative work involved a joint project to look at social work roles with older people, which both stimulated staff development in the agencies involved and produced some conceptual clarification, and achieved academic and professional developments (Lymbery et al., 2007). Critical thinking and research-mindedness are likely to blossom where there are organisational cultures that support and encourage practitioners and managers to use and engage in research in this way.

Hughes et al. (2001) also list practitioner-friendly strategies that research producers might adopt to make research more palatable, such as providing accessible research summaries, like the Joseph Rowntree's *Findings*, National Children's Bureau's *Highlights*, Barnardo's *What Works* and the Department of Health's *Messages from Research*, employing a combination of dissemination methods, for example websites, the media, seminars and targeted mailing, and using language and a style of presentation that engage interest.

Reasons for reviewing

There are three main reasons why is it important for practitioners to review evidence before deciding on an intervention and to monitor and review the intervention they have implemented, and these are each discussed in turn.

Ethics

First, it is unethical to intervene in the lives of service users without seeking to gain an understanding of how an intervention has affected or might affect them and to share this understanding, where appropriate, with service users. At the least, both need to know that the intervention has not harmed or will not harm the service user, particularly as ethical codes of practice (going as far back as the medical Hippocratic oath of Greek times) demand that professional practice should not be maleficent, that is, it should do no harm. Section 5.1 of the General Social Care Council's code of practice (GSCC, 2002) requires that social care workers 'must not harm service users'. The potential for doing harm to Sam is real. Research by McCluskey (2000) suggests that the eventual outcomes for children in care, in their educational achievement, health, self-esteem, employment and other factors, are worse than those for other children, so Carol needs to monitor Sam's progress carefully to ensure that he is not being harmed. Social workers and service users also need to know about the beneficial effects of the intervention, particularly as section 1.3 of the code expects workers to 'support service users' rights to make informed choices about the services they receive' (GSCC, 2002). For example, Judy is given advice about her alcohol consumption and the relative merits of abstinence and reduction programmes. Reviewing the effectiveness of interventions demonstrates what harms and benefits have been or are being experienced by the service user.

For practitioners, review provides the opportunity to determine whether or not what they do is worthwhile. To assess this, workers ask questions such as:

■ Did I reach the best decision in determining the intervention? Was the decision based on evidence?
■ What effect, if any, has the intervention had on the service user?
■ Have I been intervening well, or well enough?

The answers to these questions provide valuable information about what works and why it works and what does not work and why it does not work. Thus, if the answers to these questions are positive, workers can demonstrate their effectiveness to themselves and others, particularly important in a climate in which the values of professional practice are continually being challenged. If the answers to these questions are ambivalent or negative, then workers can recognise why they have not been effective, can take remedial action and modify or change their practice to make it more effective.

Requirements

The second reason for reviewing work is the existence of formal requirements for social care workers to review their work. For example, section 6 of the GSCC's code of practice states: 'As a social care worker, you must be accountable for the quality of your work and take responsibility for maintaining and improving your knowledge and skills.' Reviews are also required by legislative guidance. For example, the decisions made about Sam and Judy at the case conference must be reviewed. *Working Together to Safeguard Children* says:

> The first child protection review conference should be held within three months of the initial child protection conference, and further reviews should be held at intervals of not more than six months for as long as the child remains the subject of a child protection plan. (DfES, 2006, para 5.128)

Meanwhile, the care of Sam in the foster placement must be subject to a first review within four weeks of placement; a second review within three months of the first review and later reviews within six months of the previous review (DH, 1991c). Guidance also specifies many of the review details. For example, research by Grimshaw and Sinclair (1997) suggests questions to be asked in reviews, quoted approvingly in recent guidance from the Department for Children, Schools and Families (DCSF, 2004: 11):

- What have been the outcomes of the last review?
- Is a new assessment of need called for?
- Has the care plan been called into question by developments?
- Do its objectives need to be reformulated?
- Or is it a question of choosing new means to achieve the same ends?
- How integrated does the care plan now appear?
- How is the principle of sensitive, open and shared planning being upheld?
- How cogent is the planning process?
- How is the current planning process being recorded so that it can be monitored as part of a flexible but continuous long-term process?

This shows how review is seen as a full critical reconsideration of the case, avoiding acceptance of the assumptions that underlay the previous plan.

Government pressures

The third reason for reviewing work connects with formal requirements: government pressures towards reviewing. Social work intervention, whether directly by the social worker or indirectly by the commissioning of services from others, involves spending public money, and government at both national and local levels has a duty to ensure that public money is being spent wisely. Thus, there has been an increasing emphasis on ensuring that all public services provide 'value for money' and this is policed through a range of agencies. For example, under the Health and Social Care

Act 2008, the Commission for Social Care Inspection will merge with two other regulators to become the Care Quality Commission in 2009.

Shaw (1996: 81) notes that:

> Cost-effectiveness, joint objective setting, strengthened accountability of welfare professionals, managerial effectiveness, explicit standards, performance monitoring and customer involvement, choice and satisfaction are recurring themes in the pleas and provisions for quality in the personal social services.

Clear objectives, standards or criteria for services have been set against which the performance of the service provider can be judged and there are guidelines regarding the content and process of review. There have been a succession of government programmes aiming to develop quality of service, or particular aspects of services. These include:

- The three-year *Quality Protects* programme (DH, 1998b), which aimed to provide effective protection, better quality care and improved life chances for children.
- A variety of national service frameworks (NSFs), in which the government sets and promotes a strategy for meeting the needs of a particular group of service users (for example DH, 1999a, 2001a). Social care services are often part of a multi-agency and multiprofessional effort to help people with particular conditions. Looking at the standards they set provides a clue to the sorts of standards aspired to.
- The Performance Assessment Framework (PAF), under which local authority achievements in various aspects of social care are assessed annually and given a rating. This process aims to ensure Best Value: 'the duty to deliver services to clear standards covering both cost and quality, by the most effective, economic and efficient means available' (DH, 2002e).
- The Care Services Efficiency Delivery (CSED, www.csed.csip.org.uk/) project was developed from a review of government efficiency in 2004 to try to improve the effectiveness of commissioning of services and to deliver 'person-centred care'. It produces TRACS – Tool for Rapid Analysis of Care Services.
- The Care Services Improvement Partnership (www.csip.org.uk/), set up in 2005, integrated a number of similar projects into four core programmes – social care, National Institute for Mental Health in England, children and young people, and health and social care in criminal justice, delivered through eight regional development centres.
- The Dignity in Care project was launched in 2006 to improve the extent to which people receiving various forms of care services felt that they were treated by practitioners in a dignified way (www.dh.gov.uk/en/SocialCare/Socialcarereform/Dignityincare/index.htm).
- Similar projects exist in Scotland, for example the National Care Standards Committee develops national care standards relevant to Scotland (Scottish Government, 2008).

Looking at this long, but by no means exhaustive list of initiatives, a critical practitioner might question why they have been developed. One issue is the increasing use of managerialist approaches to social care services (see Adams et al., 2009c, Ch. 17), which emphasise performance assessment using financial and statistical indicators rather than professional judgements. Managerialism also includes an assumption that developments need to be 'driven', rather than left to professionals' judgement and discretion. It also reflects a political focus on delivering specific policies, rather than seeing health and social care services in a holistic way. Rather than seeing Sam and Judy as part of a community and as a potential family, managerialist approaches to service provision tend to focus on specific problems and issues of political concern. The constant stream of revised plans and frameworks can cause confusion for practitioners and inconsistency for service users, whose involvement in care systems is longer than any particular government's enthusiasm for a particular structure or policy.

Such initiatives can, however, highlight the need for service development and focus on needs that are not well provided for, and may help to connect individuals' care with wider elements of the social and healthcare systems. For example, as part of the promotion of better mental health within the locality, Judy is receiving help from the CMHT because research suggests that for people whose alcohol consumption exceeds recommended guidelines, brief primary care interventions, such as an assessment of alcohol intake and provision of advice, can help to reduce it (NHS Centre for Reviews and Dissemination, 1997).

These government initiatives might seem remote from individual practice and review. However, they are significant at an individual level because the objectives, indicators and targets provide a template against which the performance of an individual worker or a group can be measured, and the worker or group needs to review so they can understand why their performance has exceeded, reached or failed to reach the standard. If Sam has experienced more placements than other children, Carol needs to know why this is the case in order to reduce the number of placements that Sam has in the future. Furthermore, the data provided for and by government tend to be quantitative and describe 'how much', but not much data provide a context and explanation for the figures. Frontline workers are in an ideal position to collect this qualitative data.

Reviewing in practice

Practitioners do not always experience these formal review processes positively. They are frequently seen as the blame culture or the suspicious organisation checking up on staff and attempting to 'find them out' – part of the 'checklist and truncheon' approach (Reid, 1988: 45). The evidence they produce is seen as highly suspect because it is based on what happens during the review, not what happens in real life. For example, prior to the review, which is advertised in advance, managers ask practitioners not to work with service users but to ensure that their case files are up to date as the latter will be measured by the reviewers. Shaw (1996: 88) refers to this type of formal review as 'evaluation with a big "E"' and he speculates that this strict management by effectiveness approach creates:

> a self-defeating threat to the development of practitioners evaluating in practice competencies [and that] management by measurement risks producing a concentration on easily measurable aspects of practice; organisational behaviour will change in order to score well on measurable criteria; agency performance requirements will take precedence at the expense of the service user and the professional role of the social worker will be put at jeopardy by management by measurement.

For example, Carol was irritated because she struggled to complete the initial assessment within seven days, as specified in the *Framework for the Assessment of Children in Need and their Families* (DH/DfEE/Home Office, 2000), but her professional view was that, because of the complexity created by Judy's mental health and drug and alcohol abuse and the involvement of a number of healthcare professionals, this was too short a period within which to complete a competent assessment. Nevertheless, she was encouraged to complete it within seven days because this is a measure used to assess the effectiveness of local authority childcare services (see SSI, 2002).

Social care workers are also suspicious about the interpretation of the evidence collected by 'evaluation with a big "E"' and the use that will be made of it. The Social Services Inspectorate Report (SSI, 2002) suggests that only 39 per cent of initial assessments are completed within seven days. Social workers may believe that this will be interpreted as evidence that they are not performing their tasks efficiently and their work will be policed even more rigorously. However, other interpretations might be that it is impossible to complete 'good' assessments within seven days and time limits should be increased or scrapped altogether, or that social workers' workloads are so large that they do not have the time to complete the assessments and more staff should be employed to reduce workloads.

Care management and looked-after children reviews

Reviewing is an important aspect of care management in adult community care, and integral to the system for looked-after children and for safeguarding children. In the care management guidance documents (SSI/SWSG, 1991), reviewing aims to evaluate whether the services have provided good outcomes for users and carers, but is also seen as a way of identifying service or quality shortfalls. This is particularly important as the quality and effectiveness of commissioning services in each locality are taken forward.

The government guidance on interagency working in safeguarding children considers reviewing in three contexts:

- The child protection review conference is an example of reviewing in the context of a continuing case: the aim is to examine changes in a child's circumstances, what actions have been taken and explicitly reconsider what decisions have been taken (DfES, 2006: 126–7); comprehensive reports are prepared for a meeting at which the child and parents are represented. A crucial element is the sense of active reconsideration of past decisions, and whether current circumstances still justify them.

- Child death review processes are an example of more formal and extended consideration of actions taken in a case, to inform decisions in other cases (DfES, 2006: Ch. 7).
- Provision for serious case reviews (DfES, 2006: Ch. 8).

Childcare plans for looked-after children must be regularly reviewed, under the *Review of Children's Cases (Amendment) (England) Regulations 2004* (DCSF, 2004). These regulations also require local authorities to appoint an independent reviewing officer, among whose responsibilities is to check on the children's human rights.

What to review

Although the review of practice comes after work has started with the service user, thinking about and planning the review must be included at the beginning, as at this early stage there needs to be clarity about what will be reviewed and how it will be reviewed. Plans for review must be made as part of the initial assessment in many of the formal processes discussed above. What will be reviewed is determined by setting objectives for the intervention against which the inputs, outputs and outcomes of the intervention can be assessed. As noted by Fook (2002: 165) in her discussion of evaluating social work interviews: 'An interview cannot be understood and therefore effectively evaluated without an appreciation of its function within a particular context.' The easiest objectives to be reviewed are those that are SMART – they are specific, measurable, achievable, relevant and time limited (for SMART criteria that are set for the development of performance indicators in mental health, see DH, 1999a: 97). For example, the work with Judy aimed at enabling her to provide for her son's needs. A SMART objective derived from this would be that she would visit Sam at the foster placement twice a week for six weeks and would spend no less than an hour playing with Sam on each visit.

Formal frameworks for children's assessment have existed for many years; the *Framework for the Assessment of Children in Need* document (DH/DfEE/Home Office, 2000) is still widely used, although the Common Assessment Framework for children and young people and the single assessment process for adults (Payne, 2009) have also been developed to promote interagency cooperation. These are constantly developing and provide tools accepted locally for assessment, which also permit evaluation and a review of decisions.

Setting objectives at the assessment stage of cases can be problematic as the various stakeholders involved in a social work intervention may have different views about what the objectives of the intervention are. For example, in Sam's case, some of the stakeholders are Sam himself, Judy, Carol, the foster parents, Judy's CMHT, the children's social care department, the adult social services department and the Department of Health and perhaps the Department for Children, Schools and Families. In terms of objectives, Judy's main objective is to have Sam back at home with no more involvement from social services but this conflicts with the objective of social services, which is to be able to demonstrate that Sam is safe and his needs are being met. The conflicting objectives of parents and social services departments create tensions, particularly as the objectives of the most powerful, social services, are more likely to set the agenda than the objectives of parents, despite notions of working partnership. Efforts to redress this balance can be seen in the development of family group conferences (Marsh and Crow, 1998), in which professionals are excluded from the decision-making process and families determine the objectives against which outcomes can be measured (although where there are child protection concerns, the family's objectives require the approval of professionals).

Professionals can also have conflicting objectives. The objectives that Carol has are strongly influenced by her duty to act in the best interests of the child and she believes that, in this case, his interests may be best served by adoption. Although Judy's CMHT must also act in the best interests of the child, they are also influenced by the requirement, under the *NSF for Mental Health*, to 'strengthen individuals to enhance their psychological well-being' (DH, 1999a: 15) and see Sam's rehabilitation with Judy as crucial in helping her to regain her self-esteem, confidence and motivation. Such conflicts between childcare and mental health professionals have been explored by Stanley and Penhale (1999: 34), who note that collaboration between mental health professionals and social workers was sometimes lacking and that this might be due to 'the way in which the problems of mothers and their children are conceptualised by different services'.

Clearly, there are problems in reviewing and assessing the outcomes of interventions with service users if there are disagreements about the objectives. If the objectives are set by professionals and the outcomes are measured by professionals, the intervention may be seen as effective. However, the service users might see the intervention as ineffective because it was not what they wanted anyway. As a parent who had approached social services because of the behaviour of her son put it: 'We went to [family therapy] … everything was directed at me. He was just drawing a picture. It was a waste of time. I had better things to do' (DH, 2000e: 68).

Furthermore, there is a danger that the indicators used to assess the achievement of an objective may be used because they are measurable rather than because they truly reflect the underlying objective. Thus, measuring the amount of time Sam's mother plays with him does not provide a measure of the quality of that play. In their study of local authority indicators in relation to looked-after children, Oliver et al. (2001) note that:

Staff frequently challenged the extent to which selected performance indicators represent a suitable measure of good social work practice. For example, a good piece of social work practice, a baby moved from hospital at birth to a foster placement then on to her adoptive family, all within a year … appeared as a negative statistic under the proxy measure of 'stability', that is, number of placements in a year.

Evaluating practice

Evaluation offers a more comprehensive consideration of services. Evaluation at the end of service provision examines the worth of the services provided to the people involved during the whole period of provision: have they helped service users and, separately, carers? It contributes to considering services of similar kinds provided to everyone. In considering how to review practice, practitioners need to consider what it is they want to find out and how they will find it out. Smith (1996) and the *NSF for Mental Health* (DH, 1999a) suggest that there are three major areas for evaluators to find out about:

1 *Inputs*, such as the resources that have been put into an intervention.
2 *Process*, what happens during the work, what is the throughput?
3 *Outcome*, which includes output and the value of the output.

Examining inputs provides some information about the efficiency of the work and encourages a consideration of whether or not the outcome of the intervention was worth the cost of the input and whether or not there were more efficient ways of achieving the same output. There appears to be little evidence that, in their evaluations of their work, practitioners consider the cost of inputs (usually their time) against the value of the outcome, and the review by the Audit Commission (1994) noted that even health and social care organisations were not always aware of the costs of the services they were providing.

The second area for evaluation is concerned with the process of the intervention and seeks to discover what was done, why it was done and how it was done. For example, Lonergan (2000) provides a detailed description of his work with a young man who is moving from foster care to independent living. This type of evaluation is usually linked to a qualitative approach.

The third area for evaluation is the outcome, which is made up of the output from an intervention, for example Sam's weight increasing since he went into foster care, and the value of that output, which, from the social worker's perspective, might be that this demonstrates that Sam's safety and welfare have been enhanced. This type of evaluation more usually adopts a quantitative approach. For example, Macdonald (2000) describes a randomised controlled trial that aimed to assess whether an intensive, natural parent-focused service would enhance placement outcomes for children.

The methods available to evaluate social work interventions range from carefully controlled experiments or surveys to single case studies or reflecting on practice (see

Alston and Bowles, 1998). Information can be gathered through observations, questionnaires, interviews, discourse analysis and the analysis of documents.

Concerned with the lack of progress in relation to Judy, Carol decides to have a thorough one-off review of the case because although there have been regular formal 'reviews', these have not fully explored her work with Judy and Sam (see Figure 21.1). Carol could use a review pro forma as described by Cheetham et al. (1992) but such forms can be formulaic and generally do not capture the complexity of practice. Instead she decides to embark on a summative case review using a 'research map' developed by Layder (1993). Layder (1993: 71) argues that:

> planning and designing research (or evaluation) projects involves consideration of the different levels of social life, [each] closely interrelated, but which for analytic and research purposes can be scrutinised separately.

The research map serves as a reminder of the complexity of the intervention as it explores the intervention from macro- to micro-levels:

- *Context*, including values, traditions, social and power relations such as class, gender, race relations
- *Setting*, including the immediate environment of social activity such as school, family, team, project, community group
- *Situated activity*, including interpersonal relations and the dynamics of face-to-face interaction
- *Self*, including biographical experience and social involvements as influenced by and interacting with the above.

Thus, in relation to her intervention with Judy, Carol can generate evidence from practice to answer, for example, the following questions:

- *In relation to context:* What general distribution of power and resources in society is relevant to the analysis of state intervention in Judy's life? What values, ideas and ideologies encourage or discourage certain forms of behaviour on the part of Judy in her role as a mother?
- *In relation to the social setting:* What forms of power, authority and control are there in the organisations providing the interventions – between staff, such as Carol, her manager, the voluntary organisations providing the parenting class and the intensive family support, and the service users; and between men and women and between different ethnic groups?
- *In relation to situated activity:* Who is doing what to whom in the parenting classes and in the intensive family support? What forms of communication are being used, verbal and nonverbal? What are the relationships and interactions between Judy and the workers who are providing services?
- *In relation to the self and situated activity:* What are Judy's subjective feelings associated with the parenting class and the intensive family support: feelings of disempowerment, low self-esteem, hopelessness, distrust/dislike/fear of authority?

Carol also decides to involve her supervisor in the review using Smyth's (1991) model of supervision, which includes describing, informing, confronting and reconstructing, as an aid to reflecting on her practice:

- In *describing*, Carol provides a description of her practice and outlines the confusion, ambiguities, contradictions and concerns that she has.
- In *informing*, she explores the meanings, theories and values that help to make sense of the description.
- In *confronting*, Carol thinks about how and why the case has developed in the way that it has and reflects on who has gained and who has lost throughout her work with Sam and Judy.
- In *reconstructing*, Carol works out how further involvement with Judy and Sam may be developed in different ways in the direction of 'good' practice and how Judy can be empowered by that practice.

Everitt and Hardiker (1996: 155) argue that 'this supervision provides ways in which to interrogate practice, to make explicit evidence of practice, and to tease out the thoughts, values, intentions and aspirations of the actors involved'.

Following this supervisory evaluation, Carol decides to recommend continuing work with Judy but the approach will be different. She will adopt an 'action research' approach that will include Judy throughout the process. Hart and Bond (1995: 3) argue that the:

> combination of enquiry, intervention and evaluation which powers the action research cycle mirrors the iterative processes involved employed by professional staff in assessing the needs of vulnerable people, responding to them and reviewing progress.

The main attraction of an action research approach is that it can be used to make changes in non-hierarchical and non-exploitative ways. Together, Judy and Carol will:

- Define the problem(s) and explore ways in which the problem(s) might be addressed
- Agree on a way to address the problem(s)
- Set objectives for work on the problem(s) and agree how objectives will be measured
- Work on resolving the problem(s)
- Review the work being done and assess the extent to which it is meeting or has met the objectives
- If the work has met its objectives, consider tackling another problem or close the case; if the work is meeting objectives, continue with the work; if the work is not meeting objectives, agree a different way of working
- Continue reviewing the progress of the work until the case can be closed.

Conclusion

Monitoring, evaluation and review are more complex than is implied by many of the formal review mechanisms considered here because they explore the process, output and outcome of social work practice from a range of perspectives, including those of the social worker and the service user. Nevertheless, despite the complexity, it is essential that practitioners consider their work critically, not merely because government or agencies require it but because effective practice is built on the learning gained from the practitioner's own past practice as well as the past practice of others.

Reviewing is as important a part of social work practice as assessing and intervening, and good, competent, effective practitioners will have developed an understanding of and skills in reviewing, alongside an understanding of and skills in assessing and intervening. As stated by Williams et al. (1999: 94):

> Social work is not an exact science but this does not make it an art to be performed on the basis of flair, intuition and affiliation to a particular school. In the absence of a more certain practice it is important that social work interventions are based on the best available understanding and the best available information about what works.

For further discussion of using supervision, see Adams et al., 2009c, Chapter 15, and for aspects of evaluating practice, see Adams et al., 2009c, Chapter 24.

http://www.rip.org.uk/index.asp   Research in Practice is a useful source of publications to support evidence-based practice.

http://www.ripfa.org.uk/   Research in Practice for Adults has a government-funded knowledge base, supplying research information about work with vulnerable adults.

http://www.uea.ac.uk/swk/MRC_web/public_html/   Making Research Count is a consortium including several universities, which provides research briefings.

Clarke, A. (1999) *Evaluation Research: An Introduction to Principles, Methods and Practice*, London, Sage. Clarke introduces the reader to the fundamental principles of evaluation by demonstrating how a wide variety of social research methods can be applied in different evaluation contexts in imaginative and creative ways. He outlines some of the conceptual, methodological and practical problems that might be encountered by the would-be evaluator.

DCSF (Department for Children, Schools and Families) (2004) *Independent Reviewing Officers Guidance: Adoption and Children Act 2002: The Review of Children's Cases (Amendment) (England) Regulations 2004*, London, DCSF. An interesting example of government guidance in reviewing.

Everitt, A. and Hardiker, P. (1996) *Evaluating for Good Practice*, Basingstoke, Macmillan – now Palgrave Macmillan. The authors argue that the increasing evaluation of social work and social care practice by government and organisations has turned evaluation into a mechanism for managerial and financial control. They go on to suggest ways in which this trend can be countered by practitioners conducting evaluations that will contribute to the development of 'good' practice and empower service users.

Shaw, I. and Lishman, J. (eds) (1999) *Evaluation and Social Work Practice*, London, Sage. The first three chapters of this book provide an overview of research and evaluation in social work practice. The remaining chapters are written by a range of contributors who provide examples to demonstrate how social workers can review their practice. This 'applied' aspect of the book makes it relevant to practitioners.

Part 3

THE PRACTICE ENVIRONMENT

Part 3 of this book provides the basis for understanding how social work services are delivered. Part 1 dealt in some detail with the main areas of knowledge that underpin social work and Part 2 explored the processes enabling practitioners to carry out the work. We now consider the environments in which this work takes place. These vary considerably, given that social work provision spans not only people's life courses, including childhood and parenting (Chapter 22), but also a variety of human problems of adulthood, involving health, mental health, impairment and the vulnerabilities which accompany these (Chapter 23).

The settings for social work do not just include public sector and local authority provision, but also services provided by organisations and agencies in the private, voluntary and independent sectors (Chapter 24). It is important to prepare for social work practice in these different settings (Chapter 25) and to examine what is entailed in such preparations. The process of learning in the workplace is demanding and never stops, because organisations re-organise, legislation and regulations change, and people move from one post to another. Finally (Chapter 26), we bring together all aspects of the previous chapters in the book under the general heading of personal and professional development. Every aspect of social work knowledge, understanding and practice has implications not only for practice at work but also for how practitioners develop as people. Because social workers reflexively use their own personalities in their work, drawing on emotions and thoughts arising from their own experiences, we cannot disentangle personal and professional development.

Working with children, young people and families

22

Chapter overview

This chapter introduces an array of children's services that respond to the many problems affecting children, young people and their parents. Inevitably, given its breadth of responsibilities, social work with children and young people tends to be multiprofessional, involving health, education and social work agencies and community, residential and daycare roles. It also takes place in a variety of settings, reflecting the complexity of needs of children, young people and families and the range of services engaged with meeting them.

Social changes

Social workers deal with a range of psychological and interpersonal problems as well as with the more intractable personal and emotional consequences of the economic and social changes affecting families in the UK, including the vulnerability of children and young people to harm or neglect.

The lives of families are changing, as a reflection of wider changes in society. Apart from other less apparent changes in lifestyle, changes in the family structure of the typical household are very visible. Although in the last quarter of the twentieth century, the average number of children in a family decreased only marginally, from 2.0 to 1.8, the proportion of dependent children living in a lone-parent family increased from 1 in 14 to 1 in 4 by 2004 (www.statistics.gov.uk). Some parts of the UK, such as large tracts of Wales and Scotland, had, until the start of the twenty-first century, experienced largely static or even falling populations. Population growth here and in many urban districts of England has begun due to migration from other parts of the country and from other countries in Europe and Asia. One effect is that children in many rural as well as urban settings are now growing up in more ethnically and culturally diverse communities.

In some societies, children, particularly male children, are highly valued. For

Child socialisation refers to the processes by which the child acquires knowledge of and skills in behaving according to the culture and customs of the community in which the child lives.

Childhood has some universal characteristics, such as physical and psychological maturation and some form of transition to adulthood. Beyond this, childhood is not a universal reality, fixed by the age of the child. It is a social and cultural construction and legal measures applying to children vary from country to country.

historical and cultural reasons, the 11 million or so children and young people in the UK occupy a somewhat problematic place. The low status of children and the relatively punitive nature of child socialisation over many generations endure into the twenty-first century. Childhood and adolescence are widely perceived not just as periods of rapid development but also, in the case of teenagers, as an essential troubled and troubling period in the transition from childhood to adulthood.

Childhood is a changing phenomenon as society changes. Childhood is not fixed and universally tied to age stages and growing up, but is partly, as James and James (2004: 6–9) show, a cultural construct defined by policy and legal enactments. The ages at which children are no longer treated as children but as adults vary greatly from country to country. The aspects of childhood treated differently include the ages at which children:

- must begin and end compulsory schooling
- can vote
- are regarded as having criminal responsibility and liability to prosecution under the law
- can or cannot be subjected to physical, that is, corporal, punishment such as caning or smacking by parents or adults in charge
- can buy tobacco or alcohol or smoke or drink various types and quantities of alcoholic drinks in public or in private
- can consent to sexual relationships with other minors or with adults
- can undertake full-time work.

Childhood is not just a legal construct but is a social and cultural construct as well. As Franklin (1995: 7) acknowledges, the variety of childhoods that children experience 'are social constructs formed by a range of social, historical and cultural factors'. This means that we cannot define childhood in a simple, unambiguous way. Childhoods are experienced differently by children in different circumstances. One person's childhood is, quite literally, the happiest time of their life, while another cannot wait to escape from being a child.

Childhood is a legal category, even though within the UK, in Europe and in other countries, the legal definition of different aspects of the lives of children and young people is completely lacking in consensus.

Children's services need to be understood in the wider context of social policies aiming to tackle child and family poverty (see Chapter 7). The factors that segregate different groups of children, young people and families tend to be the social factors – often exacerbated by social class, ethnic, faith and cultural differences – which contribute to inequalities and discrimination. Prominent among these inequalities is child and family poverty, which affects almost 4.5 million children, about 2.4 million of whom are living in families on income support; they also suffer from other disadvantages such as lack of food and clothing, poor housing and worsened educational opportunities and achievements. A third of children and young people in the UK suffer directly through harm done to them by other people and indirectly through the effects of social inequalities such as poverty. Services for children and their families also struggle every year to cope with the consequences of poor housing, unemployment and exclusion. The Labour government lifted about 600,000 children out of poverty between 1997 and 2007, but is unlikely to meet its interim target of halving child poverty by 2010 and it is still an open question as to whether it will achieve its aim of abolishing child poverty by 2020. According to Hirsch's (2006) estimate, this may be achieved through benefits and tax credits but it will be hugely expensive, unless wider educational and social methods are also used.

Policy context

In the early twenty-first century, social work with children, young people and families has undergone major changes in policies, laws and procedures. These reflect in part the anti-poverty policies referred to above and partly an increasing climate of concern about safeguarding children from the sufferings they are perceived to be enduring, through abuse, neglect and failure to thrive. To some extent, these assumed evils of 'poverty' and 'abuse' are labels that simplify the complexity of problems faced by children and families and enable politicians, managers and professionals to develop pragmatic policies to tackle them.

The mass media also have played an increasingly important role in shaping public responses to professional social work (Franklin and Parton, 1991). A letter to *The Times* in 1944 by Lady Allen about the poor state of orphanages, plus the Monckton Report (1945) following the death of Dennis O'Neill in foster care, was followed by the Curtis Committee (1946), which led to the setting up of children's departments in 1948. From the early 1970s, problems of child abuse – physical, sexual and emotional, to say nothing of other aspects such as financial deprivation and child neglect – began to be recognised. The death of Maria Colwell, fostered by her aunt and uncle and killed by her stepfather, was followed by an inquiry report (Secretary of State for Social Services, 1974), which led to policy and practice changes in the Children Act 1975. This prioritised the welfare of the child in decisions about social work services for children and families. The inquiry report into child abuse in Cleveland (Butler-Sloss, 1987) led to the Children Act 1989, which consolidated previous legislation and stated that the welfare of the child was paramount. Thirty years later, the Laming Report (2003) of the inquiry into the death of Victoria Climbié, the culmination of a further series of child abuse inquiries (Munro, 2004b), led to the Children Act 2004, which brought about the reorganisation of social services and education services in England and Wales into integrated children's services.

At the same time, successive inquiries into abuses of children by staff in residential childcare (Hughes, 1986; Brannan et al., 1993; Kirkwood, 1993; Levy and Kahan, 1991; Williams and McCreadie, 1992; DH, 2000f) have indicated the need for reforms to the system of local authorities looking after children taken into care (Hobbs and Hobbs, 1999).

The responses of adults, individually and collectively through social policies, to children's problems as displayed in disturbed behaviour have traditionally been ambivalent at best and punitive at worst. This ambivalence is evident in the twin goals of justice and welfare reflected in children's legislation. The justice goal itself is divided between the purpose of meeting society's expectations of justice – imposing sanctions on parents perceived as falling short of their parental responsibilities and punishing children who transgress or exhibit problem behaviour – and meeting the requirement that children receive justice, through satisfying their rights. Some of the judicial sanctions applied to parents since the late 1990s are significantly punitive. Intervention was strengthened under the Crime and Disorder Act 1998, which granted local authorities powers to apply to courts for a parenting order, where parents were prosecuted under section 444(1) of the Education Act 1996 for failing to ensure that their child attended school. In 2003, the Anti-social Behaviour Act extended these powers of intervention, enabling local authorities to apply for a parenting order where a child was excluded from school. A parenting order is a civil court order requiring a parent to attend counselling or parenting classes, usually for up to 12 months.

The welfare goal leads to what King (2005: 65–6) identifies as three main policy responses to children's suffering – once its multitude of forms have been renamed as 'abuse' – driven by the justification of meeting the needs of children, in their best interests:

1 Through *social hygiene approaches*, where the abuse is perceived as widespread in areas of society lacking 'community spirit, neighbourliness, a social conscience, parenting skills, self-discipline, religion and education' (King, 2005: 65).
2 Through *medical approaches*, whereby pathologies are diagnosed and biological and psychological symptoms of problem behaviour are treated.
3 Through *pathological families approaches*, which involve categorising certain families as dysfunctional and developing different remedial treatments to correct this.

Returning to the justice goal, we find the focus not upon the welfare needs of the child, but upon giving the child rights, so that the child has the power to say 'no' and can state personal wishes and preferences so that adults can help them to achieve them.

Laws, policies and procedures continue to reflect the tension between these twin goals of safeguarding children and advocating their rights, as we now explore.

Safeguarding children

A vast formal apparatus of professionals, committees and procedures continues to manage the potential risks of abuse or harm to children, while overseeing the criteria for responding to children regarded as problems or at risk of becoming problems.

The Children Act 1989 in England and Wales and its equivalents in Scotland and Northern Ireland provide the legal basis for about 60,000 children to be looked after at any one time in the UK. 'Looked-after' children constitute about 16 per cent of the total of children regarded as 'in need' of social care services, including social work. The majority of looked-after children are placed in foster care and an increasing proportion of these are later adopted.

Children's rights

While the balance of children's legislation continues to prioritise the child's welfare as paramount, it contains elements of children's rights as well. For example, most of the legislation contains measures to ensure that the child's wishes and choices are heard, when decisions about the future welfare of the child are being made by professionals.

Symbolic of the increasing importance attributed to children's rights in the UK was the establishment of children's commissioners, with slightly different titles and briefs in the four devolved countries, but with the general function of promoting awareness of children's views and interests. Wales was first to appoint a children's commissioner, in 2001, under the Care Standards Act 2000. In Scotland, the commissioner for children and young people was inaugurated under the Commissioner for Children and Young People (Scotland) Act 2003 and in the same year in Northern Ireland under the Commissioner for Children and Young People (Northern Ireland) Order 2003. In England, it was not until the Children Act 2004 that a children's commissioner was made law.

Taken as a whole, these new laws and associated procedures provided the basis for children's services to be provided on an integrated basis through newly created 'children's trusts' in new local authority departments, formed by merging education and social services departments. At the same time, a number of measures have been taken to strengthen work with families, both intervention and prevention forming part of government policy. However, research by the Audit Commission (2008) indicates that progress towards the joint commissioning of services and integrated working is patchy and slow, due to the failure of children's trusts to give a clear enough lead.

Tensions exist in England between the focus of children's services on children and the historical rooting of social work with children in work with families. There is a cultural gulf between the focus on the individual child of much schooling and youth work and the focus of social work with children and families. The reality is that the lives and experiences of children and young people are shaped by a great many people, institutions and services, some of which are more apparent than others (Figure 22.1).

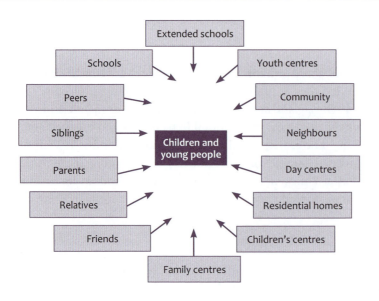

Figure 22.1 Factors shaping experiences of children and young people

Every Child Matters

Following continuing child abuse scandals in the 1990s, which exposed weaknesses in childcare and child protection in England, Wales and Scotland in particular, and then the Laming Report (2003), which contained recommendations about the priority to be given to reforming child protection and social work with children and families, the early twenty-first century has witnessed a fresh wave of childcare legislation. The immediate spur to legislation was the government Green Paper *Every Child Matters* (DfES, 2003), followed by the Children Act 2004, which provided the legal foundation in England and Wales (the legislation is complicated because some non-devolved provisions apply throughout the UK and some provisions, such as the setting up of a children's commissioner for England, do not apply in Wales) for the implementation of the recommendations of *Every Child Matters*. Under section 10 of the Act, the following outcomes were identified as necessary to each child's wellbeing: be healthy, stay safe, enjoy and achieve, make a positive contribution and achieve economic wellbeing. The Children Act 2004 established integrated children's services, creating new children's services departments from merged education and social services departments. The Childcare Act 2006 transformed early years and childcare provision in England, based on the ten-year childcare strategy published by HM Treasury in 2004. The Childcare Act 2006 prescribed the responsibilities of local authorities for early children's services and adopted a Common Assessment Framework to ensure that the five *Every Child Matters* goals were met. In line with the major recommendations of the Laming Report, measures were taken to try to update and improve the effectiveness of interagency joint working to safeguard children (DfES, 2006).

Common Assessment Framework

The Common Assessment Framework (CAF) incorporated as part of the *Every Child Matters* agenda is the basis for all assessment of children's needs, save in circumstances where there is a risk of harm. In that case, as laid down by the Children's Workforce Development Council (CWDC, 2007), the practitioner should follow the procedures prescribed by the local safeguarding children board.

The enhanced procedures for assessing children reflected the need for improved practice arising from earlier *Messages from Research* (DH, 1995a). The assessment procedures embodied in the CAF were in place by the millennium (DH/DfEE/Home Office, 2000). These entailed a 'triangle' of equally important components of systematic assessment of needs (DH/DfEE/Home Office, 2000: 17) (see Figure 16.2):

1 the child's developmental needs
2 the parental capacity of the parents
3 the family and environmental factors.

Assessment of these three aspects leads to prioritising children in three categories:

1 *High priority need:* This includes children who would be in immediate danger without help, for example through abuse, neglect or family breakdown.
2 *Medium priority need:* This includes children whose health or development could suffer without support services.
3 *Low priority need:* This includes children who need advice, information or another universally available service giving access to community resources for children and families.

The CAF contributes to the achievement of two sets of standards:

1 The five goals for children set out in *Every Child Matters*:
   ■ Being healthy
   ■ Staying safe
   ■ Enjoying and achieving
   ■ Making a positive contribution
   ■ Achieving economic wellbeing.
2 The five standards set out in the *National Service Framework for Children, Young People and Maternity Services* (DH, 2004), for improving delivery of health and social care:
   ■ Health and wellbeing
   ■ Delivering child-centred services
   ■ Safeguarding and promoting welfare
   ■ Supporting disabled children and those with complex health needs
   ■ Promoting mental health and psychological wellbeing.

Practising social work with children and families

Social work with children cannot be practised in isolation from work with their families, or in isolation from wider policies concerned with their living environment and their schooling. The rate of poverty for large families in the UK is the highest of any country in the Organisation for Economic Co-operation and Development (OECD) (Bradshaw and Mayhew, 2006). A Child Poverty Action Group (CPAG) briefing, based on measuring poverty as an income below 50 per cent of average income after housing costs are deleted, estimates that about 14 million people, 1 in 4 of the population of the UK, lived in poverty in 1997/98, in contrast with 1 in 10 in 1979, including approximately 63 per cent, nearly two-thirds, of lone-parent families (www.cpag.org.uk/info/sp_briefings/0200childpov.htm). There is ample evidence that the health of children correlates strongly with the wealth or poverty of their families (Barnes et al., 2008). About 2.4 million poor children are more likely to be born prematurely and to be less healthy and more prone to accidents and illnesses than other children (Barnes et al., 2008). They are more likely to grow up into poverty and, as adults, to be unemployed or in low paid work, to live in poor housing, to have a criminal record and to abuse alcohol and drugs. Consequently, improvements in the health of children and young people depend not only on health, social work and education interventions but on factors lying beyond these. In fact, not only are some inequalities in children's health growing more pronounced, but some healthcare interventions may increase these inequalities still further.

The Families at Risk Review *Reaching Out: Think Family* was launched by the government in 2007 (Social Exclusion Task Force, 2007). It aimed:

- to use evidence of the consequences for the life chances and outcomes of children that parental family circumstances could have, by breaking into the cycle of disadvantage passed on through the generations
- to concentrate on early intervention by agencies using a joined-up approach, focusing on trying to help the most excluded 2 per cent of families, who are living in poverty and whose needs are complex, who suffer from complex problems and have low aspirations.

EXaMPLE

Trenton is our fictitious name for a largely urban English local authority, the profile of which we have compiled from comparable actual statistics of a reasonably deprived local authority of about 100,000 people, including 30 per cent (30,000) children aged 0–19 years. According to the index of multiple deprivation (ODPM, 2004), 10 of the local authority's 15 wards (a district of the local authority) are in the top 10 per cent most deprived in England. Unemployment, at 5 per cent, is twice the national average and 20 per cent (8,200) of households have dependant children, with half of these being lone-parent households. Life expectancies in different wards vary as much as 14 years for males and 12 years for females. In 2005, Trenton had:

- 620 children in need receiving social care services
- 130 looked-after children
- 110 on the child protection register
- 475 children with a statement of special needs (indicating that the local authority recognises that their learning disabilities require additional educational resources).

Responding to needs: integrated children's services

'Integrated children's services' is the phrase commonly used to refer to the joined-up services that in English local authorities aspire to cater for the needs of children and young people, and their parents and carers, from birth to age 19, and, in the case of some vulnerable groups, to age 25. Integrated children's services provided in Nottingham (www.nottinghamics.co.uk/), for example, include:

- schools providing extended hours activities, such as before- and after-school clubs, and becoming the focus for a range of training, leisure and recreation, health and employment services for children, young people and the wider community
- a network of children and family centres for children aged 0–5 across an entire local authority
- multidisciplinary teamwork with children and families, led by one coordinating and leading professional to maximise information-sharing and service provision.

In Scotland, similar initiatives have been taken, based on the proposals in *Getting it Right for Every Child* (Scottish Executive, 2005d) since the report *For Scotland's Children* was published in 2001 (Scottish Executive, 2001b). As part of this, the social inclusion partnership programme resources a network of 54 social inclusion partnerships, which combine coordination, prevention and innovation to tackle social exclusion, by providing play and recreational childcare and extended school programmes.

EXaMPLE (cont'd)

Trenton local authority has set out the policy and practice priorities for the local authority in the children and young people's plan (Table 22.1). From this, we can see the broad scope of services provided by the children's services department.

Table 22.1 Key priorities for local authority services for children and young people

Being healthy
Improving diet through expanding leisure and sporting opportunities at school
Reducing childhood obesity, by improving school meals, providing cookery for all school pupils
Developing a programme of parental education
Improving availability of healthy food in the wards with highest illness and premature death rates
Extending cessation of smoking programmes
Reducing teenage conception rates
Reducing rates of sexually transmitted diseases among children and young people
Improving child and adolescent mental health services
Reducing incidence of children and young people with complex, persistent and severe behavioural disorders
Increasing inclusiveness of special education in mainstream schools
Staying safe
Improving the present therapeutic social work service for children and young people
Improving the running of the local safeguarding children's board
Develop preventive programme to reduce the number of child protection conferences
Reduce the number of initial and core assessments of children
Improving anti-bullying programmes in schools and the community
Improving the long term stability of looked-after children, by:
– reducing the number of long-term (more than four years) looked-after children who have changed foster parents within the past two years
– increasing the proportion of looked-after children who move towards being adopted
Enjoying and achieving
Increasing the resources allocated to supporting vulnerable children and young people in schools
Setting up learning support centres for disaffected children and young people
Improving the educational achievement of children and young people
Increasing the rates of excluded pupils who are successfully reintegrated
Improving the quality and range of recreational facilities, in partnership with private, voluntary and independent partners
Making a positive contribution
Enable children and young people to make the transition from children's to adult services
Provide emotional literacy and social development programmes for schools
Ensure that children from black and minority ethnic groups have equal access to services
Ensure that all children and young people can contribute to service development through participation strategy for children, young people and parents
Increase the proportion of looked-after children participating in their reviews
Enable looked-after children and young people to participate in appointments of care staff
Reduce criminal and antisocial behaviour through preventive and rehabilitation services
Develop restorative justice and services to victims of crime
Achieving economic wellbeing
Improving the quality of housing occupied by children and young people
Reduce the number of young people, including those with learning disabilities, not in education, training or employment
Improve the number of young people from disadvantaged groups engaged in education, training or employment (retention rates)
Increase the number of young people entering higher education (progression rates)
Increase proportion of child benefit recipients claiming child tax credit
Increase the number of families receiving direct payments
Reduce the proportion of care leavers who become homeless

Practice issues

We highlight here a number of aspects of practice that present particular issues for social work practice: family and parental support; early years services; focus on risk; child abuse and neglect; looked-after children; young carers; asylum and immigration control; young offenders; partnership and participation; and finally, the tensions between locking children up, protecting or liberating them.

Family and parental support and punitive interventions

Parents are the most important factor shaping the outcomes for their children. Child development knowledge provides crucial underpinning to enable parents, to say nothing of child and family workers, to understand the needs of children and families. The months of pregnancy and the early years, particularly the first three years, of a child's life are the most significant in terms of the vital importance of the role of the parents.

Government policies reflect ambivalence towards parents rather than unconditionally supporting them. Policy and social work with children and parents tend to be built around the twin objectives of supporting families, and imposing punitive sanctions on parents who fall short and are held responsible for perceived shortcomings in their children's behaviour. In the post-welfare state era, good citizenship is held by government to be conditional upon the parent socialising the child adequately. The dominant assumption is that the problems represented by children and young people – such as truancy from school – originate within the household and that parents are at least partly responsible for this. We shall briefly illustrate in turn the twin, contrasting aspects of family and parental support and punitive sanctions against parents.

Family and parental support

'Family support' is an umbrella term covering a wide range of activities at the different levels of individual, family, neighbourhood and community. The vast majority of families need support at one or more of these different levels at different stages of the development of children and at different points in the lives of adults in the family. Different stresses affect people in a variety of ways throughout the life course and many parents take on several tasks at once when they live in a family household; being a partner, being a parent, being a brother/sister, being a neighbour and being a friend are just a few of these. The complex challenge of juggling work, home life and education and training are not restricted to childhood or adulthood, but increasingly affect people at different points in their lives.

Family support can take many forms: financial, physical and emotional. Respite care for parents may provide parents with space to tackle issues between them. The decisions that parents make before birth can have consequences for their child's subsequent health and wellbeing. Low birth weight, for example, increases the chances of death before age one or, if the baby survives, increases the likelihood of adult heart disease and diabetes. The importance of health-led family support and the contribution of the midwife and health visitor are increasingly recognised, as are support services and parenting programmes geared to responding to the needs of parents and children.

Many activities fall under the heading of family or parental support. Parental support strategies were introduced in 2005 as part of the government's parenting strategy under the Local Government Act 2003. The term 'progressive universalism' was used to refer to a strategy ensuring that:

■ all parents receive extra support at particular points, including key transitions such as birth and the first year of a child's life
■ parents with extra needs, because of the challenging circumstances they face, receive the greatest interventions and supports.

Parent support services include a range of activities and services that focus on giving parents and carers information, advice and support in bringing up their children. This could include helping parents to:

■ bond better with their children
■ help children learn
■ develop routines with their children
■ improve their communication skills with children
■ deal with difficult behaviour.

Social workers may become involved in parenting programmes, home visits and focus group meetings with parents where difficulties have arisen.

A focus group is a group that may be suggested by the social worker after a child has become involved in challenging problems at school. The parent and the child will be present. The meeting may take place at home, at school or on neutral territory such as a children's centre or drop-in centre. The social worker may suggest that a particular teacher is invited. The parent may be able to veto this and suggest another teacher and propose which additional people are invited. The purpose of the meeting would be to discuss the behaviour and try to arrive at strategies for preventing the behaviour recurring and, in the event that it recurs, coping with similar situations in future.

Parent support advisers may be appointed to schools. Their role involves prevention or early intervention, supporting children and families and working in partnership with parents. A parenting programme may be linked with the appointment of a mentor for the parent or child and one-to-one tuition for the child. A parental support adviser may help with school attendance, support parents through the exclusion of their child from school, help their child to engage in learning and development, support transitions from one school to another, and improve relationships and communication between parents and school.

Punitive interventions

In the case of truancy, legislation – the Education Act 2000, which increased the penalty for the parent of a truanting child from £1,000 to £2,500, a community punishment or three months' imprisonment, and the Anti-social Behaviour Act 2003, which introduced parenting orders that require parents to attend counselling, guidance or residential training regarding the child's behaviour – empowers the local authority to take legal action against parents whose child persistently truants.

Early years services

The years since 2000 have seen the major reorganisation of early years services, involving the merger of educational and social services for younger children. The term used to describe childminding and daycare for children under eight is 'early education'. For decades there have been issues concerning the heterogeneous and inconsistent nature of provision in this area, much of it being informally arranged between mothers, for example through unregistered childminders and preschool playgroups, and many of the facilities employing untrained staff. Many poorer parents have been disadvantaged and forced into unsocial work through the unavailability of high-quality, state-subsidised nurseries and childminding. Improved childcare benefits for working parents (such as child tax credit and working tax credit) go some way to ameliorating these problems. The Care Standards Act 2000, amended by the Children Act 2004, has shifted responsibility for regulating this area – that is, registering and inspecting, investigating complaints and enforcing compliance with national standards of childminding, full daycare, sessional daycare, crèches and out of school care – from local authorities to Her Majesty's Chief Inspector of Schools (HMCI) at the Office for Standards in Education (Ofsted), where it now sits alongside government-funded nursery education for children aged three to four. These measures amount to central government taking a firm hold by imposing standards of services and inspection from the centre, alongside **managerialism** at the local level, through which managers now manage and professionals intervene to direct the foundation curriculum for child development and learning in the preschool sector, where formerly parents and children initiated their own activities through the self-help playgroup movement. Sure Start, a government-led initiative to provide additional services for young children and their families, is based on intensive family support initiatives in the US. Early evaluation of Sure Start was discouraging, with improved outcomes only for better off families, those in the most socially excluded circumstances actually being worse off (Tunstill et

> **Managerialism** can be understood as the faith in the applicability of management principles and techniques to the benefit of any organisation's activities. In the social sciences, including social work, the term tends to be used more critically. It draws attention to the ways in which managerial authority and control can invade the territory of professionals and undermine or distort their legitimate area of expertise with techniques such as performance management. The term 'new managerialism' is used particularly to refer to ways in which services are restructured and reorganised around principles such as efficiency and cost effectiveness. In these cases, professionals may feel deskilled and consider their professional autonomy restricted.

al., 2005). More encouragingly, later evaluation showed benefits for the most excluded families (Tunstill and Allnock, 2007).

Focus on risk

We can adopt a critical view of the weighting of priorities in children's social services since the 1980s, towards the identification and management of risk. There is an ambiguity in this, since in one way children are regarded as subject to risks – such as the risk of harm or abuse – and in another way they are regarded as sources of risks to others, through their difficult, disruptive or criminal behaviour. So, in one sense, children are viewed as victims and, in another sense, they are demonised. In response to these twin concerns, policy and practice on child protection on one hand and young offender management and treatment on the other hand remain the highest priority children's and young people's services in terms of expenditure and resources. This complex picture helps to explain why social work with children and young people remains quite controversial. Parton (1998) points out that in this way social work is always liable to be contested because it occupies the territory between respectable and potentially vulnerable people on one hand and excluded and potentially dangerous people on the other hand.

Child abuse and neglect

In no other area of social work with children, young people and adults does the actual practice – what practitioners do – influence the outcomes for children more directly than the area of child abuse and neglect. At the same time, there are wider, environmentally induced factors that affect children and families. The extent of child abuse and neglect is positively correlated with poverty. It follows that to be effective, social work needs to contribute to helping families, in one way or another, to tackle the worst effects of poverty for them. In addition, community-based initiatives may strengthen and develop support networks for parents and other family members and, directly and indirectly, may contribute towards safeguarding children (Macdonald, 2002: 211).

Looked-after children

The local authority, through the children's services department, is legally responsible for the welfare of all looked-after children. Most resources are taken up with fostering children, while adoption and children in residential care take up the bulk of the remaining resources.

Unsurprisingly perhaps, in view of the above statement, foster care is the most common placement for looked-after children. The importance of children retaining contact with their birth families, even though they may be living in temporary and longer term foster placements, has been increasingly accepted. Family placement services depend on a range of placements and it is important for these to be well supported and well resourced and for foster parents to receive adequate training. Kinship care – where a relative or friend volunteers to look after a child – is an increasingly important way forward, often culturally sensitive, offering a way out of shortages of suitable potential placements and is well regarded by children and young people (Broad et al., 2007).

Foster care may be directly through the local authority or, once the child has been with the foster parent for 28 days, through a private arrangement between a parent and someone who is not another parent or relative, when the parents and carers have a duty to inform the local authority of the arrangement, under the Children Act 1989. Adoption consists of the permanent placement of a child with adults, who take on full parental responsibility, and since 2000, the government has taken measures to accelerate the process of adoption (DH Adoption and Permanence Taskforce, 2001).

Young carers

The circumstances of young carers as a particularly vulnerable group have become better known in Britain and other European countries since the mid-1990s. Research has established that children and young people who care for a parent who is ill or long-term disabled suffer negative effects on their own education, job prospects, social life and development towards independence (Dearden and Becker, 2000).

Asylum and immigration control

Political considerations affect policy and practice in the area of asylum and immigration control. Since 2000, legislation (Nationality, Immigration and Asylum Act 2002; Asylum and Immigration (Treatment of Claimants etc) Act 2004; Immigration, Asylum and Nationality Act 2006) has imposed progressively tighter restrictions on immigration, especially for refugees and asylum seekers.

Young offenders

Social work with young offenders tends to take place through youth offending teams that work multiprofessionally (Adams et al., 2009b, Ch. 24, Adams et al., 2009c, Ch. 5). The most effective interventions with young offenders in terms of reducing the chances of future offending are not necessarily those most used by magistrates or most favoured by the general public. This is because public attitudes towards young offenders remain stubbornly punitive.

The Crime and Disorder Act 1998, linked with the growing emphasis by the government on joined-up local strategies, has led to a proliferation of initiatives aiming to promote safer communities as well as community-based programmes targeting young offenders and their offending. The Crime and Disorder Act confirmed the goal of preventing offending by children and young people, partly by using the new orders it introduced for reparation, parenting and community-based action plans aiming to tackle offending behaviour. Research confirms the necessity for early intervention, since the earlier children begin offending, the more likely they were to become career criminals (Loeber and Farrington, 1998; Rutter et al., 1998). Many young people are involved in illegal alcohol consumption and drug taking (see Adams et al., 2009c, Ch. 10).

Partnership and participation

Children's services are delivered by statutory and voluntary and, increasingly, by private agencies and organisations, working in partnership with children and families. The Children Act 1989, the Children (Scotland) Act 1995 and the Children (Northern Ireland) Order 1995 all emphasise the need to engage children and young people in direct participation (Aldgate and Seden, 2006: 231). There is a growing body of research indicating preferred ways of promoting and implementing participation by children and young people (NcNeish and Newman, 2002).

The engagement of children and young people in community development has become increasingly prominent, but this is mainly associated with the broader agenda of urban regeneration. These are frequently associated with leisure and play facilities, which we can regard as the easier areas for the participation agenda. Craig (2002: 114) observes that such work takes place 'against a context of many structural inhibitors to effective child or young person participation, such as dominant rural and urban planning trends, or generalist community approaches that do not recognise the need for children to have a separate voice'.

Putting children in custody, protecting or liberating them

To return to the tension we identified near the start of this chapter, we can regard children from a welfare perspective as targets for protection and safeguarding, or from a justice perspective as entitled to enhanced rights. Advocating children's rights is not the same as advocating treating children as miniature adults. Childhood is a part of the life course to be respected as a unique stage in its own right. Children have the right to be childish. In the 1980s, children's rights were perceived as in tension between protecting them (protectionism) and freeing them from the restrictions of childhood (liberationism) (Franklin, 1986). In the twenty-first century, the distinction tends to be posed in terms of protection versus participation (Franklin, 2005: 9). Few people would question children's right to be protected, but many would agree with John Stuart Mill that children do not have the maturity and capacity to reason, which would entitle them to take part on an equal basis with adults (Franklin, 2005: 10).

Prout (2005) identifies the tension between two trends: on one hand an increased tendency towards greater control and regulation of children and on the other hand towards treating children as having the capacity for self-realisation.

Unfortunately, the entitlement of children to 'justice' can be argued either from a progressive direction or from a punitive one. The UK offers children and young people who transgress a particularly bleak, often custodial response, and one often associated with other punitive consequences (see Adams et al., 2009b, Ch. 24). Sir Aynsley-Green, the children's commissioner for England, states that 'the UK has one of the worst records in Europe for detaining children' (*New Statesman*, 4 September 2008). A confusing mass of conventions and laws apply to children's rights in the UK, which in total do not provide inviolable protection for their rights. Basic rights for children and young people are set out in a variety of UN, European and UK laws, conventions and procedures (Table 22.2). From 1981, the UK opted out of the provision of the UN Convention on the Rights of the Child, so as to enable the government to sanction the continued detention of child migrants and asylum seekers without judicial scrutiny. Gillian Slovo writes that 'only asylum-seekers' children can be locked up without committing a crime' (*New Statesman*, 11 September 2008). This overrode the principle of the Children Act 1989 that priority should be given to the best interests of the child. In September 2008, the government ended this opt-out, thus making it more difficult for children to be locked up, sometimes for one or two months, pending deportation.

The concerns of pressure groups continued about the treatment of children held in custody for committing serious offences. The Children's Rights Alliance for England (CRAE; www.crae.org.uk/protecting/custody.html) noted that 30 children have died in custody since 1990 but there has not been one public inquiry. The CRAE continued to campaign to ban the detention of all children in custody. Following the damning findings of an inquest into the death of a restrained child, however, the campaign of CRAE and several other organisations continued to reduce the use of deliberately painful restraints on children and young people held in privately run secure training centres and prison. The judgement given by the Court of Appeal on 28 July 2008 meant that measures such as rib and nose 'distractions' and bending back thumbs, introduced on 6 July 2007, were ruled illegal and were banned from July 2008.

Table 22.2 Policy and legal bases for rights of the child

Policy and legal bases	Basic rights of the child
Children Act 1989	Paramountcy of welfare of the child
	Rights of children to participate
European Convention on Human Rights (ECHR) 1950	All people have recognised legal rights
	Article 3 Prohibits torture and cruel, inhuman and degrading treatment (for example most corporal punishment)
	Article 6 Right to a fair trial
	Article 8 Right to privacy and family life
	Article 14 Prohibits discrimination
Human Rights Act 1998	Provisions broadly follow the ECHR above
UN Convention on the Rights of the Child 1989	Article 12 Right to express views freely
	Article 13 Right of freedom to seek, receive and give information
	Article 23 Disabled children's right to dignity, independence and active participation in community
National Service Framework for Children, Young People and Maternity Services, 2004	Disabled children must be consulted about their views

This ambiguity is an appropriate ending for this chapter, because it is central to children's policies, surfaces continually in practice and provides the critical practitioner with endless material for action.

Conclusion

It is ironic that while childcare practices tend towards the welfare approach, policy and practice regarding children and young people who have committed offences remain stubbornly resistant to welfare principles. The numbers of children and young people in custody remain proportionately higher than in most other Western countries and the treatment of children and young people in custody falls short of the dignity and respect that would normally be given to vulnerable people of any age, let alone those at an early stage in their development. Arguably, in order for social work with children, young people and families to take proper account of the issues raised by research and inquiry reports, it is necessary to develop a rights-based approach. This is based on the principle that children have the right to be consulted about, and involved significantly in, decisions about them, as is required in Article 12 of the UN Convention on the Rights of the Child.

For further discussion of social work with families, see Adams et al., 2009b, Chapter 25, and for risk-aware practice, see Adams et al., 2009c, Chapter 4.

www.crae.org   Children's Rights Alliance for England (CRAE) is an organisation which campaigns to advance the rights of the child in England.

www.childpolicy.org.uk   4 Nations Child Policy Network is a partnership between Children in Scotland, Children in Northern Ireland, Children in Wales and the National Children's Bureau (NCB). It provides an information service on comparative policy and best practice in services for children.

www.cpag.org.uk/info/sp_briefings/0200childpov.htm   Child Poverty Action Group is a pressure group which carries out and publishes research and campaigns to end child and family poverty in the UK.

www.nyas.net   National Youth Advocacy Service is a charity which provides socio-legal services for children and advances children's rights.

www.unicef.org.uk/youthvoice   UNICEF UK is one of 34 national committees in this organisation dedicated to helping improve children's lives throughout the world.

Department for Work and Pensions (2003) *Measuring Child Poverty*, London, DWP; UNICEF (2005) *An Overview of Child Poverty in Rich Countries*, Report Card 6, Florence, Innocenti Research Centre; and UNICEF (2007) *An Overview of Child Wellbeing in Rich Countries*, Report Card 7, Florence, Innocenti Research Centre. These research reports are important sources of data and critical appreciation of the consequences of poverty for families in the UK, with some unflattering comparisons with other countries.

Foley, P. and Rixon, A. (eds) (2008) *Changing Children's Services: Working and Learning Together*, Bristol, Policy Press. This book, geared particularly to work with children from birth to age 12, focuses on a small number of important aspects, including integrated working and, crossing several chapters, key aspects of knowledge and understanding required for working with parents and children.

Hendrick, H. (ed.) (2005) *Child Welfare and Social Policy: An Essential Reader*, Bristol, Policy Press. Useful, wide-ranging collection of authoritative, often critical, essays on relevant aspects of child and family policy.

James, A. and James, A.L. (2004) *Constructing Childhood: Theory, Policy and Social Practice*, Basingstoke, Palgrave Macmillan. A critical text that deals in interesting detail with important aspects of the ways childhood is constructed rather than intrinsic ages or stages of child development.

Wilson, K. and James, A. (eds) (2007) *The Child Protection Handbook*, 3rd edn, London, Ballière Tindall. A more than adequate collection of essays on aspects of child abuse, neglect and protection issues, which in Part 3 gives a good introduction to relevant interventions and approaches to working with children.

23

Adult services and health-related social work

Chapter overview

This chapter deals with adult services and those aspects of social work with adults that relate closely to, or are based in, health services. The first two sections focus on important professional issues about social work models of practice in these services, and national policy and structure. Subsequent sections explore the local organisation of social and healthcare services and some important models of practice in adult and mental health social work.

Social and healthcare models of practice

Social science models offer ways of understanding health and wellbeing that focus on the uniqueness of people's experiences of their bodies' health and illness and the meanings they and their cultural or social groups attribute to those experiences. They emphasise a range of social and cultural factors that contribute to, or affect our perceptions of, illnesses, disability, long-term conditions and health.

The biomedical model is an approach to understanding the body's health and illness based on scientific research and empirical findings in biology and medicine. It sees illness as a deviation from an ideal or normal body and focuses on biological reactions to medical intervention such as surgery and drug treatment for illnesses, rather than experiential, social or cultural aspects of illness and wellbeing.

Adult social care and health-related social work are connected because they focus on help for people who have an illness or disability. Because of their close interaction, social workers are part of a partnership of professions and agencies, in which they represent a **social science model** of understanding and practice, complementing **biomedical models** of understanding. Medicine and healthcare organisations have a particular conception of the social phenomena that they deal with which reflects a medical model of practice: to identify conditions of the body and mind, illnesses or disabilities, which, through medical interventions, may be cured or reduced in their impact. This view is contested by disability and independent living movements of health and social care service users, which argue that disabled people are an oppressed group, excluded from ordinary society because it makes no allowance for the impact of their physical impairments on social participation (Oliver, 1996: 22).

There is a degree of polarisation in these views which, while it has the advantage of highlighting differences, does blur some of their respective merits. For instance, it has to be acknowledged that, from a biomedical viewpoint, some people do suffer severe physical impairments. It follows, therefore, that the social perspective cannot assume that all disablement is simply a product of socially induced barriers and that all impairment disappears through their removal. A realistic goal for professionals and services is to empower disabled people at least to achieve independent living and, in some circumstances, to attain autonomy as well.

Medical care focuses on individuals and their bodies or even on parts of their body in which the physician specialises. Processes such as ageing that are partly social or social reactions to illness and disability that may affect patients are of less concern than identifying and overcoming disease or physically disabling conditions. People invest a great deal of their identity in their bodies, their racial, sexual or social identity. For example, women may feel intense psychological reactions to mastectomy operations to cure or prevent breast cancer, since their breasts may represent important aspects of their femininity. Another example is social patterns of consumption, where metabolic illnesses such as diabetes may require restrictions in diet or regular injections of medication, and this affects involvement in ordinary social life. Wider social and family involvements in the processes of becoming ill or disabled, of being diagnosed and living an ordinary life with an illness, its cure or its management, perhaps over a long period of time, also feel less important than physical treatment to those involved in healthcare.

The development of the social model has led to a movement for social change to transform society and incorporate disability as a natural variation in social living, and has empowered disabled people to value themselves as they are, rather than seeing them as having deficits from a 'normal' ideal of the human body (Shakespeare and Watson, 2002). Critiques of the social model in its early form have led to increasing flexibility. Feminist scholars have, for example, argued that it is important to recognise the personal experience of pain and physical limitation (Crow, 1996) and the way in which disability and illness persist exhaustingly for long periods of time (Thomas, 1999). Shakespeare and Watson (2002) have also argued that the social model has become an orthodoxy, which focuses on the social consequences of disability to the exclusion of the importance of physical impairment and illness.

This debate is a good example of how critical debate in the social sciences has an impact on social work practice. While the social model critique has force, the debate suggests that health and social care services need to recognise the complexity of alternative conceptualisations of illness and disability. Social work plays an important role in ensuring that the social and family impacts of illness processes are fully included in services. Social workers should avoid becoming seduced by the specialist role and by involvement in healthcare environments, which are interesting and motivating settings to work in. Instead, social workers need to contribute to healthcare and adult social care the important broader perspective of the meaning of health conditions for people surrounding the individual patient.

Thus influencing services and care through partnership and multiprofessional work is crucial in adult services and health-related social work. Services and professionals in related but different lines of work need to be connected up. Practitioners can build and maintain an equal, cooperative relationship with adult service users and their carers, while a protective, disciplinary relationship is often necessary with children's social care. Partnership practice in adult care and health-related social work has a different and challenging character than in social care with children and families, where social care is often the lead agency. Healthcare is an economically and politically more important service than social care. Leading healthcare professions, such as nursing and medicine, have a socially accepted confident position, and may question or misunderstand social work and its role, which may challenge social workers' professional perspective.

In everyday practice, therefore, adult services and health-related social work practitioners need to retain a firm grasp of the role and contribution of social work, and are challenged to maintain a good standard of practice that produces good results for service users, their carers and colleagues.

Partnership work may involve interagency work, both involvement in strategic planning and in improving everyday communication and collaboration (see Chapter 12). It also involves work with service users and carers (see Chapter 15). Another important factor in social work in these settings is multiprofessional practice, in which practitioners take account of and respond to the different professional disciplines, the organised knowledge and research that underlies the work of their colleagues.

There are two approaches to multiprofessional teamwork practice. One focuses on improving group relations among professional colleagues, by agreeing a shared vision and mission for their work, and coordinating the flows of work and communication between them (Payne, 2000). Health services research shows that agreeing shared objectives and having a positive attitude towards innovation, improving the quality of services and maintaining active participation in regular meetings are the most effective way of improving teamwork (Borrill et al., 2001). The second approach focuses on knowledge management. This approach sees the role of teams as bringing together different knowledge and skills, allowing each profession to achieve its own objectives, while contributing to a holistic picture of and a shared action plan for the service user's needs. In this way, people learn together about how they can work to improve services to their users and carers, creating a community of practice through shared learning (Wenger, 1998). Opie's (2003) research into social workers in multiprofessional teams shows that an important feature of leadership in such teams is enabling each professional area of knowledge to make its contribution.

National structure and policy

Social care and healthcare are separated in the UK by legal, financial and administrative divisions that affect the relationship between central government policy-making and local service delivery. Central government departments are responsible for developing policy and strategy for these services, including making sure that appropriate legislation is passed, and for regulating the amount and quality of provision. Each UK country has a slightly different structure and approach to these services. In

England, Northern Ireland and Wales, the Department of Health of the relevant government is responsible. In Scotland, social work is part of the education department. Healthcare organisations are usually 'branded' NHS, to emphasise to users the range of provision they receive from this politically important care system.

Extensive research demonstrates that there are profound inequalities in health, in the UK and worldwide (Davey-Smith, 2003). Inequalities in health connect closely with socioeconomic divisions. There is a consistent health gradient: the wealthier people are, the healthier they will be.

Summarising the European research on this issue, Skalli et al. (2006) identify four different approaches to understanding inequalities in health:

- *Psychosocial factors*, in particular work-related stress and the availability of social support in people's lives, affect the overall impact of ill health on people's lives. Social work can contribute to combating, for example, social isolation among mentally ill or older people.
- Some *stages of life* in particular contribute to later ill health, for example experiences in the womb or in childhood. By concentrating on particularly dangerous transitions in life, social workers can help to combat later ill health.
- The *life course approach* (Davey Smith, 2003) proposes that small inequalities accumulate over life. By working with people vulnerable to the risks of ill health, social workers can contribute to limiting the impact of unhealthy behaviour or social factors.
- A *structural approach* (Wilkinson, 1996) argues that the extent of inequality in a society generates health inequalities. More unequal societies develop higher health inequality, for example by clustering people in areas that may generate ill health or excluding people from participation in good quality healthcare. By concentrating on families and communities that experience the most difficulties, social workers can focus on the people who need most help to avoid later ill health.

Socially progressive views suggest that ill health is a serious exclusion from ordinary participation in a happy and successful life, More conservative views focus on unhealthy behaviours, such as smoking or obesity, placing responsibility on individuals to change their behaviours, rather than accepting the impact of broader inequalities in society, such as the fact that lower status employees experience greater stress than professionals because they have less control over their work and working environment (Siegrist and Marmot, 2006). A balance between these views is necessary, but psychological and social issues are at the centre of combating health inequalities. Social work's contribution to resolving these issues is therefore important (McLeod and Bywaters, 2000).

In England, financial support for social care is separated from policy and development; this makes it difficult to coordinate the implementation of policy that affects both. The Department for Communities and Local Government administers the finance system for local councils (local authorities – LAs – in official jargon), while the Department of Health is responsible for the development of adult social care policy for services largely provided by LAs in England. Local authorities provide other services such as housing, education, planning and libraries. Because they have some powers to raise their own money through council tax and charges for services, they have some discretion over the priorities between their various responsibilities. They might prefer, for example, to spend money on education or rubbish disposal rather than social care and this means that there is somewhat more local direction and consequently variation between the services that LAs provide than local NHS organisations experience.

The Department of Health in England, and the equivalent national departments elsewhere, directly manage and fund the NHS. This has come about for two reasons: because of its political importance, and maintaining independent medical discretion in diagnosis and treatment decisions. Although funding for local NHS services is through local bodies – in England, primary care trusts (PCTs), in Northern Ireland, health and social services boards, in Scotland, NHS local boards, and in Wales, local health boards – the members of the trusts are national political appointees, rather than locally elected, as in LAs. Many services, for example major hospitals, are provided by politically independent trusts. Most PCT or equivalent money is spent on paying for hospital services for patients of the GPs in the PCTs' areas, but PCTs also organise or contract with private agencies for a range of community health services. There are mechanisms (called 'flexibilities') for PCTs and adult social services departments (ASSDs) to engage in joint planning and service provision, and also to merge elements of their services. The services most commonly merged are children's services in children's trusts and mental health and learning disabilities services.

The legal basis for social and healthcare services is a further source of division (see Chapter 8). Most healthcare legislation has been consolidated into the NHS Act 2006. This enshrines in section 1 the central political tenet of the NHS: that healthcare in the UK is free 'at the point of delivery', that is, no UK citizens pay charges when they receive services, which are funded directly from taxation. Social care legislation is older and, because it has not been consolidated, more of a patchwork of duties and enabling legislation for LAs. The main source of provision is the National Assistance Act 1948, which mainly dealt with residential accommodation for people who were homeless or 'in need of care and attention not otherwise available'. As services developed, this residential care provision was seen as less relevant, and through legislation and policy development, it has been replaced by domiciliary services, that is, care provided in people's own homes. This policy shift is the main driver of the long-standing policy of 'community care', in which social work plays an important part. Among the most important pieces of legislation were the Mental Health Acts 1959 and 1983, which started the process of closing the large old mental hospitals, originally called asylums, and replacing them with care at home or in small residential care or hospital environments; the 1983 Act has recently been substantially amended. The Chronically Sick and Disabled Persons Act 1970 required LAs to identify disabled people in their area and supply them with services at home.

The current main system of organising this home care provision was enacted in the National Health Service and Community Care Act 1990. It introduced a new system of community care provision. In a 'purchaser–provider split', LAs plan and commission services offered in their area by a range of providers, and employ care managers to assess people's needs to decide their eligibility for care and to organise a 'package of care' to meet their needs. Many such care managers are social workers.

Adult social care

Most LAs in England and Wales have an ASSD or adult social care department, but a few have other arrangements, combining social care with other elements of their services. In Scotland, adult social care is provided by LA social work departments, which merge children's social care, offender and other services together; the NHS is separate. In Northern Ireland, adult social services are provided by health and social services boards, which merge healthcare and social care services. In all countries of the UK, however, the services available are broadly similar.

Adult social care provides for four main service user groups and many ASSDs organise their staff into specialist teams for these groups:

- *Older people*, men and women of pensionable age, which is being equalised over a period to 65 years; many older people receive social care because of increasing frailty as they age. This is the largest group, incurring the greatest expenditure; because the proportion and number of older people in the population are expected to rise during the next few decades, financing and managing services for this group has steadily grown in importance. This trend seems likely to continue.
- *Younger people*, that is, under pensionable age, with disabilities, which includes physical and sensory disabilities, for example blindness and deafness, and people who are chronically sick.
- *People with learning disabilities.*
- *Mentally ill people*, including people misusing drugs or alcohol. This group is controversial because community care policy has led to mental healthcare being largely outside hospitals, but a small number of patients whose behaviour may cause risk to themselves or others raise a high degree of public concern (Reith, 1997).

Some people fall into more than one user group; in particular, many people with both learning and physical disabilities and people with mental illnesses shift into the 'older people' category when they reach 65. **Dual diagnosis** refers to people mostly in the mental health field who fall into two categories, for example people with learning disabilities and mental illness, or people who are drug misusers and also mentally ill.

Dual diagnosis is often used to refer to people who not only have a mental health problem but also have learning difficulties or who misuse alcohol or drugs alongside their mental illness. People with multiple problems often have complex needs that do not fit readily into a single medical or psychological diagnosis or social work assessment.

Social care services, therefore, may help people to meet their needs in each of these areas. They are long-term services providing for people who are very physically, psychologically or emotionally dependent on other people and who need care:

- for long periods of the day
- over a long timescale
- covering many aspects of their lives (Parker, 1981).

This requires services that are able to provide continuity, to be receptive to complex needs, interweaving their care with both service users and people in their families and communities who provide informal care for them (Payne, 2009).

In addition to its association with healthcare, adult social care is also connected with housing services, since many people's care requires specialised or adapted accommodation. Most services are domiciliary and are provided in people's own homes, contributing to the informal care provided by relatives and others in the service users' social network. Some users are helped by living in sheltered housing, which may be specially adapted for disabled people. A small number of people are helped in care homes where there is shared communal accommodation, and this may be supplemented by nursing care in care homes with nursing, although most people still call the latter by the traditional name, 'nursing homes'.

Social care has a number of characteristics (Payne, 2009):

1 It is multisectoral, that is, providers of social care operate in the public, private and voluntary, not-for-profit or third sectors of the economy. Therefore, practitioners working in social care participate in a market system of provision, in which service users may be cared for in any sector and are sometimes provided for by several sectors working together. Users may be able to have some choice between different providers, and important roles for practitioners in care management include helping people understand the system, organising 'packages' of care for users and advocating for their needs and their carers' needs within a complex quasi-market. A quasi-market is designed to work like an economic market with people purchasing services from different providers, but it is not a full market because it is substantially funded and therefore dominated by the state and public policy.

2 Social care is closely integrated with the informal sector, with the contributions of users' own self-care and their carers (the British term) or informal caregivers (the internationally recognised term). An important principle of practice is interweaving formal services with informal care, respecting and valuing carers' involvement.

3 Social care involves 'provision' of care rather than therapeutic social work. Consequently, it is designed to provide services to assist and support service users rather than to achieve social and behaviour change, although of course some users and carers may need therapeutic help with the emotional and family consequences of the care needs with which they are struggling.

The starting point of social care services, therefore, is that element of the international definition of social work that emphasises personal problem-solving (IFSW, 2000) or the 'social order' focus within social work of delivering caring services effectively (Payne, 2006). This is important because it underlies the social model of disability and care services (Barnes and Mercer, 2005).

CASE EXAMPLE

Paul, a man with a mild learning disability, was bullied by Harding, a neighbour who misuses hard drugs, to hand over money to feed Harding's habit. When this problem was identified, the practitioner did not blame Paul for failing, as an adult, to stand up to the bullying, as this inability to deal with the situation came from a lack of social skill arising from his disability. Harding wrongly misused his power, but the source of his behaviour is social and healthcare needs, which he needs help with to remove his oppressive behaviour. The social care response is to find ways of protecting Paul, not to regard him as responsible for resisting oppression, although some social skills education might help him. Instead, the social care response is to ensure that Harding's needs are met in alternative ways, so that he does not need to bully Paul.

The long-term nature of social care is a crucial element, because it means that its practice must focus on continuity and support, rather than being concerned with short-term problem-solving. However, many long-term conditions go through periods of crisis, and it is important to be able to react quickly, because this helps to give service users security that the services are responsive.

Social care covers all groups of service users, including children, but children are usually provided for separately from adults, except in physical and psychological healthcare (Payne, 2009). The division between adult and children's social care and healthcare is a political and strategic decision. Adults and people with disabilities or health problems live in families; an individual's ill health and disability affects the whole family, including, and perhaps especially, the children in the family. Also, children experience ill health and disability and therefore use healthcare services, so health-related social work includes work with children and families. There is also a transition: children become adults and the age of transition in most social care is the eighteenth birthday. Therefore, at that point, children who have previously used children's social care and healthcare become the responsibility of adult social care services. This legal and administrative change in status particularly affects children with lifelong physical disabilities and those with intellectual and learning disabilities, and there should be an organised transition between services.

Healthcare settings

Healthcare in the UK is provided through a national government agency, the NHS, which offers four types of services, each of which may involve social workers, although they are mainly to be found in the larger hospitals and health agencies.

Primary care

Primary care is called 'primary' because it is the local first point of contact between a citizen and the NHS. It aims to assess health concerns presented by patients, provide and supervise treatment in most cases, and refer patients to other services if the treatment cannot be completed locally. Primary care services in the UK are organised around a doctor called a 'general practitioner' (GP), who employs a 'primary healthcare team' (PHCT) of administrators, nurses, healthcare assistants and sometimes other staff, and might include a counsellor or social worker – GPs decide. Projects to place social workers with GPs, so that they are present in a frontline universal agency with high public credibility, have not led to any consistent pattern. Some are seconded from LAs, some employed directly by GPs and in some cases, there are liaison workers who promote relationships between ASSDs and GPs (Rummery, 2003). In most cases, GPs do not have access to social work help, and refer difficulties to the ASSD in their area.

Acute care

Acute care includes what is sometimes called 'secondary care', because it is the next place that GPs refer patients if they cannot provide all the treatment required. Most acute care is provided through a local 'district general hospital' (DGH), which often has an 'accident and emergency department' (A&E); these provide an alternative route into the hospital system in an emergency. Acute care aims to provide medical and nursing treatment to cure a patient's illness, disability or injury or to reduce the impact of the symptoms, so that patients become self-managing and return home to ordinary life. Most people are treated as outpatients or day patients; inpatient facilities provide beds for patients who need operations and nursing that cannot be completed within a day. DGHs have specialist doctors, nurses and other healthcare staff, and usually have social workers, directly employed or seconded from the LA. All these staff are organised around medical specialties, such as surgery, coronary care and renal care. Specialised facilities for complex conditions, called 'tertiary (third-level) care', are often specialist hospitals for cancer or heart conditions, or hospices providing care for people dying with hard-to-manage symptoms.

Attaching social workers to specialists creates a range of social workers within health specialties, particularly in long-term care, such as cancer, children, heart disease, geriatric care (the medical care of older people) and renal disease. Specialist services such as drug action teams and child and adolescent mental health services (CAMHS) employ social workers, who often move from LA adult social care or children's social care posts. CAMHS bridge children's social care and NHS mental healthcare.

Mental healthcare is provided by GPs and DGHs, and through specialist healthcare services. There are some DGH psychiatric units and some specialist hospitals, although most large hospitals for mentally ill people who lived in them long term have closed. Most psychiatric hospital units employ social workers or have social workers on secondment from LAs. In most areas, community mental health teams (CMHTs) are managed jointly by local NHS and ASSD bodies. Specialist 'forensic mental health services' are for people who have committed serious offences, most often murder, rape and arson, because of a mental illness. Most regions have a medium secure unit and there are maximum security hospitals for extremely dangerous patients. A specialist group of social workers works in these settings, usually after experience in general mental health services.

Intermediate care

Intermediate care is inpatient rehabilitation. Since the aim of acute care is to make people self-managing, where this is not possible, intermediate care provides more intensive rehabilitation of a period of a month or six weeks in order to return the patient to the point where they are self-managing again. Not all geographical areas have intermediate care, or they have only limited resources.

Continuing care

Continuing care is a funding mechanism for care in people's homes or in care homes. If acute and intermediate care is unsuccessful in returning a patient to being self-managing, the NHS pays for their care, provided their main needs are a 'primary health need'. Here the meaning of primary is different from primary care; it means that a health need is the main problem that the patient faces. This system of funding interacts with ASSD provision for community care. The relationship is sequential, since ASSDs cannot provide healthcare, as the Health and Social Care Act 2001 removed the power of ASSDs to provide nursing care, and continuing care funding pays for social care services if they are required by someone with a primary health need.

Adulthood as an issue in service provision

One of the features that distinguishes social work in adult services work from children's social care is that the main client is an adult. Four aspects of adulthood raise issues for the way in which social care is provided: autonomy, the idea that an adult is a fully developed person, the idea that adults should be financially independent, and that they are expected to meet their own need in most domains of living.

Autonomy

The idea of autonomy means that adults are expected to be self-managing in their care and to make their own decisions about lifestyle, medical and social care and treatment. They are entitled to give their consent for involvement by professionals, including involvement by social workers.

This has two consequences for social care. First, people cannot be compelled to accept care or treatment, even where professionals and family members think this would be desirable. The main situation where compulsion is permitted is under criminal legal jurisdiction, when someone is found guilty of crime. Also, under the Mental Health Act 1983, amended by the Mental Health Act 2007, people can be detained in hospital and compelled to accept treatment for the disorder (DH, 2008).

The second main consequence of the right to autonomy for social care is that people who have lost the capacity to exercise their autonomy, for example through brain damage, learning disabilities or dementia in old age, need someone else to exercise their autonomy. The Mental Capacity Act 2005 makes provision for various relatives or professionals to make decisions for people who are unable to do so themselves (DCO, 2007). Where care decisions are being made, an independent mental capacity advocate (IMCA) is contracted by the LA to represent their interests; IMCAs are often social workers.

Autonomy is a complex idea (Slowther, 2007); nobody is completely self-determining, because we all follow conventions of behaviour. The question to ask is: 'To what extent are we free to make a choice and what limits us?'

CASE EXaMPLE

Karim, an older man, may be free to decide to go into a residential care home, but if the care home cannot consistently provide the Asian food he has eaten all his life, this would involve such a cultural loss that his freedom is limited. On the other hand, he may be frightened of accident or injury if he stays in his own home, and this also limits his choice.

Education and personal development

An individual adult is a fully developed person and is expected to take responsibility for their own education and personal development, fulfilling ambitions and life tasks and developing personal relationships. Social care services help people where this is not so. For example, people with learning disabilities may need further social education and personal development opportunities, people with disabilities may be delayed in their education or require re-education and training after an accident or disabling illness, and older people may lose physical and mental capacities and have to relearn skills, or develop alternative interests to achieve a fulfilling lifestyle. People who are not fully developed may be vulnerable to exploitation by others, for example financial, physical and sexual abuse. However, in the UK, except in Scotland, there are no compulsory powers for ensuring that protection, as there are for children. More subtly, adults who are not fully developed or have impairments may be treated as less than human or less than fully responsible; a physically disabled person, fully capable of answering, might find their carers being asked: 'Does he take sugar?'

Providing for personal development needs and education may seem a luxury compared with meeting basic social or healthcare needs, but is integral to helping people to achieve a satisfying life. Older frail people or disabled people may find themselves treated with impatience in a hurried world. Social care services may therefore have to justify the resources allocated to personal development and education for adults.

Financial responsibility

Adults are financially responsible for their own existence. People who are financially dependent on others and the state are stigmatised for being unable to be responsible for their own needs. This is reflected, for example, in the policies that adults should pay charges for their social care and residential care (Payne, 2009).

Life competence

Adults are expected to be competent to meet their own needs in all domains of living. Where they are not able to do so, they may be stigmatised as inadequate, dependent or demanding, and the services provided for them regarded as a low priority. This assumption is clear within the organisation of NHS services, since, as we said above, the aim of acute care is to get people to the point of being self-managing, with intermediate care accepting that in some cases more work is required to get to that point. Primary and continuing care are designed to help people who are able to manage their own care.

The domains of life within which adults are expected to be responsible for meeting their own needs are: to seek their own healthcare, including mental healthcare, to be responsible for their own education, housing and maintaining their home, employment, and for obeying the law, both civil and criminal. Since they are financially responsible, they are expected to produce an income, including making appropriate transfers to provide for pensions and insurance, avoiding dependence on social security if possible and taking responsibility for mitigating their poverty (Kamerman, 2002).

Implications of adulthood for social work practice

Thinking of a service user as an adult makes clear the practitioner's responsibility for respecting and enhancing their autonomy, competence, responsibility and personal development. Health-related social work and adult social care have continued to use and develop the many models of social work practice in fieldwork and in residential care described in Adams et al., 2009b, Part 2. They continue to be relevant for helping with the psychological, interpersonal and family difficulties created by disability, frailty and illness in adulthood. However, valuing the human rights of the adults who practitioners work with means trying to develop the maximum quality of life, bearing in mind the limitations of the condition that causes their difficulties, not just crossing the threshold of an acceptable level of care (Edwards, 2005). Therefore, particular models of practice are incorporated into adult social care and health-related social work in addition to the panoply of social work practice theories and knowledge about a wide range of issues facing particular user groups, discussed in Adams et al., 2009b, Part 3 and, at a more complex level, in Adams et al., 2009c, Part 1. The following sections discuss examples of community care and mental health practice as important aspects of this.

Community care practice

Care management practice

The main social work practice associated with adult social care is care management, introduced in the 1990s after experiments in the 1980s (Payne, 1995). The processes are set out in Figure 23.1.

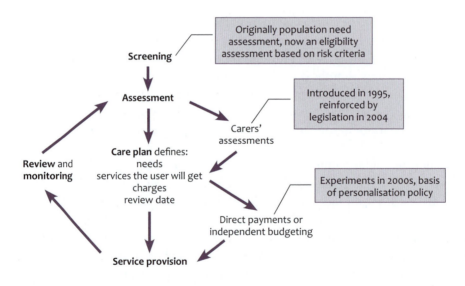

Figure 23.1 Developments in community care assessment and care management

Care management is a cycle of assessment, planning, service provision and monitoring and review. This draws on social work practice concepts of process, described earlier in Part 2, and originally based on the concept of 'case management' developed earlier, in the US. The first stage of screening originally envisaged a population-wide understanding of need, so that decisions could be placed in the context of the overall population. The government guidance on care assessment and management envisaged several different types of assessment, according to the apparent needs of the service user. However, the main political priority in the introduction of care management was to constrain the rapid increase in community care costs that took place in the 1980s (Lewis and Glennerster, 1996), and the care management role, never well defined, has become increasingly concerned with rationing access to services. Screening has consequently become a stage in which LA staff decide whether, according to nationally established criteria, an applicant for services is likely to be eligible for the level of needs that the LA is able to provide.

The assessment, service provision and review stages of the process have also become formalised in adult services care management. Although it is possible to implement them flexibly and with a concern for psychological and interpersonal issues for service users, their carers and families, the process has, in many LAs, become bureaucratised, with extensive paperwork designed to achieve fair, comprehensive and defensible assessments and to manage resources carefully. This has been regarded as a deprofessionalisation of social work, failing to use the full range of its skills and not responding flexibly and creatively to service users' needs (Simic, 1995; Davis et al., 1997; Postle, 2001, 2002). However, imaginative practice is possible. Morrison's (2001) Warwickshire study, for example, showed how an LA adult services team adapted their 'open white space' community care assessments for users with some agreed phrases to improve consistency and make the assessments easier to write.

Carers' assessments

Two new elements have been added to the care management cycle since the 1990s. Legislation in 1995 made provision for a separate assessment of the needs of informal carers of service users and the provision of services to help them, although these have been underfunded. This provision was reinforced by further legislation in 2004. This process reflects the dual responsibility in adult social care to link formal services with self-care and family and carer involvement, which usually provides the most consistent care and support in a service user's life.

Direct payments, independent budgeting and self-directed care

A further process has been added. At the outset, direct payments, originating in 1995 legislation, are provided for users to receive payments directly for the cost of the services they were assessed as needing. They organise their own care, sometimes employing their own carers (DH, 2003). The idea is an extension of case management, drawing on Canadian brokerage schemes (Brandon et al., 1995). Independent budgeting is an extension of this, with, in England, provision from the Departments of Health and of Work and Pensions aimed at providing both care and support for a more independent life, including a work life (PMSU, 2005). This strategy reflects a general approach of the Labour government during the early 2000s focusing on reducing poverty and inequality by promoting work life, rather than reliance on social care services. Behind this, lies the idea of person-centred or self-directed care, building on a US American concept, originally focused on people with or recovering from mental illnesses and alcoholism (SAMHSA, 2005). This aims for service users to control the services offered and the way in which support might best help them.

The intention of these developments is to shift the focus of the social work role in community care away from organising service provision, towards working with and supporting service users and carers in planning and managing their own services, and, more importantly, their personal fulfilment in taking up the range of life chances that are possible for them. This approach was first signalled in a government Green Paper on social care and developed as the idea of the 'person-alisation' of care. Developed by the think tank Demos (Leadbeater and Lownsborough, 2005), particularly in Scotland, this policy was designed to offer a conceptual basis for a focus on user control of and participation in planning services to be appropriate to personal needs and to promote self-care. It was made more concrete in England, in experiments in 13 areas on independent budget-ing, by a wide-ranging official statement on policy on social care: *Putting People First* (DH, 2007a) and by development work from the Care Services Improve-ment Partnership (see Web links below).

The development of personalisation as a policy and practice of participation and user control has been welcomed by many people in social work and adult social care, and by leaders in organisations representing service users and carers. Also, it seems to have broad political support. It offers a new direction for social work in support and advocacy for users' needs, moving away from service provi-sion and care management as a rationing device. However, the history of the way financial constraints in LAs led to the loss of the potential of care management for flexible and creative care suggests that personalisation may not be easy to develop, when similar financial constraints will apply, because of the rising number of older people in the population. Also, the connection made in govern-ment policy between self-control and the reduction of demands on services through greater independence of disabled people in work suggests that different interpretations of self-control may lead to tensions in the implementation of the policy in practice.

Mental health social work practice

US American case management ideas were also the basis of alternative practice devel-opments. Two particular forms of case management are used in mental health services: the care programme approach and mental health case management.

The care programme approach

The care programme approach (CPA) was introduced in 1991, supported by extensive guidance (DH, 1995b). Although initially intended to be used with a range of severely mentally ill people, it has increasingly focused on people with the most severe needs. A written plan is produced for people who are a risk to themselves or others on discharge from psychiatric treatment, particularly forensic care, and they are allocated a care worker. Special arrangements are in place for people whose freedom has been 'restricted' by the courts. More recently, there are multi-agency public protection arrangements coordinated in each area by the probation service. These are based on the idea of a single professional acting as the key worker for an individual at risk. Carpenter et al.'s (2004) survey of users' attitudes found that they valued being given involvement in decision-making, had been told about their medication and its use and side effects, they mostly knew who their key worker was, felt comfortable with them and felt treated with respect. They felt more involved where CPA was well integrated with more general care management approaches, and felt less involved where services were strongly targeted, that is, focused on the users with most needs. User satisfaction was highest where user involvement was a specific focus of the LAs approach.

Mental health case management

CMHTs (the abbreviation) can be ambiguous, because there used to be CMHTs referring to community mental handicap teams, which now no longer exist, but there is a literature.

Community mental health teams (CMHTs) have also developed case management approaches to help people with continuing mental health problems. Packages of care under the community care arrangements are supplemented by regular involvement by a worker, who may be a psychiatric nurse or social worker. There is some evidence that social workers, in a minority in such teams, feel isolated and find it hard to maintain the social work role against a healthcare ethos. Considerable efforts have been made to create effective CMHTs, although the social work experience of them is variable (Onyett, 2003). Until the reforms by the Mental Health Act 2007 of previous legislation, 'approved social workers' have had special training and a legal role in the compulsory admission of mentally ill people to hospital. The reforms have widened this role to other mental health professions, who may become 'approved mental health practitioners'; however, the training remains the responsibility of the General Social Care Council, and it is unclear how the professional social work role will develop in community mental health.

Successful experiments have been carried out with other case management techniques in community mental health, but their widespread implementation is not yet complete, and their long-term impact has not been assessed, although there has been some commentary that there are insufficient resources to adopt all elements of the models of practice (Marshall and Creed, 2000). Assertive community treatment is a US American service that actively seeks out mentally ill people who are likely to lose touch with services because of chaotic or drifting lifestyles, or failure to take anti-psychotic medication. In addition to this, it includes case sharing among the team, small caseloads, a team leader who is an active team member working with users, dedicated time from a psychiatrist, 24-hour cover and services mainly in the community. Intensive case management seeks to improve users' connections with ordinary resources in the community rather than, as in administrative case management, substituting formal services for natural support networks.

Conclusion

This chapter focuses on important issues that affect social work practice in adult services and health-related social work. These are:

- The political and social importance of healthcare and its implications for the structure of services and the role of occupational groups or professions and academic and professional disciplines.
- The status of being an adult, the autonomy and human rights that go with it and the way they may be infringed by social care and healthcare interventions.
- The effect of social and economic inequalities on people's access to and use of adult social care and healthcare.
- The medicalisation of perspectives and social processes in healthcare and its impact on perceptions and decision-making in adult social care and health-related social work, leading to the development of a social model of disability that has wide application.
- The multiprofessional and partnership work involved in adult social care and health-related social work.

To understand and practise social work in adult social care and healthcare, practitioners need to be alert to these issues as they affect service users, their carers and families. I have argued that social work practice in adult social care and health-related social work needs to respond to these issues by focusing on partnership working incorporating the values and wishes of users and carers into daily practice decisions. Social workers have a particular responsibility to incorporate social and psychological perspectives into healthcare and to develop flexible, responsive and caring practice in adult social care services in the future.

For further discussion of different aspects of working with adults, see Adams et al., 2009b, Chapters 28 to 33.

www.dh.gov.uk/en/SocialCare/Socialcarereform/index.htm   Keeping up to date with rapid policy changes on adult social care over the next few years requires close attention to the Department of Health Social Care reform website.

www.networks.csip.org.uk/personalisation/index.cfm?pid=782   Good practice guidance on personalisation is available on the Care Services Improvement Partnership website.

Davey Smith, G. (ed.) (2003) *Health Inequalities: Lifecourse Approaches*, Bristol, Policy Press. A collection of important papers on health inequalities, which, although it takes a particular (life course) approach, contains many of the most important insights in this field and many outstanding academic articles with both policy and practice implications.

Glasby, J. and Littlechild, R. (2004) *The Health and Social Care Divide: The Experiences of Older People*, 2nd edn, Bristol, Policy Press. Good general account of the structural issues between health and social care, based on interesting research on the experiences of older people.

McLeod, E. and Bywaters, P. (2000) *Social Work, Health and Equality*, London, Routledge. Good introduction to the issues of inequality that social workers face in working within the healthcare system.

Payne, M. (2009) *Social Care Practice in Context*, Basingstoke, Palgrave Macmillan. General introduction to social work practice in social care services, with a focus on adult services.

24 Working in the voluntary and independent sectors

Chapter overview

Social workers operate within a mixed economy of care, in which voluntary and private sector organisations are involved in providing social care. This chapter complements the previous two chapters by reviewing the nature and role of voluntary and private organisations as a setting for social care work. It reviews debates about the role of voluntary organisations in social provision, and discusses the importance of partnership work and commissioning in social care.

Introduction: the voluntary and independent sectors

This chapter examines social work in the setting of the voluntary and independent sectors. The UK economy may be divided into three sectors: public, private and voluntary organisations, which together create a 'mixed economy of care', with some care being provided in each sector:

■ **Public sector organisations** are set up by the authority of Parliament to carry out public policy – examples are local authorities and NHS organisations.

■ **Private sector organisations** are set up to make a profit for their owners – many care homes are owned in the private sector.

■ **Voluntary sector organisations** are set up by their members to benefit people other than themselves – examples might be the organisations providing social work and social care for children, such as the Children's Society and National Children's Homes, or for people with particular disabilities, such as Scope, the organisation for people with cerebral palsy. Members make a gift of their resources and time to other people, so they are sometimes called *charitable or not-for-profit organisations* to distinguish them from the private sector. They are also sometimes called the *third sector*, that is, not private or public. This is the term currently favoured by the UK government, which has an Office for the Third Sector as part of the Cabinet Office.

The situation of the voluntary sector has changed markedly since the last quarter of the twentieth century. In little more than 30 years it has moved from occupying a fairly marginal role as provider of social work and social care services to being regarded as an essential provider, in partnership with local authorities as the commissioning agents. In the process, perhaps ironically, some 'voluntary' organisations have become employers of managerial and professional staff which rival in size some of the local authorities that they work in partnership with.

Private and voluntary organisations are sometimes collectively called the *independent sector*, that is, independent of government and the public sector. A range of community and informal organisations are connected to but do not always see themselves as part of the voluntary sector. Community groups are created by people in particular localities to meet needs that they have identified. Informal groups are created by people to make progress with shared interests, and may include self-help and mutual support groups of people who share similar problems.

Many social workers and social care practitioners work in private and voluntary organisations, while others work for the state, financing and supporting the development of voluntary organisations. Of the more than one million people working in social care in England, two-thirds work for 25,000 employers in the private and voluntary sectors (www.dh.gov.uk/en/SocialCare/workforce/index.htm). Expenditure on social care in non-public sector settings is growing: between the financial years 2001/02 and 2005/06, the percentage of gross expenditure by local councils on care services in the voluntary and private sectors grew from 59 to 72 per cent and in the final year reached £9.3 billion (CSCI, 2008). The number of people employed in the voluntary sector increased by 26 per cent over the period 1996–2005, and the number of people employed in 'social work activities without accommodation', that is, in fieldwork roles, rose during the same period by 86 per cent to 277,000 (Reichart et al., 2008). Of 76,300 social workers registered with the GSCC in March 2007, 71 per cent were employed by local authorities, 6 per cent by the independent sector, 6 per cent by employment agencies and smaller proportions by other organisations (Eborall and Griffiths, 2008).

Because the independent sector contains many organisations and employs a large number of people, it is a significant part of social provision in the UK, even though the proportion of social workers it employs is small. Therefore, social workers will interact with it and may at some time be employed in it, so it is important to understand its role in social care and social work practice within it. It is also important historically and in public perception. The idealist philosophy that it was possible to do something about social problems and that the state should have a major role in doing so dates from the late nineteenth century (Offer, 2006); before that, care and help was paid for, by people who could afford it, for example in private madhouses, or was provided by individuals. These were often rich or socially important people accepting responsibility for charity to people less fortunate than themselves. However, with urbanisation and industrialisation, such individual social responsibility became hard to connect with the immense needs of the new cities, and people formed charitable organisations to provide care. Prior to the welfare state legislation, brought into effect during 1945–51, most hospitals and other care was provided by charities, although their resources and organisation were severely tested by the major economic depression of the 1930s and the war of 1939–45. Many present-day voluntary organisations date from the period 1850–1945. Because they have had to raise donations from the public, they promote favourable aspects of their work to the public, which generally has a higher awareness and positive view of their work compared with the work of state social services.

The next section describes examples of voluntary organisations to indicate what they are like and the roles that social workers may play in them. In the following sections, I discuss the structure, legal basis and social roles of voluntary organisations, and the debates about the part that voluntary organisations play in social provision. In the final section, I discuss commissioning and partnership work as important roles of social workers in interagency work.

Voluntary organisations

Kendall and Knapp (1996), working as part of an international research project, identified four distinguishing characteristics of voluntary organisations:

- *Formal organisation;* informal and self-help groups are not included, unless they develop structures and rules for decision-making and accountability that go beyond informal discussion among members.
- *Independence from government,* which means that their policy and practice is created internally, rather than imposed by government. However, they may receive funding from government and be regulated in their work, so there may be significant government influence on what they do and how they do their work.
- *Voluntary,* that is, a significant element of their resources of time, effort and money is provided by the choice of the members, rather than by external pressures.
- *Non-party political and non-sacramental,* that is, their purposes do not include seeking election to government bodies or providing the main infrastructure of a church.

These ideas are quite diffuse, so there are two examples below to demonstrate what kinds of organisations are considered to be voluntary, and then, in the following section, in contrast, there are four examples of private sector bodies.

EXaMPLE

A hospice

St Christopher's Hospice in southeast London, where I work, cares for people who are dying, their families and carers and people who are bereaved. It was started over 40 years ago by Dame Cicely Saunders, a nurse who became a social worker. She set it up as a voluntary organisation to pioneer her ideas for better care for dying people, outside the NHS, where she felt medical attitudes resisted these developments. It has become a worldwide movement, supported by World Health Organization policy that end-of-life care should be available to everyone.

Many social workers work in St Christopher's. The chief executive is a social worker, responsible for an annual budget of £12 million and more than 250 staff. I advise on policy issues, develop new projects, carry out research and evaluation projects, recruit, train and support volunteers, coordinate safeguarding practice for children and adults, liaise with community organisations and local authorities, organise patients' access to records and advise on family problems. A group of social workers and a manager, attached to multiprofessional teams, provide social work and psychological help to 48 patients being cared for on its inpatient wards, and around 650 patients being cared for at home; this is like the health-related social work role discussed in Chapter 23. The social workers train and support around 20 volunteers supporting bereaved people. A groupworker runs six-week programmes for current and bereaved carers, working in liaison with carers' organisations in the community. The social work manager also manages three specialist welfare rights advisers who work with patients and families. All these staff provide support to families and carers as well as to patients. All the social workers started in SSDs, working in both children and families divisions and adult services. The director of education, a social worker, organises conferences and training for some 4,000 professionals annually from across the world, including several advanced courses provided in association with universities. Another social worker leads a bereavement service for children and young people, mostly employing part-time social workers; many of them, like their colleagues working in the hospice services, have gained additional qualifications in various specialist models of counselling, psychotherapy and groupwork.

⬦⬦⬦⬦ EXaMPLE

A local voluntary organisation

Dyscover (www.dyscover.ndo.co.uk), a local organisation in my home area, supports people with aphasia (having no speech) and dysphasia (having disrupted speech). It was set up 15 years ago by a speech and language therapist who felt that not enough was done in the NHS for people who had strokes and brain damage from accidents to help them recover their language. It now has two day centres and provides social support for people with these long-term disabilities and their families. The social pressures are illustrated at a meeting I attended recently, where a dysphasic man and his wife who were members talked movingly about how an active man who gave lectures and did a lot of writing in his work was now unable to string a sentence together. He often set off to go to the toilet in his home but forgot how to get there; frustrating for both him and his wife. She had tried helping him with his speaking, but did not really know the best way to help.

Independent organisations

One of the boundaries between voluntary and other organisations is between voluntary and private sector bodies within the independent sector. Even though they do not have all the characteristics of a voluntary organisation, it is often hard to distinguish some private sector bodies from similar voluntary organisations.

◇◇◇◇ EXAMPLE ◇◇

A social enterprise

The mother of a young person with learning disabilities received direct payments for his care, and found that she was called on through local organisations to give advice to other parents doing the same sort of thing. Eventually, the local authority arranged to pay her for her time in doing this, and she set up a small company to provide mentoring to people receiving direct payments, and training to local authority and other agencies' staff in helping people to make the best use of direct payments. Much help of this kind is provided by organisations of disabled people or similar local groups, set up as voluntary organisations. However, needing an income herself and wanting the freedom of action to express her own views and act on behalf of people with care needs meant that she took the route of creating a hybrid organisation, which has social objectives, but is established as a profit-making business, a **social enterprise**. In this way, organisations can become self-sustaining through their income, rather than seeking financial support through fund-raising, donations and grants. The social enterprise model combines many of the advantages of for-profit organisations, while still aiming to achieve social objectives. It has been actively used in the field of community regeneration, because it allows deprived communities to achieve improvements that are more sustainable in the long term because they achieve a regular income.

> **Social enterprise** refers to private sector activities that engage groups and organisations in trading goods and services for collective and social purposes.

◇◇◇◇ EXAMPLE ◇◇

A social work private practice

Melinda is a private practice social worker. She worked in various aspects of children and families work, and developed her practice in adoption and fostering teams. Eventually, having taken some time off to be a full-time mother, in the 1990s, she decided to become a guardian ad litem – a person who prepares independent reports representing the interests of the child for adoption panels and divorce and family courts where childcare issues arise. This work has now been organised nationally by Cafcass, the Children and Family Court Advisory and

Support Service. This allowed her to organise her time flexibly around her own family's needs and to do most of her work directly with and on behalf of children, which she preferred to many of the child protection roles that were available to her in local government. She teamed up with Jo, whom she had known when working for social services; Jo had then become a social work lecturer. Jo was interested in ideas about loss, and during her time as a lecturer had done some private work counselling people who were struggling with bereavement. This work has become known to a large practice of local GPs, and they gave her a contract to work three days a week as a counsellor in their practice. She left her lecturing job, and as she became known in this field locally, she found that she had more than enough work to do. Eventually, Melinda and Jo set up an office with a secretary to do their administrative work and, rather than form a company, they set up a formal partnership, as many lawyers, doctors and accountants do. The government has plans to organise child protection through independent practices like this, working under contract for local authorities.

EXaMPLE

Care homes

During the 1980s, a married couple, Katie, a nurse, and Kevin, a social worker, opened a private care home after adapting a large house, using a mortgage. The house provided a home for 12 older people, while they lived in the house's converted stables. Although this was a private sector company, and some friends in the social services accused them of making a profit from providing social services, the salaries that they took for themselves were lower than they were earning in the local authority and the NHS. However, they felt they were able to provide a more personal and flexible service to the residents than the larger and more institutional style of buildings provided by the local authority.

As the community care system changed and expanded in the 1990s, they found that many of the residents received funding from the local authority community care budget and sometimes NHS, as explained in Chapter 23. This helped their business to become successful, and over the years, they bought other properties, until they owned a small chain of three homes. With the buildings attached to some of the homes, they extended their provision, first to offer daycare facilities, then to let some small independent flatlets to older people who were able to be more independent, but wanted to call on the facilities of the home if they needed it. Finally, they rented a shop in the town, and set up a domestic care agency, which employed people to provide home care services in the locality. Some older people and others needing domestic help came to them directly, but again most of their work came from local authority and NHS contracts.

Katie and Kevin found that their competitors in the care homes market were increasingly large national and international companies. One of their weaknesses compared with such organisations was that they could not offer their staff the same training and personal development opportunities. However, many potential employees preferred a more personal style of organisation, which older people and their relatives often appreciated. To improve the quality of what they offered, they started offering training courses for care assistants, which they arranged to be accredited with the local further education college, and gained extra income by offering student placements for nursing and social work courses. Eventually, they were running a sizable organisation, but still on a very personal basis, in which they had more daily contact with their homes and residents than many managers in social services and the NHS. Their income also improved markedly over the years, and the value of their company, when they come to sell it on retirement, will probably give them a good income in retirement and a feeling that they had made a big contribution to the care services and the lives of many people in their home town.

EXAMPLE

An informal community organisation

I agreed to advise a small local group that residents of a council estate had set up 20 years ago. They had been concerned about misbehaviour among young people locally, and wanted to set up youth facilities. They started by fundraising to support a youth club in a local church hall, staffed by volunteers, but found many 'difficult' young people would not become involved. Advised by the local council's area youth and community officer, they obtained funding from a government scheme for a youth worker. The youth worker became a 'detached' worker, meeting young people on the streets and in bars, encouraging them in useful social activities. However, this did not support the youth club, which failed, and several members of the committee who had been committed to voluntary work in the club resigned. The remaining members of the committee continued to support the detached worker, but when she left, they found it difficult to get along with her replacement.

I found that this conflict had arisen partly because the population had changed over the years. The new worker was concentrating on young people from minority ethnic groups who were at risk of becoming regular drug users. The committee had mixed and (I thought) possibly racist feelings about this. However, their concerns had also moved on and some of the members were more concerned about the position of older people in the community. As a well-established local group, although still mostly informal, they had been approached to be the local sponsors of a scheme, which could attract government funding to set up community-based facilities for older people, of which they had no experience.

Advantages and disadvantages

Summing up, we can identify a number of important roles that the voluntary sector plays:

- The vanguard role of innovating new services and methods of provision, which can then be adopted or adapted in the public sector.
- The role of providing alternatives and choices for both service users and professionals in the way in which services are provided and organised.
- The opportunity for participation by service users and members of the public in providing and managing social help.
- The possibility of advocating and campaigning for change and improvement in public services, which is difficult to do as a public employee.
- The opportunity for practitioners to develop their career and practice in ways that go beyond what the public sector requires.
- Alternative and additional forms of finance for social help.

While many of the advantages that we have identified in these examples could equally well have been achieved within a flexible and open-minded public sector, or a socially concerned private market sector of the economy, in practice, the different organisational structures seem to offer different opportunities for effective service provision. Part of the reason for this is that commitment to and involvement with localities and specific interests can make professionals' participation seem more genuine. This promotes a more equal relationship between professional and service user than is possible between public official and service user.

The disadvantages of having independent sector provision in social care are:

- Planning coordinated services and finance can be more complex.
- The plethora of organisations can be confusing to service users.
- Funding can feel insecure for employees because they do not have the regularity of funding and infrastructure for staff support provided by taxation to public organisations.
- While smaller, less formal organisations can be more open, they may have poor mechanisms for formal accountability to other local people. Changes in membership might lead to changes in direction and uncertainty. They may also be less good at managing conflict, disagreement and planning, which means that members are pushed this way and that by funding opportunities and are unable to define policy or manage their staff.
- Some people feel that accepting 'charity' from other people is demeaning and stigmatising, because they become dependent on the generosity of other people. Financial structures that allow people to pay for the services they receive can feel more 'normal' and acceptable to many people.
- While setting up a social enterprise or private provider allows people to do socially useful work, without the hassle of involving others setting up a charity to do it, this can be individualistic and uninvolving.

Policy on involving the independent sector in planning and regulation of their work alongside local authority structures can help to mitigate some of these problems, and enhance the contribution of independent organisations. It is therefore important for practitioners to understand the infrastructure of independent CVS organisations, their work in the locality and the area of practice that practitioners are working in, and to develop effective partnership working.

National and local infrastructure

At first sight, the independent sector looks like a mess of small organisations that it is hard to make sense of, but there is an infrastructure, which helps to find your way around and an important element of this infrastructure is coordinating organisations. These are bodies specifically set up to make connections between organisations in the sector, and to connect voluntary sector with public and private sector organisations.

At the national level, there are two main types of coordination bodies:

- UK and national generalist bodies; an example is the UK-wide National Council for Voluntary Organisations (NCVO), which is led by Stuart Etherington, a former social worker, and Volunteering England and its national equivalents, for example Volunteer Development Scotland. There are similar specialist coordinating organisations, for example the National Council of Voluntary Child Care Organisations. There are umbrella organisations for the main groups of private sector providers, social enterprise and community organisations. An important group for private practice social workers is the Independents Forum organised by the British Association of Social Workers.
- UK and national bodies concerned with particular services or needs, such as Age Concern, Alcohol Concern, MIND (the national association for mental health), and Scope, the organisation concerned with cerebral palsy.

At the local level, these two types are replicated:

- Most areas have a council for voluntary service (CVS), sometimes called a voluntary action council, community council or something similar, and a volunteer centre or volunteer bureau. These perform locally some of the same functions as the national bodies mentioned above. Sometimes they have a local name that expresses the organisation's approach, for example, a CVS in the area where I work is called 'Community Links'. Many social enterprises and community organisations link in with these arrangements, but private sector organisations usually have their own connections.
- Each area has local bodies concerned with particular services and needs: there is often, for example, a local equivalent of all the organisations mentioned above.

People may be confused that these organisations are often called councils, because they associate 'council' with the local authority. Talking to service users and members of the public, practitioners need to be specific that these organisations are represent-ative bodies for organisations with specialised interests. For example, the hospice that I work for is a member of the local CVS in each area we work in, and of the London CVS, which covers the region we are involved with, and I am the hospice's represent-ative on each of the councils of these bodies.

As with the public sector, the fact that there is a local and national infrastructure means that there are issues about the relationship between the local and national networks. The three main types of relationship are:

- *Top-down structures,* in which there is one national organisation, whose supporters form local branches to raise funds, pursue local activities such as information or discussion meetings and conferences and encourage support of the national body. Help the Aged is like this, formed by people who wanted to change attitudes and policies about older people and influence interna-tional developments; it has a national campaigning role, policy influence, information and training services.
- *Representative structures,* in which similar local bodies form a national structure to support their interests at a national level. An example is Age Concern, which was founded as the National Old People's Welfare Council (NOPWC) and is made up from representatives of local OPWCs, originally designed to set up local councils and support them with information and advice.
- *Foundations,* which may be local or national, have a funding relationship with voluntary organisations. They are organisations that have accumulated financial resources to give to other organisations for charitable purposes. A good example is the Joseph Rowntree Foundation, set up originally by the eponymous choco-late manufacturers in York, who used their profits to benefit both the local community and national social policy development.

In practice, some of these different types of organisation may look rather similar to outsiders and have often developed towards each other; as a result, Help the Aged and Age Concern have been considering a merger for some time.

Many of the examples I have given here have been of organisations set up by people who employ professionals to provide the services. However, there are two other types of personnel involved. Many voluntary organisations, as we have seen from the examples above, particularly involve people who want to take action about issues that concern them. Voluntary organisations are a way of doing so that allows a focus on particular issues, rather than the broader focus on general political poli-cies required for people who get involved in party politics. So the voluntary sector promotes participation by people in helping others in society and in seeking social change. Connected with this, voluntary organisations have a particular role in enabling people to volunteer, that is, give their time without payment to help others or to contribute to the community. A significant proportion of the population volun-teer regularly in some way and the voluntary sector attracts a large number of people to act as trustees of organisations (Davis Smith, 2001).

Legal and administrative structures

Anyone can set up a group; examples are a group of friends meeting to raise funds in their local pub, or a mutual support group of people in the area who all care for elderly parents. It becomes a voluntary organisation when it sets clear objectives, policies to achieve them and an organisational structure. The two main structures for voluntary organisations are charity and company law.

Charity law regulates how an organisation can collect donations of money and use it to benefit people other than themselves. The main basis of this is trust: the board or committee of a voluntary organisation are trustees of the money and aims of the organisation, that is, they hold the money for other people's benefit. Alternatives to charitable structures are friendly society or industrial and provident society structures; these offer broadly similar advantages for organisations with particular roles.

Company law allows an organisation to have an identity separate from the individuals involved in it, and in regulating what such organisations can do, it protects the members from having to accept complete personal responsibility for what the organisation does. For example, if the organisation goes into debt and cannot repay it, the individual members are not responsible personally for the debt. This makes it easier for organisations to grow, because they can take risks that an individual could not safely accept on their own. It was the basis of the development of capitalism in the nineteenth century because it permitted large-scale businesses to develop. As voluntary organisations grow, they face the same problem, so most large voluntary organisations are both charities and companies.

Most private sector organisations are also companies and are regulated by companies legislation. This is mainly concerned with making sure that their aims and finances are publicly known and transparent.

The mixed economy, community, civil society and social capital

Why should we have a voluntary and independent sector and therefore a mixed economy of social care? This important political issue about the voluntary and independent sectors can become a personal issue for people who work in them. They are accused of profiting from other people's misfortune, like Katie and Kevin, or using their expertise to pursue their own interests rather than the priorities that governments have identified, like Melinda and Jo. There are also ideological and planning arguments. Taking collective responsibility for meeting social need represents a shared bond between everybody in society; it is a central characteristic of citizenship in a modern society that nations provide through taxation for the needs of all citizens, who receive help according to their needs. This strengthens mutual support and loyalty in society; it therefore strengthens cooperation in society to meet other challenges, such as climate change. If we are accepting that responsibility, then the most effective and economical provision will be carefully planned to meet identified needs. If we allow and encourage organisations such as St Christopher's or Dyscover, we are taking resources away from effectively organised state services and adding to the complexity of running state services, because more effort and time has to be put into coordination.

However, against this broadly social democratic view of the role of the state in making social provision, an alternative broadly neoliberal or conservative view suggests that many needs can be met in a market economy, and the state should only provide when the market cannot. Also, in a free society, citizens should be entitled to provide services in their own way or according to their own philosophies and other citizens should be allowed to choose between alternatives; the state should not seek to direct how everyone should have highly personal needs met. In reality, it does not have a monopoly of the good ideas for providing services. This has led to debate about a number of important issues:

- *Market and state failure:* one of the reasons that the state became involved in providing social care and other social services is 'market failure', that is, markets do not provide effectively for some important aspects of life. The main reason for this is that, for markets to work, people have to pay for the goods and services they receive, but a common feature of people needing social services of all kinds is that they have reduced or no income. Therefore, the state has to step in; we all pay taxes to take collective responsibility for people who need help. However, experience of state monopoly provision is that this can become ineffective and too expensive. This is because, as with all monopolies, the providers have a financial commitment to the present provision, and find it hard to be flexible to meet new needs. Also, markets help to provide competition, which can push forward innovation and creative ways of doing things. Thus, there are aspects of both the market and the state that mean that there can be no single provider.
- *Public choice:* because markets are involved in provision, citizens and state services organising and coordinating provision have greater choice between different philosophies and types of service provision. Neoliberal political philosophy particularly identifies the failure of trust in the state as a single provider and a wish for people to be able to make their own choices within the services they receive. It is argued that people have developed higher expectations of choice in a consumer-oriented society over the past few decades.
- *Citizenship:* this is an important issue, because people who are citizens should be entitled to receive public services; on the other hand, they should be entitled to offer them through voluntary organisations and volunteering.
- *Faith groups:* the role of faith groups in providing social care has become an issue, for two reasons. Some churches or faith groups have seen the provision of social care services as a way of influencing public policy in the direction of their faith, and seeking commitment to or maintenance of faith as an aspect of providing their service. For example, some Christian groups providing services to people

with learning disabilities have sought to limit recruitment of staff to Christians, so that the guidance and advice given to people with learning disabilities should be Christian in character (BHA, 2008). Faith has also become an issue in anti-discriminatory practice, since people from some minority ethnic groups prefer help from organisations that represent their own faith, rather than secular organisations of groups representing other faiths.

■ *Contracting:* contracting has presented difficulties for voluntary organisations. Since, as we saw in Chapter 23 and in the examples discussed above, many organisations act as providers of services under contract to public bodies, much of their work may be redirected from its main objectives towards meeting the service provision requirements and demands of regulatory bodies. It also requires organisations to develop an administrative infrastructure to administer contracts, rather than receiving donations or grants from government bodies with fewer limitations. Also, this tends to lead to greater government control and surveillance of objectives and activities by voluntary organisations. This may limit them in being able to pursue campaigning or social change activities. If Dame Cicely Saunders had been required to comply with government regulations half a century ago, she would have found it more difficult to establish the first hospice and the worldwide hospice movement, which at the time was contrary to the accepted priorities in providing care for dying people.

Important social and political ideas are relevant to understanding these debates on the role of voluntary organisations in society. The first is the idea of 'community', the connections within a locality (a 'place community'), or among a group of people who share common interests (a 'community of interest') that people experience as supportive. Many people feel that capitalism and business do not provide for aspects of life such as education, infrastructure and the social development of societies, and that governments and the public sector do not generate a sense of personal support and shared identity. Therefore, we need to develop and support other social structures that create a strong identity, include people in sharing and mutually supportive relationships and create reciprocity among their members. Many people see encouraging people to volunteer to make gifts of their time and to become involved in voluntary organisations as an important way of achieving this.

Community work (see Adams et al., 2009b, Ch. 11) is a set of professional techniques for achieving the development of shared values and mutual support and security. Establishing and building up voluntary organisations is often an important aspect of community work, since it establishes organisations outside business and government that promote social solidarity and order. Communitarian ideas argue that individuals should accept personal, moral responsibility for contributing to the health and wellbeing of the community in which they live, in return for the rights that they enjoy as citizens to safety, protection and support (Etzioni, 1995). Among the critiques of such views and professional practices is that they reflect a romantic ideal of a mutually supportive and sharing rural or small town community formed through shared adversity rather than by positive mutual support. Communitarian views are often criticised because they do not acknowledge that all people have human rights to care, support and justice, which should not be dependent upon some contribution they have made – human rights cannot be taken away from a human being.

Civil society is an ideal that societies should be regulated by democracy, liberty and solidarity rather than solely by economic and political power. Therefore, organisational structures outside political and economic systems are a focus for social development and an important counterbalance to the adverse effects of globalisation. This is often taken to refer to voluntary or charitable organisations, and aspects of society that are concerned with meeting social needs, for example education, housing, health and social care. Organisations that focus on such issues form civil society. It includes social work agencies and voluntary organisations, outside the conventional structures of economic and political power. Creating and strengthening civil society is considered a way of maintaining the social order, because it stimulates commitment from citizens to their society. Promoting civil society, however, can be criticised because it is another way in which powerful people use informal structures to support their existing political and economic power. For example, the trustees and patrons of many major voluntary organisations are businesspeople and members of the royal family, and gaining their support for charitable fund-raising may mean that voluntary organisations become dependent on people with economic and social power in society. This can be just as limiting as being dependent on people in government pursuing political policies. Against this, it can be argued that elected governments, both national and local, have more accountability for their actions than unelected patrons of voluntary groups.

Social capital follows from these ideas. It proposes that active participation in communities and societies is essential to maintain the social fabric. Putnam (2000) showed how formal, political, civic and religious participation was declining in American society, and was being replaced by informal links and relationships. He refers to economic pressures on people's time and money, suburbanisation and urban sprawl, which reduced local social identity and interconnections, the way in which the electronic mass media have made leisure more private and individual, and generational change in which socially involved older people are being replaced by less involved younger generations. Commitment to social movements and the growth of a wide range of social networks, particularly through the internet, are among the factors that combat and mitigate these trends. Developing social capital might be seen as a strategy for drawing on human resources to contribute to social development and redirect and re-energise communities to respond to important social issues.

Bringing these points together, many people see an important role for volunteering, the voluntary sector and a private sector in social provision generally and in social care. In recent years, government has also supported the development of that role for a variety of political and practical reasons. There is also dissent from the favourable view that governments and many members of the public take, mainly from a social democratic or socialist view, that favours the clarity of citizens' rights to collective provision for their social needs. Even where social workers take this view, they currently have to work within a mixed economy of care, assessing service users and providing services within a quasi-market.

Commissioning and partnership work between the state and independent sectors

As the role of the voluntary and private sectors in providing social care and many other public services has developed as a result of the emphasis on developing social capital through a stronger civil society in many Western societies, ideas about how the different sectors may integrate their work have developed. From ideas that it was the responsibility of the public sector to coordinate a range of provision, the concepts of commissioning and partnership work have grown steadily more important in practice. These ideas form the basis for current processes for integrating public and independent sector provision.

Commissioning has developed from the quasi-market approach to dividing purchasers of services from providers, used particularly in adult services and the NHS. The relevant public sector bodies are encouraged to work together and in partnership with independent sector bodies to plan the range of services that should be available in any area. New services and improvements should be developed in each locality to offer a full range of services, and new and improved provision is commissioned jointly, that is, its development is financed and supported until it is able to offer the services required. In this way, Katie and Kevin were enabled to work with local authorities and NHS staff in their area to develop their day provision and home care agency in ways which connected with other services and filled gaps in provision.

While this makes services available, the other aspect of commissioning is ensuring that packages of services relevant to the needs of particular service users are provided in a coordinated way. This involves selecting from the range of services commissioned and organising the package in a way that meets the user's needs; this is usually done, as we saw in Chapter 23, by care managers in the local authority and the NHS.

Commissioning and partnership are often described as interagency processes; however, organisations do not cooperate, people do, and cooperation requires trust. This is also true in services concerned with risk and protection, such as safeguarding services. These are organised by interagency committees, involving representatives of all service sectors and the police. Procedures are jointly written to allow professionals to share concerns about people who may be at risk, either children or vulnerable adults. However, the availability of procedures does not ensure that people trust the person on the other end of the telephone to respond appropriately to the issue. For example, when adult protection procedures were introduced in St Christopher's Hospice, staff were worried about reporting concerns about potential abuse of their patients, because they feared that local authority staff would carry out a heavy-handed investigation. Only a series of sensitive responses from local authority social workers has relieved these anxieties and freed people to make contact when they need to do so.

Partnership work, therefore, involves careful development work. Among structures that may be helpful are:

- Mediators, for example coordinators in each agency, who are well acquainted with the procedures and able to support staff and deal with difficulties and are champions for the importance of their area of work.
- Clear contact information.
- Arrangements for careful participation by all professionals and a concern for the needs of all users involved. Therefore, while the concern may be for the mental health of a young mentally ill man, agencies should also be able to take on another agency's concern for the safety of his elderly mother.

All social workers need, therefore, to take responsibility for making their personal contribution to partnership between state and independent organisations. This includes:

- Being well informed about the range of organisations working in their locality and professional area, for example by keeping up to date with relevant websites and directories.
- Taking time to participate in opportunities to meet colleagues in other agencies and learn about their work and attitudes.
- Being clear about procedures and coordinators within their own agency and in interagency processes.
- Be clear about their personal stance about the debates on the role of voluntary and private sector organisations in society and in social care, discussed above, and be clear how they will work with volunteers, and with voluntary and private sector agencies in ways that benefit the people who they all serve in their different organisational structures.
- Taking part in and supporting joint training and development work.

Conclusion

This chapter has examined the different types and roles of voluntary and independent sector organisations and reviewed debates about their place in society and in social care. Social workers will inevitably work with and may, at some time in their careers, work within voluntary organisations. As part of their work, therefore, all social workers need to ensure that they operate in an appropriate partnership with colleagues in voluntary and independent sectors, while being aware of and responding to policy issues and debates about the limitations and advantages of the mixed economy of care.

For further discussion of the community sector, see Adams et al., 2009b, Chapter 11, and for partnership working, see Adams et al., 2009c, Chapter 13.

www.dsc.org.uk/Home The Directory of Social Change provides training and information for people working in the voluntary sector and publishes a wide range of practical 'how to do it' books.

www.ncvo-vol.org.uk/ The National Council for Voluntary Organisations is the national coordinating body of voluntary organisations; if you click on members, you can go to the websites of any of its members, which includes most national and many local groups.

www.cabinetoffice.gov.uk/third_sector/about_us.aspx The Office of the Third Sector is a unit of the Cabinet Office. It coordinates government policy on and support for voluntary organisations, and contains a wide range of information, including connections to all the sources of government grants for voluntary organisations.

www.volunteering.org.uk/ Volunteering England was formed from the UK coordinating body for organisations who organise and do their work with volunteers; this remains the biggest body, and provides links to organisations covering the other UK countries.

Davis Smith, J. and Locke, M. (2008) *Volunteering and the Test of Time*, London, Institute for Volunteering Research. This collection of papers, previously published in the journal *Voluntary Action*, provides a useful survey of issues and concerns about volunteering policy and practice.

Harris, M. and Rochester, C. (eds) (2001) *Voluntary Organisations and Social Policy in Britain: Perspectives on Change and Choice*, Basingstoke, Palgrave Macmillan. A good collection of articles on various aspects of the voluntary sector.

Locke, M. and Lucca, P. (2003) *Faith and Voluntary Action: Communities, Values and Resources*, London, Institute for Volunteering Research. An interesting research study on the potential and actual contribution of faith organisations to voluntary action.

Preparing for social work practice

25

This chapter deals with what in many ways is the heart of becoming a qualified practitioner – the preparation for practice. This includes what in the UK is now known as the 'practice learning opportunity' but was traditionally known as the 'placement'. It explores some of the practical difficulties involved in practice learning allocation and introduces a process of preparation that a student needs to start thinking about and engaging with long before going into practice. The more prepared you are for practice, the more you will gain from the experience.

Chapter overview

The importance of practice

The social work degree qualification is generic, enabling graduates to develop their careers in different directions once qualified, rather than being trained to work with one specific service user group or in one type of service agency. This is reflected in the academic and practice elements of the programme, which provide opportunities for variety and breadth of learning and the development of transferable skills.

Social work training and education are split equally between practice and the academic study that supports and underpins practice. Practice comprises certain periods of **experiential learning**, where students learn the job in a social work agency under supervision and in a supportive learning environment. The academic contribution of research and knowledge underpins this practice. In different countries, the structure of courses leads to different arrangements for practice experience and learning. In the UK, social work students must spend at least 200 days, or 1,200 hours, learning in a practice setting under the direction of an educator (DH, 2002f: 3).

> **Experiential learning** refers to the primary experiences of learning from life and work and to the secondary experiences of work-based learning in a practice learning setting as part of a course. Experiential learning, its critics point out, exists alongside other forms of learning – cognitively (by thinking), from studying and by consciousness-raising and social action.

Social work programmes recognise the important role of practice learning and ensure that preparation for practice and direct practice are given equal status and the same degree of investment as other areas of the course. The Quality Assurance Agency for Higher Education states that:

> Practice provides opportunities for students to improve and demonstrate under-standing through the application and testing of knowledge and skills ... [and] practice activity is also a source of transferable learning in its own right. Practice learning can transfer both from a practice setting to the classroom and vice versa. (QAA, 2000)

Practice learning opportunities

Responsibility for delivering the practice learning lies with the higher education institutions (HEIs). It is important to note that:

- HEIs have a contractual responsibility to deliver all aspects of the social work degree to students on their programmes.
- The quality, coherence and sufficiency of practice learning opportunities fall within their area of responsibility.
- It is, however, impossible to deliver the practice curriculum without having formal collaborative arrangements in place with the social work agencies that provide the practice learning opportunities.
- HEIs have no power or control over these agencies to deliver what they require.
- Similarly, the agencies are seldom, if ever, involved in decisions about the number of students that are selected onto social work programmes, or the timings of practice learning experiences, yet they are expected to be able to deliver sufficient practice learning opportunities on time and to a high standard.

Two main factors affect the quality of practice learning offered to students:

1 HEIs are driven by an agenda that requires them to keep income and therefore students to a maximum, which means that social work programmes find themselves under strong pressure to recruit larger numbers of students.
2 Social work agencies, on the other hand, have to manage a whole range of priorities, of which practice learning is one, and includes providing work-based learning for many occupational groups, not just social work.

A student may only really start to seriously think about the location of the first period of practice at the stage when the tutor discusses learning needs in relation to practice learning opportunities. However, to ensure a sufficiency of good quality practice learning opportunities, the process relies on strong collaborative foundations that have been built over time with social work agencies and their staff. It is a mistake to think that the negotiation is a discrete activity that bears no resemblance to the overall relationship of the HEI to the social work agencies within their region. Searching for new practice learning opportunities and maintaining them requires strategic thinking, good preparation and strong collaborative links. Building up mutually supportive relationships between the education provider and the practice provider is crucial to success.

A two-way process of reciprocal arrangements between HEIs and agency partners exists, with tutors and practitioners meeting regularly and contributing to each other's development, through the process of student selection and recruitment, programme design, delivery and quality assurance through to graduation. These reciprocal arrangements not only benefit the student directly, but also indirectly in the future, as they contribute to the research endeavours of the HEI and to service and workforce development among their social work agency partners.

Agencies running training events for work-based supervisors and practice teaching assessors can enrich the experience on the practice learning opportunity by drawing on the expertise within HEIs. This builds up strong working relationships where there is regular communication and interaction, better understanding and better practice experience for the students.

There is an enormous amount of learning to take on before the student is ready to embark upon the first practice period. The complexity of the role requires professionals who are highly skilled, knowledgeable and accountable. In order for the social work student to demonstrate and improve understanding through the application and testing of knowledge and skills, ensuring that you are adequately prepared for practice is important. The better prepared you are, the more rewarding practice will be. For most students, it is the hands-on practice that gives life to academic study, reading and research. It is perhaps the most enjoyable, yet the most uncertain part of the course.

The practice curriculum

The curriculum is a body of knowledge – the subject, the content. Education and training are the processes by which this knowledge is delivered to the student by the most effective method that can be devised. It encompasses all learning that is planned and guided, whether undertaken in groups, individually within or outside the university. In the UK, the practice curriculum has been adapted from the stages approach put forward by Green and Statham (2004), which identifies three stages:

1 Foundation stage: safety to practise
2 Intermediate stage: capability to practise
3 Final stage: readiness to practise.

Fitness to practise includes the criterion of safety to practise and is assessed at the foundation stage, in that, before beginning the first period of practice, the student must demonstrate safety to do so. Different programmes will use different methods of formally assessing a student's safety to practise. The involvement of service users and

Fitness to practise is judged according to the criteria of the candidate's competence, health and qualification in social work. Fit to practise is the term used by the care councils registering social workers in the UK to refer to a candidate for social work whose registration is approved.

carers is also a formal requirement, emphasising practice organised around service users' and carers' expectations of social work, to:

> ensure that all students undergo assessed preparation for direct practice to ensure their safety to undertake practice learning in a service delivery setting. This preparation must include the opportunity to develop a greater understanding of the experience of service users and the opportunity to shadow an experienced social worker. (DH, 2002f: 3)

Social work students must also have an opportunity to shadow a social worker. However, the hours/days are not prescribed, resulting in different arrangements from one to five or more days of shadowing, depending on the programme.

National Occupational Standards

However the 'safety to practise' element is delivered and assessed, it should emphasise both practice learning and relevant academic knowledge, and be placed in the programme at the appropriate stage in order to help the student to 'bridge the gap' between social work in theory and social work in practice, building on the themes introduced in the foundational social work courses. It is here that the National Occupational Standards (NOS) (Topss, 2002) should be explored, together with the benchmark statement for the honours degree in social work (QAA, 2000).

The NOS are written in a generic and straightforward way, thus enabling the student to begin to translate their learning needs and requirements into opportunities that they can explore once they go out into practice. There are six key roles that provide the basis for assessment of practice, with twenty-one supporting units of competence. Although some key roles are more detailed than others, they are all of equal importance.

Your activities during the required number of days in practice are assessed to ensure that by the end of the degree you have attained the standards for beginning professional practice, according to the six key roles. The QAA benchmark statement provides a template of the knowledge, understanding, skills and standards that might be expected of a graduate in social work.

Bringing all these different aspects together in an attempt to bridge the gap enables the student to see how all the pieces of the learning jigsaw fit together, and to understand why certain subjects are studied and how these interlink, support and inform practice. It also enables the student to see the ultimate goal in terms of competence and to plan the journey to qualification.

Beginning the practice curriculum

It is important at the beginning of the practice curriculum that the student is able to reflect on relevant experiences so far, and identify the personal skills and abilities brought to the course. It may be difficult to reflect on your own life experiences and recognise the value of these experiences in social work. Dempsey et al. (2001) developed a system of preparatory workshops to help students reflect on their motivation to become a social worker and to develop an open, honest and genuine communication rather than a false or professional presentation of oneself.

Individualised learning leads on to professional skills, enabling you to:

- Make sense of social work
- Understand the knowledge and research base
- Develop the skills base and values base
- Link the personal with the professional.

The aim of this is to encourage you to think about your own learning in conjunction with the requirements for social work and to be able to present an appraisal of your individual further learning needs and how these might be met.

Building evidence of learning

Many professions use a portfolio as a formal part of establishing evidence of learning. This is true for both qualifying and continued professional development. A portfolio enables the student to evidence the process of continuous reflective learning that underpins professional development, because the portfolio acts as a summary of learning. By building on it in each academic year, it becomes a useful resource to take into practice and eventually into employment. It also offers a relatively easy way to assess how the student has progressed by examining their succinct summaries of learning presented in one portfolio of evidence. I remember one of my lecturers saying to me when I was studying for my degree: 'If you can't evidence it, it didn't happen.'

Portfolios are not in favour with all programmes. They can become overlarge and cumbersome, but if used to produce an appraisal of the student's individual development and further learning needs that can be shared with their practice teaching assessor, they can provide the starting block for the hands-on training.

Guest speakers from social work agencies can bring a crucial element of hands-on experience, and introduce different organisational settings and contexts. Presentations from service users and carers, focusing on 'lived' experiences, bring another perspective of what makes a good social worker and what it feels like to be on the receiving end of poor practice and poor service delivery. Students should be prepared to receive and sometimes to critically analyse such feedback from service users and carers, because it will not always be positive.

The statement of expectations of social workers' practice (Topss, 2002) identifies certain aspects of practice that people on the receiving end of services and their carers considered important. These aspects are grouped together as follows:

- Communication skills and information-sharing
- Good social work practice
- Advocacy

- Working with other professionals
- Knowledge
- Values.

If these aspects are used as the focus for the input from practitioners, service users and carers, it will help the student to recognise that skills have been developed in the classroom which can then be applied to practice. This does not mean passive learning in the classroom, but interactive learning and active skill development.

EXaMPLE

In one safety to practise module, students, working in small groups, undertake class presentations. Initially, students are nervous about this activity, but the sessions are fun, creative and informative. Most importantly, they promote the development of essential skills that will enable them to present to court, in team or multiprofessional meetings and so on, gaining the confidence to argue a case effectively or to present a point of view.

You may be joining a social work course with very little, if any, practical experience and limited personal experience, in which case, your first experience of 'real' practice can present enormous challenges. In order to deal with the demands of emotionally charged situations, you need an awareness that social workers face:

- complex issues
- competing responsibilities
- conflicting professional and personal roles.

Finally, students need to think about the basics. If you have very little experience of working within a team or office environment, it may come as a shock to find that you are working in an open office, sharing a desk with another student, colleague or even with your work-based supervisor. You may find it difficult to concentrate in a busy office. It can also be disconcerting at first being overheard on the phone. Indeed, how do you answer a phone in a professional manner? A few tips from an experienced office manager will help you at this point.

Finding the right practice learning opportunity

Having been assessed as 'safe to practise', the next task is to match the student to an appropriate practice learning opportunity. In order for the student to achieve a satisfactory learning experience, the HEI will follow clear procedures that have been agreed by programmes and practice learning opportunity providers. To skimp on this all-important preparatory work could jeopardise its successful completion – delivering competent social work practice does not rely on good luck and last-minute arrangements.

Securing sufficient numbers of practice learning opportunities has always been fraught with difficulties. No matter what strategies, projects or initiatives have been funded, the demand for practice learning opportunities continuously outweighs the supply.

From the point of view of the practice learning coordinator (PLC)

It is important for the student to appreciate that the supply of appropriate practice learning opportunities is more likely than not to be limited and, on occasions, some-what uncertain. As a PLC, I have found myself in the final stages of negotiation with an agency. We have discussed the requirements and expectations, identified the learning opportunities, and allocated a student for consideration. Paperwork in place, everyone prepped, and I am sure that it is 'in the bag'. The only stage left is for the student to visit the agency. Then, quite unexpectedly, the offer is withdrawn. The reasons are many and varied. It can be due to staff movements resulting in staff shortages, organisational restructuring (which never seems to end), or changes in funding, especially in the voluntary and private sectors.

Frustratingly, the successful delivery of a practice learning opportunity can still depend heavily on one lead person within the agency. When that person leaves, the future provision of practice learning opportunities within that agency often ends until new relationships with new staff are developed. HEIs therefore encourage agencies to think about how they can deliver their own practice curriculum, so that they are able to take a more proactive approach to providing a learning environment, where all members of the team have input and are not reliant on one person.

However, the reality remains that agencies can say 'no' to a request to take a student. Larger agencies will often draw up a service-level agreement with an HEI, agreeing to offer a certain number of practice learning opportunities each year, but this does not mean that they always match up with the students you have to place in terms of geographical area, service user group or setting. The agency can then say 'that's it, no more', leaving the HEI with the seemingly impossible task of getting the rest of the students placed somewhere, somehow.

Securing practice learning opportunities requires complex, sensitive and involved negotiation. It is too simplistic to assume that the student will conveniently fit into any available practice learning opportunity, or indeed that the student's wishes are predominant. However, there is always a danger that a shortage will lead to taking any and all offers just to ensure that every student is placed. In these circumstances, allocation is often based not on individual learning needs, but on availability. This can give rise to a degree of scepticism from students about the value of some of the practice learning opportunities, especially if they do not match their perceived choice, or are seen as the only one available. Deadlines have to be met wherever possible. Allocation delays and late starts can result in severe financial difficulties for students, so every effort is made to ensure that the student starts the practice on time, and remains in sync with the other students in the group.

The first practice learning opportunity is often the easiest because the student can be matched to any service user group or setting. The challenge comes in finding future practice learning opportunities that provide a contrasting experience. Official requirements are that each student must have experience in at least two practice settings providing services to at least two user groups (such as people with mental health problems or children), one of which must contain statutory social work tasks involving legal interventions (DH, 2002f: 3).

While the bursary has helped, many students still have part-time jobs, and have a difficult balancing act between work, academic study, practice and/or family commitments. Practice learning coordinators try to accommodate all these practicalities in addition to the individual learning needs. This may mean trying to place students within a smaller geographical area while maintaining safety in terms of distance from the service user group.

The contribution of the university or college and the PLC

The university or college and the PLC have an important role to play. The PLC will have acquired specialised knowledge of the practice learning opportunities within their region. They are usually the first point of contact for agency staff seeking information about paperwork, clarification of procedures, programme expectations and requirements, and even when difficulties in practice arise. A large part of the job can be taken up with audits, initial troubleshooting, or holding a situation together until the tutor can go in and visit. An essential part of the job is to get to know the agency staff who are providing the practice learning opportunities and establishing a good working relationship.

It is impossible for one person to visit every agency and every practice learning opportunity, so support is offered to those involved in practice learning through training workshops, support groups and opportunities for questions to be addressed, enabling the PLC to clarify points, provide feedback to the university staff group, or bring back concerns that practitioners may have. This provides an effective link between academic and practice educators, and an opportunity to inform practitioners of changes, new projects or initiatives, and to help form an alliance for research and development where possible.

Intermediate stage: capability to practise

The intermediate stage of the practice curriculum starts with the first period of assessed practice, where for the first time the student will engage directly with service users and carers, demonstrating the knowledge and skills developed in the classroom. Different programmes have different timetabled periods of practice activities. Some programmes timetable the assessed practice in the last two years, whereas others spread the 200 days across all three years. Whatever the timetable, the programme is responsible for ensuring that the student has sufficient time in the classroom to develop the knowledge and skills needed to support the practice.

No matter where a practice learning opportunity takes place, it is essential that the agency understands from the start exactly what is involved, what the aims and objectives are and can identify the opportunities that it can provide for the student. Agencies also need to be supported to develop their own curriculum for practice, which provides:

■ A safe and supportive learning environment for students, with time to think, analyse, reflect and try out new ideas
■ Opportunities for students to be able to demonstrate the knowledge, skills and abilities necessary to become a critically reflective practitioner
■ Opportunities that enable students to provide evidence of competence against the National Occupational Standards
■ Opportunities that enable students to build on the academic study that supports and underpins that practice
■ Opportunities that will provide variety and breadth of learning and the development of transferable skills
■ Opportunities that allow students to build on prior practice learning, from work or previous practice learning or appropriate life experience
■ Opportunities for students to reflect on their own values and those of the social work profession
■ Opportunities for students to demonstrate their ability to work under an umbrella of anti-oppressive and anti-discriminatory practice
■ Encouragement for students to take responsibility for their own learning.

The contribution of the work-based supervisor

Increasingly, the day-to-day responsibility is managed by an on-site work-based supervisor, who takes responsibility for work allocation, oversees learning opportunities, and provides case management-type supervision, in much the same way as a line manager would for a member of staff. The practice teaching assessor can sometimes be a member of the same team, or may be a freelance off-site practice teaching assessor contracted by either the agency or the HEI providing the active teaching of theory, specific skills and anti-oppressive practice, and the assessment. The advantages of off-site practice teaching assessors are that they:

■ enable a greater diversity of practice learning opportunities to be experienced
■ provide the student with different perspectives and different role models to learn from
■ are better able to help the student reflect on their own value base and that of the organisation in which they are placed.

The disadvantages of off-site supervisors are that they:

- increase the number of people involved in the negotiation process
- are sometimes nominated by their agency without being adequately prepared to take on this role
- may not be available if there are insufficient numbers of freelance practice teaching assessors available to cover the demand.

If off-site practice teaching assessors are used, it is extremely important that the agency is fully aware of the expectations and is adequately prepared to meet the following requirements by providing:

- a work-based supervisor who will manage the day-to-day practice opportunity, and who has been appropriately trained to do so
- an induction pack with relevant information about the organisation and related organisations, also policies and procedures, health and safety issues and so on
- an induction programme that offers the student an opportunity to meet staff and visit partner organisations
- work space, stationery, computer, administrative resources, and training or guidance on recording systems and so on
- case management supervision to ensure the student has opportunities for learning and development as set out in the practice learning agreement
- observation of the student's practice, providing feedback as set out in the practice learning agreement
- feedback to the practice teaching assessor on the student's work.

The contribution of the practice teaching assessor

An important question today is who judges student competence and on what basis. The tasks, specialised nature of the work and the variety of roles and responsibilities and situations that apply to the job are determined by the workplace, the employer and the student. This will constantly evolve as you gain experience and acquire additional skills or adapt to new areas of work.

The term 'practice teacher' clings on still, but is rapidly being replaced by 'practice assessor'. This has received a cool reception by practice teachers who have undertaken training to be able to supervise, teach and assess social work students, seeing this development as once more devaluing their role and the important function they perform. Many staff prefer to use the term 'practice teaching assessor', because this is the person who plays a significant part in seeking out opportunities to encourage and facilitate learning, as well as being an effective assessor of the student's competence in practice, carrying out assessments in accordance with the practice learning agreement in a way that is:

- transparent
- relevant

- fair
- valid
- supported with evidence.

The lines of responsibility between the practice teaching assessor and work-based supervisor must be clearly stated and agreed within the practice learning agreement. The practice teaching assessor has the responsibility to ensure evidence of competence in all areas of work, by helping the student to link theory to practice and understand the legal framework, undertake direct observation of work with service users and provide regular planned professional supervision. The practice assessor will also teach areas of practice through discussion, exercises, role plays and so on.

The contribution of the tutor

Searching for a practice learning opportunity

The first stage in the search for a practice learning opportunity begins with a dialogue between tutor and student. You will have ideas of the setting and/or the service user group in which you wish to work derived from your own or others' experience. These will frequently be framed in terms of 'preference'. However, in order to make the best possible match, statements that identify your learning need such as: 'must have a statutory mental health practice learning opportunity', 'wants to work with children', are at the very least unhelpful. Until the day comes when there is a catalogue of available practice learning opportunities to select from, a student will have little choice over the service user group. For example, ten students might request statutory mental health experience, but only two such offers are on the table.

The dialogue between tutor and student should first examine the practical issues: transport, geographical location, ability to work unsociable hours, and any personal circumstances. Increasingly important is whether or not a student has an up-to-date hepatitis B vaccination. Disappointingly, this is still not a requirement for the social work profession, unlike nursing. Agencies cannot therefore demand that you have this level of protection, but I would strongly recommend it. If it was a requirement for the profession, this would give social work students readier access to it.

Tackling your learning needs

Once practical issues have been considered, focus should turn to the student's learning needs. Agencies need as much information about you as possible. A short CV is inadequate as it gives only a basic outline. What is required is the identification of the knowledge, skills and abilities you will bring to the agency, drawing on prior experience, both academic and practical, as well as what knowledge and skills you hope to acquire from this experience.

Matching learning needs to learning opportunities

From a coordinator's perspective, while it is important to appropriately match students in terms of practical issues, learning needs and the provision of contrast in terms of service user group, the ultimate goal is to have every student placed and started on time. This goal can only be achieved by having the correct information about the student and the available learning opportunities that agencies can provide.

Supporting you during the process of practice learning

The role of the tutor has not been defined by the GSCC, therefore the role of the tutor in working with and supporting the student in practice may differ from one programme to another. Tutors may only visit the practice learning opportunity at the contract setting stage, while for other programmes, the tutor will also visit at the midway point and towards the end. This resource-intensive approach is simply impractical for many programmes, however. I firmly believe that the most important contribution the tutor can make is to visit the practice learning opportunity as early as possible in order to have active involvement in the practice learning agreement to ensure that expectations, learning opportunities and outcomes are clearly identified right from the start.

Dealing with difficulties: marginal and failing students

Research undertaken by Burgess et al. (1998) in examining unsuccessful or incomplete practice learning opportunities found that practice teachers felt tutors took on a neutral, rather supportive role, protected by decision-making systems, and contributed little in the difficult process of assessing and failing students. The research also indicated that many students did not see their tutors as having a significant part to play in their overall education and training.

EXAMPLE

The University of Southampton has separated the role of the academic tutor from that of the field tutor. The academic tutor provides personal tutorials that focus on the knowledge and skills acquired in the classroom and helps students to recognise the connection between behaviour in the classroom and behaviour in practice, for example the importance of regular attendance at lectures and tutorials. Harrison and Ruch (2007) present a clear argument for the need for students to understand the close fit between the personal self and the professional self. Another aspect of the academic tutor's role is pastoral.

Field tutors, on the other hand, are qualified and active practice teaching assessors, many still working in practice. These field tutors are enthusiastic

about practice, have a good understanding of the different roles, what constitutes evidence in practice, and what opportunities would meet key roles.
They offer expert advice with failing or borderline students, understand the
demands placed upon work-based supervisors and practice teaching assessors,
and are very much in touch with practice. Their focus is on the practice
curriculum only.

Final stage: readiness to practise

The final stage of the practice curriculum links to the final year of study. There is a
big leap from the first to this final practice learning opportunity because the student
will now be working towards qualification and readiness to practice. By the end of
the final practice learning opportunity, you should be able to demonstrate that you
are able to carry out activities competently and safely. If successful, your final readiness for practice portfolio will be signed off by an experienced social worker.

Practice learning in a changing world

Social work has undergone major changes in recent years in many countries of the
world. In the UK, there have been three main areas of change:

1 Introduction of the social work degree from 2003 onwards.
2 Changes in the organisation of social work itself, with the separation of adult and
   children's services.
3 Increased emphasis on multidisciplinary models of service delivery and services
   provided not through statutory local authority facilities, but commissioned by
   them and provided by agencies and organisations in the 'third sector', that is,
   voluntary and private providers.

   In the social work degree, the word 'placement' has been replaced by 'practice
learning opportunity', although many people still use the term 'placement' or simply
'practice'. The Department of Health talks about 'experience and learning in practice
settings' (DH, 2002f: 3). A practice learning opportunity or placement is where one
student is assigned to one practice teaching assessor working in a social work setting
for a prescribed period of time.

   The recent demise of the qualification for practice teachers who are qualified
social workers and take a further course – the practice teachers award – has already
started to impact on the way practice learning opportunities are planned, delivered
and assessed. This formally accredited award, first established in 1987, moved away
from the previously mainly supervisory role to a more active approach to teaching
and supervision that we have benefited from today, and is therefore a great loss.

   The introduction of the Department of Health performance indicator for practice learning in 2003 was pivotal in refocusing local authorities on the provision of practice learning. Each local authority in England was given a star rating (zero to three), which was informed by its achievement across all 46 performance indicators, of which practice learning was one. For the first time, the number of days provided had a bearing on the local authorities' assessed performance and star rating. The calculation of performance indicators also included an element related to the number of practice learning opportunity days directly supported in the voluntary and private sector. Although many local authorities already undertook this, the introduction of the performance indicator created an environment in which this could flourish, and focused attention on this area of development. Some organisations even appointed voluntary and private practice learning coordinators, specifically to work with and support these agencies in the third sector. The removal of the performance indicator for practice learning is a retrograde move that is likely to result in the reduction of practice learning opportunities provided by local authorities and the support they offer to voluntary and private organisations.

To overcome these difficulties, it is necessary to accept a broader definition of practice learning by concentrating on how the identified learning outcomes, the knowledge, skills and values can be acquired and demonstrated through the development of a broader and more imaginative practice curriculum, for example 'skills teaching' that can be delivered partly or wholly within universities/colleges and outside conventional placements.

Conclusion

This chapter has looked at the nature of the practice curriculum, taking you through what a student needs to do in order to engage in practice. I hope this has given you an insight not only into the role and responsibilities of a student, but also has broadened the picture to include the contribution made by other key stakeholders in practice learning: social work qualifying programmes in higher education institutions, lecturers, practice learning coordinators and tutors, staff in local authorities who commission and manage services, agencies in the voluntary and private sector who provide services, and practice learning supervisors. Finally, I have discussed some of the current areas of debate and uncertainty in practice learning and the practice curriculum and indicated some of the options for future development.

For further discussion of aspects of supervision, see Adams et al., 2009c, Chapter 15, and for coping with the workload, see Adams et al., 2009c, Chapter 12.

www.gscc.org.uk The General Social Care Council is the body responsible for regulating and registering social work in England.

www.sssc.uk.com The Scottish Social Services Council is the body with responsibility for regulating the Scottish social services workforce.

www.niscc.info The Northern Ireland Social Care Council is the equivalent body in Northern Ireland.

www.ccwales.org.uk The Care Council for Wales is the equivalent body responsible for maintaining standards in Wales.

Dominelli, L. (2004) *Social Work: Theory and Practice for a Changing Profession*, London, Polity Press. Explores the contested nature of practice and the concept of service users as citizens with human rights.

Fraser, S. and Matthews, S. (eds) (2007) *The Critical Practitioner in Social Work and Health Care*, London, Sage. Takes a comprehensive and reflective look at key areas of practice and the challenges professional face in training and in their working lives.

Higham, P. (2006) *Social Work: Introducing Professional Practice*, London, Sage. Explicitly constructed around the key roles and benchmark statements. It bridges the gap between theories and real-life practice.

Limber, M. and Pestle, K. (eds) (2007) *Social Work: A Companion to Learning*, London, Sage. Written and edited by leading experts in the field, each chapter equips the student with core knowledge, values and skills to successfully complete their training.

Lishman, J. (ed.) (2007) *Handbook for Practice Learning in Social Work and Social Care: Knowledge and Theory*, 2nd edn, London, Jessica Kingsley. An updated and expanded edition of a classic text covering the traditional knowledge base for social workers.

26 Personal and professional development

Chapter overview

This chapter examines the context of personal and professional development in social work, and essential elements of personal and professional development. In particular, it reflects on our motivation for social work, and our capacity to manage complexity, change and uncertainty: these involve personal and professional development, which are discussed in turn.

Social work involves entering into the lives of people who are in distress, conflict or trouble. To do this requires not only technical competence but also qualities of integrity, genuineness and self-awareness. (Lishman, 1994)

Discussion of personal and professional development must be set in the uncertain, demanding, complex and changing context of social work. The current emphasis on vocational training and, despite the accession of the social work degree and occupational standards, the achievement of discrete technical competences in a culture that promotes market forces, consumerism and managerialism (Holman, 1993; Clark, 1995; Dominelli, 1996; Banks, 2006) is at the expense of fundamental aspects of social work, including:

- a concern about individual people and the enhancement of their lives and relationships
- a commitment to social justice and the eradication of poverty and discrimination
- a commitment to social work as a moral and ethical activity
- a holistic approach to practice, where relationships and process as well as outcomes are addressed
- a commitment to partnership and involvement with users in developing services to meet their needs
- a commitment to evaluating practice as a means of developing it
- a commitment to the 'personalisation' of services (Leadbeater, 2004)
- a recognition that the worker's use of self is integral to social work activity.

The examination of personal and professional development in this chapter is based on a definition of social work that includes these fundamental aspects. We cannot, however, ignore the tensions between this holistic approach and the current culture and context in which the professional definition and identity of social work have been challenged by the political ideology of the New Right and, interestingly and paradoxically, sustained and continued by New Labour. The government's definition involves adherence to managerialism and efficiency savings, and a competency-driven approach to training and professional development (Sheppard, 1995; Vanstone, 1995; Banks, 2006).

In this chapter, we examine the context of personal and professional development in social work and the essential elements of personal and professional development; our motivation for social work and our capacity to manage complexity, change and uncertainty, insofar as each of these involves personal and professional development. Finally, we deal with three critical aspects of professional development: the use of supervision, the articulation and promotion of good practice along with the development and evaluation of models of practice and service provision. Through all this, we need to ask how to maintain a commitment to reflective and evidence-based practice (Fook, 2007; Lishman, 2007b) with the next generation of entrants to social work.

The context and nature of personal and professional development in social work

The ideological, political, economic and financial context has already been alluded to and is hostile to the concept of reflective professional practice on which this discussion of personal and professional development is based. The complex and uncertain nature of social work – with its ethical base, legal accountability, responsibility for complex decision-making and risk assessment, public profile and constantly changing legislation, requirements, structures and organisation – requires social workers to engage in ongoing development, personal and professional, if they are to survive, respond effectively to service users and carers, and manage the uncertainty that is endemic to the profession.

The ethical issues in social work, summarised by Banks (2006), involve tensions between individual rights, public welfare, inequality and structural oppression; they lead to moral dilemmas and a balancing of rights, duties and responsibilities for which there may be no 'right answer'. An ethical response may conflict with financial accountability and resource availability; it may inform or conflict with legal accountability.

Social workers engage in complex decision-making, often about relative risks, safety, harm and protection. They do so in the context of a breakdown of a consensus about social and collective responsibility and a rise in the value accorded to individual choice and responsibility. Paradoxically, 'society' simultaneously experiences widespread economic insecurity and increasing marginalisation and vulnerability, in particular in relation to people from ethnic minorities or people (more recently) who have ethnic backgrounds not perceived either as British or from an ethnic minority (for example Polish or Lithuanian immigrants) or people who are unemployed, in poverty or homeless, or have mental health problems (Parton, 1996). Social work is closely interlinked with these changes, and social workers' dilemmas and actions reflect and symbolise these wider preoccupations with insecurity, safety, marginalisation, risk and control. The Labour government's emphasis on social inclusion has recognised and sought to address societal division, marginalisation and exclusion. However, it is not clear that social work has been seen as a major driver of this agenda (Jordan and Jordan, 2000), despite its inherent involvement with people who are vulnerable and marginalised.

Such inherent complexity in the social work task is compounded by the pace of change that social work has experienced. Change is not unique to social work, although we may feel we have been bombarded by it. Since the late 1980s, policy and legislative change has included:

■   the National Health Service and Community Care Act 1990
■   local government reorganisation, 1996
■   the Children Act 1989
■   the Children (Scotland) Act 1995
■   the overall reorganisation of social work into childcare, community care and criminal justice, with the loss in England and Wales of probation as part of social work training (Criminal Justice Act 1991; Children Act 1989; Children (Scotland) Act 1995).

Current drivers include the need for interdisciplinary practice (McLean, 2007).

In social work education and training, new initiatives for qualifying training were introduced in 1990, and revised in 1995 (CCETSW, 1995). Historic reviews of CCETSW and social work education and training (J.M. Consulting, 1999) led to qualifying education and training being set at honours degree level. The implication of changing models of service design and delivery and consequently different degrees for each of the devolved countries continue to unfold. For example, in Scotland, criminal justice remains in social work education and they have not gone down the English route of separating services for adults and services for children. Instead they have taken a holistic view that children live in families with adults who may be old, have mental health problems, be involved in criminal justice proceedings, or may have substance abuse problems.

Scotland has seen the graduation of the first students to have completed the new honours social work degree. The postgraduate/master's in social work is nearing the completion of its third cohort. Social work qualifying education in Scotland is now required to meet the *Standards in Social Work Education* (SISWE) (Scottish Executive, 2003) and *Key Capabilities in Child Care and Child Protection* (Scottish Executive, 2006b). Equivalent requirements at honours degree level underpin qualifying education in the other three countries, England, Wales and Northern Ireland. Changes in qualification requirements in social work education have implications for our continuing personal development as do the requirements of the regulatory professional councils. In Scotland, the Scottish Social Services Committee requires a newly qualified member of staff to demonstrate evidence of professional development in their first year and thereafter social workers to engage in 15 days of professional development over three years in relation to vulnerable adults and children. In the other three UK countries, the regulatory bodies have equivalent requirements.

This history suggests that the external environment of social work will constantly change. Internally led change and development in practice and service delivery, which are responsive to service user and carer views and based on the evaluation of practice and service delivery, are also essential. However, such rapid policy, legal and organisational change adds to the uncertainty and complexity we experience in our practice.

The context of social work practice historically has not been favourable to personal or professional development. As Pietroni (1995: 38) argued:

> no nationally recognised career path or consistent professional development structures, an inhibition or an antipathy towards individual authority and excellence and a context is produced which is intrinsically antagonistic to thoughtful practice.

Other barriers to professional development and learning included:

- a tension between a local authority's requirement for a technically competent worker, and a professional requirement for critical reflective practice, which may include criticism of the agency practice
- a lack of agency recognition in terms of pay and status for the achievement of professional development
- a lack of agency time allowed for professional development
- a wider lack of organisational investment in continuous professional development and 'learning organisations' (Scottish Executive, 2004).

The new requirements of social work honours degrees addressed the original problem of the two-year social work diploma being very short. The establishment of regulatory bodies for the legislation of social workers and over time all social care workers and the development of codes of conduct and practice are strategic attempts to change the organisational and cultural problems identified in relation to continuing professional development and learning in social work (see, for example, the Scottish Executive, 2000b, 2004).

There are now requirements for professional registration, but there are other clear reasons why social workers should engage in continuing professional and personal development. Professional development is essential to develop, use and promote more effective models of practice and service delivery in a context of rapid change of policy and legislation. Personal development is essential to underpin professional development, since our use of self is part of the service we offer to service users and carers. The need for continuing professional development is not the prerogative of social work. Qualifying training, in any profession and whatever the length, is inevitably limited in input, both breadth and depth, and opportunities for application to practice. Professionals therefore need to update their expertise as knowledge and methods change and develop:

> One central purpose of continuing professional education is to bring practising professionals into contact with new knowledge and ideas. Sometimes this is conceived in terms of general updating, sometimes as a stimulus to critical thinking and self evaluation, sometimes as the dissemination of a particular innovation, sometimes as part of the process of implementing a new mandatory policy. (Eraut, 1994: 25)

Put briefly, but too simply, two contrasting models appear to influence continuing professional development: the competency-based approach, which underpins the national vocational system, and an alternative approach, which values reflective practice and the learning process, stresses the role of the professional as a critical reflective practitioner (Schön, 1987; Fook, 2007) and a commitment to evidence-based and research-minded practice (Lishman, 2007b).

The 'competency' model is based on functional analysis, which:

> breaks the job down into functional units and the units into elements each of which has to be separately assessed to cover a range of situations according to a list of performance criteria. (Eraut, 1994: 118)

This model is inappropriate for education, training and professional development in social work because it results in fragmentation of the complexity of social work and lacks a holistic approach to the necessary integration of knowledge, values and skills and the processes whereby these are integrated and applied.

This chapter bases professional development on the second approach, the critical reflective practitioner model. Schön (1987) acknowledges the need for academic rigour but also its limitations in the messy reality of practice. By critical reflection and analysis, we can adapt and develop the theories we use to new, complex and out-of-the-ordinary situations. By a research-minded and evidence-based approach to practice and policy, we can draw on the best possible knowledge and research to underpin our assessment and intervention, critical for service users and outcomes for them (Lishman, 2007b).

Our motivation for social work

Why do we become social workers, and why should this be relevant to our personal and professional development?

The motivation for social work, like social work itself, is varied and complex. Cree (1996) found that the reasons for entering social work training included family background, significant life experience of loss, illness or disability, and adult choice including social work as a vocation to care for individuals, as a means of 'changing the system' and promoting social justice or as a career. Rochford (2007) drew attention to the experience of loss, both normal and exceptional, as a major factor in the motivation for social work. Cree (1996) highlighted gender differences in the motivation for social work. Men were entering a profession in which their promotion prospects were high but the qualities and abilities required of them were not stereotypically male. For women, the opposite was true.

Cree (2003: 5) further explored why we become social workers and our motivation. In relation to her own motivation, she says: 'I have been trying to resolve central contradictions in my own background and upbringing.' Cree (2003) examines personal and structural reasons for the motivation to undertake social work: personal reasons do include loss, not just in the form of personal experiences of death or disability or evacuation in the Second World War but also being an 'outsider'. This could involve structurally challenging discrimination in relation to the impact of poverty, ethnicity, gender, sexuality and disability for all users of services, voluntary or involuntary clients, service users or carers.

Whatever our present circumstances and role, we need to draw what we can from the above evidence base of research. Our particular focus will depend on our personal position. We may be just beginning the process of learning about social work, or we may be joining a professional qualifying programme with substantial social work experience.

In these differing circumstances, why does motivation matter, and why should it be an issue for personal development? Think about your own motivation. Was it political, was it your experience of racial or gender discrimination, or did it arise from your personal experience, as a child or as an adult? How do you think it influences your practice? As I reflect on my motivation, I note my huge practice commitment to children and families and helping them to improve their communication. This, I believe, stems directly from my experience in my family of origin. However, for me, focusing on this personal motivation meant that initially I unhelpfully did not pay sufficient attention to the structural and policy issues that heavily influence the practice of social work.

We need a personal element in our motivation for social work, whether it arises from our experience of structural oppression or personal difficulty. It can give us compassion, empathy and insight into the lives of people with whom we work and a commitment to challenging injustice and discrimination. However, we must not be driven in our practice by our personal experience, attempt to impose the experiences that motivate us on clients or service users, or work out our agendas (personal or political) through their lives.

How may we harness the positive and empowering aspects of our motivation and avoid the potential danger of using service users to meet our own needs rather than responding to theirs? Developing and maintaining self-awareness is one way, supervision, potentially, is another (see Adams et al., 2009c, Ch. 15).

Self-awareness and reflection

We need to develop our self-awareness and capacity for critical reflection in order to ensure that our motivation and past experience are used to enhance our practice. Self-awareness is also necessary if we are to recognise our impact on others. Do we convey authority and expertise where required? Do we convey a non-judgemental attitude to aspects of the lives of service users that are potentially shocking, for example violence, abuse or deprivation? What sense of empowerment do we convey to service users? How do we remain aware of our impact on others?

Self-awareness and critical self-reflection are also necessary to ensure confidence that our responses arise from the situation of the service user rather than our past or needs. This requires self-awareness and:

> Awareness of situations and topics which generate most personal anxiety to the worker since intense anxiety is likely to lead to inattention, poor listening, and inappropriate responses and action. (Lishman, 1994: 60)

Finally, we need to use self-awareness and reflection to meet the complex demands of social work. Carter et al. (1995) suggest that, in social work, we experience a tension between the uniqueness of each situation and the need to develop generalised responses to 'familiar social work problems':

> We have to think things through, for every case is unique. When we forget this, problems arise. If we simply label people as a 'housing problem' for example, and then go through our 'housing routine' we are liable to miss all sorts of things ... Of course, we rely on routines: it would be intolerable if we had to work things out from first principles for each and every situation. However, these routines have to be open to feedback from the situation. (Carter et al., 1995: 8)

They argue that this requires both 'reflecting-in-action' and 'reflection-on-action'.

We need to develop a discipline of reflecting on what we have done and how we have behaved – 'reflection-on-action' (Schön, 1987) – in order to learn, confirm good practice, analyse mistakes and develop alternative actions and responses. Questions contributing to reflection-on-action include:

■ How did I engage with that person or in that situation?
■ What previous experiences influenced me?
■ What did I do?
■ Why did I do it?
■ On reflection, how might I have responded differently, if at all?

By practising such discipline, we may increasingly be able to 'reflect in practice', where questions have a more immediate focus and may include the following:

■ What am I feeling?
■ How am I presenting?
■ Do I need to change my approach or focus?
■ Why do I feel uncomfortable?

Fook (2007) develops this model of reflective practice by examining 'critical reflection'. Briefly, she argues that we need to reflect on 'deeper assumptions' and how in particular they reflect power differentials. My understanding of critical reflection is that we need to challenge continuously whether we do employ 'taken-for-granted' assumptions about how our world in social work operates. This is not just about reflection in and on action but about a critical review of our espoused theories.

One tool in this critical review is research-mindedness and evidence-based practice.

Research-mindedness and evidence-based practice

As Sackett et al. (1997) and Sheldon (1998) argue, evidence-based practice requires us to draw on current best evidence, conscientiously, using our professional ethics and values explicitly, and 'judiciously (critically, analytically and carefully balancing and judging the evidence)' (Lishman, 2007b: 384). Evidence includes ethics and values, research, service users' and carers' perspectives, and professional judgement (Morago, 2006). Professional and personal development needs to ensure that we are research minded and evidence based in order that we do not rely on outdated knowledge, our own reflective practice wisdom or colleagues' anecdotes and practice wisdom.

But what might be our caution about the agenda for evidence-based practice? I argue (Lishman, 2007b: 183) that two of the concerns about evidence-based practice are that it may:

- fail to address the complex interrelationships between policy imperatives, resource allocations and practice realities
- involve a lack of attention to the complexity, messiness and individuality of social work practice.

I have also argued that while we need to use evidence about what methods of assessment and intervention are most successful in outcomes in a particular area of practice, including the experiences of service users and carers, we also need to recognise 'the range of stakeholders in social work practice and the differential power they can employ. Our concept of evidence needs to take account of different and conflicting expectations of social work and social care' (Lishman, 2007b: 387).

However, our concept of evidence also needs to use relevant research and therefore it is important in our professional development that we become more sophisticated in accessing and critiquing it and able to use systematic reviews, which use 'explicit and systematic criteria' to:

- search, identify, select and evaluate research studies applied to a specific social work focus, for example child protection, working with people with learning disabilities, or working with people with mental health problems.
- draw together and critically analyse the general findings from the review (Cochrane Collaboration, 2003).

We need to improve our focus on outcomes and evaluation and use research to inform this but we also need to be aware of the tension between this evidence-based approach and managing complexity and uncertainty.

Managing complexity

We have noted the complicated demands of social work, but its very essence is complex and ambiguous, involving tensions between a focus on the alleviation of individual distress and misery and challenging structural oppression and inequality, and between meeting individual need, promoting empowerment, ensuring the protection of vulnerable children and adults, and carrying out functions of social work control. Practice is equally complex. For example, faced with families in poverty, in isolation, with difficulties in childcare and control (Walker, 1995), what, out of the range of relevant knowledge and theory, do we draw on? What focus do we select? What methods do we employ? Equally, how do we manage the complexity of our feelings, of being overwhelmed, the feelings of inadequacy, helplessness, empathy and frustration?

Such complexity 'stirs up powerful and primitive feeling in all professionals' (Trowell, 1995: 195). One danger is that we become paralysed by attempting to manage all the complexity and our inability to do so effectively. Walker (1995: 56) warns of the dangers of the wish to be omnipotent: 'the belief that I could or should be brilliantly effective'. An alternative danger is that we attempt to limit and simplify the complexity, for example, by:

- providing 'concrete responses', such as providing a service or aid, but ignoring the feelings and relationships that surround the problem – for example, providing a Zimmer frame may be necessary for the person's functioning but not sufficient for their wellbeing, because issues about dependency and anxiety about 'failing' may need to be addressed.
- 'splitting' and 'projection':

> Splitting arises from the existence of utterly contradictory feelings that seem impossible to countenance simultaneously and which are therefore kept in separate compartments ... Projection occurs when a feeling or characteristic which in reality belongs to the self is first externalised and then ascribed to another person.
> (Brearley, 2007)

Splitting and projection are defence mechanisms that began in infancy in order to cope with the powerful good and bad primitive feelings and can be helpful essential mechanisms in coping as adults. As workers, however, if we use splitting and projection in relation to service users or our work in organisations, we are in danger of distorting a complex reality.

We have to be able to contain, for example, worry and concern for a mother on her own, depressed, in debt and without the very basic material props of parenting, such as a washing machine; our anxiety about her child's emotional and physical needs; our anger with the political and social security system that allows if not promotes this; and resonances with our past and our childhood experience of need and dependency. If we split, for example by focusing entirely on the child's needs and vulnerability, or project, for example by raging at the system, we cannot manage and balance the complex task of addressing ways of improving resources and parental care, and improving the ways in which the parent's and child's needs can be met.

How can we develop this personal capacity to contain and manage such complexity? There are several ways:

- we need to recognise this as a continuing area of personal and professional development
- it requires a commitment to the maintenance and development of self-awareness
- it requires a capacity for reflection in and on action
- we need to learn from available research in a systematic way
- we need to be able to analyse practice and therefore learn from and build on previous experience.

Practice supervision may offer the opportunity to examine our responses to complex cases with real needs, vulnerability and risks, and engage in the same processes for personal development and learning. We also need to be allowed to make mistakes and get things 'wrong', provided that we learn from the experience and are not dangerous to our clients.

Managing uncertainty

Uncertainty faces us in a number of ways. We face uncertainty about our value base as we are challenged to examine, for example, how racism, sexism, heterosexism, ageism and other forms of oppression may influence us (Fook's, 2007, deeper assumptions), without our necessarily recognising this. In working with service users and carers, we face uncertainty about how to respond appropriately, how to choose the 'right' response to the myriad of feelings, impressions, theories and experiences that form our working practice. Uncertainty is not unique to social work but is a component of 'professional' activity. More specifically:

- uncertainty in social work arises because individuals and their problems are unique
- there is no set causal link between a problem, a response and an outcome
- risk assessment is problematic (Kemshall, 2007)
- the organisational and legal context has been constantly changing
- the political context has frequently been hostile and unpredictable.

Dealing with uncertainty means realising that often there is no right response, although there may be a wrong one. The danger here is that, again, we try to simplify, which may involve:

- demanding certainty and answers where none are available

- giving answers and information that are definite but may be wrong
- dealing with the discrete parts of a problem that may have an immediate solution and ignoring the more messy and uncertain areas.

Such strategies for denying uncertainty can be dangerous as they may lead us to impose 'certain' but wrong action on service users.

How may we better deal with uncertainty? Perhaps we first have to recognise it as an essential part of life, not just social work. We need to consider how we deal with uncertainty in our own lives, what helps and what hinders. 'We need to avoid jumping to closed conclusions and keep open the possibility of change as a result of reflecting in action and dialogue with others' (Carter et al., 1995: 9). We need to use the experience of training, supervision and our colleagues to help us examine our own ways of dealing with uncertainty and, where we find they are inappropriate, to explore and practise other ways. (Adams et al., 2009c, Ch. 2 deals with uncertainty in more detail.)

Managing change

We have seen that the recent context of social work has been of rapid, constant and externally imposed change. Change is not unique to social work. In our personal lives, we have to adapt to changes of biological maturation and ageing, and life cycle social and emotional changes.

More generally, we need to be aware that any major change, be it voluntary or imposed, will involve loss for the participants – an initial loss of their previous 'taken-for-granted' view of the world, sense of security and established sense of meaning and purposes (Marris, 1974). Such loss is met with ambivalence, analogous to grief, involving conflict between contradictory impulses: to remain the same and keep what is valuable from the past, and to move on. Marris argues that the management of change necessitates the expression of ambivalence and conflicting impulses before the participants can move on to accept the change (whether it involves new perspectives, skills or organisational structures) and integrate it into a continuity of experience and meaning. Such an analysis helps us to understand why change, even where we can see that it brings rewards, is met with apparently irrational resistance. While such resistance to change is not intrinsically bad – for example, it may delay ill-thought-out or ill-advised changes (Coulshed and Orme, 2006) – change is essential if an organisation is to be responsive to its environment and develop and thereby survive, and in order to develop better services and practice.

In our personal and professional development, it is important to pay attention to how we manage change. At the extremes, do we totally resist it or embrace it without a thought for the past? We need to examine our personal responses because they will influence how we respond to service users who are facing change, for example in relationships, dependency or physical location, how we respond to changes in the organisation and delivery of social work, and how open we are to new ideas, without discarding hard-earned knowledge and skills from the past.

Managing complexity, uncertainty and change is demanding and stressful, and it is impossible to prescribe methods and techniques to do so 'successfully'. What can help? At a personal level, we have seen the need to develop and maintain an awareness of our own strengths and weaknesses, a capacity to tolerate and contain our irrational feelings and responses, and a discipline of self-critical reflection.

To support and help us in this, we can use specific training courses, discussion with colleagues, mulling over particular cases and incidents, recording, reflection and evaluation, and, perhaps potentially most important, supervision.

Supervision

> Supervision is an effective tool for professional staff development which managers would be foolish not to consider. However, many managers subvert the supervision process into a means of controlling or instructing staff, instead of as a means of developing staff. (Turner, 1995: 127)

The above quotation indicates the potential dilemma and danger of supervision. It frequently becomes a management tool of accountability and efficiency. Equally, it can be used to enhance professional development and thereby practice and service provision (Peach and Horner, 2007). Peach and Horner (2007) question whether supervision is 'support or surveillance'. According to Argyris and Schön (1996: 215), the support element occurs when organisations are 'responsible, productive and creative, and where errors are seen as vehicles for learning'. In contrast, Peach and Horner (2007: 229) argue:

> Unfortunately 'modern' social work organisations suffer from the convictions that no mistakes are tolerable and, therefore, that the sole goal of supervision is in danger of becoming the elimination of risk through micro-management and surveillance of practitioners and their outcomes.

Supervision has to include accountability but other elements are that:

- It should, ideally, be provided on a regular and reliable basis
- It should involve mutual trust and an awareness of issues of authority and responsibility
- It should provide support and an opportunity to express feelings and go 'below the surface' in the analysis of problems and situations
- It should address particular issues that workers identify as problematic, including facing pain, anxiety, confusion, violence and stress
- Its content and process should be anti-oppressive and anti-discriminatory, with a professional development focus of empowerment
- It should focus on learning and quality of work.

As Peach and Horner (2007) argue, these functions of supervision include educational, supportive, administrative and managerial ones.

There is a gap between what should happen and what actually does happen (Jones, 2001). Areas of discrepancy that hinder professional development include:

- the unavailability of supervision
- the abuse of power, for example where the dissemination of information is controlled, or supervision is used to exercise the supervisor's power or control as negative power, by blocking and restricting, or by punishment (Grimwood and Popplestone, 1993)
- a lack of emotional or feeling support:

> Supervisors often cut off from the pain in the lives of users of services. The worker, unable to share and thereby receive support from her line manager, is left on her own with the loss and grief of users of services. (Hanmer and Statham, 1988, cited in Grimwood and Popplestone, 1993: 47)

- a lack of acknowledgement and support in issues connected with violence: often as workers, we are left to deal with fears of and responses to violence as our personal responsibility rather than being offered support and the opportunity for reflection, process and analysis in supervision.

It is important to seek good supervision. In particular, it can help us to manage anxiety and confusion. Turner (1995: 126) argues that:

> Many workers feel they must appear to be coping well with their work at all times. What they see as their less acceptable thoughts, feelings and actions are suppressed, denied and avoided, for fear of being seen as not a good enough worker. It is important for supervisors to demonstrate in supervision their own capacity to contain anxiety and remain thoughtful about whatever the worker brings, rather than avoiding the painful issues, rushing for solutions, or giving 'neat' packages of instructions.

Such a capacity for containment, empathy, reflection and the encouragement of in-depth analysis can help us to cope with the pain, violence and anxiety we may encounter. It can also help us to become more able to take responsibility for our own work, to make our own judgements and then improve them. Supervision is a time for exploration, reflection, learning and problem-solving.

We do need to remember our accountability to the organisation employing us. (Adams et al., 2009b, Ch. 3 deals with different forms of accountability.) As Coulshed and Mullender (2000) argue, supervision should meet individual support needs, educational and developmental needs and managerial and administrative needs. These managerial needs include workload and caseload management, ensuring that staff work with the policies and developments of the agency and giving feedback about performance.

There is an inevitable tension between the different potential users of supervision, but in terms of professional development, it is essential to recognise the requirements of the agency, the need to perform appropriately and the need for supervision as a time to reflect and seek support.

Promoting and developing good practice and positive outcomes in service provision

The development of good social work practice and positive outcomes in social work and service delivery is a collective responsibility of all qualified social workers. We need constantly to examine critically and review practice and service delivery. We need to identify the ingredients of 'good practice' and how can they be applied elsewhere. We need to identify areas for improvement and gaps in service delivery and responses to service user need, in order to begin to change services and provide new ones. This is, of course, within the context of a lack of resources. Most social workers have to refuse services that carers and service users need because of a lack of resources. However, community care and care management also regularly provide examples of innovative developments in practice and service delivery to meet gaps in service provision or unmet need.

We need to develop and maintain ways of learning from others: we should not be reinventing wheels in each unitary authority or voluntary organisation. How can we keep abreast of new developments that we may usefully be able to apply? One problem is the overload of information we receive and the need to select from it. Conferences and training courses are specific and therefore targeted clearly for us in terms of application to our particular practice and service development needs, but they are expensive. However, they can put us in touch with other workers' relevant experience in relatively informal but productive ways.

We can engage in a range of academically credited, continuous professional development including child protection practice learning and mental health officer awards. We can also engage in relevant conferences and learning development activities.

We can also learn by reading, by using the internet, and by use of systematic reviews. The Social Care Institute for Excellence promotes the dissemination of both qualitative and quantitative research-based evidence to underpin social work practice and policy development. It recognises the complexity of social work practice and does not rely entirely on evidence from the 'gold standard' experimental research of the randomly controlled trial (see Lishman, 2007b for a critique of this approach).

We need to continue to articulate our practice in supervision in order to learn from what we do and change and develop our practice. We also need to articulate our practice to colleagues from other disciplines, and we need to articulate our practice so that other social workers can learn from what we do. We may be working on behalf of service users in excellent innovative ways that benefit them, but if we do not articulate this practice, others cannot learn from it and have to reinvent the wheel. We need to articulate practice for the political survival of the profession and for service users, in order to demonstrate to the government, press and public what we do well (even though they may not necessarily listen).

We need not simply identify good practice, but also evaluate it. As Shaw (1996) argues, evaluating practice has historically been a problematic aspect of social work. However, there are good reasons why we should engage in the evaluation of practice and service delivery. Evaluation examines our effectiveness and can help us to improve it, increases our accountability to service users, develops our knowledge and identifies gaps in knowledge, and helps us to develop new models of practice and service delivery (Shaw and Lishman, 1999).

If we develop a new method, project or service, we need to examine how well it works for its users. More problematically, the continued funding of innovative projects is often linked with the evaluation of effectiveness, where definitions of effectiveness may not necessarily be shared by the funder, the project and its users. We need to recognise that evaluation can be part of a political and resource context. Nevertheless, we need to engage with it; as Shaw (1996) argues: 'it holds the promise of keeping social work honest'.

How to evaluate our practice can appear threatening, with connotations of the scientific experimental method, although, as Everitt et al. (1992) suggest, the social work process of finding and collating evidence, forming hypotheses and assessment, intervention and testing hypotheses, review, further assessment, revision of intervention and further review is not dissimilar to qualitative research methodology. Shaw and Lishman (1999) demonstrate the range of methodologies appropriate to social work evaluation and Lishman (2007b) argues that 'evidence' is drawn from a range of service users' and practitioners' views and that evidence from randomised controlled trials needs a contextualised 'realistic' application.

Educating and training the next generation

There are inevitably many apparent reasons for not becoming involved in learning or providing input to social work education, including a lack of financial or career recognition, a lack of resources including staff, space and time, and a lack of organisational support where management is preoccupied with service delivery and cuts in resources (Bruce and Lishman, 2004).

In such circumstances, educating and training the next generation may be seen as a luxury. Why should you become involved in practice learning or any other teaching input to social work courses? Good reasons include the need to ensure the continuation of professional service delivery to service users, the professional and value component of creative investment (Erikson, 1965), that we should put back into the profession as we have received, and the enhancement of our learning and expertise. Students question and challenge us in ways that ensure we explore, examine, reflect on and evaluate our practice.

Teaching others often provides the best opportunity to articulate our own practice, to question and examine what we do and why, and, if we are open to challenge, to identify gaps and failures in practice and provision. Students then provide a challenging external scrutiny of what we do. By educating and training them, we provide the future development of our profession, and workers who can learn from and develop our experience. As argued in *Confidence in Practice Learning* (Scottish Executive, 2004), practice learning is the professional duty of all of us in social work.

Conclusion

Personal and professional development is a very broad agenda: it lasts a lifetime and depends on definitions of social work and its functions. It can be undermined by ideology, for example the emphasis on technical competence or managerialism, a lack of access by gender, class or ethnicity, a lack of organisational support and reward, and a lack of resources including time.

This chapter focuses on the themes of self-awareness, critical reflection and critical self-evaluation, and the use of an evidence base that underpins both personal and professional development. It does not adopt models of development involving discrete technical competencies because social work is a complex, uncertain and value-based activity in which we work with people from different backgrounds who are likely to have experienced structural oppression, discrimination, personal difficulty, loss or tragedy. Despite the barriers identified, we owe it to service users to maintain our personal and professional development and thereby contribute to the development and improvement of the social work practice and services they receive.

For further discussion of developing as a critical practitioner, see Adams et al., 2009b, Chapter 21, and for integrative practice, see Adams et al., 2009c, Chapter 1.

Eraut, M. (1994) *Developing Professional Knowledge and Competence*, London, Falmer. Contains a valuable multidisciplinary analysis of issues in professional development and pressures that deal with complexity.

Lishman, J. (2007) *Handbook for Practice Learning in Social Work and Social Care*, 2nd edn, London, Jessica Kingsley. Has a number of chapters relevant to professional development, in particular in relation to policy and practice links, evidence-based practice and critical reflective practice.

Lymbery, M. and Postle, K. (eds) (2007) *Social Work: A Companion to Learning*, London, Sage. A thoughtful, reflective and evidence-based book on learning in social work. Includes useful chapters on supervision and management.

Shaw, I. and Lishman, J. (eds) (1999) *Evaluation and Social Work Practice*, London, Sage. Presents critically a range of ways of evaluating social work practice, arguing that evaluation should not be just applied to practice but should be a direct dimension of practice.

Yelloly, M. and Henkel, M. (eds) (1995) *Learning and Teaching in Social Work: Towards Reflective Practice*, London, Jessica Kingsley. This edited collection addresses issues in the post-professional education of social workers and related professionals, examining the concepts of professionalism, competence, knowledge and anti-racism, with an emphasis on how professionals learn and maintain a self-critical and reflective approach to practice.

Concluding comment

The need for critical practice

This book has introduced the streams of knowledge that are required for us to maintain and develop critical practice in social work. We have described how we view these in our brief introductions to each of the three parts of this book. We can think of these knowledges as tributaries to the river of understanding that carries our practice forward. We practise and study social work in the present. Inevitably, we are conscious that the present draws from past experience and moves towards the future. This is because in practice and in understanding social work, as a profession and as an activity, we cannot deny what has formed our 'now'. Also, since all social work has purposes, it must look forward. Drawing on the past means changing some of it, because to move is to change. However, the present and future always carry with them the currents and debris of the past. Perhaps you have played one of the computer games that involves building cities, hospitals or theme parks for simulated people to live, work and play in. In these games, current pressures always make it difficult to find the time to change the basic road system or the building structures, so we are always constrained by previous decisions.

Being a student or a practitioner involves managing our day-to-day activities within the constraints of the present. We have somehow to manage the present within our practice, while keeping a strategy in mind for future change and dealing with the constraints and opportunities of the past that structure our present efforts. This chapter – and this book – moves beyond acknowledging the importance of the past for our present efforts, beyond the constraints of the present, beyond prescriptions for the future and proposes that if we are going to take action within our practice, we must always maintain a critical view of the past, present and future of social work. This affects the professional and agency context of our practice and the practice itself. A critical view of past, present and future is essential to good practice because of the way they interact. We must be able to think about when we must keep the past or change it, when we must focus on the present or avoid its constraints, and when we must reach out for the future or move cautiously towards it.

This book has, therefore, highlighted how the nature of social work always presents problems and issues to be considered and debates about contexts for practice (Part 1) and how different views of social work processes and stages of practice (Part 2) remain unresolved and unfinished. Part 3, though, shows the breadth of opportunities for creative practice and contexts that control, constrain and shape our practice. Many of the chapters have been concerned in one way or another with the twin, but sometimes opposed, themes of continuity and change. We are likely to see some of these continuities and changes as positive, others as negative, and still others as not entirely one or the other. Our position in discussions and controversies about them depends on our political stance and value position. Some aspects of our values are entirely personal, others cannot be dissociated from our practice and that of others.

The values associated with social work, explored in Part 1, are particularly associated with its traditions and distinctiveness. They introduce moral, social and political dimensions to every aspect of theory and practice. Equally, they are constant guides to present actions, because they have continuing relevance to every decision we make. Then again, they condition the future because our values influence the choices we make about our purposes.

We cannot forget either the past of social work or that of the people we encounter while we practise. Part 1 shows that how social work was formed creates and constructs our present practice and organisation. The ideas considered in Parts 2 and 3 show how these values have to be integrated into a stream of activities in our daily practice. The constant linkage and interaction between past, present and future in this book draws attention to the ways in which hopes and plans for the future continually alter our present interpretation of the constraints and possibilities to be found in the past. Although the past is amenable to examination, it is inevitably coloured by our interpretations of it. Similarly, the future is still in our minds because it lies in our ideas and plans. The crucial aspect of linking past and future, therefore, is our interpretations, which are always of the 'now' but inevitably interact with the past and our ideas for the future.

Thus, there can never be certainty and clarity of past, present or future, because the past is indistinct and overlaid by interpretation, we are bound up in the currency of the present and the future is yet to be. We can see that various factors influence these different aspects of time. But the direction that social work takes in the future is not determined by the past. Those involved can shape it in the present. The dominant ideas about the direction of health and welfare policies and practices are subject to change. We can take action individually and collectively, campaign, protest and resist where we regard it as necessary. We can all act to contribute to the development of future values, approaches and practice. Some of us may become carers or service users and we have power to act in those capacities as well.

At the outset of this chapter, we have to acknowledge that even what we think of as the past – 'set in concrete' as a student once described it – cannot be taken for granted. That so-called concrete is a subject for endless debate. What is it? What is it composed of? Is it as solid, unchanged and unchanging as it seems? How was it formed? Can we ever be certain we have described it adequately and comprehensively?

Views of histories

Reality is a question of perspective; the further you get from the past, the more concrete and plausible it seems – but as you approach the present, it inevitably seems more and more incredible. (Rushdie, 1982: 165)

With these words, Salman Rushdie's novel *Midnight's Children*, about the emergence of Indian independence from the preceding history of civil disturbances, delicately reminds us of the intrinsic paradoxes in the way we regard our past and our present. Some aspects of social work, such as civil disturbances, concern those aspects of people's lives that arouse strong feelings and views. It is often politicised, debated and controversial. Other aspects of social work are no less problematic, because they are hidden and concern people who commonly are neglected or ignored. So we can add to the paradoxes identified by Rushdie four further barriers between us and the so-called authentic account of the past and present of social work.

The first barrier is that our views of the past are framed by our assumptions and values. Just as people selecting a frame for a picture impose on it a particular set of assumptions and affect the way it is viewed, so our history is affected by how we frame it. It is easy to take history for granted as evolutionary and developmental, because we can understand how a particular decision came to be taken. That histories can be regarded from different perspectives is particularly relevant in social work. A brother pushes his sister and causes her to fall downstairs. Which is 'true'? Is it the brother's explanation of the 'accident', or the sister's view that the push was 'intentional' because she won an argument, or their father's interpretation of high spirits, or the mother's interpretation of the boy's lack of physical control? Behind these potential explanations are views of the world and the past, present and future: of the relations between the sexes and how they arise from gendered assumptions about how boys and girls should behave. Perhaps most families nowadays would not openly say that the father should always be right, but interpersonal relationships in a family, based on historical assumptions, might still linger in how people actually behave. Whose history comes to dominate? It might be the mother's because she manages the family's daily life, or the father's because of his physical power. If a social worker comes to investigate, she will select for her record particular explanations, and her selection will determine whether this incident contributes to the family being put on any 'at-risk' register subject to a child protection plan. However, that history will not prevent the sister who fell down the stairs relying on her own view of history in deciding how to deal with her brother, her parents and the social worker in future.

Similarly, for social work as a profession and activity, different views of the past and present of social work lead to distinctive portrayals of its nature and contexts in social policy and the social sciences. Liberal views might see it as a contributor to the stability of the state and emphasise the consciences of philanthropists and reformers as the main motivators for progress. Alternative views might adopt a range of social-ist and radical perspectives, arguing for the inadequacy of progressive zeal and humanitarian enlightenment as an explanation, regarding social work as a contributor to curbing the discontent of the lower classes, including the 'underclass', and contributing to the oppression and control of these classes by the state. Counter views from those in the new social movements might bring into the analysis the understandings and experiences of people receiving services, such as survivors of mental health treatment or people with disabilities, for whom state control and intervention through social work and allied professions provide the stimulus for resistance, challenging oppression and endorsing empowerment. Postmodern views might interpret social work in any particular historical context as the product of the interaction of all these aspects of social work's position in society. These varied conceptions of social work lead to different emphases being put on different aspects and issues and can lead to different responses in practice.

The second barrier between our present interpretations of the past and the events that comprise those interpretations is that our past is comprised of histories not history. There is no single, agreed history. There are histories. At school, some of us were taught 'the history' of a country with reference to its rulers. Nowadays, pupils are encouraged to put themselves into the position of various people occupying different strata of past societies and, using historical data – some based on diaries and reminiscences – imagine their histories. Social work history is often taught as a triumphant progression from uncertain beginnings to the achievement of its widely recognised role in most welfare states. This makes us despondent about present criticisms of present changes, which seem to move away from the welfare state and question the value of social work. However, there are many incidents which were setbacks in that progression, that led to reappraisals of mainstream practices, for example the state as the main provider of psychiatric hospitals. Additionally, different countries treat social work in different ways and organise it in structures that vary from country to country and subject the profession to different regulatory regimes. We can see our present position as the beginnings of a downturn, which might lead to the displacement of social work's values in our country, or as one of the setbacks to be overcome, perhaps drawing inspiration from examples provided by people from other countries. We can see the welfare state as a necessary condition of social work flourishing and defend it at all costs, or as a temporary phase of the international economy whose destruction will lead to social work arising in another form, perhaps the social development one that has been so useful in developing countries.

The third barrier between our present and our histories is that we are constantly revising these. Histories are provisional, not definitive. Our knowledge of the past of social work is not complete. As new findings emerge, we have to revise our view of the past. This process is replicated when as social workers we deal with a case and different points of view lead us to revise our assessment of it. It is also true of wider histories. For example, most histories of social work (for example Woodroofe, 1962) focus on the role of the nineteenth-century Charity Organisation Society (COS) as an origin for a set of social work methods that remain popular today. However, Laybourn's (1997) work on guilds of help suggests that there are alternative sources of practice to be uncovered. Why were they not obviously part of our histories already? It may be because the COS was based in the capital city and was run by people from social elites, whose historians dominated early interpretations of social work, while guilds of help started in the provinces and were influenced by municipal and local reformers. Similar points can be made about the silencing of the impact of the settlement movement on the profession. These other explanations provide examples of how power and influence can create particular versions of history. Some of the great revelations about the past of the way children and families have been treated by social work agencies have arisen from uncovering the memories of ordinary people, rather than through official records, which are another form of power. For example, the remarkable work by a student at Nottingham University with Philip Bean followed a chance meeting with a former Barnardo's child and led to the dramatic exposure of the enforced migration to Australia up to the 1970s of tens of thousands of Barnardo's children and the subsequent abuse of many of them (Bean and Melville, 1990).

Finally, the fourth barrier comes from our realisation that writing history retrospectively, and from people's own accounts, is intrinsically problematic. It may seem obvious but it is still important to note that just as histories written at the time in, say, a diary may lack the broader perspective of what was going on in the organisation or society, histories written in retrospect cannot be segregated from the hindsight of the backward-looking writer. So, history-taking – as any social worker who has had to interview a person in depth and use this as the basis for an account of their life knows – is notoriously difficult. A good example of these problems is the use of oral history, which is history written in the light of interviewing numbers of people involved in an event or experience. The spirit of Mass Observation in Britain during the Second World War contributed to Harrison's impressive book, *Living Through the Blitz* (Harrison, 1976). Its author pointed out that, although distinctive and unique, oral testimony is not necessarily more authentic than other records. People interviewed afterwards were prone to polish their memories as they told and retold the dramatic bits, responding, perhaps, to the astonishment of their audiences.

So, history-taking and history-making is no more straightforward than any other aspect of our construction of our experiences and perceptions of our pasts and presents. These are points well taken in social work, where we use the skills of interviewing to inform judgements about placing children and adults in households, residential homes and foster homes, and where inquiries and investigations are reliant largely on oral testimony, sometimes years after the alleged event.

Milestones in the past of social work

The past of social work may be problematic but it is marked by a number of events of significance. As we noted above, the significance of these events is likely to be debated endlessly. Not least, events that had earth-shaking significance at the time may have faded into obscurity 20 years later.

It is worth posing the question: what do those who have lived and worked through a particular era now regard as a milestone when they recall it? Everybody's memories will give a different emphasis. We can appreciate this by recalling some of the factors that may be important to social workers who lived through recent periods.

Social workers working in the 1970s, around the time that many current student social workers were born, are likely to recall the impact on policy and practice of the rediscovery of poverty in the early 1960s, the Seebohm Report (1968) and the Children and Young Persons Act 1969. The creation of social services departments and the introduction of generic social workers, economic recession and debates about the impact of youth unemployment, long-term unemployment and the social workers' strikes over declining services in local authority budget cuts of the late 1970s will still be real to them.

Social workers active in the 1980s are likely to recall the impact of Conservative government throughout the decade, Thatcherism, the New Right. They might be aware of the Black Report (DHSS, 1980) giving evidence of persistent inequalities in health, which, however, was not broadcast by the Conservative government at the time. Debates developed about whether the universalistic welfare state would be dismantled, the introduction of the contract culture in local government service provision, marketisation, privatisation, the new importance of the voluntary, private and informal sectors in health and welfare provision, the Children Act 1989 and the NHS and Community Care Act 1990.

Social workers in the 1990s may identify in particular the impact of quality assurance, standards and inspection in health and social services. The change of government to New Labour from 1997, the reality of political devolution in Scotland, Wales and Northern Ireland and the growing impact on the UK of legislation in the European Union, and the government's commitment to the modernisation of public services, including social work, are all important markers of this period. Trends towards globalisation, changing government policy affecting pensions, social security and benefits for lone parents and disabled people, public–private partnerships, the Human Rights Act 1998, legislation in criminal and youth justice and controversies concerning the treatment of refugees and asylum seekers all had their impact on social work.

Continuities and changes

Many of these events in the past continue to have an impact today. Legislative and policy changes highlight the diversity of social work in different settings, but this arises in the context of basic service organisations, social services departments, that recall the experiences of social workers from the 1970s. The pattern of community care services bears the hallmarks of the marketisation of the 1980s. Child protection work has developed from the early child abuse scandals of the 1970s, through the rise of concern about sexual abuse in the 1980s, and the reform of relations between parents and children attempted by the implementation of the Children Act 1989 in the 1990s and the amendments to it in 2004.

Yet these arrangements for delivering social work and social services have continued to change. Social services departments in England have been divided into children's and adult social care services, whereas in the rest of the UK they remain largely generic. These aspects of service are being realigned with other services, in community mental health trusts, in stronger alliances with the NHS for adult and community care services and the education services for children.

The present period brings changes and challenges of its own. Global changes are emphasising commonalities shared by social workers and social work organisations in different countries. The problems besetting people persist – poverty, criminal violence in the home, sexism, racism, discrimination against disabled people, older people, children, migrants and refugees. However, the twenty-first century has seen new attempts to devise responses to these long-standing problems. For example, conditionality, a policy development in social security during the first part of the twenty-first century, has pressed single parents and disabled people to seek employment as the main route to income security and poverty reduction; this strategy may be the most effective course for many people, but is also the most economical route for the government in providing social security. Social workers helping service users who need to claim social security allowances need to understand the policy and social imperatives and the personal responses of the people with whom they work. These policy moves partly connect to long-held prejudices about social security 'scroungers', more recent concerns about the way long-term reliance on social security allowances may exclude people from participation in ordinary work and social life, and current individualistic and communitarian ideologies. These propose that individuals should make a contribution to their own support wherever possible, rather than emphasising collective responsibility for people with social needs.

Future prospects for social work

The changes that social work is undergoing are never-ceasing, but provide the contexts in and through which we look to the future. They raise questions: Will social work have a place in health and social care? Will social work lose ground to other professions or new creations such as personal advisers? Will social work gain in importance in particular areas such as mental health and childcare? Despite the fact that social work is in a state of flux and social workers who remain in the job are disillusioned, as Vivienne Cree (Chapter 3) notes, it is probably an exaggeration to describe social work as in a state of crisis.

Nevertheless, we know from crisis theory that change offers both opportunities and risks. Becoming more closely involved in healthcare and education services offers the chance to increase the concern of healthcare services for the social needs of patients, for a wider range of social explanations and knowledge to influence healthcare. There may be advantages in being more closely associated with a more universal and less stigmatised service than social care has become. On the other hand, social explanations and needs may lose ground to more powerful medical models or educational priorities. The skills and commitment of social workers as they take up new roles in new settings offer the chance for every worker to have an impact, to make a difference not only to the lives of the people with whom they work, but also to the impact that social work might have on the societies in which we live.

Towards a critical view of the past, present and future of social work

We have emphasised in this chapter that it is important to develop a questioning attitude to the past and present and not to take for granted views handed to us as authoritative. The past may be changed in its impact by our present interpretations of it. Our present may have an impact on the future, by the plans we make and our commitment to change.

This is the point at which we leave you, the reader, and invite you to join us in the next stage of the journey – from critical debates about approaches to social work practice, to engaging critically in practice. We undertake this in the second book in the trilogy: *Critical Practice in Social Work* (Adams et al., 2009b).

Bibliography

AASW (Australian Association of Social Workers) (2003) *Practice Standards for Social Workers: Achieving Outcomes*, www.aasw.asn.au/adobe/publications/Practice_Standards_Final_Oct_2003.pdf.

Acheson, Sir D. (1998) *Independent Inquiry into Inequalities in Health Report*. London: TSO.

Adams, A. (2000) 'Introduction: the challenge of globalisation', in A. Adams, P. Erath and S. Shardlow (eds) *Fundamentals of Social Work in Selected European Countries*. Lyme Regis: Russell House Publishing.

Adams, R. (2007) 'Reflective, critical and transformational practice', in W. Tovey (ed.) *The Post-qualifying Handbook for Social Workers*. London: Jessica Kingsley.

Adams, R. (2008) *Empowerment, Participation and Social Work*. Basingstoke: Palgrave Macmillan.

Adams, R., Dominelli, L. and Payne, M. (eds) (2005) *Social Work Futures: Crossing Boundaries, Transforming Practice*. Basingstoke: Palgrave Macmillan.

Adams, R., Dominelli, L. and Payne M. (eds) (2009a) *Social Work: Themes, Issues and Critical Debates*, 3rd edn. Basingstoke: Palgrave Macmillan.

Adams, R., Dominelli, L. and Payne M. (eds) (2009b) *Critical Practice in Social Work*, 2nd edn. Basingstoke: Palgrave Macmillan.

Adams, R., Dominelli, L. and Payne M. (eds) (2009c) *Practising Social Work in a Complex World*, 2nd edn. Basingstoke: Palgrave Macmillan.

ADSS Cymru (2005) *Social Work in Wales: A Profession to Value*, the Garthwaite Report. Torfaen: ADSS Cymru.

Ahmad, B. (1990) *Black Perspectives in Social Work*. Birmingham: Venture.

Ainsworth, M. (1989) 'Attachments beyond infancy', *American Psychologist*, **44**(4): 709–16.

Ainsworth, M. (1991) 'Attachment and other affectional bonds across the life cycle', in C.M. Parkes, J. Stevenson-Hinde and P. Marris (eds) *Attachment Across the Life Cycle*. London: Routledge.

Alaszewski, A. and Walsh, M. (1995) 'Typologies of welfare organisations: a literature review', *British Journal of Social Work*, **25**: 805–15.

Aldgate, J. and Seden, J. (2006) 'Direct work with children', in J. Aldgate, D. Jones, W. Rose and C. Jeffrey (eds) *The Developing World of the Child*. London: Jessica Kingsley.

Allan, G., Hawker, S. and Crow, G. (2001) 'Family diversity and change in Britain and Western Europe', *Journal of Family Issues*, **22**(7): 819–37.

Allen, I. (ed.) (1988) *Hearing the Voice of the Consumer*. London: Policy Studies Institute.

Allen, J.P. and Hauser, S.T. (1996) 'Autonomy and relatedness in adolescent-family interactions as predictors of young adults' states of mind regarding attachment', *Development and Psychopathology*, **8**(4): 793–810.

Allen, J.P. and Land, D. (1999) 'Attachment in adolescence', in J. Cassidy and P.R. Shaver (eds) *Handbook of Attachment: Theory, Research and Clinical Implications*. New York: Guilford Press

Allen, J.P., Hauser, S.T., Bell, K.L. and O'Connor, T.G. (1994a) 'Longitudinal assessment of autonomy and relatedness in adolescent–family interactions as predictors of adolescent ego development and self-esteem', *Child Development*, **65**(1): 179.

Allen, J.P., Leadbeater, B.J. and Lawrence Aber, J. (1994b) 'The development of problem behavior syndromes in at-risk adolescents', *Development and Psychopathology*, **6**(2): 323.

Allen, J.P., Hauser, S.T. and Borman-Spurrell, E. (1996a) 'Attachment theory as a framework for understanding sequelae of severe adolescent psychopathology: an 11-year follow-up study', *Journal of Consulting and Clinical Psychology*, **64**(2): 254–63.

Allen, J.P., Hauser, S.T., O'Connor, T.G. et al. (1996b) 'The connection of observed hostile family conflict to adolescents' developing autonomy and relatedness with parents', *Development and Psychopathology*, **8**(2): 425–42.

Alston, M. and Bowles, W. (1998) *Research for Social Workers: An Introduction to Methods*. London: Allen & Unwin.

Amato-von Hemert, K. (1994) 'Should social work education address religious issues? Yes!', *Journal of Social Work Education*, **30**(1): 7–11.

Antman, E., Lau, J., Kupeltruck, B. et al. (1992) 'A comparison of the results of meta-analyses of random controlled trials and recommendations of clinical experts', *Journal of the American Medical Association*, **268**(4): 240–8.

Argyle, M. (1999) 'Causes and correlates of happiness', in D. Kahneman, E. Diener and N. Schwartz (eds) *Well-being: The Foundations of Hedonic Psychology*. New York: Russell Sage Foundation, pp. 353–72.

Argyris, C. and Schön, D.A. (1996) *Organizational Learning II: Theory, Method and Practice*. Reading, MA: Addison-Wesley.

Armsden, G.C. and Greenberg, M.T. (1987) 'The inventory of parent and peer attachment: individual differences and their relationship to psychological well-being in adolescence', *Journal of Youth and Adolescence*, **16**(5): 427–54.

Arnstein, S.R. (1969) 'A ladder of citizen participation', *Journal of the American Institute of Planners*, **35**(4): 216–24.

Arnstein, S.R. (1971) 'A ladder of citizen participation', *Journal of the Town Planning Institute*, **16**(3/4): 321–35.

Ashley, C. and Nixon, P. (2007) *Family Group Conferences: Where Next? Policies and Practices for the Future*. London: Family Rights Group.

Atkinson, D. and Warmsley, J. (1999) 'Using autobiographical approaches with people with learning difficulties', *Disability and Society*, **14**(2): 203–16.

Audit Commission (1994) *Seen but not Heard*. London: HMSO.

Audit Commission (2002) *Recruitment and Retention: A Public Service Workforce for the Twenty-first Century*. London: Audit Commission.

Audit Commission (2008) *Are We There Yet? Improved Governance and Resource Management in Children's Trusts*. London: Audit Commission.

Bailey, R. and Brake, M. (eds) (1975) *Radical Social Work and Practice*. London: Edward Arnold.

Baldwin, N. (ed.) (2000) *Protecting Children and Promoting their Rights*. London: Whiting & Birch.

Baldwin, N. and Spencer, N. (2000) 'Strategic planning to prevent harm to children', in N. Baldwin (ed.) *Protecting Children, Promoting their Rights*. London: Whiting & Birch.

Balen, R., Blyth, E., Calabretto, H. et al. (2006) 'Involving children in health and social care research: "Human becomings" or "active beings?"', *Childhood*, **13**(1): 29–48.

Banks, S. (2006) *Ethics and Values in Social Work*. Basingstoke: Palgrave Macmillan.

Bar-Haim, Y., Sutton, B.D., Fox, N.A. and Marvin, R.S. (2000) 'Stability and change of attachment at 14, 24, and 58 months of age: behaviour, representation and life events', *Journal of Child Psychology and Psychiatry and Allied Disciplines*, **41**(3): 381–8.

Barker, G. (2005) *Dying to be Men: Youth, Masculinity and Social Exclusion*. London: Routledge.

Barker, R.L. (2003) *The Social Work Dictionary*, 5th edn. Washington DC: NASW Press.

Barnes, C. (2003) 'Rehabilitation for disabled people: a sick joke?', *Scandinavian Journal of Disability Research*, **5**(1): 7–24.

Barnes, C. and Mercer, G. (2002) *Disability*. Cambridge: Polity Press.

Barnes, C. and Mercer, G. (eds) (2005) *The Social Model of Disability: Europe and the Majority World*. Leeds: Disability Press.

Barnes, C. and Mercer, G. (2006) *Independent Futures: Creating User-led Disability Services in a Disabling Society*. Bristol: Policy Press.

Barnes, M. and Shardlow, S. (1997) 'From passive recipient to active citizen: participation in mental health user groups', *Journal of Mental Health*, **6**(3): 289–300.

Barnes, M., Newman, J., Knopps, A. and Sullivan, H. (2003) 'Constituting "the public" in public participation', *Public Administration*, **81**(2): 279–399.

Barnes, M., Blom, A., Cox, K. et al. (2005) *New Horizons: The Social Exclusion of Older People*. London: DCLG.

Barnes, M., Conolly, A. and Tomaszewski, W. (2008) *The Circumstances of Persistently Poor Families with Children: Evidence from the Families and Children Study (FACS)*, Research Report No. 487. London: DWP.

Barrell, R., Guillemineau, C. and Liadze, I. (2006) 'Migration in Europe', *National Institute Economic Review*, **198**: 36–9.

Barth, R.P., Crea, T.M., John, K. et al. (2005) 'Beyond attachment theory and therapy: towards sensitive and evidence-based interventions with foster and adoptive families in distress', *Child & Family Social Work*, **10**(4): 257–68.

Bartholomew, K. and Horowitz, L.M. (1991) 'Attachment styles among young adults: a test of four-category model', *Journal of Personality and Social Psychology*, **61**(2): 226–44.

Basset, T., Campbell, P. and Anderson, J. (2006) 'Service user/survivor involvement in mental health training and education: overcoming the barriers', *Social Work Education*, **25**(4): 393–402.

Basu, M. (1997) *The Challenge of Local Feminisms: Women's Movements in Global Perspective*. Boulder, CO: Westview Press.

BASW (British Association of Social Workers) (1996) *A Code of Ethics for Social Work.* Birmingham: BASW.

BASW (British Association of Social Workers) (2003) *Code of Ethics for Social Work.* Birmingham: BASW.

Bateson, G. (1956) *Steps to an Ecology of Mind,* London: Palladin.

Bean, P. and Melville, J. (1990) *Lost Children of the Empire.* London: Unwin Hyman.

Beck, U. (1992) *Risk Society: Towards a New Modernity.* London: Sage.

Becker, G.S. (1996) *Accounting for Tastes.* Cambridge, MA: Harvard University Press.

Becker, S. (2002) '"Security for those who cannot": Labour's neglected welfare principle', *Poverty,* **112**: 13–17.

Becker, S. and Bryman, A. (2004) *Understanding Research for Social Policy and Practice: Themes, Methods and Approaches.* Bristol: Policy Press.

Beckett, C. (2006) *Essential Theory for Social Work Practice.* London: Sage.

Beckett, C., Bredenkamp, D., Castle, J. et al. (2002) 'Behavior patterns associated with institutional deprivation: a study of children adopted from Romania', *Journal of Developmental and Behavioral Pediatrics,* **23**(5): 297–303.

Beckett, C., Maughan, B., Rutter, M. et al. (2006) 'Do the effects of early severe deprivation on cognition persist into early adolescence? Findings from the English and Romanian adoptees study', *Child Development,* **77**(3): 696–711.

Beckford Report (1985) *A Child in Trust.* Wembley: London Borough of Brent.

Bell, M. and Wilson, K. (2006) 'Children's views of family group conferences', *British Journal of Social Work,* **36**(4): 671–81.

Belsky, J. (1980) 'Child maltreatment: an ecological integration', *American Psychologist,* **35**: 320–35.

Bently, T. and Wisdon J. (eds) (2003) *The Adaptive State: Strategies for Personalising the Public Realm.* London: Demos.

Benzeval, M., Judge, K. and Whitehead, M. (eds) (1995) *Tackling Inequalities in Health: An Agenda for Action.* London: King's Fund.

Beresford, P. (2000) 'Services users' knowledges and social work theory: conflict or collaboration?', *British Journal of Social Work,* **30**: 489–503.

Beresford, P. (2005) 'Theory and practice of user involvement in research: making the connection with public policy and practice', in L. Lowes and I. Hulatt (eds) *Involving Service Users in Health and Social Care Research.* London: Routledge.

Beresford, P. and Croft, S. (1993) *Citizen Involvement: A Practical Guide for Change.* Basingstoke: Macmillan – now Palgrave Macmillan.

Beresford, P. and Croft, S. (2001) 'Service users'

knowledges and the social construction of social work', *Journal of Social Work,* **1**(3): 295–316.

Beresford, P. and Croft, S. (2004) 'Service users and practitioners reunited: the key component for social work reform', *British Journal of Social Work,* **34**: 53–68.

Beresford, P., Adshead, L. and Croft, S. (2006) *Palliative Care, Social Work and Service Users: Making Life Possible.* London: Jessica Kingsley.

Beresford, P., Croft, S. and Adshead, L. (2008) '"We don't see her as a social worker": a service user case study of the importance of the social worker's relationship and humanity', *British Journal of Social Work,* **38**(7): 1388–1407.

Beresford, P., Green, D., Lister, R. and Woodard, K. (1999) *Poverty First Hand: Poor People Speak for Themselves.* London: CPAG.

BERR (Department for Business, Enterprise and Regulatory Reform) (2007) *The UK's Fuel Poverty Strategy,* fifth annual report. London: DEFRA.

Berridge, D. (2007) 'Theory and explanation in child welfare: education and looked-after children', *Child & Family Social Work,* **12**(1): 1–10.

Beveridge, W. (1942) *Social Insurance and Allied Services,* Cmnd 6404. London: HMSO.

BHA (British Humanist Association) (2008) 'Tribunal victory for employee in landmark religious discrimination case', www.humanism.org.uk/site/cms/newsarticleview.asp?article=2450.

Biehal, N. (1993) 'Participation, rights and community care', *British Journal of Social Work,* **23**(5): 443–58.

Biehal, N. (2005) *Working with Adolescents: Supporting Families, Preventing Breakdown.* London: BAAF.

Biesteck, F.P. (1961) *The Casework Relationship.* London: George Allen and Unwin.

Bishop, A. (2001) *Becoming an Ally: Breaking the Cycle of Oppression.* Halifax: Fernwood.

Black Assessors (1994) 'DipSW consultation a sham', *Community Care,* October, pp. 13–18.

Black, D. (2001) 'The limitations of evidence', in T. Heller, R. Muston, M. Sidell and C. Lloyd (eds) *Working for Health.* London: Open University/Sage.

Blanden, J., Gregg, P. and Machin, S. (2005) *Intergenerational Mobility in Europe and North America.* London: LSE Centre for Economic Performance.

Blomfield, R. and Hardy, S. (2000) 'Evidence-based nursing practice', in L. Trinder and S. Reynolds (eds) *Evidence-based Practice: A Critical Approach.* Oxford: Blackwell.

Booth, T. (2000) 'Parents with learning difficulties, child protection and the courts', *Representing Children,* **13**(3): 175–88.

Booth, T. and Booth, W. (1995) 'For better for

worse: professionals, practice and parents with learning difficulties', in T. Philpott and L. Ward (eds) *Values and Visions, Changing Ideas in Services for People with Learning Difficulties*. Oxford: Butterworth Heinemann.

Booth, T., Booth, W. and McConnell, D. (2005) 'The prevalence and outcomes of care proceedings involving parents with learning difficulties in the family courts', *Journal of Applied Research in Intellectual Disabilities*, 18(1): 7–17, doi:10.1111/j.1468-3148.2004.00204.x.

Booth, T., McConnell, D. and Booth, W. (2006) 'Temporal discrimination and parents with learning difficulties in the child protection system', *British Journal of Social Work*, 36: 997–1015.

Borrill, C.S., Carletta, J., Carter, C.S. et al. (2001) *The Effectiveness of Health Care Teams in the National Health Service*, http://homepages.inf.ed.ac.uk/jeanc/DOH-final-report.pdf.

Botting, B. (ed.) (2003) *Family Spending: A Report on the Expenditure and Food Survey*. London: ONS.

Bowl, R. (1985) *Changing the Nature of Masculinity: A Task for Social Work*. Norwich, University of East Anglia: Social Work Monographs.

Bowlby, J. (1951) *Maternal Care and Mental Health*. Geneva: World Health Organisation.

Boylan, J. and Braye, S. (2006) 'Paid, professionalised and proceduralised: can legal and policy frameworks for child advocacy give voice to children and young people?', *Journal of Social Welfare and Family Law*, 28(3/4): 233–49.

Bradshaw, J. and Mayhew, E. (2006) *Child Poverty in Large Families*. York: Joseph Rowntree Foundation.

Bradshaw, J., Hoelscher, P. and Richardson, D. (2006) 'An index of child well-being for the European Union', *Journal of Social Indicators Research*, 80(1): 133–77.

Brafman, O. and Beckstrom, R.A. (2006) *The Starfish and the Spider: The Unstoppable Power of Leaderless Organizations*. New York: Penguin Portfolio.

Brand, A.E. and Brinich, P.M. (1999) 'Behavior problems and mental health contacts in adopted, foster, and nonadopted children', *Journal of Child Psychology and Psychiatry and Allied Disciplines*, 40(8): 1221–9.

Brandon, D., Brandon, T., Barnes, C. and Brandon, A. (1995) *Advocacy: Power to People with Disabilities*. Birmingham: Venture.

Brannan, C., Jones, J.R. and Murch, J.D. (1993) 'Lessons from a residential special school enquiry: reflections on the Castle Hill report', *Child Abuse Review*, 2: 271–5.

Braverman, H. (1974) *Labor and Monopoly Capital*. New York: Monthly Review Press.

Braye, S. (2000) 'Participation and involvement in social care: an overview', in H. Kemshall and R. Littlechild (eds) *User Involvement and Participation in Social Care*. London: Jessica Kingsley.

Braye, S. and Preston-Shoot, M. (1990) 'On teaching and applying the law in social work: it is not that simple', *British Journal of Social Work*, 20(4): 333–53.

Braye, S. and Preston-Shoot, M. (1995) *Empowering Practice in Social Care*. Buckingham: Open University Press.

Braye, S. and Preston-Shoot, M. (1999) 'Accountability, administrative law and social work practice: redressing or reinforcing the power imbalance?' *Journal of Social Welfare and Family Law*, 21(3): 235–56.

Braye, S. and Preston-Shoot, M. (2006a) *Teaching, Learning and Assessment of Law in Social Work Education: Resource Guide*. London: Social Care Institute for Excellence.

Braye, S. and Preston-Shoot, M. (2006b) 'The role of law in welfare reform: critical perspectives on the relationship between law and social work practice', *International Journal of Social Welfare*, 15: 19–26.

Braye, S. and Preston-Shoot, M. (2009) *Practising Social Work Law*, 3rd edn. Basingstoke: Palgrave Macmillan.

Braye, S., Preston-Shoot, M. and Thorpe, A. (2007) 'Beyond the classroom: learning social work law in practice', *Journal of Social Work*, 7(3): 322–40.

Brearley, J. (2007) 'A psychodynamic approach to social work', in J. Lishman (ed.) *Handbook for Practice Learning in Social Work and Social Care: Knowledge and Theory*, 2nd edn. London: Jessica Kingsley.

Brewer, M., Goodman, A., Nuriel, A. and Sibieta, L. (2007) *Poverty and Inequality in the UK: 2007*, IFS Briefing Note No. 73. London: Institute for Fiscal Studies, www.ifs.org.uk.

Briner, R. (2000) 'Evidence-based human resource management', in L. Trinder and S. Reynolds (eds) *Evidence-Based Practice: A Critical Approach*. Oxford: Blackwell.

Brint, S. (1994) *In an Age of Experts: The Changing Role of Professionals in Politics and Public Life*. Princetown: Princetown University Press.

Broad, B., Hayes, R. and Rushforth, C. (2007) *Kith and Kin: Kinship Care for Vulnerable Young People*. London: National Children's Bureau.

Broadbent, J., Dietrich, M. and Laughlin, R. (1993) *The Development of Principal-Agent Contracting and Acceptability Relationships in the Public Sector: Conceptual and Cultural Problems*. Sheffield: Sheffield University.

Bronfenbrenner, U. (1977) 'Toward an experiential ecology of human development', *American Psychologist*, 32: 513–31.

Brook, E. and Davis, A. (eds) (1985) *Women, the Family and Social Work.* London: Tavistock.

Brookfield, S. (1987) *Developing Critical Thinkers.* Buckingham: Open University Press.

Brooks, G., Pugh, A.K. and Schagen, I. (1996) *Reading Performance at Nine.* Buckingham: NFER/Open University.

Brown, H.C. (1996) 'The knowledge base of social work', in A. Vass (ed.) *Social Work Competences.* London: Sage.

Brown, L.S. and Wright, J. (2001) 'Attachment theory in adolescence and its relevance to developmental psychopathology', *Clinical Psychology and Psychotherapy,* **8**: 15–32.

Bruce, L. and Lishman, J. (2004) *Agency-based Practice Learning: A Literature Review.* Aberdeen, The Robert Gordon University: Scottish Institute for Excellence in Social Work Education.

Bruni, L. and Porta, P.-L. (eds) (2005) *Economics and Happiness: Framing the Analysis.* Oxford: Oxford University Press.

Buchanan, A. (1999) *What Works for Troubled Children: Family Support for Children with Emotional and Behavioural Problems.* Ilford: Barnardo's.

Buchanan, J.M. and Tullock, G. (1962) *The Calculus of Consent: Logical Foundations of Constitutional Democracy.* Ann Arbor: University of Michigan Press.

Burgess, R., Campbell, V., Philips, R. and Skinner, K. (1998) 'Managing unsuccessful or uncompleted placements', *Journal of Practice Teaching in Health and Social Work,* **1**(1): 4–12.

Burman, E. (2007) *Deconstructing Developmental Psychology,* 2nd edn. London: Routledge.

Burnham, J.B. (1986) *Family Therapy.* London: Routledge.

Burton, J. and van den Broek, D. (2008) 'Accountable and countable: information management systems and the bureaucratization of social work', *British Journal of Social Work,* Advance Access published 26 April, 2008; doi:10.1093/bjsw/bcn027.

Burton, M. and Kellaway, M. (1998) *Developing and Managing High Quality Services for People with Learning Disabilities.* Aldershot: Ashgate.

Butler-Sloss, E. (1987) *Report of the Inquiry into Child Abuse in Cleveland,* Cm 412. London: HMSO.

Butrym, Z.T. (1976) *The Nature of Social Work.* London: Macmillan – now Palgrave Macmillan.

Bytheway, B., Keil, T., Allatt, P. and Bryman, A. (eds) (1990) *Becoming and Being Old: Sociological Approaches to Later Life.* London: Sage.

Bywaters, E. and McLeod, E. (2001) 'The impact of New Labour health policy on social services: a new deal for service users' health?', *British Journal of Social Work,* **31**(4): 579–94.

Cabinet Office (2002) *Creating Public Value: A New Framework for Public Sector Reform.* London: Cabinet Office, Strategy Unit, www/strategy.gov.uk/2001/futures/attachments/pv/publicvalue.pdf.

Cairney, J., Chettle, K., Clark, M. et al. (2006) 'Editorial', *Social Work Education,* **25**(4): 315–18.

Calder, M. (2003) 'The assessment framework: a critique and reformulation', in M. Calder and S. Hackett (2003) *Assessment in Child Care: Using and Developing Frameworks for Practice.* Lyme Regis: Russell House Publishing.

Calder, M. and Hackett, S. (eds) (2003) *Assessment in Childcare: Using and Developing Frameworks for Practice.* Lyme Regis: Russell House Publishing.

Campanini, A. and Frost, E. (eds) (2004) *European Social Work: Commonalities and Differences.* Rome: EUSW/Carocci.

Canales, M. (2000) 'Othering: towards an understanding of difference, vulnerability and empowerment', *Advances in Nursing Science,* **22**(4): 16–31.

Cannan, C., Berry, L. and Lyons, K. (1992) *Social Work and Europe.* Basingstoke: Macmillan – now Palgrave Macmillan.

Carpenter, J. (2002) 'Mental health recovery paradigm: implications for social work', *Health and Social Work,* **27**(2): 86–94.

Carpenter, J., Schneider, J., McNiven, F. et al. (2004) 'Integration and targeting of community care for people with severe and enduring mental health problems: users' experiences of the Care Programme Approach and care management', *British Journal of Social Work,* **34**(3): 313–33.

Carr, S. (2004) *Has Service User Participation Made a Difference to Social Care Services?* London: SCIE/Policy Press.

Carr, S. (2007) 'Participation, power, conflict and change: theorizing dynamics of service user participation in the social care system of England and Wales', *Critical Social Policy,* **27**(2): 266–76.

Carter, P., Jeffs, T. and Smith, M.K. (1995) *Social Working.* Basingstoke: Macmillan – now Palgrave Macmillan.

Cass, E., Robbins, D. and Richardson, A. (2008) *Dignity in Care. Adults' Services Practice Guide 9.* London: SCIE.

Cassidy, J., Kirsh, S.J., Scolton, K.L. and Parke, R.D. (1996) 'Attachment and representations of peer relationships', *Developmental Psychology,* **32**(5): 892–904.

Castells, M. (2000) *The Rise of the Networked Society.* Oxford: Blackwell.

CCETSW (Central Council for Education and Training in Social Work) (1995) *Assuring Quality: in the Diploma in Social Work – 1: Rules and Requirements for the DipSW (revised).* London: CCETSW.

Cedersund, E. (1999) 'Using narratives in social work interaction', in A. Jokinen, K. Juhila and T. Poso (eds) *Constructing Social Work Practices*. Aldershot: Ashgate.

CHAI (Commission for Healthcare Audit and Inspection) (2006) *Joint Investigation into the Provision of Services for People with Learning Disabilities at Cornwall Partnership NHS Trust*. London: CHAI.

Chan, C.L.W. (2001) *An Eastern Body-Mind-Spirit Approach: A Training Manual with One-second Techniques*. Hong Kong: Department of Social Work and Social Administration, University of Hong Kong.

Chan, C.L.W., Chan, Y. and Lou, V.W.Q. (2001) Evaluating an empowerment group for divorced Chinese women in Hong Kong, *Research on Social Work Practice*, **12**: 558–69.

Chan, C.L.W., Law, M.Y.Y. and Yeung, P.P.Y. (2000) 'An empowerment group for Chinese cancer patients in Hong Kong', in C.L.W. Chan and R. Fielding (eds) *Psychosocial Oncology & Palliative Care in Hong Kong: The First Decade*. Hong Kong: Hong Kong University Press.

Chan, H.Y., Chan, C.L.W., Ho, R.T. et al. (2004) 'Tallying the pains and gains: development of a spiritual outlook inventory for cancer survivors.' Manuscript submitted for publication.

Chapman, J. (2002) *System Failure: Why Governments Must Learn to Think Differently*. London: Demos.

Cheetham, J., Fuller, R., McIvor, G. and Petch, A. (1992) *Evaluating Social Work Effectiveness*. Buckingham: Open University Press.

Chisholm, K. (1998) 'A three year follow-up of attachment and indiscriminate friendliness in children adopted from Romanian orphanages', *Child Development*, **69**(4): 1092–106.

Chisholm, K., Carter, M.C., Ames, E.W. and Morison, S.J. (1995) 'Attachment security and indiscriminately friendly behavior in children adopted from Romanian orphanages', *Development and Psychopathology*, **7**(2): 283–94.

Christie, I., Harrison, M., Hitchman, C. and Lang, T. (2002) *Inconvenience Food: the Struggle to Eat Well on a Low Income*. London: Demos.

Church, K. (1997) 'Research in brief', *Journal of Psychiatric and Mental Health Nursing*, **4**: 307–8.

Clark, B. (1993) *Who's Life Is It Anyway?* London: Heinemann.

Clark, C. (1995) 'Competence and discipline in professional formation', *British Journal of Social Work*, **25**: 563–80.

Clark, C.L. (2000) *Social Work Ethics: Politics, Principles and Practice*. Basingstoke: Palgrave – now Palgrave Macmillan.

Clark, E.J. and Woods-Waller, G. (2005) 'Improving the profession: changing perceptions – social work in the USA', in N. Hall (ed.) *Social Work: Making a World of Difference*. Berne: IFSW/Fafo.

Clark, J. (1994) 'Should social work education address religious issues? No!', *Journal of Social Work Education*, **30**(1): 12–17.

Clarke A. and Clarke A. (eds) (1976) *Early Experience: Myth and Evidence*. New York: Free Press.

Clarke, A. and Clarke, A. (2000) *Early Experiences and the Life Path*. London: Jessica Kingsley.

Clarke, J. (1996) 'After social work?', in N. Parton (ed.) *Social Theory, Social Change and Social Work*. London: Routledge.

Clarke, J. and Newman, J. (1997) *The Managerial State: Power, Politics and Ideology in the Remaking of Social Welfare*. London: Sage.

Cleaver, H. and Department of Health (2000) *Assessment Recording Forms*. London: TSO.

Clegg, S.R. (1990) *Modern Organizations: Organization Studies in the Postmodern World*. London: Sage.

Clifford, D. (1998) *Social Assessment Theory and Practice*. Aldershot: Ashgate.

Cochrane Collaboration (2003) 'Glossary' of Cochrane Collaboration, Issue 2. Oxford: Update Software.

Cole-Hamilton, I. and Lang, T. (1986) *Tightening Belts*. London: London Food Commission.

Coleman, J. and Hagell, A. (eds) (2007) *Adolescence, Risk and Resilience: Against the Odds*. Chichester: John Wiley & Sons.

Coleman, J.S. (1988) 'Social capital and the creation of human capital', *American Journal of Sociology*, **94**: 595–621.

Coles, J. and Connors, P. (2008) 'Best practice with people with learning difficulties: being seen and heard', in K. Jones, B. Cooper and H. Ferguson (eds) *Best Practice in Social Work: Critical Perspectives*. Basingstoke: Palgrave Macmillan.

Collins, P.H. (1990) *Black Feminist Thought*. London: Routledge.

Compton, B. and Galaway, B. (1999) *Social Work Processes*, 6th edn. Pacific Grove: Brooks/Cole.

Compton, B.R., Galaway, B. and Cournoyer, B.R. (2005) *Social Work Processes*, 7th edn. Pacific Grove, CA: Brooks/Cole.

Connell, R.W. (1995) *Masculinities*. London: Routledge.

Constable, R. and Metha, U. (1993) *Education for Social Work in Eastern Europe*. Vienna: International Association of Schools of Social Work.

Cooper, A. and Hetherington, R. (1999) 'Negotiation', in N. Parton and C. Wattam (eds) *Child Sexual Abuse: Responding to the Experiences of Children*. Chichester: Wiley.

Cooper, B. (2000) 'The measure of a competent

childcare social worker?', *Journal of Social Work Practice*, **14**(2): 113–24.

Corrigan, P. and Leonard, P. (1978) *Social Work under Capitalism*. London: Macmillan – now Palgrave Macmillan.

Coulshed, V. and Mullender, A. (2000) *Management in Social Work*, 2nd edn. Basingstoke: Palgrave – now Palgrave Macmillan.

Coulshed, V. and Orme, J. (1998) *Social Work Practice: An Introduction*. Basingstoke: Macmillan – now Palgrave Macmillan.

Coulshed, V. and Orme, J. (2006) *Social Work Practice*, 4th edn. Basingstoke: Palgrave Macmillan.

Cowen, H. (1999) *Community Care, Ideology and Social Policy*. London: Prentice Hall.

Cox, M. (1998) 'Whistleblowing and training for accountability', in G. Hunt (ed.) *Whistleblowing in the Social Services: Public Accountability and Professional Practice*. London: Arnold.

Craig, C. (2002) 'Poverty, social work and social justice', *British Journal of Social Work*, **32**: 669–82.

Craig, G. (2002) 'Community development with children', in D. McNeish, T. Newman and H. Roberts (eds) *What Works for Children?* Buckingham: Open University Press.

Crawford, M., Rutter, D., Manley, C. et al. (2002) 'Systematic review of involving patients in the planning and development of health care', *British Medical Journal*, **325**: 1263–5.

Cree, V.E. (1995) *From Public Streets to Private Lives: The Changing Task of Social Work*. Aldershot: Avebury.

Cree, V.E. (1996) 'Why do men care?' in K. Cavanagh and V.E. Cree (eds) *Working with Men*. London: Routledge.

Cree, V.E. (2002) 'Social work and society', in M. Davies (ed.) *Blackwell Companion to Social Work*, 2nd edn. Oxford: Blackwell.

Cree, V.E. (2003) *Becoming a Social Worker*. New York: Routledge.

Cree, V.E. and Davis, A. (2007) *Social Work: Voices from the Inside*. London: Routledge.

Cree, V.E. and Myers, S. (2008) *Social Work: Making a Difference*. Bristol: Policy Press.

Creswell, J. (2003) *Research Design: Qualitative, Quantitative and Mixed Methods Approaches*, 2nd edn. London: Sage.

Crisp, B.R., Anderson, M.R., Orme, J. and Green Lister, P. (2007) 'Assessment Frameworks: a critical reflection,' *British Journal of Social Work*, **37**(6): 1059–77.

Croft, S. and Beresford, P. (2000) 'Empowerment', in M. Davies (ed.) *The Blackwell Encyclopaedia of Social Work*. Oxford: Blackwell.

Crow, L. (1996) 'Including all our lives', in J. Morris (ed.) *Encounters with Strangers: Feminism and Disability*. London: Women's Press.

CSCI (Commission for Social Care Inspection) (2005) *The State of Social Care in England, 2004–05*. London: CSCI.

CSCI (Commission for Social Care Inspection) (2008) *The State of Social Care in England, 2006–07*. London: CSCI.

Curtis, K., Roberts, H., Copperman, J. et al. (2004) '"How come I don't get asked no questions?" Researching "hard to reach" children and teenagers', *Child and Family Social Work*, **9**(2): 167–75.

Curtis, M. (1946) *Report of the Care of Children Committee (Curtis Report)*, Cmnd 6922. London: HMSO.

CWDC (Children's Workforce Development Council) (2007) *Common Assessment Framework for Children and Young People: Practitioners' Guide*. London: CWDC.

Cyngor Gofal Cymru/Care Council for Wales (2004) *Code of Practice for Social Care Workers and Code of Practice for Employers of Social Care Workers*, www.ccwales.org.uk/DesktopDefault.aspx?tabid=132.

D'Cruz, H. and Jones, M. (2004) *Social Work Research: Ethical and Political Contexts*. London: Sage.

Dalrymple, J. and Burke, B. (2006) *Anti-Oppressive Practice: Social Care and the Law*, 2nd edn. Buckingham: Open University Press.

Daniel, B., Wassell, S. and Gilligan, R. (1999) *Child Development for Child Care and Protection Workers*. London: Jessica Kingsley.

Davey Smith, G. (ed.) (2003) *Health Inequalities: Lifecourse Approaches*. Bristol: Policy Press.

Davies, H.T., Nutley, S.M. and Smith P.C. (eds) (2000) *What Works? Evidence-based Policy and Practice in Public Services*. Bristol: Policy Press.

Davies, M. (1985) *The Essential Social Worker*, 2nd edn. Aldershot: Gower.

Davies, M. (1994) *The Essential Social Worker*, 3rd edn. Aldershot: Arena.

Davies, M. (2004) 'Book review of social work: theory and practice for a changing profession', *Child and Family Welfare*, **34**(3): 667.

Davis, A., Ellis, K. and Rummery, K. (1997) *Accessing Assessment: Perspectives of Practitioners, Disabled People and Carers*. Bristol: Policy Press.

Davis Smith, J. (2001) 'Volunteers: making a difference', in M. Harris and C. Rochester (eds) *Voluntary Organisations and Social Policy in Britain: Perspectives on Change and Choice*. Basingstoke: Palgrave – now Palgrave Macmillan.

DCLG (Department for Communities and Local Government) (2006) *Antisocial Behaviour Intensive Families Support Projects*. London: DCLG.

DCO (Department for Constitutional Affairs) (2007) *Mental Capacity Act 2005: Code of Practice*. London: TSO.

DCSF (Department for Children, Schools and Families) (2004) *Independent Reviewing Officers Guidance: Adoption and Children Act 2002: The Review of Children's Cases (Amendment) (England) Regulations 2004*. London: DCSF.

de Beauvoir, S. (1974) *The Second Sex*, trans. H.M. Pashley. New York: Vintage Books.

de Botton, A. (2000) *The Consolations of Philosophy*. Harmondsworth: Penguin.

de Shazer, S. (1985) *Clues: Investigating Solutions in Brief Therapy*. New York: W. W. Norton.

Deacon, B. (1992) *The New Eastern Europe*. London: Sage.

Dean, M. (2005) 'Fears of the Leviathan', *Guardian*, 9 March.

Dearden, C. and Becker, S. (2000) *Growing Up Caring: Vulnerability and Transition to Adulthood – Young Carers' Experiences*. Leicester: National Youth Agency.

Delanty, G. (2005) *Social Science*, 2nd edn. Maidenhead: Open University Press.

Delgado, M. (2000) *Community Social Work Practice in an Urban Context: The Potential of a Capacity-enhancement Perspective*. Oxford: Oxford University Press.

Dempsey, M., Halton, C. and Murphy, M. (2001) 'Reflective learning in social work education: scaffolding the process', *Social Work Education*, 20(3): 631–42.

DETR (Department of Environment, Transport and the Regions) (1998) *Modernising Local Government: Improving Local Services Through Best Value*. London: DETR.

Devo, J. (2006) 'Out of Africa into Birmingham: Zimbabwean social workers talk to *Professional Social Work*', *Professional Social Work* (1 August): 12–13.

DfES (Department for Education and Skills) (2003) *Every Child Matters*, Green Paper. London: TSO.

DfES (Department for Education and Skills) (2004) *Every Child Matters: Change for Children*. London: TSO.

DfES (Department for Education and Skills) (2006) *Working Together to Safeguard Children: A Guide to Interagency Working to Safeguard and Promote the Welfare of Children*, 2nd rev edn. London: TSO.

DfES (Department for Education and Skills) (2007) *Every Parent Matters*. London: TSO.

DH (Department of Health) (1991a) *The Children Act Guidance and Regulations*, Vol. 2 *Family Support, Day Care and Educational Provision for Young Children*. London: HMSO.

DH (Department of Health) (1991b) *The Children Act Guidance and Regulations*, Vol. 3 *Family Placements*. London: HMSO.

DH (Department of Health) (1991c) *The Children Act 1989. Guidance and Regulations*, Vol. 4, *Residential Care*. London: HMSO.

DH (Department of Health) (1994) *Implementing Caring for People. Community Care Packages for Older People*. London: HMSO.

DH (Department of Health) (1995a) *Child Protection: Messages from Research*. London: TSO

DH (Department of Health) (1995b) *Building Bridges: A Guide to Arrangements for Interagency Working for the Care and Protection of Severely Mentally Ill People*. London: DH.

DH (Department of Health) (1998a) *Modernising Social Services: Promoting Independence, Improving Protection, Raising Standards*, Cm 4169. London: TSO.

DH (Department of Health) (1998b) *Quality Protects: Framework for Action and Objectives for Social Services for Children*. London: DH.

DH (Department of Health) (1999a) *National Service Framework for Mental Health: Modern Standards and Service Models for Mental Health*, LAC(99)34. London: TSO.

DH (Department of Health) (1999b) *Caring about Carers: A National Strategy for Carers*. London: TSO.

DH (Department of Health) (1999c) *Adoption Now: Messages from Research*. Chichester: John Wiley.

DH (Department of Health) (2000a) *A Quality Strategy for Social Care*. London: DH, www.doh.gov. uk/pdfs/qstrategy.pdf.

DH (Department of Health) (2000b) *The NHS Plan: A Plan for Investment, a Plan for Reform*, Cm 4818-1. London: TSO.

DH (Department of Health) (2000c) *Valuing People: A New Strategy for People with Learning Disability for the 21st Century*, Cm 5086. London: TSO.

DH (Department of Health) (2000d) *No Secrets: Guidance on Developing and Implementing Multi-Agency Policies and Procedures to Protect Vulnerable Adults from Abuse*. London: TSO.

DH (Department of Health) (2000e) *The Children Act: Messages from Research*. London: HMSO.

DH (Department of Health) (2000f) *Lost in Care: Report of the Tribunal of Inquiry into the Abuse of Children in Care in the Former County Council Areas of Gwynedd and Clwyd since 1974*. London: TSO.

DH (Department of Health) (2001a) *National Service Framework for Older People*, LAC(2001)12. London, TSO.

DH (Department of Health) (2001b) *Research Governance Framework for Health and Social Care*. London: DH.

DH (Department of Health) (2002a) *Tackling Health Inequalities: 2002 Crosscutting Review*, www. dh.gov.uk.

DH (Department of Health) (2002b) *Fair Access to Care Services: Guidance on Eligibility Criteria for Adult Social Care*, LAC(2002)13. London: DH.

DH (Department of Health) (2002c) *Requirements for Social Work Training*. London: DH.

DH (Department of Health) (2002d) *Listening, Hearing, Responding. Department of Health Action Plan: Core Principles for the Involvement of Young People*. London: TSO.

DH (Department of Health) (2002e) *PSS Perform-ance Assessment Framework*. London: DH.

DH (Department of Health) (2002f) *Requirements for Social Work Training*. London: DH.

DH (Department of Health) (2003) *Direct Payments Guidance: Community Care, Services for Carers and Children's Services (Direct Payments) Guid-ance*. London: DH.

DH (Department of Health) (2004) *The National Service Framework for Children, Young People and Maternity Services*. London: TSO.

DH (Department of Health) (2005a) *Independence, Well-being and Choice: Our Vision for the Future of Social Care for Adults in England*, Green Paper, Cm 6449. London: DH.

DH (Department of Health) (2005b) *The National Service Framework for Long-term Conditions*. London: TSO.

DH (Department of Health) (2006) *Our Health, Our Care, Our Say: A New Direction for Community Services*. London: HMSO.

DH (Department of Health) (2007a) *Putting People First: A Shared Vision and Commitment to the Transformation of Adult Social Care*. London: DH.

DH (Department of Health) (2007b) *Care Matters: Time for Change*. London: TSO.

DH (Department of Health) (2008) *Code of Practice: Mental Health Act 1983*. London: TSO.

DH Adoption and Permanence Taskforce (2001) *First Annual Report*. London: TSO.

DH/DfEE/Home Office (Department of Health/Department for Education and Employment/Home Office) (2000) *Framework for the Assess-ment of Children in Need and their Families*. London: TSO.

DH/DfES (Department of Health/Department of Education and Skills) (2004) *The National Service Framework for Children, Young People and Maternity Services*. London: TSO.

DH/DfES (Department of Health/Department for Education and Skills) (2006) *Options for Excel-lence: Building on the Social Care Workforce of the Future*. London: DH.

DH/SSI (Department of Health/Social Services Inspectorate) (1991) *Care Management and Assessment Practice Guidance*. London: HMSO.

DH/SSI (Department of Health/Social Services Inspectorate) (1995) *Planning for Life: Develop-ing Community Services for People with Complex Multiple Disabilities*, No. 3 *Good Practice in the Independent Sector* (London: HMSO).

DH/SSI (Department of Health/Social Services Inspectorate) (1996) *Planning for Life: Develop-ing Community Services for People with Complex Multiple Disabilities*, No. 2 *Good Practice in Manchester*. London: HMSO.

DHSS (1980) *Inequalities in Health: A Report of a Research Working Group* (The Black Report). London: DHSS.

Di Tella, R., MacCulloch, R. and Oswald, A. (2003) 'The macroeconomics of happiness', *Review of Economics and Statistics*, **85**(4): 809–27.

Dixon, N. (1999) *The Organisational Learning Cycle: How We Can Learn Collectively*. Aldershot: Gower.

Doel, M. and Shardlow, S.M. (2005) *Modern Social Work Practice*. Aldershot: Ashgate.

Doel, M., Carroll, C., Chambers, E. et al. (2007) *Participation: Finding out What Difference it Makes*. London: SCIE.

Dominelli, L. (1988) *Anti-Racist Social Work*. Basing-stoke: Macmillan – now Palgrave Macmillan.

Dominelli, L. (1990–91) '"What's in a name?" A comment on "Puritans and paradigms"', *Social Work and Social Sciences Review*, **2**(3): 231–5.

Dominelli, L. (1993) *Social Work: Mirror of Society or its Conscience?* Sheffield: Department of Socio-logical Studies.

Dominelli, L. (1996) 'Deprofessionalising social work: anti-oppressive practice, competencies and post-modernism', *British Journal of Social Work*, **26**: 153–75.

Dominelli, L. (1997) *Sociology for Social Work*. Basing-stoke: Macmillan – now Palgrave Macmillan.

Dominelli, L. (2000) 'Empowerment: help or hindrance in professional relationships', in D. Ford and P. Stepney (eds) *Social Work Models, Methods and Theories: A Framework for Practice*. Lyme Regis: Russell House Publishing.

Dominelli, L. (2002a) *Feminist Social Work Theory and Practice*. Basingstoke: Palgrave Macmillan.

Dominelli, L. (2002b) *Anti-oppressive Social Work: Theory and Practice*. Basingstoke: Palgrave Macmillan.

Dominelli, L. (2004a) *Social Work: Theory and Prac-tice for a Changing Profession*. Cambridge: Polity Press.

Dominelli, L. (2004b) 'Practising social work in a globalising world', in T. Ngoh-Tiong and A. Rowlands (eds) *Social Work around the World III*. Berne: International Federation of Social Workers.

Dominelli, L. (2005) 'Social work research: contested knowledge for practice', in R. Adams, L. Dominelli and M. Payne (eds) *Social Work Futures: Crossing Boundaries, Transforming Prac-tice*. Basingstoke: Palgrave Macmillan.

Dominelli, L. (2007) *Revitalising Communities in a Globalising World*. Aldershot: Ashgate.

Dominelli, L. (2008) *Anti-racist Social Work*, 3rd edn. Basingstoke: BASW/Palgrave Macmillan.

Dominelli, L. (2009) *Introducing Social Work*. Cambridge: Polity Press.

Dominelli, L. and Hoogvelt, A. (1996) 'Globalisation and the technocratisation of social work', *Critical Social Policy*, **47**(2): 45–62.

Dominelli, L. and McLeod, E. (1989) *Feminist Social Work*. Basingstoke: Macmillan – now Palgrave Macmillan.

Dominelli, L., Callahan, M., Rutman, D. and Strega, S. (2005) 'Endangered children: the state as parent and grandparent', *British Journal of Social Work*, **35**(7): 1123–44.

Dominy, N. and Kempson, E. (2006) *Understanding Older People's Experience of Poverty and Material Deprivation*, Research Report 363. London: DWP.

Douglas, M. (1970) *Natural Symbols: Explorations in Cosmology*. London: Barrie and Rockliff.

Douglas, M. (1978) 'Cultural bias', in M. Douglas, *In the Active Voice*, London: Routledge & Kegan Paul (1982).

Douglas, M. (1987) *How Institutions Think*. London: Routledge & Kegan Paul.

Downie, R.S. (1989) 'A political critique of Kantian ethics in social work: a reply to Webb and McBeath', *British Journal of Social Work*, **19**(6): 507–10.

Downie, R.S. and Telfer, E. (1969) *Respect for Persons*. London: Allen & Unwin.

Downie, R.S. and Telfer, E. (1980) *Caring and Curing: A Philosophy of Medicine and Social Work*. London: Methuen.

Driver, G. and Martell, L. (1997) 'New Labour's communitarianisms', *Critical Social Policy*, **17**(3): 27–46.

DSS (Department of Social Security) (1998) *A New Contract for Welfare*, Cm 3805. London: TSO.

DSS (Department of Social Security) (1999) *Opportunity for All: Tackling Poverty and Social Exclusion*, Cm 4445. London: TSO.

Durkheim, E. (1912) *Elementary Forms of Religious Life: The Totemic System in Australia*. London: Allen and Unwin (1915).

Durkin, K. (1995) *Developmental Social Psychology: From Infancy to Old Age*. Oxford: Blackwell Publishing.

Durlauf, S.N. and Fafchamps, M. (2004) Social Capital, working paper 10485, www.nber.org/papers/W10485.

DWP (Department for Work and Pensions) (2003) *Measuring Child Poverty*. London: DWP.

DWP (Department for Work and Pensions) (2007) *Reducing Dependency, Increasing Opportunity: Options for the Future of Welfare to Work* (Freud Report). London: DWP.

Eborall, C. and Griffiths, D. (2008) *The State of the Adult Social Care Workforce in England, 2008: Executive Summary*. Leeds: Skills for Care.

Edwards, S.D. (2005) *Disability: Definitions, Value and Identity*. Oxford: Radcliffe.

Egan, G. (1982) *The Skilled Helper*. Monterey, CA: Brooks/Cole.

Egan, G. (2002) *The Skilled Helper: A Systemic Approach to Effective Helping*, 7th edn. Pacific Grove, CA: Brooks/Cole.

Eisenstadt, S. (1956) *From Generation to Generation*. Glencoe, IL: Free Press.

Ellis, K. (2000) 'The care of the body', in K. Ellis and H. Dean (eds) *Social Policy and the Body: Transitions in Corporeal Discourse*. Basingstoke: Macmillan – now Palgrave Macmillan.

Ellis, K. (2007) 'Direct payments and social work practice: the significance of 'street-level bureaucracy in determining eligibility', *British Journal of Social Work*, **37**(3): 405–22.

EOC (Equal Opportunities Commission) (2007) *Annual Report and Accounts 2006–2007*. London: EOC/Equality and Human Rights Commission, www.equalityhumanrights.com/en/publicationsandresources/.

Eraut, M. (1994) *Developing Professional Knowledge and Competence*. London: Falmer Press.

Erikson, E. (1965) *Childhood and Society*, 2nd edn. London: Hogarth Press.

Etzioni, A. (1995) *The Spirit of Community: Rights, Responsibilities and the Communitarian Agenda*. London: Fontana.

Evans, D. and Kearney, J. (1996) *Working in Social Care: A Systemic Approach*. Aldershot: Arena.

Everitt, A. and Hardiker, P. (1996) *Evaluating for Good Practice*. Basingstoke: BASW/Macmillan – now Palgrave Macmillan.

Everitt, A., Hardiker, P., Littlewood, J. and Mullender, A. (1992) *Applied Research for Better Practice*. Basingstoke: Macmillan – now Palgrave Macmillan.

Fanon, F. (1990) *The Wretched of the Earth*. London: Penguin.

Farrall, S. (2002) *Rethinking What Works With Offenders*. Cullompton: Willan Publishing.

Felsman, D.E. and Blustein, D.L. (1999) 'The role of peer relatedness in late adolescent career development', *Journal of Vocational Behavior*, **54**: 279–95.

Ferard, M.L. and Hunnybun, N.K. (1962) *The Caseworker's Use of Relationships*. London: Tavistock.

Ferguson, H. (2008) 'Best practice in family support and child protection: promoting child safety and democratic families', in K. Jones, B. Cooper and H. Ferguson (eds) *Best Practice in Social Work*. Basingstoke: Palgrave Macmillan.

Ferguson, I. (2008) *Reclaiming Social Work: Chal-*

lenging Neo-liberalism and Promoting Social Justice. London: Sage.

Fimister, G. (ed.) (2001) Tackling Child Poverty in the UK: An End in Sight. London: CPAG.

Fine, B. (2001) Social Capital Versus Social Theory: Political Economy and Social Science at turn of the Millennium. London: Routledge.

Fisher, M. (2002) 'The role of service users in problem formulation and technical aspects of social research', Social Work Education, 21(3): 305–12.

Flaherty, J., Veit-Wilson, J. and Dornan, P. (2004) Poverty: The Facts, 5th edn. London: CPAG.

Fletcher, K. (1998) Best Value Social Sciences. Caerphilly: SSP Publications.

Follett, M.P. (1918) The New State: Group Organization the Solution of Popular Government, New York: Longmans, Green, reprinted in R.E. Pumphrey and M.W. Pumphrey (eds) (1961) The Heritage of American Social Work. New York: Columbia University Presss.

Fook, J. (2000) 'Deconstructing and reconstructing professional expertise', in B. Fawcett, B. Featherstone, J. Fook and A. Rossiter (eds) Postmodern Feminist Perspectives. London: Routledge.

Fook, J. (2002) Social Work: Critical Theory and Practice. London: Sage.

Fook, J. (2007) 'Reflective practice and critical reflection', in J. Lishman (ed.) Handbook for Practice Learning in Social Work and Social Care: Knowledge and Theory, 2nd edn. London: Jessica Kingsley.

Forrester, D., Kershaw, S., Moss, H. and Hughes, L. (2008) 'Communication skills in child protection', Child and Family Social Work, 13(1): 41–51.

Foucault, M. (1973) The Birth of the Clinic: An Archaeology of Medical Perception. London: Tavistock.

Foucault, M. (1977) Discipline and Punish. London: Allen Lane.

Francis, J., McGhee, J. and Mordaunt, E. (2006) Protecting Children in Scotland: An Investigation of Risk Assessment and Inter-agency Collaboration in the Use of Child Protection Orders. Edinburgh: Scottish Executive.

Franklin, B. (ed.) (1986) The Rights of Children. Oxford: Blackwell.

Franklin, B. (1995) 'The case for children's rights: a progress report', in B. Franklin (ed.) The Handbook of Children's Rights: Comparative Policy and Practice. London: Routledge.

Franklin, B. (ed.) (2005) The New Handbook of Children's Rights: Comparative Policy and Practice. London: Routledge.

Franklin, B. and Parton, N. (1991) Social Work, the Media and Public Relations. London: Routledge.

Fraser, M., Richman, J., and Galinsky, M. (1999) 'Risk, protection, and resilience: toward a conceptual framework for social work practice', Social Work Research, 23: 129–208.

Freeman, M. (2000) 'The future of children's rights', Children and Society, 14(4): 277–93.

Freire, P. (1972) The Pedagogy of the Oppressed. Harmondsworth: Penguin.

Frey, B. and Stutzer, A. (2002) Happiness and Economics: How the Economy and Institutions Affect Human Well-being. Princeton, NJ: Princeton University Press.

Fudge, N., Wolfe, C.D. and McKevitt, C. (2008) 'Involving older people in health research', Age and Ageing, 36(5): 492–500.

Fuller, R. and Petch, A. (eds) (1995) Practitioner Research: The Reflective Social Worker. Buckingham: Open University Press.

Garbarino, J. (1992) Children and Families in the Social Environment. New York: Aldine.

Gathorne-Hardy, F. (1995) Devising and Resourcing Personal Care Packages. London: Disablement Income Group.

Geddes, J. (2000) 'Evidence-based practice in mental health', in L. Trinder and S. Reynolds (eds) Evidence-based Practice: A Critical Approach. Oxford: Blackwell.

Geva, J. and Weinman, M.L. (1995) 'Social work perspectives on organ procurement', Health and Social Work, 20(4): 241–320.

Giddens, A. (1990) The Consequences of Modernity. Cambridge: Polity Press.

Giddens, A. (1998) The Third Way: The Renewal of Social Democracy. Cambridge: Polity Press.

Gilchrist, R. and Jeffs, T. (2001) Settlements, Social Change and Community Action. London: Jessica Kingsley.

Gilder, G. (1984) Wealth and Poverty. New York: Basic Books.

Glasby, J. and Beresford, P. (2006) 'Who knows best ? Evidence-based practice and the service user contribution', Critical Social Policy, 26(1): 268–84.

Glasby, J. and Littlechild, R. (2004) The Health and Social Care Divide: The Experiences of Older People, 2nd edn. Bristol: Policy Press.

Glaser, B. and Strauss, A. (1968) A Time for Dying. Chicago, IL: Aldine Books.

Gloor, P. (2006) Swarm Creativity: Competitive Advantage Through Collaborative Innovation Networks. New York: Oxford University Press.

Gneezy, U. and Rustichini, A. (2000) 'A fine is a price', Journal of Legal Studies, 29: 1–17.

Goffman, E. (1967) Interaction Ritual: Essays in Face-to-Face Behaviour. New York: Doubleday Anchor.

Golightley, M. (2004) Social Work and Mental Health. Exeter: Learning Matters.

Golan, N. (1978) *Treatment in Crisis Situations*. New York: Free Press.

Golombok, S. and Fivush, R. (1994) *Gender Development*. Cambridge: Cambridge University Press.

Goodinge, S. (2000) *A Jigsaw of Services: Inspection of Services to Support Disabled Adults in Their Parenting Role*. London: DH.

Gordon, D., Townsend, P., Levitas, R. et al. (2000) *Poverty and Social Exclusion in England*. York: Joseph Rowntree Foundation.

Gorz, A. (1989) *Critique of Economic Reason*. London: Verso.

Gould, N. (1990) 'A political critique of Kantian ethics: a contribution to the debate between Webb and McBeath, and Downie', *British Journal of Social Work*, **20**(3): 495–9.

Gould, N. (2008) 'The research perspective', in M. Davies (ed.) *The Blackwell Companion to Social Work*, 3rd edn. Oxford: Blackwell.

Gould, R. (1978) *Transformations: Growth and Change in Adult Life*. New York: Simon & Schuster.

Graham, M. (2002) *Social Work and African-centred Worldviews*. Birmingham: Venture Press.

Green, L. and Statham, D. (2004) *Scoping Report, East Midlands Learning Resource Centre Network*. Derby: Skills for Care East Midlands Regional Committee.

Greenberg, M.T., Siegel, J.M. and Leitch, C.J. (1983) 'The nature and importance of attachment relationship to parents and peers during adolescence', *Journal of Youth and Adolescence*, **12**(5): 373–87.

Greene, R. (ed.) (2002) *Resiliency: An Integrated Approach to Practice, Policy and Research*. Washington DC: NASW Press.

Greer, P. (1994) *Transforming Central Government: The New Steps Initiative*. Buckingham: Open University Press.

Grimshaw, R. and Sinclair, R. (1997) *Planning to Care: Regulation, Procedure and Practice under the Children Act 1989*. London: National Children's Bureau.

Grimwood, C. and Popplestone, R. (1993) *Women, Management and Care*. Basingstoke: Macmillan – now Palgrave Macmillan.

Groothues, C., Beckett, C.M. and O'Connor, T.G. (2001) 'Successful outcomes: a follow-up study of children adopted from Romania into the UK', *Adoption Quarterly*, **5**(1): 5–22.

Gross, R. (2005) *Psychology: The Science of Mind and Behaviour*. London: Hodder Arnold.

GSCC (General Social Care Council) (2002) *Accreditation of Universities to Grant Degrees in Social Work*. London: GSCC.

GSCC (General Social Care Council) (2004) *Code of Practice for Social Care Workers and Code of Practice for Employers of Social Care Workers*. London: GSCC.

GSCC (General Social Care Council) (2006) *Social Care Code of Practice on International Recruitment*. London: GSCC.

GSCC (General Social Care Council) (2007) *Roles and Tasks of Social Work in England: Consultation Paper*. London: GSCC, www.gscc.org.uk/.

GSCC (General Social Care Council) (2008) *Social Work at its Best: A Statement of Social Work Roles and Tasks for the 21st Century*. London: GSCC.

Guthrie, T. (1998) 'Legal liability and accountability for child-case decisions', *British Journal of Social Work*, **28**(3): 403–22.

Hall, D. (1985) 'Technical note: extreme deprivation in early childhood', *Journal of Child Psychology and Psychiatry and Allied Disciplines*, **26**(5): 825.

Hallett, C. (1995) *Inter-agency Co-ordination in Child Protection*. London: HMSO.

Hallett, C. and Birchall, E. (1992) *Co-ordination and Child Protection: A Review of the Literature*. Edinburgh: TSO.

Halmos, P. (1978) *The Personal and the Political in Social Work*. London: Hutchinson.

Hamer, S. and Collinson, G. (eds) (1999) *Achieving Evidence-based Practice: A Handbook for Practitioners*. London: Baillière Tindall.

Hamilton, G. (1951) *Theory and Practice of Social Case Work*, 2nd edn. New York: Columbia University Press.

Hammersley, M. (2000) 'Evidence-based practice in education and the contribution of educational research', in L. Trinder and S. Reynolds (eds) *Evidence-based Practice: A Critical Approach*. Oxford: Blackwell.

Hanley, B., Bradburn, J., Barnes, M. et al. (2004) *Involving the Public in NHS, Public Health and Social Care Research: Briefing Notes for Researchers*. Eastleigh: INVOLVE.

Hargie, O. and Dickson, D. (2004) *Skilled Interpersonal Communication: Research, Theory and Practice*. London: Routledge.

Harris, J. (2003) *The Social Work Business*. London: Routledge.

Harris, J. and Bamford, C. (2001) 'The uphill struggle: services for deaf and hard of hearing people – issues of equality, participation and access', *Disability and Society*, **16**(7): 969–79.

Harrison, T.H. (1976) *Living through the Blitz*. London: Collins.

Harrison, K. and Ruch, G. (2007) 'Social work and the use of self: on becoming and being a social worker', in M. Lymbery and K. Postle (eds) *Social Work: A Companion to Learning*. London: Sage.

Hart, E. and Bond, M. (1995) *Action Research for Health and Social Care: A Guide to Practice*. Buckingham: Open University Press.

Hart, R.A. (1997) *Children's Participation: The Theory and Practice of Involving Young Citizens in Community Development and Environmental Care*. London: Earthscan.

Hatton, C., Waters, J., Duffy, S. et al. (2008) *A Report on in Control's Second Phase: Evaluation and Learning 2005–2007*. Birmingham: in Control Publications.

Hazan, C. and Shaver, P. (1987) 'Romantic love conceptualised as an attachment process', *Journal of Personality and Social Psychology*, **52**(3): 511–24.

Healy, K. (2000) *Social Work Practices: Contemporary Perspectives on Change*. London: Sage.

Healy, K. (2005) *Social Work Theories in Context: Creating Frameworks for Practice*. Basingstoke: Palgrave Macmillan.

Healy, K. and Meagher, G. (2004) 'The reprofessionalization of social work: collaborative approaches for achieving professional recognition', *British Journal of Social Work*, **34**: 243–60.

Helliwell, J.F. (2003) 'How's life? Combining individual and national variables to explain subjective well-being', *Economic Modelling*, **20**: 331–60.

Heron, J. (1996) *Cooperative Inquiry: Research into the Human Condition*. London: Sage.

Heron, J. (2001) *Helping the Client: A Creative Practical Approach*, 5th edn. London: Sage.

Heron, J. and Reason, P. (2001) 'The practice of co-operative inquiry: research with rather than on people', in P. Reason and H. Bradbury (eds) *Handbook of Action Research: Participative Inquiry and Practice*. London: Sage.

Herzberg, F. (1959) *The Motivation to Work*. New York: John Wiley and Sons.

Hickson, D.J., Hinnings, C.R., McMillan, C.J. and Schwitter, J.P. (1974) 'The culture-free context of organization structure: a tri-national comparison', *Sociology*, **8**: 59–80.

Higham, P. (2006) *Social Work, Introducing Professional Practice*. London: Sage.

Hill, A. (in press) 'Combining professional expertise and service user expertise: negotiating therapy for sexually abused children', *British Journal of Social Work*, Advance Access published online 16 October 2007.

Hill Collins, P. (2000) *Black Feminist Thought: Knowledge, Consciousness and the Politics of Empowerment*, 2nd edn. Boston: Unwin Hyman.

Hills, J. (1995) *Joseph Rowntree Foundation Inquiry into Income and Wealth*, vol. 2. York: Joseph Rowntree Foundation.

Hills, J. (2007) *Ends and Means: The Future Roles of Social Housing in England*, CASE Report 34. London: ESRC Research Centre for Analysis of Social Exclusion.

Hirsch, D. (2006) *What Will it Take to End Child Poverty? Firing on All Cylinders*. York: Joseph Rowntree Foundation.

HM Treasury (2004) *Choice for Parents, the Best Start for Children*. London: HM Treasury.

HMRC (Her Majesty's Revenue and Customs) (2008) *Child Tax Credit and Working Tax Credit: Take-up Rates 2005–06*, www.customsand revenue.eu/stats/personal-tax-credits/cwtc-take-up2005-06.pdf.

Hobbs, G. and Hobbs, C. (1999) 'Abuse of children in foster and residential care', *Child Abuse and Neglect*, **23**(12): 1239–52.

Hodge, S. (2005) Participation, discourse and power: a case study in service user involvement, *Critical Social Policy*, **25**(2): 164–79.

Hodges, J. and Tizard, B. (1989a) 'IQ and behavioral adjustment of ex-institutional adolescents', *Journal of Child Psychology and Psychiatry and Allied Disciplines*, **30**(1): 53–75.

Hodges, J. and Tizard, B. (1989b) 'Social and family relationships of ex-institutional adolescents', *Journal of Child Psychology and Psychiatry and Allied Disciplines*, **30**(1): 77–97.

Hofstein, S. (1964) 'The nature of process: its implications for social work', *Journal of the Social Work Process*, **14**: 13–53.

Holland, S. and Rivett, M. (2006) '"Everyone started shouting": connections between the process of family group conferences and family therapy practice', *British Journal of Social Work*, **38**(11): 21–30.

Holland, S., Scourfield, J., O'Neill, S. and Pithouse, A. (2005) 'Democratising the family and the state? The case of family group conferences in child welfare', *Journal of Social Policy*, **34**(1): 59–77.

Hollis, M. and Howe, D. (1987) 'Moral risks in social work', *Journal of Applied Philosophy*, **4**: 123–33.

Hollis, M. and Howe, D. (1990) 'Moral risks in the social work role: a response to Macdonald', *British Journal of Social Work*, **20**(6): 547–52.

Holloway, M. and Lymbery, M. (2007) 'Editorial – caring for people: social work with adults in the next decade and beyond', *British Journal of Social Work*, **37**(3): 375–86.

Holman, R. (1993) *A New Deal for Social Welfare*. Oxford: Lyon Publishing.

Home Office Border and Immigration Agency (2007) *Accession Monitoring Report, A8 Countries, May 2004–June 2007*. A joint online report between the Border and Immigration Agency, Department for Work and Pensions, HM Revenue and Customs and Communities and Local Government, www.ukba.homeoffice.gov.uk/.

Honey, P. and Mumford, A. (1992) *The Manual of Learning Styles*, 3rd edn. Maidenhead: Honey.

Hood, C. (1991) 'A public management for all seasons', *Public Administration*, **69**: 3–19.

Hood, C., Rothstein, H. and Baldwin, R. (2001) *The*

Government of Risk: Understanding Risk Regulation Regimes. Oxford: Oxford University Press.

Horder, W. (2002) 'Care management', in M. Davies (ed.) *The Blackwell Companion to Social Work.* Oxford: Blackwell.

Horne, M. (1999) *Values in Social Work.* Aldershot: Ashgate.

Horner, N. (2006) *What Is Social Work?*, 2nd edn. Exeter: Learning Matters.

Howarth, C., Kenway, P., Palmer, G. and Street, C. (1998) *Monitoring Poverty and Social Exclusion: Labour's Inheritance.* York: New Policy Institute/ Joseph Rowntree Foundation.

Howe, D. (1987) *An Introduction to Social Work Theory,* Aldershot: Wildwood House.

Howe, D. (1992) *An Introduction to Social Work Theory,* 3rd edn. Aldershot: Wildwood House.

Howe, D. (1995) *Attachment Theory for Social Work Practice.* Basingstoke: Macmillan – now Palgrave Macmillan.

Howe, D. (2002) 'Relating theory to practice', in M. Davies (ed.) *Companion to Social Work,* 2nd edn. Oxford: Blackwell.

Howe, D. and Fearnley, S. (1999) 'Disorders of attachment and attachment therapy', *Adoption and Fostering,* **23**(2): 19–30.

Hudson, B. and Henwood, M. (2002) 'The NHS and social care: the final countdown?', *Policy and Politics,* **30**(2): 153–66.

Hughes, B. (1995) *Older People and Community Care: Critical Theory and Practice.* Buckingham: Open University Press.

Hughes, J. and Sharrock, W. (1997) *The Philosophy of Social Research,* 3rd edn. London: Longman.

Hughes, K., Bellis, M.A. and Kilfoyle-Carrington, M. (2001) *Alcohol, Tobacco and Drugs in the North West of England: Identifying a Shared Agenda.* Liverpool: Liverpool John Moores University.

Hughes, W.H. (1986) *Report of the Inquiry into Children's Homes and Hostels.* Belfast: HMSO.

Humphries, B. (2004) 'An unacceptable role for social work: implementing immigration policy', *British Journal of Social Work,* **34**: 93–107.

IFSW (International Federation of Social Workers) (2000) *Definition of Social Work,* www.ifsw.org/ Publications/4.6e.pub.html.

IFSW (International Federation of Social Work) (2004) *Ethics in Social Work, Statement of Principles,* www.ifsw.org/en/p38000324.html.

Innocenti Report (2007) *Child Well-being in 21 Rich Countries,* Card 7. Florence, Italy: OECD.

Institute of Medicine (2001) *Crossing the Quality Chasm: A New Health System for the 21st Century.* Washington, DC: National Academies of Sciences.

Irvine, E.E. (1966) 'A new look at casework', in E. Younghusband (ed.) *New Developments in Casework.* London: Allen & Unwin.

J.M. Consulting Ltd (1999) Review of the Delivery of the Diploma in Social Work for the Department of Health. Bristol: J.M. Consulting Ltd.

Jack, C. and Gill, O. (2003) *The Missing Side of the Triangle: Assessing the Importance of Family and Environmental Factors in the Lives of Children.* Ilford: Barnardo's.

Jackson, S., Fisher, M., and Ward, H. (2000) 'Key concepts in looking after children: parenting, partnership, outcomes', in DH, *A Child's World.* London: HMSO.

James, A. and James, A. (2004) *Constructing Childhood: Theory, Policy and Social Practice.* Basingstoke: Palgrave Macmillan.

James, A. and Prout, A. (1997) *Constructing and Reconstructing Childhood: Contemporary Issues in the Sociological Study of Childhood,* 2nd edn. London: Routledge.

James, O. (2006) *Affluenza.* London: Allen Lane.

Jessup, H. and Rogerson, S. (1999) 'Postmodernism and teaching and practice of interpersonal skills', in B. Pease and J. Fook (eds) *Transforming Social Work Practice: Postmodern Critical Perspectives.* London: Routledge.

Johnson, D.E. (2002) 'Adoption and the effect on children's development', *Early Human Development,* **68**: 39–54.

Johnson, J., Bottorff, J., Browne, A. et al. (2004) 'Othering and being othered in the context of health care services', *Health Communication,* **16**(2): 255–71.

Jones, C. (1983) *State Social Work and the Working Class.* London: Routledge & Kegan Paul.

Jones, C. (1994) Dangerous Times for British Social Work Education. Paper presented at the 27th Congress of the International Association of Schools of Social Work, Amsterdam, 11–15 July.

Jones, C. (2001) 'Voices from the front line: State social workers and New Labour', *British Journal of Social Work,* **31**(4): 547–62.

Jordan, B. (1984) *Invitation to Social Work.* Oxford: Martin Robertson.

Jordan, B. (2007) *Social Work and Well-being.* Lyme Regis: Russell House.

Jordan, B. (2008) *Welfare and Well-being: Social Value in Public Policy.* Bristol: Policy Press.

Jordan, B. and Jordan, C. (2000) *Social Work and the Third Way: Tough Love as Social Policy.* London: Sage.

JUC SWEC (Joint University Council Social Work Education Committee) (2006) *A Social Work Strategy in Higher Education.* London: Social Care Workforce Research Unit.

JUC SWEC (Joint University Council Social Work Education Committee) (2007) *A Research Strategy for Social Work: A Consultation Document.* Coventry: JUC SWEC, Research Strategy Subcommittee.

Juliusdottir, S. and Petersson, J. (2004) 'Nordic

standards revisited', *Social Work Education*, **23**(5): 567–79.

Kadushin, A. (1983) *The Social Work Interview*. New York: Columbia University Press.

Kadushin, A. (1990) *The Social Work Interview*, 3rd edn. New York: Columbia University Press.

Kahneman, D., Diener, E. and Schwartz, N. (1999) *Well-being: Foundations of Hedonic Psychology*. New York: Russell Sage Foundation.

Kamerman, S.B. (2002) 'Fields of practice', in M.A. Mattaini, C.T. Lowery and C.H. Meyer (eds) *Foundations of Social Work Practice: A Graduate Text*. Washington, DC: NASW Press.

Kant, I. (1785) 'Groundwork of the metaphysic of morals', in H.J. Paton (ed.) (1948) *The Moral Law*. London: Routledge.

Kellett. M. (2005) *Children as Active Researchers: A New Paradigm for the 21st Century?* ESRC National Centre for Research Methods Review Papers/003.

Kellett, M., Forrest, R., Dent, N. and Ward, S. (2004) '"Just teach us the skills please, we'll do the rest": empowering ten-year-olds as active researchers', *Children and Society*, **18**: 329–43.

Kempson, E. (1996) *Life on a Low Income*. York: Joseph Rowntree Foundation.

Kempson, E. (1997) 'Privatisation of utilities', in A. Walker and C. Walker (eds) *Britain Divided: The Growth of Social Exclusion in Britain 1979–1997*. London: CPAG.

Kempson E. (2002) *Over-indebtedness in Britain*. London: Department of Trade and Industry.

Kemshall, H. (2007) 'Risk assessment and management: an overview', in J. Lishman (ed.) *Handbook for Practice Learning in Social Work and Social Care: Knowledge and Theory*, 2nd edn. London: Jessica Kingsley.

Kemshall, H. (2008) 'Editorial', *British Journal of Social Work*, **38**(1).

Kemshall, H. and Pritchard, J. (eds) (1997) *Good Practice in Risk Assessment and Risk Management*, vol 2. London: Jessica Kingsley.

Kendall, J. and Knapp, M. (1996) *The Voluntary Sector in the UK*. Manchester: Manchester University Press.

Kendall, K. (2000) *Social Work Education: Its Origins in Europe*. Alexandria, VA: CSWE.

Khan, P. and Dominelli, L. (2000) 'The impact of globalisation on social work in the UK', *European Journal of Social Work*, **3**(2): 95–108.

Kiernan, K.E. (1998) 'Parenthood and family life in the United Kingdom', *Review of Population and Social Policy*, **7**: 63–81.

King, M. (2005) 'Good intentions into social action', in H. Hendrick (ed.) *Child Welfare and Social Policy*. Bristol: Policy Press.

King, M. and Trowell, J. (1992) *Children's Welfare and the Law: The Limits of Legal Intervention*. London: Sage.

Kipling, R. (1902) 'The elephant's child', in his *Just So Stories*. London: Macmillan – now Palgrave Macmillan.

Kirby, P. (2004) *A Guide to Actively Involving Young People in Research: For Researchers, Research Commissioners and Managers*. Eastleigh: INVOLVE.

Kirby, P., Lanyon, C., Cronin, K. and Sinclair, R. (2003) *Building a Culture of Participation: Involving Children and Young People in Policy, Service Planning, Delivery and Evaluation*. Nottingham: DfES.

Kirkwood, A. (1993) *The Leicestershire Inquiry 1992*. Leicester: Leicestershire County Council.

Knapp, M. and Prince, M. (2007) *Dementia UK*. London: Alzheimer's Society.

Kolb, D.A. (1976) *Learning Style Inventory: Technical Manual*. Boston, MA: McBer.

Koprowska, J., Hicks, L., McCluskey, U. et al. (1999) *Moving Images: Teaching Interviewing Skills in a University Social Work Department*, video and booklet. University of York.

Kreppner, J.M., O'Connor, T.G., Rutter, M. et al. (2001) 'Can inattention/overactivity be an institutional deprivation syndrome?', *Journal of Abnormal Child Psychology*, **29**(6): 513–28.

Kübler-Ross, E. (1969) *On Death and Dying*. London: Tavistock.

Labour Party (1997) *Manifesto*. London: Labour Party.

Laing, R.D. (1969) *Intervention in Social Situations*. London: Association of Family Caseworkers/ Philadelphia Association Ltd.

Laming, H. (2003) *The Victoria Climbié Inquiry: Report of an Inquiry by Lord Laming*. London: TSO.

Langan, M. (1998) 'Radical social work', in R. Adams, L. Dominelli and M. Payne (eds) *Social Work, Themes, Issues and Critical Debates*. Basingstoke: Macmillan – now Palgrave Macmillan.

Lawson, J. (1996) 'Framework of risk assessment and management for older people', in H. Kemshall and J. Pritchard (eds) *Good Practice in Risk Assessment and Risk Management*. London: Jessica Kingsley.

Layard, R. (2005) *Happiness: Lessons from a New Science*. London: Allen Lane.

Layard, R. (2006) 'Happiness and public policy: a challenge to the profession', *Economic Journal*, **116**(510): 24–33.

Laybourn, K. (1997) 'The guild of help and the community response to poverty 1904–c.1914', in K. Laybourn (ed.) *Social Conditions, Status and Community 1860–c. 1920*. Stroud: Sutton.

Layder, D. (1993) *New Strategies in Social Research*. Cambridge: Polity Press.

Leach, P. (1999) *The Physical Punishment of Children*. London: NSPCC.

Leadbeater, C. (2004) *Personalisation Through*

Participation: A New Script for Public Services. London: Demos.

Leadbeater, C. and Lownsborough, H. (2005) *Personalisation and Participation: The Future of Social Care in Scotland: Final Report.* London: Demos.

Leathard, A. (2003) *Interprofessional Collaboration: From Policy to Practice in Health and Social Care.* Hove: Brunner-Routledge.

Leather, S. (1996) *The Making of Modern Malnutrition: An Overview of Food Poverty in the UK.* London: Caroline Walker Trust.

Leece, J. and Bornat, J. (eds) (2006) *Developments in Direct Payments.* Bristol: Policy Press.

Leonard, P. (1976) 'The function of social work in society', in N. Timms and D. Watson (eds) *Talking about Welfare.* London: Routledge and Kegan Paul.

Leonard, P. (1997) *Postmodern Welfare: Reconstructing an Emancipatory Project.* London: Sage.

Leung, T. (2008) 'Accountability to welfare service users: challenges and responses of service providers', *British Journal of Social Work*, **38**: 521–45.

Levin, E. (2004) *Involving Service Users and Carers in Social Work Education.* London: Social Care Institute for Excellence.

Levinson, D. and Levinson, J. (1997) *The Seasons of a Woman's Life.* New York: Ballantyne.

Levinson, D., Darrow, D., Klein, E. et al. (1978) *The Seasons of a Man's Life.* New York: Knopf.

Levy, A. and Kahan, B. (1991) *The Pindown Experience and the Protection of Children: The Report of the Staffordshire Child Care Inquiry.* Stafford: Staffordshire County Council.

Lewis, J. (1996) 'What does contracting do to voluntary agencies?', in D. Billis and M. Harris (eds) *Voluntary Agencies: Challenges of Organisation and Management.* Basingstoke: Macmillan – now Palgrave Macmillan.

Lewis, J. and Glennerster, H. (1996) *Implementing the New Community Care.* Buckingham: Open University Press.

Lewis, M., Feiring, C. and Rosenthal, S. (2000) 'Attachment over time', *Child Development*, **71**(3): 707–20.

Lishman, J. (ed.) (1991) *Handbook of Theory for Practice Teachers in Social Work.* London: Jessica Kingsley.

Lishman, J. (1994) *Communication in Social Work.* Basingstoke: Macmillan – now Palgrave Macmillan.

Lishman, J. (ed.) (2007a) *Handbook of Theory for Practice Learning in Social Work and Social Care*, 2nd edn. London: Jessica Kingsley.

Lishman, J. (2007b) 'Research, evaluation and evidence based practice', in J. Lishman (ed.) *Handbook for Practice Learning in Social Work*

and Social Care: Knowledge and Theory, 2nd edn. London: Jessica Kingsley.

Lister, R. (2004) *Poverty.* Bristol: Polity Press.

Little, M. (1997) 'The refocusing of children's services: the contribution of research', in N. Parton (ed.) *Child Protection and Family Support: Tensions, Contradictions and Possibilities.* London: Routledge.

Little, M. and Mount, K. (1999). *Prevention and Early Intervention with Children in Need.* Aldershot: Ashgate.

Loeber, R. and Farrington, D.P. (eds) (1998) *Serious and Violent Juvenile Offenders: Risk Factors and Successful Interventions.* London: Sage.

Lonergan, P. (2000) 'James: moving on to independent living', in H. Martyn (ed.) *Developing Reflective Practice.* Bristol: Policy Press.

Loney, M. (1983) *Community Against Government: The British Community Development Projects, 1968–1978: A Study of Government Incompetence.* London: Heinemann.

Long, T. and Johnson, M. (eds) (2007) *Research Ethics in the Real World: Issues and Solutions for Health and Social Care.* London: Churchill Livingstone Elsevier.

Lorde, A. (1984) *Sister Outsider.* New York: The Crossing Press.

Lorenz, W. (1994) *Social Work in a Changing Europe.* London: Routledge.

Lupton, C. and Nixon, P. (1999) *Empowering Practice? A Critical Appraisal of the Family Group Conference Approach.* Bristol: Policy Press.

Lymbery, M. (2001) 'Social work at the crossroads', *British Journal of Social Work*, **31**(3): 369–84.

Lymbery, M. (2005) *Social Work with Older People: Context, Policy and Practice.* London: Sage.

Lymbery, M. (2006) 'United we stand? Partnership working in health and social care and the role of social work in services for older people', *British Journal of Social Work*, **36**(7): 1119–34.

Lymbery, M., Lawson, J., MacCallum, H. et al. (2007) 'The social work role with older people', *Practice*, **19**(2): 97–113.

Lynn, J. and Adamson, D.M. (2003) *Living Well at the End of Life: Adapting Health Care to Serious Chronic Illness in Old Age.* Washington: Rand Health.

McCarrick, C., Over, A. and Wood, P. (2000) 'Towards user friendly assessment' and 'a framework for assessment in child protection' in N. Baldwin (ed.) *Protecting Children: Promoting their Rights.* London: Sage.

McCluskey, J. (2000) *NCH: Action for Children Factfile 2000.* London: NCH Action for Children.

Macdonald, G. (1990a) 'Allocating blame in social work', *British Journal of Social Work*, **20**(6): 525–46.

Macdonald, G. (1990b) 'Moral risks? A reply to Hollis and Howe', *British Journal of Social Work*, **20**(6): 553–6.

Macdonald, G. (2000) 'Social care: rhetoric or reality?', in H.T. Davies, S.M. Nutley and P.C. Smith, (eds) *What Works? Evidence-based Policy and Practice in Public Services.* Bristol: Policy Press.

Macdonald, G. (2002) 'Child protection', in D. McNeish, T. Newman and H. Roberts (eds) *What Works for Children?* Buckingham: Open University Press.

Macdonald, G. (2008) 'The evidence based perspective', in M. Davies (ed.) *The Blackwell Companion to Social Work.* Oxford: Blackwell, pp. 435–41.

Macdonald, G. and Winkley, A. (1999) *What Works in Child Protection.* Ilford: Barnado's.

McDonald, T. and Marks, T. (1991) 'A review of risk factors assessed in child protective services', *Social Services Review*, (March): 112–32.

McGuire, J. (1995) *What Works: Reducing Reoffending.* Chichester: John Wiley.

Mackway-Jones, K. (1997) *Emergency Triage: Manchester Triage Group.* London: BMJ Publishing.

McLaughlin, H. (2006) 'Involving young service users as co-researchers: possibilities, benefits and costs', *British Journal of Social Work*, **36**(8): 1395–410.

McLaughlin, H. (2007a) *Understanding Social Work Research: Key Issues and Concepts.* London: Sage.

McLaughlin, H. (2007b) 'Ethical issues in the involvement of young service users in research', *Ethics and Social Welfare*, **1**(2): 176–93.

McLaughlin, H. (in press) 'What's in a name: 'client', 'patient', 'customer', 'consumer', 'expert by experience', 'service user' – what's next?', *British Journal of Social Work*, Advance Access published online 21 February 2008.

McLean, T. (2007) 'Interdisciplinary practice', in J. Lishman (ed.) *Handbook for Practice Learning in Social Work and Social Care: Knowledge and Theory*, 2nd edn. London: Jessica Kingsley.

McLeod, E. and Bywaters, P. (2000) *Social Work, Health and Equality.* London: Routledge.

McLeod, E., Bywaters, P., Tanner, D. and Hirsch, M. (2008) 'For the sake of their health: older service users' requirements for social care to facilitate access to social networks following hospital discharge', *British Journal of Social Work*, **38**(1): 73–90.

MacNaughton, G. and Davis, K. (2001) 'Beyond "othering": rethinking approaches to teaching young Anglo-Australian children about indigenous Australians', *Contemporary Issues in Early Childhood*, **2**(1): 83–93.

McNeill, F., Batchelor, S., Burnett, R. and Knox, J. (2005) *21st Century Social Work.* Edinburgh: Scottish Government.

McNeish, D. and Newman, T. (2002) 'Involving children and young people in decision making', in D. McNeish, T. Newman and H. Roberts (eds) *What Works for Children?* Buckingham: Open University Press.

McNeish, D., Newman, T. and Roberts, H. (eds) (2002) *What Works for Children? Effective Services for Children and Families.* Buckingham: Open University Press.

Maddock, J.W. and Larson, N. (1995) *Incestuous Families: An Ecological Approach to Understanding the Treatment.* New York: WW Norton.

Manning, C. (2002) 'Expert patients', rapid response to Crawford et al. (2002): 'Systematic review of involving patients in the planning and development of health care', *British Medical Journal*, **325**: 1263–5.

Mansfield, R. and Mayer, C.L. (2007) 'Making a difference with combined community assessment and change projects', *Journal of Nursing Education*, **46**(3): 132–4.

Markiewcz, D., Doyle, A.B. and Brendgen, M. (2001) 'The quality of adolescents' friendships: associations with mothers' interpersonal relationships, attachments to parents and friends', *Journal of Adolescence*, **24**(4): 429.

Marris, P. (1974) Loss and Change. London: Routledge & Kegan Paul.

Marsh, P. and Crow, G. (1998) *Family Group Conferences in Child Welfare.* Oxford: Blackwell.

Marsh, P. and Fisher, M. (1992) *Good Intentions: Developing Partnerships in Social Services.* York: Joseph Rowntree/Community Care.

Marsh, P. and Fisher, M. (2005) *Developing the Evidence Base for Social Work and Social Care Practice.* London: Social Care Institute for Excellence.

Marshall, M. and Creed, F. (2000) 'Assertive community treatment. Is it the future of community care in the UK?', *International Review of Psychiatry*, **12**(3): 191–6.

Marx, K. and Engels, F. ([1847] 1961) 'The German ideology', in R. Freeman (ed.) *Marx on Economics.* Harmondsworth: Penguin.

Maslow, A. (1968) *Toward a Psychology of Being.* New York: John Wiley and Sons.

Mayer, J.E. and Timms, N. (1970) *The Client Speaks.* London: Routledge & Kegan Paul.

Mayer, M.F. (1972) 'The parental figures in residential treatment', in J.K. Whittaker and A.E. Trieschman (eds) *Children Away from Home: A Sourcebook of Residential Treatment.* Chicago, IL: Aldine.

Mayo, E. (1933) *The Human Problems of an Industrial Civilization.* New York: Macmillan.

Mayo, E. (1975) *The Social Problems of an Industrial Civilization.* London: Routledge & Kegan Paul.

Meinert, R., Pardeck, J.T. and Kreuger, L. (2000) *Social Work: Seeking Relevancy in the Twenty-first Century*. New York: Haworth Press.

Mintzberg, H. (1979) *The Structuring of Organizations: A Synthesis of the Research*. Englewood Cliffs, NJ: Prentice Hall.

Mitchell, J., Mouratidis, K. and Weale, M. (2005) *Poverty and Debt, National Institute of Economic and Social Research* Discussion Paper no. 263, www.niesr.ac.uk/pubs/dps/dp263.pdf.

Monckton, W. (1945) *Report of Sir Walter Monckton on the Circumstances which led to the Boarding Out of Dennis and Terence O'Neill at Bank Farm, Minsterly, and the Steps Taken to Supervise their Welfare*. London: HMSO.

Moore, M.H. (1995) *Creating Public Value: Strategic Management in Government*. Cambridge, MA: Harvard Business Press.

Morago, P. (2006) 'Evidence based practice from medicine to social work', *European Journal of Social Work*, **9**(4): 461–77.

Morris, J. (1997) 'Care or empowerment? A disability rights perspective', *Social Policy and Administration*, **31**(1): 54–60.

Morris, J. (1998) *Don't Leave Us Out: Involving Disabled Young People and Young People with Communication Difficulties*. York: Joseph Rowntree Foundation.

Morris, J. (2005) *Minimum Income for Healthy Living: Older People*. London: Age Concern.

Morris, K. (2008) 'Setting the scene', in K. Morris (ed.) *Social Work and Multi-agency Working: Making a Difference*. Bristol: Policy Press.

Morrison, A. (2001) 'Interpreting the quality of written assessments: a participative approach', in V. White and J. Harris (eds) *Developing Good Practice in Community Care: Partnership and Participation*. London: Jessica Kingsley.

Morrison, T. (2001) *Staff Supervision in Social Care: Making a Real Difference for Staff and Service Users*. Brighton: Pavilion.

Moynagh, M. and Worsley, R. (2005) *Working in the Twenty First Century*. Leeds: The Tomorrow Project/ESRC.

Mullaly, B. (1997) *Structural Social Work, Ideology, Theory and Practice*, 2nd edn. Oxford: Oxford University Press.

Mullender, A. and Ward, D. (1991) *Self-directed Groupwork: Users Take Action for Empowerment*. London: Whiting & Birch.

Munday, B. and Lane, D. (1998) *The Old and the New: Changes in Social Care in Central and Eastern Europe*. Canterbury: European Institute of Social Services, University of Kent.

Munro, E. (1999) 'Common errors of reasoning in child protection work', *Abuse and Neglect*, **23**(8): 745–58.

Munro, E. (2002) *Effective Child Protection*. London: Sage.

Munro, E. (2004a) 'The impact of audit on social work practice', *British Journal of Social Work*, **34**(8): 1075–95.

Munro, E. (2004b) 'The impact of child abuse inquiries since 1990', in J. Manthorpe and N. Stanley (eds) *The Age of the Inquiry, Learning and Blaming in Health and Social Care*. London: Routledge.

Murray, C. (1984) *Losing Ground: American Social Policy, 1950–80*. New York: Basic Books.

Murray, C. (1990) *The Emerging British Underclass*. London: Institute for Economic Affairs.

Murray, C. (1994) *Underclass: The Crisis Deepens*. London: Institute for Economic Affairs.

Myers, D.G. (1999) 'Close relationships and quality of life', in D. Kahneman, E. Diener and N. Schwartz (eds) *Well-being: The Foundations of Hedonic Psychology*. New York: Russell Sage Foundation.

Myers, S. and Milner, J. (2007) *Sexual Issues in Social Work*. Bristol: Policy Press.

NASW (National Association of Social Workers) (1996) *Code of Ethics*, 2nd edn. Silver Spring, MD: NASW, www.naswdc.org/code.htm.

National Schizophrenia Fellowship (1992) *How to Involve Users and Carers: Guidelines on Involvement in Planning, Running and Monitoring Care Services*. Kingston Upon Thames: National Schizophrenia Fellowship.

National Treatment Agency for Substance Misuse (2006) Models of Care for Treatment of Adult Drug Misusers: Update 2006. London: National Treatment Agency for Substance Misuse.

Neimeyer, R.A. (2002) 'Mourning and meaning', *American Behavioral Scientist*, **46**: 235–51.

Neugarten, B., Moore, J. and Lowe, J. (1965) 'Age norms, age constraints, and adult socialization', *American Journal of Sociology*, **70**: 710–16.

Newman, B.M. and Newman, P.R. (2007) *Theories of Human Development*. New York: Psychology Press/Erlbaum/Taylor & Francis.

Newman, T., Moseley, A., Tierney, S. and Ellis, A. (2005) *Evidence-based Social Work: A Guide for the Perplexed*. Lyme Regis: Russell House Publishing.

NFER (National Foundation for Educational Research) (2001) *Multi-agency Working and Audit of Activity*. London: LGA.

NHS Centre for Reviews and Dissemination (1997) 'Brief intervention and alcohol use', *Effective Health Care* **3**. London: DH.

Noble, C. (2007) 'Social work, collective action and social movements: re-thematising the local–global nexus', in L. Dominelli (ed.) *Revitalising*

Communities in a Globalising World. Aldershot: Ashgate.

Nocon, A. and Qureshi, H. (1996) Outcomes of Community Care for Users and Carers. Buckingham: Open University Press.

Nolan, M., Hanson, E., Grant, G. and Keady, J. (eds) (2007) User Participation in Health and Social Care Research: Voices Values and Evaluation. Maidenhead: Open University Press.

Northern Ireland Social Care Council (2004) Code of Practice for Social Care Workers and Code of Practice for Employers of Social Care Workers, www.niscc.info/registration-2.aspx.

Nutley, S.M., Walter, I. and Davies, H.T. (2007) Using Evidence. Bristol: Policy Press.

O'Brien, S. (2003) Report of the Caleb Ness Inquiry. Edinburgh: Edinburgh/Lothians Child Protection Committee.

O'Connor, I., Hughes, M., Turney, D. et al. (2006) Social Work and Social Care Practice. London: Sage.

O'Connor, T.G., Bredenkamp, D., Rutter, M. and the English and Romanian Adoptees Study Team (1999) 'Attachment disturbances and disorders in children exposed to early severe deprivation', Infant Mental Health Journal, 20(1): 10–29.

O'Connor, T.G., Rutter, M. and the English and Romanian Adoptees Study Team (2000a) 'Attachment disorder behavior following early severe deprivation: extension and longitudinal follow-up', Journal of the American Academy of Child and Adolescent Psychiatry, 39(6): 703–12.

O'Connor, T.G., Rutter, M., Beckett, C., Keaveney, L., Kreppner, J. M. and the English and Romanian Adoptees Study Team (2000b) 'The effects of global severe privation on cognitive competence: extension and longitudinal follow-up', Child Development, 71(2): 376–90.

O'Hagan, K. (1986) Crisis Intervention in Social Services. London: Macmillan – now Palgrave Macmillan.

Oakley, A. and Williams, A.S. (eds) (1994) The Politics of the Welfare State. London: University of Central London Press.

ODPM (Office of the Deputy Prime Minister) (2004) The English Indices of Deprivation. London. ODPM.

Offer, J. (2006) An Intellectual History of British Social Policy: Idealism versus Non-idealism. Bristol: Policy Press.

Office for Public Management (1994) From Margin to Mainstream: User and Carer Involvement in Community Care, Local Authorities Changing Themselves – Manager's Manual. London: Office for Public Management.

Oliver, C., Owen, C., Statham, J. and Moss, P. (2001) Figures and Facts: Local Authority Variance on Indicators Concerning Child Protection and Children Looked After. London: Institute of Education.

Oliver, M. (1990) The Politics of Disablement: From Theory to Practice. Basingstoke: Macmillan – now Palgrave Macmillan.

Oliver, M. (1996) Understanding Disability: From Theory to Practice. Basingstoke: Macmillan – now Palgrave Macmillan.

Olsson, C.A., Bond, L., Burns, J.M. et al. (2003) 'Adolescent resilience: a concept analysis', Journal of Adolescence, 26(1): 1–11.

ONS (2006) Birth Statistics, Series FM1 no. 33. London: ONS.

Onyett, S. (2003) Teamworking in Mental Health. Basingstoke: Palgrave Macmillan.

Opie, A. (2003) Thinking Teams/Thinking Clients: Knowledge-based Teamwork. New York: Columbia University Press.

Owusu-Bempah, K. (2007) Children and Separation: Socio-genealogical Connectedness Perspective. London: Routledge.

Pain, R., Askins, K. and Kitoko, G. (2007) Connecting Places, Connected Lives: An Anti-Bullying Art Project. ACANE/Durham University, www.geography.dur.ac.uk/Projects/Default.aspx?alias=www.geography.dur.ac.uk/projects/acaneart.

Palmer, G., Carr, J. and Kenway, P. (2005) Monitoring Poverty and Social Exclusion in the UK. York: Joseph Rowntree Foundation.

Palmer, G., Macinnes, T. and Kenway P. (2007) Monitoring Poverty and Social Exclusion 2007. York: Joseph Rowntree Foundation/New Policy Institute.

Parker, J. (2007) 'The process of social work', in M. Lymbery and K. Postle (eds) Social Work: A Companion to Learning. London: Sage.

Parker, J. and Bradley, G. (2003) Social Work Practice: Assessment, Planning, Intervention and Review. Exeter: Learning Matters.

Parker, R. (1966) Decisions in Child Care: A Study of Prediction in Fostering. London: Allen and Unwin.

Parker, R. (1981) 'Tending and social policy', in E.M. Goldberg and S. Hatch (eds) A New Look at the Personal Social Services. London: Policy Studies Institute.

Parsons, T. (1942) 'Age and sex in the social structure of the United States', American Sociological Review, 7: 604–16.

Parton, N. (ed.) (1996) Social Theory, Social Change and Social Work. London: Routledge.

Parton, N. (1998) 'Risk, advanced liberalism and child welfare', British Journal of Social Work, 28: 5–27.

Parton, N. (1999) 'Reconfiguring child welfare practices: risk, advanced liberalism and the government of freedom', in A.S. Chambon, A. Irving and L. Epstein (eds) *Reading Foucault for Social Work*, Chichester: Colombia University Press.

Parton, N. (2006) *Safeguarding Children: Early Intervention and Surveillance in a Late Modern Society*. Basingstoke: Palgrave Macmillan.

Parton, N. and O'Byrne, P. (2000) *Constructive Social Work: Towards a New Practice*. Basingstoke: Palgrave – now Palgrave Macmillan.

Patel, N., Naik, D. and Humphries, B. (eds) (1998) *Visions of Reality: Religion and Ethnicity in Social Work*. London: Central Council for Education and Training in Social Work.

Pawson, R., Boaz, A., Grayson, L. et al. (2003) *Types and Quality of Knowledge in Social Care*, Knowledge Review 3, London: Social Care Institute for Excellence.

Payne, M. and Askeland, G. (2008) *Globalisation and International Social Work: Postmodern Change and Challenge*. Aldershot: Ashgate.

Payne, G. and Payne, J. (2004) *Key Concepts in Social Research*. London: Sage.

Payne, H. and Littlechild, B. (2000) *Ethical Practice and the Abuse of Power in Social Responsibility*. London: Jessica Kingsley.

Payne, M. (1991) *Modern Social Work Theory: A Critical Introduction*. Basingstoke: Macmillan – now Palgrave Macmillan.

Payne, M. (1995) *Social Work and Community Care*. Basingstoke: Macmillan – now Palgrave Macmillan.

Payne, M. (1996) *What is Professional Social Work?* Birmingham: Venture.

Payne, M. (2000) *Teamwork in Multiprofessional Care*. Basingstoke: Palgrave – now Palgrave Macmillan.

Payne, M. (2005) *Modern Social Work Theory*. Basingstoke: Palgrave Macmillan.

Payne, M. (2006) *What is Professional Social Work?* 2nd edn. Bristol: Policy Press.

Payne, M. (2009) *Social Care Practice in Context*. Basingstoke: Palgrave Macmillan.

Peach, J. and Horner, A. (2007) 'Using supervision, support or survelliance', in M. Lymbery and K. Postle (eds) *Social Work: A Companion to Learning*. London: Sage.

Perlman, H.H. (1957) *Social Casework: A Problem-Solving Process*. Chicago: Chicago University Press.

Petch, A. (2002) 'Work with adult service users', in M. Davies (ed.) *The Blackwell Companion to Social Work*. Oxford: Blackwell.

Petch, A. (2008) 'Social work with adult service users', in M. Davies (ed.) *The Blackwell Companion to Social Work*, 3rd edn. Oxford: Blackwell.

Peters, T.J. and Waterman, R.H. (1982) *In Search of Excellence*. London: Harper and Row.

Petrosino, A., Turpin-Petrosino, C. and Beuhler, J. (2003) 'Scared straight and other juvenile awareness programs for preventing juvenile delinquency', *The Campbell Collaboration Reviews of Interventions and Policy Evaluations*. Philadelphia, PA: Campbell Collaboration.

Phillips, J., Ray, M. and Marshall, M. (2006) *Social Work with Older People*. Basingstoke: Palgrave Macmillan.

Phillips, M. (1993) 'An oppressive urge to end oppression', *Observer*, 1 August.

Pierson, J. and Thomas, M. (2002) *Collins Dictionary of Social Work*, 2nd edn. London: Collins.

Pietroni, M. (1995) 'The nature and aims of professional education for social workers; a postmodern perspective', in M. Yelloly and M. Henkel (eds) Learning and Teaching in Social Work: Towards Reflective Practice. London: Jessica Kingsley.

Pinker, R. (1993) 'A lethal kind of looniness', *Times Higher Educational Supplement*, 10 September.

Pinkney, S. (1998) 'The reshaping of social work and social care', in G. Hughes and G. Lewis (eds) *Unsettling Welfare: The Reconstruction of Social Policy*. London: Routledge.

Platt, D. (2007) 'Congruence and cooperation in social workers' assessments of children in need', *Child and Family Social Work*, **12**(4): 326–35.

PMSU (Prime Minister's Strategy Unit) (2005) *Improving the Life Chances of Disabled People: Final Report*. London: PMSU.

Polanyi, K. (1944) *The Great Transformation: The Political and Economic Origins of Our Times*. Boston: Beacon Press.

Postle, K. (2001) 'The social work side is disappearing. I guess it started with us being called care managers', *Practice*, **13**(1): 13–26.

Postle, K. (2002) 'Working between "the idea and the reality": ambiguities and tensions in care managers' work', *British Journal of Social Work*, **32**(3): 335–51.

Postle, K. and Beresford, P. (2007) 'Capacity building and the reconception of political participation: a role for social care workers?', *British Journal of Social Work*, **37**(1): 143–58.

Powell, F. (2001) *The Politics of Social Work*. London: Sage.

Powell, J., Robinson, J., Roberts, H. and Thomas, G. (2007) 'The single assessment process in primary care: older people's accounts of the process', *British Journal of Social Work*, **37**(6): 1043–58.

Preston-Shoot, M. (2000a) 'What if? Using the law

to uphold practice values and standards', *Practice*, **12**(4): 49–63.

Preston-Shoot, M. (2000b) 'Making connections in the curriculum: law and professional practice', in R. Pierce and J. Weinstein (eds) *Innovative Education and Training for Care Professionals: A Providers' Guide*. London: Jessica Kingsley.

Preston-Shoot, M. (2001) 'A triumph of hope over experience? On modernising accountability in social services: the case of complaints procedures in community care', *Social Policy and Administration*, **35**(6): 701–15.

Preston-Shoot, M. (2008) 'Things must only get better', *Professional Social Work*, (March): 14–15.

Preston-Shoot, M., Roberts, G. and Vernon, S. (1998a) 'Social work law: from interaction to integration', *Journal of Social Welfare and Family Law*, **20**(1): 65–80.

Preston-Shoot, M., Roberts, G. and Vernon, S. (1998b) 'Working together in social work law', *Journal of Social Welfare and Family Law*, **20**(2): 137–50.

Preston-Shoot, M., Roberts, G. and Vernon, S. (2001) 'Values in social work law: strained relations or sustaining relationships?', *Journal of Social Welfare and Family Law*, **23**(1): 1–22.

Priestley, M. (2003) *Disability: A Life Course Approach*. Cambridge: Polity Press.

Priestley, M., Jolly, D., Pearson, C. et al. (2007) 'Direct payments and disabled people in the UK: supply, demand and devolution', *British Journal of Social Work*, **37**: 1189–204.

Prout, A. (2005) 'Children's participation: control and self-realisation in late modernity', in H. Hendrick (ed.) *Child Welfare and Social Policy: An Essential Reader*. Bristol: Policy Press.

Public Service Productivity Panel (2001) *Creating Successful Partnerships*. London: HM Treasury.

Pugh, D.S. and Hickson, D.J. (2007) *Writers on Organizations*. London: Penguin.

Putnam, R.D. (2000) *Bowling Alone: The Collapse and Revival of American Community*. New York: Simon & Schuster.

Putnam, R.D. (2000) *Bowling Alone: The Decline and Revival of American Community*. New York: Simon & Schuster.

QAA (Quality Assurance Agency for Higher Education) (2000) *Subject Benchmark Statement for Social Policy and Administration and Social Work*, www.qaa.ac.uk.

QAA (Quality Assurance Agency for Higher Education) (2008) *Subject Benchmark Statements: Social Work*. Gloucester: QAA.

Quadagno, J. (2005) *Aging and the Life Course: An Introduction to Social Gerontology*, 3rd edn. London: McGraw-Hill.

Quinton, D. and Rutter, M. (1984a) 'Parents with children in care I: current circumstances and parenting', *Journal of Child Psychology and Psychiatry and Allied Disciplines*, **25**(2): 211–29.

Quinton, D. and Rutter, M. (1984b) 'Parents with children in care II: intergenerational continuities', *Journal of Child Psychology and Psychiatry and Allied Disciplines*, **25**(2): 231–50.

Reamer, F.G. (1990) *Ethical Dilemmas in Social Service*, 2nd edn. New York: Columbia University Press.

Reamer, F.G. (2005) 'Social work values and ethics: reflections on the profession's odyssey', *Advances in Social Work*, **6**(1): 24–32.

Reder, P. and Duncan, S. (2002) 'Predicting fatal child abuse and neglect', in K.D. Browne, H. Hanks, P. Stratton, and C. Hamilton (eds) *Early Prediction and Prevention of Child Abuse*. Chichester: John Wiley.

Reder, P., Duncan, S. and Gray, M. (1993) *Beyond Blame: Child Abuse Tragedies Revisited*. London: Routledge.

Reichardt, O., Kane, D., Pratten, B. and Wilding, K. (2008) *The UK Civil Society Almanac 2008*. London: NCVO.

Reid, W. (1988) 'Service effectiveness and the social agency', in R. Patti, J. Poertner and C. Rapp (eds) *Managing for Effectiveness in Social Welfare Organisations*. New York: Haworth Press.

Reid, W.J. (2001) 'The role of science in social work: the perennial debate', *Journal of Social Work*, **1**(3): 273–94.

Reid, W.J. and Epstein, L. (1972) *Task-centered Casework*. New York: Columbia University Press.

Reith, M. (1997) *Community Care Tragedies: A Practice Guide to Mental Health Inquiries*. Birmingham: Venture.

Repper, J. and Perkins, R. (2003) *Social Inclusion and Recovery: A Model for Mental Health Practice*. London: Ballière Tindall.

Rescher, N. (2002) 'Process philosophy', in E.N. Zalta (ed.) *The Stanford Encyclopedia of Philosophy*, www.plato.stanford.edu/archives/sum2002/entries/ process-philosophy/.

Rice, S. (2002) 'Magic happens: revisiting the spirituality and social work debate', *Australian Social Work*, **55**(4): 303–12.

Richmond, M. (1917) *Social Diagnosis*. New York: Russell Sage Foundation.

Ritchie, J. (2003) 'The applications of qualitative methods of social research', in J. Ritchie and J. Lewis (eds) *Qualitative Research Practice: A Guide for Social Science Students and Researchers*. London: Sage.

Ritchie, J., Dick, D. and Lingham, R. (1994) *Report*

of the Inquiry into the Care and Treatment of Christopher Clunis. London: HMSO.

Robinson, L. (2007) Cross-cultural Child Development for Social Workers. Basingstoke: Palgrave Macmillan.

Rochford, G. (2007) 'Theory, concepts, feelings and practice: the conceptualisation of bereavement within a social work course', in J. Lishman (ed.) Handbook for Practice Learning in Social Work and Social Care: Knowledge and Theory. London: Jessica Kingsley.

Roddam, G., Simmons, J. and Charnley, H. (2007) Involving children and young people as social work educators and beyond. Paper presented at an international conference, Authenticity to Action: Service User Involvement in Higher Education, Grange over Sands.

Roe, W. (2006) Report of the 21st Century Social Work Review: Changing Lives. Edinburgh: Scottish Executive.

Roediger, D.R. (1991) The Wages of Whiteness. London: Verso.

Rogers, C. (1980) A Way of Being. Boston: Houghton Mifflin.

Rose, N. (1996) Inventing Ourselves: Psychology, Power and Personhood. Cambridge: Cambridge University Press.

Rothbaum, F., Weisz, J., Pott, M. et al. (2000) 'Attachment and culture', American Psychologist, 55(10): 1093–104.

Roy, P., Rutter, M. and Pickles, A. (2000) 'Institutional care: risk from family background or pattern of rearing?, Journal of Child Psychology and Psychiatry and Allied Disciplines, 41(2): 139–49.

Royal Commission on Long Term Care for the Elderly (1999) With Respect to Old Age: Long Term Care – Rights and Responsibilities, Cm 4192. London: TSO.

Ruch, G. (2007) 'Reflective practice in contemporary child-care social work: the role of containment', British Journal of Social Work, 37: 659–80.

Rummery, K. (2003) 'Social work and multidisciplinary collaboration in primary care', in J. Weinstein, C. Whittington and T. Leiba (eds) Collaboration in Social Work Practice. London: Jessica Kingsley.

Rushdie, S. (1982) Midnight's Children. London: Jonathan Cape.

Rushmer, R.K. and Pallis. G. (2003) 'Inter-professional working: the wisdom of integrated working and the disaster of blurred boundaries', Public Money and Management, 32(1): 59–66.

Ruskin, J. ([1860] 1985) 'Ad valorem', in J. Ruskin, Unto this Last and Other Writings, ed. C. Wilmer. Harmondsworth: Penguin.

Rutherford, J. (1992) Men's Silences: Predicaments in Masculinity. London: Routledge.

Rutter, M. (1972) Maternal Deprivation Reassessed. Harmondsworth: Penguin.

Rutter, M. (1999) 'Resilience concepts and findings: implications for family therapy', Journal of Family Therapy, 21(2): 119–44.

Rutter, M. (2000) Children in substitute care: some conceptual considerations and research implications, Children and Youth Services Review, 22(9/10): 685–703.

Rutter, M., Graham P., Chadwick O.F. and Yule W. (1976) 'Adolescent turmoil: fact or fiction?', Journal of Child Psychology and Psychiatry, 17(1): 35–56.

Rutter, M., Andersen-Wood, L., Beckett, C. et al. (1998) 'Developmental catch-up, and deficit, following adoption after severe global early privation', Journal of Child Psychology and Psychiatry and Allied Disciplines, 39(4): 465–76.

Rutter, M., Giller, H. and Hagell, A. (1998) Antisocial Behaviour by Young People. Cambridge: Cambridge University Press.

Rutter, M., Andersen-Wood, L., Beckett, C. et al. (1999) 'Quasi-autistic patterns following severe early global privation', Journal of Child Psychology and Psychiatry and Allied Disciplines, 40(4): 537–49.

Rutter, M., Kreppner, J.M. and O'Connor, T.G. (2001) 'Specificity and heterogeneity in children's responses to profound institutional privation', British Journal of Psychiatry, 179: 97–103.

Rutter, M., Beckett, C., Castle, J. et al. (2007a) 'Effects of profound early institutional deprivation: an overview of findings from a UK longitudinal study of Romanian adoptees', European Journal of Developmental Psychology, 4(3): 332–50.

Rutter, M., Colvert, E., Kreppner, J. et al. (2007b) 'Early adolescent outcomes for institutionally deprived and non-deprived adoptees I: disinhibited attachment', Journal of Child Psychology and Psychiatry, 48: 17–30.

Rutter, M., Kreppner, J., Croft, C. et al. (2007c) 'Early adolescent outcomes for institutionally deprived and non-deprived adoptees III: quasi-autism', Journal of Child Psychology and Psychiatry, 48(12): 1200–7.

Sackett, D.L., Richardson, S., Rosenberg, W. and Haynes, R.B. (1997) Evidence-based Medicine: How to Practice and Teach EBM. London: Churchill Livingstone.

SAMHSA (Substance Abuse and Mental Health Service Administration) (2005) Free to Choose: Transforming Behavioral Health Care to Self-direction. Rockville, MD: SAMHSA.

Samra-Tibbets, C. and Raynes, B. (1999) 'Assessment and planning', in M.C. Calder and J. Horwath (eds) Working for Children on the Child

Protection Register: An Inter-agency Practice Guide. Aldershot: Arena.

Save the Children (2008) Why Money Matters: Family Income, Poverty and Children's Lives. London: Save the Children.

Schaffer, R.H. (2000) 'The early experience assumption: past, present, and future', International Journal of Behavioral Development, 24(1): 5–14.

Schaffer, R.H. (2006) Key Concepts in Developmental Psychology. London: Sage.

Schön, D.A. (1983) The Reflective Practitioner: How Professionals Think in Action. New York: Basic Books.

Schön, D.A. (1987) Educating the Reflective Practitioner. San Francisco, CA: Jossey-Bass.

Schonberger, R.J. (1984) Japanese Manufacturing Techniques. New York: Free Press.

SCIE (2005) 'Helping parents with learning difficulties in their role as parents', research briefing 14, www.scie.org.uk/publications/briefings/briefing14/index.asp.

Scottish Executive (2000a) Community Care: A Joint Future. Report of the Joint Future Group. Edinburgh: Scottish Executive.

Scottish Executive (2000b) The Way Forward for Care. Edinburgh: Scottish Executive.

Scottish Executive (2001a) Guidance on Single Shared Assessment of Community Care Needs. Edinburgh: Scottish Executive.

Scottish Executive (2001b) For Scotland's Children. Edinburgh: Scottish Executive.

Scottish Executive (2003) Standards in Social Work Education (SISWE). Edinburgh: Scottish Executive.

Scottish Executive (2004) Confidence in Practice Learning. Edinburgh: Scottish Executive.

Scottish Executive (2005a) An Inspection into the Care and Protection of Children in Eilean Siar. Edinburgh: Social Work Inspection Agency.

Scottish Executive (2005b) Getting It Right For Every Child: Review of Children's Hearing System. Edinburgh: Scottish Executive.

Scottish Executive (2005c) No Fears as Long as We Work Together. Edinburgh: Social Work Inspection Agency.

Scottish Executive (2005d) Getting it Right for Every Child: Proposals for Action. Edinburgh: Scottish Executive.

Scottish Executive (2006a) Changing Lives: Summary Report of the 21st Century Social Work Review. Edinburgh: Scottish Executive.

Scottish Executive (2006b) Key Capabilities in Child Care and Child Protection. Edinburgh: Scottish Executive.

Scottish Government (2007) Effective Approaches to Risk Assessment in Social Work: An International Literature Review. Edinburgh: Scottish Government.

Scottish Government (2008) National Care Standards Committee: Background, Agenda and Minutes, www.scotland.gov.uk/Topics/Health/care/17652/ncscfoi/ncscfoiinfo.

Scourfield, P. (2007) 'Social care and the modern citizen: client, consumer, service user, manager and entrepreneur', British Journal of Social Work, 37(1): 107–22.

Secretary of State for Social Services (1974) Report of the Committee of Inquiry into the Care and Supervision Provided in Relation to Maria Colwell. London: HMSO.

Seebohm Report (1968) Report of the Committee on Local Authority and Allied Social Services. London: HMSO.

Sen, A. (1999) Development as Freedom. Oxford: Oxford University Press.

Senge, P. (1990) The Fifth Discipline: The Art and Practice of the Learning Organisation. London: Random House.

Sennett, R. (2008) The Craftsman. London: Allen Lane.

Serbin, L.A. (1997) 'Research on international adoption: implications for developmental theory and social policy', International Journal of Behavioral Development, 20(1): 83–92.

SEU (Social Exclusion Unit) (2004) Mental Health and Social Exclusion. London: SEU.

Sewpaul, V. (2005) 'Global standards: promise and pitfalls for reinscribing social work into civil society', International Journal of Social Welfare, 14(3): 210–17.

Shakespeare, T. (1999) 'When is a man not a man?', in J. Wild (ed.) Working with Men. London: Routledge.

Shakespeare, T. and Watson, N. (2002) 'The social model of disability: an outdated ideology?', Research in Social Sciences and Disability, 2: 9–26.

Shaping Our Lives (2007) The Changing Roles and Tasks of Social Work from Service Users' Perspectives. London: GSCC.

Shaw, I. (1996) Evaluating in Practice. Aldershot: Arena.

Shaw, I. (2003) 'Cutting edge issues in social work research', British Journal of Social Work, 33(1): 107–16.

Shaw, I. (2004) 'Evaluation for a learning organization', in N. Gould and M. Baldwin (eds) Social Work, Critical Reflection and the Learning Organization. Aldershot: Ashgate.

Shaw, I. (2007) 'Is social work research distinctive', Social Work Education, 26(7): 659–69.

Shaw, I. and Gould, N. (2001) 'The social work context for qualitative research', in I. Shaw and N. Gould (eds) Qualitative Research in Social Work. London: Sage.

Shaw, I. and Lishman, J. (eds) (1999) Evaluation and Social Work Practice. London: Sage.

Shaw, I. and Norton, M. (2007) *The Kinds and Quality of Social Work Research in UK Universities*. London: Social Care Institute for Excellence.

Sheldon, B. (1998) 'Evidence-based social services: prospects and problems', *Research, Policy and Planning*, 16(2): 16–18.

Sheldon, B. and Chivers, R. (2000) *Evidence-based Social Care: A Study of Prospects and Problems*. Lyme Regis: Russell House Publishing.

Sheldon, B., Chivers, R., Ellis, A. et al. (2005) 'A pre-post empirical study of the obstacles to, and opportunities for, evidence-based practice in social care', in A. Bilson (ed.) *Evidence Based Practice in Social Work*. London: Whiting & Birch.

Sheppard, M. (1995) *Care Management and the New Social Work: A Critical Analysis*. London: Whiting & Birch.

Sheppard, M. (2006) *Social Work and Social Exclusion*. Aldershot: Ashgate.

Sheppard, M. and Ryan, K. (2003) 'Practitioners as rule-using analysts: a further development of process knowledge in social work', *British Journal of Social Work*, 33(2): 157–76.

Sheppard, M., Newstead, S., Di Caccavo, A. and Ryan, K. (2000) 'Reflexivity and the development of process knowledge in social work: a classification and empirical study', *British Journal of Social Work*, 30(4): 465–88.

Shier, H. (2001) 'Pathways to participation: openings, opportunities and obligations: a new model for enhancing children's participation in decision making', *Children and Society*, 15: 107–17.

Shulman, L. (1999) *The Skills of Helping Individuals, Families, Groups and Communities*, 4th edn. New York: F.E. Peacock.

Sibeon, R. (1989) 'Comments on the structure and form of social work knowledge', *Social Work and Social Sciences Review*, 1(1): 29–44.

Siegrist, J. and Marmot, M. (eds) (2006) *Social Inequalities in Health: New Evidence and Policy Implications*. Oxford: Oxford University Press.

Simic, P. (1995) 'What's in a word? From "social worker" to "care manager"', *Practice*, 7(3): 5–18.

Simmons, J. (2006) *Involving Young People in Decisions about Service Provision and Delivery*. Norwich: Social Work Monographs.

Simmons, R. and Birchall, J. (2005) 'A joined-up approach to user participation in public services: strengthening the "participation chain"', *Social Policy & Administration*, 39(3): 260–83.

Simon, B. (1990) 'Rethinking empowerment', *Journal of Progressive Human Services*, 1(1): 27–39.

Simons, K. (1992) *'Sticking Up For Yourself': Self-advocacy and People with Learning Difficulties*. York: Joseph Rowntree Foundation.

Skalli, A., Johansson, E. and Theodossiou, I. (eds) *Are the Healthier Wealthier or the Wealthier Healthier? The European Evidence*. Helsinki: Taloustieto Oy.

Skuse, D. (1984a) 'Extreme deprivation in early childhood I: diverse outcomes for three siblings from an extraordinary family', *Journal of Child Psychology and Psychiatry and Allied Disciplines*, 25(4): 523–41.

Skuse, D. (1984b) 'Extreme deprivation in early childhood II: theoretical issues and a comparative view', *Journal of Child Psychology and Psychiatry and Allied Disciplines*, 25(4): 543–72.

Skuse, D. (1985) 'Extreme deprivation in early childhood: a reply, *Journal of Child Psychology and Psychiatry and Allied Disciplines*, 26(5): 827–8.

Slowther, A.-M. (2007) 'The concept of autonomy and its interpretation in health care', *Clinical Ethics*, 2(4): 1173–5.

Smale, G. and Tuson, G. with Biehal, N. and Marsh, P. (1993) *Empowerment, Assessment, Care Management and the Skilled Worker*. London: NISW.

Smale, G., Tuson, G. and Statham, D. (2000) *Social Work and Social Problems*. Basingstoke: Palgrave – now Palgrave Macmillan.

Smalley, R.E. (1967) *Theory for Social Work Practice*. New York: Columbia University Press.

Smalley, R.E. (1970) 'The functional approach to casework practice', in R.W. Roberts and R.H. Nee (eds) *Theories of Social Casework*. Chicago: Chicago University Press.

Smith, C. (1982) *Social Work with the Dying and Bereaved*. Basingstoke: Macmillan – now Palgrave Macmillan.

Smith, D. (1984) 'Law and order: arguments for what?', *Critical Social Policy*, 11: 33–45.

Smith, D. (1992) 'Puritans and paradigms: a comment', *Social Work and Social Sciences Review*, 3(2): 99–103.

Smith, G., Smith, T. and Wright, G. (1997) 'Poverty and schooling: choice, diversity or division?', in A. Walker and C. Walker (eds) *Britain Divided: The Growth of Social Exclusion in Britain 1979–1997*. London: CPAG.

Smith, P. (ed.) (1996) *Measuring Outcomes in the Public Sector*. London: Taylor & Francis.

Smyth, J. (1991) *Teachers as Collaborative Learners: Challenging Dominant Forms of Supervision*. Milton Keynes: Open University Press.

Snape, D. and Spencer, L. (2003) 'The foundations of qualitative research', in J. Ritchie and J. Lewis (eds) *Qualitative Research Practice: A Guide for Students and Researchers*. London: Sage.

Social Exclusion Task Force (2007) *Analysis and Themes from the Families at Risk Review*. London: Cabinet Office.

Sone, K. (1995) 'Get tough', *Community Care*, 6–12 March, pp. 16–18.

SSI (Social Services Inspectorate) (1999) *Inspection*

of Services to Support Disabled Adults in their Parenting Role. Cornwall County Council, Bristol West Inspection Group: Department of Health.

SSI (Social Services Inspectorate) (2002) Delivering Quality Children's Services. London: HMSO.

SSI/SWSG (Social Services Inspectorate/Social Work Services Group) (1991) Care Management and Assessment: Practitioners' Guide. London: DH.

SSSC (Scottish Social Services Council) (2002) Codes of Practice for Social Service Workers and Employers. Dundee: SSSC.

SSSC (Scottish Social Services Council) (2004) Code of Practice for Social Service Workers and Code of Practice for Employers of Social Service Workers, www.sssc.uk.com/Registration/Codes+of+Practice.htm.

Stanley, N. and Penhale, B. (1999) 'The mental health problems of mothers experiencing the child protection system: identifying needs and appropriate responses', Child Abuse Review, 8(1): 34–46.

Stanley, T. (2005) Making Decisions: Social work processes and the construction of risk(s) in child protection work, PhD thesis. Canterbury, New Zealand: University of Canterbury.

Stedman-Jones, G. (1971) Outcast London. Oxford: Clarendon.

Stein, M. (1997) What Works in Leaving Care. Ilford: Barnado's.

Stepney, P. (2006) 'Mission impossible? Critical practice in social work', British Journal of Social Work, 36: 1289–307.

Stevenson, O. (1988) 'Law and social work education: a commentary on the "Law report"', Issues in Social Work Education, 8(1): 37–45.

Stevenson, O. and Parsloe, P. (1993) Community Care and Empowerment. York: Joseph Rowntree Foundation and Community Care.

Stiglitz, J.E. (2002) Globalisation and its Discontents. London: Allen Lane.

Stiglitz, J.E. and Greenwald, B. (2003) Towards a New Paradigm of Monetary Economics. Cambridge: Cambridge University Press.

Stiglitz, J.E., Ocampo, J.A., Spiegel, S. et al. (2006) Stability with Growth: Macroeconomics, Liberalisation and Development. Oxford: Oxford University Press.

Stroebe, M. and Schut, H. (1999) 'The dual process model of coping with bereavement: rationale and description', Death Studies, 23(3): 197–224.

Stuart-Hamilton, I. (1991) The Psychology of Ageing: An Introduction. London: Jessica Kingsley.

Sugarman, L. (2001) Life-span Development: Concepts, Theories, and Interventions, 2nd edn. Hove: Psychology Press.

Sutton, C. (1999) Helping Families with Troubled Children: A Preventative Approach. Chichester: Wiley.

Swain, J. and French, S. (2008) Disability on Equal Terms. London: Sage

Tapscott, D. and Williams, A. (2006) Wikinomics: How Mass Collaboration Changes Everything. New York: Penguin Portfolio.

Tarleton, B. (2007) 'Specialist advocacy services for parents with learning disabilities involved in child protection proceedings', British Journal of Learning Disabilities, doi:10.1111/j.1468-3156.2007.00479.x.

Tarleton, B. and Ward, L. (2007) '"Parenting with support": the views and experiences of parents with intellectual disabilities', Journal of Policy and Practice in Intellectual Disabilities, 4(3): 194–202, doi:10.1111/j.1741-1130.2007.00118.x.

Taylor, C. (2004) 'Underpinning knowledge for child care practice: reconsidering child development theory', Child & Family Social Work, 9(3): 225–35.

Taylor, F.W. (1911) The Principles of Scientific Management. New York: Harper and Brothers.

Taylor, J., Baldwin, N. and Spencer, N. (2008) 'Predicting child abuse and neglect: ethical, theoretical and methodological challenges', Journal of Clinical Nursing, 17: 1193–200.

Tew, J. (2006) 'Understanding power and powerlessness: towards a framework for emancipatory practice in social work', Journal of Social Work, 6(1): 33–51.

Thomas, C. (1999) Female Forms: Experiencing and Understanding Disability. Buckingham: Open University Press.

Thompson, A.M. (1986) 'Adam – a severely-deprived Colombian orphan: a case report', Journal of Child Psychology and Psychiatry and Allied Disciplines, 27(5): 689–95.

Thompson, N. (2002) Building the Future: Social Work with Children, Young People and their Families. Lyme Regis: Russell House.

Thompson, R.A. (2000) 'The legacy of early attachments', Child Development, 71(1): 145–52.

Thompson, S. and Kahn, J.H. (1970) The Group Process as a Helping Technique. Oxford: Pergamon.

Timms, N. (1983) Social Work Values: An Enquiry. London: Routledge & Kegan Paul.

Titterton, M. (1999) 'Training professionals in risk assessment and risk management: what does the research tell us?', in P. Parsloe (ed.) Risk Assessment in Social Care and Social Work. London: Jessica Kingsley.

Tizard, B. (1977) Adoption: A Second Chance. London: Open Books.

Tizard, B. and Hodges, J. (1978) 'The effect of early institutional rearing on the development of eight-year-old children', Journal of Child Psychology and Psychiatry and Allied Disciplines, 19: 99–118.

Tizard, B. and Rees, J. (1974) 'A comparison of the effects of adoption, restoration to the natural mother, and continued institutionalisation on the cognitive development of four-year-old children', *Child Development*, **45**: 92–9.

Tizard, B. and Rees, J. (1975) 'The effect of early institutional rearing on the behaviour problems and affectional relationships of four-year-old children', *Journal of Child Psychology and Psychiatry and Allied Disciplines*, **16**: 61–73.

Topss (Training Organisation for the Personal Social Services) (2002) *The National Occupational Standards for Social Work*. Leeds: Topss.

Treseder, P. (1997) *Empowering Children and Young People – Training Manual: Promoting Involvement in Decision Making*. London: Save the Children.

Trevithick, P. (2000) *Social Work Skills*. Buckingham: Open University Press.

Trevithick, P. (2005) *Social Work Skills: A Practice Handbook*, 2nd edn. Maidenhead: McGraw-Hill.

Trinder, L. (1996) 'Social work research: the state of the art (or science)', *Child & Family Social Work*, 1(4): 233–42.

Trinder, L. (2000) 'A critical appraisal of evidence-based practice', in L. Trinder and S. Reynolds (eds) *Evidence-based Practice: A Critical Appraisal*. Oxford: Blackwell Science.

Trinder, L. and Reynolds, S. (eds) (2000) *Evidence-based Practice: A Critical Appraisal*. Oxford: Blackwell Science.

Triseliotis, J. (2002) 'Long-term foster care or adoption? The evidence examined', *Child and Family Social Work*, 7(1): 23–34.

Trowell, J. (1995) 'Working together in child protection, some issues for multi-disciplinary training from a psychodynamic perspective', in M. Yelloly and M. Henkel (eds) *Learning and Teaching in Social Work: Towards Reflective Practice*. London: Jessica Kingsley.

Tunstill, J. and Allnock, D. (2007) *Understanding the Contribution of Sure Start Local Programmes to the Task of Safeguarding Children's Welfare: National Evaluation Report*. London: HMSO.

Tunstill, J., Meadows, P., Allnock, D. et al. (2005) *Implementing Sure Start Local Programmes: An Integrated Overview of the First Four Years*. London: HMSO.

Turner, M. (1995) 'Supervising', in P. Carter, T. Jeffs and M.K. Smith (eds) *Social Working*. Basingstoke: Macmillan – now Palgrave Macmillan.

Turner, M. and Beresford, P. (2005) *What User Controlled Research Means, and What it Can Do*. Eastleigh: INVOLVE.

UN (1989) *UN Convention on the Rights of the Child*. Geneva: United Nations.

UNICEF (2007) *Child Poverty in Perspective: An Overview of Child Well-Being in Rich Countries*, Report Card 7. Florence, Italy: Innocenti and UNICEF.

Utting, W. (1996) 'The case for reforming social services law', in T. Harding (ed.) *Social Services Law: The Case for Reform*. London: NISW.

Vanstone, M. (1995) 'Managerialism and the ethics of management', in R. Hugman and D. Smith (eds) *Ethical Issues in Social Work*. London, Routledge.

Verschelden, C. (1993) 'Social work values and pacifism: opposition to war as a professional responsibility', *Social Work*, **38**(6): 765–9.

Vondra, J.I. and Barnett, D. (eds) (1999) *Atypical Attachment in Infancy and Early Childhood among Children at Developmental Risk*. Oxford: Blackwell.

Walker, A. (1990) 'Blaming the victims', in Institute of Economic Affairs (eds) *The Emerging British Underclass*. London: IEA.

Walker, A. and Walker, C. (eds) (1997) *Britain Divided: The Growth of Social Exclusion in Britain 1979–1997*. London: CPAG.

Walker, A. and Walker, C. (1998) 'Social policy and social work', in R. Adams, L. Dominelli and M. Payne (eds) *Social Work: Themes, Issues and Critical Debates*. Basingstoke: Macmillan – now Palgrave Macmillan.

Walker, C. (1993) *Managing Poverty: The Limits of Social Assistance*. London: Routledge.

Walker, J. (1995) 'Counselling in a social services area office: the practice behind the thoery', in P. Carter, T. Jeffs, and M.K. Smith (eds) *Social Working*. Basingstoke, Macmillan – now Palgrave Macmillan.

Walker, S. and Beckett, C. (2003) *Social Work Assessment and Intervention*. Lyme Regis: Russell House Publishing.

Walsh, F. (1998) *Strengthening Family Resilience*. New York: Guilford Press.

Walter, C. (2007) 'The story of Matthew: an ecological approach to assessment', *Scottish Journal of Residential Childcare*, **6**(1): 45–53.

Walter, I., Nutley, S., Percy-Smith, J. et al. (2004) *Improving the Use of Research in Social Care Practice: Knowledge Review 7*. London: SCIE.

Wanless, D. (2006) *Securing Good Care for Older People: Taking a Long-term View*. London: King's Fund, www.cpag.org.uk/press/120207.htm.

Wardhaugh, J. and Wilding, P. (1993) 'Towards an explanation of the corruption of care', *Critical Social Policy*, **13**(1): 4–31.

Warren, J. (2007) *Service User and Carer Participation in Social Work*. Exeter: Learning Matters.

Waterhouse, R. (2000) *Lost in Care: The Report of the Tribunal of Inquiry into the Abuse of Children in Care in the Former County Council Areas of Gwynedd and Clwyd since 1974*. London: TSO.

Waters, E. and Cummings, E.M. (2000) 'A secure base from which to explore close relationships', *Child Development*, **71**(1): 164–72.

Waters, E., Merrick, S., Treboux, D. et al. (2000) 'Attachment security in infancy and early adulthood: a twenty-year longitudinal study', *Child Development*, **71**(3): 684–9.

Watzlawick, P., Beavin, J. and Jackson, D. (1967) *Pragmatics of Human Communication*. New York: W.W. Norton.

Webb, D. (1990–91a) 'Puritans and paradigms: a speculation on the form of new moralities in social work', *Social Work and Social Sciences Review*, **2**(2): 146–59.

Webb, D. (1990–91b) 'A stranger in the academy: a reply to Lena Dominelli', *Social Work and Social Sciences Review*, **2**(3): 236–41.

Webb, S. (1994) 'My client is subversive! Partnership and patronage in social work', *Social Work and Social Science Review*, **5**(1): 5–23.

Webb, S.A. (2001) 'Some considerations on the validity of evidence-based practice in social work', *British Journal of Social Work*, **31**(1): 57–79.

Webb, S.A. (2006) *Social Work in a Risk Society: Social and Political Perspectives*. Basingstoke: Palgrave Macmillan.

Webb, S.A. and McBeath, G.A. (1989) 'A political critique of Kantian ethics in social work', *British Journal of Social Work*, **19**(6): 491–506.

Webb, S.A. and McBeath, G.A. (1990) 'A political critique of Kantian ethics in social work: a reply to Professor R.S. Downie', *British Journal of Social Work*, **20**(1): 65–71.

Weber, M. ([1947]1978) *Max Weber: Selections in Translation*, ed. W.G. Runciman, trans. E. Mathews. Cambridge: Cambridge University Press.

Weinfield, N.S., Sroufe, L.A. and Egeland, B. (2000) 'Attachment from infancy to early adulthood in a high-risk sample: continuity, discontinuity, and their correlates', *Child Development*, **71**(3): 695–702.

Weinstein, J., Wittington, C. and Leiba, T. (2003) *Collaboration in Social Work Practice*. London: Jessica Kingsley.

Weiss, R.S. (1991) 'The attachment bond in childhood and adulthood', in C.M. Parkes, J. Stevenson-Hinde and P. Marris (eds) *Attachment Across the Life Cycle*. London: Routledge.

Wendell, S. (1996) *The Rejected Body*. Toronto: Garamond Press.

Wenger, E. (1998) *Communities of Practice: Learning, Meaning and Identity*. Cambridge: Cambridge University Press.

Wheal, A. (ed.) (2002) *The RHP Companion to Leaving Care*. Dorset: Russell House Publishing.

Whitaker, D., Archer, L. and Hicks, L. (1998) *Working in Children's Homes: Challenges and Complexities*. Chichester: Wiley.

White, S. (2001) 'Auto-ethnography as self-reflexive inquiry: the research act as self surveillance', in I. Shaw and N. Gould (eds) *Qualitative Research in Social Work*. London: Sage.

White, V. (2006) *The State of Feminist Social Work*. London: Routledge.

Whittaker, J. (1974) *Social Treatment: An Approach to Interpersonal Helping*. Aldine: Chicago.

Wilcox, P. (2006) 'Communities, care and domestic violence', *Critical Social Policy*, **26**: 722–47.

Wild, J. (ed) (1999) *Working with Men*. London: Routledge.

Wilkinson, R.G. (1996) *Unhealthy Societies: The Afflictions of Inequality*. London: Routledge.

Wilkinson, R.G. (2005) *The Impact of Inequality: How to Make Sick Societies Healthier*. New York: The New Press.

Williams, F., Popay, J. and Oakley, A. (1999) *Welfare Research: A Critical Review*. London: University College London Press.

Williams, G. and McCreadie, J. (1992) *Ty Mawr Community Home Inquiry*. Ebbw Vale: Gwent County Council.

Williams, J., Toumbourou, J.W., McDonald, M. et al. (2005) 'A sea change on the island continent: frameworks for risk assessment prevention and intervention in child health in Australia', *Children and Society*, **19**(2): 91–104.

Williams, P. (2002) 'The competent boundary spanner', *Public Administration*, **80**(1): 103–24.

Wilson, K., Ruch, G., Lymbery, M. and Cooper, A. (2008) *Social Work: An Introduction to Contemporary Practice*. Harlow: Pearson Education.

Wilson, V. and Pirrie, A. (2000) 'Multi-disciplinary team-working: beyond the barriers? a review of the issues', SCRE research paper 96. Glasgow: Glasgow University Press.

Wise, S. (1995) 'Feminist ethics in practice', in R. Hugman and D. Smith (eds) *Ethical Issues in Social Work*. London: Routledge.

Woodroofe, K. (1962) *From Charity to Social Work in England and the United States*. London: Routledge & Kegan Paul.

Woodward, J. (1970) *Industrial Organizations: Behaviour and Control*. London: Oxford University Press.

World Bank (2001) *World Development Report 2000–2001: Attacking Poverty*. Washington, DC: World Bank.

Wright, P., Turner, C., Clay, D. and Mills, H. (2006) *The Participation of Children and Young People in Developing Social Care: Practice Guide 6*. London: Social Care Institute for Excellence.

Younghusband, E. (1959) *Report of the Working Party on Social Workers in the Local Authority Health and Welfare Services*. London: HMSO.

Younghusband, E. (1981) *The Newest Profession: A Short History of Social Work*. Sutton, Surrey: Community Care/IPC Business Press.

Author index

Subject index